IAN KERSHAW

Hitler, the Germans, and the Final Solution

International Institute for Holocaust Research
Yad Vashem
Jerusalem

Yale University Press
New Haven &
London

Set in Sabon type by Keystone Typesetting, Inc., Orwigsburg, Pennsylvania.
Printed in the United States of America by Vail-Ballou Press,
Binghamton, New York.

Library of Congress Control Number: 2007940635
ISBN: 978-0-300-15127-5 (pbk.)

A catalogue record for this book is available from the British Library.

10 9 8 7 6 5 4 3 2 1

Hitler, the Germans, and the Final Solution

Contents

Introduction

It seems, in writing this introduction, as if I am passing review over my life — certainly a good portion of my academic life. It is both a strange and disconcerting feeling. Strange, because at least the earlier pieces in this volume were written so long ago that I almost feel at times as if another hand, not my own, was at work. Disconcerting, because, were I to write those pieces now, I would certainly write them differently. How could it be otherwise? It would be odd indeed, and probably not very commendable, if a historian found nothing to alter or revise in his or her own work during a course of thirty years' reflection on the issues in question. So it is with a degree of unease that I look over these pieces which my friends in Yad Vashem have chosen to present in this volume. I am, nevertheless, most grateful to them for suggesting this collection of some of my work, quite especially to Otto Dov Kulka, a good 'intellectual friend' over thirty years from whom I have learned an immense amount during a prolonged and fruitful exchange of correspondence.

The contributions to the volume are presented in a thematic way. To make sense of how they fit together, and how they came to be written, it is best, nevertheless, to take them for the most part chronologically. This approach allows a clearer glimpse of the historian behind the history, of how I conceived of the pieces at the time, how they reflect the course of my own intellectual development in writing on these issues, and how in some cases my views have changed in the light of later reflection.

I should say at the outset, too, that I have always seen myself as a historian of modern Germany, specifically of Nazism, not directly of the Holocaust. I had come to German history via an increased competence in the German language — German was a subject unavailable at my school, so I was able to begin learning it only in 1969, and then for three years purely as a casual hobby — and what really, and increasingly, intrigued me, as a product of post-war British democracy, was how Germany had so completely succumbed to a dictatorship which had brought about world war and, to rational minds, a scarcely intelligible persecution and extermination of the Jews. This shaped the course of my work, and the place of my studies of German reactions to the persecution of the Jews and of the 'Final Solution,' within it.

My chief interest, when I began working on the Third Reich in the mid-1970s, was on how German society had reacted to Nazism, what the attitudes of 'ordinary' Germans had been under the Hitler dictatorship, and what had shaped their behaviour. But within this general framework of interest, I was certainly concerned especially, and from the beginning, to understand as best I could how the majority German population had responded to the increasingly ferocious persecution, then extermination, of the Jews. An early exposure to this issue came in a chance encounter with an old Nazi in 1972, when I (still at the time a committed medievalist, with a position at an English university devoted to the teaching and research of English medieval economic and social history) had nevertheless realised the urgent importance for my future in mastering German with all rapidity and was taking an intensive German-language course at the Goethe-Institut in Grafing, a small market town about twenty miles outside Munich. At one point in a conversation which had become increasingly fascinating for me through its expression of a strange, alien mentality, my coffee-table companion remarked that 'the Jew is a louse'. The expression shocked me at the time and, vivid in my memory, still does. But it posed the question in my mind about what the people of this attractive, sleepy little provincial Bavarian town had thought and done during the Nazi era. Little did I know then that only four or so years later I would be reading police reports from the same small town dating from the period immediately following Hitler's takeover of power, or, indeed, that the hostelry where I and other students from the Goethe-Institut regularly ate our midday meals had been the main meeting place of the small town's Nazi Party.

I

By 1976 I was engaged as part of the research team, based at the Institut für Zeitgeschichte in Munich, working under the direction of Professor Martin Broszat on the Bavaria Project. Astonishingly, the social history of the Third Reich was in its outright infancy in the mid-1970s, when the project was established. It was Broszat's brilliant imagination that saw the project, ostensibly set up to work on 'resistance and persecution in Bavaria during the Nazi era', as an opportunity to break free from conventional notions of opposition and to uncover patterns of behaviour not usually covered by the rubric 'resistance'. Broszat had welcomed me with open arms when I had explained to him my interest (which I had developed independently) in carrying out research on popular opinion during the Third Reich, based upon the extensive sets of reports on the 'mood of the people' sent in on a regular basis by an array of agencies of the Nazi state. Though operating within the Bavaria Project, I continued to work largely independently (and very intensively) during a twelve-month stay in Munich in 1976–7 on what I envisaged as a large monograph which would embrace both oppositional and acclamatory aspects of popular opinion.

Broszat became particularly enthusiastic about one part of this research, that which was directed at assessing popular attitudes towards Hitler. With his strong encouragement, this eventually saw life as *Der Hitler-Mythos,* published in its original German form in 1980.[1] Broszat was also extremely taken by a lengthy chapter (intended as part of the initially conceived monograph) on antisemitism and popular opinion, which dealt with Bavarian reactions to the persecution of the Jews. He had already in 1979 incorporated this in the second volume of the series of publications emanating from the Bavaria Project.[2] It gave me my first chance to publish in my new field of modern German history.

When the other part of my initially planned monograph, dealing with the oppositional side of the coin, on which I had extensive material and had drafted several chapters, then became the core of a separate publication, appearing in 1983 with Oxford University Press under the title *Popular Opinion and Political Dissent: Bavaria 1933–1945,* I included in it, as I had always intended, a slightly abridged English-language version of this essay. This is the contribution, originally composed in 1977, which appears as Chapter 7 in this volume. It was my initial attempt to examine, on the basis of the regime's own monitoring of opinion, the behaviour and attitudes of ordinary Germans with regard to the 'Jewish Question'.

It is, I think, worth understanding this genesis of the piece — how it arose as part of a widely framed analysis of different facets of popular attitudes towards the Nazi regime, positive and negative — in order to see how my interpretation took shape. I was struck, as I ploughed through an unending mass of police reports on 'the mood of the people', not by how much, but by how little the 'Jewish Question', the core of the Nazi 'worldview', appeared to figure, irrespective of whether the opinion reported was acclamatory or oppositional. Reflections of Hitler's popular image in the sources gave, for instance, little indication of the centrality of the Jews to his personal doctrine of hatred. Accordingly, when I published the original version of *Der Hitler-Mythos*, I decided against including a thematic chapter relating to Jews. (I later thought this had been a mistake, and included such a chapter, newly written, in the English-language version, *The 'Hitler Myth'*, which was published in 1987.)[3]

In the related study, *Popular Opinion and Political Dissent,* I was able to produce extensive evidence of the constant shaping of opinion by the material-ist concerns of daily life — constant complaints about wages, prices, work conditions, and specific grievances of various sectors of society — and of the huge (though politically limited) alienation that emanated from Nazi attacks on the Christian churches. In contrast, what had really surprised me when I was carrying out the research was how little the persecution of the Jews appeared to invade the daily life of the majority of the population, and how limited its impact on popular opinion seemed to be. Of course, there were major flash-points, such as the boycott of 1933, the promulgation of the Nuremberg Laws in 1935, and, especially, the terrible pogroms of November 1938, when the persecution of the Jews briefly occupied the foreground of opinion. But even during the biggest waves of anti-Jewish action in 1933, 1935, and 1938, opin-ion had seemed to be influenced in the main by other factors. Of course, this was Bavaria, not Germany as a whole. And, a point which struck me strongly, in wide swathes of Bavaria there were no Jews at all. Most of the population, that is, probably encountered no actual Jews in daily life.

I brought out the relative insignificance of the 'Jewish Question' in the shap-ing of popular opinion during the prewar years in a piece published in 1981 (and included in this volume as Chapter 5). I was attempting here to summarise my findings on the disparate strands of opinion and deployed Max Weber's concept of *'das Außeralltägliche'* — a German abstraction more weakly ren-dered in English as 'the Exceptional' — to distinguish those spheres of Nazi policy which were intermittent rather than constant, such as the pressures of daily life (in Weber's parlance, *'das Alltägliche'*, the 'everyday', or routine) in shaping attitudes. I included brief reference to the persecution of the Jews as part of the 'exceptional' sphere, and suggested, here too, that the 'Jewish Question' had 'less and less genuine relevance for the daily life of the majority German population' and that 'the consequence for the shaping of opinion was less the creation of dynamic hatred than of lethal indifference' — a lack of concern with ultimately deadly consequences.

From my approach to popular opinion in general during the Third Reich came, then, my suggestion that 'indifference' towards the fate of the Jews had characterised the stance of the majority of Germans. I summed up my interpretation in a sentence which has often been quoted since then: 'The road to Auschwitz was built by hate, but paved with indifference'.[4] Following this pointed conclusion, I made the chapter on 'Popular Opinion and the Extermination of the Jews' (included in this collection as part of Chapter 8) the shortest in the book, trying to underline the point that, while the Jews were being killed in their millions during the war of extermination unleashed by the Nazis, most Germans had other things on their minds. Of course, I scarcely meant this in any complimentary, let alone apologetic, sense. Rather, I was trying to show that the Nazi efforts at instilling 'dynamic' hatred of Jews in the population through relentless propaganda were not successful — but also not necessary. As I put it, 'latent antisemitism and apathy sufficed to allow the increasingly criminal "dynamic" hatred of the Nazi regime the autonomy it needed to set in motion the Holocaust'.

I had derived the distinction between 'latent' and 'dynamic' antisemitism from a somewhat obscure postwar tract by a German psychologist, Michael Müller-Claudius.[5] During the Nazi era, Müller-Claudius had subtly prompted a small number of party members of his acquaintance into voicing their views about the November pogroms of 1938, then the deportations in 1941. Through this technique, and on the basis of this tiny, scarcely representative and obliquely constructed sample, he drew his conclusions about opinion towards the persecution of the Jews. Much of it, he indicated, could be summed up as 'indifference', a term which he used to describe reserved or noncommittal reactions. Müller-Claudius had, in fact, come to influence not just me, but the small number of others at that time who had carried out work on popular reactions to the persecution of the Jews. The latter included Marlis Steinert, whose impressive examination of wartime opinion as reflected in the reports of the SD (*Sicherheitsdienst*, or Security Service) I had found particularly stimulating.[6] Steinert's large book of more than six hundred pages included just one chapter, of twenty-seven pages, on German attitudes towards the Jews, and that at a time when the regime was taking the steps that would lead to the 'Final Solution', including the deportation of thousands of Jews to the death camps. Again, both the sense that most Germans had other things on their minds during the war (reflected in the small proportion of the book devoted to reactions to the persecution of Jews) and her adoption from Müller-Claudius of the notion of 'indifference' seemed to me convincing.

At the time (though this was to change) the concept of 'indifference', emanating from Müller-Claudius, had, I think, left its mark on another scholar, working independently and, in the mid-seventies, completely unknown to me, on German popular opinion and the persecution of the Jews. This was Otto Dov Kulka, whose name was first mentioned to me by an Israeli friend, Benjamin Kedar, later a distinguished medieval historian at the Hebrew University of Jerusalem, but in 1976–7, like me, researching in Munich, thanks to the generous financial support of the marvellous German institution, the Alexander von Humboldt-Stiftung. I was, of course, eager to learn what my 'rival' researcher in Israel, of whose work I knew nothing at that point, was doing. Benjamin agreed to go through one of Kulka's publications, linguistically inaccessible for me, to clarify what common ground we might have. So I spent a long evening in a Munich beer hall — no great hardship, I readily concede, and not such a rare occurrence either — making notes while Benjamin translated from an article which Kulka had published in Hebrew of direct relevance to my own work.[7] It was the beginning of what would turn into a lasting dialogue between Kulka and me, which began in earnest when we met as I was giving a presentation at Harvard in the early 1980s. By that time, however, if not before, Kulka was already critical of the notion of 'indifference', especially with regard to the years of the 'Final Solution', and, together with a former student of mine, Aron Rodrigue, wrote a constructively critical review of my interpretation on the appearance of my book *Popular Opinion*.[8]

In their review, Kulka and Rodrigue thought the concept of 'indifference' might be 'more confusing than helpful' and was 'especially problematic when applied to the interpretation of popular attitudes towards the Jews during the war years', not least since it was an argument derived from the relative silence of the SD reports on this matter. They pointed to some reports from 1941 and 1942 which indicated widespread approval for the imposition of the 'Yellow Star' and for a 'radical solution of the Jewish problem' at the time of the deportations, concluding that 'the concept of "indifference", suggesting as it does only a lack of concern, is too limited in scope and does not convey the full complexity of popular opinion'. Their preference was to replace 'indifference' by 'an attitude that might best be characterized as passive complicity'.[9]

The disagreement caused me to rethink the validity of the notion of 'indifference', and an opportunity soon arose to present my 'second thoughts' at an important conference staged by the Leo Baeck Institute in Berlin in 1986, which both Kulka and I attended. These further ruminations are included as Chapter 9 of this volume.

I conceded some ground in accepting that interest in the fate of the Jews was greater, certainly at specific junctures such as the introduction of the 'Yellow Star' and the deportations, than I had allowed. I agreed, too, that 'indifference' was a difficult, less than ideal, concept. Yet I continued to prefer it, as a descriptive term of attitudes that shaped behaviour, to 'passive complicity'. In fact, I took the view that no one term could adequately encapsulate the variations in opinion (insofar as it is possible at all to assess prevailing attitudes in conditions of repressive dictatorship and absence of free speech). Beyond that, it seemed to me that the more I revisited the sources and the issues arising, the closer rather than the more divergent Kulka and Rodrigue's and my own interpretations of behaviour turned out to be, despite apparent conflict over definitional terms.

The term 'indifference', I insisted, did not mean neutrality, but carried negative overtones — those of shrugging one's shoulders or turning one's back on an evil in recognition that one can do nothing about it, and in the feeling that other concerns are more pressing or overwhelming. It is scarcely a heroic stance, nor morally commendable, but, I was claiming, it probably amounts to a commonplace attitude (and even in democracies, let alone in a dictatorship at war). To strengthen the term, I turned it into 'moral indifference', which I thought was perfectly compatible with the growing depersonalisation of Jews during the war and the hardening of attitudes towards the 'Jewish Question' in the population. In essence, therefore, I was holding to the view that 'at the time that Jews were being murdered in their millions, the vast majority of Germans had plenty of other things on their mind' and that the 'Jewish Question' was relatively unimportant in the overall shaping of popular opinion.

In this piece, I also addressed more directly than I had done in my work on Bavaria the major difficulties of interpreting the reports on opinion from within the Nazi regime. While Kulka and Rodrigue criticised the 'argument from silence', for instance, I pointed to the problems of assessing what *was* presented in the reports as the opinion of the population. Though I agreed that a hardening of attitudes towards Jews, as reflected in the reports, most likely *had* occurred, it did seem fairly self-evident to me that the *reported* views voicing, for example, outright approval of the 'Yellow Star' were almost certain to have been those of the nazified section of the population. What proportion of the total population that amounted to is in the nature of things impossible to quantify. Despite the obvious dangers involved in expressing criticism of measures against Jews, moreover, the sources do indicate that Nazi policies did not meet with total approval, even during the war, though certainly this applied to only a small (and equally unquantifiable) minority. Between the extremes, and here we return to the 'argument from silence', I took the view that it is impossible to know with any precision what people thought. An inference that most people were probably preoccupied with the mounting personal anxieties during the war seemed reasonable. That would, in turn, bring us back to a sense of moral indifference towards the fate of a generally disliked minority.

I returned to the passivity, which I saw as reflecting the low level of priority in German consciousness accorded to the fate of the Jews, in a paper presented to a conference in Haifa in 1986, included in this volume as Chapter 6. Here, as earlier, I suggested that lack of interest in discrimination against a generally disliked minority, coupled with the latent antagonism that had existed even in democratic conditions before the incomparably greater difficulties of speaking out under a dictatorship arose, provided a prerequisite for the process of genocide by allowing the fanatical hatred of part of the population to gather pace unchecked and unhindered. Pessimistically, I alluded to the questionable liberal assumptions that human beings under threat will be defended in an open society. In this, my last attempt to wrestle with the intractable sources on popular opinion and the fate of the Jews, I tried to distinguish between what people could and did know (quite a lot), what they made of the information (an awareness that genocide, even if the word was not then in currency, was taking place, though ignorance of scale and detail led to only partial comprehension), and reactions (a spectrum from overt approval to blank condemnation, though with an apathetic turning away from unpalatable knowledge and events which could not be averted as the most widespread).

By this time, I felt I could take my own investigations of popular attitudes towards the persecution of the Jews no further. Since then, nevertheless, other historians have extended the exploration, and on the basis of a much wider selection of sources than had been available to me in the 1970s and early 1980s. The most notable, among a growing array of studies on this theme, have been David Bankier's wide-ranging analysis, a recently published book by Peter Longerich, and the magnificent edition of all known police reports on popular opinion and the 'Jewish Question' by Otto Dov Kulka and Eberhard Jäckel.[10] Relevant, too, if not directly based upon the opinion reports, is the detailed study of Nazi wartime propaganda about the Jews by Jeffrey Herf.[11] I need briefly to comment here on the ways in which my own views, compiled so long ago and represented in the unrevised essays in this volume, still stand up or have been totally supplanted by later research.

Bankier spoke of 'moral insensibility to the Jews' fate' by the German population during the deportations and mass murder, of which there was widespread knowledge, adding that 'many deliberately sought refuge from the consciousness of genocide' (which implied responsibility). He accepted that 'the public did not assign antisemitism the same importance as the Nazis did' but that preexisting, deep-seated anti-Jewish feeling meant that there was widespread support for the aim of ridding Germany of Jews, even when methods, and particularly open violence, were criticised.[12] In these judgements I found nothing with which I could not concur.

Longerich moved the debate on by arguing that the regime's reports on reactions to anti-Jewish policy represented not authentic but rather 'artificially produced' 'official' public opinion, and that their role was 'to document that the population, in its daily behaviour, expressed its approval for regime policy'. As such, opinion was largely reported only in phases of intense antisemitic propaganda accompanying anti-Jewish measures, and not in the relatively quiet intervening periods. In this approach, silence in the reports cannot be taken to mirror the indifference of the population. Rather, it reflected the fact that the propaganda machine itself had little interest in certain phases of stressing the anti-Jewish theme and thus equally little interest in trying to monitor responses. Longerich focused, therefore, less on the reports as indicators of opinion than on the efforts of propaganda to shape it — efforts which, he admitted, were only a partial success. A consequence of this focus on the monitoring of steered (and therefore distorted) opinion is, he suggested, that it becomes pointless to try to establish the existence of a 'true' popular opinion. The regime's interest, he argued, was to implicate the population, whose awareness of atrocities on a huge scale was extensive, into complicity in the mass murder, something it did by making the 'Final Solution' a sort of open secret. As the fortunes of war turned sharply against Germany, this changed and the regime endeavoured to suppress discussion of the murder of the Jews. Fearful of 'Jewish revenge', the population was now less than ever ready to concern itself with details of genocide and increasingly tended to suppress what knowledge it had. He concluded that 'the most simple and dominant attitude' by this time amounted to openly apparent 'indifference and passivity towards the "Jewish Question"', which was not to be mistaken for disinterest, but rather reflected demonstrative ignorance as a retreat from responsibility.[13]

There is much in this analysis that rings true. And yet much still rests upon inference and surmise rather than empirically demonstrated fact. Anyone familiar with the entire gamut of opinion reports, not just on the 'Jewish Question', and coming from simple local police as well as more sophisticated central agencies of the regime, would have reservations about claims that the views recorded were merely manufactured and 'artificial', that there was no 'authentic' sphere of opinion, however difficult to recapture, beyond the product of propaganda. If that were so, it is difficult to know why the reports so readily recorded dissenting views — in contrast to the reports from propaganda leaders to Goebbels' ministry, where conformity was very much 'encouraged' and negative reportage criticised — and why the regime leadership halted the central SD digests in 1944. The fact that from Stalingrad onwards dissenting views also increasingly included criticism of Hitler himself, if of course carefully and often obliquely expressed, also speaks in favour of an 'authentic' opinion beneath the propaganda construct and reported approval of government policy. There remains in Longerich's analysis the problem of interpreting the silences of the reports on attitudes towards the Jews. He sees these as mirroring simply the relative lack of propaganda activity, not relative lack of interest in the genocide until the last phase of the Third Reich when it amounted to a self-protective 'cultivated' lack of interest. He may be right. But how can he (or we) be sure? The mentalities behind opinions left unsaid are anybody's guess. Arguments from silence remain open to objections whichever way they fall.

In his detailed study of wartime propaganda on the 'Jewish Question', which consciously shifts the emphasis from what ordinary Germans thought to how the Nazis presented it to them, Jeffrey Herf offers what seems to me a sensible admonition to those wanting to draw conclusions about popular attitudes from such problematical sources as the SD reports. As regards German knowledge or thought about the Holocaust, and how ordinary people responded to the barrage of anti-Jewish agitation, he remarks that 'the beginning of wisdom in these matters is a certain restraint and much less certainty regarding what "ordinary Germans" made of Nazi propaganda'. I agree with this, and, were I writing on this topic today rather than thirty years ago, I would probably be more cautious and 'agnostic' than ever about generalised conclusions on opinion in the German population towards the fate of the Jews. I also concur with a further comment of Herf about the opinion reports: 'The most plausible reading of the evidence is that a fanatical, but no small, minority embedded in or hovering around the front organizations of the Nazi party' was fully persuaded by the radical propaganda of Jewish responsibility for the war, 'and that these fanatics were surrounded by a society in which milder forms of anti-Semitism had become commonplace'.[14] This matches fairly well with the rough and ready division I suggested in my own work between a sizeable minority of radical antisemites (though one, it is important to stress, backed by all the powerful organs of a ferociously repressive regime), an infinitesimally tiny minority disapproving of the persecution and prepared in some ways to support Jews, and a large proportion which was latently antisemitic but passively tolerant towards the ever more radical persecution.

The edition by Kulka and Jäckel differs from the above works in that it is a superb and comprehensive edition of Nazi reports on attitudes towards the Jews, but one containing no more than a textual introduction which refrains from analysis or interpretation. The editors nevertheless raise the question of 'indifference' as part of the major problem of interpreting the newly assembled sources, suggesting — perhaps optimistically — that 'the material now allows a more precise framework of questions and well-grounded answers'.[15] In an essay published before the completion of this remarkable edition, Kulka was bolder. Raising once more the differing weightings to be attached to the extensive silence in the reports on the 'Final Solution' and the depersonalisation of Jews, he contrasted the notion of 'general passivity' as 'the result of indifference, of not knowing or not wishing to know, or alternatively of a repression of such knowledge' with 'general passivity' as 'the expression of a broad consensus on the government's policy, a kind of tacit agreement that there was no need to take an active stand on the subject'. Extending his consideration to the statements approving of the regime's antisemitism in the postwar opinion surveys carried out in occupied Germany by the Americans, Kulka concludes: 'it is obvious that the interpretation that the German population was generally indifferent to the genocidal policy against the Jews does not pass the test of the confrontation with the additional sources. It is also plain enough that identification with the "Final Solution" was quite widespread among the public in the Third Reich'.[16]

I doubt myself whether the postwar surveys bear the strength of this interpretation. On the figures which Kulka provides from one of the surveys, 20 percent 'went along with Hitler on his treatment of the Jews', and a further 19 percent 'were generally in favor but felt that he had gone too far'.[17] Appalling though these findings are, they do little to address the 'indifference' issue. My own correspondence with Kulka has continued, and our nuanced disagreements continue. They do not seem to me to be very great. But nor are they ultimately resolvable. In the end, I am willing — as I have been throughout — to accept and acknowledge extensive and, probably down to the mid-war period, increasing approval of policies to remove Jews from Germany. But whether the passivity of the majority reflected moral indifference, bad conscience, suppression of uncomfortable knowledge, fear of the consequences, or tacit approval for what was being done seems to me, truth to tell, impossible to establish. I have the feeling, as I did already by the mid-eighties, that interpretations of the German population's stance on the 'Final Solution' cannot be taken any further. Sometimes historians simply have to accept that they cannot find the hard and fast answers they seek in the inadequate remnants of the past with which they have to deal. New work will, I fear, be susceptible to the likelihood of diminishing returns.

II

By the mid-eighties my own interests were, in any case, moving away from this problem. What had started to engage me over the previous few years was less the issue of how Germans had reacted to the 'Final Solution' than the question of how the regime that brought this about actually worked.

My interest in the structures of power in the Nazi state, and quite especially the place of Hitler within those structures, had gained particular impetus through my attendance in 1979, when I was still no more than a novice in research on the Third Reich, at a conference at Cumberland Lodge, in Windsor Great Park, just outside London. The conference gained a certain notoriety for its bitter disputes among leading German historians revolving around the terms — which began life at the conference and polarised debate on the character of the Nazi regime for years to come — of 'intentionalism' and 'structuralism' (or 'functionalism').

Somewhat nervously, I gave my first ever conference paper on my new field of study at the gathering. My paper, on 'The Führer Image and Political Integration: The Popular Conception of Hitler in Bavaria during the Third Reich' (a foretaste of my *Hitler-Mythos,* to be published the following year), was well received, to my great relief. But my main fascination with the conference was in the apparently unbridgeable gulf in interpretations about the structures of power in the Nazi state among the assembled leading German historians. The insistence on the one hand on Hitler's complete domination of all that mattered, the equal insistence on the other of a 'polycratic' system of rule which functioned chaotically and in good measure independently of Hitler's sporadic interventions, intrigued me. And when, plucking up courage, I tentatively suggested, as a newcomer and outsider, that there were fairly obvious ways of bridging the gap between the interpretations, I was gently and humorously put down by one of the luminaries present, who informed me that I was a '*Doppelgänger*' who wanted it both ways. Nevertheless, the stimulation of the conference prompted me to try to look more closely at the historiographical developments that had led to this, to my mind, strange polarisation of views which provoked unusually vehement and polemical assertions.

This formed the background to the short book on which I started work in the early eighties. The first edition of *The Nazi Dictatorship: Problems and Perspectives of Interpretation* appeared in 1985 with, at its heart, three chapters directly devoted to the role of Hitler in the power structures of the Third Reich, covering domestic affairs, the persecution of the Jews, and foreign policy. The contributions included in Part III of this volume (Chapters 10–12) comprise three sections of the revised fourth edition of this work, published in 2000.

It is worth underlining the point here that when the first edition had come out fifteen years earlier, detailed empirical research on what had come to be called 'the Holocaust' was only just beginning. Remarkably, the published contributions to the Cumberland Lodge Conference in 1979 on the Nazi state did not include a single paper on the Holocaust.[18] Nor, to my recollection, did the 'Final Solution', or the persecution of the Jews more generally, figure centrally in any of the discussions during the conference. This had not struck me at the time. The main focus of attention then had been on the internal structure of the regime during the 1930s, rather than on the period of war and genocide. Broszat's 'structuralist' account of the 'genesis of the "Final Solution"', prompted by David Irving's apologist claims in *Hitler's War*, had, it is true, appeared in 1977, followed by Christopher Browning's impressive rejoinder.[19] But these essays marked the very beginning of serious attempts to uncover the complex stages of emergence of the 'Final Solution'. Surprising as it sounds today, the symposium staged by Eberhard Jäckel at Stuttgart in 1984, at which leading historians advanced their differing interpretations of the complicated evidence for the decision-making process leading to the 'Final Solution', was the first time an academic conference in Germany had ever been devoted to the persecution of the Jews.

During the 1980s and 1990s, however, immense advances were made in this field, in Germany as well as outside. Part III tries to do justice to the quality of much of this work, as well as to the legitimate variants in interpretation which have emerged. Anyone troubling to compare the four editions of *The Nazi Dictatorship* will be able to follow there not just the burgeoning research but also the ways in which I revised my own interpretation in the light of the new findings as they arose. Chapter 10, 'Hitler and the Holocaust', encapsulates the picture as I saw it when I was preparing the fourth edition. Were I to refine the chapter now for a fifth edition (which I have declined to do), then I would have to incorporate still further important editions to the historiography (touched upon here in Chapter 4).

The belated, but then intensive, focus on the Holocaust in German historiography played its part in the extraordinary eruption of the 'Historians' Dispute' (*Historikerstreit*) in 1986, in which many of Germany's leading historians openly (and heatedly) debated the singularity of the Holocaust in the pages of leading newspapers. Subsumed in this dispute (which cast more heat than light and was political rather than actually historical in content) was a related but separable issue, and one which was to my mind more interesting from a scholarly perspective. This was the debate about whether the time had arrived to treat the Nazi era as a 'normal' part of history, and by 'normal' historical methods, much as one would, for example, analyse, say, the French Revolution or the Reformation. This meant with cool rationality, free from emotion. It also meant ending the way the Third Reich was almost exclusively seen as a resort for lessons of political morality and properly integrating it into German history to promote better understanding and a sharpened historical consciousness in postwar democratic German society. And, thirdly, it meant looking to those parts of National Socialism which might be detachable from the criminal side of the regime and could be incorporated, even positively, in continuities stretching beyond the end of the Third Reich.

These bold suggestions arose from what became a famous (or notorious) 'plea for the historicisation of National Socialism' advanced by Martin Broszat in 1985.[20] I included an evaluation of the 'historicisation' debate (which involved the leading Israeli historians Saul Friedländer, Otto Dov Kulka, and Dan Diner) in the second edition of my *Nazi Dictatorship,* presented here as Chapter 11.

Behind the debate lay the increasing attention paid over the previous decade in German work on the Third Reich to '*Alltagsgeschichte*' ('the history of everyday life') — the attempt to explore the social history of the Nazi era from below, from its grass roots. The Bavaria Project had played a major part in stimulating the new avenues of 'history from below' that took off in Germany like a bush fire by the late seventies. Some aspects of this history of daily life seemed to depict, even under conditions of the Nazi dictatorship, a 'normality' distinct from the criminal characteristics of the regime — repression, persecution, terror, concentration camps, war — that had dominated in the historiography. But could these be written about as 'normal' history, ignoring their setting in a criminal regime and the context of criminality within which the 'normality' appeared to exist? Was Auschwitz unconnected with 'normal life' in the Third Reich? This was ultimately the key issue.

My own assessment of the issue at the time can be read here in Chapter 11. In retrospect, I think it is plain that Broszat's critics had the better of the debate. It should probably also be added that Broszat's 'plea' had been rather hurriedly written and was somewhat ill-conceived. It was certainly convoluted, and in some senses misleading in expression. Its intention was more limited than it appeared to be. What Broszat was trying to do was to locate the Nazi era in the continuities that led on beyond 1945 and into the Federal Republic (something which was engaging his attention in his scholarly work at the time) and to emphasise the need to build genuine *historical* understanding rather than mere moral condemnation into the (West) German political consciousness. But his 'plea' had the unfortunate effect of seeming to dislocate the daily experience of Nazism from the regime's crimes.

Looking back on it twenty years later, the debate, for all its seriousness at the time, seems to have little methodological or programmatic importance. It reflected a particular juncture in historiography, and perhaps also a generational response from a historian who had himself experienced the Hitler era as a young man and presumably seen facets of daily life which had appeared 'normal' and not part of the criminality at the heart of Nazism. As far as I can see, the methodological issues at stake in the debate have had no real influence on the subsequent writing of the history of the Nazi era.

A striking feature, in fact, even of '*Alltagsgeschichte*', as time went on, was how much, not how little, it came to embrace the criminality of the regime — how much the criminality left its mark on so many seemingly 'normal' aspects of life. The Bavaria Project itself, beginning by researching multifaceted manifestations of daily opposition, increasingly uncovered complicity and collaboration. And this turned out to be a precursor of the way some of the best products of '*Alltagsgeschichte*' took shape.[21] In the meantime, we have also seen the publication of a number of general histories of the Third Reich which have had no difficulty in combining social history 'from below' with the full weight accorded to the destructive, criminal, and genocidal essence of the Hitler regime.[22] In practice, therefore, the acute division of interpretations which the debate over 'historicisation' appeared to signify has not materialised. Nor, it could be added, has a split between German and Jewish interpretations of the Third Reich developed, despite the implication at the time that this was an unavoidable outcome of separate and conflicting memories.

Soon, in any case, the preoccupations of the *Historikerstreit* and the concerns about 'historicisation' of National Socialism were swept away by the dramatic events, unforeseen I think by any of the historians taken up in the disputes, that saw the fall of the Berlin Wall, the reunification of Germany, and the collapse of the Soviet bloc. Within a short time, new perspectives on the Nazi past began to emerge. Chapter 12 amounts to my attempt to assess them, at a time when the trends were still fresh.

Here, too, what I wrote then has to be seen as a *pièce d'occasion* — reflections at a specific juncture which, looking back, have a transitory air to them. Since reunification, Germany has become a 'normal' European nation-state more smoothly than perhaps anyone imagined, even if one labouring more than any other under the strain of its own recent past (that of a second German dictatorship, the German Democratic Republic, as well as of the Nazi regime) and still facing difficulties in the full integration of the 'new *Länder*'. The potential dangers of attempts to instil a sense of national identity which either blended out the Nazi past or, even worse, emphasised 'positive' aspects of that past while playing down its crimes against humanity have simply evaporated, even if neo-Nazism (like new forms of fascism elsewhere in Europe) is something not to be viewed with complacency or equanimity.

One of these 'positive' aspects could again be linked to the 'plea for the historicisation' of Nazism: the notion that Hitler's dictatorship could chiefly and best be viewed as an attempt, admittedly brutal, to force through a modernisation of Germany which came fully to fruition in the Federal Republic. It seemed a very German perspective. I recall attending a conference in Berlin in 1990 where the question of Nazism as an agency of modernisation — consciously or unwittingly a sort of 'developmental dictatorship' — was discussed.

A Jewish colleague, who had fled from Nazism in the 1930s, left partway through the discussions. He told me later, with no small amount of irony, that it had never occurred to him then, as he suffered the torment of Hitler's hordes, that what Nazism was really about was the modernisation of Germany. It was a telling point. Even leaving aside any apologetic intent, the tendency implicit in trying to focus upon Nazism's presumed 'modernising' credentials was to mistake the accidentals of the phenomenon for its essence. It can, however, be immediately added that this type of approach, too, had a short shelf life. It turned out to be a passing strand of historical writing, which in practice left little mark on historiography.

A third strand which I highlighted will certainly have greater longevity. This is the increased readiness to compare National Socialism with other forms of terroristic and inhumane regimes, most notably with Stalinism. But while crude nonscholarly statements that 'Stalin had more people killed and was worse than Hitler' are almost certainly more commonplace, not just in Germany, than they used to be, my impression is that inside the 'academy' the heyday of the revitalised 'totalitarianism' theorem which often made for simplistic comparisons has passed. Instead, some sophisticated, but not value-loaded, empirical analysis has been undertaken which, while accepting some shared ground in the Stalinist and Nazi systems, highlights the differences rather than the similarities.[23] Much the same could be said of a good deal of excellent work on the German Democratic Republic which easily avoids the trap of bracketing the regimes, and the extent of their crimes, through the crude label of 'totalitarianism'.[24] Banal truism that it might be, comparison of regimes is necessary to establish singularity. And the same applies to the need to specify the singularity of the Holocaust by placing it within a framework of comparative genocide.[25]

All in all, looking back on the period since German reunification, most of the worries that I voiced about trends in historiography, and that arose during the heated disputes of the mid-1980s, have dissipated. Instead, the Holocaust and attendant crimes of the Nazi regime have loomed ever larger both in historical writing and in popular consciousness — so much so, indeed, that the Holocaust can now plainly be seen (something not so plainly apparent in the 1970s or even 1980s) as a defining episode of the twentieth century. Among the various reasons for this development is the opening of the archives of the former Soviet bloc which has prompted a much sharper focus than had ever been possible during the Cold War on Nazi crimes in eastern Europe — the epicentre of the horror. It was in a climate already altered by the revelations emerging from access to new material that the emphasis in historiography, belatedly, turned away from purely 'functional' or materialist explanations and started to lay the emphasis squarely upon race ideology as a central driving force of Nazism's attempt to build a new Germany and a new Europe, one purged of its racial enemies.

The sensational impact, in Germany above all, of Daniel Goldhagen's book *Hitler's Willing Executioners*, on its publication in 1996, has partly to be explained by this new atmosphere, of which it was both a reflection and an intensification.[26] In my critical remarks about Goldhagen's book, reprinted below in Chapter 12, I suggested that it would occupy only a limited place in future historiography. Looking back, I think that this is technically correct but underplays the spur that Goldhagen's flawed book gave to new research, not least by German scholars, on antisemitism. Of course, this remains a necessary but insufficient cause of the Holocaust, but much is now being done to understand in more detailed fashion than earlier the penetration of parts of German society by lethal antisemitism even before Hitler began his meteoric climb to power. A comprehensive social history of antisemitism in Germany during the Weimar Republic — during, that is, the period of a liberal democracy, when the seeds of the later genocide were sewn, were fertilised, and started to germinate — has yet to be written. But a beginning has been made.[27]

III

In the later 1980s, a new phase in my own work began. The historiographical exploration I had undertaken earlier in the decade, stimulated by my wish to develop a greater understanding of the workings of the Nazi dictatorship, now started to lead me in a direction which I would earlier not have thought possible.

I had accepted, I think in 1986 or 1987, an invitation to contribute a short analysis of Hitler's power to a series of publications in England, then in its initiatory phase, called 'profiles in power', aimed primarily at a student readership and framed around an examination of how major political leaders in different countries and in different historical epochs had exercised power. I had never worked directly on Hitler, but the idea appealed to me, not in terms of writing a biography, but as a chance to situate the German dictator within the power structures of the Nazi state, and, methodologically, to deploy Max Weber's concept of 'charismatic domination'. This had for long seemed to me a fruitful way of looking at the Third Reich, but I had so far used the concept only in conjunction with the 'Hitler Myth', not Hitler himself.

Soon afterwards an even more remarkable development (given my trajectory as, in essence, a historian of German society in the Third Reich) occurred: I agreed to write a full-scale new biography of Hitler. I had initially, in fact, declined the publisher's request to undertake this. I was not greatly taken with biography as a genre and thought that a biography of Hitler could not avoid the pitfalls (all of which I had until then been trying to avoid) of an unduly personalistic interpretation of complex developments in the Third Reich. In any case, I was more than aware that Alan Bullock, then, a generation later, Joachim Fest, had written justly praised biographies of Hitler (leaving aside a myriad of lesser biographies) and felt that there was probably not a lot more to be said.[28] The publisher (Penguin, in London) accepted my decision but asked to be informed should I change my mind.

I did. I reread both Bullock and Fest and decided that, after all, they had far from said the last word. On the persecution, then murder, of the Jews and on the war itself—both completely inextricable from the history of Nazism—I was astonished to see how little Bullock and Fest had said. The essence of Hitler's 'vision' and how it had become translated into practical policy had not been to my mind adequately examined. Vital phases in the radicalisation of anti-Jewish policy, in the build-up to the Nuremberg Laws in 1935, preceding and immediately following the '*Reichskristallnacht*' pogroms in 1938, and, not least, in the emergence of the 'Final Solution' itself, had received surprisingly little detailed treatment. In my own biography, by contrast, as it took shape, antisemitism (not just of Hitler himself), the course of anti-Jewish policy (in which initiatives often came from others), and then the 'twisted' path to the 'Final Solution' ran as a crucial 'red thread'.[29]

The gestation period, even before I began work on the biography in earnest, was a lengthy one. But it was essential for the ripening of my ideas on how to undertake it. One preliminary piece of work emerged from research which I carried out in Polish archives in 1989. I learnt a good deal from my immersion in the files of Arthur Greiser, the horrendous *Gauleiter* of the Wartheland, later expanding my sources in a stay in Ludwigsburg to work in the war crimes archive there (where at lunch each day Daniel Goldhagen, Philippe Burrin, and I would discuss our latest research findings).

My interest was in trying to understand as thoroughly as possible the way in which the establishment of the first systematic killing installation of what became the 'Final Solution', at Chelmno in the Warthegau, had come about. I was not persuaded by arguments, first advanced by Broszat, that the 'Final Solution' had arisen out of a series of unplanned initiatives by regional or local Nazi leaders in the eastern territories, only subsequently gaining sanction and becoming centrally coordinated in a genocidal programme. On the other hand, I had always found the straightforward 'Hitler-centric' line of much of the literature unconvincing. The article (Chapter 3 in this volume) was my attempt to investigate this issue in a specific, regional case study. The Warthegau was a pivotal area, given the Nazi attempts to 'germanise' the province with all haste, which involved the brutal deportation of the unwanted sections of the population, first and foremost Jews, but also huge numbers of non-Jewish Poles. What I tried to show was that initiatives for the moves to genocide there were indeed taken by the regional leadership. However, Greiser and the region's security police leaders, most notably the police chief of the region, Wilhelm Koppe, were taking their initiatives in the full knowledge, and with the full approval, of their bosses in Berlin. And, though his presence was shadowy, Hitler, it seemed clear, was the ultimate instance in the authorisation of genocide in the province.

A second preliminary to the writing of my Hitler biography (included here as Chapter 2) arose from an invitation to speak at the Institut für Zeitgeschichte in Munich in 1992 at the publication launch of the first three volumes of what would become an indispensable fourteen volumes of Hitler's speeches, writings, and ordinances between the refoundation of the Nazi Party in February 1925 and his takeover of power eight years later.[30] I had already some years earlier reviewed the superb edition of Hitler's early speeches and writings assembled by Eberhard Jäckel with the assistance of Axel Kuhn.[31] I now took the opportunity systematically to review the changing content of Hitler's public presentations between 1925 and 1928, while the Nazi Party floundered in the political doldrums but while Hitler was largely still speaking to the converted, before the surge in popularity demanded an alteration in propaganda methods. What this investigation clearly showed, to my mind, was that Hitler was far more than the propagandist and loud-mouthed beer hall bigot of so much dismissive portrayal. There *was*, however repulsive, a consistent mind at work — something much earlier accepted by Eberhard Jäckel and, more intuitively before him, also by Hugh Trevor-Roper.[32] Moreover, there seemed no need to choose between the two versions — Hitler as ideologue or Hitler as propagandist. He was both. This — and his often underrated skill in political manoeuvring — was his danger. He was an ideological fanatic who did not retreat into cranky but alienating obsessions, but knew how to mobilise politically. It was a fatal mix.

By now, thanks to a period of research leave spent at the incomparable Wissenschaftskolleg in Berlin in 1989–90, where I could follow with my own eyes the astonishing events of that extraordinary year, I had been able to complete my short profile of Hitler's power.[33] In this brief study I developed my ideas of 'charismatic domination' as the basis of Hitler's leadership position. I also introduced a related concept as an integral part of my analysis. This was taken from the superb translated documentary collection by Jeremy Noakes (with assistance in the first of the four volumes from Geoffrey Pridham), which I had regularly used with my students in England. I was very struck with a document in the second volume citing a routine speech by a Nazi functionary in 1934, who had declared that 'it is the duty of everybody to try to work towards the Führer along the lines he would wish'.[34] I had not at this point started my biography, but I now knew what the explanatory leitmotiv would be.

I developed the notion further in a paper prepared for a conference at Philadelphia in 1991. This paper, reproduced in this book as Chapter 1, was another important preparatory step towards undertaking the biography. The theme of the conference was a comparison between Germany and Russia (then the Soviet Union) in the first half of the twentieth century.[35] So, in the first part of my paper, I compared the nature of leadership in the Hitler and Stalin dictatorships before going on to develop my thesis that 'charismatic domination' formed the key to the exceptionality of Hitler's position. I saw the radical dynamic of the regime rooted in Hitler's embodiment of a utopian vision of national redemption through racial purification within Germany as the platform for imperial conquest through racial extirpation. The final section of the paper then introduced the related concept of 'working towards the Führer' to try to show how the radical dynamic worked, how the drive to put into practice the vision symbolised by Hitler operated. This was in essence a preview of the interpretative thrust of my two-volume biography of Hitler, written in the second half of the 1990s.

'Working towards the Führer' has, then, as I see it, particular relevance to the radicalisation of policy in the 'Jewish Question'. I had emphasised this in the relevant parts of my biography. Some time after its completion, I developed the analysis in an essay on Hitler's role in the 'Final Solution', initially commissioned as a contribution to a multi-volume Italian compilation, *Storia della Shoah,* then printed in its original English form in *Yad Vashem Studies* and appearing in this work as Chapter 4.[36]

The remit of the commission included a survey of existing historiographical interpretations. This formed the first part of the essay (updating, therefore, to some extent the historiographical analysis in Chapter 10 below). The second part then went on to unfold my understanding of the 'dialectic of radicalisation' in Nazi anti-Jewish policy before the war. Hitler himself later acknowledged that during the earlier part of his rule he had been forced (for tactical, not principled reasons, of course) to remain 'inactive' in the 'Jewish Question'.[37] Yet the radicalisation had continued unabated. I tried to explain how this could happen. This dialectic, as I depicted it, had its driving force in the vision of national salvation which Hitler represented—a distant utopian goal which could be attained only by the 'cleansing' to be brought about through the 'removal' of the Jewish archenemy. What 'removal' meant, of course, was open to different interpretations. I suggested that the dialectic ran along the following lines: Hitler would signal a 'green light' to party radicals to step up measures against Jews; 'action' would inevitably build from below, putting pressure on the regime to sanction it, and ultimately demanding Hitler's intervention; this would 'legitimate' the radical action before starting the process once more, but at a higher level of discrimination and persecution.

I then went on to illustrate how Hitler operated in the genesis of the 'Final Solution'. A key seemed to me (as it had done when I was writing the biography) to be found in the use of his infamous 'prophecy', first announced to the Reichstag in 1939, that in the event of another war the Jews would be destroyed. As the 'Final Solution' was being ushered in, Hitler used this 'prophecy' on several telling occasions to signal the need for radical action by his underlings. They, in turn, understood the 'prophecy' to indicate the 'wish of the Führer' without any need for explicit orders. The 'prophecy' had an additional function: to spread to the general public an awareness, while avoiding detailed or explicit information, that the destruction of the Jews was inexorably taking place. In this way, the 'prophecy' became a key metaphor for the 'Final Solution' and, functionally, served to indicate how in this crucial area the presumed 'wish of the Führer' activated this most terrible of the regime's crimes.

IV

The final two essays in this collection (Chapters 13 and 14) are more reflective pieces which try to come to grips with the question of the essential singularity of Nazism.

Whether and, if so, in what ways the Third Reich could be seen as an 'exceptional' or 'unique' system of rule was an issue which had always implicitly, and sometimes explicitly, raised itself in the historiography. Often, such a question was dealt with through models of comparative fascism or totalitarianism (both of them concepts with serious definitional problems). An invitation to deliver a Trevelyan Lecture at Cambridge in 2002, in which I was asked to survey relevant historiography, gave me the opportunity to tackle the question head-on.

After a brief overview of how the problem had been treated in some influential strands of historiography, I returned to the nature of Hitler's 'charismatic authority', which had been a constant theme of my work on the Third Reich since I had worked on the 'Hitler Myth' back in the 1970s. I briefly compared the character of the Führer cult in Germany with the leadership cults in Italy, the Soviet Union, and Spain to underline the peculiar strength of Hitler's position. I emphasised the way in which he could embody in his public image important pseudo-religious strains of German political culture which had pre-dated the First World War but had through war and defeat received an enormous boost. This embodiment in Hitler of a dynamic, revolutionary thrust, unachievable without war and a colossal gamble for world power and demanding national salvation through racial 'purification' — a chiliastic goal that became institutionalised in every facet of political organisation in the Third Reich — distinguishes the Third Reich from every other known political dictatorship, however terrible the specific forms of gross inhumanity in each of these was.

The final essay in this volume widens the perspective far beyond Germans and Jews. It also attempts to link an evaluation of the past with a few reflections about the future from the vantage point of the beginning of the twenty-first century. The piece began life as a talk in German delivered at a specific occasion — a gathering on the edge of the beautiful Lake Starnberg in Bavaria in late 2000 to celebrate Hans Mommsen's seventieth birthday. For me, the timing was not propitious. I was so frequently away from home around then giving lectures related to my Hitler books that I was able to prepare my talk only in airport lounges and on planes. A couple of years later, I decided to work up the paper somewhat more thoroughly in English. This is the version that was eventually published in *Contemporary European History* in 2005, and is reprinted here.

I asked in the essay what, beyond advances in the technology of killing, had spawned such a colossal expansion of mass political violence in the twentieth century; what propelled societies towards violence or restrained them from perpetrating it; and, finally, what was intrinsically 'modern' about modern mass violence. I found answers in the combination of Janus-faced popular sovereignty (used to justify, in different conditions, both liberal democratisation and populistic attacks on democracy coupled with the demonisation of minorities) with the potential for bureaucratic planning and technological advances (both again holding positive and negative potential). I parted company, however, from the full implications of Zygmunt Bauman's influential thesis locating the propensity to genocide (and the Holocaust in particular) in the highly developed bureaucratic rationality of the modern state machine.[38] The lack of sophistication in planning and implementation but magnitude and speed of the mass killing in the Rwanda genocide, carried out in the main with little more than guns and machetes, should alone give pause for thought about such an argument. Rather, I suggested, the decisive factor was the nature of a new kind of ideology, which, whatever its varied form and expression, was absolutist in its total claim to determine who should have the right to inhabit the earth in the building of a mooted coming utopia. To be a Jew under Hitler, a Kulak under Stalin, or an intellectual under Pol Pot was, as I put it, tantamount to a death sentence. The Nazi state, however, produced the most absolutist form of ideology of all in that the biological exclusion of Jews was more lethally uncompromising than the often brutally arbitrary socially deterministic exclusivism of Stalinism or Pol Pot. And this most extreme manifestation of absolutist ideology thoroughly permeated the most advanced state machinery and exploited the most developed technology in Europe. The 'Final Solution' arose from this unholy combination.

The essay ended with a rather gloomy look into the crystal ball. Historians are, of course, no better than anyone else when it comes to dealing with the future rather than the past. How things will turn out is impossible to foretell. At least, a replication of the conditions which produced the Holocaust is, mercifully, nowhere in sight. The problems are now very different to those which gave rise to Hitler and genocidal antisemitism. Even so, it is difficult to view the future with great optimism. The threat from an international order in disarray, most obviously in the Middle East, is palpable. And humankind's capacity to combine new forms of ideological demonisation with bureaucratic refinement and unparalleled technological killing power is far from eradicated. So far, with great effort, the combination, which would be truly dangerous if marshalled by a powerful state entity, has been held in check. Will it continue to be?

Notes

1. *Der Hitler-Mythos. Volksmeinung und Propaganda im Dritten Reich,* Stuttgart, 1980.

2. 'Antisemitismus und Volksmeinung. Reaktionen auf die Judenverfolgung', in Martin Broszat and Elke Fröhlich (eds.), *Bayern in der NS-Zeit,* vol. 2: Herrschaft und Gesellschaft im Konflikt, Munich/Vienna, 1979, pp. 281–348.

3. *The 'Hitler Myth': Image and Reality in the Third Reich,* Oxford, 1987. Chapter 9 (pp. 229–52) was titled 'Hitler's Popular Image and the "Jewish Question"'. Apart from this added chapter, and an introduction, eliminated from the initial German edition, which framed my enquiry around Max Weber's concept of 'charismatic domination', this version of my book widened the initial Bavarian emphasis to include further material from other parts of Germany. A German translation of this revised edition was published under the title *Der Hitler-Mythos. Führerkult und Volksmeinung,* Stuttgart, 1999.

4. *Popular Opinion and Political Dissent in the Third Reich. Bavaria, 1933–1945,* Oxford, 1983, p. 277.

5. Michael Müller-Claudius, *Der Antisemitismus und das deutsche Verhängnis,* Frankfurt am Main, 1948, pp. 162–75 (who had referred to 'static' and 'dynamic' hatred).

6. Marlis Steinert, *Hitlers Krieg und die Deutschen,* Düsseldorf/Vienna, 1970, pp. 236–63.

7. Otto Dov Kulka, ' "Public Opinion" in National Socialist Germany and the "Jewish Question" ', *Zion,* 40 (1975), pp. 186–290. Only the English abstract and the German documentation were accessible to me. The translation concerned the analysis, published in Hebrew.

8. Otto Dov Kulka and Aron Rodrigue, 'The German Population and the Jews in the Third Reich', *Yad Vashem Studies,* 16 (1984), pp. 421–35.

9. Quotations from Kulka and Rodrigue, pp. 430–5.

10. David Bankier, *The Germans and the Final Solution. Public Opinion under Nazism,* Oxford, 1992; Peter Longerich, *"Davon haben wir nichts gewußt!". Die Deutschen und die Judenverfolgung 1933–1945,* Munich, 2006; Otto Dov Kulka and Eberhard Jäckel (eds.), *Die Juden in den geheimen NS-Stimmungsberichten 1933–1945,* Düsseldorf, 2004 (English translation forthcoming).

11. Jeffrey Herf, *The Jewish Enemy: Nazi Propaganda during World War II and the Holocaust,* Cambridge, Mass., 2006.

12. Bankier, quotations pp. 155–6.

13. Longerich, pp. 313–28, quoted phrases, p. 317.

14. Herf, pp. 275–7, quotation p. 277.

15. Kulka and Jäckel, p. 9.

16. Otto Dov Kulka, 'The German Population and the Jews: State of Research and New Perspectives', in David Bankier (ed.), *Probing the Depths of German Antisemitism: German Society and the Persecution of the Jews, 1933–1941,* New York/Oxford/Jerusalem, 2000, pp. 271–81, quotations, pp. 277, 280.

17. Quoted in Kulka, 'The German Population', p. 279.

18. Gerhard Hirschfeld and Lothar Kettenacker (eds.), *Der "Führerstaat": Mythos und Realität. Studien zur Struktur und Politik des Dritten Reiches,* Stuttgart, 1981. For the slow development of research on the Holocaust, see Otto Dov Kulka, 'Major Trends and Tendencies of German Historiography on National Socialism and the "Jewish Question" (1924–1984)', *Yearbook of the Leo Baeck Institute,* 30 (1985), pp. 215–42.

19. Martin Broszat, 'Hitler und die Genesis der "Endlösung". Aus Anlaß der Thesen von David Irving', *Vierteljahrshefte für Zeitgeschichte,* 25 (1977), pp. 739–75 (Engl., 'Hitler and the Genesis of the "Final Solution" ', *Yad Vashem Studies,* 13 [1979]); Christopher Browning, 'Zur Genesis der "Endlösung". Eine Antwort auf Martin Broszat', *Vierteljahrshefte für Zeitgeschichte,* 29 (1981), pp. 97–109 (Engl., 'A Reply to Martin Broszat regarding the Origins of the Final Solution', *Simon Wiesenthal Center Annual,* 1 [1984], pp. 113–32); David Irving, *Hitler's War,* London, 1977.

20. Martin Broszat, 'Plädoyer für eine Historisierung des Nationalsozialismus', *Merkur,* 39 (1985), pp. 373–85.

21. Perhaps, though it does not in detail deal with the persecution of the Jews, the brilliant book of Detlev Peukert, *Volksgenossen und Gemeinschaftsfremde. Anpassung, Ausmerze und Aufbegehren unter dem Nationalsozialismus,* Cologne, 1982, could be singled out in this regard.

22. Examples are Hans-Ulrich Thamer, *Verführung und Gewalt. Deutschland 1933–1945,* Berlin, 1986; Jost Dülffer, *Deutsche Geschichte 1933–1945. Führerglaube und*

Vernichtungskrieg, Stuttgart, 1992; Ludolf Herbst, *Das nationalsozialistische Deutschland 1933–1945,* Frankfurt am Main, 1996; Michael Burleigh, *The Third Reich: A New History,* London, 2000; and Richard Evans, *The Third Reich in Power,* London, 2005 (the second of a three-volume general history, covering the years 1933–9. The third volume, dealing with the war years, is in preparation).

23. See, for example, the excellent comparative study by Richard Overy, *The Dictators: Hitler's Germany, Stalin's Russia,* London, 2004.

24. In English, the work of Mary Fulbrook might be singled out, especially her *Anatomy of a Dictatorship: Inside the GDR, 1949–1989,* Oxford, 1995; and *The People's State: East German Society from Hitler to Honecker,* New Haven/London, 2005.

25. An impressive work in this regard, in my view, is Michael Mann, *The Dark Side of Democracy: Explaining Ethnic Cleansing,* Cambridge, 2005.

26. Daniel Jonah Goldhagen, *Hitler's Willing Executioners,* New York, 1996.

27. See, for example, Dirk Walter, *Antisemitische Kriminalität und Gewalt. Judenfeindschaft in der Weimarer Republik,* Bonn, 1999; Michael Wildt, ' "Der muß hinaus! Der muß hinaus!" Antisemitismus in deutschen Nord- und Ostseebädern 1920–1935, *Mittelweg 36,* 10 (2001), pp. 3–25; Michael Wildt, ' "Wir wollen in unserer Stadt keine Juden sehen." Antisemitismus und Volksgemeinschaft in der deutschen Provinz', *Mittelweg 36,* 13 (2004), pp. 84–102 (and especially, *Volksgemeinschaft unf Selbstermächtigung. Gewalt gegen Juden in der deutschen Provinz 1919 bis 1939,* Hamburg, 2007).

28. Alan Bullock, *Hitler: A Study in Tyranny,* London, 1952 (revised ed., Harmondsworth, 1962); Joachim Fest, *Hitler. Eine Biographie,* Frankurt am Main/Berlin/Vienna, 1973.

29. Ian Kershaw, *Hitler, 1889–1936: Hubris,* London, 1998; *Hitler, 1936–1945: Nemesis,* London, 2000. The notion of a 'twisted road' to the 'Final Solution' was coined by Karl Schleunes, *The Twisted Road to Auschwitz: Nazi Policy Toward German Jews, 1933–1939,* Urbana/Chicago/London, 1970.

30. *Hitler. Reden, Schriften, Anordnungen: Februar 1925 bis Januar 1933,* ed. Institut für Zeitgeschichte, 5 vols. in 14 parts, Munich, 1992–8.

31. *Hitler. Sämtliche Aufzeichnungen 1905–1924,* ed. Eberhard Jäckel with Axel Kuhn, Stuttgart, 1980.

32. Eberhard Jäckel, *Hitlers Weltanschauung. Entwurf einer Herrschaft,* Tübingen, 1969; H. R. Trevor-Roper, 'The Mind of Adolf Hitler', introduction to *Hitler's Table Talk 1941–1944,* London, 1953, pp. vii–xxxv.

33. Ian Kershaw, *Hitler: A Profile in Power,* London, 1991.

34. Jeremy Noakes and Geoffrey Pridham (eds.), *Nazism 1919–1945: A Documentary Reader,* 4 vols., Exeter, 1983–98. The quotation is taken from vol. 2, 'State, Economy and Society 1933–1939', document 144, p. 207. The original is in the Niedersächsisches Staatsarchiv, Oldenburg, Best. 131, Nr. 303, Fol. 131v.

35. A selection of papers from the conference were printed in Ian Kershaw and Moshe Lewin (eds.), *Stalinism and Nazism: Dictatorships in Comparison,* Cambridge, 1997.

36. *Storia della Shoah,* vol. 1, ed. Marina Cattaruzza et al., Turin, 2005.

37. *Adolf Hitler. Monologe im Führerhauptquartier 1941–1944,* ed. Werner Jochmann, Hamburg, 1980, p. 108.

38. Zygmunt Bauman, *Modernity and the Holocaust,* Cambridge, 1989.

PART I

Hitler and the Final Solution

'Working towards the Führer': Reflections on the Nature of the Hitler Dictatorship

The renewed emphasis, already visible in the mid-1980s, on the intertwined fates of the Soviet Union and Germany, especially in the Stalin and Hitler eras, has become greatly intensified in the wake of the upheavals in Eastern Europe. The sharpened focus on the atrocities of Stalinism has prompted attempts to relativise Nazi barbarism — seen as wicked, but on the whole less wicked, than that of Stalinism (and by implication of communism in general).[1] The brutal Stalinist modernising experiment is used to remove any normative links with humanising, civilising, emancipatory or democratising development from modernisation concepts and thereby to claim that Hitler's regime, too, was — and intentionally so — a 'modernising dictatorship'.[2] Implicit in all this is a reversion, despite the many refinements and criticisms of the concept since the 1960s, to essentially traditional views on 'totalitarianism' and to views of Stalin and Hitler as 'totalitarian dictators'.

There can be no principled objection to comparing the forms of dictatorship in Germany under Hitler and in the Soviet Union under Stalin and, however unedifying the subject matter, the nature and extent of their inhumanity.[3] The totalitarianism concept allows comparative analysis of a number of techniques and instruments of domination, and this, too, must be seen as legitimate in itself.[4] The underlying assumption that both regimes made *total* claims upon society, based upon a monopolistic set of ideological imperatives and resulting in unprecedented levels of repression and attempted indoctrination, manipulation and mobilisation — giving these regimes a dynamic missing from more conventional authoritarian regimes — again seems largely incontestable. But the fundamental problem with the term 'totalitarianism' — leaving aside its non-scholarly usage — is that it is a descriptive concept, not a theory, and has little or no explanatory power.[5] It presumes that Stalinism and Hitlerism were more like each other than different from each other. But the basis of comparison is a shallow one, largely confined to the apparatus of rule.[6]

My starting point in these reflections is the presumption that, despite superficial similarities in forms of domination, the two regimes were *in essence* more *unlike* than like each other. Though seeing greater potential in comparisons of Nazism with other fascist movements and systems rather than with the Soviet system, I would want to retain an emphasis upon the unique features of the Nazi dictatorship and the need to explain these, alongside those characteristics which could be seen as generic components of European fascism in the era following the First World War, through the specific dominant features of German political culture. (In this I admit to a currently rather unfashionable attachment to notions of a qualified German *Sonderweg*.)[7]

Sometimes, however, highlighting contrasts can be more valuable than comparing similarities. In what follows I would like to use what, on an imperfect grasp of some of the recent historiography on Stalinism, I understand to be significant features of Stalin's dictatorship to establish some important contrasts in the Hitler regime. This, I hope, will offer a basis for some reflections on what remains a central problem of interpretation of the Third Reich: what explains the gathering momentum of radicalisation, the dynamic of destruction in the Third Reich? Much of the answer to this question has, I would suggest at the outset, to do with the undermining and collapse of what one might call 'rational' structures of rule, a system of 'ordered' government and administration. But what caused the collapse and, not least, what was Hitler's own role in the process? These questions lie at the centre of my enquiry.

First, however, let me outline a number of what appear to me to be significant points of contrast between the Stalinist and Hitlerist regimes.

• Stalin arose from *within* a system of rule, as a leading exponent of it. He was, as Ronald Suny puts it, a committee man, chief oligarch, man of the machine;[8] and, in Moshe Lewin's phrase, 'bureaucracy's anti-Christ', the 'creature of his party',[9] who became despot by control of the power which lay at the heart of the party, in its secretariat. In a sense, it is tempting to see an analogy in the German context in the position of Bormann rather than

Hitler. Is it possible to imagine Stalin echoing Hitler's comment in 1941: 'I've totally lost sight of the organisations of the Party. When I find myself confronted by one or other of these achievements, I say to myself: "By God, how that has developed!" '?[10]

At any rate, a party leader and head of government less bureaucratically inclined, less a committee man or man of the machine, than Hitler is hard to imagine. Before 1933 he was uninvolved in and detached from the Nazi Movement's bureaucracy. After 1933, as head of government he scarcely put pen to paper himself other than to sign legislation put in front of his nose by Lammers. The Four-Year Plan Memorandum of 1936 is a unique example from the years 1933–45 of a major policy document composed by Hitler himself — written in frustration and fury at the stance adopted during the economic crisis of 1935–6 by Schacht and some sectors of business and industry. Strikingly, Hitler only gave copies of his memorandum to two persons, Göring and Blomberg (much later giving a third copy to Speer). The Economics Minister himself was not included in the short distribution list! Business and industrial leaders were not even made aware of the existence of the memorandum.[11]

Hitler's way of operating was scarcely conducive to ordered government. Increasingly, after the first year or two of the dictatorship, he reverted to a lifestyle recognisable not only in the party leader of the 1920s but even in the description of the habits of the indolent youth in Linz and Vienna recorded by his friend Kubizek.[12] According to the post-war testimony of one of his former adjutants:

> Hitler normally appeared shortly before lunch, quickly read through Reich Press Chief Dietrich's press cuttings, and then went into lunch. So it became more and more difficult for Lammers [head of the Reich Chancellory] and Meissner [head of the Presidial Chancellory] to get him to make decisions which he alone could make as head of state. . . . When Hitler stayed at Obersalzberg it was even worse. There, he never left his room before 2.00 p.m. Then, he went to lunch. He spent most afternoons taking a walk, in the evening straight after dinner, there were films. . . . He disliked the study of documents. I have sometimes secured decisions from him, even ones about important matters, without his ever asking to see the relevant files. He took the view that many things sorted themselves out on their own if one did not interfere.[13]

At this comment points out, even Lammers, the only link between Hitler and the ministries of state (whose heads themselves ceased definitively to meet around a table as a cabinet by early 1938), had difficulty at times with gaining access to Hitler and extracting decisions from him. Lammers him-self, for example, wrote plaintively to Hitler's adjutant on 21 October 1938 begging for an audience to report to the Führer on a number of urgent matters which needed resolution and which had been building up since the last occasion when he had been able to provide a detailed report, on 4 September![14]

Hitler's increasing aloofness from the State bureaucracy and the major organs of government seems to mark more than a difference of style with Stalin's *modus operandi*. It reflects, in my view, a difference in the essence of the regimes, mirrored in the position of the leader of each, a point to which I will return.

- Stalin was a highly interventionist dictator, sending a stream of letters and directives determining or interfering with policy. He chaired all important committees. His aim appears to have been a monopolisation of all decision-making and its concentration in the Politburo, a centralisation of state power and unity of decision-making which would have eliminated Party–State dualism.[15]

  Hitler, by contrast, was on the whole a non-interventionist dictator as far as government administration was concerned. His sporadic directives, when they came, tended to be delphic and to be conveyed verbally, usually by Lammers, the head of the Reich Chancellory, or, in the war years (as far as civilian matters went), increasingly by Bormann.[16] Hitler chaired no for-mal committees after the first years of the regime, when the Cabinet (which he hated chairing) atrophied into non-existence.[17] He directly undermined the attempts made by Reich Interior Minister Frick to unify and rationalize administration, and did much to sustain and enhance the irreconcilable dualism of Party and State which existed at every level.[18]

  Where Stalin appeared deliberately to destabilise government (which of-fered the possibility of a bureaucratic challenge),[19] Hitler seems to have had no deliberate policy of destabilisation, but rather, as a consequence of his non-bureaucratic leadership position and the inbuilt need to protect his deified leadership position by non-association with political infighting and potentially unpopular policies, to have presided over an inexorable erosion of 'rational' forms of government. And while the metaphor of 'feudal anar-chy' might be applied to both systems,[20] it seems more apt as a depiction of the Hitler regime, where bonds of personal loyalty were from the beginning the crucial determinants of power, wholly overriding functional position and status.

- Personalities apart, Hitler's leadership position appears to have been struc-turally more secure than Stalin's. If I have followed the debates properly, it would seem that there was some rational basis for Stalin's purges even if the dictator's paranoia took them into the realms of fantasy.[21] As the exponent of one party line among several, one set of policies among a number of alternatives, one interpretation of the Marx-Lenin arcanum among others, Stalin remained a dictator open to challenge from within. Kirov, it appears, had the potential to become a genuine rival leader in the early 1930s, when dissatisfaction and discontent with Stalin's rule was widespread.[22] Stalin's exaggerated feeling of insecurity was then to some measure grounded in reality. The purges which he himself instigated, and which in many instances were targeted at those closest to him, were above all intended to head off a bureaucratic challenge to his rule.

Hitler thought Stalin must be mad to carry out the purges.[23] The only faint reflections in the Third Reich were the liquidation of the SA leadership in the 'Night of the Long Knives' in 1934, and the ruthless retaliation for the attempt on Hitler's life in 1944. In the former case, Hitler agreed to the purge only belatedly and reluctantly, after the going had been made by Himmler and Göring, supported by the army leadership. The latter case does bear comparison with the Stalinist technique, though by that time the Hitler regime was plainly in its death-throes. The wild retaliation against those implicated in the assassination attempt was a desperate measure and aimed essentially at genuine opponents, rather than being a basic technique of rule.

Down to the middle of the war, Hitler's position lacked the precarious-ness which surrounded Stalin's leadership in the 1930s. Where Stalin could not believe in genuine loyalty even among his closest supporters, Hitler built his mastery on a cultivated principle of personal loyalty to which he could always successfully appeal at moments of crisis.[24] He showed a marked reluctance to discard even widely disliked and discredited satraps like Streicher, who had in Hitler's eyes earned his support through indispensable loyalty and service in the critical early years of the movement.[25] And he was in the bunker visibly shaken by news of Himmler's treachery — the 'loyal Heinrich' finally stabbing him in the back.[26]

A dangerous challenge to Hitler, especially once Hindenburg was dead, could effectively come only from within the armed forces (in tandem with an emergent disaffected, but unrepresentative, minority among the conserva-tive élites) or from a stray attack by a lone assassin (as came close to killing Hitler in 1939).[27] Even in 1944, the leaders of the attempted coup realised their isolation and the lack of a base of popular support for their action.[28] Hitler, it has to be accepted, was, for most of the years he was in power, outside the repressed and powerless adherents of the former working-class

movements, sections of Catholicism, and some individuals among the traditional élites, a highly popular leader both among the ruling groups and with
the masses.

And within the Nazi Movement itself, his status was quite different from
that of Stalin's position within the Communist Party. There are obvious
parallels between the personality cults built up around Stalin and Hitler. But
whereas the Stalin cult was superimposed upon the Marxist-Leninist ideology and Communist Party, and both were capable of surviving it, the 'Hitler
myth' was structurally indispensable to, in fact the very basis of and scarcely
distinguishable from, the Nazi Movement and its *Weltanschauung*.

Since the mid-1920s, ideological orthodoxy was synonymous with ad-
herence to Hitler. 'For us the Idea is the Führer, and each Party member has
only to obey the Führer,' Hitler allegedly told Ôtto Strasser in 1930.[29] The
build-up of a 'Führer party' squeezed heterodox positions onto the sidelines, then out of the party. By the time the regime was established and
consolidated, there was no tenable position within Nazism compatible with
a fundamental challenge to Hitler. His leadership position, as the font of
ideological orthodoxy, the very epitome of Nazism itself, was beyond question within the movement. Opposition to Hitler on fundamentals ruled
itself out, even among the highest and mightiest in the party. Invoking the
Führer's name was the pathway to success and advancement. Countering
the ideological prerogatives bound up with Hitler's position was incompatible with clambering up the greasy pole to status and power.

- Stalin's rule, for all its dynamic radicalism in the brutal collectivisation
programme, the drive to industrialisation and the paranoid phase of the
purges, was not incompatible with a rational ordering of priorities and
attainment of limited and comprehensible goals, even if the methods were
barbarous in the extreme and the accompanying inhumanity on a scale
defying belief. Whether the methods were the most appropriate to attain the
goals in view might still be debated, but the attempt to force industrialisation at breakneck speed on a highly backward economy and to introduce
'socialism in one country' cannot be seen as irrational or limitless aims.

And despite the path to a personalised dictatorship, there was no inexorable 'cumulative radicalisation'[30] in the Soviet Union. Rather, there was even
the 'great retreat' from radicalism by the mid-1930s and a reversion towards some forms of social conservatism before the war brought its own
compromises with ideological rectitude.[31] Whatever the costs of the personal regiment, and whatever the destructiveness of Stalin in the purges of
the party and of the military, the structures of the Soviet system were not
completely broken. Stalin had been a product of the system. And the system

was capable of withstanding nearly three decades of Stalin and surviving him. It was, in other words, a system capable of self-reproduction, even at the cost of a Stalin.

It would be hard to claim this of Nazism. The goal of national redemption through racial purification and racial empire was chimeric, a utopian vision. The barbarism and destructiveness which were inherent in the vain attempt to realise this goal were infinite in extent, just as the expansionism and extension of aggression to other peoples were boundless. Whereas Stalinism could 'settle down', as it effectively did after Stalin's death, into a static, even conservative, repressive regime, a 'settling down' into the staid authoritarianism of a Francoesque kind, is scarcely conceivable in the case of Nazism. Here, the dynamic was ceaseless, the momentum of radicalisation an accelerating one incapable of having the brakes put on — unless the 'system' itself were to be fundamentally altered.

I have just used the word 'system' of Nazism. But where Soviet communism in the Stalin era, despite the dictator's brutal destabilisation, remained recognisable as a *system* of rule, the Hitler regime was inimical to a rational order of government and administration. Its hallmark was *systemlessness,* administrative and governmental disorder, the erosion of clear patterns of government, however despotic.

This was already plain within Germany in the pre-war years as institutions and structures of government and administration atrophied, were eroded or merely bypassed, and faded into oblivion. It was not simply a matter of the unresolved Party–State dualism. The proliferation of 'special authorities' and plenipotentiaries for specific tasks, delegated by the Führer and responsible directly to him, reflected the predatory character and improvised techniques immanent in Nazi domination.[32] Lack of coherent planning related to attainable middle-range goals; absence of any forum for collective decision-making; the arbitrary exercise of power embedded in the 'leadership principle' at all levels; the Darwinian principle of unchecked struggle and competition until the winner emerged; and the simplistic belief in the 'triumph of the will', whatever the complexities to be overcome: all these reinforced each other and interacted to guarantee a jungle of competing and overlapping agencies of rule.

During the war, the disintegration of anything resembling a state *system* rapidly accelerated.[33] In the occupied territories, the so-called Nazi 'new order' drove the replacement of clearly defined structures of domination by the untrammelled and unco-ordinated force of competing power groups to unheard of levels. By the time Goebbels was writing in his diary, in March 1943, of a 'leadership crisis'[34] — and speaking privately of a 'leader crisis'[35] —

the 'system' of rule was unrescuable. Hitler's leadership was at the same time absolutely pivotal to the regime but utterly incompatible with either a rational decision-making process or a coherent, unified administration and the attainment of limited goals. Its self-destructive capacity was unmistakeable, its eventual demise certain.

Hitler was irreplaceable in Nazism in a way which did not apply to Stalin in Soviet Communism. His position was, in fact, irreconcilable with the setting up of any structures to select a successor. A framework to provide for the succession to Hitler was never established. The frequently mooted party senate never came about.[36] Hitler remained allergic to any conceivable institutional constraint, and by 1943 the deposition of Mussolini by the Fascist Grand Council ruled out once and for all any expectation of a party body existing quasi-independently of the Leader in Germany. Though Göring had been declared the heir apparent, his succession became increasingly unlikely as the Reich Marshal's star waned visibly during the war. None of the other second-rank Nazi leaders was a serious alternative candidate to succeed Hitler. It is indeed difficult to see who could have taken over, how the personalised rule of Hitler could have become systematised. The regime, one is compelled to suggest, was incapable of reproducing itself.

The objection that, but for a lost war there was nothing to prevent this happening, seems misplaced. The war was not accidental to Nazism. It lay at its very core. The war had to be fought and could not be put off until a more favourable juncture. And by the end of 1941, even though the war dragged on a further three and a half years, the gamble for 'world power' was objectively lost. As such, the dynamism of the regime and its self-destructive essence could be said to have been inseparable.

This brings me back to the questions I posed at the beginning of the paper. If my understanding of some of the recent discussion on Stalinism is not too distorted, and if the points of contrast with the Hitler regime I have outlined above have some validity, then it would be fair to conclude that, despite some superficial similarities, the character of the dictatorship, that is, of Stalin's and Hitler's leadership positions within their respective regimes, was fundamentally different. It would surely be a limited explanation, however, to locate these differences merely in the personalities of the dictators. Rather, I would suggest, they should be seen as a reflection of the contrasting social motivations of the followers, the character of the ideological driving force and the corresponding nature of the political vanguard movement upholding each regime. The Nazi Movement, to put the point bluntly, was a classic 'charismatic' leadership movement; the Soviet Communist Party was not. And this has a bearing on the self-reproducing capacity of the two 'systems' of rule.

The main features of 'charismatic authority' as outlined by Max Weber need no embroidering here: the perceptions of a heroic 'mission' and presumed greatness in the leader by his 'following'; the tendency to arise in crisis conditions as an 'emergency' solution; the innate instability under the double constant threat of collapse of 'charisma' through failure to meet expectations and of 'routinisation' into a 'system' capable of reproducing itself only through eliminating, subordinating or subsuming the 'charismatic' essence.[37] In its pure form, the personal domination of 'charismatic authority' represents the contradiction and negation of the impersonal, functional exercise of power which lies at the root of the bureaucratic legal-rational authority of the 'ideal type' modern state system.[38] It cannot, in fact, become 'systematised' without losing its particular 'charismatic' edge. Certainly, Max Weber envisaged possibilities of institutionalised 'charisma', but the compromises with the pure form then become evident.

The relevance of the model of 'charismatic authority' to Hitler seems obvious.[39] In the case of Stalin it is less convincing. The 'mission' in this latter case resides, it could be argued, in the Communist Party as the vehicle of Marxist-Leninist doctrine. For a while, it is true, Stalin hijacked the 'mission' and threatened to expropriate it through his personality cult. But this cult was a gradual and belated product, an excrescence artificially tagged on to Stalin's actual function. In this sense, there was a striking contrast with the personality cult of Hitler, which was inseparable from the 'mission' embodied in his name practically from the beginning, a 'mission' which from the mid-1920s at the latest did not exist as a doctrine independent of the leader.

Weber's model of 'charismatic authority' is an abstraction, a descriptive concept which says nothing in itself of the content of any specific manifestation of 'charismatic authority'. This is determined by the relationship of the leadership claim to the particular circumstances and 'political culture' in which it arises and which give it shape. The essence of the Hitlerian 'charismatic claim' was the 'mission' to achieve 'national rebirth' through racial purity and racial empire. But this claim was in practice sufficiently vague, adaptable and amorphous to be able to mesh easily with and incorporate more traditionalist blends of nationalism and imperialism, whose pedigree stretched back to the *Kaiserreich*.[40] The trauma of war, defeat and 'national disgrace', then the extreme conditions of a state system in a terminal stage of dissolution and a nation wracked by chasmic internal divisions, offered the potential for the 'charismatic claim' to gain extensive support, stretching way beyond the original 'charismatic community', and for it to provide the basis for an altogether new form of state.

In a modern state, the replacement of functional bureaucracy through personal domination is surely an impossibility. But even the co-existence of 'legal-rational' and 'charismatic' sources of legitimacy can only be a source of tension and conflict, potentially of a seriously dysfunctional kind. What occurred in the Third Reich was not the supplanting of bureaucratic domination by 'charismatic authority', but rather the superimposition of the latter on the former. Where constitutional law could now be interpreted as no more than 'the legal formulation of the historic will of the Führer — seen as deriving from his 'outstanding achievements'[41] — and where Germany's leading constitutional lawyer could speak of 'state power' being replaced by unrestrained 'Führer power',[42] the result could only be the undermining of the basis of impersonal law on which modern 'legal-rational' state systems rest and the corrosion of 'ordered' forms of government and institutionalised structures of administration through unfettered personal domination whose overriding source of legitimacy was the 'charismatic claim', the 'vision' of national redemption.[43]

The inexorable disintegration into 'systemlessness' was, therefore, not chiefly a matter of 'will'. Certainly, Hitler was allergic to any semblance of a practical or theoretical constraint on his power. But there was no systematic 'divide and rule' policy, no sustained attempt to *create* the administrative anarchy of the Third Reich. It was, indeed, in part a reflection of Hitler's personality and his style of leadership: as already pointed out, he was unbureaucratic in the extreme, remained aloof from the daily business of government and was uninterested in complex matters of detail. But this non-bureaucratic style was itself more than just a personal foible or eccentricity. It was an inescapable product of the deification of the leadership position itself and consequent need to sustain prestige to match the created image. His instinctive Darwinism made him unwilling and unable to take sides in a dispute till the winner emerged. But the need to protect his infallible image also made him largely incapable of doing so.

It was not in itself simply the undermining of 'rational' structures of government and proliferation of chaotic, 'polycratic' agencies that mattered. It was that this process accompanied and promoted a gradual realisation of ideological aims which were inextricably bound up in the 'mission' of the 'charismatic' Leader as the 'idea' of Nazism, located in the person of the Führer, became translated between 1938 and 1942 from utopian 'vision' into practical reality. There was, in other words, a symbiotic relationship between the structural disorder of the Nazi state and the radicalisation of policy.

The key development was unquestionably the growth in autonomy of the authority of the Führer to a position where it was unrestrained in practice as well as theory by any governmental institutions or alternative organs of power, a stage reached at the latest by 1938.[44] After the Blomberg–Fritsch affair of February 1938 it is difficult to see where the structures or the individuals capable of applying the brakes to Hitler remained. By this date, the pressures unleashed in part by the dictator's own actions, but even more so by diplomatic and economic developments beyond his control, encouraged and even conditioned the high-risk approach which was in any case Hitler's second nature.

Meanwhile, in conjunction with the expansion into Austria and the Sudetenland in 1938, race policy, too, shifted up a gear. The *Reichskristallnacht* pogrom in November, instigated by Goebbels not Hitler—though carried out with the latter's express approval[45]—was the culmination of the radicalisation of the previous year or so, and ended by handing over effective centralised co-ordination of the 'Jewish Question' to Heydrich.

Territorial expansion and 'removal of the Jews', the two central features of Hitler's *Weltanschauung*, had thus come together in 1938 into sharp focus in the foreground of the picture. The shift from utopian 'vision' to practical policy options was taking shape.

It would be mistaken to look exclusively, or even mainly, to Hitler's own actions as the source of the continuing radicalisation of the regime. Hitler was the linchpin of the entire 'system', the only common link between its various component parts. But by and large he was not directly needed to spur on the radicalisation. What seems crucial, therefore, is the way in which 'charismatic authority' functioned in practice to dissolve any framework of 'rational' government which might have acted as a constraint and to stimulate the radicalisation largely brought about by others, without Hitler's clear direction.

The function of Hitler's 'charismatic' Führer position could be said to have been threefold: that of unifier, of activator, and of enabler in the Third Reich.

As *unifier,* the 'idea' incorporated in the quasi-deified Führer figure was sufficiently indistinct but dynamic to act as a bond not only for otherwise warring factions of the Nazi Movement but also, until it was too late to extricate themselves from the fateful development, for non-Nazi national-conservative élites in army, economy and state bureaucracy. It also offered the main prop of popular support for the regime (repeatedly giving Hitler a plebiscitary basis for his actions) and a common denominator around which an underlying consensus in Nazi policy could be focused.[46]

As *activator,* the 'vision' embodied by Hitler served as a stimulant to action in the different agencies of the Nazi Movement itself, where pent-up energies and unfulfilled social expectations could be met by activism carried out in Hitler's name to bring about the aims of Leader and Party. But beyond the movement, it also spurred initiatives within the state bureaucracy, industry and the armed forces, and among the professionals such as teachers, doctors or lawyers where the motif of 'national redemption' could offer an open door to the push for realisation of long-cherished ambitions felt to have been held back or damaged by the Weimar 'system'.[47] In all these ways, the utopian 'vision' bound up with the Führer — undefined and largely undefinable — provided 'guidelines for action'[48] which were given concrete meaning and specific content by the voluntary 'push' of a wide variety of often competing agencies of the regime. The most important, most vigorous and most closely related to Hitler's ideological imperatives of these was, of course, the SS, where the 'idea' or 'vision' offered the scope for ever new initiatives in a ceaseless dynamic of discrimination, repression and persecution.

Perhaps most important of all, as *enabler* Hitler's authority gave implicit backing and sanction to those whose actions, however inhumane, however radical, fell within the general and vague ideological remit of furthering the aims of the Führer. Building a 'national community', preparing for the show-down with Bolshevism, purifying the Reich of its political and biological or racial enemies, and removing Jews from Germany, offered free license to initiatives which, unless inopportune or counter-productive, were more or less guaranteed sanction from above. The collapse in civilised standards which began in the spring of 1933, and the spiralling radicalisation of discrimination and persecution that followed, were not only unobstructed by but invariably found legitimation in the highest authority in the land.

Crucial to this 'progress into barbarism'[49] was the fact that in 1933 the barriers to state-sanctioned measures of gross inhumanity were removed almost overnight. What had previously been unthinkable suddenly became feasible. Opportunities rapidly presented themselves; and they were readily grasped. The Sterilisation Law of July 1933 is an early instance of such a dropping of barriers. Ideas long cherished by proponents of eugenics in biological-social engineering found all at once a climate in which they could be put into practice without the constraints still taken for granted in proposals — in themselves inhumane enough, but still confined to *voluntary* sterilisation — for legislation put forward by the German Doctors' Association just weeks before Hitler's takeover of power.[50]

By 1939 the erosion of civilised values had developed far enough to allow for the possibilities of liquidating as 'useless life' those deemed to be harmful to the propagation of 'healthy comrades of the people'.[51] And, illustrating how far the disintegration of the machinery of government had progressed, when written authorisation was needed, it took the form not of a government law or decree (which Hitler expressly ruled out) but a few lines typed on Hitler's private headed paper.[52] The few lines were enough to seal the fate of over 70,000 mentally ill and physically disabled persons in Germany by mid-1941 in the so-called 'euthanasia action'.

After 1939, in the parts of Poland annexed by Germany and incorporated into the Reich, prompted by Hitler's exhortation to brutal methods in a 'racial struggle' which was not to be confined by legal considerations,[53] the constraints on inhumanity to the Polish population, and of course to the Jewish minority in Poland, disappeared completely. Hitler needed to do nothing to force the pace of the rapidly escalating barbarism. He could leave it to the satraps on the spot. Characteristically, he said he asked no more of his *Gauleiter* in the East than that after ten years they should be able to announce that their territories were completely German.[54] The invitation was in itself sufficient to spark a competition in brutality — though allegedly this was the opposite of what Hitler wanted — between the arch-rival provincial chieftains Albert Forster in West Prussia and Arthur Greiser in the Warthegau to be able to report to the Führer in the shortest time that the 'racial struggle' had been won, that complete Germanisation had been achieved.[55]

The licence which Hitler as 'enabler' offered to such party bosses in the East can be illustrated graphically through the 'initiative' taken by Greiser in May 1942 recommending the liquidation of 35,000 Poles suffering from incurable tuberculosis.[56] In the event, Greiser's suggestion encountered difficulties. Objections were raised that it would be hard to maintain secrecy — reference was made here to the impact of the earlier 'euthanasia programme' in Germany itself — and was likely, therefore, to arouse unrest among the Polish population as well as presenting foreign propaganda with a gift. It was regarded as necessary to consult Hitler himself if the 'action' were to go ahead. Greiser's enlightening response ran: 'I myself do not believe that the Führer needs to be asked again in this matter, especially since at our last discussion with regard to the Jews he told me that I could proceed with these according to my own judgement'.[57] This judgement had already, in fact, been to recommend to Himmler the 'special treatment' (that is, killing) of 100,000 Jews in the Warthegau — the start of the 'final solution' there.[58]

Greiser thought of himself throughout as the direct agent and instrument of the Führer in the crusade to create his 'model Gau'. Any hindrance was met by the claim that his mandate to Germanise the Warthegau rested on plenipotentiary powers bestowed on him personally by the Führer himself.[59]

The relationship between the Führer, serving as a 'symbol' for actionism, and ideological radicalisation, and the drive 'from below' on the part of so many agencies, non-Nazi as well as Nazi, to put the 'vision' or parts of it into operation as practical policy is neatly captured in the sentiments of a routine speech of a Nazi functionary in 1934:

> Everyone who has the opportunity to observe it knows that the Führer can hardly dictate from above everything which he intends to realise sooner or

later. On the contrary, up till now everyone with a post in the new Germany has worked best when he has, so to speak, worked towards the Führer. Very often and in many spheres it has been the case — in previous years as well — that individuals have simply waited for orders and instructions. Unfortunately, the same will be true in the future; but in fact it is the duty of everybody to try to work towards the Führer along the lines he would wish. Anyone who makes mistakes will notice it soon enough. But anyone who really works towards the Führer along his lines and towards his goal will certainly both now and in the future one day have the finest reward in the form of the sudden legal confirmation of his work.[60]

These comments hint at the way 'charismatic authority' functioned in the Third Reich — anticipation of Hitler's presumed wishes and intentions as 'guidelines for action' in the certainty of approval and confirmation for actions which accorded with those wishes and intentions.

'Working towards the Führer' may be taken in a literal, direct sense with reference to party functionaries, in the way it was meant in the extract cited. In the case of the SS, the ideological executive of the 'Führer's will', the tasks associated with 'working towards the Führer' offered endless scope for barbarous initiatives, and with them institutional expansion, power, prestige and enrichment. The career of Adolf Eichmann, rising from a menial role in a key policy area to the manager of the 'Final Solution', offers a classic example.[61]

But the notion of 'working towards the Führer' could be interpreted, too, in a more indirect sense where ideological motivation was secondary, or perhaps even absent altogether, but where the objective function of the actions was nevertheless to further the potential for implementation of the goals which Hitler embodied. Individuals seeking material gain through career advancement in party or state bureaucracy, the small businessman aiming to destroy a competitor through a slur on his 'aryan' credentials, or ordinary citizens settling scores with neighbours by denouncing them to the Gestapo were all, in a way, 'working towards the Führer'. Doctors rushing to nominate patients of asylums for the 'euthanasia programme' in the interests of a eugenically 'healthier' people; lawyers and judges zealous to co-operate in the dismantling of legal safeguards in order to cleanse society of 'criminal elements' and undesirables; business leaders anxious to profit from preparations for war and, once in war, by the grabbing of booty and exploitation of foreign slave labour; thrusting technocrats and scientists seeking to extend power and influence through jumping on the bandwagon of technological experimentation and modernisation; non-Nazi military leaders keen to build up a modern army and restore Germany's hegemony in central Europe; and old-fashioned conservatives with a distaste for the Nazis but an even greater fear and dislike of the Bolsheviks: all were, through their many and varied forms of collaboration, at least indirectly 'working towards the Führer'. The result was the unstoppable radicalisation of the 'system' and the gradual emergence of policy objectives closely related to the ideological imperatives represented by Hitler.

Time after time, Hitler set the barbaric tone, whether in hate-filled public speeches giving a green light to discriminatory action against Jews and other 'enemies of the state', or in closed addresses to Nazi functionaries or military leaders where he laid down, for example, the brutal guidelines for the occupation of Poland and for 'Operation Barbarossa'. But there was never any shortage of willing helpers, far from being confined to party activists, ready to 'work towards the Führer' to put the mandate into operation. Once the war — intrinsic to Nazism and Hitler's 'vision' — had begun, the barbarism inspired by that 'vision' and now unchecked by any remnants of legal constraint or concern for public sensitivities plumbed unimaginable depths. But there was no prospect, nor could there have been, of the 'New Order' settling into a 'system' of government. Competing fiefdoms, not structured governments, formed the grim face of Nazi rule in the occupied territories. The rapaciousness and destructiveness present from the start within Germany now became hugely magnified and intensified with the conquered peoples rather than the Germans themselves as the main victims.

Through the metaphor of 'working towards the Führer', I have tried to suggest here that the 'vision' embodied in Hitler's leadership claim served to funnel a variety of social motivations, at times contradictory and conflicting, into furthering — intentionally or unwittingly — Nazi aims closely associated with Hitler's own ideological obsessions. The concept of 'charismatic authority' in this interpretation can be taken as useful in helping to depict the bonds with Hitler forged by various social and political forces, enabling the form of personalised power which he represented to free itself from all institutional constraints and to legitimise the destructive dynamic intrinsic to the Nazi gamble for European hegemony through war.

The model of 'charismatic authority', which I have suggested is applicable to the Hitlerian but not to the Stalinist dictatorship, not only helps to characterise the appeal of a quasi-messianic personalised form of rule embodying national unity and rebirth in the context of the collapse of legitimation of the democratic system of Weimar. It also, given the irreconcilable tension between 'charismatic authority' and bureaucratic rule in the Third Reich, offers insights into the inexorable erosion of anything resembling a *system* of domination capable of reproducing itself. Within this 'Behemoth' of governmental disorder,[62] 'working towards the Führer' amounted to a selective push for the radicalisation and implementation of those ideological lines most closely associated with Hitler's known broad aims, which could gradually take shape as policy objectives rather than distant goals.

Above all, the 'charismatic' model fits a form of domination which could never settle down into 'normality' or routine, draw a line under its achievements and come to rest as conservative authoritarianism, but was compelled instead to sustain the dynamism and to push ceaselessly and relentlessly for new attainments in the quest to fulfil its chimeric goal. The longer the Hitler regime lasted, the more megalomaniacal the aims, the more boundless the destructiveness became. But the longer the regime went on, the less it resembled a governmental *system* with the capacity to reproduce itself.

The inherent instability of 'charismatic authority' in this manifestation — where the specific content of the 'charismatic claim' was rooted in the utopian goal of national redemption through racial purification, war and conquest — implied, then, not only destructiveness but also self-destructiveness. Hitler's own suicidal tendencies could in this sense be said to reflect the inbuilt incapacity of his form of authoritarian rule to survive and reproduce itself.

Notes

1. Ernst Nolte's contributions to the *Historikerstreit* reflect this tendency. See '*Historikerstreit*'. *Die Dokumentation der Kontroverse um die Einzigartigkeit der national- sozialistischen Judenvernichtung*. (Munich: Piper, 1987), 13–35, 39–47, and his book *Der europäische Bürgerkrieg 1917–1945* (Frankfurt am Main/Berlin: Proplyäen Verlag, 1987).

2. See, for instance, the essay collection produced by Michael Prinz and Rainer Zitelmann, eds, *Nationalsozialismus und Modernisierung* (Darmstadt: Wissenschaft- liche Buchgesellschaft, 1991), especially the editors' foreword (vii–xi) and Zitelmann's own essay, 'Die totalitäre Seite der Moderne', 1–20.

3. See on this the thoughtful comments of Charles Maier, *The Unmasterable Past. History, Holocaust, and German National Identity* (Cambridge, MA/London: Harvard University Press, 1988), 71–84.

4. The Deutsche Forschungsgemeinschaft is currently investigating the structures of differing authoritarian systems in twentieth-century Europe in a major research project, 'Diktaturen im Europa des 20. Jahrhunderts: Strukturen, Erfahrung, Überwindung und Vergleich'.

5. I argue this case in chapter 2 of my *Nazi Dictatorship. Problems and Perspectives of Interpretation*, 3rd edn (London: Edward Arnold, 1993).

6. The comparison becomes even more shallow where the focus shifts from Stalin's own regime to later 'Stalinist' systems. The revelations of the extent of repression in the German Democratic Republic have, for example, prompted simplistic notions of essen- tial similarities between the Honecker and Hitler regimes. See on this the comments of Eberhard Jäckel, 'Die doppelte Vergangenheit', *Der Spiegel*, 23 Dec. 1991, 39–43.

7. On the *Sonderweg* debate, see the sensible comments of Jürgen Kocka, 'German History before Hitler: The Debate about the German *Sonderweg*', *Journal of Contemporary History,* Vol. 23 (1988), 3–16.

8. Ronald Grigor Suny, 'Stalin and his Stalinism: power and authority in the Soviet Union, 1950–53', in Ian Kershaw and Moshe Lewin, eds., *Stalinism and Nazism: Dictatorships in Comparison* (Cambridge: Cambridge University Press, 1997), 30.

9. Moshe Lewin, 'Bureaucracy and the Stalinist State', in *ibid.,* 70.

10. Werner Jochmann, ed., *Adolf Hitler. Monologe im Führerhauptquartier* (thereafter Jochmann, *Monologe*) (Hamburg: Albrecht Knaus Verlag, 1980), 158; trans. *Hitler's Table Talk* thereafter *Table Talk*, intro. H. R. Trevor-Roper (London: Weidenfeld and Nicolson, 1953), 153.

11. Dieter Petzina, *Autarkiepolitik im Dritten Reich* (Stuttgart: Deutsche Verlags-Anstalt, 1968), 48–53; Peter Hayes, *Industry and Ideology. IG Farben in the Nazi Era* (Cambridge: Cambridge University Press, 1987), 164–7.

12. See August Kubizek, *Adolf Hitler, mein Jugendfreund,* 5th edn (Graz/Stuttgart: Leopold Stocker Verlag, 1989).

13. Fritz Wiedemann, *Der Mann, der Feldherr werden wollte* (Kettwig: Velbert, 1964), 69; trans. Jeremy Noakes and Geoffrey Pridham, eds, *Nazism 1919/1945. A Documentary Reader* (thereafter Noakes and Pridham, *Nazism*) (Exeter: Exeter University Press, 1984), ii. 207–8.

14. Institut für Zeitgeschichte, Munich, Nuremberg Document no. NG-5428; trans. Noakes and Pridham, *Nazism,* ii. 245.

15. Suny, 33–4, 42, 47, 50–1.

16. Dieter Rebentisch, *Führerstaat und Verwaltung im Zweiten Weltkrieg* (thereafter, Rebentisch, *Führerstaat*) (Stuttgart: Franz Steiner Verlag Wiesbaden, 1989), has clearly shown that Hitler involved himself in civilian affairs to a far greater extent than was once thought. However, when he intervened it was usually at the prompting of one of the few favoured Nazi leaders graced with regular access to his presence, and providing him with one-sided information on specific issues of concern to them. He remained at all times alert to any extension of their power which could undermine his own. Other than this, there was nothing in his haphazard interventions to indicate any systematic grasp of or clear directives for coherent policy-making. In military matters and armaments production, from the middle of the war onwards, Hitler's involvement was on a wholly different scale. Here, his interventions were frequent — at daily conferences — and direct, though his dilettante, arbitrary and intransigent interference was often disastrously counter-productive. See Helmut Heiber, ed., *Hitlers Lagebesprechungen. Die Protokollfragmente seiner militärischen Konferenzen 1942–1945* (Stuttgart: Deutsche Verlags-Anstalt, 1962), and Willi A. Boelcke, ed., *Deutschlands Rüstung im Zweiten Weltkrieg. Hitlers Konferenzen mit Albert Speer 1942–1945* (Frankfurt am Main: Verlagsgesellschaft Athenaion, 1969).

17. See Lothar Gruchmann, 'Die "Reichsregierung" im Führerstaat', in Günther Doecker and Winfried Steffani, eds., *Klassenjustiz und Pluralismus* (Hamburg: Hoffmann und Campe Verlag, 1973), 192.

18. See Peter Diehl-Thiele, *Partei und Staat im Dritten Reich* (Munich: Beck Verlag, 1969), 61–9.

19. Suny, 47–9.

20. *Ibid.*, 30; Robert Koehl, 'Feudal Aspects of National Socialism', *American Political Science Review'*, Vol. 54 (1960), 921–33.

21. My main orientation was gleaned from the debates in *The Russian Review*, Vols 45–6 (1986, 1987), as well as from J. Arch Getty, *Origins of the Great Purges. The Soviet Communist Party Reconsidered* (Cambridge: Cambridge University Press, 1985); Moshe Lewin, *The Making of the Soviet System* (New York: Methuen, 1985); Robert C. Tucker, ed., *Stalinism: Essays in Historical Interpretation* (New York: Norton, 1977); and the papers by Ronald Suny and Moshe Lewin (see above notes 8–9).

22. Suny, 42, 47.

23. Elke Fröhlich, ed., *Die Tagebücher von Joseph Goebbels* (Munich: K. G. Saur Verlag, 1987), iii. 198 (entry for 10 July 1937).

24. A good example was his successful appeal to his old comrades, the *Gauleiter*, to close ranks at the moment of deep crisis following the sudden departure of Gregor Strasser in December 1932. See Noakes and Pridham, *Nazism,* i. 112–14 (based on an unpublished vivid, post-war account by Hinrich Lohse held in the Forschungsstelle für die Geschichte des Nationalsozialismus, Hamburg). I am grateful to Jeremy Noakes for letting me see a photocopy of this document.

25. See Jochmann, *Monologe,* 158–60; *Table Talk,* 153–6.

26. H. R. Trevor-Roper, *The Last Days of Hitler* (London: Pan Books, 1973), 202.

27. See Anton Hoch, 'Das Attentat auf Hitler im Münchner Bürgerbräukeller 1939', *Vierteljahrshefte für Zeitgeschichte,* Vol. 17 (1969), 383–413; and Lothar Gruchmann, ed., *Autobiographie eines Attentäters. Johann Georg Elser* (Stuttgart: Deutsche Verlags-Anstalt, 1970).

28. See Hans Mommsen, 'Social Views and Constitutional Plans of the Resistance', in Hermann Graml, *et al., The German Resistance to Hitler* (London: Batsford, 1970), 59.

29. Noakes and Pridham, *Nazism,* i. 46.

30. The term is that of Hans Mommsen. See his article, 'Der Nationalsozialismus: Kumulative Radikalisierung und Selbstzerstörung des Regimes', in *Meyers Enzyklopädisches Lexikon,* Vol. 16 (1976), 785–90.

31. Suny, 44–5.

32. See Martin Broszat, *Der Staat Hitlers* (thereafter Broszat, *Staat*) (Munich: dtv, 1969), esp. chs. 8–9.

33. The internal government of Germany during the war has now been systematically examined by Rebentisch, *Führerstaat* (see n. 16 above).

34. Louis D. Lochner, ed., *Goebbels Tagebücher aus den Jahren 1942–43* (Zürich: Atlantis Verlag, 1948), 241, 274, 296.

35. Albert Speer, *Erinnerungen* (Frankfurt am Main/Berlin: Propyläen Verlag, 1969), 271.

36. See Broszat, *Staat,* 262, 361–2; Rebentisch, *Führerstaat,* 101, 421–2.

37. Max Weber, *Economy and Society,* ed. Guenther Roth and Claus Wittich (Berkeley/Los Angeles: University of California Press, 1978), 241–54, 266–71, 1111–57.

38. See André Gorz, *Farewell to the Working Class* (London: Pluto Press, 1982), 58–9, 62–3.

39. The model is interestingly deployed by M. Rainer Lepsius, 'Charismatic Leadership: Max Weber's Model and its Applicability to the Rule of Hitler', in Carl Friedrich

Graumann and Serge Moscovici, eds, *Changing Conceptions of Leadership* (New York: Springer-Verlag, 1986). My own attempt to use it is in my recent short study *Hitler. A Profile in Power* (London: Longman, 1991).

40. For the imperialist traditions on which Nazism could build, see Woodruff D. Smith, *The Ideological Origins of Nazi Imperialism* (Oxford: Oxford University Press, 1986). The ways in which Nazism could exploit 'mainstream' nationalism are stressed by William Sheridan Allen, 'The Collapse of Nationalism in Nazi Germany', in John Breuilly, ed., *The State of Germany* (London: Longman, 1992), 141–53.

41. Hans Frank, *Im Angesicht des Galgens* (Munich/Gräfelfing: Beck Verlag, 1953), 466–7; trans. Noakes and Pridham, *Nazism*, ii. 200.

42. Ernst Rudolf Huber, *Verfassungsrecht des Großdeutschen Reiches* (Hamburg: Hanseatische Verlagsanstalt, 1939), 230; trans. Noakes and Pridham, *Nazism*, ii. 199.

43. For a compelling analysis of 'national rebirth' as the essence of the fascist doctrine, see Roger Griffin, *The Nature of Fascism* (London: Pinter, 1991).

44. See Broszat, *Staat*, ch. 8.

45. See *Die Tagebücher von Joseph Goebbels,* ed. Elke Frölich, Pt. I, *Aufzeichnungen,* Vol. 6, Munich, 1998, 180–2.

46. I have attempted to present the evidence in my study *The 'Hitler Myth'. Image and Reality in the Third Reich* (Oxford: Oxford University Press, 1987).

47. For an excellent study of how the medical profession exploited the opportunities offered by National Socialism, see Michael H. Kater, *Doctors under Hitler* (Chapel Hill/London: University of North Carolina Press, 1989).

48. Martin Broszat, 'Soziale Motivation und Führer-Bindung des Nationalsozialismus', *Vierteljahrshefte für Zeitgeschichte,* Vol. 18 (1970), 405.

49. Michael Burleigh and Wolfgang Wippermann, *The Racial State. Germany 1933–1945* (Cambridge: Cambridge University Press, 1991), back cover.

50. See Jeremy Noakes, 'Nazism and Eugenics: The Background of the Nazi Sterilisation Law of 14 July 1933', in R. J. Bullen, *et al.*, eds., *Ideas into Politics* (London/Sydney: Croom Helm, 1984), 75–94, esp. 84–5.

51. See the documentation by Ernst Klee, *'Euthanasie' im NS-Staat. Die 'Vernichtung lebensunwerten Lebens'* 2nd edn (Frankfurt am Main: Fischer Verlag, 1983).

52. *Ibid.,* 100–1.

53. Martin Broszat, *Nationalsozialistische Polenpolitik 1939–1945* (Frankfurt am Main: Fischer Verlag, 1965), 11, 25.

54. *Ibid.,* 200 n. 45.

55. *Ibid.,* 122.

56. The correspondence between Greiser and Himmler on the subject, dated between 1 May and 3 Dec. 1942, is in the personal file of Arthur Greiser in the Berlin Document Center (thereafter BDC). For a more extended discussion, see my article, 'Improvised Genocide? The Emergence of the "Final Solution" in the "Warthegau"', *Transactions of the Royal Historical Society,* 6th Series, Vol. 2 (1992), 51–78, here 71–3.

57. BDC, Personal File of Arthur Greiser, Greiser to Himmler, 21 Nov. 1942.

58. BDC, Personal File of Arthur Greiser, Greiser to Himmler, 1 May 1942.

59. Examples in the Archive of the Polish War Crimes Commission, Ministry of Justice, Warsaw, Greiser Trial Documents, File 11, fol. 52, File 13, fol. 15. According to the post-

war testimony of one of the heads of regional administration in the Warthegau, Greiser never missed an opportunity in his speeches to insist that he was 'persona gratissima' with the Führer (File 36, fol. 463). Another contemporary commented that his gratitude knew no bounds once Hitler had granted him this special plenipotentiary authority. See Carl J. Burckhardt, *Meine Danziger Mission 1937–1939* (Munich: dtv, 1962), 79. I have provided a short pen-picture of Greiser for the forthcoming second volume of Ronald Smelser, *et al.*, eds, *Die braune Elite und ihre Helfer* (Darmstadt: Wissenschaftliche Buchgesellschaft, 1993).

60. Niedersächsisches Staatsarchiv, Oldenburg, Best. 131, nr. 303, fol. 131v, speech by Werner Willikens, State Secretary in the Ministry of Food, 21 Feb. 1934; trans. Noakes and Pridham, *Nazism,* ii. 207.

61. See Hannah Arendt, *Eichmann in Jerusalem* (London: Faber and Faber, 1963).

62. See Franz Neumann, *Behemoth. The Structure and Practice of National Socialism* (London: Victor Gollancz, 1942).

2

Ideologue and Propagandist: Hitler in Light of His Speeches, Writings and Orders, 1925–1928

The difficulty inherent in locating and assembling the scattered texts authored by Adolf Hitler is probably the principal factor that has impeded progress on their collation and publication. A full half century after the end of the Third Reich, when the present project is targeted to be completed, we will finally have a scholarly edition of Hitler's extant speeches and writings dating from the period between his entry onto the political stage and his seizure of power on January 30, 1933.

In perusing the now-available volumes of this important work, covering the period between the refounding of the NSDAP (National Socialist German Workers' Party) in February 1925 and the Reichstag election of May 1928,[1] it is sometimes difficult to keep in mind just how insignificant the Hitlerian movement actually was during those years. It constituted nothing more than a tiny, inconsequential, marginal phenomenon on the political scene.

At that time, the Weimar Republic was experiencing its so-called "golden age" — years marked by an economic upswing and Stresemann's successes in foreign policy and social-political progress. There appeared to be a consolidation afoot in the unquiet republic. Even when it came to Bavaria, where the NSDAP had done better at the polling booths than anywhere else in Germany, both the semi-monthly official reports of the district superintendents and the daily press reflect just how marginal the Nazi movement was as a political factor during this phase. It is essential to keep this salient fact in mind when embarking on an analysis of the present volumes.

The significance of this edition, then, lies principally in its value in assisting us in grasping the internal development of the NSDAP in a period when it had no realistic expectations of gaining power and was initially bogged down in a welter of serious internal disputes and wrangling. In particular, the edition provides us the first opportunity to systematically trace the development of Hitler's political ideas during the mid-1920s.

The edition begins with the refounding of the NSDAP on February 26, 1925. The early difficulties Hitler encountered in overcoming the fragmentation of the old party, which had broken up in 1924, and the various rivalries in the far-right folk-national (*völkisch*) camp were quite substantial, especially since the Bavarian authorities had issued a ban in March 1925 prohibiting Hitler from speaking in public. This muzzling had temporarily robbed him of his most powerful weapon, namely, his prodigious talents for demagogy. The first part of the edition illuminates these problems — the slow and laborious construction of the party base in Saxony, Thuringia and Württemberg, Hitler's confrontation with his rivals Graefe and Reventflow in northern Germany, and, above all, the conflicts in his own party ranks. These disputes involved not only the controversial figures in Hitler's Munich circle and elsewhere in Bavaria, particularly Hermann Esser and Julius Streicher. They also resulted from discordant interpretations of the direction of foreign-policy thinking in the movement; differences of opinion regarding the relation of the NSDAP to other *völkisch* groups; widely divergent views on strategy when it came to the burning issues of the day, such as the dispossession of the princes; and even possible changes in the party program — changes that might, after all, also have created a challenge to Hitler's position and authority. The present edition enables us to trace better the course of these disputes — with one proviso: they are viewed only from Hitler's point of view.

During these months Hitler was largely occupied with the task of solidifying his base of authority within the National Socialist movement. He insisted that party central headquarters should remain in Munich, where his personal power remained unassailable; he defended Esser and Streicher, the *Franken-führer* ("leader of the Franks") so indispensable for the party stronghold of Franconia, against their critics. Apart from that, Hitler's main goal at this stage was to eliminate his rivals in the *völkisch* camp. During his 1924 Landsberg incarceration, he had consciously kept aloof from the fragmented folk-national movement and watched from the sidelines while his political rivals foundered. None could gain the upper hand. Even before the abortive Beer Hall Putsch, there were unmistakable first signs of a personal cult in the making, a tendency that rapidly intensified after the propaganda coup of the Munich trial. In his capacity as a propagandist and mass agitator, Hitler was absolutely necessary for the movement. Although until March 1927, he had been banned in Bavaria from speaking at public meetings, he was permitted to address closed party gatherings. According to his own judgment, after the first few weeks he was able even to capitalize on the ban, further enhancing his prestige.

It is well known that Hitler's speech at the party leaders' convention in Bamberg on February 14, 1926 — unfortunately reconstructable only on the basis of a brief newspaper report (I, 294ff.) — was a milestone on the road to consolidation of his authority and the rejection of the reformist tendencies espoused by Gregor Strasser, Joseph Goebbels and others. There were the first initial indications of the development of a "*Führer* party," in which the guiding "idea" was embodied by the "*Führer*" rather than enshrined in the mutable planks of a party program.

By the time of the party plenum on May 22, 1926, Hitler had gained the upper hand. He spoke triumphantly at that meeting about the "internal consolidation" of the movement and was able, with some justification, to contend that the "homogeneity" of the party had been restored (I, 446, 448). The Weimar party convention held shortly thereafter, at which the party program of 1920 was declared unalterable, underscored his dominant position. The *Führer* cult found its external expression in the Hitler salute, from then obligatory in the movement.

The next party convention, held in Nuremberg in August 1927, proved to what extent the myth of the *Führer* had become the fulcrum of a movement in which the "idea" and party leader were inseparably fused. All other folk-national groupings were largely sapped of their energy, if not in a state of total collapse. These sectarian quarrels and bickerings would probably have continued to remain a sideshow for the development of Weimar democracy had it not been for the worldwide economic depression that took hold in 1929. Nonetheless, this was a phase in which the Nazi movement was able to successfully expand its organization and mobilize a relatively large core of activists, despite the still feeble power of attraction the movement possessed for the broader electorate.[2] In this way, and far better than before 1923, an organizational and ideological basis was forged. It was that foundation that enabled the movement, beginning in 1929, to exploit successfully the death throes of the republic.

The edition reflects salient aspects of the organizational structure and build-up of the Nazi movement as contained in the orders decreed by Hitler as party leader. However, its major importance undoubtedly lies in the fact that it provides us with the first possibility to undertake a systematic and chronological investigation of the path taken by Hitler's own thinking during this crucial period. In 1927, he himself commented on one occasion that he required more than two hours to fully expound his ideological program (II/I, 178). In this succinct overview, I hope to summarize the essential points with greater brevity.

A volume published some years ago sheds ample light on the development of Hitler's ideas up to 1924.[3] The global rabble-rousing anti-Semitism, which is the dominant chord in virtually all of Hitler's early speeches, was initially aimed at the Jews primarily in their alleged role as "financiers," "capitalists," "black marketeers" and "profiteers." In contrast, there had been a shift in perspective by the mid-1920s. Under the impact of the Russian civil war, identification of the Jews with Bolshevism had largely supplanted the emphasis on Jewish finance capital in Hitler's thinking. Or, to put it more precisely, "Jewish Bolshevism" had become his second main target and had even been transposed to center stage. However, beginning in about 1922, there was another shift: anti-Marxism gradually began to emerge as a stronger factor, outweighing anti-Semitism, though Hitler left no doubt that in his eyes the struggle against Marxism was indeed identical with that against the Jews.

A second change in Hitler's worldview in this period was the development of the concept of *Lebensraum* ("living space"), which replaced the initially rather conventionally espoused idea of colonialism by continental conceptions of conquest over Russia with England's assistance. Nonetheless, the volume edited by Jäckel and Kuhn contains only a single document pertinent to this question (from the autumn of 1922),[4] a geopolitical idea which was soon to assume a central role in the Hitlerian conceptual scheme.

Finally, the Jäckel–Kuhn edition shows that, as far as I can judge, Hitler's own self-image was undergoing a process of change by 1922–1923. Albrecht Tyrell has stressed just how crucial the period of incarceration in Landsberg had been for Hitler's shifting self-image, i.e., for the insight he gained that he was not just the "drummer" preparing the way for a future "great leader," but was himself that great leader of the future Germany.[5]

Yet that specific idea is present at least in rudimentary form even earlier than his imprisonment, in speeches given by Hitler in 1922 and 1923, when (evidently influenced by the example of Mussolini) he repeatedly referred to the institution of the heroic leader and the importance of the historical personality, increasingly emphasizing its centrality — at times, it would appear, with obvious reference to his own person.

It can be argued that by 1924, the central core of Hitler's worldview — history as racial struggle and the annihilation of both Judaism (whatever that might mean in concrete terms) and its most dangerous political and ideological manifestation, Marxism — was a conception firmly planted in his thinking.

By contrast, the notion of *Lebensraum,* although already broached, as yet occupied no special position within the matrix of his thought. And the idea of the "heroic *Führer*" was still not fully crystallized.

It is well known that in *Mein Kampf* these ideas are bundled together into an amalgam — less so in the first volume, issued in July 1925, than in the second, published in December 1926. The second volume was written in 1925–1926, and thus during the period covered by the present edition. Immediately there-after, in the summer of 1928, Hitler dictated the text of his so-called *Zweites Buch* ("Second Book"), which dealt far more than *Mein Kampf* with questions of foreign policy and *Raumfragen* ("territorial issues").[6] A major attraction of the present edition is that it covers this specific period in the development of Hitler's ideas, namely, the years spanning the second volume of *Mein Kampf* and the *Zweites Buch.*

A striking feature is Hitler's clearly deepening involvement with the "ques-tion of territory" and "land policy" during the period from 1926 to 1928, even though he expressly used the term *Lebensraum* only once, as far as I can discern, namely, on March 30, 1928 (II/I, 761). Up to the end of 1926, Hitler touched only rarely on the question of "land policy." In a speech on December 16, 1925, he characterized the "acquisition of land and soil" as the best way "to mold German fate in economic terms" (I, 240). At the Weimar party convention in July 1926, he picked up the issue once again. Yet it was not until about March 1927 that it began increasingly to appear in his speeches as a central component. Between the summer of 1927 and May 1928, Hitler spe-cifically underscored the *Raumfrage* in almost all his major speeches — *ad nauseam,* one might add, utilizing virtually the same words again and again. Several passages from these speeches are likewise repeated nearly verbatim at key points in his *Zweites Buch.*

The content can be summarized as follows: German resurgence must travel the path of economic upswing. The prerequisite for this is a solution to the "shortage of territory" (*Raumnot*), which can be attained only by the use of force. Hitler extols "eastern colonization" in the Middle Ages, imperialism, and the principle of conquest by the sword. Although he rarely mentions Russia, the ultimate aim of this territorial policy is unmistakably clear. His belief in Social Darwinism and its racial "theory of history" "is an *iron princi-ple:* the weaker must fall so that the stronger can live" (II/2, 552). In his view, three values remain decisive when it comes to the fate of a people: (a) the value of blood or race; (b) the value of personality; and (c) its warring spirit or drive for self-preservation. These three values, embodied in the "Aryan race," were, in Hitler's view, mortally endangered by the three "vices" of "Jewish Marx-ism" — democracy, pacifism, and internationalism.

By using the documentation under discussion, it can be shown for the first time that the ideas dominating the *Zweites Buch* — including the issue of South Tyrol and his interest in the growing economic power of the United States — were already present in basic form a year earlier and were repeatedly broached in Hitler's speeches in 1927–1928.

Emphasis on the importance of personality played a central role in Hitler's rhetoric. The theme of personality and of the role of the *Führer* is a recurrent leitmotif in all the speeches and writings collected in this edition. Thus, his strong emphasis in 1925–1926 on the unity of the movement that can only be achieved through a *Führer* is not surprising. In the speech on the occasion of the refounding of the NSDAP on February 27, 1925, for example, Hitler views his "role as *Führer*" in "bringing together again all those who now are diverging" (I, 150). The "art of the *Führer*" in assembling the "stones of the mosaic" (I, 100), the *Führer* as "focal point" (I, 102) or as "preserver of the idea" (II/1, 408) were repeatedly underscored, especially in the initial months after the party's refounding.

Even later Hitler never missed an opportunity to stress the importance of personality — and thus indirectly the myth of the *Führer,* functioning as the central integrating mechanism of the movement. Again and again he hinted at his own claims to grandeur and greatness, barely disguised by allusions in particular to Bismarck and Frederick the Great. One example is his remarks on Bismarck in May 1926: "It was necessary to implant the national idea within the masses of the people," and "a giant had to complete this task." As "lengthy applause" indicated, the implications of this remark were not lost on Hitler's audience (I, 426).

Quite naturally, the edition has little new to offer when it comes to the development of Hitler's anti-Semitism. As is well known, hatred for the Jews was far more than a mere propaganda theme for Hitler. Nonetheless, the consciously tactical employment of anti-Semitism within the framework of propaganda purposes is in clear evidence here. Thus, for example, Hitler made no mention whatsoever of the Jews in his notorious speech delivered before the Hamburg National Club in February 1926. The sole aim of the Nazi movement, he underscored then, was the "total and complete" annihilation of Marxism (I, 297–330). This contrasts with remarks made when speaking before his "own" audience in the Munich beer halls, where almost every speech was replete with brutal attacks on Jews as the "masterminds behind financial capital," "polluters of the people," and adherents of the "subversive doctrine of Marxism."

With mounting emphasis on the "issue of territory," beginning in 1927–1928, there is a slight drop in the frequency of expressly anti-Semitic tirades, which now often have a somewhat ritualistic ring; in part, they are replaced by emphasis on Marxism as the principal adversary. Yet this certainly did not mean that there had been any changes with respect to the pathological hatred for the Jews that Hitler harbored. For Hitler, the destruction of Marxism and the destruction of the Jews were identical goals. "The Jew is and remains the world enemy," he asserted in typical form in February 1927, "and his weapon, Marxism, is a plague afflicting mankind" (II/1, 158; cf. also I, 20f.).

The "positive" content of the many hundreds of speeches and writings reproduced in this edition is extremely scant. The sole "social" component of the "idea" consisted in doing away with the divided class society of a nationalistic but purportedly debilitated and "decadent" bourgeoisie and a socialist proletariat "polluted by Marxism," to fuse nationalism and socialism and to overcome the class antagonisms between "headworkers" and "handworkers" by the establishment of a "community of struggle." It was envisaged that this would generate the new spirit, which would in turn guarantee the success of the people's "struggle for existence."

Over and over again, Hitler declared that he had no interest in day-to-day politics and issues. In actual fact, what he formulated were distant goals. At this juncture, such goals probably had a more visionary or even metaphorical meaning for his audiences, far removed from any basis in reality. In this voluminous edition, one can search in vain for any suggestion of a medium-term, "rational" policy and hierarchy of priorities. Clarity and precise objectives were neither desired nor possible; the sole and exclusive goal was mobilization for the struggle for power.

Naturally, Hitler likewise was at a loss when it came to exactly how the utopian final aim might be achieved. The conquest of *Lebensraum* could only mean aggression against Russia. However, in the mid-1920s, it was probably little more than a militant slogan for Hitler's audiences — though not necessarily when it came to Hitler himself. Even regarding the Jews, the real aim remained fuzzy. It is true that he called for chasing "that *pack of Jews* . . . from our fatherland . . . with an iron broom" (I, 62). Yet elsewhere his remarks suggest that perhaps not all Jews should be arbitrarily expelled from Germany: "the Jew" had to be shown, he stated in February 1928, "that we're the bosses here; if he behaves well, he can stay — *if not, then out with him*" (II/2, 67). And even the fundamental prerequisite for racial struggle, the overcoming of Marxism in Germany and the establishment of a socially and racially homogeneous "folk community" (*Volksgemeinschaft*) remained at this point nothing more than a utopian vision — one that, from the vantage of the time, appeared practicable solely in the eyes of absolute fanatics.

What Hitler had to offer in contrast with all other *völkisch* leaders was an absolutely unaltering and solidly girded ideological vision. This was a vision that derived its power and persuasiveness precisely from its simplicity, internal consistency and comprehensiveness — an all-encompassing character that integrated apparently contrary and contradictory elements. Hitler combined the conviction of a fanatical believer with a demagogic talent unparalleled in the National Socialist camp. As the self-proclaimed adherent of a fixed worldview, he was always able to present his public with a crude choice of either/or, black or white, victory or total destruction.

He appealed, of course, masterfully and quite consciously, to his audience's basest instincts. In his speech at the Hamburg National Club, he declared that the masses did not want intellectual ideas; rather, what they desired was a faith, because "the broad masses of people are blind and stupid and don't know what they're doing . . . The masses have a primitive view. What abides is the feeling of hatred" (I, 3 1 5, 3 2 0). Precisely by dint of his matchless abilities to stir up hatred and his talents as a demagogue — with persuasiveness nourished by an unshakeable worldview — Hitler proved able by 1928 to consolidate his preeminent position within the extremist folk-national camp and to strengthen his colossal aura as a *Führer* among his followers.

In conclusion, I wish to point out briefly what I believe this new edition contains that is especially relevant for the current discussion among historians about Hitler and the Third Reich.

The edition makes it abundantly clear that, notwithstanding the scant intellectual substance and disgusting moral content of his ideas, Hitler had, by the mid-1920s, developed a consistent and coherent worldview that was far more than mere hollow propagandistic phrase-mongering. The fact that Hitler was nothing but an "unprincipled opportunist," as the time-worn thesis advanced by Rauschning and still in occasional currency contends,[7] appears to be untenable — as does the reductionist notion that his "ideas" were nothing but propaganda. Moreover, such an interpretative tack is hardly in a position to grasp Hitler's personal motivation and the psychological forces that powered it.

After perusing this new edition of materials, I believe there can no longer be any doubt that Hitler was both a profoundly dedicated ideologue and a masterful propagandist; and there was no contradiction whatsoever between the two. In this sense the edition strengthens those interpretations based on the assumption that it is necessary to accord Hitler's personal ideological goals central significance, particularly in connection with developments in the realm of racial and foreign policy in the Third Reich. Hitler cannot merely be reduced to the function of a system that was growing cumulatively more and more radical.[8]

On the other hand, what is contained here is no "blueprint for rule"[9] — if "blueprint" is supposed to signify something other than the formulation of

distant utopian goals. Concentrating on Hitler's personal worldview, no matter how fanatically he was inspired and motivated by it, cannot readily serve to
explain why a society, which hardly shared the arcanum of Hitler's "philosophy," gave him such growing support from 1929 on — in proportions that rose
with astonishing rapidity. Nor can it account for the reasons why, from 1933
on, the non-National Socialist élites were prepared to play more and more into
his hands in the process of "cumulative radicalization."

It is evident that an edition of Hitler's speeches and writings from the period
1925 to 1928 can contribute only indirectly to explanations of such a complex
problem. Nonetheless, it does suggest that the interpretative approach adopted
by Martin Broszat could be usefully pursued and expanded. In that view,
Hitler's "secret vision" was able to serve as an "orientation for action," or even
as an "ideological metaphor" for the masses, who were prepared, without
sharing his fanatical convictions, "to work towards the *Führer* in accordance
with his wishes"[10] — whatever their underlying motives and reasons.

An interpretation of the Third Reich currently in vogue tends to portray
Hitler as a "conscious modernizer" who had a more-or-less coherent program
for the revolutionary restructuring of German society.[11] That view is intended
to be a contribution to the "historicizing" of Hitler and National Socialism.
After examining more than 1,350 pages of his speeches, writings and orders
from this period — and I must add that aside from his biting sarcasm, there is
not a single joke in this entire corpus! — I am unable to see any basis for such a
reading. Hitler's "social idea" remained totally diffuse: "destruction of Marxism" — yes, but this is followed by a notion little more concrete than the afore-
mentioned overcoming of the division between nationalism and socialism and
the creation of a *Volksgemeinschaft* based on race and struggle.

Admittedly, there are indications in 1927–1928 that Hitler admired the
motorization and advanced technology of the United States. But he argued
again and again that Germany's possibilities for competing with — and ultimately defeating — the United States rested on a geographical prerequisite:
territorial conquest by the sword in continental Europe. To my mind this is the
most primitive form of nineteenth-century Social-Darwinistic imperialism. I
am at a loss to discover anything "modern" in such a notion. Hitler promised
"modernization" solely in the sense of a society transformed by struggle, war
and conquest. From my perspective it is an abuse of concepts to present this as
some sort of intentional social modernization. Yes, Germany's modernization
did in fact partially result from Hitler's war. But to trace this process of modernization in any way back to Hitler's intentions is, I would counsel, highly
misleading. Hitler did view himself as a revolutionary, but his revolution was
strictly and exclusively racial, a revolution of annihilation.

What makes the present edition so significant is that it documents a decisive stage not only in the shaping of Hitler's thoughts, but also in the transformation of the NSDAP into a *Führer* movement that attached itself increasingly to the visionary goals embodied in the person of the charismatic leader. As a mechanism of integration, mobilization and legitimation, the Hitler myth was indispensable for the unfolding dynamics of the NSDAP. On the basis of this edition, its development as a "charismatic community" (Max Weber) can be clearly attested.

The functional consequence is implicit: already as early as February 1925, Hitler stressed that he could not create unity as a "party within the party" (I, 25). The building up of a colossal, inviolable nimbus surrounding the *Führer,* the necessity to protect his prestige by keeping his distance from any and every conflict, and the concomitant need to maintain a distance from the daily affairs of the party — and later from the daily business of government (to say nothing about his personal preferences) — necessarily had to result in an immanent and unbridgeable contradiction in the Third Reich. This was the contradiction between the "legal-rational," i.e., the legally constituted, bureaucratic state, on the one hand, and the destructive and ultimately self-destructive system of *Führer* rule, founded on an extra-legal, "charismatic" basis, on the other hand.

Of course, the latter is far removed in time from the period covered by the materials in this edition; it will, however, be fascinating to observe in subsequent volumes just how these perspectives develop in the years of the Nazi rise to power, beginning in 1929. Yet even for these later years, the reader should bear in mind that Hitler and the NSDAP were in no position to achieve state power solely by dint of their own strength and that the actions of the non-National Socialist "power-brokers," little influenced by Hitler's personal worldview, were of crucial importance for that ascent to power. It should be recalled that even the massive influx of new members into the NSDAP was not owing primarily to Hitler's *Weltanschauung*. Finally, it is important to keep in mind that it was not so much National Socialism which sentenced the first German republic to death; on the contrary, the undermining of the Weimar democracy was a key prerequisite for the rise of the NSDAP.

Even in the face of the unsettling neo-Nazi phenomena that can be observed in the aftermath of events since 1989, there would appear to be little likelihood for a repetition of that specific structural context which facilitated a takeover of state power by a rabid demagogue and racial ideologue, as we encounter him in this edition — unless a totally unforeseen catastrophe should befall Europe.

The present edition and the project of which it is a part will make a substantial contribution to a more profound understanding of Hitler's ideas and actions in the period preceding the takeover of state power. The gap between the paltriness of his ideas and Hitler's dynamic effectiveness will remain a puzzling factor. Perhaps this suggests that any future study about the man should be conceived less as a classic biography than as a "social history of Hitler."

Notes

1. *Hitler. Reden, Schriften, Anordnungen. Februar 1925 bis Januar 1933. Band I: Die Wiedergründung der NSDAP. Februar 1925–Juni 1926*, edited and annotated by Clemens Vollnhals; *Band II: Vom Weimarer Parteitag bis zur Reichstagswahl. Juli 1926–Mai 1928*, edited and annotated by Bärbel Dusik. 2 vols., Munich, 1992. Citations in the text as follows: (II/2, 761) indicates Band II, vol. 2, p. 761.

2. Wolfgang Horn, *Führerideologie und Parteiorganisation in der NSDAP (1919–1924)*, Düsseldorf, 1972; Albrecht Tyrell, ed., *Führer befiehl . . . Selbstzeugnisse aus der "Kampfzeit" der NSDAP. Dokumentation und Analyse*, Düsseldorf, 1969.

3. Eberhard Jäckel/Axel Kuhn, eds., *Hitler, Sämtliche Aufzeichnungen 1905–1924*, Stuttgart, 1980.

4. *Ibid.*, p. 773.

5. Albrecht Tyrell, *Vom "Trommler" zum "Führer". Der Wandel von Hitlers Selbstverständnis zwischen 1919 und 1924 und die Entwicklung der NSDAP*, Munich, 1975, pp. 170–74.

6. *Hitlers zweites Buch. Ein Dokument aus dem Jahr 1928*, eingeleitet und kommentiert von Gerhard L. Weinberg, Stuttgart, 1961.

7. The formulation, which can also be found in Alan Bullock, *Hitler. A Study in Tyranny*, 2nd. rev. ed., London, 1965, p. 804, is based principally on Hermann Rauschning, *Die Revolution des Nihilismus. Kulisse und Wirklichkeit im Dritten Reich*, Zurich/New York, 1938, esp. Part I.

8. The concept of "cumulative radicalization," a notion nonetheless fruitful and apt in my view, stems from Hans Mommsen, cf. "Der Nationalsozialismus. Kumulative Radikalisierung und Selbstzerstörung des Regimes," in: *Meyers Enzyklopädisches Lexikon*, vol. 16, Mannheim/Vienna/Zurich, 1976, pp. 785–90.

9. Subtitle of the standard work by Eberhard Jäckel, *Hitlers Weltanschauung. Entwurf einer Herrschaft*, Tübingen, 1969.

10. "Rede von Werner Willikens, 21.2.1934," Niedersächsisches Staatsarchiv, Oldenburg, Best. 131, Nr. 303, fol. 131ᵛ.

11. This is, for example, the basic tenor of the interpretation by Rainer Zitelmann, cf. *Hitler. Selbstverständnis eines Revolutionärs*, Hamburg/New York, 1987, and his "Die totalitäre Seite der Moderne," in: Michael Prinz/Rainer Zitelmann, eds., *Nationalsozialismus und Modernisierung*, Darmstadt, 1991, pp. 1–20, esp. pp. 12f.

3

Improvised Genocide? The Emergence of the 'Final Solution' in the 'Warthegau'

The 'Warthegau' — officially the 'Reichsgau Wartheland', with its capital in Posen (Poznań) — was the largest of three areas of western Poland[1] annexed to the German Reich after the defeat of Poland in 1939. In the genesis of the 'Final Solution' it plays a pivotal role. Some of the first major deportations of Jews took place from the Warthegau. The first big ghetto was established on the territory of the Warthegau, at Lodz (which the Nazis renamed Litzmann-stadt). In autumn 1941, the first German Jews to be deported at the spearhead of the combing-out process of European Jewry were dispatched to the War-thegau. The possibility of liquidating ghettoised Jews had by then already been explicitly raised for the first time, in the summer of 1941, significantly by Nazi leaders in the Warthegau. The first mobile gassing units to be deployed against the Jews operated in the Warthegau in the closing months of 1941. And the systematic murder of the Jews began in early December 1941 in the first extermination camp — actually a 'gas van station'[2] — established at Chelmno on the Ner, in the Warthegau.

Despite the centrality of the Warthegau to the unfolding of what the Nazis called 'the Final Solution of the Jewish Question' — the systematic attempt to exterminate the whole of European Jewry — the precise course of development of Nazi anti-Jewish policy in the Warthegau, though mentioned in every ac-count of the origins of the 'Final Solution', has not been exhaustively explored.[3]

To focus upon the Warthegau in the genesis of the 'Final Solution' can, however, help to contribute towards answering the central questions which have come to dominate scholarly debate on the emergence of systematic genocide: how and when the decision to wipe out the Jews of Europe came about, whether at the moment of German triumph in mid-summer 1941, or later in the year when the growing probability of prolonged war in the east ruled out an envisaged 'territorial solution'; Hitler's own role in the shift to a policy of outright genocide; and whether the 'Final Solution' followed a single order or set of directives issued from Berlin as the culmination of a long-held 'programme' of the Nazi leadership, or unfolded in haphazard and piecemeal fashion, instigated by 'local initiatives' of regional Nazi bosses, improvised as a largely ad hoc response to the logistical difficulties of a 'Jewish problem' they had created for themselves, and only gradually congealing into a full-scale 'programme' for genocide.[4]

The deficiencies and ambiguities of the evidence, enhanced by the language of euphemism and camouflage used by the Nazis even among themselves when dealing with the extermination of the Jews, mean that absolute certainty in answering these complex questions can not be achieved. Close assessment of the Warthegau evidence, it is the contention of this essay, nevertheless sheds light on developments and contributes towards an interpretation which rests on the balance of probabilities.

When the rapidly improvised boundaries of the newly created Reichsgau Posen (from 29 January 1940 Reichsgau Wartheland or, for short, the Warthegau — taking its name from the Warthe, the central river of the province) were eventually settled, they included an extensive area centring upon the large industrial town of Lodz, which had formerly been in Congress Poland and had never been part of Prussian Poland.[5] The borders of the Reich were thereby extended some 150–200 kilometres eastwards of the boundaries existing before 1918. For Nazi aims at 'solving the Jewish Question', the significance of this extension was that it brought within the territory of the Warthegau — which was to be ruthlessly germanised — an area containing over 350,000 Jews (some 8% of the total population of the region). The most important figures in the Warthegau scene after 1939 were Arthur Greiser, Reich Governor and at the same time Gauleiter of the Nazi Party, and Wilhelm Koppe, the SS and police chief of the region. Greiser, born in the Posen province in 1897, was utterly ruthless and single-minded in his determination to make his region the 'model Gau' of Nazi rule.[6] He called upon a 'special commission', given to him by Hitler personally, whenever he encountered difficulties or obstructions.[7] He also stood high in Himmler's favour, and was given on 30 January 1942 the honorary rank of Obergruppenführer in the SS.[8] Koppe, born in

Hildesheim in 1896, nominally subordinate to Greiser but in practice possessing a high degree of independence as the leading SS functionary in the region, had effective control over deportation policy in the Warthegau.[9] He was well up in Himmler's good books and had the ready ear of the Reichsführer-SS. At the same date as Greiser's promotion within the SS, 30 January 1942 and precisely at the point when the killing of the Warthegau Jews had begun, Koppe was promoted by Himmler to the rank of SS-Obergruppenführer and General der Polizei.[10] Like Greiser, he was notorious for his cold ruthlessness.

The tone for the administration of Poland was provided by Hitler himself. Admiral Canaris pointed out to General Keitel on 12 September 1939 that he had knowledge that extensive executions (Füsilierungen) were planned for Poland 'and that the nobility and clergy especially were to be exterminated (ausgerottet)'. Keitel replied that this had already been decided by the Führer. The Wehrmacht had to accept the 'racial extermination' and 'political cleansing' by the SS and the Gestapo, even if it did not itself want anything to do with it. That was why, alongside the military commanders, civilian commanders were being appointed, to whom the 'racial extermination' (Volkstums-Ausrottung) would fall.[11] On 17 October, Hitler spoke to a small group of those leaders most directly concerned of a 'hard racial struggle' which did not allow any 'legal constraints' or comply with principles otherwise upheld. The new Reich territories would have to be purged 'of Jews, Polacks, and rabble', and the remainder of the former Poland (the Generalgouvernement) would serve as the dumping ground for such groups of the population.[12] Hitler was involved at an early stage in schemes for a 'solution' to the 'Jewish Question' in Poland, though the ideas themselves emanated from Himmler (presumably in close collaboration with chief of the Security Police Reinhard Heydrich). At a meeting on 14 September 1939, Heydrich explained his own views on the 'Jewish problem' in Poland to the assembled Security Police leaders, adding that suggestions from the Reichsführer were being placed before Hitler, 'which only the Führer could decide'.[13] These were presumably the suggestions which became incorporated in Heydrich's directions to leaders of the Einsatzgruppen on 21 September 1939 for the concentration of Jews in the larger towns as a preparatory measure for a subsequent 'final goal' (to be kept 'strictly secret'.)[14] The 'final goal' was at this time evidently the eventual deportation of the Jews from Reich territory and from Poland to the intended reservation east of the Vistula, as Hitler himself indicated on 29 September to Alfred Rosenberg.[15] Hitler's views accorded precisely with guidelines which Heydrich drew up on that same day. The intention was to create a type of 'Reich Ghetto' to the east of Warsaw and around Lublin 'in which all the political and Jewish elements, who are to be moved out of the future German

Gaue, will be accommodated'.[16] The plans for Poland, as they were gradually congealing in September and early October 1939, amounted, therefore, to a three-fold division: of those parts to be incorporated into the Reich and eventually wholly Germanised, and sealed off by an eastern fortification; of a German-run 'foreign-speaking Gau' under Hans Frank outside a proposed 'East Wall', centring on Cracow and coming to be called the 'General Government', as a type of buffer zone; and of a Jewish settlement to the east of this area, into which all Jews from Poland and Germany would be dumped.[17] The initial expectations, both of a Jewish reservation in the Lublin area and of the mass deportation of German Jews to the General Government rapidly, however, proved illusory. The organisational and administrative difficulties involved had been hopelessly underestimated. Eichmann's immediate attempt, in October 1939, to deport Vienna's Jews to the Lublin area was rapidly stopped.[18] And in the event, apart from small-scale deportations from Stettin and Schneidemühl in Pomerania to the Lublin area in February and March 1940—an SS 'initiative' which Frank's administration could not cope with, prompting a protest from the General Governor and a temporary ban announced by Göring on 24 March 1940 on deportation of Jews into Frank's domain[19]—Jews from the Altreich (Germany of the pre-1938 boundaries) were not deported to the east until autumn 1941.[20] From the measures for occupied Poland decided by the central Nazi leadership in September 1939, it can be seen that Hitler set the tone, and provided the ultimate authority for the brutality of racial policy; and that he had far-reaching but imprecise notions of future developments, drawing at least in part on policy initiatives suggested by Himmler, which rapidly proved unfeasible and impracticable. Precisely because Hitler's barbarous imperatives offered no more than broad but loosely formulated aims and sanction for action of the most brutal kind, they opened the door to the wildest initiatives from agencies of Party and State, and above all, of course, from the SS. The authorities on the spot in the Warthegau did not, in fact, reckon that they would have too much difficulty in tackling the 'Jewish Question', and consequently grossly underestimated the self-created logistical problems. The view prevailed that the real problem was Polish, not Jewish.[21] At the outset of the occupation, the Jews were seen by the Warthegau leadership as a sideshow.[22] The main issue in the Warthegau was thought to be less the 'Jewish' than the 'Polish question'.

Initially, it seemed that things were running more or less according to expectation. In his new capacity as Reich Commissar for the Strengthening of German Nationhood, under powers bestowed on him by Hitler on 7 October, Himmler on 30 October ordered all Jews to be cleared out of the incorporated territories in the months November 1939 to February 1940.[23] On the basis of the discussions on 8 November 1939 in Cracow, at which he was present, about 'the evacuation of Jews and Congress Poles from the Old Reich and from the Reich Gaue of Danzig, Posen' and other areas,[24] Koppe issued instructions on 12 November 1939 for the deportation from the Warthegau between 15 November 1939 and 28 February 1940 of, initially, 200,000 Poles and 100,000 Jews.[25] This appears to have been subjected to slight delay and an amendment of the numbers involved. For on 28 November, Heydrich ordered an initial 'short-term plan' (Nahplan) to deport 80,000 Jews and Poles from the Warthegau to the General Government between the 1st and the 16th of December 1939 at a rate of 5,000 per day, to make way for 40,000 Baltic Germans.[26] These expulsions were immediately put into effect. Discussions with Eichmann in Berlin on 4 January 1940 then indicated the goal for the Warthegau as the deportations of 200,000 Jews and 80,000 Poles.[27] But at a meeting in Berlin on 30 January 1940, the first murmurings of complaint from the General Government about the number of expellees being deported from the Warthegau over the border could be registered.[28] By the time Koppe was forced to reply, in spring 1940, to the ever louder complaints, the total number of Jews and Poles deported had reached 128,011.[29]

By February 1940, deep divisions on deportation policy were apparent. While Himmler pressed for speedy deportation of Poles and Jews to make room for the planned influx of ethnic Germans into the annexed territories, Göring opposed the loss of manpower useful to the war effort and was backed by Frank, anxious to block the expanding numbers of expellees being forced into his domain.[30] In April, Greiser's request to deport the Warthegau Jews was deferred until the coming August.[31] But by the summer of that year it was plain that the intended deportations from the Warthegau into the General Government could not be carried out. An important meeting on the issue took place in Cracow on 31 July 1940.[32] Greiser emphasised at the meeting the growing difficulties in the Warthegau. He spoke of the 'massing' of Jews as the construction of a ghetto in Litzmannstadt (Lodz) had concentrated around 250,000 Jews there. This was, he declared, merely a provisional solution.[33] All these Jews had to leave the Warthegau, and it had been envisaged that they would be deported to the General Government. He had imagined that the modalities would be discussed at the meeting. But now a new decision — that is, to deport the Jews overseas, to Madagascar — had emerged. Clarification was crucial. The difficulties of feeding the Jews forced into the ghetto as well as the mounting problems of disease meant, he claimed, that they could not be kept there over the coming winter. A temporary solution had at all costs to be found which would allow for the deportation of these Jews into another territory. The Governor General, Hans Frank, reminded Greiser that Himmler had given him the assurance, on Hitler's command, that no more Jews were to be sent into the General Government. Koppe brought the discussion back to the looming crisis in the Warthegau. The position regarding the Jews was deteriorating daily, he claimed, repeating that the ghetto in Litzmannstadt had only been set up on the presumption that the deportation of the Jews concentrated there would commence in mid 1940. Frank replied that the germanisation of Litzmannstadt could not take place overnight and might well last fifteen years. The situation in the General Government, he stated, was in any case worse than that in the Warthegau. Greiser correctly drew the conclusion from the discussion that there was no prospect, even as an interim solution, of the General Government receiving the Warthegau's quarter of a million Jews. It was again stressed, however, by his entourage that there could be no question of the Jews remaining in Litzmannstadt and that 'the Jewish question must, therefore, be solved in some way or other'.[34] On 6 November 1940, Frank informed Greiser by telegram that further deportations of Poles and Jews from the Warthegau into the General Government were impossible before the end of the war. He had informed Himmler of this position, and given instructions to turn back any transports.[35]

Meanwhile, conditions for the Jews in the improvised ghettos and camps of the Warthegau were unspeakable. Outbreaks of epidemic diseases were inevitable. At Kutno, where 6,500 Jews were confined in a former sugar factory, spotted fever (Fleckfieber) broke out on 30 October 1940. Breaking up the camp or dispersal of the inmates into buildings in adjoining streets was ruled out for fear of infecting Germans. Even fresh straw for bedding and hot water for delousing could not be provided. It was reported to Greiser that as things stood any possibility of combating the spotted fever in the camp could be ruled out. Worries were expressed about the situation in the coming winter. The epidemic was predictably unstoppable. By the summer of 1941 there had been 1145 cases, 280 of them fatal. The camp was finally closed in March 1942, by which time there had been 1369 cases, 313 leading to deaths.[36] A fate worse than spotted fever, of course, awaited the survivors. In the huge Lodz ghetto, whose Jewish population when hermetically sealed off from the rest of the city on 1 May 1940 numbered 163,177 persons, starvation went hand in hand with disease.[37] The problems of administration and control, of food provision and epidemic containment — that is the difficulties of coping with the internment of the Warthegau Jews which the Nazi leadership both in Berlin and in Posen had been in such a rush to bring about — were only too apparent to Greiser, Koppe, and other heads of the Warthegau administration, not least the Gestapo and the local government leaders in Lodz itself. The pressure which Greiser and Koppe had sought to put on Frank mirrored the pressure they were under from their own subordinates to do something about the mounting and apparently insoluble 'Jewish problem' in the province. But by mid 1941, there was no solution in sight.

It was at this juncture, however, in the summer of 1941, that talk began of new possibilities which might be contemplated. And the first evidence of such possibilities being envisaged can be witnessed in remarks issuing from the top echelon of the Warthegau administration. On 16 July 1941, the head of the Security Service (SD) in Posen, SS-Sturmbannführer Rolf-Heinz Höppner—a man close to both Greiser and Koppe—sent to Adolf Eichmann in the Reich Security Head Office in Berlin a summary, headed 'Solution of the Jewish Problem', of discussions, involving a variety of agencies, in the Reich Governor's headquarters. A possible solution to the 'Jewish Question' in the Reichsgau Wartheland had been broached. This amounted to the concentration of all Warthegau Jews in a huge camp for 300,000 persons close to the centre of coal production, where those Jews capable of working could be exploited in a number of ways with relatively easy policing (as the Police Chief in Lodz, SS-Brigadeführer Albert vouchsafed) and without epidemic danger to the non-Jewish population. The next item addressed the issue of what to do about those Jews incapable of working. A new, ominous, note was struck, offering a cynical rationalisation for genocide. 'There is the danger this winter', ran the minute, 'that the Jews can no longer all be fed. It is to be seriously considered whether the most humane solution might not be to finish off those Jews not capable of working by some sort of fast-working preparation. This would be in any event more pleasant than letting them starve'. Additionally, it was recommended that all Jewesses still capable of bearing children be sterilised, so that 'the Jewish problem' would be completely solved within the current generation. Reich Governor Greiser, it was added, had not yet commented on the matter. Government President Uebelhoer in Litzmannstadt had, however, given the impression that he did not want the ghetto there to disappear because it was so lucrative. Just how much could be made from the Jews had been explained to Höppner by pointing out that the Reich Labour Ministry was prepared to pay six marks a day from a special fund for each Jewish worker, whereas the actual cost amounted to only eighty pfennige a day. Höppner's covering note asked for Eichmann's opinion. 'The things sound in part fantastic', Höppner concluded, 'but would in my view be quite capable of implementation'.[38]

The Höppner memorandum demonstrates that there were still in July 1941 divergent views—even among the Lodz authorities themselves—about the treatment of the ghettoised Jews, now that the ghettos appeared to be a long-term prospect rather than a transient solution.[39] But above all, the memorandum highlights the idea of genocide at an embryonic stage.

By July 1941, events elsewhere were already pushing German policy towards the Jews strongly in the direction of genocide. The preparations for the 'war of annihilation'[40] with the Soviet Union marked, it has been noted, a 'quantum jump' into genocide.[41] Certainly, a genocidal climate was now present as never before. But orders for a general killing of Jews were, recent research indicates, not, as is often presumed, transmitted orally by Heydrich to the leaders of the Einsatzgruppen before the invasion of the Soviet Union. The Einsatzgruppen did not initially behave in a unified fashion, and there was a gradual escalation of killing during the first weeks of the campaign. Only after clarification of the tasks of the Einsatzgruppen had apparently been sought and provided by Himmler in August 1941 was there a drastic extensification of the slaughter to all Jews, irrespective of age or sex.[42] Outside the Soviet Union, too, the obvious impasses in anti-Jewish policy were, from a number of differing directions, now developing a rapid, and accelerating, momentum towards outright and total genocide.

On 31 July 1941, Göring, who had been nominally in charge of coordinating the forced emigration of German Jews since the aftermath of the great pogrom of November 1938, commissioned Heydrich with undertaking the preparations for the 'complete solution of the Jewish question within the German sphere of influence in Europe'.[43] All Göring did, in fact, was to sign a document drawn up in Heydrich's office, almost certainly drafted by Eichmann.[44] The initiative came, in other words, from the Reich Security Head Office. The Göring mandate has frequently been interpreted as the direct reflection of a Hitler order to kill the Jews of Europe. Such an interpretation is open to doubt.[45] It seems more probable that the mandate still looked to a territorial solution, envisaging the removal of German and other European Jews to a massive reservation in the east — somewhere beyond the Urals. The war, it was thought, would soon be over. The opportunity of such a territorial solution would then present itself. The result, needless to say, would itself have amounted to a different form of genocide in the long run. But it was not the actual 'final solution' which historically emerged in the closing months of 1941 and the beginning of 1942. The territorial solution which was still being pressed for in the summer of 1941 was predicated upon a swift German victory. By September, this prospect was already dwindling. Before this time, Hitler, holding to his notion that the Jews could serve as 'hostages', had resisted pressure, especially from Heydrich and Goebbels, to deport the German Jews to the east.[46] In mid September, a Foreign Office enquiry about deporting Serbian Jews to the east was turned down by Eichmann on the grounds that not even German Jews could be moved to Russia or the General Government. Eichmann recommended shooting.[47] But around the same time, in mid September 1941, Hitler was persuaded to change his mind about deporting the German Jews.[48] In the next months, the crucial steps which culminated in the 'Final Solution' proper were taken. In October and November 1941 the threads of the extermination net were rapidly pulled together.

In this development, events in the Warthegau played a crucial role. Notification of the Führer's wish that the Old Reich and the Protectorate (Bohemia and Moravia) should be cleared of Jews, as a first stage to Poland and then in the following spring further to the east, was sent by Himmler to Greiser on 18 September 1941, four days after Rosenberg's apparently successful intervention in persuading Hitler to deport the German Jews. Evidently because of the immediate implications for the Warthegau of the deportation order, the letter was sent directly to Greiser as head of the province's government and administration. Himmler reported the intention to deport 60,000 Jews to Litzmannstadt for the duration of the winter. Further details, added Himmler, would be provided by Heydrich, either directly or via Koppe.[49] Whether the figure of 60,000 Jews was an error, or was rapidly revised, is unclear. But within a week the number concerned was referred to as 20,000 Jews and now 5,000 Gypsies.[50] Possibly, they were intended as the first 'instalment'. But even this number was far too great for the authorities in Litzmannstadt. The ghetto administration vehemently protested at the intended influx, and the protest — on the grounds of existing massive overcrowding, provisioning problems, economic dislocation, and danger of epidemics — was conveyed by the Government President of Litzmannstadt, Uebelhoer, in the strongest terms to Berlin.[51] But it was to no avail. Heydrich stated — though his telegram to Uebelhoer was overtaken by events and never sent — that the deportation was 'absolutely necessary and no longer to be delayed', and that Greiser had given his permission to receive the Jews in Litzmannstadt.[52] Himmler demanded the same understanding from Uebelhoer that he had received from Greiser. He sharply upbraided Uebelhoer, for whom Greiser intervened, for his objectionable tone.[53]

From this exchange, it is clear that the pressures for deportation were coming from Berlin, that Greiser was willing to comply despite the already mounting impossibility of 'solving' the Warthegau's own 'Jewish question', and that opposition from Litzmannstadt itself was simply ruled out by Reich Security Head Office. The stated aim, the further expulsion of the Jews the coming spring to the east, does not appear at this point to have been concealing an actual intention to exterminate the Jews in death camps in Poland. Clearly, Uebelhoer knew nothing of any such intention.[54] Hitler himself spoke at the end of the first week in October of transporting Czech Jews directly 'to the east' and not first into the General Government,[55] and both Heydrich and Himmler referred in early October to German Jews being sent to camps in the Baltic.[56] Here, of course, their fate, in view of the murderous onslaught of the Einsatzgruppen in the Soviet Union, would have been all too predictable. The decision to deport Jews into areas where they had already been killed in their tens of thousands was plainly in itself genocidal.[57] By this time, in late September or early October 1941, it would appear that the decision for physical extermination — at least of Jews incapable of working — had in effect been taken, though Russia rather than Poland was still foreseen as the area of implementation. The option of deporting the Jews 'farther east' to the Soviet Union rapidly vanished, however, in the next weeks with first transport difficulties, then the stalling of the German advance and the deteriorating military position in Russia. Far from a quick blitzkrieg victory, the end of the war in the east was nowhere in sight. And towards the end of October Eichmann was making it clear that the mooted further deportation to the east of Jews deported from Germany to Litzmannstadt referred only to Jews 'fit to work'.[58] Since Jews in the east incapable of working were already being earmarked for extermination, the implication was obvious.

New approaches to 'solving the Jewish Question' were meanwhile beginning to emerge. In circles closely connected with the 'Jewish Question', there was now ominous talk of 'special measures' for extermination.[59] Viktor Brack, of the Führer Chancellory and formerly the inspiration of the 'euthanasia action' (whose personnel, after the halting of the 'programme' in the Reich in late August, were now available for redeployment and carried with them 'expertise' derived from the gassing of the incurably sick), offered advice on the potential of poison gas as a means for tackling the 'Jewish problem', again at precisely this juncture.[60] In October, too, the SS commandeered Polish labourers at Belzec in eastern Poland to undertake the construction of the extermination camp there — one of the three camps (the others were Sobibor and Treblinka) which developed into 'Operation Reinhard', directed by the Lublin police chief Globocnik.[61] The former euthanasia personnel dispatched to liaise with Globocnik arrived in Lublin around the same time.[62] The first experimental gassings at Auschwitz (of Soviet prisoners-of-war) took place in late summer and autumn 1941, and construction of the extermination camp at Auschwitz-Birkenau was underway by the end of the year.[63] On 16 December 1941, Hans Frank spoke openly in a meeting of leaders of the General Government about the need to 'exterminate the Jews wherever we find them', pointing out that the Gauleiter of the eastern territories were saying they too did not want the Jews. They were asking why there was not a resort to 'self-help' to liquidate the Jews, rather than sending them to the east. Frank commented that he did not know how the extermination of the 3.5 million Jews in the General Government could come about, since they could not be shot or poisoned.[64] A comprehensive plan for the extermination of the Jews had evidently not yet been established. Physical extermination was, however, now unmistakably the intention.[65] The Jewish transports from Berlin, Prague, Vienna, and elsewhere had meanwhile been rolling into Lodz. The first German Jews arrived on 16 October 1941. By 4 November 1941, there had already been twenty transports, and the deportation target was reached.[66] With the number of Jews sharply increasing and the prospects of reductions through further deportations eastwards even more rapidly diminishing, killing the Jews of the Warthegau now emerged as a practical option.

The option was rapidly seized upon. Already in autumn 1941, and weeks before the transports from the Lodz ghetto to systematic extermination at Chelmno began, there were mass killings of Jews at locations in the southern part of the Warthegau. Polish underground sources smuggled out information, published in the United States in 1942, of the slaughter in October 1941 of the entire Jewish population — reputedly some 3,000 persons — of the Konin district, who had been gathered together in Zagarow (a village the Germans renamed 'Hinterberg') and then driven in truckloads into the Kaszimir woods where all trace of them ended.[67] Postwar German investigations corroborated the essence of the report. They concluded that in an indeterminate period, probably between autumn 1940 and late summer or autumn 1941, and in various 'actions', a large number of Jewish men, women and children were driven into the woods between Kazimierz Biskupi and Kleczew and either shot or killed in a gas van. Most of the victims, it was noted, were from Zagorow (Hinterberg), where beforehand a large number of Jewish families from the Konin district had been concentrated. Witnesses said the killings were carried out by police and Gestapo.[68] Further postwar trial investigations in Germany established that, beginning on 26 November 1941 and lasting several days, an SS extermination squad had killed perhaps some 700 Jews — mainly elderly, ill, or feeble Jews and children — interned in a camp at Kozminek (Bornhagen in German) near Kalisch, by means of a gas van.[69]

Probably such killings were envisaged by the security police and liquidation squads as experiments in the extermination techniques which would soon need to be deployed for the far larger numbers in the Lodz ghetto. The major operation was not long delayed. At the beginning of December 1941,[70] regular and systematic extermination began at the site which had been selected specifically for the purpose, Chelmno, by a special 'task squad' which had already accumulated much expertise in gas van extermination.

In the framework of the 'euthanasia programme', which ran in the Reich between autumn 1939 and summer 1941, a 'special unit' under Herbert Lange had operated in the annexed areas of the east from a base in Posen. The most extensive of its mass killings had been the murder, between 21 May and 6 June 1940, of 1,558 mental patients from asylums in and around Soldau in East Prussia.[71] The technique used by Lange's Sonderkommando was the gassing of victims by carbon monoxide poisoning in a large van.[72] Lange's chauffeur, Walter Burmeister, recorded in postwar testimony that he had driven Lange around the Warthegau in autumn 1941, accompanied by other members of the Stapo-Leitstelle of Posen and a guard drawn from the Schutzpolizei looking for a suitable location to carry out killings of Jews. He then, presumably once an appropriate spot had been found, drove Lange to security police headquarters in Berlin and back. In November 1941, shortly after returning from Berlin, Lange's unit — now increased in size — moved from Posen to Chelmno, and at the beginning of December 1941 began the use of two gas vans (a third gas van arrived during the course of the month) sent from Berlin.[73] Thus began the killing process in the first of the extermination establishments to begin its operations.[74]

Did the initiative to begin the killing come from Berlin, or from within the Warthegau? In one postwar trial, it was accepted that orders for the 'resettle-ment' (that is, killing) of Jews from the Lodz ghetto to the extermination camp at Chelmno went directly from the Reich Security Head Office in Berlin to the Gestapo office in Lodz.[75] Even if correct, this could be taken as consonant with a request emanating from within the Warthegau, then sanctioned in Berlin. However, neither a request from Lodz nor a general order coming from Berlin for 'resettlement' of the Lodz Jews could have by-passed the heads of the civil and police administration in the Warthegau, Greiser and Koppe. Moreover, the 'resettlement' of the Lodz Jews began only on 16 January 1942, more than a month after the killings in Chelmno had started.[76] If orders were transmitted direct from Berlin to Lodz, they must have been subsidiary to an initial deci-sion to initiate the genocide in the Warthegau by exterminating the Jews inca-pable of work. And the balance of probabilities points towards seeing the initial impulses coming from within the Warthegau itself, and not directly from Berlin. The emergence of a genocidal 'solution' in the Warthegau corre-sponds exactly with the weeks in which the authorities there were having to cope with the reception of 20,000 Jews, accepted only under protest by the local authorities in Litzmannstadt. With the collapse of hopes of deporting the province's own Jews, then the forced reception of Jews from Germany, and finally the cutting off of an exit route for any of the Jews, Warthegau anti-Jewish policy had run ever further into a cul-de-sac.

Killing offered a way out. And, it will be remembered, it had already been talked of seriously among the Warthegau ruling elite as early as July 1941. The means, with the redeployment of Lange's special unit, were by autumn 1941 now to hand to implement what in July had been referred to in the Höppner memorandum as 'fantastic notions'. The mention in that memorandum of the names of the Lodz police chief Albert and the Government President Uebelhoer (who came, it will be recalled, in September to protest in the strongest terms about the orders for a new influx of Jews to the Lodz ghetto) indicates the centrality of the Lodz authorities to the internal Warthegau debate on the fate of the region's Jews. It is possible, as has been suggested (though there is no direct evidence to prove it), that when the position, from the point of view of the Nazi bosses in Lodz, became critical following the order to take in the tens of thousands of new deportees from the Reich in the autumn, the suggestion to liquidate them came initially from the Gestapo at Lodz.[77] On the other hand, the Sonderkommando Lange drew mainly for its personnel on the security police headquarters at Posen, where it was based before moving to Chelmno, and continued to liaise directly with the Posen office, not with Lodz.[78] Whatever part was played by the security police authorities in Lodz and Posen, the key role was almost certainly that of the overall head of the security services in the Warthegau, Higher SS and Police Chief Wilhelm Koppe.[79]

Koppe's own version of his involvement in the emergence of a genocidal 'solution' was given in connection with his trial in Bonn in 1960.[80] He portrays himself as the conscience-stricken recipient of orders from Berlin. Quite apart from the apologetics, the account has to be treated with caution. Koppe claimed he heard, either in 1940 or in 1941, that a Commissar (whose name he later learned was Lange) and a special SS unit were to be sent to him from Berlin to carry out the physical extermination of the Jews in the Wartheland. His understanding at the time, he said, was that this would apply only to Jews incapable of work — the impression, he added, also of Greiser. Koppe's view was that the Sonderkommando would carry out 'experiments', trying out gassing methods already devised by Brack of the Führer Chancellory. Koppe was adamant that he had heard of the deployment of the Lange unit from Ernst Damzog, Inspector of the Security Police and SD in the Wartheland, based in Posen, and learnt further from a telephone conversation with Dr. Rudolf Brandt from Himmler's personal office that an 'action' against the Jews was being prepared, and that Brack's gassing experiments, reaching completion in Berlin, were now to be deployed by Sonderkommando Lange, under Brack's direction, in the Wartheland. In a crisis of conscience, alleged Koppe, he consulted Greiser who, it was immediately obvious, was fully in the picture and stated that it was a matter of a 'Führer order' which could not be 'sabotaged' (since Koppe purportedly opposed such 'experiments' as inhumane).

In this account, it seems plain, Koppe is conflating the beginnings of the 'euthanasia action' in the Warthegau with the decision to kill the province's Jews. He could not possibly have heard of a decision to exterminate the Jews of the Warthegau in 1940. But nor did he encounter the name of Herbert Lange and existence of his Sonderkommando for the first time in 1941, and in connection with an 'action' against the Jews. For Lange and his men had by then already been stationed in Posen and at Koppe's behest for over a year, employed in the gassings of mental patients in the annexed areas of Poland. And whether in connection with the 'euthanasia action' or the extermination of the Jews, it seems unlikely that Koppe learnt of the deployment of the Sonderkommando Lange from Damzog, a subordinate. Finally, assuming that the telephone conversation with Brandt took place in autumn 1941 and along the lines Koppe described, it might still be doubted whether it should be seen as relaying an order from Berlin as opposed to complying with a request from within the Warthegau to deploy the 'Brack methods' to exterminate the Jews. Without minimising the indispensability of empowering orders from Berlin, and accepting that by October 1941 a decision had been taken or sanctioned by Hitler to exterminate European Jewry—certainly those Jews incapable of working—it seems, nevertheless, probable, as we shall see, that Koppe was far more active in initiating the 'action' against the Jews in the Warthegau than his postwar account suggests.

At any rate, for well over a year before the killing of the Jews began, Koppe was in overall command of Lange's unit. Later, when it was renamed Sonderkommando Kulmhof (the German name for Chelmno) and placed under a new leader, Hans Bothman, Koppe had general control of the unit's personnel and economic matters,[81] delegating the practical running of the unit to Damzog's office.[82] In the summer of 1941 Koppe was among the circle of recipients—including by no means all the Higher SS and Police Leaders—of the 'Reports on Events' (Ereignismeldungen), explicitly detailing the killings of Jews in the Soviet Union.[83] He knew, therefore, of the ravages of the Einsatzgruppen in Russia, and, of course, at first hand of the gassings of mental patients in the annexed Polish territories (since he had 'lent out' Sonderkommando Lange for that purpose). He was, as his own testimony shows, aware of Brack's experiments with techniques of mass killing by use of poisonous gas. There can be no doubt that he was involved in the deliberations which led to the Höppner memorandum in July 1941. He was in every way, then, well attuned to the progressively radical thinking on the possible 'solution to the Jewish Question' in the top echelons of the SS and at Reich Security Headquarters in Berlin.

The central role played by the regional command of the security police in the emergence and implementation of a policy of genocide in the Warthegau is obvious. But where did the overlord of the Warthegau, Reich Governor and Gauleiter Arthur Greiser, fit in to the decisions to move to outright genocide? Despite Koppe's assertion that Greiser was supinely carrying out a 'Führer Order' imposed on the Warthegau from Berlin, the evidence suggests, in fact, that the request to begin killing the Jews came directly from Greiser himself. As the letter from Himmler to Greiser of 18 September 1941, informing him of the decision to deport 60,000 Jews to the Lodz ghetto, shows, communication on such matters between the head of the SS and the leader of the Warthegau did not need to pass through the hands of Koppe.[84] Greiser himself had excellent relations with Himmler. But, as Koppe's testimony indicated, the Reich Governor and the regional police chief were of one mind on the 'Jewish Question', while the rounding up of Jews from the smaller ghettos of the Warthegau needed evident close cooperation between the security police and the administrative organs under Greiser's control.[85] It is clear that Greiser contacted Himmler directly in a number of instances relating to Chelmno and the Sonderkommando operating there.[86] And when, after a temporary end to the killing, the work of the Sonderkommando was recommenced in early 1944, it was on the basis of an agreement between Himmler and Greiser in which, it seems plain, the initiative was taken by the latter.[87] Something of Greiser's role can be gathered, too, from references to the killing of the Jews in mid 1942. A report of the Lodz Gestapo from 9 June 1942 noted that 'all Jews not capable of work' were to be 'evacuated' — a euphemism for liquidated — 'according to the directions of the Gauleiter'.[88] This is probably to be linked with the killing of 100,000 Jews which Greiser himself had requested and referred to in a letter to Himmler dated 1 May 1942.[89] Greiser spoke in this letter of the completion, within the next two to three months, of 'the action, approved by you in agreement with the Head of the Reich Security Head Office, SS-Obergruppenführer Heydrich, for the special treatment [another camouflage term for killing] of around 100,000 Jews in the area of my Gau'. Although Greiser spoke of the 'action' being completed within two to three months, according to a memorandum from the Reich Security Head Office dated 5 June 1942, a total of 97,000 Jews had in fact already been killed in Chelmno since December 1941.[90] Greiser's request for permission to carry out the 'special treatment' must, therefore, have been made considerably earlier. Indeed, it conceivably marked the actual request to begin the killing before the commencement of operations in Chelmno at the beginning of December 1941.[91] Greiser went on in his letter of 1 May 1942 to request Himmler's approval of a further 'initiative' on his part: the use of the Sonderkommando, directly following on the 'Jewish action', to liquidate 35,000 Poles in the Gau suffering from incurable tuberculosis.[92] The tuberculosis episode is revealing in a number of respects for the light it casts on the likely decision-making process in the killing of the Jews. Greiser's letter to Himmler was immediately followed by a letter to the latter's personal adjutant SS-Sturmbannführer Rudolf Brandt from Koppe, recommending that the case be verbally explained to the Reichsführer and offering his own approval of the 'solution striven for by the Gauleiter'.[93] Brandt's reply to Koppe stated that he had passed on Greiser's suggestion for an opinion from Heydrich, but that 'the last decision in this matter must be taken by the Führer'.[94] Soundings were, in fact, taken a week later, on 21 May, from Heydrich, who replied on 9 June, stating that he had no objections, subject to thorough discussion of the necessary measures with the security police.[95] Himmler then wrote to Greiser, using Heydrich's wording as the basis of his own letter, towards the end of June.[96]

There matters appear to have rested until the autumn. Preparations for the 'action' presumably took some time.[97] In November 1942, however, before the 'action' had commenced, Greiser received a letter from Dr. Kurt Blome, deputy head of the Nazi Party's health office (Hauptamt für Volksgesundheit) in Berlin, raising objections on the grounds that it would be impossible to maintain the necessary secrecy, thereby arousing unrest and providing enemy propaganda with a gift. He specifically referred to the lessons to be learnt from the mistakes of such a kind made in the 'euthanasia action' in Germany. Consequently, he thought it necessary to consult Hitler, to ask whether, in the light of the 'euthanasia action' which Hitler had stopped (if only partially) for such reasons, the 'tuberculosis action' should go ahead.[98] Greiser wrote again to Himmler on 21 November in the light of Blome's objections. His comment is enlightening. He wrote: 'I myself do not believe that the Führer needs to be asked again in this matter, especially since at our last discussion with regard to the Jews he told me that I could proceed with these according to my own judgement'.[99] Himmler nevertheless regarded Blome's objections as serious enough to advise against the implementation of Greiser's suggestion.[100]

From this exchange, a number of points seem clear. The initiative for killing 100,000 Jews and the later suggestion for the liquidation of 35,000 tuberculosis victims came directly from Greiser.[101] Approval in both cases was sought from Himmler, who in the latter case, certainly, then consulted Reich Security Head Office. The Warthegau head of security, Koppe, paved the way for the approval of the 'tuberculosis action' and probably did the same with regard to the 'initiative' on the Jews. It cannot be proved, but seems distinctly possible, that the initial suggestion came from him. In the case of the tuberculose Poles, it was pointed out that a decision could only come from Hitler, whose authorisation was essential, at which point doubts arose leading to

Himmler's blocking of an initiative he had earlier approved. It seems inconceivable that the killing of the Jews could have been decided upon without some equivalent blanket authorisation by Hitler.[102] But it also appears plain that, as in the tuberculosis matter, all that would have been required of Hitler was authorisation for the implementation of initiatives coming from others. And, as Greiser pointed out, Hitler's response to his own request for authorisation on 'solving the Jewish Question' in the Warthegau had been to grant him permission to act according to his own discretion. Hitler's role here, as elsewhere, was to set the tone and then to provide the broad sanction for actions prompted and set in motion by others.

In the implementation of genocide in the Warthegau, it can be concluded that responsibility for the personnel and economic matters connected with the Sonderkommando at Chelmno rested with the Higher SS and Police Chief, Koppe, and was delegated by him to the Inspector of the Security Police and SD, Damzog, while general responsibility lay in the hands of Reich Governor and Gauleiter Greiser, operating with the permission of Reichsführer SS Himmler, and head of Reich Security Heydrich, and with the blanket authorisation to act as he saw fit provided by Hitler himself.[103]

This examination of the emergence of genocide in the Warthegau — admittedly tentative in places, and necessarily resting at times on the balance of probabilities — has suggested that improvisation by the German authorities on the spot played a decisive role in the autumn of 1941. It was only in the immediate aftermath of Himmler's order to receive tens of thousands of new Jews into the Warthegau and there into the overcrowded Lodz ghetto — following Hitler's authorisation to deport German and Czech Jews — that earlier 'fantasy' talk of liquidating Jews became transformed into a realisable prospect of extermination. The rapid conversion of the Sonderkommando Lange, conveniently to hand but before that date having no special link with a proposed 'solution' to the 'Jewish Question,' into a unit deployed specifically in the systematic extermination of Jews, the prompt search for a suitable killing ground, the initial — seemingly experimental — slaughter of Jews at Zagorow and Bornhagen, and the establishment of Chelmno itself, all smack of improvisation. In this, the initiatives by the Warthegau rulers were highly important. Permission to kill a hundred-thousand Jews was actively sought by Reich Governor Greiser; no order to that effect was forced upon him by Himmler or Heydrich. Such a mandate had been requested by spring 1942 at the latest, but almost certainly well before this time and in all probability before the end of 1941. It is Greiser, too, who discusses the Warthegau Jews with Hitler himself at an unspecified date — at the latest by autumn 1942, but probably earlier — and is told to deal with them as he thinks fit. And, as we have seen, the Gestapo at Lodz recorded the fact that they were acting on Greiser's direct instructions in the liquidation of Jews incapable of work. Greiser was subsequently evidently well informed about what took place at Chelmno, and took a keen interest in the developments and in the work of Sonderkommando Kulmhof.[104] And, finally, it was Greiser who on 7 March 1944 sent a telegram to Hitler, proudly reporting that in the Warthegau 'Jewry [had] shrunk to a tiny remnant.'[105]

Nevertheless, it seems more likely that Koppe, rather than Greiser, took the lead in initiating the move to outright genocide in the Warthegau.[106] Most probably it was Koppe, au fait with the thinking of Heydrich and Himmler, already having cooperated in Brack's gassing experiments through the use of the gas van by Lange's men to kill 'euthanasia' victims, and well aware of the antagonism in Litzmannstadt caused by the order to take in the new influx of Jews — possibly even prompted by the Gestapo there — who suggested to Berlin that a way out of the self-imposed problem would be to deploy the Lange unit to liquidate at least the Jews of the smaller ghettos where the problems in Nazi eyes were even greater than those of Lodz and where the possibility of moving them to Lodz was ruled out. It will be recalled that at the time that Höppner had sent his memorandum, in July, Greiser had not voiced an opinion on the solutions suggested. Evidently they had come from within the Security Police rather than from Greiser himself. And it seems likely that, several months later in the autumn, when the 'fantastic' notions mentioned by Höppner were being turned into reality, it was not Greiser, but Koppe, who was the actual initiator, with the Reich Governor approached when approval at the Gau level was needed.

It would be mistaken to conclude from this that 'local initiatives' acted in independence of central policy in Berlin; and even more so to imagine that central policy merely 'grew out of' practical improvisations at local or regional level.[107] An abundance of evidence has now been assembled, demonstrating beyond reasonable doubt that by the late summer and early autumn 1941 the decision physically to exterminate the Jews of Europe must have been taken by the Nazi leadership.[108] But the contrast between central planning and local initiative can easily be too sharply drawn. Whatever the nature of any central decision already reached, the fateful developments of autumn 1941 do have, within the overall goal of extermination of the Jews of Europe, an unmistakable air about them of improvisation, experimentation, and rapid adaptation to new policy objectives and opportunities. The 'Final Solution', as it came to emerge, formed a unity out of a number of organisationally separate 'programmes', one of which, arising from conditions specific to the Warthegau and remaining throughout under the direction of the province's own leadership rather than the central control of the Reich Security Head Office, was the extermination programme at Chelmno.[109]

At the time of Hitler's decision in mid September — against his earlier reluctance — to deport the German Jews to the east, knowledge of any already determined central extermination policy was clearly still confined to an extremely small circle of initiates. Plainly, Uebelhoer and the Litzmannstadt authorities were unaware in late September 1941 that the aim of anti-Jewish policy was systematic genocide. Otherwise, the vehemence of the objection to the influx of more Jews to the Lodz ghetto would be hard to comprehend.[110] But Koppe would have known, if anyone in the Warthegau did. His role as the police chief 'on the ground' aware of thinking at the centre was pivotal.

Hitler's own role in the emergence of a policy of systematic genocide was mainly to voice the need for a radical 'solution' to the 'Jewish Question', and to sanction and approve initiatives presented to him by those — above all Heydrich and Himmler — keen to translate the Führer's wishes into practical policy objectives. The evidence from the Warthegau — not least the authorisation to Greiser to act as he saw fit in the 'Jewish Question' — fits the picture of a Dictator whose moral responsibility is not in question but who was content to provide carte blanche for others to turn ideological imperatives into concrete directives for action.

By the date of the Wannsee Conference on 20 January 1942 the killing in the Warthegau had been in operation for over six weeks. By March 1942 the 'Final Solution' as it is known to history was in full swing.[111]

The killings at Chelmno began with the Jews from the neighbouring small ghettos and camps.[112] Transports from the Lodz ghetto began on 16 January 1942. Some 55,000 Jews from the Lodz ghetto itself had been killed by the end of May 1942.[113] By the end of 1942, the number of transports had declined, and at the end of March 1943 operations at Chelmno were ended and the camp dissolved. Greiser appeared in Chelmno, thanked the men of the Sonderkommando 'in the name of the Führer' for their work, invited them to a festive meal in a hotel in Warthbrücken, and attained through intercession with Himmler their further deployment, according to their wishes, as a unit attached to the SS volunteer division 'Prinz Eugen' in Yugoslavia.[114] The killings were restarted in April 1944, when Bothmann and the Sonderkommando were brought back to Chelmno for a second stint which ended on 17–18 January 1945.[115]

Of the leading provincial perpetrators of Nazi genocide in the Warthegau, Inspector of the Security Police and SD Ernst Damzog was killed in action in 1945. Head of the Posen SD Rolf-Heinz Höppner was sentenced in March 1949 in Poznań (Posen) to life imprisonment and released under an amnesty in

April 1956. The Government President of Lodz, Dr. Friedrich Uebelhoer, disappeared after American internment under a false name. The Police President of Lodz, Dr. Wilhelm Albert, died in 1960. The Gestapo head in Lodz from April 1942 and, at the same time, Lord Mayor of the city of Lodz, Dr. Otto Bradfisch, responsible also for Einsatzgruppen shootings in Russia, was sentenced in Munich in 1951 to ten years in a penitentiary, and in Hanover in 1963 to thirteen years, less the time spent from his Munich imprisonment, for complicity in the murder of 15,000 and 5,000 persons. The head of the Jewish desk in Lodz, Günter Fuchs, was sentenced in Hanover in 1963 to life imprisonment for nine cases of murder and complicity in the murder of at least 15,000 persons. The head of German administration of the Lodz ghetto, Hans Biebow, was hanged in Lodz in 1947. Herbert Lange was killed in action near Berlin in 1945. His successor as head of the Sonderkommando Kulmhof, Hans Bothmann, hanged himself in British custody in 1946. Of the 160 men suspected of participating in the Chelmno murders, 105 could not be found; 22 were established as dead or missing in action, and two had been hanged in Poland. A total of 33 were located and interrogated, of whom 12 eventually stood trial in Bonn in 1962. The result of the trial and appeal was, finally, that on 23 July 1965, eight were found guilty of involvement in murder and sentenced to periods of between thirteen months two weeks in prison and thirteen years in a state penitentiary. In another three cases, the involvement was regarded as so slight that no punishment was fitting. The last case was stopped because the accused was unfit to stand trial.[116]

Arthur Greiser was condemned to death by a Polish court and hanged in Poznań in 1946—after a last-minute plea for intercession by the Papacy had failed.[117] Wilhelm Koppe escaped after the war and lived under a pseudonym for over fifteen years as a successful businessman, becoming director of a chocolate factory in Bonn before being captured in 1960 and finally, in 1964, being arraigned for his involvement in mass murder in Poland. He was deemed unfit to stand trial.[118] He died peacefully in his bed on 2 July 1975.[119]

The nearest estimates are that a minimum of 150,000 Jews and about 5,000 gypsies were murdered in Chelmno between 1941 and 1945.[120] Four Jews survived.[121]

Notes

I would like to express my warmest thanks and appreciation to the following for their most helpful contributions to the research for this article: Christopher Browning, Philippe Burrin, Lucjan Dobroszycki, Gerald Fleming, Czesław Madajczyk, Stanisław Nawrocki, Karol Marian Pospieszalski, and the staffs of the Archiwum Państwowe

Poznań, the Berlin Document Center, the Główna Komissa Badni Zbrodni Hitlerowskich w Polsce Archiwum Warsaw, the Instytut Zachodni in Poznań, and the Zentrale Stelle der Landesjustizverwaltungen, Ludwigsburg. I owe grateful thanks, too, to the British Academy and the Polish Academy of Sciences for their generous joint support of the research I undertook in Poznań and Warsaw in September 1989.

1. The others were West Prussia and part of Upper Silesia. In addition, in the north of Poland substantial tracts of territory were added to the existing German province of East Prussia. In each of the incorporated territories (least in Gau Danzig-Westpreußen, most by far in the Warthegau), the new boundaries included areas which had never hitherto belonged to Prussia/Germany. See Martin Broszat, *Nationalsozialistische Polenpolitik 1939–1945* (Frankfurt am Main, 1965), 36–41; Czesław Madajczyk, *Die Okkupationspolitik Nazideutschlands in Polen 1939–1945* (Berlin, 1987), 30–6.

2. *Der Mord an den Juden im Zweiten Weltkrieg,* eds. Eberhard Jäckel and Jürgen Rohwer (Stuttgart, 1985), 145.

3. Two essays appeared in Polish in the 1970s, but before much recent scholarly literature on the genesis of the 'Final Solution'; Julian Leszczyński, 'Ż dziejów zagłady Żydów w Kraju Warty: Szkice do genezy ludóbojstwa hitlerowskiego', *Biuletyn Zydowskiego Instytutu Historycznego* 82 (1972), 57–72; and Artur Eisenbach, 'O należyte zrozumienie genezy zagłady Zydów', *ibid.* 104 (1977), 55–69.

4. For summaries and evaluations of the debate, see: Saul Friedländer, 'From Anti-Semitism to Extermination', *Yad Vashem Studies* 16 (1984), 1–50; Michael Marrus, *The Holocaust in History* (1988), chap. 2; and Ian Kershaw, *The Nazi Dictatorship, Problems and Perspectives of Interpretation* (3rd edn., 1993), chap. 5.

5. Broszat, *Polenpolitik*, 37–8.

6. I have contributed a brief character sketch of Greiser to the forthcoming second volume of Ronald Smelser, Enrico Syring, and Rainer Zitelmann (eds.), *Die braune Elite und ihre Helfer*. A character description by the prosecution counsel at Greiser's trial can be found in Zentrale Stelle der Landesjustizverwaltungen, Ludwigsburg (= ZSL), Anklageschrift aus dem Prozeß gegen Arthur Greiser, German translation (= Prozeß Greiser), Bl. 74–82. (A copy of the Polish text is in Polen-365h, Bl. 677–828).

7. See, for example, Główna Komisa Badania Zbrodni Hitlerowskich w Polsce (= GK), (Archive of the Central Commission for the Investigation of Hitlerite Crimes in Poland, Ministry of Justice, Warsaw), Process Artura Greisera (= PAG), vol. 11, Bl. 52; and see also the comment by Carl J. Burckhardt, *Meine Danziger Mission* (Munich, 1962), 79.

8. Berlin Document Center (= BDC), Personalakte (= PA) Arthur Greiser, unfoliated, Führer decree awarding the promotion, 30 Jan. 1942. Greiser's telegram to Himmler of the same date, thanking the Reichsführer-SS for his nomination to Hitler, stated that 'I am at your disposal at all times and without reservation in all my areas of work'.

9. Directly on Koppe, there is Szymon Datner, *Wilhelm Koppe — nie ukarany zbrodniarz hitlerowski* (Warsaw, 1963). Koppe figures prominently in Ruth Bettina Birn, *Die Höheren SS- und Polizeiführer, Himmlers Vertreter im Reich und in den besetzten Gebieten* (Düsseldorf, 1986). There is much valuable information on him in his personal file in the BDC. His trial indictment, ZSL, Landgericht Bonn 8 Js 52/60, Anklageschrift gegen Wilhelm Koppe wegen Beihilfe zum Mord (= Prozeß Koppe), Bl. 49–55, summarises his

career and personality. He was said to have been unbureaucratic and unconventional in his work-style — 'ruling through the telephone', as one witness put it — and to have combined a propensity for unfolding new, sometimes fantastic, schemes, with pedantic attention to detail. *Ibid.,* Bl. 54.

10. BDC, PA Koppe, unfoliated, effusive handwritten letter of thanks to Himmler for the latter's good wishes on his promotion, 5 Feb. 1942. The headed notepaper already bore Koppe's new grade, which had been bestowed on him only a week earlier.

11. Broszat, *Polenpolitik,* p 20.

12. *Ibid.,* 25.

13. ZSL, Verschiedenes, 301 Ar., Bl. 32.

14. ZSL, Polen 365n, Bl. 635–9. Printed in Broszat, *Polenpolitik,* 21.

15. Hans-Günther Seraphim, *Das politische Tagebuch Alfred Rosenbergs 1934/35 und 1939/40* (Munich, 1964), 99.

16. ZSL, Verschiedenes, 301 Ar., Bl. 39–40.

17. *Verfolgung, Vertreibung, Vernichtung. Dokumente des faschistischen Antisemitismus 1933 bis 1942* ed. Kurt Pätzold (Leipzig, 1983), 239–40.

18. See Seev Goschen, 'Eichmann und die Nisko-Aktion im Oktober 1939', *Vierteljahrshefte für Zeitgeschichte* 29 (1981), 74–96; and Jonny Moser, 'Nisko, the First Experiment in Deportation', *Simon Wiesenthal Center Annual* 2 (1985), 1–30.

19. Pätzold, 262.

20. Some Jews were sent westwards in 1940. On 22–3 Oct. 1940, with Hitler's approval, 6,504 Jews from Baden and the Saarpfalz were deported into Vichy France. Hitler also authorised, at the prompting of von Schirach in October 1940, the deportation of Viennese Jews to Poland. These began in January 1941 but were stopped again in March. See Christopher Browning, 'Nazi Resettlement Policy and the Search for a Solution to the Jewish Question, 1939–1941', *German Studies Review,* IX (1986), 513.

21. A memorandum from the Reichsleitung of the Rassepolitisches Amt of 25 November 1939, for example, establishing guidelines for the treatment of the conquered population 'from a racial-political viewpoint', commented that the Jews in the rump of Poland (Restpolen) posed a less dangerous problem than the Poles themselves. 'The Jews here could certainly be given a freer hand than the Poles,' the memorandum ran, 'since the Jews have no real political force such as the Poles have with their Greater Polish ideology'. ZSL, Polen 365p, Bl. 449, 453.

22. Already in November 1939, on a visit to Lodz, Greiser spoke of meeting 'figures who can scarcely be credited with the name "person" ', but assured his audience that the 'Jewish Question' was no longer a problem and would be solved in the immediate future. GK, PAG, vol. 27, Bl. 167.

23. Instytut Zachodni (= IZ), Poznań, I-441, Bl. 144.

24. Institut für Zeitgeschichte, Munich (= IfZ), Eichmann 1458; and see Werner Präg and Wolfgang Jacobmeyer (eds.), *Das Diensttagebuch des deutschen Generalgouverneurs in Polen 1939-1945* (Stuttgart, 1975), (= DTB Frank), 60ff. The Lodz Jews, however, the greatest number in what became the Warthegau, were not included in the first wave of deportees since it was at this stage not clear whether Lodz would belong to the Warthegau or *Generalgouvernement.* — Christopher Browning, 'Nazi Ghettoization Policy in Poland, *Central European History,* xix (1986), 346 and n.9.

25. IZ, I-441, Bl. 145–9.

26. IfZ, Eichmann 1460.

27. ZSL, Prozeß Koppe, Bl. 156. For deportation policy in general, see Robert Koehl, *RKFDV. German Resettlement and Population Policy 1939–1945* (Cambridge, Mass., 1957). For the most reliable guide to the numbers of Poles expelled from the Warthegau under Nazi rule, see Madjczyk, *Okkupationspolitik,* appendix, Table 15.

28. ZSL, Prozeß Koppe, Bl. 158.

29. ZSL, Polen 179, Bl. 653–4. Koppe to Greiser (17 May 1940), enclosing a 'Stellung-nahme' to the complaints, dated 20 April 1940, compiled by the Umwandererzentral-stelle Posen. The expulsion figures (which do not differentiate between Jews and Poles) comprised 87,883 persons deported between 1 and 16 December 1939, and 40,128 from 10 Feb. to 15 March 1940.

30. Browning, 'Resettlement', 506.

31. Browning, 'Ghettoisation', 347.

32. All following from DTB Frank, 261–4, entry for 31.7.40.

33. DTB Frank, 261. Greiser had ordered the Lodz Jews to be ghettoised in December 1939 as an interim measure prior to their expulsion — he mentioned a figure of 'some 250,000' — 'over the border'. The empty ghetto would then, he added, be burnt to the ground. BDC, PA Greiser, Besuchs-Vermerk/Akten-Vermerk, Stabsleiter of the Reichs-schatzmeister, 11 Jan. 1940, Bl. 3. At the establishment of the ghetto, the Government President of Lodz, Dr. Friedrich Uebelhoer, proposed in a communication to party and police authorities dated 10 December 1939 a 'temporary' solution to the problem of Lodz's Jews (which he numbered at about 320,000). He emphasised that 'the establish-ment of the ghetto is, it goes without saying, only a transitional measure'. Jüdisches Historisches Institut, Warsaw, *Faschismus — Getto — Massenmord* (Frankfurt am Main, n.d. [1961]), 81.

34. DTB Frank, 264.

35. GK, PAG, vol. 36; Bl. 559–60.

36. Details in this paragraph based on reports in Archiwum Państwowe Poznań (= APP), Reichsstatthalter 2111.

37. *The Chronicle of the Lodz Ghetto, 1941–1944,* ed. Lucjan Dobroszycki (New Haven/London, 1984), xxxix, l–li. APP, Reichsstatthalter 1855 contains statistics of disease in the ghetto in 1941. And, for evidence of rocketing death-rates from summer 1940, see also Browning, 'Ghettoisation', 349.

38. GK, PAG vol. 36, Bl. 567–8v.

39. See Browning, 'Ghettoisation', 349–51, for disputes between 'productionists' and 'attritionists' in Lodz. Dr. Karl Marder, the mayor of Lodz, signified in a letter to Uebel-hoer of 4 July 1941 — less than a fortnight before the Höppner memorandum — that the character of the ghetto in Lodz had changed, and that it should remain as an 'essential element of the total economy'. *Ibid.,* 350.

40. Hitler's description, prior to the invasion of the USSR, as noted by his Chief of Staff, Franz Halder, *Kriegstagebuch,* 3 vols. (Stuttgart, 1962–4), II, 336–7.

41. Christopher Browning, *The Final Solution and the German Foreign Office* (New York/London, 1978), 8.

42. These comments follow the analyses of Alfred Streim, *Die Behandlung sowje-*

tischer Kriegsgefangener im 'Fall Barbarossa' (Heidelberg/Karlsruhe, 1981), 74–93; and Philippe Burrin, *Hitler et les Juifs. Genèse d'un génocide* (Paris, 1989), 112–28. The counter-argument, that a general order to exterminate all Soviet Jews was orally given to the Einsatzgruppen leaders before the invasion of the Soviet Union, is most vehemently expressed by Helmut Krausnick, in Helmut Krausnick and Hans-Heinrich Wilhelm, *Die Truppe des Weltanschauungskrieges* (Stuttgart, 1981), 158–66, and in Jäckel and Rohwer, 120–1.

43. *International Military Tribunal: Trial of the Major War Criminals,* 42 vols. (Nuremberg, 1949), XXVI, 266–7, Doc. 710-PS.

44. That the document emanated from the *Reichssicherheitshauptamt* is certain, that Eichmann drafted it, very probable: see Raul Hilberg, *Die Vernichtung der europäischen Juden* (Frankfurt am Main, 1990), 1064 n.7; Jäckel and Rohwer, 15; Christopher Browning, *Fateful Months. Essays on the Emergence of the Final Solution* (New York/London, 1985), 21–2; Hans Mommsen, 'Die Realisierung des Utopischen: Die "Endlösung der Judenfrage" im "Dritten Reich" ', in Hans Mommsen, *Der Nationalsozialismus und die deutsche Gesellschaft* (Reinbek bei Hamburg, 1991), 207; and Richard Breitman, *The Architect of Genocide. Himmler and the Final Solution* (1991), 192.

45. See Burrin, 129–34; Mommsen, *Der Nationalsozialismus,* 207; and Arno Mayer, *Why did the Heavens not Darken? The 'Final Solution' in History* (New York, 1988), 290–2. See also Uwe Dietrich Adam, *Judenpolitik im Dritten Reich* (Düsseldorf, 1972), 308–9, though Adam presumes a Hitler directive behind the mandate, for which there is no evidence. Gerald Fleming, *Hitler und die Endlösung. 'Es ist des Führers Wunsch . . .'* (Wiesbaden/Munich, 1982), 78, Browning, *Fateful Months,* 21–2, Breitman, 193, Krausnick in Jäckel and Rohwer, 201, with differing emphasis, hold to the view that the mandate inaugurated the 'Final Solution'. Hilberg in Jäckel and Rohwer, 137–8, rather agnostically suggests a decision might have been taken around the date of the mandate, but that the evidence is inconclusive.

46. Burrin, 136–9; Christopher Browning, 'Zur Genesis der "Endlösung" ', *Vierteljahrshefte für Zeitgeschichte* XXIX (1981), 103; Martin Broszat, 'Hitler und die Genesis der "Endlösung" ', in *ibid.* XXV (1977), 750.

47. Browning, *Fateful Months,* 26.

48. Though impossible to be certain, it is probable that Rosenberg's influence was decisive in pressing Hitler to approve the immediate deportation of German Jews in retaliation for the Soviet deportation of Volga Germans to Siberia. See Burrin, 138–9; Browning, 'Zur Genesis', 103.

49. ZSL, USA 2, Bl. 310. Both Heydrich and Koppe were in receipt of copies of Himmler's letter to Greiser, which is, in fact, the only direct record of Hitler's deportation order.

50. *Ibid.,* Bl. 286, Gettoverwaltung to Regierungspräsident Uebelhoer, 24 Sept. 1941, signed by Werner Ventzki, the Oberbürgermeister of Lodz.

51. *Ibid.,* Bl. 286–309, Gettoverwaltung to Uebelhoer, 24 Sept. 1941; Bl. 277–9, Uebelhoer to Himmler, 4 Oct. 1941.

52. *Ibid.,* Bl. 280–2, Heydrich telegram to Himmler, 8 Oct. 1941; Brandt reply to Heydrich, same date.

53. Entire correspondence in the Uebelhoer case in *ibid.,* Bl. 257–85.

54. Broszat, 'Genesis', 751; Browning's reply, 'Zur Genesis', 103–4, seems weak on this point.

55. Cited Broszat, 751, n. 24.

56. Jäckel and Rohwer, 126.

57. Burrin argues (139–41), correctly in my view, that the deportation decision was tantamount to the decision to kill the European Jews.

58. Fleming, 83, letter from Dr. Wetzel, from the Ministry of the Occupied Eastern Territories, to Hinrich Lohse, Reich Commissar for the Baltic (Ostland), 25 Oct. 1941. The letter states categorically that there are no objections to the gassing of Jews unfit for work.

59. Browning, *Fateful Months*, 27.

60. Fleming, 81–3 (see note 58).

61. Jäckel and Rohwer, 127–8; Browning, *Fateful Months*, 30–1.

62. Browning, *Fateful Months*, 31.

63. Jäckel and Rohwer, 172–6; Browning, 'Zur Genesis', 107.

64. DTB Frank, 457 (entry for 16 Dec. 1941). 'Self-help' was, in fact, already being resorted to in the Baltic, where — among many mass shootings — the first German Jews had been shot in Lithuania and Latvia in late November 1941. See Fleming, 14, 77–104.

65. Further confirmation is the reply from the Eastern Ministry in Berlin, on 18 December, to a request for clarification made the previous month by Gauleiter Lohse, the Reich Commissar in the Baltic, that economic considerations were deemed to be irrelevant to the settling of the 'Jewish problem'. Browning, *Fateful Months*, 33.

66. *NS-Vernichtungslager im Spiegel deutscher Strafprozesse*, ed. Adalbert Rückerl (Munich, 1977), S. 257 n. 39 (henceforth cited as *NS-Vernichtungslager*). APP, Reichsstatthalter 1214, Bl. 7–9 has a statistical breakdown of the 17th and 20th transports on 1st and 4th Nov. 1941. For details of point of origin, date of arrival, and numbers involved, see Dobroszycki, *Chronicle*, lvii.

67. *The Ghetto Speaks*, 5 Aug. 1942 (Bund Archives of the Jewish Labor Movement, New York), 1. I am grateful to Prof. Lucjan Dobroszycki for a copy of this document. And see Dobroszycki, *Chronicle*, liv (where it is stated they were shot, though this is not stipulated in the report in *The Ghetto Speaks*).

68. ZSL, Verfahren 206 AR-Z 228/73. I am grateful to Dr. Wacker of the ZSL for providing me with this information.

69. *Justiz und NS-Verbrechen*, VII, Amsterdam, 1971, no. 231 b-2, 217–18, 230–1.

70. The date of 5 December 1941 was accepted at the Chelmno trial in Bonn (*Justiz und NS-Verbrechen*, XXI, Amsterdam 1979, 280), and at Koppe's trial (ZSL, Prozeß Koppe, Bl. 218) as the date of the first arrival of transports in Chelmno. Browning, *Fateful Months*, 30, dates the first gassing to 8 December 1941, as does Madajczyk, *Okkupationspolitik*, 380 (apparently, though not explicitly stated, based on early postwar Polish testimony). In a letter he sent me, dated 25 June 1991, Christopher Browning writes: 'I have seen no evidence given for either date, nor have I seen the discrepancy addressed'.

71. *NS-Vernichtungslager*, 258–9.

72. The killing was carried out by bottled carbon monoxide gas being released into the van. Lange's unit was to introduce at Chelmno a refined version of gassing, using the vehicle's exhaust. See Browning, *Fateful Months*, 59, 101 n. 8.

73. Eugen Kogon et al. (eds.), *Nationalsozialistische Massentötungen durch Giftgas* (Frankfurt am Main, 1986), 113–14, 310 n. 10; *Justiz und NS-Verbrechen*, XXI, 246. According to the evidence assembled for Koppe's trial (ZSL, Prozeß Koppe, Bl. 194), the initial drivers of the vehicles were SS men from the unit who were subsequently replaced by two drivers coming from the RSHA in Berlin. Walter Burmeister, Lange's chauffeur, stated, however, that the drivers came together with the gas vans. Kogon, 114.

74. For the extermination at Chelmno, see above all *NS-Vernichtungslager*, Part 2. An important independent source is the account, compiled in 1945, of the Forest Inspector of the area, Heinz May. Part Three, 'Der große Judenmord', is printed (in German and Polish) in Karol Marian Pospieszalski, 'Niemiecki Nadleśniczy o Zagładzie Żydów w Chełmnie nad Nerem', *Przeglad Zachodni Poznań* 18 (1962), 85–105. I am greatly indebted to Prof. Pospieszalski for providing me with a copy of this article, and with a translation into German of his introduction. An extract in English can be found in Dobroszycki, *Chronicle*, lv–vi.

75. *NS-Vernichtungslager*, 252.

76. *Justiz und NS-Verbrechen*, XXI, 280.

77. As claimed, though he cites no direct evidence, by Madajczyk, *Okkupationspolitik*, 380. Prof. Madajczyk acknowledges in a letter to me, dated 27 August 1991, that the assertion rested on inference. Christopher Browning (letter to me of 25 June 1991) points to the greater role of the Posen Security Police than the Lodz Gestapo in the build-up to the exterminations in Chelmno.

78. ZSL, Prozeß Koppe, Bl. 194–7; *NS-Vernichtungslager*, 262–4.

79. The centrality of Koppe's role is taken for granted in Birn, 181.

80. Printed in Kogon, 111–12. See also, for Koppe's dubious testimony, note 106 below.

81. *NS-Vernichtungslager*, 251, 258. See also ZSL, Prozeß Koppe, Bl. 212, 216–17.

82. According to one postwar witness, formerly a civil servant in Damzog's office, both Lange and Bothmann visited Damzog on a number of occasions, there was a special file on Chelmno in the office, and reports on the numbers killed were sent there. *NS-Vernichtungslager*, 252 & n. 22. Written reports of the Sonderkommando on the liquidation of the Jews were sent to Koppe, and Damzog and Bothmann were from time to time summoned by him to present verbal reports. ZSL, Prozeß Koppe, Bl. 197, 211, 216.

83. ZSL, Prozeß Koppe, Bl. 172.

84. *NS-Vernichtungslager*, 252 n. 25.

85. *NS-Vernichtungslager*, 252.

86. *NS-Vernichtungslager*, 252–3. See, for example, ZSL, USA-1, Bl. 91–4, the exchange of letters Greiser-Himmler, 19–27 March 1943, relating to the end of the operations of the 85 men of Sonderkommando Lange in Kulmhof.

87. *NS-Vernichtungslager*, 252–3; BDC, PA Greiser, for correspondence involving Pohl, Greiser, and Himmler, 9–17 Feb. 1944.

88. *Faschismus-Getto-Massenmord*, 285; *NS-Vernichtungslager*, 252, 290.

89. BDC, PA Greiser, Greiser to Himmler, 1 May 1942; printed in *Faschismus-Getto-Massenmord*, 278.

90. *NS-Vernichtungslager*, 290–1. Possibly, Greiser's request — through not specified as such — related to Jews from the Lodz ghetto, whereas the RSHA figure was a general

one for the Warthegau. Around 55,000 Jews from the Lodz ghetto had been killed by 9 June 1942. Attention was turned in the summer to 'clearing' the surrounding rural districts, from where at least 15,000 Jews were transported to their death in Chelmno. A further 15,700, mainly weak and sick, Jews were taken from the Lodz ghetto in September 1942, bringing the total to around 70,000 Lodz Jews killed in Chelmno by the beginning of October 1942. *Ibid.*, 288–90.

91. This is presumed by Raul Hilberg, *The Destruction of the European Jews* (New York, 1973), 561, and — slightly more cautiously expressed — in the revised German edition (see above, note 44), 508.

92. BDC, PA Greiser, Greiser to Himmler, 5 May 1942. The number of Poles with tuberculosis was said to be around 230,000, those with the disease in an 'open' condition around 35,000.

93. BDC, PA Greiser, Koppe to Brandt, 3 May 1942.

94. *Ibid.*, Brandt to Koppe, 14 May 1942.

95. *Ibid.*, RFSS Persönlicher Stab-Untersturmführer Rutzen, 21 May 1942, with request from Brandt to Heydrich; Heydrich-Himmler, 9 June 1942.

96. *Ibid.*, Himmler-Greiser, 27 June 1942.

97. *Ibid.*, Greiser-Himmler, 21 Nov. 1942.

98. *Ibid.*, Blome-Greiser, 18 Nov. 1942.

99. *Ibid.*, Greiser-Himmler, 21 Nov. 1942. The date of this discussion between Hitler and Greiser cannot be precisely determined. Gerald Fleming, *Hitler und die Endlösung*, 35, states (though gives no supporting evidence) that Greiser had last seen Hitler on 1 Oct. and 8 Nov. 1942 (the English version of Fleming's book, *Hitler and the Final Solution* [Oxford, 1986], 22, has 11 Nov. 1942, but this seems a translation error). Fleming is followed in this by Friedländer, 'From Anti-Semitism to Extermination', 41, and by Czesław Madajczyk, 'Hitler's Direct Influence on Decisions Affecting Jews during World War II', *Yad Vashem Studies* XX (1990), 63–4. Both the dates mentioned by Fleming were large gatherings — a meeting of Gauleiter and Reichsleiter addressed by Hitler on 1 October, and the annual assembly of the Party faithful to commemorate the 1923 Putsch on 8 November (see Milan Hauner, *Hitler. A Chronology of his Life and Time* [1983], 179). Whether Greiser, presuming he attended both, had the opportunity for a private discussion with Hitler might be doubted. Since Greiser had requested, and been given, Himmler's permission to exterminate 100,000 Jews well before 1 May 1942, and these killings had already taken place before October-November 1942, the purpose of seeking a mandate from Hitler at such a date is not immediately obvious. The only explanations seem to be: a) that Greiser, for reasons which are unclear but were possibly directly to do with the proposed 'tuberculosis action', was trying at a late stage to obtain Hitler's retrospective dispensation for a free hand in liquidating the Jews; b) that he was asking Hitler for permission to extend the initial figure of 100,000, though it is scarcely imaginable that he would have needed to go beyond Himmler for such permission, nor that any permission at all would have been needed to widen the killing within the scope of what had by spring 1942 emerged as the fully-fledged 'Final Solution' programme; or, c) and perhaps most likely, that his discussion with Hitler relating to the Jews took place at a significantly earlier date, and was simply being evoked by Greiser in autumn 1942 as a weapon in the tuberculosis matter.

100. BDC, PA Greiser, Himmler-Greiser, 3 Dec. 1942.

101. In other policy areas, such as the persecution of the Church, the instigation of draconian measures also came from Greiser and his subordinates rather than from central directives from Berlin. ZSL, Prozeß Greiser, 96.

102. As was necessary — finally even in written form — in the 'euthanasia action' (see Ernst Klee, *'Euthanasie' im NS-Staat. Die 'Vernichtung lebensunwerten Lebens'* (Frankfurt am Main, 1983), 100–1) as well as being called for in the case of the tuberculosis victims. The point is made by Burrin, 172.

103. *NS-Vernichtungslager,* 253.

104. ZSL, Prozeß Greiser, 99–102; USA-1, Bl. 91–4, exchange of letters Greiser-Himmler about Sonderkommando Lange; UdSSR-411, Bl. 13–15, testimony of Hermann Gielow from 15 May 1945 about Greiser's involvement in the work of Sonderkommando Bothmann at Chelmno between March 1944 and January 1945; Prozeß Koppe, 210, 216.

105. BDC, PA Greiser (also in IfZ, MA-303), telegram to Himmler, 7 March 1944, thanking him for his generous support and giving the text of the 'proud report' he had sent the same day to the Führer. See also Fleming, *Endlösung,* 34.

106. Koppe's claims at his trial were both contradictory and incredible. Having claimed (see above note 80) that he heard in 1940 or 1941 from Rudolf Brandt in Himmler's office of the forthcoming 'action' against the Warthegau Jews, he then alleged that — apart from rumours — he first heard of the 'Final Solution' and of the existence of the extermination camp at Chelmno from Greiser (following a telephone call to the latter from Philip Bouhler at the Führer Chancellory). He went on to claim that he had even successfully persuaded Himmler to end the 'Final Solution', but that Göring and Keitel had opposed it being halted. — ZSL, Prozeß Koppe, Bl. 290–1, 294.

107. See Broszat, 'Genesis', 753 n. 26.

108. See Browning, *Fateful Months,* chap. 1, esp. 32; Burrin, chap. 5; Jäckel and Rohwer, 125–98; Breitman, chap. 6–9.

109. ZSL, Prozeß Koppe, Bl. 297, emphasised the regional control of the Sonderkommando Lange/Bothmann. The Lodz ghetto was a 'Gaughetto' (*Faschismus-Getto-Massenmord,* 285) — a status Greiser was able to retain in February 1944 when Oswald Pohl, from the SS-Verwaltungshauptamt, was aiming to turn it into a concentration camp (BDC, PA Greiser, Greiser to Pohl, 14 Feb. 1944).

110. See Broszat, 'Genesis', 751.

111. Browning, *Fateful Months,* 30–4; chronology in Kogon, 328.

112. *NS-Vernichtungslager,* 268.

113. *Ibid.,* 276–7, and n. 69.

114. *Ibid.,* 280–2.

115. *Ibid.,* 282–6. Some 7000 Jews were killed at Chelmno in this second spell, though all between 23 June and 14 July 1944. *Ibid.,* 292–3. There were still at that time over 68,000 Jews in the Lodz ghetto, almost all of whom were, by 28 August 1944, sent to Auschwitz-Birkenau. Dobroszycki, *Chronicle,* lxiii–v.

116. *NS-Vernichtungslager,* 246–50, 257 n. 38; letter of ZSL, dated 20 June 1989 to Prof. Dr. Stanisław Nawrocki (State Archives Poznań). I am most grateful to Prof. Nawrocki for a copy of this letter with details of the fate of some of the chief perpetrators.

117. GK Warsaw, Process Artura Greisera (36 files); ZSL, Prozeß Greiser (transl. of Anklageschrift); Polen-365h, Bl. 677–828, Anklageschrift; Polen-3650, Bl. 88–136, Greiser's final plea. The appeal for papal intercession was reported in *L'Osservatore Romano*, 22–3 July 1946. (I owe this information to the kindness of Dr. Gerald Fleming.) According to Dr. Marian Olszewski of the Instytut Zachodni in Posnań, currently working on a life of Greiser (letter to me from Prof. Nawrocki, Poznań, dated 15 May 1991), Greiser's defence lawyer, Heymowski, wrote intercession letters not only to the Pope, but also to President Truman. No response from either has come to light.

118. *NS-Vernichtungslager*, 251; ZSL, Prozeß Koppe. On Koppe's arrest, trial, and release on grounds of being unfit to stand: *Quick*, 15 July 1960; *Neue Zürcher Zeitung*, 21 Jan. 1965; *Frankfurter Allgemeine Zeitung*, 29 May 1965; *Allgemeine: Unabhängige jüdische Wochenzeitung*, 17 Feb. 1967 (copies in IfZ, Munich).

119. Date of Koppe's death according to information from ZSL (see n. 116 above).

120 *NS-Vernichtungslager*, 288–93. While these figures provide a minimum estimate, they are far more accurate than the figure of 300,000 given at Greiser's trial (ZSL, Prozeß Greiser, Bl. 58).

121. *NS-Vernichtungslager*, 293 n. 96.

4

Hitler's Role in the 'Final Solution'

Hitler's Mentality: The "Removal"
of the Jews as Germany's Salvation

Hitler's very first and last recorded political statements concerned the "Jewish Question." In a letter written as early as September 1919, using biological terminology he would frequently deploy, he spoke of the activities of Jews producing "a racial tuberculosis among nations." He stated emphatically that Jews were a race, not a religion. Antisemitism as a political movement, he declared, should be based on "reason," not emotion, and must lead to the systematic removal of the rights of Jews. However, he concluded, the "final aim," which could only be attained in a "government of national strength," had to be the "removal of the Jews altogether."[1]

In his "Political Testament," dictated on the eve of his suicide, with the Red Army at his gates, Hitler declared: "I left no doubt that if the nations of Europe are again to be regarded as mere blocks of shares of these international money and finance conspirators, then that race, too, which is really guilty of this murderous struggle, will be called to account: Jewry! I further left no one in doubt that this time millions of children of Europe's Aryan peoples would not die of hunger, millions of grown men would not suffer death, and hundreds of thousands of women and children not be burnt and bombed to death in the towns, without the real culprit having to atone for his guilt, even if by more humane means."[2]

Almost twenty-six momentous years separate the two statements. These were no propaganda ploys. There can be no doubt that they represent fervently held core beliefs. At their heart was the link in Hitler's mind between war and the Jews — there from beginning to end of his political "career". In a terrible passage in *Mein Kampf,* Hitler expressed his belief that "the sacrifice of millions at the front" would not have been necessary if "twelve or fifteen thousand of these Hebrew corrupters of the people had been held under poison gas."[3] It was not a prescription for future action. But the thought never left him.

Hitler's writings and speeches illustrate the striking continuity of a small number of basic, unchanging ideas that provided his inner driving-force. Whatever the vagaries of opportunistic policy and the necessary adjustments of propaganda over the years, these ideas remained a constant from his entry into politics down to his death in the bunker. It is seldom that a politician holds with such tenacity to a core body of ideas over such a lengthy period of time. And, however repulsive, and whatever their irrational basis, they did constitute a circular, self-reinforcing argument, impenetrable by rational critique, something which we can genuinely call a *Weltanschauung,* or ideology.[4] This ideology was formed in full no later than 1925. There were really no more than three core elements, each of them a long-term goal rather than a pragmatic middle-range political aim, resting on an underlying premise of human existence as racial struggle: 1) securing Germany's hegemony in Europe; 2) attainment of "living space" (*Lebensraum*) to ensure the material basis for Germany's long-term future; and 3) removal of the Jews. It amounted to a vision of Germany's salvation — a glorious future in waiting. It could be achieved, Hitler repeatedly stated, only by heroic leadership that, by 1924, he had come to see as represented by himself. And all three strands of the vision could be attained at one fell swoop with the destruction of the Soviet Union — and with it the eradication of "Jewish Bolshevism". The war in the east that would eventually begin in June 1941 was, therefore, intrinsic to this vision.

The *Weltanschauung,* was, however, itself a rationalization of a deeper, more profound, feeling within Hitler: a burning thirst for revenge against those who had destroyed all that he held good. The war of 1914–18, when he had experienced the immense carnage as a committed and courageous soldier, fanatical about the German cause, had given him a purpose for the first time in his life. In one of the few letters he wrote from the front, in 1915, he spoke of the huge sacrifice in human life being worthwhile to produce a postwar homeland "purer and cleansed of alien influence."[5] This was how he saw the colossal slaughter—not in terms of human suffering, but as worthwhile for the making of a better Germany. This was why the news, unexpected for him as for so many others, of Germany's capitulation in November 1918, which reached him while he was hospitalized at Pasewalk in Pomerania recovering from mustard gas poisoning, was so utterly traumatizing. He had identified his personal fate wholly with that of the German Reich. An acute sense of national humiliation now merged with his own misery. His searing bitterness and visceral hatred, of a rare intensity, reflected this identification, and was now directed at perceived enemies he had begun to identify years before, scapegoats first for his own ills, now responsible for those of the nation. He could not accept the failure of the army in which he himself had fought. Dark forces of sedition at home had to be responsible. Revenge, even though he was in no position to bring it about, gripped him with the power of an obsession. Those who had undermined Germany's national prestige, had reduced her to this shame, would have to pay for it. This was the personal fire within him that was never extinguished.

It was wholly consistent, then, that from the beginning of his "career" in 1919, Hitler fanatically pursued two interlinked goals: to restore Germany's greatness; and in so doing to avenge and make good the disgrace of the capitulation in 1918, punishing those responsible for the revolution that followed and the national humiliation that was fully revealed in the Treaty of Versailles of 1919. The goals could only be attained, as he repeatedly said, "by the sword"; that is, by war. Since in his eyes the Jews were responsible for these most terrible crimes of all time—for the "stab in the back" of 1918, the capitulation, the revolution, for Germany's misfortune; since in his perverted perception they were the main carriers of capitalism in Wall St. and the City of London as they were of Bolshevism in Moscow; and since in his belief in the legend of the "Jewish World Conspiracy" they would always block his path and pose the most dangerous enemy to his plans, it followed logically that war for him had to be a war against the Jews. Moreover, it was equally logical, in Hitler's mind, that, when that war was recognized as irredeemably lost, continuation of the struggle to the point of self-destruction, with the exhortation to future generations to continue the fight against international Jewry, would be needed as the final demonstration of Germany's defiance, the last act of sacrifice necessary to expiate the shame and infamy inflicted by the Jews in 1918.

The tenacity with which he held to his dogmatic belief that the Jews had caused the First World War but that, in the event of them plunging the world once more into war, they would perish, is truly striking. He repeated the sentiment over and again, publicly and privately. He saw himself as the agent of Germany's national salvation. And that salvation would only be achieved through destroying the power of the Jews.

The consistency of Hitler's aim "to remove" Jews, and the fact that, during the years of his dictatorship, the Jews were indeed "removed," first from Germany, then from the whole of German-occupied Europe, through ruthless persecution and ultimately physical annihilation, seems to offer a straightforward answer to the question of Hitler's role in the "Final Solution". However, this role is less obvious than it might at first sight appear. While his continued personal hatred of Jews can be plainly demonstrated, how that translated into policies of persecution, then extermination, is not always easy to discern. Hitler himself remarked in one of his wartime monologues that "even regarding the Jews, I had for long to remain inactive" — for tactical reasons, of course.[6] Yet even without Hitler's close involvement in the direction of policy, continual radicalization of anti-Jewish policy took place. And as one seminal study pointed out long ago, "the figure of Adolf Hitler is a shadowy one."[7] This in itself has given rise to differing interpretations among historians. How far Hitler had to intervene directly in order to steer policy, and whether the "Final Solution" followed a long-term, ideologically driven plan of annihilation or arose as the end of a process of "cumulative radicalization" out of unplanned, *ad hoc* improvisation and local barbaric initiatives in attempts to cope with the self-inflicted logistical problems arising from Nazi anti-Jewish policy, have been longstanding issues of legitimate disagreement. The nature and timing of any Führer order, or even whether it was necessary for one to be given, have been a central component of the debate.

Interpreting the Decision for the "Final Solution"

With few exceptions, notably the early study by Gerald Reitlinger[8] and the monumental work of Raul Hilberg,[9] detailed research on the decisions and policies of genocide began as late as the 1970s, expanding greatly over subsequent decades, especially once the archival repositories in the former eastern bloc were opened. Only in the light of such research has it become possible to evaluate more precisely the role Hitler played in the emergence of the "Final Solution". Yet even now, after exhaustive analysis, much remains obscure or contentious. The problems of interpretation arise from the complexities and deficiencies of the surviving fragmentary evidence, reflecting in good measure the obfuscatory language of the Nazi leadership as well as the extreme unbureaucratic leadership style of Hitler, who, especially once the war had begun, placed a high premium upon secrecy and concealment, with orders on sensitive issues usually passed on verbally, and on a "need-to-know" basis.[10]

Until the 1970s it was generally taken for granted that a single, direct Hitler order launched the "Final Solution". The presumption emanated from a Hitler-centric approach to the Third Reich, which placed heavy emphasis upon the will, intentions, and policy-directives of the dictator. This sometimes went hand in hand with the claim, as voiced in Lucy Dawidowicz's influential book, that Hitler had followed a "grand design" or "program of annihilation" dating back to his traumatic experience of the end of the First World War, and that, though there had on occasion been necessary tactical adjustments, the implementation of the plan merely awaited the right opportunity, which then came in 1941.[11] Gerald Fleming, one of the first historians to investigate systematically the evidence for Hitler's involvement in the implementation of the "Final Solution," concurred in seeing "a strategic plan" for the realization of Hitler's aim, dating back to his experience of the German revolution of 1918.[12] Early biographers of Hitler followed a similar line.[13] A "psychohistorical" explanation for this pathological aim was offered by Rudolph Binion, who saw Hitler entering politics in order to kill the Jews as revenge for Germany's defeat, in subliminal association with the death of his mother in 1907 under treatment from a Jewish doctor.[14]

A reaction to this pronounced Hitler-centrism gained ground in the 1970s. It formed a general alternative approach to interpreting the Third Reich — what came to be known as the "structuralist," or sometimes "functionalist," in distinction from the "intentionalist," approach. Rather than looking to Hitler's personal direction of policy, the fragmentation of policy-making in a "polycratic" system of government with confused and chaotic lines of administration, led by a "weak dictator"[15] concerned primarily with propaganda and upholding his prestige, came to be emphasized. As regards anti-Jewish policy, too, "structuralist" approaches looked away from the role of the individual — not that Hitler's paranoid antisemitism, indispensability to the barbaric persecution that led to genocide, or moral responsibility were doubted — to the "structures" of rule in the Third Reich, and the "functions" of competing agencies as they strived to implement hateful, but vaguely couched "guidelines" for action. In a seminal article published in 1977, stirring a debate that has rumbled on ever since, Martin Broszat argued that Hitler had given no "comprehensive general extermination order" at all. Rather, problems in undertaking deportation plans, arising from the unexpected failure swiftly to defeat the Soviet Union during the summer and autumn of 1941, had prompted Nazi satraps in the occupied territories of the east to start taking the initiative in killing the Jews in their regions. The killing gained retrospective sanction from above, but only gradually, by 1942, turned into a comprehensive extermination program. There had been, therefore, no long-term design for the physical annihilation of Europe's Jews. And there had been no specific Hitler order.[16]

In an influential essay published in 1983, Hans Mommsen presented a forceful argument pushing in much the same direction. Mommsen accepted without question Hitler's knowledge and approval of what was taking place. But he saw a direct Hitler order as incompatible with the dictator's endeavors to distance himself from direct personal responsibility and reluctance to speak of the "Final Solution," even among his close entourage, except in oblique terms or propaganda statements. For Mommsen, the key to the emergence of the "Final Solution" was not to be found in the implementation of Hitler's will to exterminate the Jews but in improvised bureaucratic initiatives whose dynamic prompted a process of "cumulative radicalization" in the fragmented structures of decision-making in the Third Reich.[17]

In the late 1970s and early 1980s, at the time that these programmatic essays by Broszat and Mommsen appeared, detailed research into the decisions that launched the "Final Solution" was still little developed. Important works, beyond Hilberg, had in the meantime, of course, appeared, damaging beyond repair the notion of a "grand design" for extermination, a plan reaching back to 1918. Yehuda Bauer, one of the foremost Israeli experts on the Holocaust, summed up the general revision by pointing to a number of stages of development in anti-Jewish policy, all of them rooted in the unchanging notion of removing the Jews from Germany, though not following any long-term extermination program.[18] This verdict followed two penetrating analyses of anti-Jewish policy by Karl Schleunes and Uwe Dietrich Adam which pursued the vagaries and cul-de-sacs of Nazi persecution, ruling out the notion of a simple strategy of implementing a longstanding extermination plan determined by Hitler. Far from being a straight path, the road to Auschwitz, according to Schleunes, was a "twisted" one.[19]

Directly prompted by Broszat's hypotheses, one of the first researchers to explore the intractable and highly complex source material for the crucial months in 1941 which saw the emergence of the "Final Solution" (meaning not just the mass killing of Jews in the Soviet Union in the wake of "Operation Barbarossa," but a program to exterminate all the Jews of Europe in Nazi occupied areas) was Christopher Browning—in the early stages of a career which saw him advance to become one of the world's leading experts on the Holocaust. Rejecting Broszat's emphasis upon local initiatives only gradually

congealing into a program, Browning insisted upon central direction and returned to an emphasis upon a decision by Hitler, which, like Hilberg and
others, he placed in summer 1941. He saw this decision crucially reflected in
the mandate given by Göring to Heydrich on July 31, 1941, ordering him to
prepare a "total solution of the Jewish question."[20] The novelty of Browning's
interpretation, however, was that he envisaged Hitler commissioning Göring
to work out a plan for the "Final Solution" to be confirmed at a later date — in
effect the first part of a two-staged order. The next months witnessed radicalization at various levels, during which the killing of Jews escalated greatly.
There was confusion, contradiction at times, and much improvisation. But
none of this was incompatible, in Browning's view, with a mandate to work
for the extermination of the Jews dating back to the previous July. Browning
concluded that in late October or November 1941, with the attack on the
Soviet Union stalled, Hitler approved "the extermination plan he had solicited
the previous summer."[21] In numerous impressive detailed studies that he has
published on the topic since this early essay, Browning has never substantially
revised this interpretation.[22]

The timing, as well as the nature, of any Führer decision for the "Final
Solution" had by now become a central issue of interpretation. It was extensively debated at an important conference in Stuttgart in 1984.[23] Most —
though not all — of the experts participating accepted that there must have
been a Führer order. However, on the date of such an order (which all agreed
was at some point in 1941) interpretation varied considerably. The dominant
view was that the crucial decision — mainly seen as linked to the Göring mandate — for the extension to the whole of Europe of the physical annihilation of
the Jews already raging in the Soviet Union took place in summer, while the
end of the war seemed imminent. Some, however, placed a Hitler decision not
in the "euphoric" phase of the summer, but in the autumn, when it was realized that the war in the Soviet Union would drag on, and when the possibility
of deporting Jews into Soviet territory, as earlier envisaged, had evaporated.
The question of the timing of any Hitler decision had acquired wider significance. The "euphoria" interpretation had him planning to destroy the Jews
from a position of strength, when ultimate triumph seemed within his grasp. It
pointed in the direction of a determining intention to kill the Jews when the
opportunity arose. The alternative, a decision taken from effective weakness,
when the prospect of victory had receded and the problems of a protracted
and bitter war were mounting, was more suggestive of a reaction to circumstances that had spiraled out of control, a response to the inability to bring
about the desired territorial solution of the "Jewish question" by deporting

Jews to the arctic wastes of the Soviet Union, and a vengeful determination to succeed in the "war against the Jews" even should ultimate victory in the military war prove impossible to attain.

The case for placing a Hitler decision not in the euphoria of high summer expectations of imminent victory, but some two months later, when pessimism over a long war in the east was starting to grip the dictator, was most cogently advanced by Philippe Burrin, writing in the late 1980s. In contrast to Browning and others, Burrin argued — a point meanwhile more widely accepted — that it would be mistaken to see in the Göring mandate of 31 July 1941 a reflection of a fundamental order by Hitler for the "Final Solution", that is, to extend the genocide already taking place in the Soviet Union into a program for the physical extermination of the whole of European Jewry. Rather, according to Burrin, the Göring mandate still fell within the remit of attaining a territorial settlement in the east once the war was over. The mandate, which had been drafted in Heydrich's own office for Göring's signature, was aimed at establishing the authority — in an issue where there were many competing instances — of the head of the *Reichssicherheitshauptamt* in all matters pertaining to the solution of the "Jewish Question". The lack of clarity that evidently still prevailed among Nazi authorities in the late summer and early autumn of 1941 meant, for Burrin, that no decision for the "Final Solution" had yet been made. He argued that such an order in September 1941 was synonymous with the decision to deport the Jews to the east — one unquestionably made by Hitler, and at a time when he was gloomy about the slowing advance in the Soviet Union and the growing prospect of a long conflict.[24]

Soon after Burrin's study appeared, the archives of the former eastern bloc started to divulge their secrets. Predictably, a written order by Hitler for the "Final Solution" was not found. The presumption that a single, explicit written order had ever been given had long been dismissed by most historians. Nothing now changed that supposition. In fact, little was discovered in Moscow or other east-European archives that cast new light directly on Hitler's role in the "Final Solution." Indirectly, nevertheless, new perspectives on the emergence of a genocidal program did provide fresh insights into Hitler's own role.

One outstanding work which profited from the new research opportunities was Götz Aly's study, published in 1995, of the interconnection of Nazi plans to resettle hundreds of thousands of ethnic Germans in the occupied territories of Poland and the twists and turns of policy to deport the Jews. In his detailed reconstruction of racial policy-making in the eastern territories between 1939 and early 1942, Aly was able to show how increasingly radical anti-Jewish measures resulted from blockages produced by the brutally unrealistic resettlement plans of the Nazi authorities. Aly concluded that there was no single, specific decision to kill the Jews of Europe. Rather, analogous to Mommsen's notion of a system of "cumulative radicalization," he posited a "long and complex *process* of decision-making," with notable spurts in March, July, and October 1941, but continuing still as a series of "experiments" down to May 1942. Hitler's role, according to this interpretation, was confined to decisions as an arbiter between competing Nazi leaders whose own schemes to deal with the "Jewish question" had created insoluble problems.[25]

Aly's argument that there had been no precise point at which Hitler had given a single decision for the "Final Solution" has gained backing from a number of detailed regional studies into the emergence of genocide in the occupied territories. One outcome has been a clearer understanding of how, in the critical months of autumn 1941, regional Nazi authorities resorted to increasingly radical "self-help" and local initiatives to free their areas of Jews. While there were evidently signals from Berlin indicating an approaching comprehensive "solution" to the "Jewish problem" and prompting regional Nazi leaders to adopt drastic measures to resolve their own difficulties, the conflicting interpretations of the aims of anti-Jewish policy in this phase seem to imply that a fundamental decision had not yet been taken. Some local extermination programs, set in motion by local Nazi satraps in coordination with Berlin, did commence. In November 1941 construction began of a small extermination camp at Bełżec, in the Lublin District of the *Generalgouvernement,* instigated by the SS Police Chief of the area, Odilo Globocnik, with the aim of liquidating Jews in that area incapable of working.[26] In the "Warthegau", the annexed part of western Poland, the regional police chief, Wilhelm Koppe and the Gauleiter, Arthur Greiser, liaised with Berlin about locating gas-vans at Chełmno. These began operations in early December to kill Jews from the overcrowded Łódź ghetto and elsewhere in the region as part of a deal to compensate for the influx of yet more Jews sent eastwards as part of the first wave of deportations from the Reich.[27] But localized "solutions", including the shooting of Jews on arrival from Germany in the Baltic in autumn 1941, did not yet form part of a fully-devised, comprehensive program. A "Final Solution" was still evolving, still in an "experimental" phase.

Research had, in certain ways, then, moved away from the differing hypotheses about the date of Hitler's decision for the "Final Solution" by implying — or explicitly stating — that no such decision had been made. By a different route, and on the basis of more profound research findings, this was returning to the broad thrust of the programmatic "structuralist" hypotheses of Broszat and Mommsen from the late 1970s and early 1980s. But the conclusions were far from universally accepted. The emphasis upon local initiatives, improvised measures, unsteered "processes" unfolding until they metamorphosed into an "unauthored" program of extermination was not convincing to many historians. Some experts — prominent among them Christopher Browning — felt that, for all the undoubted advances that detailed regional studies of emerging genocide had brought, the central direction of policy had been underplayed. The role of Hitler, too, seemed scarcely to figure in the new explanations. Was it likely, or plausible, that the most radical of radical antisemites had played no direct part in shaping the policies aimed at destroying his perceived archenemy?

As David Bankier then, in a magisterial survey, Saul Friedländer had demonstrated, even in the 1930s Hitler had been more active in anti-Jewish policy, down to points of detail, than the earlier work by Karl Schleunes, in particular, had implied.[28] It was not easy, therefore, to accept that he had remained detached from decision-making at precisely the time when his long-professed aim of "removing" the Jews was turning into practical reality. Browning continued in an array of important publications also to maintain the importance of a Führer order, and to date this (as he always had done) to summer 1941 – the time of "euphoria." He remained unmoved by the objections raised to this dating, though he emphasized that he was not positing a single decision, but envisaging "the point at which Hitler inaugurated the decision-making process," the first move in developments that would stretch over the subsequent months.[29]

Other historians, equally anxious to emphasize Hitler's direct role in steering policy towards an intended and planned "Final Solution," reached different conclusions about the timing of a Führer order. Richard Breitman dated "a fundamental decision to exterminate the Jews" by the dictator to as early as January 1941, adding, however, that "if the goal and basic policies were now clear, the specific plans were not," and followed only after some time, with the first operational decisions in July.[30] In other words, Breitman was not positing an incisive policy-decision, rather a statement of intent. But Hitler had long held the view that another war would bring about the destruction of the Jews. And at this point, in early 1941, in the context of planning "Operation Barbarossa," deportation of the Jews to the arctic wastes of the Soviet Union was opening up as a realistic prospect. There, over time, the presumption was that they would perish. It is difficult to see a Hitler decision in January 1941 stretching beyond that ultimate, though still vague, notion of a territorial solution. Though this was itself implicitly genocidal, the vagaries of policy over the following months speak against seeing January 1941 as the date when Hitler took *the* decision for the "Final Solution."

An entirely different suggestion for the date of a Hitler order came from

Tobias Jersak. In Jersak's view, the declaration of the Atlantic Charter by Roosevelt and Churchill on August 14, 1941 (meaning that Germany would soon be at war with the USA) was the trigger for Hitler, suffering at that point from a nervous collapse and reeling from the recognition of the failure of his strategy to defeat the Soviet Union, to take the fundamental decision that the Jews of Europe should be physically destroyed.[31] However, Jersak probably exaggerates the impact of the Atlantic Charter on Hitler. It is doubtful that this in itself was sufficient to provide the vital spur for such a momentous decision — one in Jersak's interpretation, taken swiftly and without any consultation. Jersak is left, in fact, with little but speculation to support his claim that Hitler had already taken the decision when he met Goebbels on August 19, to agree to proposals put to him by the Propaganda Minister to force Jews in Germany to wear the Star of David.

Another interpretation of a fundamental decision by Hitler to launch the "Final Solution" was proposed by Christian Gerlach. For him, the disparities in implementing anti-Jewish measures ruled out a specific central order by Hitler in summer or early autumn. Despite the evident escalation of genocidal actions, there was still a lack of clarity about the treatment of the deported Reich Jews, and the various regional liquidation measures were not yet coordinated. The need to provide precisely this clarification and coordination lay, he claimed, behind Heydrich's invitation to significant figures in those agencies concerned to a meeting at the Wannsee on December 9, 1941. Pearl Harbor then intervened and the meeting was postponed. According to Gerlach's interpretation, by the time the meeting eventually took place, on January 20, 1942, Hitler's "basic decision" to kill all the Jews of Europe had taken place. In the context of a war that had now become global, Gerlach sees a speech made by Hitler to Reichsleiter and Gauleiter on December 12, and an accompanying series of private meetings with Nazi leaders during the following days, as tantamount to Hitler's "basic decision" for the "Final Solution."[32] Gerlach certainly makes a good case for a further radicalization of extermination policy in December 1941.[33] But it is difficult to imagine Hitler, who refrained from speaking on the extermination of the Jews in other than vague generalizations even to his intimate entourage, choosing to announce a "basic decision" to instigate the "Final Solution" to a meeting of around fifty Nazi leaders. None of those present later referred to this meeting as of any particular significance with regard to the "Final Solution." And Goebbels, whose diary notes form the source for Hitler's reported comments, summarized the remarks on the Jews in a few lines of an otherwise extensive diary entry without highlighting them as of special importance.[34]

A recent, meticulous examination of the complex evidence of decision-making on anti-Jewish policy between 1939 and 1942 offers yet another variant. Florent Brayard places the date of Hitler's order to commence the "Final Solution" as a comprehensive program later than any other historian had done, to June 1942, immediately following the assassination of Reinhard Heydrich in Prague.[35] At Heydrich's funeral, June 9, Himmler told SS leaders that they would have completed the "migration" (*Völkerwanderung*) of the Jews within a year.[36] This is the point, infers Brayard, linking Himmler's comments to reported draconian remarks about the Jews by Hitler around that time, that the "Final Solution" — meaning the program for the complete and rapid eradication of all Europe's Jews — was initiated. It perhaps seems more plausible, however, to see it as the last major escalatory push in establishing a Europe-wide killing program. Peter Longerich's magisterial study of the "politics of annihilation" had, in fact, already established — something by now widely accepted, also by Brayard — that a comprehensive program of extermination of European Jewry developed as an incremental process, with a number of acceleratory spurts, between summer 1941 and summer 1942.[37] Already by March and April 1942, as Longerich shows, plans were being elaborated to deport the Jews from western Europe to the east, and to extend the killing in Poland and central Europe. Probably Heydrich's assassination provided the impetus to draw the threads together.

It seems certain, given the fragmentary and unsatisfactory evidence, that all attempts to establish a precise moment when Hitler decided to launch the "Final Solution" will meet with objections. And, of course, much depends upon what is envisaged as a Führer order. Was it a precise and clear directive, or merely a "green light" or "nod of the head?" Interpretation rests additionally upon whether decision-making on the "Final Solution" is regarded as a continuum, with adjustments and acceleratory phases over the period of a year or so, or whether a point is sought where one precise quantum leap can be distinguished as forming *the* decision.

And yet, structuralist or functionalist accounts in which Hitler's role is minimized or marginalized also seem unsatisfactory. Aly's emphasis, for instance, on the link between blockages in the Nazi plans for population transfer and resettlement of ethnic Germans and the radicalization of anti-Jewish policy, though valid, do not explain why the failure of deportation plans led to genocide solely in the case of the Jews.[38] This leads directly back to the role of ideology, often underplayed in structuralist accounts. Building on long anti-semitic tradition, the Jews occupied a quite singular place in Nazi demonology, and in plans for racial "cleansing." The Jews had been the number one ideological enemy of the Nazis from the beginning, and their murderous treatment in 1941 followed not only years of spiraling persecution but also re-

peated statements by Nazi leaders, most prominently Hitler himself, advocating their "removal." So we are back to Hitler, and to his role in the way the
Nazi system of rule operated.

It seems impossible to isolate a single, specific Führer order for the "Final
Solution" in an extermination policy that took full shape in a process of
radicalization lasting over a period of about a year. At the same time, much
indicates that the extermination program did not develop without a decisive
role being played by Hitler himself. To reconcile these two statements, we
should look *both* for a *series* of secret authorizations for particular radicalizing steps, which can only be deduced from indirect or secondary evidence, *and*
for a *number* of public signals or "green lights" for action. We should also
recognize that Hitler was the supreme and radical spokesman of an ideological
imperative that, by 1941, had become a priority for the *entire* regime leadership. Within that framework, we now need to consider how Hitler shaped the
path to genocide.

The Dialectic of Radicalisation in Nazi Anti-Jewish Policy Before the War

With Hitler's takeover of power on 30 January 1933, a proto-genocidal
elite, backed by huge mass movement—the Nazi Party and its multifarious
sub-organizations—held together by the utopian vision of national salvation,
to be achieved through racial cleansing at the core of which was the "removal"
of the Jews, gained control over the instruments of a modern, sophisticated,
state system. The vision, both in its "positive" aspects (creation of a unified
"people's community"; rebuilding of national pride, grandeur, and prosperity)
and its "negative" elements (destruction, not just defeat, of political opponents; "elimination" of those whose physical or mental weakness or disability
were seen to threaten the health and strength of the population; exclusion of
Jews from public life, and their physical removal from Germany) was embodied in the figure of the Leader. Hitler's *Weltanschauung*—a set of visionary
aims rather than precise policy objectives—now served, therefore, to integrate
the centrifugal forces of the Nazi Movement, to mobilize the activists, and to
legitimate policy initiatives undertaken to implement his expressed or implied
will. The very looseness of the ideological imperatives encouraged functionaries of the regime, in myriad ways, to "work towards the Führer"[39] to contribute to the accomplishment of the visionary goals which Hitler represented.
Among these goals, the "removal" of the Jews was a tangible objective, and
one in which the pathological fixation of Hitler himself accorded with the
central conviction of the ruling Nazi elite and also fuelled the widespread and

often bitter antisemitism at the Party's grass roots — a seething pot of hatred into which a poisonous concoction of socio-economic grievances, anger, and resentments was poured. And among the antisemitic elite now running the German state, no one took a more radical stance on the "removal" of the Jews than Hitler himself. Countless speeches during the 1920s had demanded that the Jews, whom he often associated with vermin or bacilli, should be "removed," sometimes likening the removal to that of a parasite, or a germ, excised in order to leave a healthy organ. Such imagery implied that "removal" meant destruction or "annihilation" (*Vernichtung*), a term Hitler used in his bacteriological similes. The language is not just extreme but points also to a proto-genocidal mentality. The man with this mentality was now in charge of the German state. And countless Germans were seeking at every turn to implement what they interpreted to be his wishes.

Hitler was a shrewd enough politician to know when to tone down his violent antisemitism. In the early 1930s as the Nazi Party exploited conditions of economic depression and political collapse to soar towards power, his speeches focused less on antisemitism. The huge electoral gatherings, as he knew, were scarcely to be won over to the NSDAP solely by verbal assaults on the Jews. So Hitler adjusted to circumstances. His inner convictions — most notably the central place of the "removal" of the Jews in his ideological vision — had, however, not altered one jot. Once in power, Hitler knew he had to be tactically alert, particularly to the international pressures on Germany's still weak economic and military position, to press ahead with measures against the Jews — measures which he personally wanted, and which the Nazi Movement was demanding. When necessary, he could, and did, keep the Party radicals in check. At other times, it was useful to unleash their pent-up violence on the Jews. This produced a characteristic process of radicalization during the 1930s: in accordance with Hitler's expressed or presumed wishes, a "green light" to step up measures against Jews would be given to Party radicals; pressure for action would build from below, which Hitler, though remaining aloof, would approve; when, for domestic or external reasons, violent forms of persecution became counter-productive, Hitler would intervene to channel the attacks into highly discriminatory anti-Jewish legislation, at each stage placating the radicals by ratcheting up the radicalization of the measures adopted. There was, therefore, a continuing "dialectic" between "wild" actions from below and orchestrated discrimination from above. Each phase of radicalization was more intense than its predecessor. The momentum in this way was never allowed to die.

It is well to keep in mind Hitler's pre-war role in the "Jewish Question" when considering the part he played in the emergence of the "Final Solution." It is plain that between 1933 and 1939 the decisive steps in the increasingly radical persecution of the Jews were taken with his approval and authorization — even where, for tactical reasons, he remained publicly detached or concealed the nature of his own interventions. Letting it be known that he favored action (invariably signaled through vicious public statements) and verbal approval of the most radical measures in confidential, unminuted discussions formed the usual pattern. Hitler was certainly involved when vital decisions (with regard, for example, to the boycott in 1933, the Nuremberg Laws in 1935, and the pogrom of 1938) were needed. Crucial shifts in policy required his approval. It is hard to imagine that this was not the case during the months in 1941–1942 when extermination of the Jews began to take shape as a concrete policy option.

As German expansionism led to acute tension in foreign affairs and the threat of war grew ever closer, Hitler evidently began to dwell upon the consequences for the Jews. His obsession with what he saw as the guilt of the Jews for the immense but futile "blood-sacrifice" of Germany during the war of 1914–1918, and for the calamitous defeat and revolution that had ensued, had never left him. He was already blaming "Jewish war-mongers" in Great Britain and the USA, as well as the pernicious "Jewish-Bolshevik" Soviet Union, for any new conflagration that might ensue. And the growth and spread of German might now meant that notions of "removing" the Jews no longer had to be confined to the Reich itself. "The Jews must get out of Germany, yes out of the whole of Europe," he told Goebbels at the end of November 1937. "That will take some time yet, but will and must happen."[40]

In the anti-Jewish climate in Germany around the time of the *Reichskristallnacht* pogrom of November 9–10, 1938 — a climate more menacing than ever before — "marks of a genocidal mentality" were in clear evidence in the Nazi leadership. Threats to the existence of the Jews were specifically linked to the outbreak of another war.[41] Hitler himself still connected this with revenge for 1918. Speaking to the Czechoslovakian Foreign Minister František Chvalkovský on January 21, 1939, he stated: "The Jews here will be destroyed. The Jews did not bring about November 9, 1918 for nothing. This day will be avenged."[42] He was not, of course, announcing to a foreign diplomat a preconceived extermination plan or program. But the sentiments were not merely rhetoric or propaganda. There was substance behind them.

In his long Reichstag speech on January 30, 1939, in the main a defiant tirade against what he portrayed as Jewish-inspired western war-mongers, Hitler declared:

> In the course of my life I have very often been a prophet, and have usually been ridiculed for it. . . . Today I will once more be a prophet: if the international Jewish financiers in and outside Europe should succeed in plunging the

nations once more into a world war, then the result will not be the Bolshevising of the earth, and thus the victory of Jewry, but the annihilation of the
Jewish race in Europe![43]

This was not "the decision to proceed with [the] irreversible mission" — effectively a prior announcement of the "Final Solution."[44] Nor was it simply "a
rhetorical gesture designed to put pressure on the international community."[45]
The speech, though not inaugurating an extermination program which would
only fully materialize over three years later, can nevertheless be seen to hold a
key to Hitler's role in the "Final Solution". The frequency of his later repetition
of the "prophecy" (which, significantly, he consistently misdated to September
1, 1939, the day that war began), and at decisive junctures in the unfolding of
genocide, shows how it was etched on his mind. Between 1941 and 1945, in
the years when the "Final Solution" engulfed the Jews of Europe, Hitler referred publicly and privately to his "prophecy" of 1939 on more than a dozen
occasions. No Nazi leader was left unaware in these years of the "prophecy"
the Führer had made about the Jews. Joseph Goebbels, Hans Frank, and
Alfred Rosenberg were among his underlings who alluded to it at different
times. The German public, too, heard Hitler openly speak of it in major public
addresses broadcast to the nation on no fewer than four occasions in 1942
alone, at the very time that the grisly operations in the death-mills in Poland
were going ahead at full tilt. For Hitler, the "prophecy" denoted the indelible
link in his mind between war and revenge against the Jews. Its repetition also
served a wider purpose. Without ever having to use explicit language, the
"prophecy," beyond its propaganda effect to condition the general population
against humanitarian sympathy for the Jews, signaled key escalatory shifts,
acted as a spur to radical action by conveying the "wish of the Führer," and
indicated to "insiders" Hitler's knowledge and approval of the genocide.

Hitler's "Prophecy" and the Implementation of the "Final Solution"

Hitler returned to his "prophecy" on January 30, 1941, as *his* war
against the "Jewish-Bolshevik" archenemy was taking concrete shape in his
mind. In the very weeks prior to the speech, he had agreed to Heydrich developing a new plan to deport the Jews from the German sphere of domination
to replace the short-lived and now defunct notion of deporting them to Madagascar. Ideas of deporting the Jews of Europe to a conquered Soviet Union
after an anticipated quick victory over Bolshevism were already being aired by
the SS leadership.[46] The repeat of the "prophecy" at this juncture, then, was a
veiled hint that the hour of the showdown with the Jews was approaching.

By the time Hitler's "prophecy" next leaves a mark in the records, in the summer, genocide was already raging in the Soviet Union. The slaughter, initially confined in the main to male Jews, which had begun with the German march into the USSR on June 22, 1941, had been widened massively from August onwards to include Jewish women and children. This crucial extension of the killing followed a series of one-to-one discussions in mid-July between Hitler and Himmler. No record of the talks was kept. But the outcome, we can reasonably infer, was that Hitler gave Himmler authorization to extend greatly the number of killing units in the east.[47] Hitler wanted to be kept informed on the progress of the killing. According to a message from the head of the Gestapo, Heinrich Müller, on August 1: "Continual reports from here on the work of the Einsatzgruppen in the east are to be presented to the Führer."[48]

By mid-summer 1941, Party fanatics and police leaders were vehemently pressing for Jews, portrayed as dangerous agitators on the home front, to be removed from German cities. A step on the way was to compel them to wear some form of identification on their clothing. Hitler alone, it was accepted, could take the decision. Goebbels undertook to present the case. He found the dictator, on visiting the *Führerhauptquartier* on August 18, recovering from illness. Despite the astonishing successes of the Wehrmacht in the first weeks of the attack on the Soviet Union, there were ominous signs already in August that victory would not be attained before winter set in. After the first major dispute with his army leaders, Hitler was in a state of nervous tension. Goebbels had come at a good moment to put his case for permission to compel Jews to wear the "Yellow Star." Hitler granted the Propaganda Minister what he requested. In so doing, he once more had recourse to his Reichstag "prophecy," voicing his conviction that this was coming true with uncanny certainty. "The Jews will not have much cause to laugh in future," Hitler said.[49] A key moment of radicalization of anti-Jewish policy within Germany was plainly interpreted by Hitler as a step towards the fulfillment of his "prophecy."

The decision — which again all Nazi leaders acknowledged could only come from Hitler — to deport Reich Jews to the east, taken in September 1941, constituted a major step in the direction of total genocide. Hitler had until this point insisted on awaiting final victory in the east. Now, aware that the war would drag on and conscious that the USA would probably soon be involved, he agreed to demands from a number of Nazi leaders — exploiting Stalin's deportation of hundreds of thousands of ethnic Germans from the Volga region to the wastes of western Siberia and Kazakhstan to press for retaliatory measures — to deport German, Austrian, and Czech Jews to the east even though the war was not over. It was a vital shift in policy. And the decision, indicated by Himmler on September 18, 1941, was taken by Hitler himself.[50] At precisely this point the Nazi Party's Propaganda Department distributed posters to all Party branches containing the words of Hitler's "prophecy."[51] Evidently, the "prophecy" had by now acquired symbolic status, serving as a weapon of propaganda in preparing the German population for the deportation of the Jews through hardening the climate of opinion.

The self-created logistical problems following from the deportation decision gave the genocidal impulses in Poland, the Baltic, and other conquered eastern territories a strong and irreversible push. In the autumn, the steps into all-out genocide began to follow quickly, one after the other, as the German advance faltered and plans for full-scale deportation to the Russian wastes had to be postponed, then abandoned.

A month or so after giving the order to deport Jews from the Reich, with Himmler and Heydrich as his dinner-table guests in his field headquarters, and in the context of comments betraying his knowledge of the SS's attempts to drown Jewish women in the Pripet marshes, Hitler reminded his entourage of his "prophecy" of destruction for the "criminal race" which had been responsible for the dead of the First World War and "now again hundreds of thousands" in the current war.[52]

Genocide was by now in the air. As preparations were under way to deport the first batches of Jews from Berlin and other German cities, Goebbels, who continued to be one of the most vehement advocates of the deportation, sustained the poisonous atmosphere with a menacing article on November 16, 1941, in his newspaper *Das Reich,* headed "The Jews are Guilty." Here, too, in an article widely circulated among the troops on the eastern front as well as within Germany, Goebbels directly invoked Hitler's "prophecy" of the "annihilation of the Jewish race in Europe," commenting that "we are experiencing right now the fulfillment of this prophecy." Probably, given the centrality of the issue, the article had been discussed with Hitler. An added remark by Goebbels, that any sympathy with the Jews was misplaced, certainly mirrored a sentiment forcibly voiced by Hitler on more than one occasion, as the "Final Solution" became reality.[53]

On December 11, 1941, following the Japanese bombing of Pearl Harbor four days earlier, Hitler announced Germany's declaration of war on the United States. By then, as we have noted, the killing of Jews in the Warthegau in western Poland was beginning and the construction of a small extermination camp at Bełżec in eastern Poland was under way, while deported Reich Jews had already been shot on arrival in Kowno and Riga. But these were as yet local, rather than general, solutions. The changed situation after December 11 now provided new impetus towards a comprehensive solution.

The following day, Hitler addressed his Party leaders in the Reich Chancellery in Berlin in a speech which, as we have noted, Christian Gerlach took to be the announcement of his "basic decision" to exterminate the Jews. We have seen reason to doubt this interpretation. Even so, the speech was important. Goebbels summarized next day in his diary what Hitler had said. His brief report indicates how, in the fundamental issue of anti-Jewish policy, crucial phases of radicalization could be initiated. "With regard to the Jewish Question," Goebbels noted, "the Führer is determined to make a clean sweep. He prophesied that if they brought about another world war, they would experience their annihilation. This was no empty talk. The world war is here. The annihilation of the Jews must be the necessary consequence. This question is to be viewed without sentimentality" — a repeat of the point expressed in his newspaper article a month earlier. "We're not to have sympathy with the Jews, but only sympathy with our German people. If the German people has again now sacrificed around 160,000 dead in the eastern campaign, the instigators of this bloody conflict will have to pay for it with their own lives."[54]

In the atmosphere immediately following such a decisive moment as the entry of the USA into the war, Hitler's repetition of his "prophecy" was, to go from Goebbels' account of it, more menacing than ever. Four days later, on December 16, Hans Frank, Governor General of Poland, speaking to his own minions in Krakow, repeated Hitler's "prophecy" in almost the identical words that Hitler himself had used in Berlin. "What is to happen to the Jews?," he then asked, rhetorically. "Do you believe they'll be accommodated in village settlements in the *Ostland?* They said to us in Berlin: why are you giving us all this trouble? . . . Liquidate them yourselves!" He concluded: "We must destroy the Jews wherever we find them." But he did not know how this would come about. Obviously a comprehensive extermination program still had to be developed. He reckoned there were 3.5 million Jews in his domain. "We can't shoot these 3.5 million Jews," he declared, "we can't poison them, but we must be able to take steps leading somehow to a success in extermination."[55]

Over the following weeks, the steps were taken. Hans Frank and his underlings did not need any specific Hitler order. They understood perfectly well what the repetition of his "prophecy" had meant: the time for the final reckoning with the Jews had arrived. The "prophecy" had served as the transmission belt between Hitler's own inner conviction that the war would bring about the final destruction of European Jewry and the actions of his underlings, determined to do all they could to "work towards the Führer," in turning Hitler's presumed wishes into reality.

Little over a month later, at the Wannsee Conference on January 20, 1942, to discuss the organization of what Heydrich called "the coming final solution of the Jewish question," Hans Frank's right-hand man, Josef Bühler, State Secretary in the *Generalgouvernement,* asked directly if a start could be made in his area. He wanted the Jews there, most of them as he emphasized incapable of work, "removed" and the "Jewish question" there "solved" as soon as possible. The authorities there would do all that they could to cooperate.[56] Bühler, and behind him Hans Frank, had their way. By spring 1942, what was now rapidly emerging as a comprehensive extermination program was extended from certain districts to the whole of the *Generalgouvernement* as train-loads of Jews were ferried to the newly erected camps of Bełżec, Sobibor, and, a little later, Treblinka, in what soon came to be called *Aktion Reinhard.*[57]

Ten days after the Wannsee Conference, speaking on January 30, 1942, at the Sportpalast in Berlin, Hitler again invoked his "prophecy." "I already stated on 1 September 1939 in the German Reichstag," he declared (as always, deliberately misdating his "prophecy"), "that this war will not come to an end as the Jews imagine, with the extermination of the European-Aryan peoples, but that the result of this war will be the annihilation of Jewry. For the first time the old Jewish law will now be applied: an eye for an eye, a tooth for a tooth."[58] Monitoring reactions to the speech, the SD (*Sicherheitsdienst*) remarked that Hitler's statement had been taken to mean "that very soon the last Jew would disappear from European soil."[59]

At the end of March 1942, Goebbels wrote explicitly in his diary of the liquidation of Jews in the Lublin District of the General Government. "A judgment is being carried out on the Jews which is barbaric, but fully deserved," he noted. "The prophecy which the Führer gave them along the way for bringing about a new world war is beginning to come true in the most terrible fashion." He added: "Here, too, the Führer is the unswerving champion and spokesman of a radical solution."[60]

During spring and summer of 1942 the deportation to the death-camps in Poland — now including the biggest of all, Auschwitz-Birkenau — was extended to the whole of the *Generalgouvernement* and to Slovakia, and finally to the occupied countries of western Europe. Previous important decisions concerning the "solution of the Jewish Question," such as the introduction of the Yellow Star or the deportation of Reich Jews, had required Hitler's authorization. It is unimaginable that it was not again sought and given for the massive extension of the killing program.[61] As Florent Brayard has argued, this feasibly occurred during discussions with Himmler under the impact of Heydrich's assassination.[62]

The head of the SS, Heinrich Himmler, who bore the chief responsibility for the implementation of the extermination program, repeatedly claimed that he was acting on Hitler's authority.[63] In a secret memorandum of July 28, 1942, to *SS-Obergruppenführer* Gottlob Berger, head of the *SS-Hauptamt,* for instance, Himmler stated: "The occupied eastern territories are being made free of Jews. The Führer has placed the implementation of this very difficult order on my shoulders."[64] He certainly spoke privately with Hitler on several documented occasions directly about extermination policy.[65] According to postwar testimony provided by his former personal adjutant, Otto Günsche, and his manservant, Heinz Linge, Hitler showed a direct interest in the development of gas-chambers and spoke to Himmler about the use of gas-vans.[66] Though their testimony is inaccurate in a number of ways and cannot be trusted with regard to detail, Adolf Eichmann, in effect the "manager" of the "Final Solution," Dieter Wisliceny, one of his deputies, and Rudolf Höss, the Commandant of Auschwitz, all asserted after the war that the orders passed on to them to implement the "Final Solution" derived from Hitler himself.[67] Second- and third-tier SS leaders directly implicated in the "Final Solution" were in no doubt themselves that they were fulfilling "the wish of the Führer."[68] There is no reason to doubt that they were correct, and that Hitler's authority — most probably given as verbal consent to propositions usually put to him by Himmler — stood behind every decision of magnitude and significance.

Hitler was kept informed of the scale of the "removal" of the Jews — sometimes in detail. On December 29, 1942, for example, Himmler gave him a report, one of a series, of "bandits" liquidated in southern Russia and the Ukraine over the previous three months. The total "executed" numbered 387,370. Of these, 363,211 were Jews.[69] It was a clear indication that, as Hitler had agreed with Himmler a year earlier, the Jews were being exterminated in the east "as partisans."[70] But by the end of 1942 the killing was no longer confined to the east, and now extended over much of Nazi-occupied Europe. And as Hitler repeated his "prophecy," in his speech to the Party's "Old Guard" in Munich on November 8, according to the SS's reckoning close to four million Jews were dead.[71]

Hitler continued to be closely involved in the "Final Solution." The pattern is by now familiar. In line with his "prophecy," Hitler's aim to "remove" — which now, no one was in doubt, meant kill — the Jews of Europe set the framework. Within this general remit, a radicalizing proposal would then be put to Hitler to deal with some specific aspect of the overall problem. Hitler would give his approval. The action would follow. In this way, he agreed in September 1942 to a request by Goebbels to remove Jews from the armaments industry and have them transported to the east. The roundup of these Jews followed in January 1943.[72] In December 1942, Hitler acceded to Himmler's request to have 600,000–700,000 Jews in France, where the southern part of the country was now also under German (and partly Italian) occupation, "done away with." Only diplomatic difficulties over the deportation with both the Italians and the French prevented the implementation of the order.[73]

As the war turned against Germany, such diplomatic difficulties intensified. Hitler's allies, looking to a post-Nazi future, became increasingly unwilling to deport their Jews to the gas-chambers. In the wake of the German military crisis following the catastrophe at Stalingrad, Hitler took a direct hand in trying to persuade them to be more cooperative. Obsessed as ever with the notion of demonic Jews presumed to be behind the war, he pressed his Romanian and Hungarian allies to sharpen the persecution. His language, when addressing the Hungarian leader, Admiral Horthy, in mid-April 1943, was particularly vicious. Hitler urged him — to no avail — to adopt a harsher stance towards the Jews, mentioning that the Polish Jews were being dealt with like a tubercular bacillus that attacks healthy bodies.[74] A month later, speaking to Goebbels, Hitler likened Jews to insects and parasites, declaring "there is nothing else open to modern peoples than to exterminate the Jews."[75]

The "prophecy," by now essentially a cliché used to legitimate to others and to himself that the war he had launched, which was driving Germany ever closer to perdition, had been inevitable and warranted, was still evidently deeply embedded in Hitler's psyche. On May 26, 1944, he addressed a large gathering of senior officers on the Obersalzberg, above Berchtesgaden. In a central passage of his lengthy speech, he referred to the treatment of the Jews. The old notion that had possessed him since 1918 of Jews as a treacherous fifth-column of seditionists and revolutionaries on the home front was again voiced. The removal of the Jews had eliminated this danger within Germany, he declared. He defended himself against suggestions that it might have been achieved more humanely by emphasizing once more the war as an all-or-nothing, life-or-death struggle, giving an apocalyptic vision of what would happen if Germany's enemies were victorious, and speaking of the horrors of the bombing of Hamburg and other cities, summing up: "This entire bestiality has been organized by the Jews." Humanitarian feelings were, therefore, he argued, "cruelty towards one's own people." He went on to hint at the action about to be taken against the Jews in Hungary — the horrific destruction of Hungarian Jewry would indeed unfold within weeks, following pressure directly imposed by Hitler[76] — to remove what he called "a seamless web of agents and spies." It was at this point that he turned once more to his "prophecy" of 1939 that in the event of war not the German nation but Jewry itself would be "eradicated." The audience of Wehrmacht officers responded with storms of applause.[77]

In the last weeks of the war, the "prophecy" served Hitler's need for self-justification. Although his last recorded monologues from early 1945 survive only in dubious form,[78] the comments about the Jews on February 13 certainly sound authentically Hitlerian, and are fully in line with the repetitions of his "prophecy" that we have noted. "I have fought openly against the Jews," the text runs. "I gave them a last warning at the outbreak of war. I never left them in uncertainty that if they were to plunge the world into war again they would this time not be spared—that the vermin in Europe would be finally eradicated."[79] And as we saw at the outset, his very last political manifesto was still urging the relentless persecution of the Jews.

Conclusions

Hitler's "prophecy" of January 30, 1939, which he was to invoke so frequently in the following years, has claim to be regarded as a key both to Hitler's mentality, and to the ways he provided "directions for action"[80] in the core element of his ideology. As such, it highlights the central ideological driving-force of National Socialism, and also shows the ways in which fundamental and unchanging ideas were accommodated to shifting forms of draconian persecution and translated into ever more radical policy-decisions. It illustrates, in fact, how "charismatic leadership"[81] operated in the crucial area of genocidal policy, and how Nazi activists at different levels of the regime were adept in knowing how to "work towards the Führer" without having to wait for a precise Führer order. It seems unlikely that Hitler ever gave one single, explicit order for the "Final Solution." Within the unchanging framework of his "prophecy," he needed do no more than provide requisite authorization at the appropriate time to Himmler and Heydrich to go ahead with the various escalatory stages that culminated in the murder of Europe's Jews.

In speaking, as he had done in March 1942, of Hitler as "the unswerving champion and spokesman of a radical solution" to the "Jewish Question," Goebbels was correctly summarizing Hitler's role in the "Final Solution." This role had often been indirect, rather than overt, frequently granting approval rather than initiating. The unparalleled outpourings of hatred were a constant amid the policy shifts. They often had a propaganda or mobilizing motive, and usually remained generalized. Even so, there cannot be the slightest doubt: Hitler's role was decisive and indispensable to the unfolding of the "Final Solution." Had another form of nationalist government been in power at the time in Germany, it would probably have introduced discriminatory legislation against Jews. But without Hitler, the creation of a program to bring about the physical extermination of the Jews of Europe is unimaginable.

Notes

I would like to thank the Leverhulme Trust for support in the preparation of this essay.

1. Eberhard Jäckel and Axel Kuhn, eds., *Hitler Sämtliche Aufzeichnungen 1905–1924* (Stuttgart: Deutsche Verlags-Anstalt, 1980), pp. 88–90; trans. Jeremy Noakes and Geoffrey Pridham, eds., *Nazism 1919–1945. A Documentary Reader,* vol. 1 (Exeter: University of Exeter Press, 1983), pp. 12–14.

2. Werner Maser, ed., *Hitlers Briefe und Notizen. Sein Weltbild in handschriftlichen Dokumenten* (Düsseldorf: Droste Verlag, 1973), pp. 360–361; translated in *Nazi Conspiracy and Aggression,* edited in the Office of the United States Chief of Counsel for Prosecution of Axis Criminality (Washington: US Government Printing Office, 1946–1948), vol. 6, p. 260.

3. Adolf Hitler, *Mein Kampf* (Munich: Zentralverlag der NSDAP, 876–880th reprint, 1943), p. 772; translated as *Hitler's Mein Kampf,* with an Introduction by D. C. Watt (London: Radius Books, 1972), p. 620.

4. See Eberhard Jäckel, *Hitlers Weltanschauung, Entwurf einer Herrschaft,* 4th ed. (Stuttgart: Deutsche Verlags-Anstalt, 1991).

5. Jäckel and Kuhn, *Hitler. Sämtliche Aufzeichnungen,* p. 69.

6. Werner Jochmann, ed., *Adolf Hitler. Monologe im Führerhauptquartier 1941–1944* (Hamburg: Albrech Knaus Verlag, 1980), p. 108.

7. Karl A. Schleunes, *The Twisted Road to Auschwitz. Nazi Policy toward German Jews 1933–1939* (Urbana: University of Illinois Press, 1970), p. 258.

8. Gerald Reitlinger, *The Final Solution* (London: Vallentine, Mitchell & Co. Ltd., 1953).

9. Raul Hilberg, *The Destruction of the European Jews* (Chicago: Quadrangle, 1961).

10. See Leni Yahil, "Some Remarks about Hitler's Impact on the Nazis' Jewish Policy," *Yad Vashem Studies,* 23 (1993), pp. 282–286.

11. Lucy Dawidowicz, *The War against the Jews 1933–45* (Harmondsworth: Penguin, 1977), pp. 193–208.

12. Gerald Fleming, *Hitler und die Endlösung. "Es ist des Führers Wunsch"* (Wiesbaden/Munich: Limes Verlag, 1982), pp. 13–27; English edition: *Hitler and the Final Solution* (Berkeley: University of California Press, 1994 paperback edition), pp. 1–16.

13. Alan Bullock, *Hitler. A Study in Tyranny* (Harmondsworth: Penguin, 1962), pp. 702–703; Joachim C. Fest, *Hitler. Eine Biographie* (Ullstein: Frankfurt am Main/Berlin/Vienna, 1976), vol. 2, p. 930; John Toland, *Adolf Hitler* (New York: Doubleday, 1976), pp. 88–89.

14. Rudolph Binion, *Hitler among the Germans* (New York/Oxford/Amsterdam: Elsevier, 1976), pp. 1–35.

15. For this term, see Hans Mommsen, *Beamtentum in Dritten Reich* (Stuttgart: Deutsche Verlags-Anstalt, 1966), p. 98 note 26.

16. Martin Broszat, "Hitler und die Genesis der 'Endlösung'. Aus Anlaß der Thesen von David Irving," *Vierteljahrshefte für Zeitgeschichte,* 25 (1977), pp. 737–775. An English version was published as "Hitler and the Genesis of the 'Final Solution': An Assessment of David Irving's Theses," *Yad Vashem Studies,* 13 (1979), pp. 73–125.

17. Hans Mommsen, "Die Realisierung des Utopischen: Die 'Endlösung der Juden-frage' im 'Dritten Reich'," *Geschichte und Gesellschaft,* 9 (1983), pp. 381–420.

18. Yehuda Bauer, *The Holocaust in Historical Perspective* (London: Sheldon Press, 1978), p. 11.

19. Schleunes, *Twisted Road;* Uwe Dietrich Adam, *Judenpolitik im Dritten Reich* (Düsseldorf: Droste, 1972).

20. Peter Longerich, ed., *Die Ermordung der europäischen Juden. Eine umfassende Dokumentation des Holocaust 1941–1945.* (Munich/Zurich: Piper, 1989), p. 78.

21. Christopher R. Browning, "Zur Genesis der 'Endlösung'. Eine Antwort an Martin Broszat," *Vierteljahrshefte für Zeitgeschichte,* 29 (1981), pp. 97–109; English edition: "A Reply to Martin Broszat regarding the Origins of the Final Solution", *Simon Wiesenthal Center Annual,* 1 (1984), pp. 113–132.

22. See, notably, Christopher Browning, *Fateful Months: Essays on the Emergence of the Final Solution* (New York: Holmes & Meier, 1985); *The Path to Genocide. Essays on Launching the Final Solution* (Cambridge: Cambridge University Press, 1992); and *The Origins of the Final Solution: The Evolution of Nazi Jewish Policy, September 1939– March 1942* (Jerusalem and Lincoln: Yad Vashem and University of Nebraska Press, 2004).

23. Eberhard Jäckel and Jürgen Rohwer, eds., *Der Mord an den Juden im Zweiten Weltkrieg* (Stuttgart: Deutsche Verlags-Anstalt, 1985).

24. Philippe Burrin, *Hitler et les Juifs. Genèse d'un génocide* (Paris: Seuil, 1989), pp. 129–139, pp. 164–174. English edition: *Hitler and the Jews: The Genesis of the Holocaust* (London: Edward Arnold, 1994).

25. Götz Aly, *Endlösung. Völkerverschiebung und der Mord an den europäischen Juden* (Frankfurt am Main: Fischer, 1995), pp. 398–399 and back cover. Published in English as *The Final Solution: Nazi Population Policy and the Murder of the European Jews* (London: Arnold, 1999).

26. Dieter Pohl, *Von der "Judenpolitik" zum Judenmord. Der Distrikt Lublin des Generalgouvernements 1939–1944* (Frankfurt am Main: Peter Lang, 1993), pp. 105ff.

27. Ian Kershaw, "Improvised Genocide? The Emergence of the 'Final Solution' in the 'Warthegau'," *Transactions of the Royal Historical Society,* 6th Series (1992), pp. 51–78.

28. David Bankier, "Hitler and the Policy-Making Process in the Jewish Question," *Holocaust and Genocide Studies,* 3 (1988), pp. 1–20; Saul Friedländer, *Nazi Germany and the Jews: The Years of Persecution, 1933–1939* (London: Weidenfeld & Nicolson, 1997).

29. Christopher R. Browning, "Hitler and the Euphoria of Victory: The Path to the Final Solution," in David Cesarani, ed., *The Final Solution: Origins and Implementation* (London and New York: Routledge, 1994), pp. 137–147; and *The Origins of the Final Solution,* pp. 314–316, pp. 426–427.

30. Richard Breitman, *The Architect of Genocide: Himmler and the Final Solution* (London: The Bodley Head, 1991), pp. 153, 156.

31. Tobias Jersak, "Die Interaktion von Kriegsverlauf und Judenvernichtung," *Historische Zeitschrift,* 268 (1999), pp. 311–349.

32. Christian Gerlach, "Die Wannsee-Konferenz, das Schicksal der deutschen Juden und Hitlers politische Grundsatzentscheidung, alle Juden Europas zu ermorden," *Werkstattgeschichte,* 18 (1997), pp. 7–44, reprinted with amendments in Christian Gerlach,

Krieg, Ernährung, Völkermord: Forschungen zur deutschen Vernichtungspolitik im Zweiten Weltkrieg (Hamburg: Hamburger Edition, 1998), pp. 85–166.

33. See Peter Longerich, *Politik der Vernichtung. Eine Gesamtdarstellung der nationalsozialistischen Judenverfolgung* (Munich and Zurich: Piper, 1998), p. 467.

34. See Ulrich Herbert, " 'Führerentscheidung' zur 'Endlösung'?," *Neue Zürcher Zeitung,* March 14–15, 1998, pp. 69–70.

35. Florent Brayard, *La "solution finale de la question juive". La technique, le temps et les catégories de la décision* (Paris: Fayard, 2004).

35. Bradley F. Smith and Agnes F. Peterson, eds., *Heinrich Himmler. Geheimreden 1933 bis 1945* (Frankfurt am Main, Berlin, Vienna: Proplyäen Verlag, 1974), p. 159.

37. Longerich, *Politik der Vernichtung,* pp. 579–584.

38. See Ulrich Herbert, ed., *Nationalsozialistische Vernichtungspolitik 1939–1945. Neue Forschungen und Kontroversen* (Frankfurt am Main: Fischer, 1998), p. 27; English edition: *National Socialist Extermination Policies. Contemporary Perspectives and Controversies* (New York/Oxford: Berghahn Books, 2000).

39. See, for this concept, Ian Kershaw, *Hitler, 1889–1936. Hubris* (London: Penguin, 1998), pp. 529–531.

40. Elke Fröhlich, ed., *Die Tagebücher von Joseph Goebbels* (Munich: Saur, 1993), Part I, Vol. 4, p. 429.

41. See Ian Kershaw, *Hitler, 1936–1945. Nemesis* (London: Penguin, 2000), pp. 129–153.

42. *Akten zur Deutschen Auswärtigen Politik 1918–1945* (Göttingen: Vandenhoeck & Ruprecht, 1971), Series D, Vol. IV, p. 170, Doc. 158.

43. Max Domarus, ed., *Hitler. Reden und Proklamationen 1932–1945* (Wiesbaden: R. Löwit, 1973), vol. 3, p. 1058; translated in Jeremy Noakes and Geoffrey Pridham, eds., *Nazism 1919–1945. A Documentary Reader,* vol. 3 (Exeter: Exeter University Press, 1988), p. 1049.

44. Dawidowicz, *War Against the Jews,* p. 206.

45. Hans Mommsen, "Hitler's Reichstag Speech of 30 January 1939," *History and Memory,* 9 (1997), pp. 150–151.

46. Aly, *Endlösung,* pp. 272–273.

47. Browning, "Hitler and the Euphoria of Victory," p. 140.

48. Fleming, *Hitler und die Endlösung,* p. 86.

49. *Die Tagebücher von Joseph Goebbels,* Part II, Vol. 1, pp. 265–266, 269.

50. *Die Ermordung der europäischen Juden,* p. 157.

51. Reproduced in Kershaw, *Hitler. Nemesis,* plate 45.

52. *Adolf Hitler: Monologe,* p. 106.

53. *Das Reich,* November 16, 1941.

54. *Die Tagebücher von Joseph Goebbels,* Part II, Vol. 2, pp. 498–499.

55. Werner Präg and Wolfgang Jacobmeyer, eds., *Das Diensttagebuch des deutschen Generalgouverneurs in Polen 1939–1945* (Stuttgart: Deutsche Verlags-Anstalt, 1975), pp. 457–458.

56. *Die Ermordung der europäischen Juden,* p. 91. The authoritative study of the Wannsee Conference is that of Mark Roseman, *The Villa, the Lake, the Meeting: Wannsee and the Final Solution* (London: Penguin, 2002).

57. See Yitzhak Arad, *Belzec, Sobibor, Treblinka: The Operation Reinhard Death Camps* (Bloomington: Indiana University Press, 1987); and Bogdan Musial, *Deutsche Zivilverwaltung und Judenverfolgung im Generalgouvernement. Eine Fallstudie zum Distrikt Lublin 1939–1944* (Wiesbaden: Harrassowitz, 1999), Part III, esp. pp. 229ff.

58. *Hitler. Reden und Proklamationen,* vol. 4, p. 1829.

59. Heinz Boberach, ed., *Meldungen aus dem Reich. Die geheimen Lageberichte des Sicherheitsdienstes der SS 1938–1945* (Herrsching: Pawlak Verlag, 1984), vol. 9, p. 3235.

60. *Die Tagebücher von Joseph Goebbels,* Part II, Vol. 3, p. 561.

61. See Peter Longerich, *The Unwritten Order: Hitler's Role in the Final Solution* (London: Tempus, 2001), p. 106.

62. Brayard, *La "solution finale de la question juive,"* pp. 16–18, 465–473.

63. Fleming, *Hitler und die Endlösung,* pp. 62–68, 163–165.

64. "Reichsführer-SS to Gottlob Berger," July 28, 1942, Berlin Document Center, SS-HO, 933.

65. Czesław Madajczyk, "Hitler's Direct Influence on Decisions Affecting Jews during World War II", *Yad Vashem Studies,* 20 (1990), pp. 61–65; Hermann Graml, "Zur Genesis der 'Endlösung'," in *Das Unrechtsregime II,* edited by Ursula Büttner (Hamburg: Christians Verlag, 1986), p. 14; Peter Witte et al., eds., *Der Dienstkalender Heinrich Himmlers 1941/42* (Hamburg: Christians Verlag, 1999), p. 294.

66. Henrik Eberle and Matthias Uhl, *Das Buch Hitler* (Bergisch Gladbach: Gustav Lübbe Verlag, 2005), pp. 196–197. The passages in question make no mention of Jews and convey the impression that the victims of the gassing were Soviet citizens. The text, whose provenance and intended recipient — Stalin — makes it problematical in a number of respects, goes on (see p. 197 and note 195) to claim that gas chambers were first established, on Hitler's personal order, at Charkow, though, in fact, no gas chambers were erected on the occupied territory of the Soviet Union.

67. Browning, *Fateful Months,* pp. 23–26; David Cesarani, *Eichmann: His Life and Crimes* (London: William Heinemann, 2004), pp. 91, 98–103; Martin Broszat, ed., *Kommandant in Auschwitz. Autobiographische Aufzeichnungen des Rudolf Höß* (Munich: Deutscher Taschenbuch Verlag, 1978), pp. 157, 180–181; Karin Orth, "Rudolf Höß und die 'Endlösung der Judenfrage'. Drei Argumente gegen deren Datierung auf den Sommer 1941," *Werkstattgeschichte,* 18 (1977), pp. 45–57; Richard Overy, *Interrogations. The Nazi Elite in Allied Hands, 1945* (London: Penguin, 2001), pp. 357, 359–360.

68. Fleming, *Hitler und die Endlösung,* pp. 119–126.

69. Berlin Document Center, SS-HO, 1238, Reichsführer-SS, December 29, 1942, "Meldung an den Führer über Bandenbekämpfung," a report presented to Hitler on December 31, 1942; reproduced in Fleming, *Hitler und die Endlösung,* plate 4 (between p. 128 and p. 129).

70. *Der Dienstkalender Heinrich Himmlers,* p. 294.

71. *Hitler. Reden und Proklamationen,* vol. 4, p. 1937; *Der Dienstkalender Heinrich Himmlers,* p. 73.

72. Longerich, *The Unwritten Order,* pp. 109, 114.

73. Madajczyk, "Hitler's Direct Influence on Decisions Affecting Jews," p. 64; Longerich, *The Unwritten Order,* pp. 115, 120.

74. Andreas Hillgruber, ed., *Staatsmänner und Diplomaten bei Hitler. Vertrauliche Aufzeichnungen über Unterredungen mit Vertretern des Auslandes 1942–1944* (Frankfurt am Main: Bernard & Graefe, 1970), pp. 256–257.

75. *Die Tagebücher von Joseph Goebbels,* Part II, Vol. 8, p. 288.

76. Fleming, *Hitler und die Endlösung,* p. 173; Madajczyk, "Hitler's Direct Influence on Decisions Affecting Jews," p. 67.

77. Hans-Heinrich Wilhelm, "Hitlers Ansprache vor Generalen und Offizieren am 26. Mai 1944," *Militärgeschichtliche Mitteilungen,* 2 (1976), p. 156; and idem, "Wie geheim war die Endlösung?" in *Miscellanea: Festschrift für Helmut Krausnick zum 75. Geburtstag,* edited by Wolfgang Benz (Stuttgart: Deutsche Verlags-Anstalt, 1980), pp. 134–136.

78. See Kershaw, *Hitler. Nemesis,* pp. 1024–1025, note 121.

79. *Hitlers politisches Testament. Die Bormann-Diktate von Februar und April 1945* (Hamburg: Knaus, 1981), p. 69.

80. A term taken from Martin Broszat, "Soziale Motivation und Führer-Bindung des Nationalsozialismus," *Vierteljahrshefte für Zeitgeschichte,* 18 (1970), p. 403.

81. For the way in which I apply this term to Hitler's rule, see Ian Kershaw, *Hitler. A Profile in Power* (London: Longman, 1991), pp. 10–14.

PART II

Popular Opinion and the Jews in Nazi Germany

5

The 'Everyday' and the 'Exceptional':
The Shaping of Popular Opinion, 1933–1939

Generalisations about attitudes of the German people towards the Nazi regime tended in the early postwar years to polarise around diametrically opposed interpretations. On the one hand — especially outside Germany — the emphasis was laid upon enthusiastic mass backing. On the other — among Germans themselves — the stress fell upon the helplessness of a population which for the most part rejected the regime but in the face of unparalleled terror and repression could do little but engage in 'passive resistance'. Since the social history of Nazi Germany began in earnest in the 1970s — as late as thirty years after the end of the war — a voluminous literature has wholly amended such crude generalisations. Even so, the tendency in the initial phase of '*Alltagsge-schichte*' ('the history of everyday life') which set in during the 1970s was to underline the extent of 'popular opposition'. This sometimes came close, it seemed, to playing down or grossly underestimating the spheres of consensus which provided the regime with an extensive basis of support and at times enthusiastic approval. Both elements — nonconformity and consent, opposition and approval — were features of attitudes of the German people during the Third Reich. They are two sides of the same coin. Most Germans were neither died-in-the-wool Nazis nor convinced anti-fascists. Partial rejection of Nazism existed in large parts of the population alongside partial approval of the Nazi regime. In what follows an attempt is made to explore how far varied reactions to what we might call, drawing on Max Weber, 'everyday' and 'exceptional' factors might help to explain this Janus face of popular opinion.

A few remarks about the concept of 'popular opinion' and about the sources that have to serve to reconstruct it are necessary at the outset.

Research on Popular Opinion: Sources and Problems

The term 'public opinion' is scarcely usable for the Third Reich. At any rate, we have to accept that 'public opinion' in the sense of opinion that was publicly expressed was from 1933 onwards practically only that of the regime, or rival entities among the leadership elite. Nevertheless, the regime recognised the continued existence of spontaneous, nondirected expressions of 'unofficial' opinion beneath the surface conformity. The very absence, indeed, of freely expressed 'public opinion' encouraged the regime to set up its own agencies to register and test the 'mood' of the population, if only to be able to improve the framing of propaganda. So instead of 'public opinion', a term suited to the pluralistic formation of attitudes in a liberal democracy, it seems more appropriate to speak of 'popular opinion' to embrace the unquantifiable, often generalised, diffuse and uncoordinated, but still genuine and widespread, views of ordinary citizens.[1]

Trying to reconstruct trends in opinion is difficult enough for historians — especially before opinion polls — even in democracies where opinion is shaped by pluralistic political parties, interest groups, trades unions and mass media. In conditions of repressive dictatorship, where nonconformist opinion is subjected to draconian persecution and where monopolistic propaganda determines 'official' views, such an attempt faces severe problems.

The first of these is obviously the lack of surviving authentic expressions of opinion in their original form. Open statements of political opinion in contemporary diaries, letters and private papers are, given the fear of reprisals, unsurprisingly rare. So reconstructing opinion trends in the Third Reich necessarily has to fall back in large measure upon sources from agencies of the regime or oppositional sources, in both cases serving directly political purposes and subject to evident but unquantifiable internal bias. Beyond that, evaluation has to take into account the fact that people were intimidated into concealing their true views or at best expressing them only obliquely or in camouflaged form. It can, consequently, be taken for granted that critical views registered in sources favourable to the regime represent the tip of the iceberg. Equally, pro-Nazi views recorded in oppositional sources are probably minimised and, when they occur, are to be taken as significant indicators of support for the regime. A final general difficulty in trying to assess opinion in the Third Reich is that there is no possibility of quantifying attitudes. Trends of opinion after 1933 can, therefore, only be impressionistically reconstructed. And interpretations can scarcely do justice to the multiplicity of individual motives of approval or rejection of specific measures. Conclusions are necessarily, then, limited and hypothetical, not definitive.

Even so, if we want to grasp anything about the attitudes of the German people towards the Hitler regime, we have to establish, at least in broad contours, those aspects of Nazi policy which found substantial popular appeal and those which met with notable criticism. Despite the interpretative problems, not least that of the representative nature of registered opinion, systematic and critical analysis of surviving sources allows for significant insights into mentalities and behavioural patterns of the German people during the Nazi era.

Two types of source are of special importance in reconstructing popular opinion in the Third Reich: the regular confidential reports of Nazi agencies on the 'mood and bearing' (*Stimmung und Haltung*) of the people (compiled, for example, by party offices, local government offices, the judicial administration, the Gestapo and the SD); and the detailed and extensive reports on the situation in Germany produced by exiled left-wing oppositional groups (especially by the Social Democratic Party [SPD] leadership based in Prague, then Paris, and now known as the Sopade), based upon information smuggled out of the Reich by the illegal opposition.

The regular 'situation reports' or 'reports on mood' (*Lage- und Stimmungsberichte*) from Nazi agencies constitute a source of primary importance for the social history of the Third Reich.[2] This extraordinarily voluminous and varied, if widely scattered, material compiled by the lower tiers of the regime's administration — such as local police stations, government offices, and party and SD offices at society's grass roots — is less attuned than reports produced higher up the ladder to stylised propaganda and as such permits glimpses beyond the standardised picture of manufactured opinion.

Certainly, analysing this material is no simple matter. First of all its survival is very uneven, both in quality and quantity. Continuous reports for the entire prewar period can be found at the regional level only in Bavaria and the Palatinate (at that time part of Bavaria). Even there, the position is uneven. At the local level, some reports survive in full sequence and are of extraordinary value. But for other localities they are intermittent, sparse in content and of limited use, and in many places they are missing altogether.[3] So there are huge gaps in the overall picture. Moreover, before 1938 there was no regular central reporting by the SD, and reports became frequent only once war broke out. An evaluation of the material that remains — despite the gaps still extremely voluminous — has to contend, alongside other problems, with that of selection and representative content.

Secondly, there is no certain or unobjectionable way of eliminating the bias and inherent subjective nature of the reports. The aim and character of the specific series of reports have naturally to be borne in mind. But even more important is to develop a familiarity with the style of reporting which allows a critical sense of where registered comment is contrived or authentic. The sheer quantity of surviving reports from scattered localities and from differing provenance provides some level of control on reported comment. And thanks to the unrefined and unpolished expression of many of those reporting at the grass roots, their reports give a relatively firm notion of the main trends of opinion.

Thirdly, it is not easy to contend with the problem of fear and intimidation within the population. Those compiling the reports were themselves fully conscious of the difficulty in penetrating the reluctance of people to express their true feelings openly. Quite apart from the bias of the sources, it is essential, therefore, to be able to read between the lines, to recognise the silences, the sentiments left unexpressed. Even so, it is astonishing given the circumstances how many people *were* prepared, despite the possible dangers, to risk pointed criticism of the regime, and that such criticism was so extensively and often so plainly reported. In this respect, it is in some ways more difficult to interpret reporting of expressions of approval for the regime, where an intrinsic readiness to say what was expected prevailed and where conformity might have been less than freely displayed, than oppositional comments and actions which often speak for themselves. The implicit danger is an overestimation of oppositional leanings and a tendency at the same time to play down conformist and acclamatory attitudes.

Also invaluable for the reconstruction of popular opinion, and for the social history of the Third Reich in general, are the extensive reports of the Sopade which survive between 1934 and 1940.[4] These focus naturally on the situation and attitudes of the industrial working class, but are also extremely informative on other groups of the population and on issues such as the 'Church struggle', the persecution of the Jews and, quite especially, the state of the economy. The central 'Germany Reports', which the Sopade circulated each month from May 1934 to April 1940 in Prague (1934–8) and Paris (1938–40) on thin green paper (hence the alternative name 'Green Reports'), were compiled on the basis of regular and extensive reports submitted from 'border secretaries' stationed around Germany's border — in Czechoslovakia, Switzerland, Belgium and Denmark, for instance. These in turn drew on contacts with the illegal opposition within Germany. The information emerging from the Reich, obviously at great danger to those smuggling it out, touched upon many varied facets of daily life in Nazi Germany, above all, conditions within

German factories. Especially for the years 1935 to 1938 the material is very extensive. The 'Germany Reports', reproduced in two parts, 'Reports' and 'Overviews', are themselves no more than a fraction of the total material. Reports, especially those of the border secretaries, almost completely preserved in Bonn, contain a mass of detailed information which, for security reasons, could not be included in the 'Germany Reports'.

The 'colouring' of this material is easy to see, leaning as it does towards a natural tendency to exaggerate the alienation of the mass of the population from the Nazi regime. It conveys the impression that the regime rapidly lost any basis of popularity and was forcibly sustained only by terror. Both the border secretaries and, quite especially, the Sopade leadership nonetheless tried to avoid simplistic generalisations about popular opinion, qualifying the readiness of some reporters to resort to undifferentiated assessments and at times pointing to the subjectivity and unreliability of the information received. Even with regard to the working class, they emphasised the variance in political attitudes and avoided resort to the type of one-dimensional, 'heroic' view of working-class resistance which might have been expected (and which frequently appeared in reports by the exiled Communist Party of Germany [KPD] organisation). The Sopade reports amount to an extremely valuable source, therefore, and, together with the inferences to be drawn from the reports of regime agencies, enable the construction of a nuanced depiction of trends of opinion in the Third Reich.

The Significance of 'Everyday' Conflict in the Formation of Opinion

Detailed analysis of such sources plainly shows how significant everyday experiences were to the formation of political experience. The material conditions of daily life directly and continually determined the attitude of the population to National Socialism. The extent of the disillusionment and discontent with Nazi rule which arose from subjective experience of socio-economic conditions and was mirrored in political nonconformity and oppositional behaviour is truly striking. At the same time, it is equally clear that it was often superficial and of no political significance. In fact, as the reports show, oppositional attitudes were often infiltrated and distorted by ideas revealing at least partial acceptance of Nazism. Consent and dissent could be apparent within the same individual. All sections of the population, even parts of the working class that had imbued socialism, showed the impact in ideological disorientation of relentless exposure over years to publicly unchallenged propaganda. In the absence of the counter-exposure to the public criticism of government policy which is the basis of pluralistic opinion formation in a democracy, the political horizons of the masses increasingly narrowed while the effect of at least parts of Nazi ideology both widened and deepened. The discontent produced by the worries and cares of daily life were therefore often accompanied by acceptance and approval of the essential thrust of Nazi policy.

The first clear signs of extensive discontent, largely rooted in economic disappointment, could already be glimpsed in 1934. The initial wave of optimism about economic recovery, especially the work-creation measures, gave way in the spring of 1934 to increasing criticism of the regime. This manifested itself most vehemently among those who before the takeover of power had been numbered among the fervent supporters of the NSDAP. Numerous reports, for instance, record the dissatisfaction in the middle classes about the unfilled promises to the *Mittelstand*. Small traders complained about the disadvantages arising from the regime's economic policies — lack of credit, absence of orders placed by the state, the burden of taxation, the excessive compulsory donations for the party, the exploitation of the *Mittelstand* in favour of big industry and, not least, the failure to eliminate the department stores and consumer associations. Material self-interest was plainly at the root of such criticism.

A change of mood against the regime could also be observed among farmers. The disadvantages of the Reich Entailed Farm Law (*Reichserbhofgesetz*) of September 1933, the increasing intervention of the Reich Food Estate (*Reichsnährstand*) in the marketing of agricultural produce — recalling the hated 'coercive economy' of the First World War — and other purely sectoral concerns prompted the farmers' discontent and dissatisfaction with the regime in rural areas. The head of the regional administration (*Regierungspräsident*) in one part of Bavaria spoke of 'a dangerous loss of confidence in broad sections of the peasantry'.[5] According to one report, at party meetings in his region directed at 'grumblers' and 'miseries', seen as responsible for the downturn in mood, negative attitudes had surfaced 'at a flash'. Farmers were critical of everything 'which could in any way be criticised'. The general mood, it was reported, bore comparison with that of 1917–18.[6]

This was unquestionably a gross exaggeration. It would be a mistake to overrate the significance of grass-roots critical opinion in the summer of 1934. Even the Sopade's 'Germany Reports', whose general tenor, as we have noted, was self-evidently oppositional, pointed out that, apart from the limited nature of the complaints motivated by economic grievances, the regime could still depend upon extensive reserves of support, especially the idealism of younger Germans, and the fact that Hitler still captivated the masses even though the party was increasingly in the firing line of criticism. According to

Sopade reports, the middle-class disillusionment, based as it was on no more than material dissatisfaction, was 'far removed from political aim' and wholly devoid of significance.[7] Fear of Bolshevism and lack of political education sufficed to underpin support for the regime despite economically motivated complaints. The main characteristics of popular opinion in the summer of 1934, adjudged Sopade informants, were passivity and grumbling, 'but beyond that, to oppose the regime — it doesn't go that far'.[8]

'Shrugging the shoulders', political cluelessness, fear and the atomisation of society, meaning that there was 'not only no public opinion in Germany', but 'also no sectional opinion any longer', were said to characterise the attitude of the people in 1934.[9] Even without taking account of the repressive power of the regime, the all-embracing propaganda, and the hundreds of thousands of beneficiaries of the system who constituted its hard-core support, the Sopade reached a pessimistic evaluation of the fractured popular opinion, even among opponents of the regime:

> The weakness of the opposition is the strength of the regime. Its opponents are ideologically and organisationally weak. They are ideologically weak because the vast number of them are mere discontents, grumblers whose dissatisfaction derives purely from economic causes. This is especially so among the middle classes and peasantry. These sections of the population criticise more loudly and strongly than any others, but their criticism mainly arises from personal interests. They are least ready to fight the regime in any serious way because they know least of all what they should be fighting for . . . Fear of Bolshevism, of the chaos which, in the opinion of the vast majority especially in the middle classes and peasantry would follow the fall of Hitler, still forms the negative basis of the regime's mass support.
>
> Its opponents are organisationally weak because it is in the essence of the fascist system not to allow any organisational concentration of its opponents. The forces of 'reaction' are extraordinarily splintered. . . . The working-class movement is still split between socialists and communists. . . . The attitude of the church-based opponents of the regime is disunited. Their struggle is evidently not least directed towards improving the position of the Churches *within* the regime.[10]

A new high-point of discontent was reached in winter 1935–6. Severe food shortages — especially of butter, fats, eggs and meat — together with a corresponding steep rise in food prices while wages fell or at most were held stable, led to hardship and suffering especially among the working population of large cities. In contrast to the wave of criticism of 1934, which largely emanated from the peasantry and middle classes, a bitter mood in 1935–6 made itself felt above all within the industrial working class.

Serious working-class unrest was recorded with concern in the reports of all Nazi authorities.[11] They noted an increase in derogatory comments about the state and a revitalisation of illegal opposition, whose agitation in factories and motorway construction sites (known centres of unrest) now found growing appeal. A rise in the numbers of cases of 'protective custody' and those coming before the 'Special Courts' (set up in 1933 to deal speedily with cases of 'subversive' comment or action) seemed to reflect the discontent, not least since for the most part the workers arrested had no history of political activism. Bitter criticism was rampant, attacking working conditions in factories, the German Labour Front, the Nazi Party and the state leadership, the injustice of a system where workers were paid 'starvation wages' though industrialists still drew their massive salaries and profits, the corrupt 'bossdom' (*Bonzokratie*) of the regime, and the wastage of money on grand Nazi building projects while an acute shortage of housing and falling standard of living prevailed. The regime's own internal reports in Bavaria spoke of 'a growing discontent with regime and party' in the working class.[12] The Sopade reports from industrial areas were more expressive. According to one report from the Ruhr district, 'the shortage of foodstuffs . . . [had] provoked enormous tension in the entire population. It is possible to speak of a feverish unrest in all sections of the population. At the least opportunity in daily life the most varied sorts of Nazis (SS, SA, NSV, DAF etc.) have the bitter anger directly thrown in their faces'.[13] In Saxony the bitterness was said to have found vent in 'furious insults'. Throughout the whole province, 'the mood against the regime has intensified in such a way that it would now only need a light in the powder-keg to produce the explosion'.[14] In Rhineland-Westphalia, it was said that 'all sections of the population are opposed to the system. You have to be amazed that this government can still keep going at all'.[15]

This was plainly a complete misjudgement. Other Sopade reports, in fact, were concerned not to exaggerate the significance of the critical mood. They stressed instead the divided opinion about the regime and the naivety of most critics, who were too short-sighted to draw ideological or political deductions from their discontent. They depicted, too, the prevailing conditions of fear, intimidation and atomisation which in practice excluded the possibility of directing the discontent into organised political aims. One report from Saxony called the extensive anger 'a purely emotional matter, without political reflection'.[16] A Bavarian report explained that 'it would be wrong to regard the generally prevalent poor mood as direct hostility to the ruling forces' and pointed out 'that despite the criticism to be heard everywhere the orders of the rulers are carried out without any thought of resistance'. It frequently happened 'that people who poured out their complaints about the state of affairs then shouted the loudest when filled with enthusiasm again by Nazi speakers at some rally or other'.[17]

In the last years of peace the morale of the peasantry and industrial workers caused the regime most concern because of their key importance to the economy. All sources indicate the widespread and growing discontent in farming circles between 1936 and 1939 as the needs of farming took second place to those of armaments production and pressure on the peasantry intensified. Beyond all other concerns in the countryside, the ever more acutely critical shortage of agricultural workers caused bitterness, anger and demoralisation. The SD spoke in 1938 of a mood among the peasantry approaching 'complete despair'. The 'flight from the land', becoming an avalanche as rural workers sought better-paid jobs in the armaments industry, gave farmers 'the feeling of being crushed' and produced a mood which turned 'partly to resignation and partly into an attitude of outright revolt against the farmers' leadership'.[18] The provincial farmers' leadership in Bavaria even reported a protest demonstration in February 1939 of around fifty peasants in Munich, adding: 'the shortage of hired hands [*Dienstboten*] has reached indescribable levels. . . . The mood of the peasants has risen to boiling point'.[19]

The ambivalence of the farmers' political attitude was nevertheless obvious. The same farmers who so vehemently demanded state help to prevent the flight from the land complained the loudest about the oppressive state intervention in agriculture. Indeed, the Nazi state had provided the peasantry, despite organisational disadvantages and mounting bureaucratic controls, with stable prices and protected marketing.[20] The overall picture is not altogether straightforward. On the one hand, especially among older farmers, the criticism of the regime could be extraordinarily blunt. On the other hand, important elements of Nazi ideology undoubtedly found favour among the peasantry, so that specific dissatisfaction could never be channelled into a serious political danger for the regime. As Sopade reporters continually pointed out, outweighing the economic bitterness was the acute fear of communism, constantly reinforced by Nazi propaganda. The peasants, it was noted, 'fear that Bolshevism would take their land and property from them, so they prefer to come to terms with the Nazis who only half-expropriate them'.[21]

Within the working class, the critical labour shortage and the stress of an oppressive work rate led to an increase, rather than decrease, of industrial unrest during the last prewar years.[22] This found expression in absenteeism and falling 'discipline' in the workplace. It was countered by intensified controls over the workforce, limits on movement of labour and tougher action against recalcitrant workers, backed by the power of the state and its organs of repression. Industrial conflict in the Third Reich was inevitably politicised, and the attitude of large sections of the industrial working class towards the Nazi regime was reflected in their actions. Even so, the Sopade reporters tried to avoid simple generalisations about workers' political views and stressed that opinion was influenced by varied 'objective' factors such as the composition of the workforce, the relations with the employer, working conditions in the factory or the conduct of local party representatives.[23] The differences between various industrial plants and their workers were too great, thought the Sopade leadership, to rule out subjective distortions in evaluating opinion.[24] Apart from this difficulty, it could repeatedly be seen 'that the working class was more reserved, more careful and more sceptical than other sections of society', not because it was nonpolitical, but because 'workers and their entire existence stood in a different relationship to the power of the regime than did peasants or tradesmen'. It was also impossible to ignore the fact 'that the enormous increase in the work rate not only physically, but also psychologically, exhausts many workers'.[25] The superficial apathy and political indifference of the mass of the workers were said to be results of the repression and terror, the over-long working hours and an inhumane work rate.[26]

In contrast to the view of some reporters, who wanted to interpret the sagging productivity by workers in some industries as the result of sabotage and passive resistance, the leadership of the Sopade was inclined to conclude on the basis of the majority of the reports 'that the drop in productivity is less the consequence of conscious action than the expression of the widening grip of weariness'.[27] The entire tenor of the Sopade reports matches the impression gleaned from the regime's internal reporting. This was, that down to 1939 the Nazi regime had almost wholly alienated the industrial working class but had politically largely neutralised it. The Nazi success, in the view of the Sopade, was to have atomised the working class and smashed its leadership, which had earlier been capable at least in part of transcending the divisions among workers:

> This unifying force of the workers' movement no longer exists. The National Socialists have consciously destroyed it and instead directed their policy at atomising the working class. They have done something even beyond that: they have tried to break the psychological and moral force of resistance of workers through excessively long working hours and an attritional work rate. Superficially, it looks as if they have succeeded; the great mass of workers are exhausted and worn down. But, in fact, this method has only deepened the differentiation within the working class: those who used to think still think today, and those who did not think then, think now even less. Only that the thinkers are today no longer able to lead the non-thinkers. . . .[28]

Everyday reality in the Third Reich gave practically every sector of the population cause, if in different degree, to be discontented. Reports in the prewar years both from opponents of the regime and from Nazi authorities indicate disappointment, bitterness and disillusionment — mainly arising from personal or sectoral material interests. This was the case among the lower civil service, teachers, parts of the 'free professions', people in business and the trades, among the 'bourgeoisie' and even among German youth. In all cases, the dissatisfaction had at its root the gap between the expectations that had been placed in National Socialism and the reality of the Third Reich — the true face of the 'people's community'.

There was no need, however, for the regime to be too worried about the discontent — except where poor morale among peasants or, especially, industrial workers had implications for economic production. The bitter complaints of primary-school teachers, for instance, about low pay, teacher shortages, poor conditions in schools, attacks by the party and Hitler Youth on teachers' pronounced status-consciousness, and the lack of recognition of their 'selfless work' in education as well as in numerous honorary positions of service for their local communities were in political terms utterly unimportant. This was all the more so, since a high proportion of teachers evidently sympathised broadly with Nazi ideological aims and, despite their discontent, were often prepared to act in the service of the party in onerous 'honorary' offices.

Nazi social policy prompted an astonishing level of open criticism and deep antipathy. The attitude of the population towards the regime nevertheless remained fragmented. Even within specific social groups there was little unity of opinion. And it was naturally the case that concrete 'everyday' experiences of a particular social group seldom had relevance for other groups. A critical, and even in places a hostile, popular opinion was not silenced in the Third Reich. But it was completely atomised and as a result rendered largely harmless. Without organised political opposition or a vehicle capable of orchestrating opinion, there was no possibility of creating 'horizontal' opinion around a coalition of varied interests with the potential for political action.

The Significance of the 'Führer Myth' for Popular Opinion

The indications of growing discontent in varied sectors of the population between 1933 and 1939 are, if not quantifiable, nevertheless unmistakeable. The Nazi regime was evidently by 1939 far from realising its ideal of a united 'people's community'. Daily life under National Socialism was characterised by social tensions and discord.

The shaping of opinion towards developments beyond the experiences of 'everyday' life was, however, quite a different matter. In what we might call the 'exceptional' sphere of politics, the regime was able to manufacture the desired national unity to an extraordinary extent through the exploitation of 'anti-symbols' and the fixation on distant, utopian goals, both of which diverted concern, at least temporarily, from the arena of 'everyday' conflict. In the 'exceptional' sphere, rejection of National Socialism and opposition to its policies played as good as no role whatsoever. An example is the 'Jewish Question' — the core of the Nazi 'worldview'.

When non-Jews were directly confronted, before their very eyes, with outright Nazi brutality and savagery towards the Jewish minority, or felt their economic interests or even livelihoods threatened by the tightening boycott of Jewish businesses, they often reacted in a negative fashion, even in anger or disgust (though seldom, it seems, out of humanitarian sympathy for the victims).[29] Such critical reactions, plainly visible during the antisemitic wave of 1935, reached a peak after the pogrom of 9–10 November 1938, the so-called *Reichskristallnacht* — probably the only time that the 'Jewish Question', if only briefly, played a central role in the formation of opinion. In the years after 1933, the 'Jewish Question' had actually less and less genuine relevance for the daily life of the majority German population. Increasingly, Jews were depersonalised, forced out of social and economic contact with non-Jews, largely removed from the daily life of the ordinary citizen, and reduced in effect to an ideological anti-symbol. The consequence for the shaping of opinion was less the creation of dynamic hatred than of a lethal indifference towards the fate of the Jewish population. The further Jews were removed from the 'real world' of everyday life, the more apparent was the indifference of the non-Jewish population. The relatively smooth course of anti-Jewish policy in the early war years reflected an ideological sphere of Nazi policy — the utopian goal of the 'removal of the Jews' — which met with broad approval and hardly any rejection, not least because it scarcely touched in any direct sense the daily experiences of the vast majority of the population.

In the 'exceptional' — 'non-everyday' — sphere, a potentially wide consensus was available as compensation for the travails and disaffection of daily life. The more the 'people's community' revealed itself to be an empty propaganda slogan, the more it had to be artificially manufactured. A type of pseudo-integration took place through projecting the 'positives' in National Socialism on to Hitler, the 'charismatic' leader, through focusing upon the ideals which he appeared to embody, and upon his 'achievements'.[30]

The greatest achievement of Nazi propaganda — Goebbels himself thought so — was the creation of the 'Führer myth'.[31] But that is only part of the truth of the matter. The supra-dimensional image of the Führer was not only a propaganda product injected into the population, but to a large extent the result of naive popular expectations of national salvation to be brought about by a coming 'great leader'. The combination of suggestivity through propaganda and pre-existing belief in a 'great leader' among extensive sections of the population led to an increasing readiness to dissociate the image of Hitler not only from that of the party, but also from the system itself. Just how far popular images of Hitler had detached themselves from his thoughts and actions can be seen, for example, in the acclamation he gained from the 'Röhm affair' in 1934. Röhm's murderous action on 30 June 1934 was in the main completely misinterpreted, according to contemporary reports on popular opinion, allowing Hitler to appear as a leader standing above vested interests, concerned only for his people, ready to intervene when necessary against corruption, misuse of power, and injustice within the system. In reality, he had the leaders of the storm troopers slaughtered to bolster his own power. In a phase of growing discontent, Hitler was able inordinately to strengthen, at the cost of part of his own movement, his public esteem as the 'people's leader', standing above and transcending the negative or distasteful aspects of his own party.[32]

The image of the Führer, far removed from reality, was crucial as an element of integration since it was ever more plain that the party itself was divisive rather than unifying, and incapable of overcoming the grievances and resentments of 'everyday' life. The hopes and expectations vested in Hitler have to be seen in part as a 'safety valve' for the discontents of wide swathes of the public, reflecting the need for a point of 'salvation' despite the unpalatable realities of daily life dominated by the party. The Führer stood for so many people *beyond* the party, *beyond* the 'everyday'. His 'charisma' remained largely untouched by the miseries and vexations of the 'everyday'. Hitler's undoubted popularity in the prewar years lay outside the 'everyday' political sphere. In fact, it was in part a direct reaction against it.

Hitler's popularity naturally rested in the first instance upon 'his' perceived great 'achievements'. Much of what he had to offer in spring 1933 had attractions for wide sections of the population, not just dyed-in-the-wool Nazis. This was the basis of the massive extension of his popularity. Once he could claim successes in tackling *national* problems, he could start to win acceptance not as a party leader (with all its divisive connotations), but as a *national* leader of stature, an emblem of unity.

More than anything in the first phase of his chancellorship — far more than the slight improvement in the economy — Hitler owed the rise in his popular standing to the ruthless attack on the Left, especially on the Communists. The selective wave of terror directed at the left-wing parties, regarded in bourgeois circles not just as opponents of the Nazis but as enemies of Germany, gained Hitler enormous recognition. The leading article of a Bavarian provincial newspaper — not Nazi, though with Nazi leanings — on 28 February 1933 gives a vivid flavour of the prevailing atmosphere. The article was commenting, under the headline 'An End to Moscow', on the emergency decree of that day — the day after the Reichstag fire — which in one fell swoop legislated out of existence the liberal freedoms and basic rights of the Weimar Constitution:

> This emergency decree will find no opponent despite the quite draconian measures which it threatens. Against murderers, arsonists and poisoners there can only be the most rigorous defence, against terror the call to account through the death penalty. The fanatics who would like to make a robbers' cave out of Germany must be rendered harmless. The consequences of the most acute struggle against communism have finally been drawn . . . It concerns more than parties, it concerns Germany, in fact the entire Western culture built upon Christianity. And for this reason we welcome the recent emergency decree.[33]

The smashing of the Left was terrain where the regime in its initial stage could build upon a broad if imprecise consensus which, despite the deep social, ideological and political divisions in German society, already existed outside the third or so of the population which had supported the SPD and KPD. The same applied to two other aspects of popular opinion. For one thing, there was a general conviction that only a strong state leadership could transcend the damaging and divisive conflicts, overcome Germany's deep-seated crisis and bring about new unity and prosperity. Beyond this, there was the perhaps even more widespread feeling that Germany had not only been unfairly treated in the Versailles Treaty, but was also ringed by enemy states ready to take advantage of the nation's weakness in order to destroy the German people. A government which held out hope of restoring Germany's power and, with that, could appeal to national pride as well as guarantee greater security towards Germany's enemies, had good prospects of winning massive popularity. Both spheres of consensus — inner unity and external strength — merged in the popular image of Hitler.

Compared with the situation in 1932, the internal achievements of the regime (all personalised as *Hitler's* achievements) — work creation, restoration of 'order', economic recovery — seemed hugely impressive. Counter-arguments to the Nazi interpretation that the Führer had rescued Germany were — other than within parts of the working class, which had paid the lion's share of the price for the 'economic miracle of the Third Reich' — hard to formulate convincingly. Anyone disagreeing with the 'official' version could easily be denigrated as a 'grumbler' and 'griper', a sour malcontent.

Above all in the realm of foreign policy, Hitler's achievements seemed incomparable. Though his aims were mainly misinterpreted, he was unquestionably able to win overwhelming backing for the attainment of a new international standing for Germany which had seemed unimaginable at the time of the 'seizure of power'. The genuinely popular foreign-policy successes down to 1939 drew extensively upon the resentments and hopes of most Germans. Hitler seemed in this to be the representative not of specifically Nazi, but of *nationalist* values.[34] And it was as *national* triumphs that the remilitarisation of the Rhineland, the '*Anschluss*' of Austria and — to a lesser extent — the 'homecoming' of the Sudeten Germans were cheered by most Germans, also by those who were highly critical of the regime's attacks on the Christian churches or its social policy. The defusing and neutralisation of army opposition through Hitler's 'success' in the Munich Settlement of 1938 is well known.[35] The left-wing opposition, for its part, repeatedly acknowledged how much Hitler's run of diplomatic coups had undermined their attempts at subversive propaganda. A report soon after the remilitarisation of the Rhineland from the border secretary for northern Bavaria provides a typically pessimistic assessment. From contacts in Upper Franconian industrial districts, he had learnt of a 'mood of the great mass . . . that nothing could be done against Hitler if things became serious.' People were completely convinced by the modern armaments and striking capability of the German armed forces. It had to be admitted, the border secretary added, 'that this consideration occupied the entire thoughts of the great majority of the population and that poor business trends, low wages, stability of the Mark, and so on, were not much discussed. The great mass of the population believes that he [Hitler] will put that right. In short, it's a very bad time for us again.'[36]

The pseudo-integration of German society, which was to a large extent the product of the 'Hitler Myth', served not only to defuse potential internal points of crisis, but also to legitimise the Nazi regime abroad. The recognised plebiscitary acclamation for Hitler's foreign policy was not least of significance in the development of appeasement thinking. The unity of leadership and people, constantly trumpeted by Nazi propaganda, appeared abroad to represent something not far from the truth.

The Nazi regime was unable to put its social promises into practice. Attainment of the 'people's community', from the outset a utopian idea, retreated ever farther into the distance as all sections of the population came under the pressure of the armaments economy. The social backbone of National Socialism — the petty bourgeoisie and rural population — was by the end of the 1930s largely resentful and disillusioned. The working class was politically neutralised by repression and remained alienated from the regime.

Disaffection and discontent were, however, only one facet of popular opinion. More important was its accompaniment: 'the growing depoliticisation, the increasing indifference, the astonishing apathy of the great mass of the people'. In the view of the Sopade, the 'entirely powerless whingeing' was underpinned by 'neither political insight nor political will'.[37]

In March 1938 the Sopade sought to summarise the main characteristics of German popular opinion. Simply to judge external impressions would lead to wrong conclusions, thought the Sopade leadership. But 'insofar as it is possible to generalise about the attitude of an entire people at all', the report stated, the following could be concluded:

> 1) Hitler had approval of a majority of the people in two essential issues: he has provided work, and he has made Germany strong.
>
> 2) There is extensive discontent about prevailing conditions, but this affects only the daily concerns and until now has not led to fundamental hostility to the regime among most people.
>
> 3) Doubts about the continued existence of the regime are widespread. But equally widespread is the cluelessness about what could replace it.[38]

The 'achievement' of the Nazi regime with regard to popular opinion is well summarised in this appraisal. Terror and intimidation on the one hand and the massive, but superficial, politicisation that embraced all public life on the other promoted in reality a pervasive *depoliticisation* of the masses, reflected in the sense of futility among opponents of the regime and the atomisation of opinion. The vacuum that arose from this depoliticisation was filled with the pseudo-integrative force of the 'Führer myth'.

In Max Weber's conceptualisation, charismatic authority faces the constant danger of routinisation — *Veralltäglichung* (becoming the 'everyday' instead of remaining something 'exceptional'). Only the dynamism of unbroken, recurring success could sustain such authority. In the context of the Third Reich, the pseudo-integration of the 'community of fate' of the German people could be sustained only by national 'successes'. In Hitler's own view, only constantly renewed national success could prevent stagnation and the feared social unrest that would result from it.[39] The more domestic policy revealed disunity and conflict, the greater was the need for the transcendental unity which foreign policy triumphs, if always of short duration in their effect, could produce. The progressive dynamism was, however, not endless: the end was war and destruction. Hans Dill, the Sopade's border secretary of northern Bavaria from 1934 to 1938, based in the Sudetenland not far from the German frontier, recognised already in 1936 at the remilitarisation of the Rhineland the connection between the pressure of acclamation and the dynamic of German foreign policy. In a letter to the former chairman of the SPD, Otto Wels, on 7 March 1936, Dill wrote: 'Hitler can no longer escape from his policy. He has removed the possibility of that through the dissolution of the Reichstag and the new election. With more than 90 per cent of the votes he will get approval for this, his policy, on 29 March. Then the ring is sealed and he can no longer step out of it. The dictator lets himself be bound by the people to the policy which he wanted.'[40]

The links between the 'everyday' sphere of conflict and the 'consensus sphere' which emanated from the 'exceptional', charismatic determinants of Nazi policy formed an essential part of the unstable dynamism of the Nazi regime.

Notes

The research for this essay, mainly carried out during a stay in Munich in 1976–7, was supported by the Alexander von Humboldt-Stiftung, for which, now as then, I am immensely grateful. In recouching my original German text into English I have left it unaltered apart from the occasional inclusion, within square brackets, of references to more recent relevant literature and a couple of minor interpolations necessary for a non-German readership.

1. For a distinction between 'public opinion' (*öffentliche Meinung*) and 'opinion of the public' (*Publikumsmeinung*), the latter referring to unofficial attitudes, see Marlis G. Steinert, *Hitlers Krieg und die Deutschen,* Düsseldorf/Vienna, 1970, p. 46. [Steinert's excellent book, alongside the unpublished doctoral dissertation of Lawrence D. Stokes, 'The *Sicherheitsdienst* (SD) of the *Reichsführer* SS and German Public Opinion, September 1939–June 1941', Johns Hopkins University, 1972, constituted, I think, the first general assessments of wartime attitudes among the population on the basis of the SD reports, of which an early selection had been published by Heinz Boberach (ed.), *Meldungen aus dem Reich,* Neuwied/Berlin, 1965, before the same editor went on to bring out a complete edition of the reports, *Meldungen aus dem Reich. Die geheimen Lageberichte des Sicherheitsdienstes der SS 1938–1945,* 17 vols., Herrsching, 1984.]

2. An early attempt to utilise such reports was made in Martin Broszat, Elke Fröhlich and Falk Wiesemann (eds.), *Bayern in der NS-Zeit. Soziale Lage und politisches Verhalten der Bevölkerung im Spiegel vertraulicher Berichte,* Munich/Vienna, 1977. [Since then, they have been extensively used and analysed in numerous works. Most importantly, with regard to attitudes towards the persecution of the Jews, they have been assembled in the superb edition by Otto Dov Kulka and Eberhard Jäckel, *Die Juden in den geheimen NS-Stimmungsberichten 1933–1945,* Düsseldorf, 2004. Kulka, an early pioneer in their usage, has evaluated their potential in a number of essays, including 'The German Population and the Jews: State of Research and New Perspectives', in David Bankier (ed.), *Probing the Depths of German Antisemitism,* New York/Oxford/Jerusalem, 2000, pp. 271–81. David Bankier, *The Germans and the Final Solution: Public Opinion under Nazism,* Oxford, 1992, and Peter Longerich, *'Davon haben wir nichts gewusst!' Die deutschen und die Judenverfolgung 1933–1945,* Munich, 2006, present full-scale studies based upon the reports, if with differing interpretations.]

3. Early editions of non-Bavarian material for the period 1933–9 include Bernhard Vollmer (ed.), *Volksopposition im Polizeistaat. Gestapo- und Regierungsberichte 1934–1936*, Stuttgart, 1957 (for Aachen); Franz Josef Heyen (ed.), *Nationalsozialismus im Alltag*, Boppard am Rhein, 1967 (for Koblenz-Trier); Robert Thévoz et al. (eds.), *Pommern 1934/35 im Spiegel von Gestapo-Lageberichten und -Sachakten*, Cologne/Berlin, 1974; Jörg Schadt (ed.), *Verfolgung und Widerstand unter dem Nationalsozialismus in Baden*, Stuttgart, 1976. [Since this article was published, other editions of similar material have appeared. An idea of the extent but scattered nature of the sources related to the persecution of the Jews can be gleaned from the edition by Kulka and Jäckel mentioned in note 2.]

4. The Sopade reports, both the central and regional ones on which the digest draws, are to be found in the Archiv der Sozialen Demokratie in Bonn. [Since the publication of the seven-volume reproduction of the central *Deutschland-Berichte der Sozialdemokratischen Partei Deutschlands ['Sopade'] 1934–1940*, Frankfurt, 1980 (hereafter *DBS*), these reports have become well known, which was not the case when this article was written. In particular, they serve as the basis of the work by Bernd Stöver, *Volksgemeinschaft im Dritten Reich. Die Konsensbereitschaft der Deutschen aus der Sicht sozialistischer Exilberichte,* Düsseldorf, 1993.]

5. Geheimes Staatsarchiv München (hereafter GStA) [Bayerisches Hauptstaatsarchiv, Abt. II], MA 106 682, Fortnightly report of the Government President of Swabia, 4.5.34.

6. GStA, MA 106 765, Situation Report of the Donauwörth Labour Exchange, 11.6.34.

7. *DBS*, 26.6.34, p. A34.

8. Ibid., p. A20.

9. Ibid., p. A21.

10. Ibid., pp. B22–3.

11. Broszat et al., *Bayern in der NS-Zeit*, vol. 1, pp. 256–60. [I subsequently explored this more extensively, with examples from various parts of Germany, in 'Social Unrest and the Response of the Nazi Regime, 1934–1936', in Francis R. Nicosia and Lawrence D. Stokes (eds.), *Germans against Nazism: Essays in Honour of Peter Hoffmann,* New York/Oxford, 1990, pp. 157–74.]

12. GStA, MA 106 682, Monthly report of the Government President of Swabia, 9.10.36.

13. *DBS*, 12.11.35 (actually 12.12.35), p. A2.

14. Ibid., p. A5.

15. Ibid., p. A3.

16. Ibid., p. A1.

17. Ibid., p. A3.

18. Bundesarchiv Berlin [formerly Koblenz], R58/1096, fols. 9–10, Annual report of the Security Service (*Sicherheitsdienst*), 1938. [Now printed in *Meldungen* (see note 1), vol. 2, p. 161.]

19. GStA, Reichsstatthalter 563, fols. 13–14.

20. For the objective position of the peasantry, see in general John E. Farquharson, *The Plough and the Swastika: The NSDAP and Agriculture in Germany 1928–45*, London, 1976 [and, appearing since this article was written, Gustavo Corni, *Hitler and the Peas-*

ants: Agrarian Policy of the Third Reich, 1930–1939, New York/Oxford/Munich, 1990; and Gustavo Corni and Horst Gies, *Brot-Butter-Kanonen. Die Ernährungswirtschaft in Deutschland unter der Diktatur Hitlers,* Berlin, 1997].

21. *DBS,* 18.9.37, p. A40.

22. This was explored above all in the path-breaking work of Timothy W. Mason, *Arbeiterklasse und Volksgemeinschaft,* Opladen, 1975. [Just as my article appeared, Mason summarised his arguments in 'The Workers' Opposition in Nazi Germany', *History Workshop Journal,* 11 (1981), pp. 120–37. (A German version was published in the same essay collection as my article.) He went on to modify them somewhat in 'Die Bändigung der Arbiterklasse im nationalsozialistischen Deutschland', in Carola Sachse et al., *Angst, Belohnung, Zucht und Ordnung. Herrschaftsmechanismen im Nationalsozialismus,* Opladen, 1982, pp. 11–53. Later research has qualified them in much greater measure. See, for instance, Gunther Mai, 'Arbeiterschaft zwischen Sozialismus, Nationalismus und Nationalsozialismus', in Uwe Backes et al. (eds.), *Die Schatten der Vergangenheit. Impulse zur Historisierung des Nationalsozialismus,* Frankfurt am Main/Berlin, 1990, pp. 195–217; and Ulrich Herbert, ' "The Real Mystery in Germany": The German Working Class during the Nazi Dictatorship', in Michael Burleigh (ed.), *Confronting the Nazi Past: New Debates on Modern German History,* London, 1996, pp. 23–36.]

23. Ibid., 14.4.39, p. A85–6. [At the time that this article appeared, in 1981, though quite independently of it, Michael Voges produced an extensive analysis of the Sopade reports in connection with industrial unrest: 'Klassenkampf in der "Betriebsgemeinschaft". Die "Deutschland-Berichte der 'Sopade'" (1934–1940) als Quelle zum Widerstand der Industriearbeiter im Dritten Reich', *Archiv für Sozialgeschichte,* 21 (1981), pp. 329–84. Voges tended, however, in similar fashion to Mason, to exaggerate the political significance of the industrial unrest.]

24. Ibid., 12.7.39, p. A77.

25. Ibid., 10.10.38, pp. A79–80.

26. Ibid., 14.4.39, pp. A85–6.

27. Ibid., 12.7.39, pp. 83–4.

28. Ibid., p. A77.

29. See the documentation in Broszat, *Bayern in der NS-Zeit,* vol. 1, pp. 427ff; Ian Kershaw, 'Antisemitismus und Volksmeinung. Reaktionen auf die Judenverfolgung', in *Bayern in der NS-Zeit, vol. 2: Herrschaft und Gesellschaft im Konflikt,* ed. Martin Broszat and Elke Fröhlich, Munich/Vienna, 1979, pp. 281–348; Ian Kershaw, 'The Persecution of the Jews and German Popular Opinion in the Third Reich', in *Year Book of the Leo Baeck Institute,* 26 (1981), pp. 261–89; and Otto Dov Kulka, ' "Public Opinion" in National Socialist Germany and the "Jewish Question" ', in *Zion Quarterly for Research in Jewish History,* 40 (1975), pp. 186–290 (analysis in Hebrew, documentation in German, abstract in English). [Later research—see note 2 for references to some of the most important work—has greatly extended the range of sources and basis of information without fundamentally altering the generalisation made here. It should nevertheless be added, of course, that the boycott, the so-called aryanisation which was its logical successor, and the plunder of Jewish property at the time of the deportations, beginning in 1941, were directly in the material interest of substantial parts of the non-Jewish population.]

30. See here my study *Der Hitler-Mythos. Volksmeinung und Propaganda im Dritten Reich,* Stuttgart, 1980. [An extended English version, *The 'Hitler Myth': Image and Reality in the Third Reich,* was published by Oxford University Press in 1987, with a chapter, 'Hitler's Popular Image and the "Jewish Question"', which was not included in the initial German volume. This English edition in turn appeared in German as *Der Hitler-Mythos. Führerkult und Volksmeinung,* Stuttgart, 1999 — a version which supplants the original German version cited in this article.] See, too, my essay 'The Führer and Political Integration: The Popular Conception of Hitler in Bavaria during the Third Reich', in Gerhard Hirschfeld and Lothar Kettenacker (eds.), *Der 'Führerstaat': Mythos und Realität,* Stuttgart, 1981, pp. 133–63.

31. Rudolf Semmler, *Goebbels: The Man Next to Hitler,* London, 1947, pp. 56–7.

32. See my *Der Hitler-Mythos* (1980 edition), pp. 72–89, for a fuller account.

33. *Miesbacher Anzeiger,* 2 March 1933.

34. See Lothar Kettenacker, 'Sozialpsychologische Aspekte der Führer-Herrschaft', in Hirschfeld and Kettenacker, *Der 'Führerstaat',* pp. 98–132.

35. See Steinert, p. 79. [Peter Hoffmann, *Widerstand, Staatsstreich, Attentat. Der Kampf der Opposition gegen Hitler,* Munich-Zurich, pb. edn., 1985, p. 130, points out that through the Munich Conference and the abandonment of Czechoslovakia by the Western powers, the opposition to Hitler suffered a blow from which it could not recover.]

36. Archiv der Sozialen Demokratie, Bonn, Emigration 'Sopade', M33/18.3.36, p. 4.

37. *DBS,* 27.8.38, pp. A19–20.

38. Ibid., 12.3.38, p. A1.

39. See Kershaw, 'The Führer and Political Integration', pp. 157–8.

40. Archiv der Sozialen Demokratie, Bonn, Emigration 'Sopade', M33/Hans Dill an Otto Wels, 7.3.36.

6

German Popular Opinion during the 'Final Solution': Information, Comprehension, Reactions

"One is left with the troublesome thought that there may not have been much resistance at all to involvement in genocide, that it is by no means foreign to man-in-society, and that many features of contemporary 'civilized' society encourage the easy resort to genocidal holocausts." This was Leo Kuper's concluding sentence to his chapter on the German genocide against Jews, placed in a comparative perspective in his book, *Genocide. Its Political Use in the Twentieth Century*.[1] I would like to bear this comment in mind in the following reflections on German popular opinion during the Third Reich, and its responses to the Final Solution. It seems to me that Kuper's remark directly poses the open question, going beyond historical research and beyond German-Jewish relations, of whether the perceptible German patterns of opinion and behavior toward the Jews are consonant with what could conceivably take place in other advanced societies, and involving minority groups other than Jews, where, for whatever reasons, a paranoid ideological thrust levelled at a recognizable, and largely unpopular, ethnic minority could be turned into a central focus of government policy.

Not long ago it would have seemed futile to pose any questions about the nature of popular opinion in Nazi Germany, widely regarded as a monolithic, totalitarian, "mass society", manipulated and repressed into uniformity by a powerful combination of propaganda and coercion. The "mass society" image had links with two radically opposed sets of generalized impressions of the position of the German people in the Third Reich which thrived in and immediately after the war. On the one hand, there was the distorted image prevalent in Allied wartime propaganda, and continuing to some extent even in the postwar period, of a population won over almost in its entirety by Nazi ideas, and, therefore, of a more or less direct equation of German and Nazi. The apologetic counter-picture placed the emphasis not on propaganda but on repression: this was the self-image of the Germans as the helpless victims of totalitarian terror incapable of voicing their dissent from Nazi policies.

Recent research on German society under Nazism has had no difficulty in demonstrating the palpable absurdity of both types of generalization. It has become increasingly clear that attitudes and behavior of "ordinary" Germans in the Third Reich, on a whole range of issues, were far from uniform, and that a plurality of political, social, moral-ethical, intellectual, and religious influences continued to exist, posing at least partial blockages to Nazi ideological penetration. The very wide variety and extent of political non-conformity and dissent has been amply demonstrated, particularly in issues affecting the spheres of interest of the Christian churches and daily economic concerns, especially labor relations.[2] In such cases, collective protest and forms of civil disobedience were far from unknown. In the most celebrated instance, the so-called "euthanasia action" — a genuine issue of humanitarian concern — a halt (at least in part) was called in August, 1941, to the liquidation of hereditary and incurably sick persons in asylums within Germany itself, as a result of the growing popular unease and objections articulated by leading churchmen.[3] The fact that protest could and did take place in a range of issues, even including, as in the "euthanasia action", a directly humanitarian issue, itself indicates the hollowness of the apologetics that the terroristic repression of a totalitarian system was sufficient in itself to deter any dissent.

Of course, the fear element as a genuine deterrent from opposing anti-Jewish policy has to be highly rated. But terror alone would not have sufficed to quell objections, had the so-called "Jewish Question" been an issue of importance, relevance, and above all self-interest to a large number of Germans. The apologetics that people did not know the fate of the Jews can be fairly rapidly dispelled. But what I would like especially to suggest in this paper is that the general passivity which marked the most pervasive reaction — or perhaps one should say non-reaction — to the persecution and extermination of the Jews reflected above all the low level in the ranking of priorities which the fate of the Jews occupied in German consciousness. The lack of interest in or exclusion of concern for the fate of racial, ethnic, or religious minority groups marks, I would argue, at the societal level a significant prerequisite for the genocidal process, allowing the momentum created by the fanatical ideological hatred of a section of the population to gather pace, especially, of course, when supported by the power of the state itself.

The following comments concern themselves with popular opinion in Germany only at the time, between 1941 and 1943, when the genocidal process had reached its climax. It is hard to imagine that any expression of public concern could by this stage have presented a major obstacle to the determination of the Nazi leadership to exterminate the Jews, even if the extreme emphasis upon the secrecy of the Final Solution itself suggests the regime's uncertainty about its public reception. But the difficulties for the Nazis in arriving at that stage would have been incomparably greater had the position of the Jews been incorporated into the sphere of humanitarian self-interest and self-defense at a much earlier stage by the Christian churches, and, before 1933, also by the trade unions and the anti-Nazi political parties.

In what follows, I want to consider briefly, and by way of a few selected examples from the available evidence, three aspects of popular opinion and the Final Solution: whether the information in circulation was of a kind which allowed people to deduce the nature of Nazi anti-Jewish policy in eastern Europe; whether the genocidal character of the policy was comprehended; and what sort of reactions the Final Solution provoked among the German people.

Information

The notion that there was an effective wall of silence around information about the Final Solution inside Germany — the postwar apologia that no one had been aware of what was happening to the Jews — has been thoroughly disposed of, not least in Walter Laqueur's book, *The Terrible Secret.*[4] Of course, it goes without saying that it is impossible to establish how many people knew of the extermination of the Jews, and what degree of knowledge they possessed. There is no good reason to doubt that many people *were* genuinely shocked at the postwar revelations about the scale and nature of the Holocaust, and at the disclosed horrors of the extermination camps, and that they had never possessed genuine and exact information about what was going on in the occupied territories. But what *can* be established beyond question is that widespread rumors were in circulation about the fate of the Jews, and that the information contained in the rumors was often explicit enough to provide an unmistakable indication that Jews were being killed in great numbers in the east. No less than Hitler himself referred to public rumors about the extermination of the Jews in one of his "Table Talk" monologues in October, 1941.[5] And a year later, Martin Bormann felt it necessary to counter rumors about "very sharp measures" taken against Jews in the east which had been, as he said, a topic of discussion among the population.[6] Such evidence is sufficient in itself to suggest that information pointing to genocidal policies was widely available in Germany and certainly not confined to a tiny minority of the population. How many chose to close their ears to such rumors cannot of course be elicited. Many doubtless became skilled at knowing how not to know.

What was the nature of the rumors referred to? Some fragmentary local *SD* reports which have survived confirm the existence of rumors of mass shootings of Jews as early as autumn, 1941, and indicate that ordinary Germans who were keen to find out could ascertain with some accuracy what was happening. According to a report from Minden in December, 1941, it was being said in the district that all the Jews were being deported to Russia, the transport being carried out in cattle cars once they had reached Warsaw, and that once in Russia the Jews were being put to work in factories, while the old and sick were being shot.[7] Rumors in the Erfurt area in April, 1942, where there was said to have been considerable interest in acquiring information, stated that the *Sicherheitspolizei* had been given the task of "exterminating Jewry" in the occupied territories, with thousands of Jews having to dig their own graves before being shot, and shootings reaching such an extent that members of the extermination squads were suffering nervous breakdowns.[8]

An extraordinary record both of the nature of the rumors in circulation, and of the information open to those interested in acquiring it, is provided by the remarkable diary notes kept by Karl Duerckefaelden, son of a worker in the Celle district of Lower Saxony, who himself later became a skilled technician and engineer.[9] He heard of the deportation of the Jews of Holland from a conversation with a Dutch lorry driver in July, 1942, and a few months later recorded the news of deportations of French Jews which he heard from the BBC. The wife of a Jew in the area told him details in July, 1942, of the transportation of the last Jews from Peine, in Lower Saxony, to Theresienstadt, and of the conditions of other Jews from the area who had been deported earlier to Warsaw. In autumn, 1942, he heard again on the BBC of the gassing of Jews in motor vans. A soldier who had formerly worked in the same firm provided him in January, 1943, with information about the shooting and gassing of Jews from France and other countries who had been shipped off to Poland, and he learnt from the same source that only a fraction — a tenth, it was said — of the former Jewish population still survived in the town of Vilna. His brother-in-law, a construction engineer who had helped build a bridge across the Dnieper near Kiev, visiting him on June 6, 1942, on leave from the front, gave him a graphic description, recounted in the diary in detail, of the shooting of 118 Jews from the work force—Jews who had been ill-provisioned and had become too ill and weak to work. Asked if he had seen it himself, his informant told Duerckefaelden that he had stood twenty meters away. He spoke further of the mass burial of 50,000, on another occasion of 80,000 Jews, and on a further trip home from the front declared that there were no more Jews in the Ukraine; they "were now all dead."

Compared with information on shootings, rumors of gassing seem to have been relatively sparse. As in the case of Duerckefaelden, some information was available by listening to foreign broadcasts—an audience estimated to have been, despite the draconian penalties, in the millions rather than the thousands.[10] Here too, rumors were spread by soldiers on leave from the front. Surviving records, it can be confidently asserted, can hardly bear sufficient testimony to the extent of knowledge of the gassing operations. Even so, the silence, compared with the availability of information on the shootings, suggests that knowledge of the gassings, and in particular of the conveyor-belt extermination of the death camps, was relatively limited in extent. It might be expected that information on the camps would be more extensive in the eastern regions of the Reich than in the far west. According to a report from Upper Silesia in mid-1943, the slogan "Russland-Katyn, Deutschland-Auschwitz" had been chalked up on walls in parts of Upper Silesia. An explanatory note pointed out that "the concentration camp, Auschwitz, generally known in the east, is meant,"[11] though I have not encountered the name of Auschwitz or of any other extermination camp in documents emanating from western parts of Germany at that time.

Clearly, not everyone in Germany was hearing stories about the Jews in the east. But even the few examples from a far more extensive array of evidence which I have quoted here demonstrate categorically that hard information, not just vague rumor, was being brought back to the Reich and was available. Its extent was considerable, the information itself often impressive in its detail. Only those anxious to shut their ears to the rumors in circulation could have been utterly ignorant. And only the willfully ignorant could have imagined a drastically different fate for the Jews than was actually in store for them, even if the exact character and scale of the Final Solution was scarcely conceivable. The question of the comprehension of what was happening, partly answered on the above evidence, will detain us only for a short while longer.

Comprehension

What people made of the information coming their way, how far they comprehended the full significance of the information and grasped the magnitude of the developments unfolding in the east, are questions which by their nature can scarcely be answered in any precise way by the historian. As Walter Laqueur has said: "Those who had witnessed the murder of a thousand people or heard about it from an unimpeachable source could still persuade themselves that this had been an exceptional case. They might even forget it; after all, a great many people were killed in the war, human life was cheap."[12] However, it is difficult to imagine that the evidence we have already seen and the further examples I am about to provide left much doubt in the minds of the purveyors and the recipients of the information that the "radical solution" to the "Jewish Question", which Hitler himself, Goebbels, and others were openly hinting was under way, meant more than simple resettlement of the Jews. It is difficult to imagine, in fact, that it could have been taken to mean anything other than what it was: systematic physical annihilation — genocide.

To return to Karl Duerckefaelden for a moment: At the beginning of February, 1942, he had heard on the BBC a broadcast by Thomas Mann, who had mentioned that 400 young Dutch Jews had been killed in Germany through the testing of poisonous gas. Duerckefaelden put this information, as he did on other occasions, in his diary notes in the context of official statements by the Nazi leadership. On February 24, 1942, Hitler delivered a major speech on the anniversary of the Nazi Party's foundation in which, as in several other speeches that year, he alluded to the destruction of the Jews with reference to his baleful "prophecy" of January 30, 1939, when he had forecast the destruction of European Jewry in the event of another war. The report of the speech on the following day in the *Niedersaechsische Tageszeitung* had one paragraph relating to the "prophecy" part of Hitler's speech, under the heading: "The Jew is being exterminated" (*Der Jude wird ausgerottet*). It was precisely this page of the newspaper which Duerckefaelden kept in his diary.[13]

The extreme anti-Jewish sentiments expressed in some letters from soldiers at the front, which at times gave explicit details of mass shootings of Jews — one surviving letter speaks of the shooting of 30,000 Jews in one town[14] — also included direct references to Hitler's stance on the "Jewish Question", interpreting the war in classical Nazi fashion as a struggle brought about by the Jews and destined to end in their destruction. Comprehension about what was taking place is evident in the comments. One, stating that "the great task imposed on us in the struggle against Bolshevism resides in the annihilation of eternal Jewry," went on: "Only when you see what the Jew has brought about here in Russia, can you really understand why the Fuehrer began the struggle against Jewry. What sort of suffering would not have fallen upon our Fatherland if this beast of mankind had retained the upper hand?"[15] Another, this time from a lance-corporal serving on the western front and evidently of an extreme Nazi mentality, expressly referred to Hitler's "prophecy" in a malevolent tirade in which, among other things, he thanked the *Stuermer* for remaining true to its principles in the "Jewish Question". He added: "Things have now finally reached the point which our Fuehrer at the outbreak of this struggle prophesied to world Jewry in his great speech. . . . Gradually, this race is being ever more reminded of these words. . . . All its efforts won't any longer be able to alter its fate."[16] Other soldiers sent letters with similar sentiments direct to the *Stuermer*, which still had a circulation during the war estimated at over 300,000.[17]

Surviving sources from the "home front", too, indicate that comprehension of what was happening to the Jews went beyond belief that the reported atrocities were isolated incidents. As the war started to turn sour for Germany, "situation reports" of the *SD* and other Nazi agencies recorded awareness that Jews were suffering a dire fate in the occupied territories, and the fears that there would be retaliatory measures taken against Germany in the increasingly likely event of a lost war. An *SD* report from Franconia in December, 1942, pointed out unequivocally that "one of the strongest causes of unease among those attached to the church and in the rural population is at the present time formed by news from Russia in which shooting and extermination (*Ausrottung*) of the Jews is spoken about," adding the "widely held opinion in the rural population" that "if the Jews come again to Germany they will exact dreadful revenge upon us."[18] Nazi propaganda exploiting the discovery of Polish officers' graves at Katyn was also countered, according to *SD* reports, by remarks that the Germans had no right to condemn Soviet atrocities when "on the German side Poles and Jews have been done away with in much greater numbers."[19] Clergy in Westphalia were reported as declaring that "the terrible and inhumane treatment meted out to the Jews by the *SS* demands nothing short of God's punishment for our people. If these murders do not bring bitter revenge upon us, then there is no longer any divine justice! The German people has taken such blood guilt upon itself that it cannot reckon with mercy and pardon."[20]

These selected examples from the available evidence provide incontrovertible testimony to a plain awareness of the genocidal nature of Nazi policy toward the Jews, even though the actual details of the Final Solution were known only to a relatively small number of people. Those who closed their ears to the available information doubtless closed their minds to the unmistakable significance of that information. And many who heard and even understood had, it seems certain, been affected by years of dehumanizing Nazi propaganda and the increased brutalization of the wartime period, and grasped reality only in an abstract or remote sense, along the lines that terrible things happen in war. Such partial comprehension was still reconcilable with genuine expressions of shock at the postwar exposure of the reality of the Final Solution.

Lastly, we move on to a brief attempt to place the evidence I have so far surveyed in the context of overall reactions of the German people to the radicalization of anti-Jewish policy.

Reactions

The lack of uniformity in reaction, which had been perceptible in the pre-war era in popular responses, for example, to the promulgation of the Nuremberg Laws in 1935,[21] or the *Reichskristallnacht* pogrom in 1938,[22] is still plainly discernible in the period of the Final Solution. On the one hand, there are reflections in the available sources of a hardening of attitudes toward Jews in verbal expressions of hatred and of approval of Nazi policies (though one should bear in mind here the probability that outrightly Nazified senti-ments are over-represented in *SD* reports and the like). Contrasting reac-tions — verbal expressions of sympathy and solidarity with Jews, existing amid the general climate of hostility — were also registered among a small minority of the population. The liberal intelligentsia, active church-goers, and left-wing opponents of the regime, as before the war, were the groups most likely to be sympathetic to Jews.

Three examples referring to the deportations will illustrate the mixed re-corded reactions. The Gestapo in Bremen indicated in November, 1941, that "while the politically educated section of the population generally welcomed the imminent evacuation of the Jews, . . . church-going and commercial circles especially . . . show no sympathy for it and still believe today that they have to stick up for the Jews. . . ." Both Catholics and Protestant supporters of the Confessing Church were said to have vehemently expressed their pity for the Jews.[23] The deportation of Jews from Minden, a few weeks later, reportedly prompted the "great concern" of a large proportion of the population, and the voicing of two basic viewpoints: the likely retaliation abroad, especially in America, with reference to the way the "Crystal Night" pogrom had harmed rather than helped Germany; and secondly, a more humanitarian standpoint which, it was said, could not be widely registered, but could be heard in a large section of the better-off circles, especially among the older generation, that the deportation was far too "hard", that many Jews could not be expected to survive the journey to the East in the middle of winter, and that they were all Jews who had lived in the district since time immemorial. A third response was then noted, "among the people's comrades who understand the Jewish Question," which was that "the entire action is absolutely approved of," and the "German identity feeling" brought into prominence.[24] Finally, the transport of the last Jews from Lemgo in July, 1942, also attracted considerable attention and provoked mixed responses. The deportation, it was observed, "was generally negatively criticized" by a large proportion of the older population, among them Party members. It was objected that the hardship now to be imposed upon the Jews was unnecessary, since they were in any case dying out in Germany. Even people who had previously demonstrated their "National Socialist attitude" were said to have upheld the interests of the Jews, and people in church-going circles spoke of the coming "punishment of God". Although those with confirmed Nazi views sought to explain that the "action" was fully justified and absolutely necessary, this argument was countered by the opinion that the old Jews could not do any damage, would in fact "not harm a fly", and that there were many among them who had done much good.[25]

As we have already suggested, the fairly widespread knowledge of the mass shootings of Jews was also compatible with a spectrum of responses ranging from overt approval to blank condemnation, and above all with an apathetic shrug of the shoulders, the feeling of impotence, or the turning of the face from unpalatable truths.

Much suggests, in fact, that this last type of reaction — that is, non-reaction — was the most commonplace of all. If one term above all sums up the behavioral response of the German people to the persecution of the Jews, it is: passivity. The passivity was consonant with a number of differing internalized attitudes toward Jews. Most obviously, it corresponded to latent antisemitism, and arguably, to a mentality of "moral indifference". It also mirrored apathy, a deliberate turn away from personal concern, and a willingness to accept uncritically the state's right to take radical action against its "enemies". Above all, I would argue, passivity, as the most general "reaction", was a reflection of a prevailing lack of interest in the "Jewish Question", which ranked low in the order of priorities of most Germans during the war and played only a minor role in the overall formation of popular opinion. At the time that Jews were being murdered in their millions, the vast majority of Germans had plenty of other things on their mind.

Let me return now to the considerations I raised at the outset. I hope I have sufficiently demonstrated that information about the Final Solution was widely available, and that the significance of that information was often well comprehended. I have also attempted to illustrate the varied reactions to the "Jewish Question", and have argued that the momentous scale of the inhumanity carried out in the occupied territories was of relatively little concern to most Germans. Given the access to information on genocide and comprehension of

that information, should people have reacted differently? Would the populations of other countries have responded in more "honorable" fashion in similar
circumstances? I suspect not. Certainly, the decline of basic humanitarian and
moral values among a sizeable proportion of the population of Nazi Germany
was an extremely steep one, even before their almost collapse during the war
itself. But the liberal assumption that people will instinctively defend other
human beings against mass slaughter seems at least questionable. To cite Leo
Kuper again, it may be that "one must allow for the possibility that there are
historical situations or periods in which genocide is taken for granted."[26] In the
case we have been considering it seems clear that, although the "Jewish Question" was not an issue of the greatest moment to the majority of the population,
the widespread latent antisemitism which itself conditioned the absence of any
serious and organized opposition to antisemitism from non-Jewish institutions
before the Nazi takeover of power, was quite sufficient to allow the anti-Jewish
radical momentum of the Nazi regime from 1933 onwards to gather pace until,
given the existential conditions of the war years, it was as good as unstoppable.
Self-preservation is not a particularly admirable instinct, but especially in a
climate of repression and terror it is usually stronger than the instinct to
preserve others. It goes hand in hand with moral indifference and apathetic
compliance. But there may be little in it which is peculiarly German, or specific
only to the "Jewish Question". The most obvious conclusion would seem to me
that the "failure", if that is the right word, of German popular opinion with
regard to the Jews during the Third Reich was really the failure of the pluralist
society of the pre-Nazi era to anchor the defense of Jewish interests in its
organizational and institutional structures. For, it seems to me, only the incorporation of minority interest into the organized defense of majority interest
against authoritarian inroads provides the structural framework where the
processes which can culminate in genocide are blocked from the outset.

Notes

1. L. Kuper, *Genocide. Its Political Use in the Twentieth Century.* Harmondsworth:
1981, p. 137.
2. Among an extensive body of literature, see e.g. *Bayern in der NS-Zeit.* Edited by M.
Broszat *et al.*, 6 vols., Munich & Vienna: 1977–83; *Die Reihen fast geschlossen. Beit-
raege zur Geschichte des Alltags unterm Nationalsozialismus.* Edited by D. Peukert and J.
Reulecke, Wuppertal: 1981; *Arbeiterklasse und Volksgemeinschaft.* Edited by T. W.
Mason, Opladen: 1975; T. W. Mason, "The Workers' Opposition in Nazi Germany",
History Workshop Journal, 11 (1981); I. Kershaw, *Popular Opinion and Political Dissent
in the Third Reich. Bavaria, 1933–1945.* Oxford: 1983.
3. It should be noted, however, that unrest about the "euthanasia action" did not

emanate alone or even chiefly from humanitarian concern, but arose in good measure from doubt — reaching into Nazi circles — about the lack of clear legal guidelines and sanctions for the taking of "useless life"; that the well-known public protest by Bishop von Galen was voiced only in August, 1941, after the "action" had been in operation for close on two years (though letters of protest by church leaders to the Nazi authorities had begun almost a year earlier); that by August, 1941 the numbers murdered in the "action" had already exceeded the initial target figure for potential victims; that "euthanasia" murders did in fact continue in Germany itself (and even more extensively in the occupied territories), especially in concentration camps, after the supposed halt, terminating the action in selected asylums, had been called in August, 1941; and that, according to one piece of post-war testimony, the "halt" of August, 1941 amounted to a rumor put around by the Propaganda Ministry, suggesting that the Fuehrer had just discovered the truth of what was going on, and had immediately ordered its cessation. See, definitively now on the "euthanasia" issue, E. Klee, *"Euthanasie" in NS-Staat. Die "vernichtung lebensunwerten Lebens"*. Frankfurt am Main: 1983, and *Dokumente zur "Euthanasie"*. Edited by E. Klee, Frankfurt am Main: 1985.

4. W. Laqueur, *The Terrible Secret. Suppression of the Truth about Hitler's "Final Solution"*. Harmondsworth: 1980, esp. pp. 17–40.

5. *Adolf Hitler. Monologe im Fuererhauptquartier 1941–1944*. Edited by W. Jochman, Hamburg: 1980, p. 44. The guests on this particular evening were Himmler and Heydrich.

6. Cit. in M. G. Steinert, *Hitlers Krieg und die Deutschen*. Duesseldorf: 1970, p. 252.

7. SD-Außenstelle Minden, Dec. 12, 1941, in Otto Dov Kulka and Eberhard Jäckel (eds.), *Die Juden in den geheimen NS-Stimmungsberichten 1933–1945*, Düsseldorf, 2004, doc. 604, p. 477. I am most grateful to Prof. Kulka for his kindness in allowing me to use this material in advance of its publication.

8. SD-Hauptaußenstelle Erfurt, April 30, 1942, in ibid., doc. 628, p. 491.

9. The following details are taken from H. Obenaus, "Haben sie wirklich nichts gewusst? Ein Tagebuch zum Alltag von 1933–1945 gibt eine deutliche Antwort," *Journal fuer Geschichte*, 2 (1980), Heft 1, pp. 28–9; and H. and S. Obenaus, *"Schreiben, wie es wirklich war!" Aufzeichnungen Karl Duerckefaeldens aus den Jahren 1933–1945*. Hanover: 1985, pp. 107ff.

10. See Laqueur, p. 28.

11. O. D. Kulka, " 'Daat Kahal' beReich Hashlishi ve 'Habayah Hayehudit' — Mekorot uBaayot" ("Public Opinion" in National Socialist Germany and the "Jewish Question"), *Zion*, 40 (1975), p. 289.

12. Laqueur, p. 31.

13. Obenaus, "Haben sie wirklich nichts gewusst?", pp. 28–9; Obenaus, *Schreiben wie es wirklich war!*", pp. 107–8.

14. *Das andere Gesicht des Krieges. Deutsche Feldpostbriefe 1939–1945*. Edited by O. Buchbender and R. Sterz, Munich: 1982, p. 173, no. 354, July 27, 1943.

15. Ibid., p. 171, no. 351, July 18, 1942.

16. Ibid., p. 172, no. 352, July 22, 1942.

17. F. Hahn, *Lieber Stuermer. Leserbriefe an das NS-Kampfblatt 1924 bis 1945*. Stuttgart: 1978, pp. 114, 149, 188–227.

18. Staatsarchiv Nuernberg, LRA Hilpoltstein 1792, report of *SD*-Aussenstelle Schwabach, Dec. 23, 1942.

19. *Meldungen aus dem Reich. Auswahl aus den geheimen Lageberichten des Sicherheitsdienstes der SS 1939–1944.* Edited by H. Boberach, Neuwied: 1965, p. 383; and see L. D. Stokes, "The German People and the Destruction of the European Jews," *Central European History,* 6 (1973), p. 186.

20. Kulka, "Public Opinion", p. 290.

21. See O. D. Kulka, "Die Nuernberger Rassengesetze und die deutsche Bevoelkerung im Lichte geheimer *NS*-Lage- und Stimmungsberichte," *Vierteljahreshefte fuer Zeitgeschichte,* 33 (1984), pp. 582–624, esp. pp. 601ff.

22. See W. S. Allen, "Die deutsche Oeffentlichkeit und die 'Reichskristallnacht' — Konflikte zwischen Werthierarchie und Propaganda im Dritten Reich," in Peukert and Reulecke, pp. 397–411; and Kershaw, *Popular Opinion,* pp. 257 ff.

23. Stapostelle Bremen, Nov. 11, 1941, in Kulka and Jäckel, doc. 595, p. 471.

24. *SD*-Aussenstelle Minden, Dec. 6, 1941, in ibid., doc. 604, p. 477.

25. *SD*-Aussenstelle Detmold, July 31, 1942, in ibid., doc. 648, p. 503.

26. Kuper, p. 85.

7

Reactions to the Persecution of the Jews

The significance of the Jewish Question for the 'broad mass' of the German population in the Third Reich is a complex issue which has prompted frequent speculative generalization but little systematic exploration.[1] Alongside the apologetic, much heard in Germany since the end of the war, that the persecution of the Jews could be put down to the criminal or insane fixations of Hitler and the gangster clique of top Nazis around him in the face of widespread disapproval by the mass of Germans in so far as they knew and understood what was going on, exists the counter-generalization, much favoured by Jewish historians, of a German people thirsting for a 'war against the Jews', in which anti-Semitism, based on a centuries-old tradition of persecution, played a central role in providing Hitler's support from the German people and in motivating the popular adulation of the Führer.[2] According to this interpretation, the central role of anti-Semitism in Hitler's ideology is echoed by its central role in the mobilization of the German people.

Far from emphasizing a more or less spontaneous eruption of popular anti-Semitism in the socio-psychological crisis of Weimar, contrasting interpretations have stressed the conscious manipulative exploitation of anti-Semitism, which thus functioned as a tool of integration and mass mobilization by the Nazi regime, whether in the interests of imperialist finance-capital,[3] or as the cementing element which guaranteed the continuing ceaseless 'negative' dynamic diverting from the inevitable failures of socio-economic policy and holding the antagonistic forces of the Nazi movement together.[4]

This chapter seeks to confront such interpretations with as exhaustive an examination as possible of the empirical evidence from Bavaria for the reactions of 'ordinary' people to the anti-Jewish policies of the Nazi regime. By examining dissent from and approval of various facets of the persecution of the Jews, we are attempting to explore the spheres of penetration of Nazi racial ideology in the consciousness of 'ordinary' Germans, and to ask to what extent anti-Semitism served to integrate the German people and mobilize them behind the Nazi leadership during the Third Reich.

At the outset of our enquiry we can do no more than touch upon the pattern of Jewish settlement in Bavaria, the regional distribution and socio-economic structure of the Jewish population, and the traditional framework of its relations with the non-Jewish sector of the population in Bavaria, all of which helped to shape the context in which the radical anti-Semitism of the Nazis has to be placed.

The regional distribution of Jews in Bavaria was very uneven. As a consequence of Wittelsbach policies in the sixteenth and seventeenth centuries, in which the Jews had been driven out of the Bavarian heartlands, there were few resident Jews in *Altbayern* (Upper and Lower Bavaria and the Upper Palatinate) even deep into the nineteenth century. By contrast, the diversified structure of landownership and lordship in Franconia and Swabia had tended since the sixteenth century to promote settlements of Jewish communities in the countryside and in small towns.[5] Since the early nineteenth century the Jewish proportion of the total population had been in decline. In 1818, after Lower Franconia and the Palatinate had been incorporated into Bavaria, the 53,208 Jews accounted for 1.45 per cent of the entire Bavarian population (including the Palatinate). The restrictive legislation of 1813, the so-called *Judenedikt,* which severely limited Jewish mobility, seriously contributed, however, to continued demographic decline. By the time of German unification the number of Jews had fallen to 1.04 per cent of the entire population, by the turn of the century to 0.9 per cent, and by the beginning of the Third Reich to a mere 0.55 per cent.[6]

As many as 88 per cent of Bavaria's Jews still resided in 1840 in country districts or small towns. Only following the ending of the restrictive legislation in 1861 did Jewish migration to the larger towns and cities make great headway, and in so doing help foster the nascent anti-Semitism of the urban communities. But by 1919 the geographical distribution of Jews had fundamentally altered: now as many as 78 per cent lived in the cities and larger towns.[7] The overwhelmingly urban character of the domiciled Jewish population is

The Jewish Population of Bavaria, 1933 (incl. Palatinate)

A. Distribution of the Jewish population in the Bavarian administrative regions, 1933

Administrative region	Of Jewish faith (*Glaubensjuden*) Absolute	Percentage of total population
Upper Bavaria	9,522	0.54
Lower Bavaria	293	0.04
Upper Palatinate	1,004	0.15
Upper Franconia	2,133	0.27
Middle Franconia	11,621	1.12
Lower Franconia	8,520	1.07
Swabia	2,359	0.27
Palatinate	6,487	0.66
Bavaria	41,939	0.55

B. Distribution of the Jewish population according to size of municipality in which domiciled, 1933 (%)

Size of municipality	% of entire population	% of Jewish population
Under 10,000 inhabitants	66.4 (50.7)[a]	28.4 (15.5)[a]
Between 10,000 and 100,000 inhabitants	13.7 (19.9)	22.1 (13.6)
Above 100,000 inhabitants	19.9 (30.4)	49.5 (70.9)

[a] Figures in parentheses are the corresponding percentages for the German Reich.
Sources: 'Die Glaubensjuden in Bayern', pp. 447, 451–2; 'Die Juden im Deutschen Reich', p. 150.

clearly shown in the results of the census of 1933 provided in the table above. One implication of this is obvious: the population of large tracts of Bavaria had no, or at best minimal, contact with Jews. For very many, therefore, the Jewish Question could be of no more than abstract significance.

As the 1933 census shows, only in Middle and Lower Franconia was the proportion of Jews in the total population higher than the Reich average of 0.76 per cent.[8] Almost a half of Bavaria's Jewish population lived in the four cities of Munich (9,005), Nuremberg (7,502), Augsburg (1,030), and Würzburg (2,145). Fürth, adjoining Nuremberg, was the other major Jewish community. Even so, the urban concentration of Jews in Bavaria was far weaker than in Germany as a whole.[9] In Lower Franconia the proportion of the Jewish population living in villages and small towns (of less than 10,000 inhabitants) was exceptionally large, at 60 per cent. Alongside the five major Jewish communities of over 1,000 souls there were a further eight communities with between 300 and 1,000 members each (in all 4,116 Jews).[10] The remaining 10,694 Jews in Bavaria — roughly a quarter of the total number — formed in all 186 small, mainly very small, communities or lived as individuals in country districts.[11]

Large stretches of Bavaria had, therefore, no resident Jews. Of the sum total of 293 Jews in the whole of Lower Bavaria, as many as 73 per cent lived in the four provincial towns of Straubing, Landshut, Passau, and Deggendorf. Of the few Jews in the Upper Palatinate, 77 per cent lived in the towns of Regensburg, Weiden, Neumarkt in der Oberpfalz, Amberg, and Schwandorf.[12] Outside Franconia, where, on account of the relatively prominent presence and high population density of the Jews, a history of sporadic animosity, and the effect of the anti-Semitic tirades of Julius Streicher and his following in the 1920s, the Jewish Question acquired a peculiar importance, the non-Jewish population of Bavaria came into contact with Jews mainly in the towns — especially the big cities — in spa and tourist resorts, and in some rural areas where Jews dominated agricultural trade.[13]

Anti-Jewish violence was part of the scene of traditional social conflict in some parts of Bavaria, especially in Franconia, in the nineteenth century. Synagogue arson, the desecration of cemeteries, attacks on Jewish property, the hanging of effigies, and other outrages were prompted not only by economic rivalry or social envy, but reflected, too, still existent religious antagonism of Christian towards Jew. Allegations of ritual murders or well-poisonings and the ancient slur attached to the 'crucifiers of Christ' or 'murderers of Christ' — sentiments sometimes inflamed by comments of Catholic priests or Protestant pastors — all occasioned isolated outbreaks of violence against Jews throughout the nineteenth century.[14] For most people, however, feelings probably did not go much further than an abstract dislike or distrust of Jews and there seems to have been a good deal of indifference to what was already being dubbed the 'Jewish Question'. In 1850, for example, partly at the prompting of the Catholic lower clergy, about 13 per cent of the entire population of Bavaria signed petitions opposing Jewish emancipation. When, however, the State authorities made further investigations into the 'true mood' of the people it turned out that many petitioners were wholly indifferent on the issue, had no contact with Jews, knew little of any Jewish Question, and had often added their signatures only at the prompting of the priest.[15]

Elements of this archaic hostility towards Jews undoubtedly lasted in Franconia into the Third Reich. However, the 'traditional' anti-Semitism was already in the later nineteenth century giving way to or merging with the newer, more strongly ideological currents of the *völkisch*-nationalist, racial anti-Semitism which came to provide the basis of Nazi racial thinking. Above all in the crisis-ridden years following the end of the First World War, the Revolution, and the *Räterepublik*, racial anti-Semitism in Bavaria, especially in the cities of Munich and Nuremberg, found conditions in which it could thrive. Favoured for a time even by the Bavarian government, racial anti-Semitism was the main prop of demagogues such as Streicher in Nuremberg and of course Hitler in Munich, whose speeches in the early 1920s poured forth an unending torrent of anti-Jewish filth, much to the approval of those finding their way to Nazi meetings in Munich's beer halls — prominent among them already sections of the *Mittelstand* and lumpen-bourgeoisie, fearful of the socialist Left and resentful of the influence of 'Jewish' profiteers and financiers.[16]

'Old' and 'new' anti-Semitism existed side by side and provided mutual support for each other. The 'traditional' hostility only surfaced for the most part where there was an actual physical presence of Jews and where the local population came into direct contact, especially economically, with Jews. The racial-*völkisch* variety, although fuelling appalling outrages against Jews, was in essence capable of existing independent of direct contact with Jews as an 'abstract' racial hatred whose target was only superficially a specific Jewish shop or trader, and in reality Jewry itself.

Following a calmer period in the middle years of the Weimar Republic, the climate for Jews all over Germany obviously worsened dramatically during the period of the Nazis' rapid rise to power. However, research has done much to counter and qualify the notion of a society driven by pathological hatred of the Jews, in which 'generations of anti-Semitism had prepared the Germans to accept Hitler as their redeemer'.[17] Though Hitler himself apparently regarded anti-Semitism as the most important weapon in his propaganda arsenal,[18] it seems in fact, far from being the main motive force in bringing Nazism to power, to have been secondary to the main appeal of the Nazi message. A contemporary Jewish assessment of the spectacular gains in the 1930 Reichstag elections emphasized that millions of Nazi voters were in no sense anti-Semites, adding pointedly however that their rejection of anti-Semitism, on the other hand, was evidently not great enough to prevent them giving their support to an anti-Semitic party.[19] Analysis of the ideological motivation of a selection of 'Old Fighters' in joining the NSDAP suggests anti-Semitism was decisive only in a small minority of cases.[20] And in his perceptive study of the rise of Nazism in Northeim in Lower Saxony, where the NSDAP polled almost double the national average in 1932, W. S. Allen reached the conclusion that the Jews of the town were integrated on class lines before 1933 and that people 'were drawn to anti-Semitism because they were drawn to Nazism, not the other way round.'[21]

Anti-Semitism cannot, it seems, be allocated a significant role in bringing Hitler to power, though, given the widespread acceptability of the Jewish Question as a political issue — exploited not only by the Nazis — nor did it do anything to hinder his rapidly growing popularity. However, the relative indifference of most Germans towards the Jewish Question before 1933 meant that the Nazis did have a job on their hands after the 'take-over of power' to persuade them of the need for active discrimination and persecution of the Jews. The following pages consider the extent of Nazi success in transforming latent anti-Jewish sentiment into active-dynamic hatred.[22] The first section concentrates on popular reactions to Nazi attempts to oust Jews from economic activity, and to the terror and violence employed in the exercise, between 1933 and 1938. The second part then goes on to consider the role played by the lower clergy in influencing opinion on the Jewish Question. In the final section, the varying reactions to the November pogrom of 1938 are examined.

(i) Boycott and Terror, 1933–8

The nation-wide boycott of Jewish shops carried out on 1 April 1933 was, as is generally known, in Bavaria as elsewhere in the Reich less than a total success from the Nazi point of view. If it met with no opposition to speak of, the response of the public had been markedly cool.[23] A repeat performance across the whole country was never attempted. Though in Franconia localized boycotts and attacks on Jews continued to be an all too prominent feature of the political scene during 1933–4, elsewhere, in the context of a deteriorating economic situation and the need to avoid making gratuitous enemies on the diplomatic front, a relative calm in anti-Jewish activity set in towards the end of 1933. The calm was an uneasy one and lasted no more than a year before a new series of verbal tirades by rabid anti-Semites such as *Gauleiter* Streicher in Franconia and, outside Bavaria, *Gauleiter* Kube (Kurmark) and *Gauleiter* Grohé (Köln-Aachen), together with an intensified campaign of filth in Streicher's paper, the *Stürmer,* set the tone for the renewed and heightened violence which afflicted the whole of Germany in 1935. The renewal of anti-Jewish agitation was in large measure the reflection of the discontent of the Nazi Party, or the leadership of individual sections of it, with the progress (all too sluggish in their view) made by the State in solving the Jewish Question. One aim of their activity was to push the State much more rapidly in that direction.

The new wave of anti-Jewish violence reached its climax in Bavaria with the anti-Semitic disturbances in the streets of Munich's city centre in May 1935, to which we will shortly return.

Before then, quite contrary to the situation in Franconia, the Jewish Question had played in general an insignificant role both for the population at large and even for the Nazi Party in southern Bavaria where, outside Munich, few Jews were resident. The Government Presidents of the non-Franconian regions came to include a section of their reports dealing specifically with Jews only in 1935 (in the case of Lower Bavaria and the Upper Palatinate in fact only in 1938), and even then had frequently nothing to record.[24] This was a reflection of the fact that most reports from the localities were providing 'nil return' (*Fehlanzeige*) entries on the Jewish Question, since no Jews were resident in their areas. Typical for the situation in much of rural southern Bavaria is the comment, in summer 1935, from Bad Aibling (Upper Bavaria) — a locality which, in common with all other districts, was by this time plastered with advertisements for the *Stürmer*, sported notices put up by the local Party carrying the slogan 'Jews not wanted here', and was experiencing a non-stop campaign of scurrilous agitation against the Jews perpetrated by local activists. All this hardly corresponded with the real concerns of the local population, as the District Officer laconically pointed out: 'Actually, the Jewish Question is not a live issue for the district itself because only one Jewish family of Polish nationality lives in the entire district and among the summer visitors only one long-standing summer guest in Feilnbach and a spa visitor in Aibling have been observed.'[25] The Government President of Upper Bavaria added himself a month later that the Jewish Question was insignificant for the rural areas since outside Munich there were only 602 Jews in his entire region.[26]

The situation was of course different in Munich itself, as well as in the other major city of southern Bavaria, Augsburg, in a number of the Swabian small towns with prominent Jewish minorities, in Upper Bavarian tourist areas like Garmisch or Bad Tölz, and in rural districts where Jews plied the cattle or wood trade. But even here serious cases of violence towards Jews seldom occurred before 1938. Such boycotts and harassment of Jews as took place were invariably instigated by local Party organizations quite irrespective of the interests and wishes of the bulk of the local population.[27] The 'boycott movement' and anti-Jewish agitation of spring and summer 1935 tended in fact to alienate rather than win support for the Nazi Party in Munich and southern Bavaria.

A major exception to the relative absence of outbreaks of open violence against Jews in southern Bavaria in the first years of the Third Reich occurred on 18 and 25 May 1935, when anti-Jewish 'demonstrations' took place in the centre of Munich among the crowds of the city's busy Saturday shoppers. There was nothing spontaneous about the riotous disturbances. They were the culmination of a long campaign, initiated and stirred up by no less a figure than *Gauleiter* Adolf Wagner who, as Minister of the Interior, was actually responsible for order in Bavaria. Wagner, as it later transpired, had used two employees of the *Stürmer,* working in collaboration with sections of the Munich police force, to instigate the action — carried out largely by some 200 members of an SS camp near Munich and by members of other Party affiliations. The response of the public, as the Munich police felt compelled to report, was wholly opposed to this sort of anti-Semitism and strong antagonism was felt in the city and its environs. With the mood in the city very heated, Wagner was forced to denounce in the press and on the radio the 'terror groups' who were the cause of the trouble.[28]

The distaste felt by the Munich public was more probably evoked by the hooliganism and riotous behaviour of the Nazi mob than by principled objections to anti-Semitism, for such primitive violence found condemnation deep into the ranks of the Party itself. Even *Gauleiter* Karl Wahl of Swabia — certainly no friend of the Jews — condemned what he called the 'aping of Franconian methods'.[29] The anti-Jewish 'boycott' formed in fact only one part of a whole series of disturbances initiated by Party activists in the spring and summer of 1935. The population reacted even more sharply towards the attacks on Catholic associations taking place at the same time, the accompanying disturbance of *Caritas* collections,[30] and the numerous unruly incidents surrounding the traditional Bavarian white-and-blue flag during the customary May celebrations in rural areas. Popular feeling was certainly incensed, but much more as a result of the disturbance of order than the fact that the Jews had been a target of attack. The outcome was hostility towards the Party rather than sympathy for the Jews or rejection of the anti-Jewish policies of the regime. Even so, it seems clear from such reactions that the aggressive, dynamic hatred of the Jews which the Nazi formations were trying to foster was not easy to instil in a population whose feelings towards the Jews went little further for the most part than traditional antipathy.

In Franconia the situation was different. Leaving aside the Palatinate, 62.8 per cent of Jews in Bavaria at the time of the 1933 census were to be found there, especially in Middle and Lower Franconia. Even before the First World War, Franconian North Bavaria had been known as prime anti-Semitic territory, and Streicher was able to play on much existing resentment in making the Jewish Question a prominent feature of agitatory politics to a far greater extent than in most other regions of Germany during the Nazi rise to power.[31] Nuremberg and Coburg in particular developed into centres of the most vitriolic anti-Semitism during the 1920s and Jews there, made to bear the brunt of the economic resentments of small traders or farmers, were already given during the Depression a foretaste of what was to come.[32] Following the 'seizure of power', the position of Jews, especially in Middle Franconia but also to a large extent in the neighbouring parts of Upper and Lower Franconia, was as bad as anywhere in Germany.

The overwhelmingly Protestant Middle Franconia, heavily under Streicher's influence, saw the most vicious forms of anti-Semitism. Although even here the local Party leadership, or alternatively the SA, SS, or HJ, directed and perpetrated almost all the outrages, the notorious Gunzenhausen pogrom of March 1934 — the worst expression of anti-Jewish violence in the whole of Bavaria before the horrific events of 'Crystal Night' in 1938 — showed that in extreme circumstances a wider public could be whipped up into a hysterical mood against local resident Jews.[33]

Political conflict in Gunzenhausen — a small provincial town of 5,600 inhabitants in 1933, among them 184 Jews — seems to have been particularly bitter before the 'take-over of power', and the local Nazi Party — according to the comments of functionaries in the post-pogrom investigations — had built up a store of especial hatred towards the town's Jews who, supported by 'a certain lack of character of a broad section of the population in the Gunzenhausen district', had backed the socialists and communists and had stirred up feeling against the NSDAP even after the 'seizure of power'. A whole series of violent outbursts, set in motion and executed by a particularly unsavoury local SA leadership, punctuated the following months, so that by March 1934, in the SA's own interpretation, 'the mood of the population in Gunzenhausen had reached such a pitch that the smallest incident would be enough to prompt a demonstration against the Jews.'[34] The incident which turned the small town on Palm Sunday 1934 into an inferno of murderous hatred towards its Jewish inhabitants occurred after a young local leader, Kurt Bär, along with other SA men, had entered a public house run by a Jewish couple, had mishandled and 'arrested' them, and had gratuitously beaten up and badly injured the couple's son. Bär then addressed the mob which had begun to gather outside in a hate-filled speech in which he called the Jews 'our mortal enemies' who had 'nailed our Lord God to the Cross' and were 'guilty of the deaths of two million in the World War and the four hundred dead and ten thousand seriously injured in the Movement.' He also spoke of innocent girls who had been raped by Jews. The speech was heard by some 200 bystanders.[35] It lit the touchpaper to the quasi-medieval pogrom which followed. In groups of between fifty and several hundred people, the inhabitants of Gunzenhausen roamed the streets of the town for two hours, going from one Jewish home to another and shouting 'the

Jews must go'. In brutal fashion some thirty-five male and female Jews were dragged to the town prison, where some were gravely maltreated by Kurt Bär. One Jew was found hanged in a shed; another stabbed himself in the heart before the bellowing mob could get at him.[36] Between 1,000 and 1,500 people were said to have taken part in the pogrom.[37] If without doubt the ringleaders were SA men, it is none the less clear that in this case a considerable number of non-Party members must also have taken part in the wild orgy of violence. It provided, however, a case unique in its horror even for Middle Franconia: 'In no other administrative district of the fifty-three belonging to my governmental region has such an array of infringements taken place as in Gunzenhausen', wrote Government President Hofmann to the Bavarian Ministry of the Interior after the pogrom. He attributed the peculiarly tense situation in Gunzenhausen, where there had been at least eight more or less serious violent incidents between the 'seizure of power' and the pogrom directly to the agitation of the Special Commissioner, SA-*Obersturmbannführer* Karl Bär (uncle of Kurt), 'who himself has no sense of discipline and order'.[38]

Most reports from the lower administrative authorities in Middle Franconia in the years 1933–5 contain no critical comments of the population about violence shown towards Jews. This must be juxtaposed with the open anger and protest registered in precisely this part of Bavaria at the Nazi intervention in the running of the Protestant Church in 1934. Obviously, the degree of intimidation in the Jewish Question was acute, as is shown by the arrest of a photographer from Gunzenhausen for allegedly making critical remarks about Kurt Bär, the instigator of the Gunzenhausen pogrom and himself arraigned before a court of law for the offence.[39] The level of intimidation was also largely responsible for the fact that already in spring 1933 few dared to engage in economic dealings with Jews, in contrast to the situation in most parts of Germany.[40] 'Friends of Jews' were exposed to practically the same danger as Jews themselves.

Intimidation, however, does not explain quite everything. Since intimidation itself was closely related to and dependent upon denunciation of neighbours or work-mates for their remarks or actions, its effectiveness presupposes that a considerable proportion of the population were, or were thought to be, in basic agreement with the broad contours of the persecution of the Jews.

An example of the poisoned atmosphere in one mid-Franconian village is provided by Altenmuhr, near Gunzenhausen. There were thirty-one Jews among the 800 inhabitants, and when an elderly Jew died in 1936 the construction of a coffin and transportation of the body to the cemetery, even though permission from the local police had been granted, was refused by the local joiner and undertaker. The coffin had eventually to be made by a cartwright and the corpse carried to Gunzenhausen by a hearse ordered from Nuremberg. As the report says, it had once been usual 'for a fair number of aryan mourners to attend a Jewish funeral. Since the takeover of power this fact has however fundamentally altered. Today in Altenmuhr it is inconceivable that Germans would pay last respects to a Jew.'[41]

In the second half of 1935 the wild *'Einzelaktionen'* — individual measures taken against Jews without any legal base — declined sharply after being banned by the State authorities, and especially following the promulgation of the notorious Nuremberg Laws in September 1935, which in providing anti-Jewish legislation went a long way towards meeting the aims of the Party's summer anti-Semitic campaign.[42] With one eye on the approaching Olympics and the other on the foreign and economic situation, the regime needed a period of relative calm. In August 1935 Hitler and Deputy Führer Hess had expressly banned 'individual actions' against Jews.[43] Even after the murder of Wilhelm Gustloff, the Leader of the Nazi *Auslandsorganisation* in Switzerland, by a young Jew in February 1936 there were no outbreaks of anti-Jewish violence following another firm ban by the Reich Minister of the Interior, together with Hess, on any prospective sallies against Jewish targets.[44]

The largely negative attitude of the population, especially in South Bavaria, to the open violence of Nazi thugs in the summer of 1935 was perfectly compatible with broad approval of the anti-Jewish legislation passed at the Nuremberg Party Rally in September 1935 by a specially summoned assembly of the Reichstag.[45] Probably the Government President of Upper Bavaria was not far from the mark when he distinguished between rejection of the 'inexpedient' slogans and posters of the 1935 campaign, together with fears of economic repercussions in tourist areas, and approval 'in every respect' of the 'objective struggle against Jewry'.[46] Indifference seems, in fact, to have been the most common response to the Nuremberg Laws.[47] A wide range of reports from Bavarian localities do not even mention the promulgation of the laws, and the reports of the Government Presidents, summarizing opinion at the regional level, indicate only in the briefest terms that the legal regulation of the Jewish Question had been generally welcomed and had met with the approval of the population, not least in its contribution towards the elimination of 'the recently prevailing intense disturbance'.[48] However, even where they had been unpopular, the 'individual actions' had not been without influence on people's attitudes towards Jews. As the alleged provocation of the disturbances, many were glad to see the back of the Jews, as a report in December 1936 from Bad Neustadt, an almost wholly Catholic district of Lower Franconia which the Nazis had scarcely penetrated before the 'seizure of power', shows:

Altogether there has been an almost complete change in the attitude of the population towards the Jews. Whereas people used to side in unmistakable fashion with the persecuted Jews, one now hears: 'if only they would all soon be gone!' Solely from the point of view of the tax shortfall and thus of damage to communal finances is the departure of the Jews regarded in Unsleben as unfortunate.[49]

Racial anti-Semitism met its greatest obstacle, and came up against notable resistance, where the Nazis tried to break commercial relationships between Jews and the non-Jewish population. In 1936–7 the Party, together with the Nazified trade and agricultural organizations, made renewed attempts to destroy trading contacts with Jews. The revitalized boycott encountered little sympathy, it seems, even in Streicher territory. Those who stood to gain economically through trading in Jewish shops, trafficking with Jewish cattle-dealers, providing accommodation for Jewish visitors to tourist resorts, or finding work in Jewish-owned firms were not eager to break off their contact and to boycott the Jews. Economic self-interest clearly prevailed over ideological correctitude. Here were obvious limits of Nazi ideological penetration.

Alzenau, a relatively industrialized district on the northwestern border of Lower Franconia, provides an example of how the ideological norm preached by the Party came to grief in the face of pragmatic material self-interest of workers at the Jewish-owned cigar factories which dominated local industry. Though the Nazis had made no great headway in this area before 1933,[50] the Party was responsible for not infrequent acts of violence against Jews and their property in the years after the 'seizure of power'.[51] The 'boycott movement' had, as the focus of its attack, the Jewish ownership of the cigar factories. Jews in fact owned most of the twenty-nine factories with a combined work-force of 2,206 women and 280 men.[52] Enquiries into the position of the tobacco firms following allegations that the boycott was threatening their existence and the jobs of their employees met with a more or less unanimous response: the people were glad to have work and did not ask whether the employer was an 'aryan' or a Jew; 'the relationship between the firms and the local residents is a thoroughly good and friendly one; complaints about the employers have not been heard so far.'[53]

The boycott problems of the Nazis were even greater in the countryside. Here, the main issue was the remaining dominance in many areas of the Jewish cattle-dealer, the traditional middle-man and purveyor of credit for untold numbers of German peasants. Despite vicious intimidation and ceaseless propaganda, however, the Nazis found it an uphill struggle. Most peasants were unconcerned about the racial origins of the cattle-dealer as long as his prices were good and his credit readily forthcomig. 'Aryan' cattle-dealers, complained many peasants, had little capital and could not offer prices comparable to those of their Jewish rivals. The consequence was that the ousting of the Jewish cattle-dealers made remarkably slow progress. The wholesale cattle trade in the Ebermannstadt area was in 1935 still 'to a good ninety per cent' in Jewish hands, and enquiries in autumn 1936 came to the 'regrettable' conclusion that, especially in the hill-farm districts of the Jura, nothing at all had changed: 'Here the cattle-Jew trafficks just as ever in the farmhouses. When questioned, the peasants explain almost in unison that the Jew pays well, and pays cash, which is not the case with the aryan dealers; in some instances there are no aryan dealers at all in the outlying communities.'[54] Even Party members and village mayors were not adverse to keeping ideological precepts and practical profits separate. There are numerous instances on record of functionaries and local dignitaries trafficking with Jews.[55]

Every form of chicanery, especially the withdrawal of trading permits, was used to bring about the almost complete exclusion of Jewish dealers from Middle Franconia as early as the end of 1934, though that was only possible in the peculiar conditions of Streicher's *Gau,* and even here was not always welcomed by the peasants.[56] Elsewhere in Bavaria the Jews could largely maintain their dominance in the cattle trade, despite harassment, down to the end of 1937. A not untypical report from a village in Lower Franconia shows the position clearly. The major stated that it was difficult to provide a list of names of peasants dealing with Jews, as requested, since apart from Party members almost all peasants still carried out their transactions with Jews. Recognition of the necessity of avoiding contact with Jews was hardly existent, and 'the currently expected attitude of rejection of Jews' was therefore lacking. Some peasants stood out in fact 'on account of their friendliness towards Jews'.[57] Gestapo findings were even more alarming to Nazi eyes. Even as late as 1937 the Gestapo at Munich were forced to concede 'shocking results' arising from their enquiry into relations of peasants and Jews. In Swabia along there had been 1,500 cases of peasants trafficking with Jews in 1936–7, and although this had been put down to the lack of reliable 'aryan' dealers with sufficient capital, the real reason, claimed the Gestapo, was 'the attitude of the peasants which lacked any sort of racial consciousness.'[58] Part of the problem, in the Gestapo's view, was that numerous peasants, 'who mainly have no idea of the racial problem', were of the opinion that commercial dealings with Jews were in order since the State had given them a trading licence.[59] The withdrawal of trading licences, refusal to insure cattle bought from Jews, expulsion from the Cattle Farming Association and not least exposure of those continuing to traffick with Jews in the pages of the *Stürmer* were all part of an intensified campaign to break the Jewish contact with the farming world, and by the end of 1937 the

Nazis were approaching their goal.[60] The reactions of peasants from the Lower Franconia village of Bischofsheim an der Rhön mirror the complaint of many farmers, that their economic situation had deteriorated as a result of the exclusion of the Jews since there was no longer anyone who would buy up the cattle: 'The Jews are not allowed to engage in the cattle trade any longer and there are apart from them no cattle-dealers to speak of resident in this district.'[61]

Peasant attitudes were determined almost wholly by material considerations and economic self-interest. Nazi racial propaganda played no great part. The fourfold increase in sales of the *Stürmer* during the first ten months of 1935, despite the widespread distaste the newspaper provoked, was testimony none the less to the fact that anti-Semitism was gradually gaining ground in popular opinion.[62] And certainly the fact that peasants continued to trade with Jewish dealers does not make them pro-Jewish. But it does suggest that the racial origins of the purchaser of their cattle was for them a matter of complete indifference: the only question that mattered was the price for the cow.

Negative reactions to anti-Jewish placards and slogans posted at the entry and exit in most villages by the local Nazi Party were probably also prompted more by economic than humanitarian motives. Even Nazis themselves recognized that the anti-Jewish slogans — 'Jews are our misfortune', 'Jews not wanted here', and even more threatening and offensive varieties — were guaranteed to damage the tourist trade. An anonymous letter to Reich Governor Epp in August 1934, allegedly coming from a long-serving Party member who undoubtedly had his own economic interest in the matter, pointed out that the anti-Jewish notices made the worst possible impact on foreigners travelling down the '*Romantische Straße*' through Franconia to the Passion Play in Oberammergau, and that as a result the tourist industry in towns such as Rothenburg, Dinkelsbühl, Nördlingen, and Ansbach was suffering greatly.[63] With the massive extension of the notices in 1935 — up to then they had been largely a Franconian speciality — came grave misgivings in other tourist areas such as Garmisch-Partenkirchen, where serious economic consequences were feared.[64] In some rural areas peasants expressed their distaste for the anti-Jewish boards by removing them altogether, or altering the wording to express welcome to the Jews. In one Upper Bavarian village, where some peasants were worried that the anti-Jewish notices set up by the Hitler Youth would deter Jews from coming to buy up their hops, the boards — 'Jews not wanted here' — disappeared for a short time before being replaced with an amended text: 'Jews very much wanted here'.[65]

In its patronage of Jewish shops the rural population in particular was regarded by the authorities as 'ideologically unteachable'. In one report about the boycott of Jewish shops in Cham (Upper Palatinate) in December 1936, it was pointed out that the rural population especially, 'despite repeated and thorough instruction at Party meetings and on other occasions', still preferred to buy in Jewish shops. Even being photographed for the *Stürmer*'s rogues' gallery was not enough to deter them, and many were prepared even to take sides with the Jews.[66] In Munich, the police interpreted the massive success of the annual sales at a leading Jewish clothing store as a sign that many women still 'had not understood, nor want to understand, the lines laid down by the Führer for solving the Jewish Question.'[67] Such complaints were common the length and breadth of Germany in these years.[68]

Nevertheless, in the long run the intimidation did not fail to do its work. As early as December 1935 the Government President of Swabia could provide several examples to show how the economic position of Jewish dealers in Swabia had drastically deteriorated. Ichenhausen, where Jews formed a higher proportion of the population (12.4 per cent) than almost anywhere else in Germany and where commercial life revolved around Jewish trade, was described as 'a dying town', since many no longer wanted to buy in Jewish shops and preferred to travel to Günzburg or Ulm to do their shopping — a process which was also damaging Christian shops, added the report.[69] Not a few 'aryan' businessmen saw in the 'Jewish boycott' a chance to damage or even ruin rivals by reporting their Jewish background to the local Party.[70] Under constant pressure, countless Jewish businesses had by the end of 1937 seen their customers driven away, had sold out or gone into liquidation, had emigrated or moved to larger cities where they could continue a shadowy existence for some time to come on the fringes of society, withdrawn, threatened, and persecuted.

(ii) The Influence of the Clergy on Attitudes to the Jewish Question

Following their detailed enquiries into the continuing commercial contact between peasants and Jewish dealers, the Gestapo attributed the limited penetration of the Nazi *Weltanschauung* in rural areas chiefly to the influence of the Christian Churches. If 'despite enlightenment through the National Socialist Movement' there were still those 'who think they have to stand up for the Jewish people', claimed the Gestapo, this was above all the fault of the clergy. It was often the case in rural parishes in fact, continued the report, that the priest or pastor would represent the Jews as the 'chosen people' and directly encourage the people to patronize Jewish shops:[71]

> The enquiries, which are not yet concluded, show already that in exactly those districts where political Catholicism still holds sway the peasants are so infected by the doctrines of belligerent political Catholicism that they are deaf

to any discussion of the racial problem. This state of affairs further shows that the majority of peasants are wholly unreceptive to the ideological teachings of National Socialism and that they can only be compelled through material disadvantage to engage in commercial links with aryan dealers.[72]

After more than four years of Nazi rule, then, the Nazi *Weltanschauung*, and in particular racial anti-Semitism, its central feature, had in the view of the Gestapo been able to make little headway among the Catholic rural population, which had no 'racial consciousness' and was 'deaf' to the 'racial problem'. The tendency of the Gestapo, like the SD, to exaggerate the opposition of the Churches is well known. Even so, there is no doubting the fact that the Christian Churches, especially the Catholic Church, were able to exercise very considerable influence on the population, particularly in rural areas. The Churches remained practically the only non-Nazified bodies in Germany which retained enormous influence upon the formation of opinion and the potential — as the 'Church struggle' shows — to form and foster an independent public opinion running counter to Nazi propaganda and policy. Furthermore, it was evident that the racial theories on which Nazi anti-Semitism was grounded amounted to a hatred of part of mankind which was diametrically opposed to the Christian Commandment to 'love thy neighbour': racism, as the central element of the Nazi *Weltanschauung*, stood in irreconcilable conflict with the Christian basic tenet of the equality of all men before God.

However, the attitude of the Churches and of the leaders of both denominations to racism was highly ambivalent. This ambivalence had deep roots. Against the fundamental rejection of racism stood the Christian tradition of anti-Judaism which, though in decline since the Enlightenment, retained some force as a Christian undercurrent of anti-Semitism well into the twentieth century.[73]

Steeped in such traditions, and also in the contemporary commonplaces of racial prejudice, many Church leaders were unable or unwilling to speak out forcefully and unambiguously against anti-Semitism. Even, on the Catholic side, Cardinal Faulhaber who had in 1923 been labelled 'the Jewish Cardinal' by Nazi sympathizers at Munich University for his criticism of anti-Semitic agitation, shied away from an outright public condemnation of Nazi racism. In his bold and justly famous Advent sermons of 1933, which enjoyed a wide readership outside Germany, he stressed that 'the love of one's own race' ought never to be turned into 'hatred towards other people'. He added, however, that the Church had no objections to 'racial research' (*Rassenforschung*) and 'racial welfare' (*Rassenpflege*), 'nor to the endeavour to keep the individuality of a people as pure as possible and, through reference to the community of blood, deepening the sense of national community.' A year later the Cardinal felt compelled to make clear that in his Advent sermons he had 'defended the old Biblical Scripture of Israel, but not taken a stance on the Jewish Question of today.'[74]

The even more strongly featured nationalist leanings in the Protestant Church allowed racial and anti-Semitic thinking to surface all the more readily — quite apart from the 'German Christians', the thoroughly racist Nazified wing of the Church.[75] Both Churches accepted in essence the principle of racial differentiation, rejecting — again apart from the 'German Christians' — only the outrightly aggressive hatred of Jews by the Nazis. Günther Lewy used sharp but fitting words to emphasize the consequences of such an ambivalent stance in the case of the Catholic Church: 'A Church that justified moderate anti-Semitism and merely objected to extreme and immoral acts was ill prepared to provide an effective antidote to the Nazis' gospel of hate.'[76]

The difference in attitude towards the Jewish Question, which we have already witnessed, between Franconia and South Bavaria certainly had something to do with the denominational divide between Protestant and Catholic areas. The particularly pronounced national feeling in Franconia which was closely coupled with fervent Protestantism undoubtedly tended to foster acceptance of Nazi racial stereotypes, and the piously Protestant rural population of Middle Franconia, which defended its Church and bishop so demonstratively and effectively in 1934, revealed in the same period hardly a trace of opposition to the racial idea. However, it would be easy to take the denominational distinction too far. The position of the Jews was by no means rosy in the adjacent, and largely Catholic, Lower Franconia. Catholicism provided no protection in itself against anti-Semitism (as of course is plain from the example of Austria and other central European countries). Nevertheless, given the generally stronger social cohesiveness of the Catholic Church's following, the Christian teaching which ran counter to the Nazi doctrine of race hatred certainly played a part in influencing opinion on the Jewish Question in the Catholic regions of Bavaria.

While the ambivalent and hesitant attitude of the Papacy, of the Catholic hierarchy, and of the leadership of the Evangelical Church to the Jewish Question has been the subject of thorough enquiry,[77] the stance adopted by the parochial clergy has been little touched upon. Yet it was the parish clergy who were most able to exert direct influence upon their congregations. The extent to which they attempted to influence opinion on the Jews is an important one, therefore, requiring detailed examination.

Few clergymen of either denomination seem to have spoken publicly (mainly in sermons) on the 'racial problem' in a fully-fledged Nazi sense. As the Nazi authorities themselves often reported, they were the exceptions. One Protestant pastor — 'a rare bird amongst his sort' according to the Government President of Upper and Middle Franconia — was said to have claimed in a sermon in April 1937 that the Jew had nothing in common with the Christian Church, was a foreign element, and must be regarded as the enemy of the Christian faith. The Jew sought to introduce Bolshevism into the Church and by so doing to destroy the religious community. 'The Jews are the destroyers and deserved to be whipped out', he reportedly concluded.[78] An equally 'honourable exception' was the Catholic Redemptorist from Cham who in April 1939 paid tribute to the Nazi State, touched on the Jewish Question, and described the Jews as murderers because they had crucified Christ.[79] Another Catholic priest from the Bamberg district, whose pro-Nazi comments in a sermon in March 1939 had caused such offence among his congregation that some thirty people left the Church in protest, was said to have called out as they went: 'Let them go, they're nothing but Jew-servers.'[80]

Such unrestrained Nazified remarks seldom occurred. Much more frequent were instances where members of the clergy, while not preaching racial hatred, betrayed signs of a racist attitude and of basic acknowledgement that there was indeed a 'racial problem'. In his well-attended sermons in the *Frauenkirche* in Munich in December 1936, the well-known Jesuit Hermann Muckermann, speaking on the personality of the historic Jesus, drew the conclusion that the teaching of Christ was not Jewish in origin but stood rather in opposition to Jewry. He upheld expressly 'the facts of heredity and race' and stated that the Church approved in principle of the eugenic and racial policies of the government.[81] Muckermann had already formulated his ideas about eugenics and race in spring 1936 in a series of lectures in Bamberg, in which he described a 'healthy racial stock' as 'a lofty, magnificent gift of heaven' and regarded it as Christian duty to uphold and increase the 'home race' (*Heimrasse*). Though not in itself against the Divine Order, mixing the 'home race' with 'alien races' was to be rejected.[82] Muckermann's views were based upon his theoretical concern with racial and eugenic problems, upon which subjects he had written a number of tracts. Other clergymen tended rather to reveal in their comments an unreflected acceptance of racial premises. Such attitudes were also betrayed by the eagerness with which a number of Protestant pastors retaliated in denying the 'calumny' that the clergy was 'Jew-ridden' (*verjudet*).[83] When *Gauleiter* Kube of the Kurmark attacked pastors of the 'Confessing Front' as 'Jews' accomplices' in June 1935, for instance, an array of protest telegrams landed in the offices of the Nuremberg police and protestations were also made during services in and around Nuremberg.[84]

Even such a leading figure in the Protestant Church as Helmut Kern, head of the 'People's Mission', who otherwise described concepts of race, blood, and nationality as no more than secular values and recognized the connections between 'new heathenism', racism, and the attack on Christian values, showed — probably in an unreflecting way — undercurrents of anti-Semitism when, in his campaign against the 'community school', he described it as 'a product of the Enlightenment and of Jewish liberalism', or spoke in the same context of the ideas 'of Jew-ridden Marxism and liberalism'.[85] Though it was not the intention in these or similar instances to attack the Jews directly, such comments of pastors and priests could only help to legitimize and strengthen the existing anti-Semitic climate of opinion.

Far more numerous, however, to go from the report material, were instances where clergy of both denominations — though Catholics more frequently than Protestants — took issue with the racial policy of the regime or even sided openly with the persecuted Jews.

The authorities were informed, for example, of a Protestant missionary preacher in the Weißenburg district of Middle Franconia who, in a sermon in 1935, referred disparagingly to the name of the former SA leader Ernst Röhm, shot in 1934, in connection with the notion of race 'in order to show that the aryan race was not to be regarded as better than any other.'[86] Another Protestant preacher was said to have stated that in a time when race and blood were being elevated to the status of idols people needed above all the badge of faith.[87] During a Catholic mission in Bamberg a speaker was alleged to have declared in a sermon: 'For God there are no *völkisch* matters and no national laws . . . For him there are no racial differences.'[88] A Jesuit, also in Bamberg, was reported as saying that the Catholic Church had no use for a national or racial church 'because it preaches its doctrine to all people, whatever their race.'[89]

Some clergymen of both denominations supported the Jews publicly and openly condemned their persecution. A Catholic priest in Neustadt an der Saale (Lower Franconia), for example, spoke, following a series of terroristic acts against local Jews, in a sermon in October 1934 about human hatred and lack of charity in connection with anti-Jewish actions, referred to an anti-Jewish song of the Hitler Youth, and commented that 'in this way the hatred towards the Jews is planted in the hearts of young people.'[90] The courageous Father Förtsch, a Catholic priest in the Bamberg district and clever opponent of the regime who had long been a thorn in the flesh of the authorities, declared in sermons in February 1936 'that the Jews also did a very great deal of good and were not therefore to be spurned.'[91] In the same month a Protestant pastor at Hersbruck (Middle Franconia) expressly emphasized that according to the Bible the Jews were 'the chosen people'.[92] *Dompfarrer* Kraus of Eichstätt, who battled with the authorities about the attack on Catholicism,[93] also defended the Jews in one of his sermons and strongly criticized an article in the *Stürmer* entitled 'Why I hate the Jews'.[94] Another known opponent of the regime, the brave Protestant pastor Karl Steinbauer, who paid for his courage by forfeiting his liberty, castigated anti-Semitism and the entire *völkisch* way of thinking in a sermon in September 1935 in which he boldly repeated the biblical words: 'Salvation comes from the Jews.'[95] Other pastors prayed for the Jews, or requested the congregation to pray for them.[96] Even during the war some clergymen were prepared to support the Jews. One Catholic priest in the district of Neustadt an der Aisch in Middle Franconia was served with a summons in summer 1940 for allegedly saying in a sermon that 'the Jews should not be cast out since they too are human beings.'[97] Particularly courageous and noteworthy were the remarks of the Catholic priest Josef Atzinger in Landshut in November 1940, in which he condemned the racial legislation of the Third Reich as 'godless, unjustified, and harmful'.[98]

Neither the Catholic nor the Evangelical Church leadership took any official stance towards the November pogrom of 1938. The undoubted deep disapproval of the bulk of the clergy of both denominations was voiced therefore only in the isolated comments of individual priests and pastors. Their courage in speaking out amid the official silence was all the greater in that they could expect no support from above, from their bishops and hierarchies, and little or no protection from any possible retribution by local Party activists. Four Catholic and two Protestant clergymen in the district of Wunsiedel in Upper Franconia, for example, were the targets of violent attacks because of their alleged pro-Jewish attitude during the 'Crystal Night'.[99]

Reports of the Bavarian authorities contain several instances where the 'Jewish Action' was openly denounced by members of the clergy of both denominations. A Protestant pastor in the Bamberg area, for example, was indicted with offences against the 'Malicious Practices Act' for saying in sermons in November 1938 that the actions carried out against the Jews were from a Christian point of view in no sense deserving of approval but were rather to be condemned and stating: 'A Christian person does not do such things. These were sub-humans (*Untermenschen*).[100] A priest in Neumarkt in der Oberpfalz compared those who smashed Jewish windows with 'the purest Bolsheviks'.[101] Another priest, from Pfarrkirchen in Lower Bavaria, was arraigned before the Munich 'Special Court' for allegedly saying to an eleven-year-old schoolboy following the murder of embassy official Ernst vom Rath — the spur to the pogrom — that many innocent Jews had to suffer with the one guilty of vom Rath's assassination.[102] And at St Lorenz's church in the centre of Nuremberg on the Sunday following the pogrom, all the clergy of the parish followed the pastor's remarks of sympathy for the Jews by chanting the Ten Commandments in unison before the altar.[103]

Further critical remarks of the clergy about the pogrom could not be found in the report material. Most priests and pastors kept silent, yet as in the neighbouring Württemberg their general rejection of the pogrom was easily recognizable by the authorities.[104] This was confirmed by the comment of the Government President of Upper Bavaria about reactions to the pogrom: 'Only those circles influenced by the Church do not yet go along with the Jewish Question.'[6]

Examination of remarks made by members of the Bavarian parish clergy about the Jews suggests that attitudes were divided on the 'race question'. Some clergymen adopted an outright Nazi stance and fully approved of the exclusion of Jews from German society. They were, however, exceptions. Most rejected the Nazi dogma of hate towards part of mankind. Nevertheless, latent anti-Semitic feelings occasionally found expression. There was also some ambivalence in a number of statements which appeared to condemn not discrimination itself but merely the methods of discrimination, the deplorable excesses of the persecution of the Jews. The clearest conclusion of all from the evidence surveyed would seem to be, however, that the parish clergy had on remarkably few occasions anything at all to say on the Jewish Question. The overwhelming majority of priests and pastors, like their superiors, refrained from any public comment and let the persecution of the Jews pass them by in silence. Such comments as have been cited in this chapter were therefore themselves exceptional in being made at all. And the fact that most examples derive from Franconian parishes is itself no accident, again showing that the Jewish Question was for the most part only in this area a live issue.[106]

In asking why the clergy commented so rarely on the inhumanities of the persecution of the Jews, we have of course immediately to take into account their exposed position in the Third Reich, the intimidation of the police State, the probability of recriminations, and the general pervading atmosphere of fear and repression. This explains much, but not everything. In other matters, especially when it was a case of defending immediate concerns of the Church against the regime, priests were prepared to act despite the obvious dangers involved. Defence of the Church had its own legitimacy for priests and pastors. The Jewish Question, on the other hand, belonged in the realm of 'politics' which the Church, from its leaders down, conscientiously eschewed from 1933 onwards. Even apart from any principle of non-interference in 'politics', however, there are grounds for strong suspicion that the Jewish Question was not regarded by the clergy as a central theme of interest. The narrower field of denominational issues and defence of the Church's rights and practices consumed in great measure the potential energy of the parish clergy to oppose the regime. In this sphere, the priest was able decisively to influence the opinion and behaviour of the population and to manipulate it in the struggle against the anti-Church measures of the regime. He could generally count on popular support of churchgoers in response to Nazi intervention in Church affairs, and on the maximum backing from his superiors. In the Jewish Question things were different. The clergy encountered mainly indifference or feelings of sullen helplessness, when not a widespread if abstract and latent anti-Semitism even among churchgoers. Whereas the clergy tried actively to influence popular opinion in Church matters, in the Jewish Question they gave little lead and tended to follow and reflect rather than mould popular opinion. As Christians the majority of the clergy rejected the inhumanities of the Nazi regime; but as individuals living amid a climate of opinion hostile to Jews they tended largely to mirror the latent anti-Semitism and indifference of their society.

Since the Jewish Question appears to have been relatively unimportant to the Church,[107] and since—as we have seen—the clergy rarely took a direct part in shaping opinion on the Jews, the Gestapo's interpretation, linking the lack of penetration of Nazi racial doctrines in rural areas to the active influence of the clergy, seems a dubious one. The lack of 'racial consciousness' in the Bavarian peasantry which the Gestapo bemoaned was undoubtedly often founded on traditional Christian precepts of basic humanity which continued to stand for many Christians in crass opposition to Nazi barbarity. Of at least equal importance, especially in Catholic rural areas, was the widespread rejection of the Nazi Party, above all for its assault on the Catholic Church itself, which brought with it increased solidarity with the priest and rejection of Nazi values. More important still, however, in explaining the unwillingness of the peasantry to go along with Nazi boycott demands was not so much 'lack of racial consciousness' as direct material self-interest.

Nazism had only limited success in breaking down the conventional mentality of the population, built partly on self-interest, and replacing it with an ideological dogma of hatred towards Jews. Though Christian teaching often provided the basis of the antipathy towards the Nazi *Weltanschauung*, the hierarchy and lower clergy did little directly to foster anti-racist attitudes. Only indirectly, through the closer bonds of the population to the Church as a consequence of the 'Church struggle' was immunity to Nazi ideological penetration reaffirmed. The ambivalent attitude of the Church towards race allowed, however, the retention of anti-Semitic views by the faithful. If, according to the teaching of the Church, Jews were not to be hated and persecuted, they did not necessarily have to be loved. The words of the Catholic preacher cited earlier, that in the eyes of God there were no *völkisch* matters, national laws, or racial differences,[108] denoted an uncompromising attitude adopted by a few clergymen even during the war. Such a stance ran, of course, completely counter to the very core of Nazi ideology. As was implicitly recognized here, the Nazi 'new heathenism' was grounded on the principle of racial inequality, which stood in contradiction to the Commandments of God.[109] The defence against the anti-Church component of Nazism ought theoretically, therefore, to have found one of its central points in the rejection of the concept of race. In practice, however, from the point of view of the Church the ideological struggle was regarded mainly as a struggle for the faith in the narrower sense of the word, and as a defence of Church institutions, in which the racial issue was seldom touched upon, and then only tangentially. The isolated voices of protest raised by a few courageous individuals from both denominations acquired, therefore, no significance within the framework of the 'Church struggle' and found little support from the Church leaderships.

One can hardly avoid the conclusion that the Jewish Question was on the whole a matter of just as much indifference to the clergy as it was to the churchgoing population of Bavaria. The courageous stand taken on denominational issues was never matched by anything like the same fervour on matters of so much greater human significance.

(iii) 'Crystal Night'

Only once in the twelve years of the Third Reich was the German people directly confronted with the full savagery of the anti-Jewish terror. This was on the morning of 10 November 1938, following the so-called 'Crystal Night' (*'Reichskristallnacht'*), the quasi-medieval orgy of destruction, plunder, burning of synagogues, and wild devastation carried out by the Party and the SA at the call of Propaganda Minister Goebbels — in his words as a 'spontaneous answer' of the population to the killing of Legation Secretary Ernst vom Rath by a seventeen-year-old Jewish boy, Herschel Grynszpan, in Paris.[110]

After the relative calm of the years 1936–7 the position of the Jews in Germany had worsened visibly since the beginning of 1938.[111] Following the *Anschluß* of Austria, and especially in connection with the Sudeten crisis, serious outbreaks of anti-Jewish violence had occurred in numerous Franconian localities as Party activists exploited the tension and the eventual triumphs of the Nazi State to unleash a wave of terror against the Jews.[112] Seen through Jewish eyes, the situation in the Middle Franconia was threatening in the extreme during the weeks before the pogrom:

> Already for a few weeks there had been decided signs of unrest among the masses . . . There also appeared on various shops, cinemas etc. the notices: 'Jews not wanted' etc. In Ansbach, seat of the district administration, for

example, this notice was to be seen weeks beforehand on every shop of whatever sort without exception. In smaller places and in the countryside conditions were worse still. Through terror acts or by being compelled to sign, people were forced to sell all their belongings for a bargain price within a few hours and to go away. Where to? Naturally, into the next big town. The same question, where to? which now confronts all of them.[113]

According to the report of the District Officer of Alzenau (Lower Franconia) at the end of October 1938, the area had experienced a constant spate of night attacks on Jewish buildings. Windows had been smashed in many houses, the walls smeared with red paint, and two synagogues damaged by stone-throwing.[114] Attacks by Party activists on synagogues were sharply increasing in number long before the pogrom. The tone was set by the festive demolition of the main synagogues in Munich and Nuremberg in summer 1938.[115] In Leutershausen (Middle Franconia) the synagogue was plundered by SA men in mid-October and the windows of nearby houses smashed amid tumultous scenes.[116] At the end of the month a tear-gas bomb was hurled into the Ansbach synagogue and slogans daubed on Jewish houses: 'Jew, clear off before 1.1.39.'[117] The Government Presidents reported ever increasing numbers of outrages against Jews throughout 1938.[118] Only in Upper Bavaria were conditions relatively quiet in the months before the great pogrom. And in contrast to the situation following the murder of Gustloff in February 1936, the dangerously volatile climate inside the country combined with Germany's new dominance in Europe since the Munich settlement to provide more or less ideal circumstances for the anti-Jewish 'retaliatory measures' of November 1938.

The methodically whipped-up hate campaign of 1938, together with the intensified boycott and exclusion of Jews from certain sections of the economy, had accelerated Jewish emigration, especially from small towns and villages where Jews had been particularly exposed. The relatively high proportion of Bavarian Jews living in such areas as compared with the Reich as a whole was one reason why emigration rates from Bavaria were higher than in Germany in general. Whereas the 370,000 Jews still remaining in Germany (leaving aside Austria and the Sudetenland) on 1 October 1938 represented 74 per cent of the recorded number of 1933, in Bavaria (here including the Palatinate) the Jewish population formed only 67.5 per cent of its 1933 level.[119] There were significant regional differences within Bavaria. In Upper and Middle Franconia there was a drop to 59 percent and in Lower Franconia to as little as 55 per cent, whereas the inflow from internal migration *to* Munich almost compensated for the city's losses and there was only a slight drop to 95 per cent of the 1933 figure. The quarterly statistics of the authorities show

clearly the increase in emigration since 1937 following the stepped-up boycott. In the period of almost four years from June 1933 to March 1937 the
Jewish population in Bavaria had decreased by about 8,500 persons, in the
one-and-a-half years from 1 April 1937 to 1 October 1938 by as much as
5,200 persons.[120]

Even this was not fast enough for the Nazi regime. Towards the end of
October 1938 around 17,000 Jews of Polish extract were expelled — among
them the parents of Herschel Grynszpan, whose revenge killing of vom Rath[121]
triggered off the 'Crystal Night' pogrom, the subsequent temporary internment
of some 30,000 Jews in concentration camps,[122] and — as one consequence —
the massive acceleration of Jewish emigration.[123] Jews now left Germany in
droves. By May 1939 more than 40 per cent of those Jews still in Bavaria on the
eve of the pogrom had left.[124]

So far as Goebbels had reckoned with spontaneous popular support for the
pogrom, however, he was disappointed. The disapproval of large sections of
the population was abundantly clear, even if open protest was in the circumstances hardly conceivable.

Though in accordance with Goebbels's instructions the press carried relatively few details about the nature and scale of destruction — in contrast to the
extensive coverage of the 'legal' measures introduced immediately after the
pogrom[125] — shocked inhabitants of the cities and larger towns had the appalling evidence of smashed windows, demolished property, and burnt-out synagogues before their very eyes on the morning of 10 November.[126] Outside the
towns there were fewer signs of destruction, though word of the devastation in
the cities travelled rapidly. The pogrom was throughout the Reich largely an
urban phenomenon, except in the few areas where rural Jewish settlement was
still prominent,[127] and the scale of the pogrom corresponded largely to the size
of the resident Jewish population and the level of radicality of the local Party
organizations.

In Upper Bavaria few cases of violence and destruction were recorded outside the city of Munich. Jews were often forced to leave their place of residence
immediately or within a few hours, to offer their property for sale, and to sign
an agreement never to return. Many were handed over to the police and kept
in custody.[128] The attitude of the local Party leadership was crucial in determining the limits of the 'action'. In Garmisch-Partenkirchen, for example,
where Party and SA hotheads demanded 'energetic action' against the Jews,
the local Party functionaries were able to cool things down, 'avoid excesses',
and direct the matter 'into orderly channels'. The forty or so Jews in the
district were summoned by the District Leader and forced to sign a declaration
that they would depart from the area immediately.[129]

In Lower Franconia, on the other hand, where so many Jews still lived in the countryside, the pogrom split into a myriad of local actions in small towns and rural districts. The population in this area was to a far greater extent witness to the devastation and many experienced at first hand the merciless fate of the Jews. In Swabia, Lower Bavaria, and the Upper Palatinate the horrific scenes took place, outside Augsburg and Regensburg, mainly in small towns like Memmingen, Altenstadt, Amberg, Straubing, and Neumarkt in der Oberpfalz.[130] In Streicher-dominated Middle Franconia the pogrom was especially brutal. Provisional and incomplete figures listed 42 synagogues, 115 shops or businesses, and 594 residences destroyed.[131] The events in Streicher's own city of Nuremberg were as terrible as anywhere in Germany.[132] In contrast to Munich, where for a big city there was relatively little destruction but widescale arrests of male Jews, in Nuremberg — according to Jewish eye-witnesses — there were few arrests but hundreds of houses and dwellings were laid waste.[133] Four weeks after the pogrom, the Government President of Upper and Middle Franconia could register with satisfaction the fact that the towns of Dinkelsbühl, Eichstätt, Schwabach, Zirndorf, and the rural districts of Hersbruck, Neustadt an der Aisch, Nuremberg, Pegnitz, Rothenburg ob der Tauber, and Staffelstein were 'Jew-free'.[134]

Reports of the Government Presidents which spoke of people's 'disgust', 'indignation', and even 'sheer fury' at the news of vom Rath's murder were probably accurate enough.[135] Even stronger emotions were released, however, by the ensuing pogrom. A broad swell of disapproval, unmistakable despite the intimidation, found muted expression in the comments of reporters. Most people were too afraid to speak openly, but muttered invectives and words of disgust at the barbarity of the action and shame and horror at what had taken place could be observed in Munich as in other major German cities.[136] In a smaller town like Memmingen, where the organized destruction of the synagogue and accompanying outrages took place a day later than everywhere else in the Reich, both approving and disapproving voices could be heard from the assembled crowd, though most were careful to hold their tongues.[137] Mixed reactions — partly approval, partly indifference, partly silent sympathy for the Jews — could, it was claimed, be perceived among the inhabitants of Heilbrunn, near Bad Tölz, in Upper Bavaria.[138] The *Gendarmerie* officer in the Upper Palatinate district of Vilseck felt able to establish only a single type of reaction: 'The action carried out a short time ago against the Jews was here ignored and passed over.'[139] This may well have been a not untypical reaction in many districts where the pogrom hardly left a mark.

Goebbels's claim that the pogrom had been the 'spontaneous answer' of the German people to the murder of vom Rath was universally recognized as ludicrous. It was perfectly obvious that the whole affair had been directed and orchestrated by the Party — all the more so where the demolition had been carried out by SA squads brought in from outside.[140] Most 'non-organized' Germans knew nothing about the pogrom until confronted with the debris-laden streets the following morning. If there were no signs of spontaneity, willing helpers from the public were not lacking in some places, usually where radical anti-Semites had held leading positions in the local Party for years and had been able successfully to poison the atmosphere against the Jews.[141] By-standers could sometimes be prompted into joining in the work of destruction, or into anti-Jewish abuse which added to the evil climate and spurred on the demolition teams. While the Nuremberg synagogue burned, for instance, 'the hysterical voice of a woman' was heard from the crowd by one eye-witness (a non-Jew) crying: 'Sling the Jewish pack into the fire.'[142] A similar cry of 'throw them in the fire' was said to have come from among the assembled crowd in Kitzingen as the arrested Jews were being led past the still burning synagogue, and schoolchildren showered choruses of scorn and abuse on the unhappy internees all along the way to the prison house.[143] The youth of Memmingen amused themselves by making fun of the Jewish hats removed from the synagogue while groups of spectators spoke approvingly of the demolition of the building, remarking that it should have been carried out long ago.[144]

Some *Gendarmerie* reports went so far as to suggest that the population had for the most part regarded the 'retaliatory measures' against the Jews as wholly justified. Fanatical Party and Hitler Youth members in some Upper Franconian villages were even said to have regarded the 'action' as too mild.[145] In one Lower Franconian district, where people with a macabre curiosity went on sightseeing tours of the wreckage, the local police reported that the attacks on Jews and their property had been 'greeted with joy' by the majority of the population.[146] Some of these reports are barely credible as generalizations and were obviously written with a view to providing superiors with the story it was thought they wanted to hear. In so doing they were justifying too, the propaganda myth of the demonstrated unity of leadership and people in the anti-Jewish 'demonstrations'. What percentage of the population approved of the deplorable events is impossible to assess. Critical evaluation of the reports, however, hardly permits any doubt that few other than wild fanatics in the Party and its affiliations unreservedly welcomed the 'Jewish Action'. On the basis of an admittedly small and unrepresentative sample of Party members, Michael Müller-Claudius's subtly executed private survey of opinion suggested in fact that only about 5 per cent fully approved of the pogrom as against 63 per cent who displayed some form of disgust or anger and 32 per cent who were reserved or indifferent in their comments.[147] Bavarian reports support the view that the torrent of violence and destruction not only met with little sympathy, but was 'condemned deep into the ranks of the Party'.[148] According to a report from the Amberg district of the Upper Palatinate, 'not one person up to now has said that the Jews got what they deserved.'[149] Reports from Upper Bavaria indicate that criticism of the violence employed against the Jews was especially prevalent in Catholic circles and among the 'upper classes'.[150] Catholic peasants and the bourgeoisie were said to have regarded the show of violence as an affront to 'culture and decency', going too far even for those who were glad to see the Jews driven out of the country.[151] Even in Franconia voices were heard to the effect that 'the older Jews ought not to have been treated like that.'[152]

In Franconia too, as Jewish 'eye-witness reports' compiled soon after the event point out, it was in Catholic rural districts that the most vociferous condemnation of the barbarity was heard. The Catholic population of Lohr, a small town in Lower Franconia, was said to have been 'very angry about these atrocities'; one woman protested openly and was threatened with arrest.[153] Many Catholics in Gaukönigshofen made what was described as 'a true pilgrimage' to the burnt-out synagogue on the Sunday after the pogrom, making open show of their disgust. Peasants from the neighbouring villages boycotted a public house in Ochsenfurt when they heard that the son of the owner had taken part in the destruction in Gaukönigshofen.[154] In Höchberg, not far from Würzburg, the peasants protested in vain at the burning of the synagogue by a detachment of sixteen SA men who had been detailed to the village, expressed regret and disgust over what had happened, and viewed the sudden death of one of the participants six months later as a just punishment of God.[155] In Fischbach in Swabia, in the Augsburg area, even the mayor had taken a stance against the intended burning of the synagogue, declaring that 'we are no incendiarists', and was actually able to prevent the destruction taking place. Four days after 'Crystal Night' Jewish services were held there again.[156]

Though Catholic peasants were particularly prominent in their denunciation of the pogrom, critical comments came from members of all social classes, as the records of the Munich 'Special Court' show. A master cobbler from Ruhpolding was denounced by SA men for saying that the demolition of property amounted to robbery of the Jews by the Führer.[157] A salesman, once a Party and SA member, was accused of telling three soldiers in a Munich public house that burning the churches of the Jews was a wrongful act, and that in his view all men were equal.[158] A former *Freikorps* leader and high-ranking Munich police officer who had fought against the *Räterepublik* was also denounced for condemning the burning of the synagogues as a scandal.[159] A well-to-do lady from the Füssen area had her letter to a friend in America, in which she referred to the pogrom as a 'cultural disgrace' (*Kulturschande*) and reported widespread unhappiness about it, intercepted by the border police.[160] The impressions of a Munich Jew who lived through the pogrom confirm the feelings of disgust, apparent in all sections of society. One 'aryan lady of the best social class', previously completely unknown to him, declared herself ashamed to be a German, and 'one of the top Munich bankers' begged him to spread the word abroad 'that 90 per cent of the German people is opposed to these ill-deeds. It is only a small clique which has caused this disaster.'[161] Reports reaching the *Sopade* and other exiled left-wing groups were also unanimous about the sharp condemnation of the outrages by the great majority of the German people, and eye-witnesses recounted the unmistakable abhorrence and many expressions of sympathy for the Jews.[162] Though the exiled anti-Nazi groups were keen to illustrate a broad popular front against the regime, such comments concur wholly with those from all other sources.

Examples abound, both in the Jewish eye-witness accounts and in the *Sopade* reports, of expressions of sympathy, abhorrence, and shame coming in particular from members of the bourgeoisie.[163] Many who sympathized with much of what Nazism stood for obviously felt this was going too far. A feeling of 'cultural disgrace' and damage to the German image abroad, as in the examples given above, combined with anger at the senseless destruction of property and with humanitarian feelings. One anonymous letter, apparently from a conservative bourgeois Nazi sympathizer in Schweinfurt and addressed to Goebbels, bitterly attacked the spoliation, plunder, useless waste, and endangering of German farm property in the vicinity of the burning synagogues. The writer also pilloried, however, the gratuitous violence and inhumane treatment even of the elderly and infirm. Not least he was concerned about the damage to Germany's reputation as a civilized nation. His letter ended:

> One could weep, one must be ashamed to be a German, part of an aryan noble people (*Edelvolk*), a civilized nation guilty of such a cultural disgrace. Later generations will compare these atrocities with the times of the witch-trials. And nobody dares to say a word against them, though 85 per cent of the population is angry as never before. Poor Germany, wake up properly at last![164]

Other sources make equally clear that a strong motive for the condemnation of the pogrom in the eyes of many people was the futile destruction of property. According to some reports, people deplored such destruction in the light of the needs of the Four Year Plan and said it would have been better to impose a second milliard Reichmarks as a 'fine' on top of the milliard which had been 'legally' claimed as retribution for the damage 'caused' by the Jews.[165] Given raw material shortages and intense pressure to save and conserve, the wanton demolition and casual wastage — even to the extent of hurling foodstuffs onto the streets — met with a mixture of incomprehension and rage.[166] As one report put it: 'On the one hand we have to collect silver paper and empty toothpaste tubes, and on the other hand millions of marks' worth of damage is caused deliberately.'[167]

As this and other evidence shows, objections to the spoliation and plunder of 'Crystal Night' were wholly compatible with unreserved approval of the draconian but 'legal' form of 'punishment' which the State itself decreed in the immediate aftermath of the pogrom. The response to the 'legal' measures[168] of 1938 was as positive and uncritical as it had been to the Nuremberg Laws of 1935. The Government President of Swabia reported, for example, that the decrees of the government, especially the imposition of the 'expiation payment' and the measures to remove Jews from the economy were 'generally appreciated and — especially the economic measures — approved in principle by ever more national comrades.'[169] In contrast to the pogrom itself, the 'legal' measures against the Jews also found 'fullest understanding' in Lower Bavaria and the Upper Palatinate.[170] In Lower Franconia, where there was also general approval, it was said to be the 'expiation fine' which was particularly welcomed.[171] These generalizations of the Government Presidents find frequent confirmation in the reports of the lower authorities.

A widespread hostility to the Jews, uncritical approval of the anti-Semitic decrees of the government, but sharp condemnation of the pogrom because of its material destruction and the tasteless hooligan character of the 'action' perpetrated by 'gutter elements' characterized the reactions of considerable sections of the population. Even many anti-Semites, including Party members, found the pogrom itself distasteful while approving of the root cause of it and of its consequences.

The picture of responses to the 'Crystal Night' seems for the most part, therefore, a rather dismal one in which material self-interest and legal rectitude prevailed over humanitarian considerations. Yet to leave it there would be to ignore another, more appealing, side of the popular reaction to the pogrom: its rejection on grounds of Christian compassion and common humanity. Jewish eye-witness accounts abound with references to the kindness of 'aryan' and 'Christian' neighbours and are anxious to point out the overwhelming rejection of the pogrom by the vast majority of the population. Even the Government President of Lower Bavaria and the Upper Palatinate had to admit that the pogrom had 'unnecessarily' allowed 'sympathy for the Jews in town and countryside' to emerge.[172] Especially in Catholic country districts it was clear that the Nazi message of racial hatred had made only limited inroads. Numerous witnesses from Lower Franconia and the Catholic parts of Upper Franconia confirm that help and sympathy was afforded Jews by 'aryan' neighbours during and after the night of terror. In Prichsenstadt, for example, a farmer ordered a taxi and accompanied a Jewish lady in his village to Schweinfurt to warn her husband that he was being sought out for arrest. The farmer was denounced by the owner of the taxi and spent a fortnight in prison as a result. In Schweinfurt, 'Christian neighbours' brought the children of a Jewish family fresh milk and bedding. In Burgsinn Jews were given money, fresh clothing, bread, and other foodstuffs by local inhabitants. An 'aryan' in Unteraltertheim near Würzburg prevented the house of a Jewish neighbour from being destroyed by threatening the SA men with a revolver if they did not disappear. They left. Peasants in Nördlingen gave a Jewess, whose husband had been arrested, a sack of potatoes and asked whether she was otherwise well provided for. Even the Nazi leader in Asbach, near Bamberg, was said to have shown concern for the Jews, and in other instances Nazi mayors prevented destruction or offered assistance to Jews.[173] Jews who experienced the pogrom in Munich were lavish in their praise of the sympathetic response they encountered among non-Jewish people, as in the following comment by a Jewish emigrant written a few days later:

> The mood among the Christian population in Munich is wholly against the action. I encountered the most expressive sympathy and compassion from all sides. It had been generally presumed that the houses would be attacked on the Friday evening (11 November). Aryan people from the area, unknown to me, offered to accommodate my family for the night. Despite the ban on sales to Jews, grocers asked Jews whether they needed anything, bakers delivered bread irrespective of the ban etc. All Christians behaved impeccably.[174]

There were few occasions, if any, in the Third Reich which produced such a widespread wave of revulsion — much of it on moral grounds — as the 'Crystal Night' pogrom.[175] Even the SD had to admit in its general retrospective survey that from this point of view the 'actions against the Jews' had been less than successful: 'From a basic liberal attitude many believed they had openly to stand up for the Jews. The destruction of the synagogues was declared to be irresponsible. People stood up for the "poor repressed Jews".'[176] As this and much other evidence indicates, reactions to 'Crystal Night' in Bavaria were little different in essence from those registered all over Germany.[177]

The clumsy alienation of German popular opinion through the pogrom seems to have persuaded the Nazi leadership that such a tactic should never again be tried, and that anti-Jewish measures should take a more 'rational' course. Though, from the regime's point of view, the pogrom was successful in forcing the pace of a solution to the Jewish Question, the hostility which leading Nazis showed towards Goebbels, the instigator of the pogrom, may well have been influenced by the negative public response. Similarly, Hitler's announcement — against the pressure of the radicals — that there should be no public identification badge for Jews was possibly a veiled reflection of the negative reactions to anti-Jewish measures.[178] And a year later, following the attempt on Hitler's life in the Munich *Bürgerbräukeller* in November 1939, on the anniversary of the pogrom, Rudolf Hess specifically prohibited a repetition in order to prevent any unrest in the first critical months of the war.[179]

The influence of popular opinion extended no further. This was in great measure a reflection of the conditions of extreme terror and intimidation in which people lived, and which were of themselves sufficient to deter any *organized* pressure of opinion on the regime. Reports of arrests and recrimination for pro-Jewish comments, assistance to Jews, or criticism of Nazi actions abound in the sources.[180] Summarizing the impressions of their reporters, the *Sopade* admitted 'that however great the general indignation might be, the brutalities of the pogrom hordes had increased their intimidation and consolidated the notion in the population that all resistance was useless against the unrestrained National Socialist power.'[181] Moreover, without support *from above* popular opinion was bound to remain inchoate and inarticulate. The one source this could — and arguably ought — to have come from was the leadership of the Christian Churches. Apart from much success in orchestrating popular opposition in the 'Church struggle', the Churches came, in 1941, to lead a victory without parallel for public opinion in halting the 'euthanasia action'. It happened because the Churches made a public cause of concern their own. In the case of the Jews, the Churches took no such stance.

Despite the largely negative response to the pogrom, popular opinion on the Jewish Question remained in any case divided. As the evidence we have examined clearly suggests, the Nazis had been unable to instil an active hatred for the Jews into the bulk of the population — in Müller-Claudius's terminology, to transform the latent 'static hatred' into 'dynamic hatred'[182] — and to this extent had met with less than success in a key area of their ideology. On the other hand, the unceasing barrage of anti-Jewish propaganda had not been without effect. People's minds were increasingly poisoned against the Jews in at least an abstract way; the conviction was spreading that there *was* a Jewish Question.[183] In November 1938, as earlier, it was therefore the method rather than the aim of Nazi policy which most people were condemning. Just as the Nuremberg Laws of 1935 had been widely acclaimed in contrast to the condemnation of the primitive brutality of the 'individual actions', so now approval for the 'legal measures' was juxtaposed with wide condemnation of the brutality and destruction of the pogrom itself. 'Anti-Semitism — o.k., but not like that'[184] seems to sum up much of the mainstream response to 'Crystal Night', and to the chequered course of Nazi radical attempts to solve the Jewish Question before 1938. Despite the widespread rejection of the archaic 'pogrom anti-Semitism', there was, therefore, extensive acceptance of the 'rational anti-Semitism' whose victory was sealed by the public reactions to 'Crystal Night'.

Furthermore, dissent at the method of proceeding on the Jewish Question was also perfectly compatible with general approval of Hitler's leadership and of the main aims of German policy under Nazi rule. As one *Sopade* observer pointed out, the view continued to be expressed that the extremes of Jewish policy took place against Hitler's wishes. 'Hitler certainly wants the Jews to disappear from Germany, but he does not want them to be beaten to death and treated in such fashion': such comments could be frequently heard and, it had to be admitted, continued to carry weight.[185] Though this *Sopade* report came from Berlin, the detachment of Hitler from the misdeeds of his underlings was equally a prime feature of the Führer image in Bavaria as elsewhere.[186]

However negative the instant reactions to 'Crystal Night' were, the pogrom had no lasting impact on the formation of opinion. Reactions to events of major importance, whether of euphoria or of revulsion, gave way remarkably quickly to the sullen apathy and resigned acceptance which characterized the day-to-day existence of most Germans in the Third Reich. 'Daily routine again already' (*Schon wieder Alltag*), the heading of the December report of the *Sopade,* summed it up neatly.[187] The Jewish Question was at the forefront of popular opinion on very few occasions during the Nazi dictatorship. The most spectacular occasion was 'Crystal Night'. But everything points to the fact that this event receded within a few weeks into the dim background of people's consciousness.[188] It had not been something which concerned them directly, nor was it of continuing intensity, and it had been perpetrated on a tiny and basically unloved social minority. Increasingly from November 1938 the Jews were forced to emigrate or to retire wholly into isolation on the fringes of society. Either way, Germans saw less and less of Jews. The dehumanization and social isolation of Jews after the November pogrom could, therefore, only increase the extent of the indifference of the German people towards the fate of the Jews, an indifference which had been but momentarily disturbed by the atrocities of 'Crystal Night'.

Popular opinion on the Jewish Question formed a wide spectrum running from the paranoid Jew-baiters at the one extreme, undoubtedly a tiny minority; through a wide section of the population whose existent prejudices and latent anti-Semitism, influenced in varying degrees by the virulence of Nazi propaganda, accepted legal restrictions on Jews amounting to economic exclusion and social ostracism whilst rejecting the blatant and overt inhumanity of the Jew-baiters; and finally embraced another minority imbued with a deeply Christian or liberal-humanitarian moral sense, whose value-system provided the most effective barrier to the Nazi doctrine of race hatred.

In its attempt to infuse the German people with a dynamic, passionate hatred of the Jews, the Nazi propaganda machine was less than successful. Except on isolated occasions when the Jewish Question directly confronted them, most obviously following the 1938 progrom, Germans seldom had Jews on their mind. The constant barrage of propaganda failed to make the Jews the prime target of hatred for most Germans, simply because the issue seemed largely abstract, academic, and unrelated to their own problems. The result was, for the most part, widespread disinterest in the Jewish Question. Amid the widespread apathy and disinterest, however, the 'dynamic' hatred of the few, whose numbers included some of the leaders of the Third Reich and among them the Führer himself, could flourish. 'Dynamic' Jew-haters were certainly a small percentage of the population; but active friends of the Jews formed an even smaller proportion. Furthermore, even when opinion was widely antagonistic towards Nazi actions, as in November 1938, it was impossible to articulate it. No political party, interest group, trade union, or Church had made it its job before 1933 to combat openly the dangerous growth of anti-Semitism. After 1933 the task was incomparably more difficult — perhaps impossible. Divisions of opinion, including widespread latent anti-Semitism, were reflected in the Churches themselves. But the reluctance of the Church hierarchies, for whatever motives, to oppose the inhumanity towards the Jews in the 1930s at the same time that they were often vigorously and successfully combating Nazi anti-Church measures, did much to prevent any possibility of anti-Semitism becoming an issue.

Where the Nazis were most successful was in the depersonalization of the Jew. The more the Jew was forced out of social life, the more he seemed to fit the stereotypes of a propaganda which intensified, paradoxically, its campaign against 'Jewry' the fewer actual Jews there were in Germany itself. Depersonalization increased the already existent widespread indifference of German popular opinion and formed a vital stage between the archaic violence of the pogrom and the rationalized 'assembly-line' annihilation of the death-camps.

It would go too far to deny anti-Semitism any 'objective function' of diverting from acute socio-economic problems and especially of translating pseudo-revolutionary energy into apparently realizable goals which in turn could keep alive the utopian vision of a German-dominated 'New Order' in Europe. In this sense, perhaps, one can speak of anti-Semitism functioning as an integrating element. But this was mainly within the ranks of the Nazi Movement itself, above all within the SS. Anti-Semitism provided a common denominator, necessary in a movement which was so obviously a loose coalition of interests as the Nazi Party, and which after 1933 was devoid of any real active political role apart from indoctrination and social control. The energies galvanized within the Movement in the so-called 'years of struggle' could not simply be phased out from 1933, and were necessary to retain the dynamism of Nazism and prevent it from sagging into stagnation. This more or less aimless energy could be manipulated and channelled, as in 1935 and 1938, into attacks on the Jews, and the Jewish Question could function, too, in giving ideological purpose to the 'enforcement agency' of the regime — the SS-Gestapo-SD organization. Party activists needed activity: and anti-Semitism went a long way towards providing the SA and, in practical terms, otherwise useless sections of the Party with something to do, at the same time binding them propagandistically more closely to the apparent 'aims' of Führer and Movement.

In the light of the Bavarian evidence and that from other parts of Germany, however, it would be mistaken to translate this functionalist explanation to the relationship between the regime and the broad mass of the German people. There was certainly extensive manipulation of opinion, and Nazi propaganda could claim some success. But the ideological function of anti-Semitism with regard to the mass of the population consisted at most in strengthening the German identity-feeling and sense of national-consciousness by associating the Jews with Bolshevism and plutocracy and otherwise caricaturing the non-German character of Jewry. Popular support for National Socialism was based in ideological norms which had little directly to do with anti-Semitism and persecution of Jews, and which can be summed up most adequately by the sense of social, political, and moral order embodied in the term *Volksgemeinschaft* ('National Community'), ensured by a strong state which would suppress conflict to guarantee strength through unity.[189] While Jews and other minority groups, it is true, found no place in the Nazi concept of this 'national community', their exclusion was hardly a leading feature of the hopes and aspirations of the millions who, in the chaos of the Depression, were prepared to entrust the building of this new Germany to Hitler.

The permanent radicalization of the anti-Jewish policies of the regime can hardly be said, on the evidence we have considered, to have been the product of, or to have corresponded to, the strong demands of popular opinion. It led in 1935 and 1938 to a drop in prestige for the Party, which might even have had repercussions for Hitler's own nimbus had he been seen to have supported and sided with the radicals. The radicalization of the negative dynamism, which formed the essential driving-force of the Nazi Party, found remarkably little echo in the mass of the population. Popular opinion, largely indifferent and infused with a latent anti-Jewish feeling further bolstered by propaganda, provided the climate within which spiralling Nazi aggression towards Jews could take place unchallenged. But it did not provoke the radicalization in the first place. The road to Auschwitz was built by hate, but paved with indifference.

Notes

BA	*Bezirksamt (svorstand)* ([Head of]) District Office, the unit of local government administration, from 1939 *Landrat [samt]*)
BAK	Bundesarchiv Koblenz
Bayern I–IV	*Bayern in der NS-Zeit. Soziale Lage und politisches Verhalten der Bevölkerung im Spiegel vertraulicher Berichte,* ed. M. Broszat, E. Fröhlich and F. Wiesemann, Munich/Vienna, 1977; *Bayern in der NS-Zeit. Herrschaft und Gesellschaft im Konflikt,* vols. ii–iv, ed. M. Broszat, E. Fröhlich, and (for vols. iii–iv) A. Grossman, Munich/Vienna, 1979–81
BPP	*Bayerische Politische Polizei* (Bavarian Political Police, after 1936 Gestapo)
BVP	*Bayerische Volkspartei* (Bavarian People's Party)
DBS	*Deutschland-Berichte der Sopade (Germany Reports of the Sopade)*
GBF	*Gendarmerie-Bezirksführer* (head of district police)
GHS	*Gendarmerie-Hauptstation* (district main police station)
GL	*Gauleitung*
GS	*Gendarmerie-Station* (local police station, name changed to GP in 1939)
GStA	Bayerisches Hauptstaatsarchiv, Abteilung II, Geheimes Staatsarchiv, Munich
HJ	*Hitlerjugend* (Hitler Youth)
HStA	Bayerisches Hauptstaatsarchiv, Abteilung I, Allgemeines Staatsarchiv, Munich
KL	*Kreisleiter* (Nazi Party District Leader)
KLB	*Die kirchliche Lage in Bayern nach den Regierungspräsidentenberichten 1933–1943,* ed. H. Witetschek and (vol. iv) W. Ziegler: vol. i, *Regierungsbezirk Oberbayern,* Mainz, 1966; vol. ii, *Regierungsbezirk Ober- und Mittelfranken,* Mainz, 1967; vol. iii, *Regierungsbezirk Schwaben,* Mainz, 1971; vol. iv, *Regierungsbezirk Niederbayern und der Oberpfalz,* Mainz, 1973.
KPD	*Kommunistische Partei Deutschlands* (German Communist Party)
KW	*Kreiswaltung* (district administrative unit of NSLB)
LB	*Lagebericht* (situation report)
LRA	*Landratsamt* (office of government district administration, before 1939 *Bezirksamt*)

MF	Mittelfranken (Middle Franconia)
NB	Niederbayern (Lower Bavaria)
NSDAP	*Nationalsozialistische Deutsche Arbeiterpartei* (Nazi Party)
NSLB	*Nationalsozialistischer Lehrerbund* (Nazi Teachers' Association)
OB	Oberbayern (Upper Bavaria)
OF	Oberfranken (Upper Franconia)
OP	Oberpfalz (Upper Palatinate)
Pd	*Polizeidirektion* (city police administration)
RP	*Regierungspräsident* (Government President, head of State regional administration, controlling a governmental region [*Regierungsbezirk*])
S	Schwaben (Swabia)
SA	*Sturmabteilung* (Nazi Storm Troop, paramilitary organization)
SD	*Sicherheitsdienst* (Security Service)
SGM	*Sondergericht München* (Munich 'Special Court' dealing mainly with political offences)
SPD	*Sozialdemokratische Partei Deutschlands* (German Social Democratic Party)
StA	Staatsarchiv
StAA	Staatsarchiv Amberg
StAB	Staatsarchiv Bamberg
StAM	Staatsarchiv München
StAN	Staatsarchiv Nürnberg
StAW	Staatsarchiv Würzburg
UF	Unterfranken (Lower Franconia)
VfZ	*Vierteljahrshefte für Zeitgeschichte*
WL	Wiener Library, London (since removed to Tel Aviv, leaving only a microfilm library in London)
ZdBSL	*Zeitschrift des Bayerischen Statistischen Landesamts*

1. The only studies to date which have concerned themselves directly with the problem are: M. G. Steinert, *Hitlers Krieg und die Deutschen,* Dusseldorf, 1970, pp. 236–63; L. D. Stokes, 'The German People and the Destruction of the European Jews', *Central European History,* vi (1973), 167–91; and O. D. Kulka, ' "Public Opinion" in National Socialist Germany and the "Jewish Question" ', *Zion,* xl (1975), 186–290 (in Hebrew, documents in German, and with an English summary). There is now also the dissertation by S. A. Gordon, 'German Opposition to Nazi Anti-Semitic Measures between 1933 and 1945, with Particular Reference to the Rhine-Ruhr Area', State University New York/Buffalo, D. Phil. thesis, 1979. The present chapter is a modified and shortened version of my contribution to *Bayern II,* pp. 281–348. I have attempted to survey also the non-Bavarian evidence in a recent essay, 'The Persecution of the Jews and German Popular Opinion in the Third Reich', *Leo Baeck Institute Year Book,* xxvi (1981), 261–89.

2. L. Dawidowicz, *The War against the Jews 1933–45,* Harmondsworth, 1977, esp. pp. 77, 209–11.

3. K. Pätzold, *Faschismus, Rassenwahn, Judenverfolgung,* Berlin, 1975, pp. 28–32.

4. M. Broszat, 'Soziale Motivation und Führer-Bindung des Nationalsozialismus', *VfZ,* xviii (1970), 392–409, esp. pp. 400 ff.

5. S. Schwarz, *Die Juden in Bayern im Wandel der Zeiten,* Munich, 1963, pp. 57 ff.; B. Z. Ophir and F. Wiesemann, *Die jüdischen Gemeinden in Bayern 1918–1945. Geschichte und Zerstörung,* Munich, 1979, p. 13; *Bayern I,* p. 429.

6. J. Toury, *Soziale und politische Geschichte der Juden in Deutschland 1847–1871,* Düsseldorf, 1977, pp. 12 ff.; B. Z. Ophir and F. Wiesemann, *Die jüdischen Gemeinden in Bayern 1918–1945. Geschichte und Zerstörung,* Munich, 1979, p. 14. *Bayern I,* p. 428.

7. Ophir, *Die jüd. Gemeinden,* p. 14.

8. The census of 16 June 1933 comprised only those of Jewish faith (*Glaubensjuden*). The number of *Glaubensjuden* in Munich was given as 9,005, though police registration of Jews on 1 Feb. 1933 amounted to a total of 10,737, a discrepancy of 19.23 per cent. The number of Jews leaving Munich between February and June 1933 cannot, however, be established. (Police data in HStA, MInn 73725. Details for areas outside Munich have not survived.)

9. Jewish settlement in small towns and in the countryside was particularly a feature of south-western Germany. Cf. 'Die Juden im Deutschen Reich 1816 bis 1933', *Wirtschaft und Statistik,* xv (1935), 150.

10. Ibid., p. 148; 'Die Glaubensjuden in Bayern auf Grund der Volks- und Berufszählung vom 16. Juni 1933', *ZdBSL,* lxx (1938), 451 ff.

11. From data in B. Z. Ophir, *Pinkas Hakehillot. Encyclopedia of Jewish Communities from their Foundation till after the Holocaust (Germany-Bavaria),* Jerusalem, 1972 (in Hebrew with English introduction), p. XIV.

12. 'Die Glaubensjuden in Bayern', p. 451.

13. Expressing the sparseness of the Jewish population in another way, there was on average one non-Jewish citizen of Bavaria for every 0.99 square kilometre, one Jew for every 181.21 square kilometres — Calculated from data in ibid., pp. 447, 451 and GStA, Reichsstatthalter 578.

14. Cf. E. S. Sterling, *Judenhaß. Die Anfänge des politischen Antisemitismus in Deutschland (1815–1850),* Frankfurt/Main, 1969, pp. 12, 55–62, 171–4 and *passim.* The notorious Deggendorf popular celebrations of the medieval burning of the town's Jews by pious Catholic citizens as revenge for the alleged defiling of the consecrated host were only abolished in 1969 — Cf. G. Lewy, *The Catholic Church and Nazi Germany,* London, 1964, pp. 272–3; Ophir, *Die jüd. Gemeinden,* p. 66. Streicher, who — perhaps not just coincidentally — grew up as a schoolboy in Deggendorf, exploited such sentiments in the *Stürmer.* For the disgusting 'ritual murder' issue, cf. ibid., p. 22.

15. Sterling, pp. 159–62.

16. See the comprehensive collection of Hitler's early speeches and writings edited by E. Jäckel, *Hitler. Sämtliche Aufzeichnungen, 1905–1924,* Stuttgart, 1980.

17. Dawidowicz, pp. 210–11.

18. H. Rauschning, *Hitler Speaks,* London, 1939, pp. 233–4.

19. Cit. in A. Paucker, *Der jüdische Abwehrkampf gegen Antisemitismus und Nationalsozialismus in den letzten Jahren der Weimarer Republik,* 2nd edn., Hamburg, 1969, pp. 194–5.

20. P. Merkl, *Political Violence under the Swastika. 581 Early Nazis,* Princeton, 1975, pp. 33, 446 ff., and *passim.*

21. W. S. Allen, *The Nazi Seizure of Power. The Experience of a Single German Town,*

Chicago, 1965, p. 77. Similar conclusions about the relative lack of importance of anti-Semitism in bringing new converts to Nazism were reached in the excellent study by D. L. Niewyk, *The Jews in Weimar Germany,* Manchester, 1980, pp. 79–81. Cf. now also Gordon, ch. 3, for a thorough survey of the evidence.

22. Cf. M. Müller-Claudius, *Der Antisemitismus und das deutsche Verhängnis,* Frankfurt/Main, 1948, pp. 76–9, 119, 157 for the equivalent formulation '*statischer Haß — dynamischer Haß*'.

23. Cf. Pätzold, pp. 77–9; K. A. Schleunes, *The Twisted Road to Auschwitz. Nazi Policy towards German Jews 1933–1939,* Chicago, 1970, pp. 88–9; H. Krausnick, 'The Persecution of the Jews', in H. Krausnick *et al., Anatomy of the SS State,* London, 1968, p. 26; and specifically for Bavaria, *Bayern I,* pp. 433 ff.; P. Hanke, *Zur Geschichte der Juden in München zwischen 1933 und 1945,* Munich, 1967, pp. 83–6.

24. Special sections on the Jews were first included in the monthly reports of 11 June 1935 (Upper Bavaria), 6 Nov. 1935 (Swabia), and 8 June 1938 (Lower Bavaria and the Upper Palatinate): GStA, MA 106670, MA 106682, MA 106673.

25. StAM, LRA 47140, BA Bad Aibling, 3 Oct. 1935; cf. also the reports of 6 June, 6 July, 5 Aug., and 2 Nov. 1935 in which it was stated that the Jewish Question was 'not acute' in the district and played 'no role' at all.

26. GStA, MA 106670, RPvOB, 11 Nov. 1935.

27. For a good example of a planned disturbance at the abattoir in Regensburg in 1936, where the Gestapo established that the 'indignation' of the 'aryan' dealers about the presence of Jews had been 'obviously arranged and prepared accordingly in advance' by dealers from Nuremberg without any locals taking part at all, cf. GStA, MA 106411, fols. 84–7.

28. Cf. *Bayern I,* pp. 442 ff.; Pätzold, pp. 216–21; GStA, MA 106411, fols. 361, 373, 382 for Wagner's press notice about 'terror groups'. Reports and investigations about the affair are contained in: GStA, MA 105618, MA 106411, MA 106685 (Pd München, 26 May 1935), Reichsstatthalter 447. For Wagner's direct implication in initiating the trouble, cf. Berlin Document Center, Personal File of SS-Oberf. Frhr. Hermann von Schade, betr. Adolf Wagner, minutes of a meeting in Munich which took place on 25 Jan. 1936.

29. GStA, MA 106411, fol. 394.

30. KLB, i. 68–71, 73. For similar sentiments, cf. StAM, LRA 76887, GS Hohenlinden, 31 May 1935; GS Zorneding, 31 May 1935; LRA 61613, BA Garmisch, 4 June 1935; GS Oberammergau, 31 May 1935; KLB, iii. 61.

31. Cf. R. Hambrecht, *Der Aufstieg der NSDAP in Mittel- und Oberfranken* (1925–1933), Nuremberg, 1976, pp. 5 ff., 249 ff. and *passim;* G. Pridham, *Hitler's Rise to Power: the Nazi Movement in Bavaria, 1923–1933,* London, 1973, pp. 237, 244; Ophir, *Pinkas,* p. X.

32. Cf. Hambrecht, pp. 252–4; Pridham, pp. 242–4; Stadtarchiv Coburg, A7870, A8521.

33. The following account is based upon the extensive description of the events in HStA, MInn 73708 and the trial of Kurt Bär in GStA, MA 106410. Cf. also E. N. Peterson, *The Limits of Hitler's Power,* Princeton, 1969, pp. 256–9.

34. HStA, MInn 73708, fol. 15; GStA, MA 106410, fols. 100 f.

35. HStA, MInn 73708, fols. 46 f. Cf. also Peterson, p. 257.

36. Bär and another eighteen ringleaders, most if not all SA men, were given prison sentences of between three and ten months. The sentences of all except Bär (who received ten months) were quashed on appeal. In mid-July, Bär — obviously still at large — returned to the inn where he had started the original outrages and shot the publican and his son, killing one and badly wounding the other. Bär was sentenced to life imprisonment, but apparently put on probation, and reportedly died in a Russian prison camp — GStA, MA 106410, trial of Bär *et al.;* Ophir, *Die jüd. Gemeinden,* p. 190; Peterson, p. 259.

37. GStA, MA 106410, fol. 210. Another estimate, that of SA-*Obersturmbannführer* Karl Bär, made in the late evening towards the end of the pogrom, put the number at 700–800 persons — HStA, MInn 73708, fol. 18.

38. HStA, MInn 73708, fols. 22 f.

39. StAN, 212/13/II, 654, BA Neustadt an der Aisch, 2 May 1934.

40. StAN, 212/8/V, 4266, interrogation of Max Strauß, 16 Dec. 1933.

41. GStA, MA 106411, fols. 153 f., GHS Gunzenhausen, 28 Mar. 1936.

42. Cf. U. D. Adam, *Judenpolitik im Dritten Reich,* Düsseldorf, 1972, pp. 114–31.

43. *Bayern I,* p. 453, n. 17; Ophir, *Pinkas,* pp. XVIII f.

44. GStA, MA 106411, fol. 216.

45. For the chaotic immediate background to the promulgation of the Nuremberg Laws, see Schleunes, pp. 120–5; Peterson, pp. 135–40.

46. GStA, MA 106670, RPvOB, 11 June 1935.

47. For varying reactions in different parts of the Reich, cf. Kershaw 'Persecution', pp. 272–3; Kulka, p. XLIII.

48. GStA, MA 106770, RPvOB, 9 Oct. 1935; MA 106672, RPvNB/OP, 8 Oct. 1935; MA 106677, RPvOF/MF, 10 Oct. 1935; MA 106680, RPvUF, 8 Oct. 1935; MA 106682, RPvS, 7 Oct. 1935; StAW, LRA Bad Neustadt 125/3, BA Bad Neustadt, 29 Sept. 1935.

49. StAW, LRA Bad Neustadt 125/4, BA Bad Neustadt, 1 Dec. 1936.

50. The votes had been mainly divided among the BVP (46.7 per cent in March 1933), SPD (20 per cent), and KPD (7.2 per cent). The 25.2 per cent which the NSDAP gained in the March 1933 election was below the average for Lower Franconia — Data in M. Hagmann, *Der Weg ins Verhängnis,* Munich, 1978, pp. 18 f., 26.

51. E.g., StAW, LRA Alzenau Bd. 5, BA Alzenau, 26 Oct. 1934.

52. StAW, GL Mainfranken XII/1, BA Alzenau, 18 Oct. 1935.

53. Ibid., GS Geiselbach, 2 Oct., GS Schöllkrippen, 2 Oct., GHS Alzenau, 7 Oct. 1935.

54. StAB, K8/III/18472, BA Ebermannstadt, 29 Dec. 1936. Cf. also K8/IV/1476.

55. E.g., StAM, LRA 76887, Bgm. Egmating, 31 Aug. 1935, GS Egmating, 31 Aug. 1935; StAW, GL Mainfranken II/41, KL Würzburg, 20 July 1936; StAN, 212/8/V,4241, GS Heidenheim, 15 Nov. 1934.

56. Cf. e.g., StAN, 212/17/III,8444, GBF Schwabach, 2 Mar. 1936, which mentions expressions of regret because the absence of Jewish tobacco dealers meant lack of competition and low prices. For the exclusion of Jewish dealers in Middle Franconia, see Ophir, *Pinkas,* pp. XXI f., and for the whole question as it affected Bavaria, most recently, F. Wiesemann, 'Juden auf dem Lande: die wirtschaftliche Ausgrenzung der jüdischen Viehhändler in Bayern', in D. Peukert and J. Reulecke (eds.), *Die Reihen fast geschlossen. Beiträge zur Geschichte des Alltags unterm Nationalsozialismus,* Wuppertal, 1981, pp. 381–96.

57. StAW, GL Mainfranken XII/6, Bgm. Dittlofsroda, 19 June 1937; cf. also in the same file Bgm. Schwärzelbach, 18 June 1937; and the commentary of the Government President, GStA, MA 106680, RPvUF, 8 Feb. 1937.

58. GStA, MA 106689, Gestapo München, 1 June 1937, p. 54; MA 106690, Gestapo München, 1 Aug. 1937, pp. 43 f.

59. GStA, MA 106690, Gestapo München, 1 Sept. 1937, p. 40.

60. Cf. Ophir, *Pinkas*, pp. XXII f.

61. StAW, LRA Bad Neustadt 125/5, GS Bischofsheim, 28 Jan. 1938.

62. 'How popular was Streicher?' (no author), *Wiener Library Bulletin*, v–vi (1957), 48.

63. GStA, MA 106410, fol. 91; the Reich Minister of Economics had already in July 1934 sought the banning of notices 'in the interests of preventing further unrest in the economy' (ibid., fol. 28), but without much effect in practice.

64. GStA, MA 106670, RPvOB, 11 June 1935.

65. StAM, LRA 76887, GS Glonn, 30 June 1935; LRA 58130, GS Höhenkirchen, 5 Jan. 1936; LRA 72055, GS Hohenwart, 3 June 1935, and HJ-Gefolgschaft to KL-Schrobenhausen, 27 May 1935.

66. GStA, MA 106411, fols. 103 f.; MA 106689, Gestapo München, 1 Jan. 1937, pp. 54 f.

67. GStA, MA 106697, Pd München, LB, 5 Feb. 1936.

68. Cf. e.g., the *Sopade*'s reports on continued trading in Jewish shops, DBS, 21 Sept. 1935, A29–37, 16 Oct. 1935, pp. 21–5. This and other evidence is summarized in Kershaw, 'Persecution', pp. 266–7.

69. GStA, MA 106682, RPvS, 7 Dec. 1935; cf. Ophir, *Die jüd. Gemeinden*, p. 472.

70. E.g., GStA, MA 106411, fols. 122–39 for the case of an 'aryan' owner of a sausage grillery in Nuremberg who was driven to ruin by his trade rivals under the cover of the anti-Semitic campaign, since his wife was Jewish. Certificates from the Reich Ministry of the Economy confirming the 'aryan' status of his business were of no help.

71. GStA, MA 106689, Gestapo München, 1 July 1937, pp. 53 f.

72. GStA, MA 106690, Gestapo München, 1 Aug. 1937, pp. 42 f.

73. Cf. Lewy, pp. 268–74.

74. M. Faulhaber, *Judentum, Christentum, Germanentum*, Munich [1934], p. 116; cf. L. Volk, 'Kardinal Faulhabers Stellung zur Weimarer Republik und zum NS-Staat', *Stimmen der Zeit*, clxxvii (1966), pp. 183 ff., and Lewy, pp. 275–76.

75. Cf. J. S. Conway, *The Nazi Persecution of the Churches, 1933–45*, London, 1968, pp. 10–12, 32, 339–46, 353–7; see also I. Arndt, 'Machtübernahme und Judenboykott in der Sicht evangelischer Sonntagsblätter', in W. Benz *et al.* (eds.), *Miscellanea. Festschrift für Helmut Krausnick*, Stuttgart, 1980, pp. 15–31.

76. Lewy, p. 274.

77. E.g., ibid., ch. 10; Conway, *passim;* and, most recently, B. van Schewick, 'Katholische Kirche und nationalsozialistische Rassenpolitik', in K. Gotto and K. Repgen (eds.), *Kirche, Katholiken und Nationalsozialismus*, Mainz, 1980, pp. 83–100.

78. KLB, ii. 174.

79. Ibid., p. 317.

80. Ibid., p. 314.

81. KLB, i. 175 ff.

82. KLB, ii. 90.

83. Ibid., pp. 195, 227, 231; KLB, iii. 155.

84. KLB, ii. 58.

85. Ibid., pp. 73, 104–5; KLB, iii. 28.

86. KLB, ii. 76.

87. Ibid., p. 237.

88. Ibid., p. 218.

89. Ibid., p. 274.

90. StAW, LRA Bad Neustadt 125/2, GSH Bad Neustadt, 24 Oct. 1934, BA Bad Neustadt, 27 Oct. 1934.

91. KLB, ii. 80.

92. Ibid., p. 76.

93. Cf. Peterson, pp. 309–12.

94. KLB, ii. 146.

95. StAN, Pol.-Dir. Nürnberg-Fürth 357, BPP, 1 Oct. 1935, pp. 21 f. For Steinbauer, cf. K. Tenfelde, 'Proletarische Provinz. Radikalisierung und Widerstand in Penzberg/ Oberbayern 1900 bis 1945', in *Bayern IV*, pp. 348–56.

96. KLB, ii. 33, 117, 147, 390.

97. Ibid., p. 353.

98. KLB, iv. 276.

99. KLB, ii. 300.

100. Ibid., p. 309 and cf. also p. 301.

101. KLB, iv. 224.

102. Ibid., p. 219; StAM, SGM 4731, GS Tann, 1 Dec. 1938. According to GS Tann's record of the interrogation of 2 Jan. 1939, the priest nevertheless defended himself with anti-Semitic arguments. He claimed the schoolboy had misunderstood him, that he had meant the German people was punishing all the Jews for the crime of one person because they did not know 'how many are behind it'.

103. A. Müller, *Geschichte der Juden in Nürnberg 1146–1945,* Nuremberg, 1968, p. 245.

104. Cf. StA Ludwigsburg, K110 Nr. 44, report of SD-*Abschnitt* Stuttgart, 1 Feb. 1939 for the rejection of the pogrom by the Protestant and Catholic clergy of Württemberg. There are no similar SD reports of this date surviving for Bavaria.

105. KLB, i. 301.

106. Comments of the Lower Franconian clergy on the Jewish Question are far less plentiful than those of priests and pastors in Upper and Middle Franconia. This is probably in the main reflection of the less detailed nature of the reports of the Government President of Lower Franconia.

107. An indication of this was the decision of the Fulda Bishops' Conference in summer 1938, faced with alternative draft pastoral letters, the one refuting racial ideology, the other condemning 'the struggle against Church and Christianity', to choose the latter. 'Obviously the majority of the bishops regarded the threat to Christianity as so great, in the summer of 1938, that they preferred a clear word on this issue to a public condemnation of racism' — Van Schewick, pp. 90–1.

108. KLB, ii. 218.

109. Cf. the comments of Helmut Kern, KLB, iii. 28.

110. For details and for the course of the pogrom, cf. among other works, L. Kochan, *Pogrom. 10 November 1938,* London, 1957, and R. Thalmann and E. Feinermann, *Crystal Night: 9–10 November 1938,* London, 1974.

111. Cf. Adam, pp. 172 ff.; Schleunes, pp. 133 ff.

112. Cf. Ophir, *Pinkas,* p. XXVII, note.

113. WL, B155 (without date, but from content written in November 1938 or very shortly afterwards).

114. StAW, LRA Alzenau Bd. 5/2, BA Alzenau, 31 Oct. 1938.

115. Ophir, *Pinkas,* p. XXVI; Müller, pp. 236–9; Hanke, pp. 204 ff.

116. WL, PIIe/765, pp. 29, 62 f.

117. WL, 'Der 10. November 1938' (typescript of collected short reports of persecuted and émigré Jews, compiled in 1939 and 1940 by S. Brückheimer), pp. 29 f. The volume contains short descriptions of the pogrom events in seventy-two Bavarian localities, mainly in Lower Franconia.

118. GStA, MA 106681, RPvUF, 9 Apr. 1938, 10 Oct. 1938; MA 106673, RPvNB/OP, 8 Aug. 1938, 7 Oct. 1938, 7 Nov. 1938; MA 106678, RPvOF/MF, 7 Oct., 7 Nov. 1938; MA 106683, RPvS, 6 Aug., 7 Nov. 1938.

119. For the Reich figure, cf. BAK, R58/1094, SD-Jahresbericht für 1938, p. 35.

120. From data in HStA, MInn 73725, MInn 73726.

121. See Thalmann and Feinermann, pp. 45 ff; H. Heiber, 'Der Fall Grünspan', VfZ, v (1957), 139.

122. See Thalmann and Feinermann, pp. 167 ff.; Kochan, pp. 76 ff. Following decrees of 12 Nov. 1938 the Jews were also burdened with payment of one milliard RM as 'atonement' and with the costs of the damage caused by the pogrom. They were also completely ousted from the German economy. Cf. H. Genschel, *Die Verdrängung der Juden aus der Wirtschaft im Dritten Reich,* Göttingen, 1966, pp. 186 ff.

123. BAK, R58/1094, SD-Jahresbericht für 1938, pp. 25–34.

124. The number of Jews resident in Bavaria (excluding the Palatinate) was given as 14,684 in the 1939 census, i.e. 59.7 per cent of the number of Jews (24,580) in Bavaria on 1 Oct. 1938. Cf. Ophir, *Die jüd. Gemeinden,* p. 24; HStA, MInn 73726.

125. Cf. BAK, Zsg.102/13, fol. 19 for Goebbels's press directive. There is a translation in *Documents on Nazism,* ed. J. Noakes and G. Pridham, London, 1974, pp. 335–6. The newspapers were allowed to state 'that here and there windows had been broken and that synagogues had gone up in flames' but there were to be no front-page headlines, no pictures, and no collective reports from the Reich.

126. For Munich, see Hanke, p. 218; for Nuremberg, cf. F. Nadler, *Eine Stadt im Schatten Streichers,* Nuremberg, 1969, pp. 10 f.

127. This was especially the case in Lower Franconia, where on the eve of the pogrom Jews were still resident in every administrative district, as opposed to the other regions where large tracts were already being recorded as 'free of Jews'–HStA, MInn 73726.

128. GStA, MA 106671, RPvOB, 10 Dec. 1938.

129. StAM, LRA 61616, BA Garmisch, 10 Nov. 1938. The few Jews still resident in the Berchtesgaden district were similarly ordered to leave the area within an hour— StAM, LRA 29655, BA Berchtesgaden, 5 Dec. 1938. Cf. also E. R. Behrend-Rosenfeld,

Ich stand nicht allein. Erlebnisse einer Jüdin in Deutschland 1933–1944, Hamburg, 1949, p. 69.

130. GStA, MA 106683, RPvS, 7 Dec. 1938; MA 106673, RPvNB/OP, 8 Dec. 1938; D. Linn, *Das Schicksal der jüdischen Bevölkerung in Memmingen von 1933–1945*, Stuttgart, 1968, pp. 41–7.

131. GStA, MA 106678, RPvOF/MF, 8 Dec. 1938.

132. WL, PIIe/765, B. Kolb, 'Juden in Nürnberg' (typescript), pp. 22 ff., 51 ff.; Müller, pp. 240–5 (largely based on Kolb); Nadler, pp. 11 ff.

133. WL, B28, 15 Nov. 1938; B65, 22 Nov. 1938; cf. also B74 and PIId/37 for further descriptions of events in Nuremberg. For Wagner's provisional estimates of damage in Munich, see GStA, Reichsstatthalter 823 and MA 106412, fos. 3–6.

134. GStA, MA 106678, RPvOF/MF, 8 Dec. 1938. Four of these districts had no resident Jews in the weeks preceding the pogrom — HStA, MInn 73726.

135. GStA, MA 106671, RPvOB, 10 Dec. 1938; MA 106673, RPvNB/OP, 8 Dec. 1938; MA 106683, RPvS, 7 Dec. 1938; MA 106678, RPvOF/MF, 8 Dec. 1938; MA 106681, RPvUF, 9 Dec. 1938.

136. Behrend-Rosenfeld, p. 72; cf. also, R. Andreas-Friedrich, *Der Schattenmann*, Berlin, 1947, pp. 28 ff. for reactions in Berlin, and *Docs, on Nazism*, pp. 472–4 for Leipzig.

137. Linn, pp. 43 ff.

138. StAM, LRA 134059, GS Heilbrunn, 26 Nov. 1938.

139. StAA, BA Amberg 2399, GS Vilseck, 23 Nov. 1938. Many *Gendarmerie* reports from rural areas did not mention the pogrom at all.

140. Linn, pp. 42 f.; StAW, LRA Bad Neustadt 125/4, BA Bad Neustadt, 28 Nov. 1938. The Government President of Upper Bavaria reported that 'the protest action was widely regarded as organized' — GStA, MA 106671, RPvOB, 10 Dec. 1938. That the whole affair had been seen to be directed and orchestrated by the Party was recognized even by the Nazi Party's Supreme Court in its investigations of murders committed during the pogrom — Cf. H. Graml, *Der 9, November 1938. 'Reichskristallnacht'*, Bonn, 1953, p. 16.

141. Graml, *Der 9. Nov.*, pp. 7–14.

142. Nadler, p. 13, eye-witness report of the Nuremberg journalist Otto Fischer.

143. WL, 'Der 10. November', p. 14.

144. Linn, p. 42.

145. StAB, K8/III/18473, GS Muggendorf, 26 Nov. 1938; GS Waischenfeld, 25 Nov. 1938.

146. StAW, LRA Bad Neustadt 125/5, GS Sandberg, 28 Nov. 1938.

147. Müller-Claudius, pp. 162 ff.

148. GStA, MA 106673, RPvNB/OP, 8 Dec. 1938.

149. StAA, BA Amberg 2399, GS Freihung, 23 Nov. 1938.

150. GStA, MA 106671, RPvOB, 10 Dec. 1938; StAM, LRA 29654, GS Reichenhall, 30 Nov. 1938; GS Markt Schellenberg, 30 Nov. 1938; LRA 29655, BA Berchtesgaden, 5 Dec. 1938.

151. StAM, NSDAP 983, KW Traunstein, Abschn. Haslach, 19 Nov. 1938; Abschn. Marquartstein, 19 Nov., 13 Dec. 1938; LRA 61616, GS Wallgau, 26 Nov. 1938; LRA 113813, GS Feilnbach, 17 Nov. 1938; LRA 47140, GS Bad Aibling, 20 Nov. 1938.

152. StAB, K8/III/18473, GS Heiligenstadt, 25 Nov. 1938.

153. WL, 'Der 10. November', p. 12; cf. ibid., pp. 6, 33 for Schweinfurt and Bamberg.

154. Ibid., pp. 18 f.

155. Ibid., p. 26.

156. Ibid., p. 38.

157. StAM, SGM 4656.

158. Ibid., 4700.

159. Ibid., 4604.

160. Ibid., 4655.

161. WL, B66, eye-witness account of Arthur Berg of Munich, recorded in Amsterdam, 22 Nov. 1938.

162. DBA, 10 Dec. 1938, pp. A44 ff.; *Deutsche Mitteilungen*, 19 Nov., 22 Nov. 1938, 7 Jan., 25 Feb. 1939 (copies in WL). The newly published article by W. S. Allen, 'Die deutsche Öffentlichkeit und die "Reichskristallnacht" — Konflikte zwischen Werthierarchie und Propaganda im Dritten Reich', in Peukert/Reulecke (eds.), *Die Reihen fast geschlossen*, pp. 397–411, makes much use of the *Sopade* material.

163. Cf. Kershaw, 'Persecution', pp. 278–9.

164. GStA, Reichsstatthalter 823.

165. E.g., StAW, LRA Alzenau Bd.5/2, GS Alzenau, 28 Nov. 1938.

166. StAW, LRA Bad Neustadt 125/4, BA Bad Neustadt, 28 Nov. 1938; LRA Bad Neustadt 125/5, GS Bad Neustadt, 28 Nov. 1938; GS Oberelsbach, 28 Nov. 1938; GS Sandberg, 28 Nov. 1938; StAB, K8/III/18473, GS Waischenfeld, 25 Nov. 1938; BA Ebermannstadt, 2 Dec. 1938; GStA, MA 106681, RPvUF, 9 Dec. 1938; MA 106673, RPvNB/OP, 8 Dec. 1938; MA 106671, RPvOB, 10 Dec. 1938.

167. StAA, BA Amberg 2399, GS Hirschau, 23 Nov. 1938.

168. For these measures cf. *Reichsgesetzblatt* (1938), 1579 ff.

169. GStA, MA 106683, RPvS, 7 Dec. 1938.

170. GStA, MA 106673, RPvNB/OP, 8 Dec. 1938.

171. GStA, MA 106681, RPvUF, 9 Dec. 1938.

172. GStA, MA 106673, RPvNB/OP, 8 Dec. 1938. An Upper Bavarian NSLB functionary reported similarly: 'The action against the Jews awakened great sympathy in these [church] circles — the poor Jews' (the last three words underlined in red) — StAM, NSDAP 983, Kreisamtsleiter Erding, 21 Nov. 1938.

173. WL, 'Der 10. Nov.', pp. 5 f, 8, 28 f, 35 ff.

174. WL, B66; cf. also Behrend-Rosenfeld, pp. 73, 76 ff. and Hanke, p. 218.

175. Kulka's view that 'most did not denounce the atrocities against the Jews, but protested against the destruction of German property' is, as we have seen, a far too sweeping generalization — Cf. Kulka, p. XLIV.

176. BAK, R58/1094, fol. 109.

177. Cf. the evidence surveyed in Kershaw, 'Persecution', pp. 275–81; Allen, 'Die deutsche Öffentlichkeit', pp. 397–411, and Gordon, pp. 184 ff.

178. Cf. D. Orlow, *The History of the Nazi Party, ii, 1933–1945*, Newton Abbot, 1973, pp. 250–1.

179. Ibid., p. 265, n. 8.

180. E.g., WL, PIId/760; PIId/40; PIId/528; 'Der 10. Nov.', p. 5.

181. DBS, 10 Dec. 1938, p. A44 and cf. also p. A46.

182. Müller-Claudius, pp. 76–9, 157 ff.

183. A *Sopade* report from Berlin in 1936 concluded: 'In general terms one can say that the Nazis have indeed brought off a deepening of the gap between the people and the Jews. The feeling that the Jews are another race is today a general one' — DBS, 11 Feb. 1936, pp. A17–18.

184. Andreas-Friedrich, p. 32.

185. DBS, 10 Dec. 1938, p. A48.

186. Cf. I. Kershaw, *Der Hitler-Mythos. Volksmeinung und Propaganda im Dritten Reich*, Stuttgart, 1980, esp. ch. 3.

187. DBS, 10 Dec. 1938, p. A1.

188. Critical comments about the Jewish Question formed only slightly more than one per cent of the *Heimtücke* cases of the Munich 'Special Court'. Of all the cases concerning the Jews, more than two-thirds were begun in 1938–9, almost a half — overwhelmingly related to 'Crystal Night' — in the five months between November 1938 and the end of March 1939.

189. Though couched in populist-nationalist language, the class nature of these sentiments implied by the *Volksgemeinschaft* concept needs no emphasis.

8

Popular Opinion and the Extermination of the Jews

The fate of Bavarian Jews after 'Crystal Night' mirrors closely that of Jews from other parts of the Reich. By the beginning of the war, following the massively accelerated emigration after the pogrom, some 10,000 Jews — less than a third of the Jewish population of 1933 — remained in Bavaria (excluding the Palatinate).[1] The social isolation of these Jews was all but completed during the first war years. The physical presence of the Jew in the countryside or in small towns was now — except for certain parts of Swabia and Lower Franconia — largely a memory of the past, as the persecuted outcasts found their way to the slightly greater security of Jewish communities in the big cities of Munich, Nuremberg, Augsburg, and Würzburg. Following the law of 30 April 1939 preventing Jews and non-Jews from living in the same tenement blocks, the social isolation was increased by the creation of 'Jew houses' and the formation of ghettos in the large cities.[2] Munich provides an example of what was happening.[3] Between May and December 1939 some 900 Jewish dwellings were confiscated, the best of which were given over to Party functionaries, civil servants, or officers. At the start of the war, the city's Jews (numbering about 4,000) had to make room in their increasingly cramped accommodation for several hundred Jews moved to Munich from Baden. From 1939, too, Munich's Jews, like Jews elsewhere, were compelled to perform hard labour in a variety of degrading jobs, frequently as quasi-slave

197

work-parties in armaments factories. By early 1941 many were put to work constructing ghetto barracks for the 'Jewish settlement' in the north of the city. By October that year the barracks were accommodating 412 of Munich's Jews, eventually holding 1,376 persons although it was only meant to house a maximum of 1,100. The Milbertshofen Jewish settlement served from November 1941 as a collecting point for the deportation of Munich's Jews to the death-camps of the east.

The depiction of Jews as the pariahs of the 'National Community' found its symbolic expression in the introduction of the compulsory wearing of the yellow 'Star of David' in September 1941. Only the actual physical removal of the Jews from the sight of Germans now remained. This was not long delayed.[4] The first deportations of 1,820 Jews to Riga from collection points in Munich, Nuremberg, and Würzburg took place in late November 1941. In Spring 1942 further deportations of almost 3,000 Jews to the Lublin area of Poland followed, and during the remainder of 1942 and the first half of 1943 another three-and-a-half thousand Jews were transported to Auschwitz and (the large majority) to Theresienstadt. In all, 8,376 Jews were deported from Bavaria, almost all of them by September 1943. Their fate in the camps of the east merged with that of the other Jewish victims of the Nazis from within and outside Germany. Those deported to Riga were most likely among the vast numbers shot by the *Einsatzkommandos* of the *Sicherheitspolizei* between February and August 1942; those sent to Lublin probably perished in the gas-chambers of Sobibor and Belzec; very few survived the war. The post-war Jewish communities in Bavaria (numbering 5,017 Jews in 1971) have no direct line of continuity with the historic communities extinguished by Nazi terror.

How did the Bavarian population, which was capable in the war years of significant expressions of popular feeling and opposition to Nazi measures, react to the persecution and deportation of the Jews? What did they know of the horrors taking place in the occupied territories of Poland and the Soviet Union?

Remarkable as it may sound, the Jewish Question was of no more than minimal interest to the vast majority of Germans during the war years in which the mass slaughter of Jews was taking place in the occupied territories. The evidence, though surviving much more thinly for the war years than for the pre-war period, allows no other conclusion.

Above all, the war seems to have encouraged a 'retreat into the private sphere'[5] as regards political opinion in general and the Jewish issue in particular. Such a retreat into concerns of private interest and welfare to the exclusion of all else in conditions of crisis and danger is neither specific to Germany nor to societies under dictatorial rule, but the level of repression and the increasingly draconian punishment for politically nonconformist behaviour enhanced this trend in the German population during the war. Under the growing pressures of war, the worries about relatives at the Front, fears about bombing raids, and the intensified strain of daily existence, great concern for or interest in a minority social group was unlikely to be high. Moreover, the Jews, a generally unloved minority, had become, as we have just seen, almost totally isolated from the rest of German society. For most people, 'the Jew' was now a completely depersonalized image. The abstraction of the Jew had taken over more and more from the 'real' Jew who, whatever animosity he had caused, had been a flesh-and-blood person. The depersonalization of the Jew had been the real area of success of Nazi policy and propaganda on the Jewish Question. Coupled with the inevitable concern for matters only of immediate and personal importance, mainly the routine day-to-day economic worries, and the undoubted further weakening that the war brought in questions of moral principle, it ensures that the fate of the Jews would be far from the forefront of people's minds during the war years.

During the first two years of the war mention of the Jewish Question hardly occurs in the opinion reports of the Nazi authorities. SD informants in Bad Kissingen overheard conversations after the Polish campaign in late 1939 about the planned 'settlement' of Polish, Czech, and Austrian Jews in the Lublin area 'from which there would be no return', and from where it was presumed that the Jews concerned would go or be sent to Russia. This was said to have been 'welcomed by Party comrades and by a great proportion of the national comrades, and suggestions were heard that the Jews who still live in Germany should also set out on their march into this territory'.[6] Such comments clearly emanated from Party circles. They are practically the sole recorded comments about the Jews from Bavarian sources during the first phase of the war. A more positive account, though from a non-Bavarian source, of a Rabbi written towards the end of 1940, went so far as to claim that the Jewish Question had become less important during the war, and that anti-Jewish feeling among the ordinary population had declined. He pointed to the active clandestine help which thousands of Jews living in their ghetto-like conditions still received daily from ordinary Germans.[7]

Whether or not this account was over-generous to the state of opinion towards the Jews, there is no doubt that conditions for the tiny Jewish minority deteriorated drastically following the invasion of Russia in June 1941. Apart from the introduction of the 'Yellow Star' in September, a whole series of new restrictions in the autumn deprived Jews of telephones, newspapers, and ration cards for meat, milk, fish, white bread, and many other consumer items. Jewish living conditions were reduced to a level far beyond the tolerable in the same months that the first mass deportations to the east got under way. This combination of anti-Jewish measures occurred in one of the few short periods in the war when public reactions found a muted and distorted echo in the reports of the authorities.

According to a report of the Mayor of Augsburg, the decree ordering the wearing of the 'Yellow Star' brought expressions of 'great satisfaction among all national comrades'. A ban imposed in December on Jews attending Augsburg's weekly market was, it was claimed, equally welcomed.[8] Similar reactions to the introduction of the 'Yellow Star' were recounted in the central SD report of 9 October 1941.[9] Summarizing responses, a later SD report emphasized that the decree had met a long-cherished wish of large sections of the population, especially where Jews were numerous, and that many were critical of the exceptions made for Jewish wives of 'aryans', saying this was not more than a 'half-measure'. The SD added that 'for most people a radical solution of the Jewish problem finds more understanding than any compromise, and that there existed in the widest circles the wish for a clear external separation between Jewry and German national comrades.' It was significant, it concluded, that the decree was not seen as a final measure, but as the signal for more incisive decrees with the aim of a final settlement of the Jewish Question.[10] It seems difficult to accept such comments as they stand. The tone is redolent only of the overtly Nazi element of the population, and it is more than likely that the SD was in this case as in other instances repeating comments made by Party members as general popular opinion. Understandably, those critical of the measure were far less open in their comments, though the SD reports themselves point out that 'isolated comments of sympathy' could be heard among the bourgeoisie and Catholics — the two groups most vociferous in their condemnation of earlier anti-Jewish measures — and 'medieval methods' were spoken of.[11] Almost certainly, those condemning the 'Yellow Star' decree were in a minority, as were those openly lauding the public branding of Jews. For the majority of the population, the decree passed without comment, and very likely without much notice.[12]

The deportations, beginning in autumn 1941, were also apparently accompanied by remarkably little attention of the non-Jewish population. Most reports fail to mention any reactions, confining their comments to a cold, factual account of the 'evacuations'.[13] In one or two instances stereotype 'approval', 'satisfaction', or 'interest' of the local population is mentioned. The Nuremberg population was said to have 'noted approvingly' the first deportations from the city on 15 November 1941, and 'a great number' of Forchheim's inhabitants allegedly followed the departure of eight Jews from the town 'with interest and great satisfaction'.[14] Such generalized statements of approval, sceptical though one must be of their representative value, practically exhaust the Bavarian evidence on reactions to the deportations. For the rest, the silence is evocative.[15] The absence of registered reactions in the sources is probably not a grotesque distortion of popular attitudes. Not only intimidation but widespread indifference towards the remaining tiny Jewish minority explains the lack of involvement in their deportation. And where real interest was awakened on the part of the non-Jewish population it was less a product of human concern or moral principle than self-interest and the hope of material advantage. Such was the case when a complainant in Fürth near Nuremberg wrote to the Reich Governor of Bavaria in 1942 on behalf of the co-tenants of her apartment block protesting at the sequestration of Jewish property by the local Finance Office when so many were crying out for it. 'Where is the justice and *Volksgemeinschaft* in that?', she lamented.[16]

Such blatant self-interest existed alongside the widespread passivity and emotionless acceptance of the deportations. There can be little doubt that strong reactions would have left their mark in the reports of the authorities. Such reports contain a mass of comment critical of the regime. And at the very same time as the deportations were proceeding with minimal response from the population, the force of angry and concerned popular opinion was bringing to a halt the removal of crucifixes from Bavarian schools and — of incomparably greater importance — the gassing of thousands of mentally defective persons in the 'euthanasia action'. Compared with the popular interest in the film *I Accuse,* which attempted a justification of euthanasia, the obnoxious 'documentary' film *The Eternal Jew* was apparently badly attended.[17] A second disguised private survey of opinion by Michael Müller-Claudius in 1942 revealed that whereas just under a third of his selected group of Party members had been indifferent or non-commital about the Jewish Question following the November pogrom of 1938, the figure was now 69 per cent.[18]

Though people often knew about the deportations before they took place, their knowledge of the fate of the Jews in the east has inevitably been the subject of much speculation and debate. Documentary evidence can hardly provide an adequate answer to the question: 'how much did the Germans know?', and given the generally prevailing silence and the difficulties of interpretation only tentative suggestions can be made. Undoubtedly, however, the generalization of one historian that 'people were acquainted with the ultimate fate of the deported Jews' is far too sweeping.[19] Most people in fact probably thought little and asked less about what was happening to the Jews in the east. The Jews were out of sight and literally out of mind for most. But there is incontrovertible evidence that knowledge of atrocities and mass shootings of

Jews in the east was fairly widespread, mostly in the nature of rumour brought home by soldiers on leave. If most rumour was unspecific, eye-witness accounts of shootings and also broadcasts from foreign radios provided material which was sufficiently widely circulated for Bormann to feel obliged in autumn 1942 to give new propaganda directives for countering the rumours of 'very sharp measures' taken against Jews in the east.[20] Concrete details were seldom known, but an awareness that dire things were happening to the Jews was sufficient to make people already worried about possible retaliatory measures of the enemy should Germany lose the war, as the Government President of Swabia pointed out in November 1942 in the light of 'a further rumour about the fate of the Jews taken to the east.'[21] A month later an SD report from Middle Franconia stated:

> One of the strongest causes of unease among circles attached to the Church and in the rural population at the present time is formed by news from Russia in which shooting and extermination (*Ausrottung*) of the Jews is spoken about. This communication frequently leaves great anxiety, care, and worry in those sections of the population. According to widely held opinion among the rural population, it is not at all certain now that we will win the war and if the Jews come to Germany again they will exact dreadful revenge on us.[22]

A Catholic priest in the same locality also referred directly to the extermination of the Jews in a sermon in February 1943. He was reported as saying that Jesus was descended from the Jews and that it was therefore 'not right if Jewry was persecuted or exterminated (*ausgerottet*) since the Catholic faith was based upon the same.'[23]

It was, however, above all the attempts by Goebbels to exploit the discovery of mass graves of Polish officers at Katyn in April 1943 which suddenly cast a ray of light on knowledge among the German people of the murder of Jews in the eastern territories. The regional headquarters of the SD in Würzburg reported in mid-April:

> The thorough and detailed reportage about the murder of 12,000 Polish officers by the GPU [Soviet secret police] had a mixed reception. Especially among sections of the intelligentsia, the propaganda put out by radio and press was rejected. Such reportage was regarded as exaggerated. Among those associated with the Churches the view was put forward that it could be a matter of mass graves laid out by Germans for the murdered Polish and Russian Jews.[24]

The Government President of Swabia also noted that, according to one report he had received, the Katyn propaganda had provoked 'discussion about the treatment of the Jews in Germany and in the eastern territories.'[25] Such comments were typical of remarks being noted in many parts of Germany. According to the SD's central digest, people were saying that Germans 'had no right to get worked up about this action of the Soviets because from the German side Poles and Jews have been done away with in much greater numbers.'[26] Party reports reaching Bormann spoke also of comments of clergy referring to the 'terrible and inhumane treatment meted out to the Jews by the SS' and to the 'blood guilt of the German people.'[27] Similar comments were heard after the uncovering at Winniza in July 1943 of mass graves of Ukrainian victims of the Russian secret police.[28] Soon afterwards, Bormann, commissioned directly by Hitler, provided new directives about treatment of the Jewish Question, stating now that in public 'all discussion of a future complete solution (*Gesamtlösung*)' had to cease, and it could only be said 'that Jews had been conscripted *en bloc* for appropriate deployment of labour.'[29] The Nazi leadership was clearly aware that public feeling in Germany was not ready for frank disclosures on the extermination of the Jews.

Recorded comments about the murder of Jews refer almost invariably to mass shootings by the *Einsatzgruppen,* which in many cases were directly witnessed by members of the *Wehrmacht.*[30] The gassing, both in mobile gas-units and then in the extermination camps, was carried out much more secretly, and found little echo inside Germany to go by the almost complete absence of documentary sources relating to it.[31] Even so, the silence was not total. Rumours did circulate, as two cases from the Munich 'Special Court' dating from 1943 and 1944 and referring to the gassing of Jews in mobile gas-vans, prove. In the first case a middle-aged Munich woman admitted having said in autumn 1943: 'Do you think then that nobody listens to the foreign broadcasts? They have loaded Jewish women and children into a wagon, driven out of the town, and exterminated (*vernichtet*) them with gas.' For these remarks, made to her neighbour's mother, and for derogatory comments about Hitler she was sentenced to three years in prison.[32] In the other case, an Augsburg furniture removal man was indicted of having declared in September 1944 that the Führer was a mass-murderer who had Jews loaded into a wagon and exterminated by gas.[33]

These appear to be the only instances in the Munich 'Special Court' files which touch upon the gassing of Jews in the occupied territories. They were presumably the tip of the iceberg, but on the available evidence one can take it no further. Whether there was anything like hard information circulating about the extermination camps in Poland is again a question which cannot be satisfactorily answered on the basis of available sources. The silence of the documents on this point has to be viewed critically. One might assume that knowledge — or at very least highly suggestive rumour — of the systematic extermination of the Jews in the camps was more widely circulating than is apparent from surviving documentation. On the other hand, many people genuinely first learnt about the nature and purpose of the camps in the horrifying disclosures at the Nuremberg Trials. It is quite likely, in fact, that there were differences in the degree of knowledge or surmise between the eastern regions bordering on Poland and areas in the west and south of the Reich. At any rate, according to a report of the *Gauleitung* of Upper Silesia in May 1943, following the Katyn disclosures, the Polish resistance movement had daubed up the slogan 'Russia-Katyn, Germany-Auschwitz' in public places of the industrial region of Upper Silesia. 'The concentration camp Auschwitz, generally known in the east, is meant', added the report.[34] An exhaustive search of the extensive Bavarian materials, on the other hand, reveals no mention of the name Auschwitz, or of the name of any other extermination camp in the east. There was some knowledge of the camps among leading members of the group which plotted the attempt on Hitler's life in 1944 and among Church leaders, and the extent of auxiliary services to the camps meant that total secrecy was a practical impossibility.[35] The extent of knowledge will never be known. The judicious, if inconclusive, assessment of one historian that 'it may be doubted . . . whether even rumours of Auschwitz as a Jewish extermination centre had circulated widely throughout Germany — and if they had, whether they were believed', is probably as far as one can take it.[36]

All the evidence points towards the conclusion that for the people of Bavaria, as for the German population as a whole, the Jewish Question was hardly a central topic of concern during the war years. And most of what few comments survive from this period touch mainly upon the imagined connection between the persecution of the Jews and the war itself. A Munich waiter, for instance, was denounced for allegedly having said in May 1940 with typically Bavarian finesse: 'If they had left the Jews here and not chucked them out this bloody war would not have happened.'[37] A hair-dresser, also from Munich, sentenced to four years in a penitentiary for repeatedly 'malicious, hateful, agitatory, and base-minded comments' about Führer, Party, and State in spring 1942 was said to have called Hitler 'a crazy mass-murderer' and blamed him for the war 'because if he had left the Catholic Church and the Jews alone things would not have come to this pitch.' She added for good measure 'that she preferred Jewish women as customers to the wives of the SS men. In the course of time she had become sick to death of the latter.'[38] A number of comments betray the fact that many people regarded the allied bombing-raids as revenge and retaliation for the treatment of the Jews. A labourer in Weißenburg was condemned by the Munich 'Special Court' to eighteen months in prison for allegedly saying:

You will see alright. Weißenburg will have to put up with the flyers in good measure. The English haven't forgotten that so many from Weißenburg were in Dachau. In fact there were hardly any others in Dachau apart from those from Weißenburg. If only they had let the Jews go. They don't fly into the bishopric [of Eichstätt] because they [the people of Eichstätt] haven't done anything.[39]

In Lower Franconia, too, comments could be heard in the summer of 1943 relating the allied terror-bombing to retaliation for the November pogrom of 1938. People were asking whether the Jews would return to their former homes if Germany lost the war and pointed to the absence of air-raids on 'outright Jewish cities' like Fürth and Frankfurt.[40] The raids on Schweinfurt gave the inhabitants of Bad Brückenau renewed occasion in May 1944 to relate the bombing to Nazi anti-Jewish policies. Contrasts were drawn with the handling of the Jewish Question in Hungary, whose government had not followed the Nazi pattern of persecution of the Jews until March 1944:

> Many national comrades are of the opinion that the Jewish Question has been solved by us in the most clumsy way possible. They say quite openly that Hungary has learnt from our failure in this matter. And certainly our cities would still be intact if we had only brought the Jews together in ghettos. In that way we would have today a very effective means of threat and counter-measure at our disposal.[41]

Similar sentiments also found expression in the files of unbelievably inhumane letters sent to Goebbels from all over Germany, themselves a witness of the success of years of propaganda, suggesting for example that Jews should not be allowed in air-raid shelters but should be herded together in the cities threatened by bombing and the numbers of their dead published immediately after each air-raid; or that the Americans and British should be told that ten Jews would be shot for each civilian killed in a bomb-attack.[42]

Comments about the relationship between the Jews and the war demonstrate that the methods of the persecution of the Jews were often criticized at the same time as the basic principles behind the persecution were found acceptable. Furthermore, talk of 'retaliatory' air-raids, or the 'revenge of the Jews' descending upon Germany if the war were lost,[43] all point unmistakably towards the traces of belief in a 'Jewish World Conspiracy' theory, present before the Third Reich and massively boosted by Nazi propaganda.[44]

The last two years of the war saw the 'broad mass' of 'ordinary' Germans preoccupied less than ever with the Jewish Question, despite an unceasing barrage of propaganda on the issue. By mid-1944 there were a mere 1,084 Jews left in Bavaria, in Germany as a whole fewer than 15,000.[45] Though slogans about the Jew being the world enemy continued to be pumped into young Germans, Party propagandists reckoned that hundreds of thousands of them were now hardly in a position to know 'what the Jew is'. Whereas the elder generation knew 'it' from their own experience, the Jew was for the young only a 'museum-piece', something to look at with curiosity, 'a fossil wonder-animal (*fossiles Wundertier*) with the yellow star on its breast, a witness to bygone times but not belonging to the present', something one had to journey far to see.[46] This remarkable admission is testimony at one and the same time to the progress of abstract anti-Semitism, and to the difficulty of keeping alive the hatred of an abstraction. To be anti-Semitic in Hitler's Germany was so commonplace as to go practically unnoticed.[47] And the hallmarks of anti-Semitic attitudes outlasted the Third Reich, to be detected in varying degrees of intensity in three-fifths of those Germans in the American Zone tested by public opinion researchers of the occupying forces in 1946.[48]

Very many, probably most, Germans were opposed to the Jews during the Third Reich, welcomed their exclusion from economy and society, saw them as natural outsiders to the German 'National Community', a dangerous minority against whom it was legitimate to discriminate. Most would have drawn the line at physical maltreatment. The Nazi Mayor of Mainstockheim near Kitzingen in Lower Franconia no doubt spoke for many when, in preventing violence and destruction by SA and Party fanatics during the pogrom of November 1938, he reportedly said: 'You don't have to have anything to do with the Jews. But you have got to leave them in peace.'[49] Such an attitude was not violent. But it was discriminatory. And such 'mild' anti-Semitism was clearly quite incapable of containing the progressive radical dynamism of the racial fanatics and the deadly bureaucratization of the doctrine of race-hatred. Our examination of popular opinion on the Jewish Question has shown that in its anti-Jewish policies the Nazi regime acted not in plebiscitary fashion, but with increasing autonomy from popular opinion until the extermination policy in the east was carried out by the SS and SD as a 'never to be written glorious page of our history', as Himmler put it, whose secret it was better to carry to the grave.[50] The very secrecy of the 'Final Solution' demonstrates more clearly than anything else the fact that the Nazi leadership felt it could not rely on popular backing for its extermination policy.

And yet it would be a crass over-simplification to attribute simply and solely to the criminal ideological paranoia of Hitler, Heydrich, and a few other leading personalities of the Third Reich the implementation of policies which led to the death-camps. The 'Final Solution' would not have been possible without the progressive steps to exclude the Jews from German society which took place in full view of the public, in their legal form met with widespread approval, and resulted in the depersonalization and debasement of the figure of the Jew. It would not have been possible without the apathy and widespread indifference which was the common response to the propaganda of hate. And it would not have been possible, finally, without the silence of the Church hierarchies, who failed to articulate what opposition there was to Nazi racial policies, and without the consent ranging to active complicity of other prominent sections of the German élites — the civil service bureaucracy, the armed forces, and not least leading sectors of industry. Ultimately, therefore, dynamic hatred of the masses was unnecessary. Their latent anti-Semitism and apathy sufficed to allow the increasingly criminal 'dynamic' hatred of the Nazi regime the autonomy it needed to set in motion the holocaust.

Notes

AS	*Außenstelle* (local SD office)
BAK	Bundesarchiv Koblenz
Bayern I–IV	*Bayern in der NS-Zeit. Soziale Lage und politisches Verhalten der Bevölkerung im Spiegel vertraulicher Berichte,* ed. M. Broszat, E. Fröhlich and F. Wiesemann, Munich/Vienna, 1977; *Bayern in der NS-Zeit. Herrschaft und Gesellschaft im Konflikt,* vols. ii–iv, ed. M. Broszat, E. Fröhlich, and (for vols. iii–iv) A. Grossmann, Munich/Vienna, 1979–81
GenStA	*Generalstaatsanwalt* (Chief State Attorney in an OLG [*Oberlandesgericht;* Higher Regional Court] region)
GStA	Bayerisches Hauptstaatsarchiv, Abteilung II, Geheimes Staatsarchiv, Munich
HAS	*Hauptaußenstelle* (main SD office of a region)
KL	*Kreisleiter* (Nazi Party District Leader)
RP	*Regierungspräsident* (Government President, head of State regional administration, controlling a governmental region [*Regierungsbezirk*])
S	Schwaben (Swabia)
SD	*Sicherheitsdienst* (Security Service)
SGM	*Sondergericht München* (Munich 'Special Court' dealing mainly with political offences)
StAB	Staatsarchiv Bamberg
StAM	Staatsarchiv München
StAN	Staatsarchiv Nürnberg
StAW	Staatsarchiv Würzburg
WL	Wiener Library, London (since removed to Tel Aviv, leaving only a microfilm library in London)

1. B. Z. Ophir, and F. Wiesemann, *Die jüdischen Gemeinden in Bayern 1918–1945. Geschichte und Zerstörung,* Munich, 1979, pp. 24–5, 27.

2. Ibid., p. 27.

3. Ibid., pp. 27, 54–5; cf. pp. 213–16 for Nuremberg.

4. Ibid., pp. 28–9.

5. M. G. Steinert, *Hitlers Krieg und die Deutschen,* Dusseldorf, 1970, p. 242.

6. StAW, SD/11/1, HAS Würzburg, 27 Nov. 1939.

7. WL, PIIa/625, cited in A. Rodrigue, 'German Popular Opinion and the Jews under the Nazi Dictatorship', Univ. of Manchester, B.A. thesis, typescript, 1978 (copy in WL), p. 43.

8. GStA, MA 106683, RPvS, 8 Oct. 1941; 12 Jan. 1942; BAK, NS 26/1410, Oberbgm. Augsburg, 6 Jan. 1942.

9. Steinert, pp. 239–40.

10. Ibid., p. 240; *Meldungen aus dem Reich,* ed. H. Boberach, Neuwied, 1965, pp. 220 ff.

11. Steinert, p. 239.

12. Cf. ibid., p. 240, where it is pointed out that *NS-Frauenschaft* reports from different parts of the Reich mention reactions to the decree in only two areas, Hesse and Berlin (both of which still had relatively sizeable Jewish communities).

13. Cf. *Bayern I,* pp. 484 ff.

14. BAK, R22/3381, fol. 90v, GenStA Nürnberg, 10 Dec. 1941; StAB, K9/XV, 995, Kriminalpolizei Forchheim, 27 Nov. 1941.

15. Evidence from regions outside Bavaria is summarized by L. D. Stokes, 'The German People and the Destruction of the European Jews', *Central European History,* vi (1973), pp. 189 ff.

16. In: GStA, Reichsstatthalter 823.

17. Steinert, p. 243, citing a report from KL Kiel from December 1941; cf. also Stokes, 'The German People', p. 183, n. 64. On the other hand, the film did apparently run in sixty-six Berlin cinemas simultaneously in the autumn of 1940 (D. Singleton and A. Weidenfeld, *The Goebbels Experiment,* London, 1942, p. 213), and the anti-Semitic film *'Jud Süß'* was a popular success (R. E. Herzstein, *The War that Hitler Won. Nazi Propaganda,* London, 1979, p. 426).

18. M. Müller-Claudius, *Der Antisemitismus und das deutsche Verhängnis,* Frankfurt am Main, 1948, pp. 167–76.

19. O. D. Kulka, ' "Public Opinion" in National Socialist Germany and the "Jewish Question" ', *Zion,* xl (1975), p. XLIV. Contrast Stokes, 'The German People', p. 181 and the sources listed in n. 57. A recent article by H.-H. Wilhelm, 'Wie geheim war die Endlösung?', in W. Benz et al. (eds.), *Miscellanea. Festschrift für Helmut Krausnick,* Stuttgart, 1980, pp. 131–8, goes even farther than Kulka in arguing that anyone with ears to hear and eyes to read could hardly fail to grasp the broad hints of extermination given in speeches and editorials by Nazi leaders during the war.

20. Cited by Steinert, pp. 252 f.

21. GStA, MA 106684, RPvS, 10 Nov. 1942.

22. StAN, 212/11/VI, 1792, SD-AS Schwabach, 23 Dec. 1942.

23. Ibid., 6 Mar. 1943.

24. StAW, SD/37, HAS Würzburg, 17 Apr. 1943.

25. GStA, MA 106684, RPvS, 10 May 1943.

26. *Meldungen,* p. 383; Stokes, 'The German People', p. 186; Steinert, p. 255; Kulka, pp. 288–9.

27. Kulka, p. 290, based on reports from North Westphalia.

28. Stokes, 'The German People', p. 187; Steinert, p. 255.

29. Cited in Steinert, p. 257.

30. Cf. *Documents on Nazism*, ed. J. Noakes and G. Pridham, London, 1974, pp. 611 ff.

31. Cf. Steinert, p. 261; Stokes, 'The German People', pp. 184–5.

32. StAM, SGM 12719.

33. StAM, SGM 6501. The proceedings were abandoned when it transpired that he had been denounced out of sheer revenge for having denounced his accuser at an earlier date. This does not alter the fact that the case is proof of rumours circulating about gassing of Jews.

34. Printed in Kulka, p. 289.

35. Cf. Stokes, 'The German People', p. 184; Steinert, pp. 258–9.

36. Stokes, 'The German People', p. 185.

37. StAM, SGM 12539.

38. StAM, SGM 12573.

39. StAM, SGM 12520.

40. StAW, SD/37, HAS Würzburg, 7 Sept. 1943; cf. also SD/22, AS Schweinfurt, 6 Sept. 1943. Fürth and Frankfurt did not escape the bombing for much longer.

41. StAW, SD/12, AS Bad Brückenau, 8 May 1944.

42. Steinert, p. 260.

43. StAM, SGM 12443.

44. Cf. N. Cohn, *Warrant for Genocide*, London, 1967, for the spread of the 'world conspiracy' theory.

45. B. Z. Ophir, *Pinkas Hakehillot. Encyclopedia of Jewish Communities from their Foundation till after the Holocaust. Germany-Bavaria*, Jerusalem, 1972 (in Hebrew with an introduction in English), p. XL; Steinert, p. 259.

46. Cited in Steinert, p. 259.

47. Cf. A. Speer, *Erinnerungen*, Frankfurt am Main, 1969, p. 126.

48. *Public Opinion in Occupied Germany. The OMGUS Surveys, 1945–1949*, ed. by A. J. Merritt and R. L. Merritt, Urbana, 1970, pp. 146 f.; cf. pp. 239 f. for a second survey in April 1948.

49. WL, 'Der 10. Nov.', pp. 28 f.

50. *International Military Tribunal*, xxix, pp. 145 ff (Doc. PS-1919); H. Buchheim, 'Command and Compliance', in H. Krausnick *et al., Anatomy of the SS State*, London, 1968, p. 359.

9

German Popular Opinion and the 'Jewish Question', 1939–1943: Some Further Reflections

Remarkable as it may seem, little systematic work was carried out until relatively recently on analysing what seems an obviously central issue: the behaviour, attitudes, and opinion of the German non-Jewish population towards the Jews during the era of Nazi persecution: Only in the last decade or so have both Jewish and non-Jewish scholars, working within the context of a growing body of research on, and more differentiated understanding of, various facets of German society in the "Third Reich", systematically explored extensive but complex source materials and provided new perspectives of interpretation on the attitudes of "ordinary" Germans on the "Jewish Question" and relations between Germans and Jews during the Nazi dictatorship.[1] This recent research has had little difficulty in breaking down, with regard to the "Jewish Question" as to other aspects of "grass-roots" opinion and behaviour, the rather undifferentiated picture of a monolithic "totalitarian society" which prevailed in the 1950s and 1960s. Beneath the propaganda construct of a unified "people's community", it has now become perfectly clear that strands of opinion which did not conform to Nazi guidelines continued to exist, if often inchoate and inarticulate; and that attitudes pre-formed through a plurality of political, social, moral-ethical, intellectual, and religious influences, doggedly prevailed, offering at least a partial barrier to Nazi ideological penetration. Simplistic generalisations based on out-dated notions of a "mass society" under Nazism can, therefore, be ruled out. But this poses new problems for the historian, not least in an attempt to analyse attitudes in German society on such a sensitive issue as the "Jewish Question". Clearly, the "German people" cannot be treated as an undifferentiated whole; a plurality of attitudes towards the Jews existed throughout the Nazi years, shaped by variants of geography, class, religion, political background and by other factors, such as the level of organisation (or avoidance of organisation) within the multi-structured Nazi Movement. A major problem is, however, that while the sources enable us to recognise this, they are seldom differentiated enough to allow for fine nuances of interpretation or wholly definitive judgements. Despite the advances in scholarship, therefore, the contours of popular opinion towards the Jews have inevitably to be painted with a broad brush, with fewer fine touches than one would wish.

This is particularly the case with regard to the war years, where the main areas of scholarly difference in interpretation are to be found — a reflection in part of a more unhelpful source base compared with the pre-war period. The deviating interpretations centre, as Otto Dov Kulka and Aron Rodrigue have recently pointed out, around the meaning attached to concepts of "depersonalisation" of the Jews and the alleged "indifference" of the mass of the German population, and around assessments of the extent and significance of knowledge of the "Final Solution" and what people grasped of the "basic principles" of the persecution of the Jews.[2] Kulka and Rodrigue presented the interpretative differences in polarised form: while one line of interpretation, advanced some years ago by Marlis Steinert and more recently in my own work, suggests that the progressive "depersonalisation" meant decreasing interest in the Jews, furthered by a retreat into the "private sphere" and the general harshening of attitudes during the war years, the other, favoured by Kulka and Rodrigue, emphasises "the cumulative effect of the abstraction of the Jewish Question in the anti-Semitic war propaganda and . . . the possible internalization by the population at large of the abstract slogans and demands for the 'elimination' of the Jews".[3]

The alternative interpretation was advanced by Kulka and Rodrigue in a recent very thoughtful review article evaluating the current state of scholarship on the German population's attitudes to the Jews under the Nazi regime, and focusing largely on my own work.[4] This had attempted to analyse reactions to the persecution of the Jews as *one* strand of a broader study of popular opinion in the "Third *Reich*", in which the major concentration was on the pre-war, rather than the war years. The shortness of the chapter I included on attitudes towards the "Jewish Question" in the war years was not merely a reflection of the relative paucity of the source materials, but was consciously intended to emphasise a main point of my argument, that at the time when such momentous developments were taking place in Poland and Russia, the "Jewish Question" was of no more than marginal importance in the formation of popular opinion within Germany.

This indicated in turn to me a discrepancy between the centrality of anti-semitism to Hitler's world-view, and the relatively unimportant place it appeared to occupy in the scale of values and ranking of priorities of most ordinary Germans. I summed up the argument in the claim that "the road to Auschwitz was built by hate, but paved with indifference".[5] The implications were, I thought, well summarised by one perceptive reviewer, when he commented:

> While it was always frightening to imagine a nation swept away and dominated by the Nazis, it is surely no less frightening to consider that the Nazis were able to accomplish most of what they set out to do without acquiring unquestioning allegiance or imposing complete control. Apparently they did not need to: it was not necessary for Germans to believe, nor even necessary for them to approve; compliance, not conviction was required. For the Nazi state to thrive, its citizens had to do no more than go along, maintaining a clear sense of their own interests and a profound indifference to the suffering of others.[6]

Kulka and Rodrigue are critical of this line of interpretation, particularly as applied to the war years, and especially sceptical about the weight attached to the notion of "indifference". Their stimulating criticism has prompted me to reconsider the evidence relating to popular attitudes towards the "Jewish Question" during the war years. This paper is the product of those "second thoughts", and indeed represents more of a process of "thinking aloud" than any attempt to come up with definitive answers on such a complex issue. To provide the gist of my argument in advance: While I think the critical evaluation of the concepts of "depersonalisation" and "indifference" has been justified and has proved fruitful, and while I think I did underplay to some extent the interest which "ordinary" Germans showed at certain junctures in aspects of anti-Jewish policy, I see no cause to abandon the basic tenor of the interpretation which I put forward. It seems to me, too, that the alternative concept of "passive complicity" favoured by Kulka and Rodrigue[7] — a term more moral-normative than behavioural-descriptive in its connotations — introduces additional problems of interpretation. And finally, the polarised interpretations suggested by Kulka and Rodrigue do not in my view amount to irreconcilable opposites at all, but are in fact closely complementary.

In what follows, I shall first indicate very briefly the main developments in

popular opinion on the "Jewish Question" in the pre-war period, where research has been more heavily concentrated, the sources more plentiful and in
some respects better — in part a reflection of the greater contact in these years
between Jews and non-Jews, and where there is a fairly high degree of unan-
imity (despite a few differences in nuance) among those historians who have
researched the field. I shall then focus directly on the war-time period, within
the context of the differing interpretations outlined above. It will be useful to
bear in mind during the discussion the rough-and-ready (but in my view sensible and helpful) typology suggested by Konrad Kwiet, distinguishing between
attitudes reflecting various levels of solidarity and sympathy with the Jews in
the period of their greatest isolation and exposure to Nazi barbarism; attitudes
revealing outright and open hate and varying degrees of aggression and active
support for Nazi anti-Jewish actions; and attitudes suggestive of passivity and
indifference.[8] I shall devote most attention to the third area, where the greatest
problems of interpretation lie. It is important to emphasise here what I am
excluding from the following discussion. I am not concerned directly with the
behaviour and attitudes of the elites in the military, civil service, economy, and
Christian Churches, nor with those of apparatchiks of the Nazi regime in the
bureaucracy and judiciary, nor with "official" attitudes within the Party and
heavily indoctrinated affiliates like the SS. The attitudes I am attempting to
evaluate here are "popular" attitudes in the sense that they are deducible from
more or less spontaneous reactions and behaviour or comment of wide sections of the German people and are reflective of opinion existing outside the
"organised" channels of "official" orthodoxy.

For the pre-war era, there can be little fundamental disagreement with the
broad categorisation suggested by Kulka and Rodrigue. This divides attitudes
of the non-Jewish population towards the "Jewish Question" into four main
types: attitudes of a violently aggressive kind, prevalent particularly within the
Nazi Movement among antisemitic radicals, criticising the "moderation" of
the regime's anti-Jewish policy; acceptance of the broad principles of legal
discrimination and exclusion on racial grounds, attitudes which gained in
currency during periods of outright antisemitic violence, prompted by the
need to restore "law and order"; critical attitudes deriving from moral and
religious objections of committed Christians, ethical and humanistic considerations of the liberal intelligentsia, ideological rejection of the Marxist Left,
and economic disadvantages felt by some business circles; finally, indifferent
attitudes — perhaps part of a general ideological and political indifference —
reflected in lack of reaction to the "Jewish Question".[9]

Of course, the sources — a whole range of opinion reports, massive in quantity, from the various agencies of the Nazi regime; detailed and informative

reports on conditions within Germany smuggled out by the illegal resistance groups to exile organisations; Jewish eye-witness accounts and memoirs; and court and police records on arrests, denunciations and the like — do not allow any statistical weighting to be attached to the four categories. Even so, the accumulated weight of evidence speaks strongly in favour of the second and fourth types of attitude–acceptance of the principle of discrimination, and indifference — greatly predominating over either outrightly violent or openly critical attitudes. Indeed, the distinction between passive acceptance of the principle of discrimination (arising from widespread latent antisemitism pre-dating Nazism) and indifference and apathy is arguably one only of nuance and emphasis. Apathy is defined in one dictionary reading as "insensibility to suffering", while indifference denotes unimportance and can carry negative as well as neutral connotations.[10] Given these meanings, the distinction would come close to disappearance point.

Furthermore, in my work to date on this subject, I have used the term "indifference" to characterise non-Jewish attitudes towards the "Jewish Question" in an attempt to emphasise a point which Kulka and Rodrigue appear to accept,[11] that the "Jewish Question" did not rank prominently on the scale of priorities of the German population during the Nazi era. This is not to say that at certain periods, it did not temporarily come into prominence, and that at those times a basic lack of interest in the "Jewish Question" as a major concern was partially replaced by more pronounced antisemitic attitudes — less in the form of open violence than in the acceptance of the need for legislative discrimination against the Jews. Thus in the spring of 1933, far more so in the summer of 1935, and above all in the autumn of 1938, the "Jewish Question" had a high profile, and the basic lack of involvement of the mass of the population revealed a spectrum of attitudes, prominent among which, however, was the acceptance of discriminatory "legal" measures against Jews, themselves legitimating the "wild" Nazi violence and accommodating the spiral of radicalisation in anti-Jewish policy.[12]

What I am suggesting, therefore, is that apathetic and latent discriminatory attitudes (in which the need for "legal" discrimination against Jews was accepted, not least in order to put an end to unseemly disturbances and disorder) were closely related, and formed together a broad and fluid spectrum — unquestionably the majority opinion in the 1930s.

Within this spectrum, we can of course also point to the well-known, if somewhat loosely-drawn, structural distinctions — that big-city, Catholic, South- (except for Austria, especially Vienna) and West-German areas tended on the whole to be less rabidly antisemitic than small towns and country districts, and Protestant, especially northern and eastern, areas. Along class lines, the social group most favourably inclined towards Jews were the bourgeois liberal intelligentsia, but class distinctions of a hard and fast kind are hard to make among those helping Jews. Given the essentially middle-class social background of most German Jews, it is not surprising that those assisting them came rather more from the middle class than from among manual workers, where contact with Jews was less frequent. Evidence on gender distinction seems too sparse to allow any valid conclusions. Young Germans, brought up in the Depression or the Dictatorship itself, were by most accounts far more likely to be rabidly antisemitic than were the higher age-groups. And a basic and fairly obvious point is certainly that organisations within branches of the Nazi Movement itself produced higher and increasing levels of aggression towards Jews from Germans who had previously not been particularly antisemitic.

What we appear to have for the 1930s, therefore, is something close to Kwiet's three-fold typology of a relatively small group of sympathisers with Jews or critics of Nazi anti-Jewish policy, a larger group of violent radicals, and by far the largest sector of opinion ranging from outright lack of interest in the "Jewish Question", as being a matter of no central concern, to the — certainly growing — feeling that it was proper to discriminate legally against Jews and that it was justified Nazi policy to attempt to remove the Jews from Germany. A recent local case-study of a small Rhineland town arrives at a similar rough three-fold division of attitudes, noting that

> there were approximately several hundred persons . . . sympathetic to the Jews; these were counterbalanced by about one hundred firm and committed Nazis . . . ; between these two extremes was the remainder of the population, which was by and large apathetic toward the Jewish issue and which obeyed the regulations and edicts of the Nazi regime. These people kept their mouths shut and their thoughts to themselves, and they did nothing to disturb the status quo.[13]

By the eve of the war, it seems plain that attitudes towards the Jews had hardened even among the broad apathetic sector of the population. Coupled with the growing pariah status of Jews, whose social contacts with non-Jews had been significantly reduced, the six years of Nazi propaganda had undoubtedly taken its toll, in particular in its association of the Jews with the foreign policy tension and the growing menace of war — dreaded by so many Germans — in 1938–1939. The feeling that there *was* a "Jewish Question",[14] that the Jews *were* another race, and that they deserved whatever measures had been taken to counter their undue influence, and should be excluded from Germany altogether, had spread ominously. But the spread in passive discriminatory attitudes had taken place largely subconsciously, as the mode of discourse relating to Jews had itself shifted. On the verge of war, as in the previous years of Nazism, the "Jewish Question" appears to have ranked low in the concern of most Germans, to go by the factors which influenced the formation of daily opinion.[15]

We must now turn to consider the development of the attitudes we have outlined for the war-time period.

I will relate my comments on attitudes towards the Jews during the war years primarily to the contentious issues of depersonalisation, knowledge of the fate of the deported Jews, and lack of interest in the "Jewish Question".

It is striking how little the "Jewish Question" figures in the vast numbers of opinion reports emanating from the various agencies of the Nazi regime during the first two years or so of the war, down to the period following the invasion of the Soviet Union and the introduction of the Yellow Star and the first wave of deportations from Germany in the autumn of 1941. Reflections of popular attitudes towards the Jews in this period are found only rarely in these sources. One set of recorded comments from Lower Franconia in late 1939, welcoming the removal of Polish, Czech, and Austrian Jews to the Lublin reservation and hoping that the same would be done with German Jews, was said to have represented the view of "Party comrades" and the great proportion of "people's comrades".[16] There is no way of testing the accuracy of such reports. It seems fair to presume, however, that such comments emanated chiefly from Party circles, and it is inherently unlikely that sympathetic noises from the non-organised population were sufficiently extensive to justify the generalisation of the SD informant that this was majority opinion.

Other sorts of sources are not much more forthcoming at this period. The last *Sopade* report from April 1940 has a section on the persecution of the Jews, but deals mainly with Poland and points out that comments on the situation of the Jews inside Germany itself were now sparse. The general interpretation of the *Sopade* analysts on the basis of the information they were receiving was that the Nazis were consciously attempting to stir up hatred of the Jews through attributing to them the exclusive guilt for the war "because the majority of the German people is today less sympathetic than ever to the antisemitic excesses". As far as the effectiveness of propaganda could be assessed, it was said, "this war guilt manoeuvre is making little impression on the German people, and the persecutions of Jews are rejected now as before", though the report made a significant exception for those young Germans who had grown up under Nazism, had largely swallowed Nazi propaganda on the Jews, and were always ready to take part in excesses against them.[17] Despite this qualification, the report sounds one-sided and over-optimistic about the state of German opinion, as do the assessments of the *Neu Beginnen* group, emphasising the "amazingly friendly" attitude towards Jews encountered in various parts of Germany in reports stretching to autumn 1941.[18] Such reports were not infrequently based on the experiences of Jews who had managed to leave Germany, and the emphasis upon assistance and friendliness from "Aryans" is matched in Jewish memoirs and eye-witness reports.[19] Presumably, acts of friendliness or sympathy in a generally hostile environment made a particularly strong impression and could easily lead from a Jewish perspective to a distortedly positive evaluation of prevailing attitudes.[20] Even so, such a balanced account as that of Inge Deutschkron documents, in the context of a climate determined by aggression and ringed by a wide band of apathy, an impressive extent of help and sympathy in this period for Jews in Berlin, where conditions for the relatively large Jewish population were probably more favourable than in any other German city.[21]

The evidence on which to assess attitudes in the period before the invasion of the Soviet Union is, therefore, meagre in extent and conflicting and inconclusive in content. An assessment has to be largely a matter of tentative, hypothetical inferences rather than firm deductions. Such inferences point firstly to the low level of importance of the "Jewish Question" in this phase as a factor in the framing of popular opinion. Comments such as Inge Deutschkron's that "Germans who did not want to know what was going on around them had indeed no idea of how we lived among them",[22] are suggestive, secondly, of a deliberate or subliminal exclusion of the treatment of Jews from popular consciousness — a more or less studied lack of interest or cultivated disinterest, going hand in hand with what can indeed fairly be described as an accentuated "retreat into the private sphere" and increased self-centredness in the more difficult and worrying war-time conditions. Thirdly, frequent acts of solidarity and sympathy occurred, but formed, it is clear, impressive islands of humanitarian concern amid an atmosphere impregnated with menace and aggression. Fourthly, despite the claims of the *Sopade* that antisemitic propaganda had been largely ineffective in the first phase of the war, it seems hardly conceivable that the intensified hate campaigns purveyed in the *Stürmer*, other Nazi newspapers, on the radio, and through the disgusting "documentary" *Der Ewige Jude*[23] remained without impact in intensifying anti-Jewish attitudes in growing sections of the public. It seems, if these inferences are correct, possible to argue, therefore, that, in the months before the Russian campaign brought a qualitatively new dimension to conditions for German Jews in the autumn of 1941, there had been *both* a decrease in interest in the "Jewish Question" (compared, for example, with 1938–1939 and relative to other more pressing issues) enhanced by a "retreat into the private sphere", *and,* in the face of a barrage of Nazi propaganda, the absence of any alternative "mode of discourse", and the growing detachment of Jews from regular contact with non-Jews, an intensification of negative attitudes towards an increasingly abstract—that is, depersonalised, and ever more dehumanised—image of the Jew.

Amid the welter of incisive restrictions which afflicted Jews in the autumn of 1941, the introduction of the Yellow Star, the outward badge of Jewishness, caused the greatest stir and produced the most overt reflection in the opinion reports of the regime. Pressure from within the Party for the wearing of the Yellow Star had been resisted before the war as being inexpedient.[24]

It is evident, however, that in the period of stepped-up hatred towards the "Jewish-Bolshevik" arch-enemy and heightened tension with the opening of the new war front in the East in the summer of 1941, Party activists at home were stirring up renewed pressure for the introduction of methods to exclude Jews from access to increasingly scarce material commodities and services, and to brand them as outcasts for all to see.

An indication of the threatening mood is provided by a report from the *SD-Hauptaußenstelle* at Bielefeld on 5th August 1941, alleging general approval for the announcement in the local papers at the end of July that Jews would receive no compensation for damage suffered through the war, and claiming such growing strong feeling about the "provocative behaviour" of Jews that the town administrations of Bielefeld and Minden had already felt obliged to ban attendance at the weekly markets for Jews "in order to avoid acts of violence". The report added that even these measures did not satisfy the population, who were demanding "that compulsory identifying marks should finally be introduced, similar to what has been common in the *Generalgouvernement* since the beginning of the war" to prevent Jews from avoiding such restrictions. It was further claimed that even in Paderborn, where because of Catholic influence there had so far been little hatred of Jews to speak of, demands had grown that Jews and Poles should only be attended to in shops when German customers had already been served. Nazi circles were reported as saying that one should resort to self-help and apply force against Jews and Poles if official measures were not taken straightaway.[25]

Further SD reports from the area following the introduction of the Yellow Star in September 1941 emphasise not only the general approval for the measure, but the allegedly widespread feeling that it did not go far enough, and that *Mischlinge* as well as full Jews should be forced to wear the Star, preferably also on the back.[26] Similar reactions were reported from many parts of Germany and summarised in central SD digests in October 1941 and February 1942.[27]

I think in retrospect that Kulka and Rodrigue are right to place more weight on such comments than I had previously been prepared to attribute to them. The public nature of the branding produced by the Yellow Star decree evidently did elicit considerable attention and comment—much of it, as I acknowledged, vicious in tone. Such comment no doubt reflects a further hardening of attitudes towards Jews. At the same time, it still appears to me that Kulka and Rodrigue are inclined to treat such reports too uncritically. One such report which I have just mentioned, from the Bielefeld area, begins for instance by saying that extensive discussion about the introduction of the Yellow Star had not taken place. It then, nevertheless, goes on to interpret the general mood as being approving and viciously aggressive towards the Jews.[28] The point I made in my remarks on the SD reporting on the Yellow Star was that the tone of the reportage was above all redolent of the overtly Nazi element of the population, whose comments probably provided the dominant public voice on the issue. Doubtless, such rabid sentiments found a greater echo than had earlier been the case. But whether they were the overwhelming majority opinion might be open to doubt. At any rate, I still question "the reliability of this thoroughly documented report"[29] as an accurate reflection of majority attitudes on the "Jewish Question" in autumn 1941.

And there certainly was a significant minority critical voice, according to the SD, especially in Catholic and bourgeois circles abhorring the measure. Demonstrative shows of sympathy from strangers feature prominently in numerous Jewish eye-witness accounts, especially from Berlin, where, according to such memoirs, as Monika Richarz puts it, "hidden shows of sympathy were the more frequent reaction, in so far as the population showed any reaction at all".[30] In the context of Berlin, Inge Deutschkron again provides a balanced account, in which the unpleasant experiences—especially of children forced to wear the Star—are given due prominence, and where the discriminatory isolation accentuated by the wearing of the Star is emphasized. Her summary of the mixed attitudes she encountered notes that "there were people who looked at me with hate; there were others whose glances betrayed sympathy; and others again looked away spontaneously".[31] It is impossible to attach proportions to these behavioural types, but my speculation from the unsatisfactory evidence in that the third category—keeping quiet, avoiding involvement, apathy and indifference mingling with passive compliance—was still far larger than Kulka and Rodrigue are inclined to accept on the basis of the SD reports alone.

As with the introduction of the Yellow Star, I think in retrospect and in the light of some further interesting SD reports which have come to light, that I may have overemphasised the lack of interest in the deportations when they began in the autumn of 1941, and in the subsequent fate of those deported,

possibly at the cost of underplaying the inhumane responses towards the removal of the Jews and the level of hostility towards those remaining. At the
same time, it is necessary to repeat the point: compared with other events at
home and on the military front which were preoccupying the German people
in the autumn of 1941 and winter of 1941–1942, the deportation of the Jews
elicited remarkably little comment and, it is fair to conclude, was clearly of
minor significance among the factors shaping popular opinion. In relation to
other issues, therefore, this points towards a distinct lack of interest in the
"Jewish Question". This seems confirmed by Müller-Claudius's long-known,
but still interesting evidence, to which I shall return.[32] Secondly, the point must
again be made that the SD reports and other such material need to be read with
a critical and sceptical eye, not least on such a sensitive issue as attitudes
towards the Jews, where it seems certain that people would be increasingly
cautious about expressing critical comment on the regime's anti-Jewish measures, so that comment coming to the ears of SD informants would be predominantly that of loyal Nazis who basically shared the official standpoint, or
even took a more aggressive attitude. Thirdly, although knowledge about the
mass shootings of Jews undoubtedly became fairly widespread (knowledge of
the gassings less so, but even so was also spreading in rumours), this knowledge was compatible with a spectrum of attitudes ranging from overt approval to blank condemnation, and above all with the apathetic shrug of the
shoulders—the feeling that "horrible things happen in war, and I can't do
anything about it anyway" and the turning of the face from unpalatable
truths, the deliberate exclusion of "knowing in order to know what not to
know".

Few reports have come to light which cast any detailed light on attitudes
towards the deportations. Generally, the "evacuation" of Jews was coldly and
factually recorded, and sometimes the "approval", "satisfaction", or "interest" of the local population was noted.[33] Occasionally, however, a report went
beyond such uninformative stereotypes. For instance, the *Gestapo* in Bremen
indicated in November 1941 that "while the politically educated section of the
population generally welcomed the imminent evacuation of the Jews . . .
especially church-going and commercial circles . . . show no sympathy for it
and still believe today that they have to stick up for the Jews . . ." Both
Catholics and Protestant adherents of the Confessing Church were said to
have vehemently expressed their pity for the Jews. In one Protestant parish,
where the largely bourgeois and intelligentsia population supported the Confessing Church, the Jews had been provided with material support. And in the
business world, it was said, firms employing Jews did not want to lose them.
Even "well-respected" firms were not hesitating to file petitions saying they

could carry on no longer if their Jews were to be deported.[34] Another report, from Bielefeld, summarised reactions to the deportation of 400 Jews from the Minden district in December 1941. Though the "action" had been kept secret, word had got round, and a number of comments were registered from which it could be gathered that the "action" found the approval of the great majority of the population. One or two wholly nazified comments — e.g. thanking the *Führer* for freeing the people of the plague of Jewish blood, claiming it should have been done half a century earlier and then the First World War would have not been necessary, or bemoaning the fact that the town's buses had been laid on to bring the Jews to the station — were recorded. The report then mentioned a few critical remarks, registering incomprehension "that the Jews could be handled so brutally" since "whether Jew or Aryan, all are human beings created by God". Informed rumours (to which I will return) about the fate of the deported Jews were also described in the report, along with rumours that the *Führer* wanted to hear by 15th January 1942 that there were no more Jews in Germany. Rumours were also in circulation that as revenge for the treatment of the Jews, all Germans in America had to wear a swastika on the left side of the breast. The rumours were said to have emanated "solely from denominational circles, as has become customary with all actions of the State".[35]

The Bielefeld report was built up from two reports from Minden itself about the evacuation, dating respectively from 6th and 12th December. Comparison of the Minden reports and the Bielefeld summary is instructive. The Minden report of 12th December contains the rumours about the destination of the Jews in Russia, Hitler's supposed order to clear out all Jews by mid-January 1942, and the alleged swastika badges in the USA. It is not said that such comments were confined to "denominational circles"; only that "through this prattling, the vein of sympathy (*Mitleidsdrüse*) of various people with Christian attitudes is indeed being strongly activated".[36] The slightly earlier report of 6th December started by pointing out the "great concern" of a large proportion of the population about the "evacuation" of the Jews. Two basic viewpoints were then singled out: the likely retaliation abroad, especially in America, with reference to the way the *Kristallnacht* pogrom had harmed rather than helped Germany; and secondly, a more humanitarian standpoint which, it was said, could not be widely registered, but could be heard in a large section of the better-off circles, especially among the older generation, that the measure was far too "hard", that many Jews could not be expected to survive the journey to the East in the middle of winter, and that they were all Jews who had lived in the district since time immemorial. Only the third and final paragraph of the report added the rider that "among the *Volksgenossen* who understand the Jewish Question . . . the entire action is nevertheless absolutely approved of" and the "German identity feeling" brought into prominence.[37]

The suggestion of the Minden reports, therefore, in contrast to the Bielefeld digest of them, is that concern (from a number of motives) and criticism were more prominent reactions than Nazi-style approval. This reading is supported, too, by a report from the same area, this time from the SD station at Detmold, about a later transport of the last Jews from Lemgo in July 1942. The assembly of the Jews in the market place at Lemgo on 28th July had excited much attention, and the deportation, it could be observed, "was generally negatively criticised" by a large proportion of the "older *Volksgenossen*", among them some Party members. Various "arguments" were "more or less openly" advanced against the deportation, for instance, that the hardship now to be imposed on the Jews was unnecessary, since they were in any case dying out in Germany. Even people who had previously demonstrated their "National Socialist attitude" were said to have supported the interests of the Jews, and people in church-going circles spoke of the coming "punishment of God". Although those with confirmed Nazi views sought to explain that the "action" was fully justified and absolutely necessary, this argument was countered by the opinion that the old Jews could not do any damage, would in fact "not harm a fly", and that there were many among them who had done much good.[38]

The indications of such reports, exceptional as they are in the extent of the reported comment they provide on the deportations, are that expressed attitudes of a Nazi character towards the removal of the Jews were by no means universal and could even be in a minority. And although opinion was clearly divided, there evidently *was* at least temporarily some direct interest taken in the removal of the Jews and in their fate. Of course, nowhere did it come to anything more than expressions of the sort recounted here, with the single exception of the successful week-long protest demonstration of more than 200 non-Jewish women in Berlin in March 1943 against the deportation of their Jewish husbands, where the Nazi leadership, sensitive to public feeling in the post-Stalingrad atmosphere, backed down and released the Jews.[39]

The unique public protest against anti-Jewish actions was, of course, carried out by those who were most directly interested — the wives of those to be deported. This instance where *active* opposition paid dividends again suggests, therefore, that where Germans were *not* directly affected by the "Jewish Question" — as they were, at least potentially, by, for example, the "Euthanasia Action" — then the prevailing attitude was basically one of passivity and apathy, apart from those anxious to profit materially from the removal of the Jews by staking a claim to their property or requesting the use of their apartments.[40]

Even the level of involvement in the deportation of the Jews shown in the reported responses which we noted of the population in the Bielefeld area might not have been typical of the reactions to deportations in the big cities. Although Inge Deutschkron points out that the first deportations from Berlin had been accompanied by some critical comments of bystanders, so that future deportations were carried out from the suburban station of Grunewald and not from the central Lehrter *Bahnhof*, the main type of response she singled out was one of reserve, of not wanting to be involved. "It was strange", she wrote, "how the Berliners knew how to avoid such actions taking place in their city. How many of them stood behind the curtains can only be guessed. Sometimes we saw how a head behind them suddenly disappeared."[41]

Also on the question of how far the German people knew about the fate of the deported Jews, and if they did whether they approved of it, variants of interpretation have revolved around the notion of "indifference". I have myself suggested that most Germans probably thought little and asked less about what was happening to the Jews in the East, that Jews were out of sight and literally out of mind for most. However, I stressed the incontrovertible evidence that knowledge of atrocities and mass shootings of Jews in the East was fairly widespread, mostly in the nature of rumour brought home by soldiers on leave, and the rumours were also circulating about gassings in mobile gas-units, and probably to a far lesser extent about the operations of the death-camps. I mentioned Bormann's provision of new propaganda directives in autumn 1942 to counter rumours about the "very sharp measures" taken against the Jews in the East, the rumours referred to in SD and other reports about the possible revenge of the Jews and of Germany's other enemies should Germany lose the war, the reactions about German inhumanity towards the Jews in the light of the regime's anti-Russian propaganda following the discovery of the Katyn massacre, and other indications that, even where concrete details were not known, the awareness that dire things were happening to the Jews in the East was fairly widespread.[42] Kulka and Rodrigue added to this the growing number of Jewish suicides once the deportations had begun, and also the outspoken hints by Hitler in his public speeches as further evidence of knowledge of the fate of the Jews, putting it "beyond doubt that the drastic nature of the path taken by the 'Jewish Question' was not a secret to the public".[43] They draw the debatable conclusion from this, however, that "what was actually reported to the regime should not be understood as 'indifference', but as an attitude that might best be characterized as passive complicity".[44] This does seem to allow for a distinction between what was reported to the regime, and other non-reported attitudes. But even so, it is not unproblematic in its generalisation of the basic attitude, and probably overdismissive of the notion of "indifference".

Additional fragments of evidence which have recently come to light confirm the existence of the rumours of mass shootings as early as autumn 1941, illustrate accurate rumours and some aroused interest in the activities of the *Sicherheitspolizei* in the occupied territories in April 1942, and indicate that fairly precise information could be acquired by ordinary Germans who were keen to find out what was happening. The report mentioned earlier from the *SD-Außenstelle* Minden noted on 12th December 1941 that it was being said in the district that all the Jews were being deported to Russia, the transport being carried out in cattle waggons once they had reached Warsaw, and that once in Russia the Jews were being put to work in factories while the old and sick were being shot.[45] A report in April 1942 to the *SD-Hauptaußenstelle* Erfurt, following a report in the *Völkischer Beobachter* about the deployment of the SD in combating partisans in the Soviet Union, indicated "a still wholly unclear picture about the happenings behind our fronts in Soviet territory", but a considerable interest in obtaining more information, and "the wildest rumours" that the *Sicherheitspolizei* had been given the task of "exterminating Jewry" in the occupied territories, with thousands of Jews having to dig their own graves before being shot, and shootings reaching such an extent that members of the extermination squads were suffering nervous breakdowns. All these rumours were providing the activities of the *Sicherheitspolizei* with "a horrible image" (*ein grausiger Nimbus*).[46] In addition to such "official" evidence, a remarkable set of extant diary notes from the Nazi era which has recently come to light reveals how, a few months later, an ordinary worker near Celle in Lower Saxony, Karl Dürkefälden, was acquiring detailed information about the mass shootings in the Soviet Union through questioning of a relative home on leave.[47] And according to her recollections, it was in November 1942 that Inge Deutschkron and her mother first heard via the British Broadcasting Corporation of the gassings and shootings of Jews — news which they inwardly suppressed, since it was so shocking and so hard to grasp.[48]

The testimony of Karl Dürkefälden and Inge Deutschkron points to difficulties of interpreting generalised attitudes of the population from knowledge about the fate of the Jews. Dürkefälden's case indicates the difficulty of presuming that accurate knowledge of the fate of the Jews among "ordinary Germans" necessarily implied "passive complicity". As far as is known, Dürkefälden (who had belonged to no political party, though he probably sympathised with the *Sozialdemokratische Partei Deutschlands* [SPD], and clearly disliked the Nazi regime, even casting a no-vote in the 1933 plebiscite) made no use of the information he acquired about the Jews. His behaviour can, therefore, be regarded as passive in the Jewish issue as in practically every other sphere. But it was "complicity" only in the sense that he did not openly risk his neck to denounce what he knew was taking place. And Deutschkron demonstrates what is otherwise known from Jewish sources, that the reported information from the East was too horrific for Jews to appreciate in any rational sense. It seems at least reasonable speculation, quite apart from post-war apologetics, to presume that many non-Jews, faced with mounting problems of their own as the war turned against Germany, reacted in not dissimilar fashion by rejecting the horror stories as allied propaganda or simply excluding the truth from their consciousness as being unpalatable or causing too much anxiety. There seems something in Walter Laqueur's point: "Quite likely that while many Germans thought that the Jews were no longer alive, they did not necessarily believe that they were dead. Such belief . . . is logically inconsistent, but a great many logical inconsistencies are accepted in war time." Certainly, his conclusion on this question is apposite, that the fate of the Jews "was an unpleasant topic, speculation was unprofitable, discussions of the fate of the Jews were discouraged. Consideration of this question was pushed aside, blotted out for the duration."[49]

Evidence about knowledge of the fate of the Jews is, therefore, overwhelming in indicating that the availability of that knowledge was widespread. It is less straightforward, however, in demonstrating what attitudes followed from the knowledge. Kulka and Rodrigue take the view that "the composite picture that the regime obtained from popular opinion reports pointed toward the general passivity of the population in the face of persecution of the Jews", thus proving the "objective complicity of the population in the 'Final Solution' ", but reject the concept of "indifference" as too limited in scope and not conveying the "full complexity of popular opinion".[50] As I have attempted to argue, no single term can do justice to the various strands of opinion on the final stages of Nazi anti-Jewish policy. Doubtless, as I conceded earlier for the first phases of the war, there was a further radicalisation of opinion in an already hostile climate, so that in the period following the invasion of the Soviet Union it seems almost certain that one can speak of some hardening of attitudes towards the Jews, and a feeling among a growing number of people that the Jews were getting what they deserved, even if they did not wholly rationalise what exactly that meant. At the same time, however, the SD reports on which Kulka places such reliance cannot be uncritically read, and stereotype generalisations in response to draconian, but well-worn, Hitler threats to annihilate the Jews, as in his speech on 30th January 1942, are a less than sophisticated guide to the complexity of opinion.[51] Certainly, the SD reports provided the regime with an impression of general approval for the anti-Jewish policy, and especially with an impression of passivity, as Kulka and Rodrigue claim. But the leadership does not appear to have been entirely sure of its standing with the public on the issue, as the caution shown by Goebbels in Berlin following the Stalingrad defeat and the concern of Bormann to ban discussion within the Party of the future "solution" of the "Jewish Question" in 1943 seem to indicate.[52]

Above all, however, the SD reports must have given the regime the impression that the "Jewish Question" was a matter of low concern to the general public compared with the numerous issues on which opinion was heated and anxiety great. In this sense, indifference towards the "Jewish Question" in relation to other issues still seems an appropriate depiction of overall attitudes, even though, when for short periods the "Jewish Question" was brought into the limelight, the bulk of vocal opinion was antagonistic to the Jews and expressed little dissent and much approval for the regime's attempts to find a "solution". In this context, the replies summarised by Michael Müller-Claudius based on his unique, camouflaged small sample of opinion of sixty-one Party members in 1942 still offer a nuanced analysis of attitudes which rings true.[53]

According to Müller-Claudius, 42 of the Nazis (69% of his "sample") he prompted with his opening statement that "the Jewish problem still hasn't been cleared up" and "we hear nothing at all about what sort of solution is imagined" provided responses which could be classed as "indifference of conscience". Characteristic replies were: (1) "I prefer not to speak of it. It's simply not possible to form an opinion on it." (2) "It's too risky to speak about it, and anyway nobody has any influence on these things." (3) "There's no point in thinking about it. The decision lies with Hitler alone." (4) "Actually, I'm not at all for solutions of force — but the problem as such is probably not ripe for decision in a political sense." (5) "To be frank, I've heard some very unpleasant things, but are they true? How much can you believe of rumours, anyway? Nobody can test them, so it's best to keep out of it." (6) "I've had nothing to do with Jewish policy and know as little as you do, how it's going to develop. Ultimately, we've got a total state. It has the sole responsibility." (7) "Actually, I'm not against the Jews altogether. But I keep miles away from the topic. The *Gestapo* is very sensitive about it. Talk about the subject is not wanted." (8) "Have a cigarette instead. I'm busy 12 hours a day, and can't be concerned with that as well. I need to keep all my thoughts on my work, and the rest of the time for relaxation." (9) "I'm just about up to here with the war. I want a regulated situation. What part the Jews play in that isn't my concern." And, (10) "What are you interested in that for? That's purely a question for the State . . . And we have no influence on politics."

Of the remainder of Müller-Claudius's "sample" of 61 persons, all of whom had joined either the NSDAP or the Hitler Youth before 1933, only three (5%)

expressed open approval of the right to exterminate the Jews, with comments such as: "The *Führer* has decided upon the extermination of Jewry and promised it. He will carry it out." Thirteen persons (21%) showed some signs of ethical and moral sense, speaking for instance of a future Jewish state, but accepting much of the Nazi claim that the Jews had caused Germany harm, and seeing a Jewish state as a way to prevent this in future by allowing for separate German and Jewish development. These replies also revealed resigned attitudes — washing of the hands for whatever brutalities were taking place. One characteristic reply, for instance, ran: "What can one do? An SS man told me that in the East the Jews have to dig their own graves and are then shot in them. He says it's so horrible that there is already a hospital for soldiers who have gone mad from it. But can one imagine that soldiers are really misused for such disgraceful acts?" Another reply dealing with rumours of barbarous acts towards Jews in the East concluded: "If the war so brutalises people, then one must indeed be prepared for the worst." Müller-Claudius's final "reaction group" comprised three persons (5%) who revealed what he called a "clear detachment from antisemitism", as in comments such as: "The rigid racial standpoint will not be able to be maintained in a genuine peace. We cannot deny that we have obligations towards Jewry", and suggesting it would only be fair to give Jews the choice of living in Germany or in a Jewish national state.

The conclusion which Müller-Claudius, himself formerly a professional psychologist, reached about the majority "indifferent" group was that it comprised those who "evaded responsible and sympathetic thought and feeling and persisted in a situation of moral indifference". There was no activation of aggressive hatred, but "the function of conscience was paralysed by lack of participation", enhanced through acceptance of the "total state" depriving the individual of his responsibility for what takes place.

For all its evident weaknesses, Müller-Claudius's analysis is, so far as I am aware, the nearest we can come to a differentiated assessment on psychological grounds of attitudes towards the Jews in the year that the deportations and extermination were in full swing. That the responses came from Nazis who had been in the Party since before Hitler's "seizure of power" suggests that the predominant attitude of "moral indifference" probably applied *a fortiori* to "non-organised" Germans. It is worth noting that the most recent investigation of relations between Jews and non-Jews, taking the case-study of a small Rhineland town and basing the findings largely on oral history techniques, also reached the conclusion that "because of the general fear and suspicion that surrounded their lives, few people probably gave more than a passing thought to the fate of the Jews. Trying to survive under a repressive regime was the uppermost concern for the Gentile population."[54] That there is nothing heroic or praiseworthy about such an attitude goes without saying. But, regrettably, it seems a very human response. And on basic common sense grounds, too, the dulling of the moral senses into indifference seems likely to have been an attitude with a wide currency in the "Third *Reich*".

Let me try to sum up briefly, as a series of tentative hypotheses, the argument I have been advancing.

(1) The evidence on which to base an analysis of attitudes of the non-Jewish population towards the Jews is particularly unsatisfactory for the war-time period. A sophisticated level of differentiation cannot be obtained.

(2) The SD reports, in particular, need critical analysis and cannot be taken at face value. They do indicate some hardening of attitudes towards the Jews and provide indications of distinct interest in the persecution, deportation, and ultimate fate of the Jews at certain specific junctures where the "Jewish Question" was temporarily brought into prominence. But it is *a priori* likely that vocal comment on the Jews coming to the attention of the SD tended to overrepresent the nazified attitudes in the population.

(3) The SD material shows, nevertheless, that attitudes towards the radicalisation of anti-Jewish policy were far from uniform, and that amid the general atmosphere of alienation and hostility there were pockets of sympathy or solidarity. Assistance or acts of friendliness from non-Jews presumably made a striking impact on Jews who experienced them and forms a correspondingly prominent part in their recollections. Undoubtedly only a small minority of the population was involved.[55] Class, gender, geographical or other factors cannot be precisely analysed. As in the pre-war era, church-going Catholics, pious Protestants (especially attached to the Confessing Church), the liberal intelligentsia, and committed Socialists and Communists were the most likely groups to be critical of Nazi anti-Jewish policy and action, as part of their general antipathy to the Nazi regime. But most acts of "friendliness" appear, not suprisingly, to have come not from strangers, but from personal contacts. Given the social milieu of most German Jews, these contacts were more likely to be with the bourgeoisie than with the working class. Geographically, the Jews of Berlin were more likely to encounter assistance or friendly attitudes than the Jews of any other large city it seems, and certainly more than the exposed Jewish populations of small towns. Given the size of the Jewish population of war-time Berlin, it was presumably statistically more likely that acts of sympathy towards Jews would occur. But the liberal cultural and political traditions of the city, its large bourgeoisie and intelligentsia, its cowed but recalcitrantly anti-Nazi blocks of the former Socialist and Communist working class, and the scarcely veiled (and increasing) antagonism towards the

regime in substantial proportions of the population, meant that the situation for Jews, appalling though it was, compared favourably with anywhere else in the *Reich*.[56]

(4) Evidence from Jewish eye-witness accounts and recollections, from the relatively sophisticated psychological analysis of attitudes by Michael Müller-Claudius, and from a critical reading of the silences as much as the actual content of SD and other regime-internal material, suggests that apathy and "moral indifference" to the treatment and fate of the Jews was the most wide-spread attitude of all. This was not a neutral stance. It was a deliberate turning away from any personal responsibility, acceptance of the state's right to decide on an issue of little personal concern to most Germans (contrasting with the protests on denominational issues and even on the single humanitarian issue of the "euthanasia action"), the shying away from anything which might pro-duce trouble or danger. This apathy was compatible with a number of inter-nalised attitudes towards Jews, not least with passive or latent antisemitism — the feeling that there *was* a "Jewish Question" and that something needed to be done about it.

(5) What seems to be certain is that the "Jewish Question" played only a minor role in the overall formation of opinion for the German population during the war. At the time that Jews were being murdered in their millions, the vast majority of Germans had plenty of other things on their mind. The "Jewish Question", as a component in framing popular opinion, was generally unimportant. In this sense, there was a relative indifference to the "Jewish Question". The low ranking of the "Jewish Question" in the scale of priorities of most Germans, before and during the war, suggests strongly a basic contrast between the centrality of antisemitism in Hitler's world view and the apathy towards the "Jewish Question" of the bulk of the population.

(6) To this extent, it seems to me that the dichotomy posed by Kulka and Rodrigue, between "depersonalisation" meaning decreasing interest in the Jews by a retreat into the "private sphere" together with a general harshening of attitudes, and the cumulative effect of the abstraction of the "Jewish Ques-tion" and "internalisation" of demands for the "elimination" of the Jews, is a false, or at least an overdrawn one.[57] Both sets of attitudes existed, side by side and sometimes probably together. Decreasing interest in general in the "Jew-ish Question" was compatible with latent dislike for Jews and even with occa-sional shows of outrightly aggressive attitudes. What proportions of the pop-ulation tended more towards passive reserve or more towards occasional articulation of aggression cannot, from the nature of the evidence, be known.

(7) Ultimately, the difference in interpretation of popular attitudes appears to be neither wide, nor significant in explaining the regime's "freedom of

action to push for a radical 'Final Solution' ".[58] Clearly, by the beginning of the war the regime could presume a high degree of consensus in the acceptance of a "Jewish Question" and the need to find a solution to it, even if views about the solution differed, the more openly brutal methods met with criticism, and the consensus — on my interpretation — was based on the passivity and apathy of the vast majority of the population in the face of the dynamic aggression of a minority (which, however, was probably growing in size and had the broad backing of Party and State at its disposal). Though the "Jewish Question" was not an issue of great moment to the majority of the population, the widespread latent antisemitism and absence of any serious and organised opposition to antisemitism from non-Jewish institutions *before* 1933 was quite sufficient to allow the anti-Jewish radical momentum of the regime to gather pace until, given the existential conditions of the war years, it was as good as unstoppable. Once in power, the Nazi regime had not the slightest difficulty in finding among elites and among "ordinary" Germans collaborators, who, for a variety of motives, many of which had little to do with antisemitism, were prepared to push through and implement discriminatory policies which created their own spiral of radicalisation. And, of course, in the "Jewish Question" as in other matters, the conditions of Nazism encouraged the full flourishing of denunciation as an effective form of social control, in which neighbours and workmates collaborated with "active" not "passive complicity" in building the climate of repression and terror in which self-preservation goes hand in hand with moral indifference and apathetic compliance. In this there may well be little which is peculiarly German, or specific only to the "Jewish Question". A high level of passivity and "moral indifference" is arguably a common characteristic of attitudes towards "outsider" minorities in most authoritarian states, and to some extent even in "liberal democracies". Though not an "active" consensus, it is consensus nevertheless.

At the same time — and a point which I make as the only speaker at the Conference who is neither German nor Jewish — it is plain that so far in history no other advanced society has experienced a collapse of collective moral consciousness and individual civil morality approximating to the steepness of the decline in Germany after 1933. It was above all the absence of a choice against evil. Willy Brandt's concluding remarks in his foreword to a recent book on German-Jewish relations seem apposite, if banal:[59] "If there is any lesson to be learned from the extermination of millions of Jews, it is that decent men and women learn to make choices in favour of the good, and to do this before criminal power is established and gets stabilised. It is the one lesson history must teach, so that it does not repeat itself."[60]

Notes

1. See Otto Dov Kulka and Aron Rodrigue, 'The German Population and the Jews in the Third Reich. Recent Publications and Trends in Research on German Society and the "Jewish Question" ', in *Yad Vashem Studies*, 16 (1984), pp. 421–435, here esp. pp. 421–425.

2. *Ibid.*, p. 433.

3. *Ibid.*, pp. 426–427.

4. See note 1; and Ian Kershaw, *Popular Opinion and Political Dissent in the Third Reich. Bavaria 1933–1945*, Oxford 1983, chs. 6 and 9 (a modified version of 'Antisemitismus und Volksmeinung. Reaktionen auf die Judenverfolgung', in Martin Broszat and Elke Fröhlich (eds.), *Bayern in der NS-Zeit*, vol. 2, Munich–Vienna 1979, pp. 281–348), and 'The Persecution of the Jews and German Popular Opinion in the Third Reich', in *Year Book XXVI of the Leo Baeck Institute*, London 1981, pp. 261–289.

5. Kershaw, *Popular Opinion, op. cit.*, p. 277.

6. James J. Sheehan, 'National Socialism and German Society. Reflections on Recent Research', in *Theory and Society*, 13 (1984), pp. 851–867, here pp. 866–867.

7. Kulka and Rodrigue, *loc. cit.*, p. 434.

8. Konrad Kwiet, 'Zur historischen Behandlung der Judenverfolgung im Dritten Reich', in *Militärgeschichte Mitteilungen*, 27 (1980), pp. 170 ff.; Konrad Kwiet and Helmut Eschwege, *Selbstbehauptung und Widerstand. Deutsche Juden im Kampf um Existenz und Menschenwürde 1933–1945*, Hamburg 1984, pp. 42ff.

9. Kulka and Rodrigue, *loc. cit.*, p. 426.

10. *Concise Oxford Dictionary*, 5th edn., Oxford, 1964, pp. 52, 619. The adjective "apathetic" is defined as "insensible to emotion; indifferent", while "indifferent" can be both a neutral "neither good nor bad", and a negative "rather bad".

11. Kulka and Rodrigue, *loc. cit.*, p. 435.

12. See now the interesting demonstration of this in 1935 in Otto Dov Kulka, 'Die Nürnberger Rassengesetze und die deutsche Bevölkerung im Lichte geheimer NS-Lage- und Stimmungsberichte', in *Vierteljahrshefte für Zeitgeschichte*, 33 (1984), pp. 582–624.

13. Frances Henry, *Victims and Neighbors. A Small Town in Nazi Germany Remembered*, South Hadley, Mass. 1984, p. 106.

14. See Kershaw, *Popular Opinion, op. cit.*, p. 272 and note 85.

15. This conclusion is also reached by William Sheridan Allen, 'Die deutsche Öffentlichkeit und die "Reichskristallnacht" — Konflikte zwischen Werthierarchie und Propaganda im Dritten Reich', in Detlev Peukert and Jürgen Reulecke (eds.), *Die Reihen fast geschlossen . . .*, Wuppertal 1981, pp. 401–402.

16. Cited in Kershaw, *Popular Opinion, op. cit.*, pp. 360–361.

17. *Deutschland-Berichte der Sozialdemokratischen Partei Deutschlands 1934–1940*, Frankfurt a. Main 1980, vol. 7 (1940), pp. 257–258.

18. Wiener Library, London, *Deutsche Inlandsberichte/Reports from Inside Germany*, issued by the Auslandsbureau of Neu Beginnen, London, No. 64 (10th September 1941), p. 24; No. 65 (14th December 1941), pp. 17–19.

19. See e.g. Kershaw, *Popular Opinion, op. cit.*, p. 361.

20. Pointed out by Kulka and Rodrigue, *loc. cit.*, p. 432 note 32.

21. Inge Deutschkron, *Ich trug den gelben Stern,* 4th edn., Cologne 1983, pp. 60–62.

22. *Ibid.,* p. 80.

23. For this film, released in 1940, see David Welch, *Propaganda and the German Cinema 1933–1945,* Oxford 1983, pp. 292ff.

24. Dietrich Orlow, *The History of the Nazi Party,* vol. 2, 1933–1945, Newton Abbot 1973, pp. 250–251.

25. SD-Hauptaußenstelle Bielefeld, 5th August 1941, in Otto Dov Kulka and Eberhard Jäckel (eds.), *Die Juden in den geheimen NS-Stimmungsberichten 1933–1945,* Düsseldorf 2004, doc. 560, pp. 452–3. I am most grateful to Prof. Kulka for his kindness in allowing me to use this material in advance of his publication.

26. SD-Außenstelle Höxter, 25th September 1941; SD-Hauptaußenstelle Bielefeld, 30th September 1941; and see also SD-Außenstelle Minden, 21st February 1942, all in Kulka and Jäckel, doc. 567, pp. 456–7; doc. 569, pp. 458–9; doc. 619, pp. 486–7.

27. See Kershaw, *Popular Opinion, op. cit.,* p. 362; Marlis G. Steinert, *Hitlers Krieg und die Deutschen,* Düsseldorf 1970, pp. 239–240; Heinz Boberach (ed.), *Meldungen aus dem Reich,* Neuwied 1965, pp. 220–225; Kulka and Rodrigue, *loc. cit.,* p. 433.

28. SD-Außenstelle Höxter, 25th September 1941, in Kulka and Jäckel, doc. 567, pp. 456–7.

29. Kulka and Rodrigue, *loc. cit.,* p. 433.

30. Monika Richarz (ed.), *Jüdisches Leben in Deutschland. Selbstzeugnisse zur Sozialgeschichte 1918–1945,* Stuttgart 1982, Veröffentlichung des Leo Baeck Instituts, p. 63 and the eye-witness accounts p. 381 (" . . . Die Judensterne sind nicht populär. Das ist ein Mißerfolg der Partei . . . "), and p. 402.

31. Deutschkron, *op. cit.,* p. 87.

32. Michael Müller-Claudius, *Der Antisemitismus und das deutsche Verhängnis,* Frankfurt a. Main 1948, esp. pp. 166ff.

33. See Kershaw, 'Persecution', *loc. cit.,* p. 283.

34. Stapostelle Bremen, 11th November 1941, in Kulka and Jäckel, doc. 595, pp. 471–2.

35. SD-Hauptaußenstelle Bielefeld, 16th December 1941, *ibid.,* doc. 605, p. 478.

36. SD-Außenstelle Minden, 12th December 1941, *ibid.,* doc. 604, p. 477.

37. SD-Außenstelle Minden, 6th December 1941, *ibid.,* doc. 603, pp. 476–7.

38. SD-Außenstelle Detmold, 31st July 1942, *ibid.,* doc. 648, p. 503.

39. Kurt Jakob Ball-Kaduri, 'Berlin is "Purged" of Jews. The Jews in Berlin in 1943', in *Yad Vashem Studies,* 5 (1963), pp. 271–316, here pp. 279ff.; Richarz, *op. cit.,* p. 64; and see Wiener Library London, 'P' Collection Eye-Witness Accounts, PIIIc, No. 1143; PIIId, No. 854.

40. See Kershaw, 'Persecution', *loc. cit.,* pp. 283–284; Kulka and Rodrigue, *loc. cit.,* p. 434 note 40.

41. Deutschkron, *op. cit.,* p. 106 and see also p. 128.

42. Kershaw, *Popular Opinion, op. cit.,* pp. 364–368; *idem,* 'Persecution', *loc. cit.,* pp. 284–286.

43. Kulka and Rodrigue, *loc. cit.,* p. 434, though it appears to me difficult to draw firm inferences about the knowledge and reactions of non-Jews from the number and frequency of Jewish suicides.

44. *Ibid.,* p. 434.

45. SD-Außenstelle Minden, 12th December 1941, repeated in SD-Hauptaußenstelle Bielefeld, 16th December 1941, in Kulka and Jäckel, docs. 604–5, pp. 477–9.

46. SD-Hauptaußenstelle Erfurt, 30th April 1942, in *ibid.*, doc. 628, p. 491.

47. Herbert Obenaus, 'Haben sie wirklich nichts gewußt? Ein Tagebuch zum Alltag von 1933–1945 gibt eine deutliche Antwort', in *Journal für Geschichte*, 2, Heft 1 (1980), pp. 26–31, here esp., pp. 28–30. And see now, Herbert and Sibylle Obenaus, '*Schreiben, wie es wirklich war!' Aufzeichnungen Karl Dürkefäldens aus den Jahren 1933–1945*, Hannover 1985, pp. 107ff.

48. Deutschkron, *op. cit.*, pp. 107, 109–110, 140, 198. And see p. 170 for the comment of a Nazi betraying knowledge of extermination policies.

49. Walter Laqueur, *The Terrible Secret*, London 1980, p. 201.

50. Kulka and Rodrigue, *loc. cit.*, p. 435.

51. *Ibid.*, pp. 433–434. According to the SD report itself, the main interest of the population in Hitler's speech lay in his assessment of the military situation in the East. In the report of 2nd February 1942, which covers almost four printed pages in Boberach, *Meldungen*, pp. 216–220, the generalised response to Hitler's vicious but unspecific remarks about the Jews is summed up in five lines.

52. See Kershaw, 'Persecution', *loc. cit.*, pp. 284–285; Ball-Kaduri, *loc. cit.*, pp. 282–283; and cf. Müller-Claudius, *op. cit.*, pp. 165–166.

53. For what follows, see Müller-Claudius, pp. 166–176.

54. Henry, *op. cit.*, p. 143.

55. For notable instances of aid to Jews, see Kwiet and Eschwege, *op. cit.*, pp. 159 ff.; and also H. D. Leuner, *When Compassion was a Crime*, London 1966; and Anton Maria Keim (ed.), *Yad Washem. Die Judenretter aus Deutschland*, Mainz–Munich 1983.

56. For Berlin, see Deutschkron, *op. cit.*, and more recently the graphic account by Leonard Gross, *The Last Jews in Berlin*, London 1983.

57. Kulka and Rodrigue, *loc. cit.*, p. 427.

58. *Ibid.*, p. 435.

59. Henry, *op. cit.*, p. viii.

60. An additional comment upon a few of the points which were raised in the discussion of my paper would seem to me essential.

It does not seem sufficient to me to claim simply that Nazi propaganda had achieved its goal, opposition was neutralised, and that "moral indifference" is an unsatisfactory concept because "the very occasional acts of solidarity really tell us what we have to know about the response of the German people". My paper used the concept in an attempt to get behind crude generalisations and to consider the motives which underlay passive behaviour. The concept of "popular opinion", also criticised, is in my view necessary, despite the obvious inability to measure opinion precisely, to denote attitudes which, however inarticulate, continued throughout the "Third *Reich*" to exist in large measure independent of the "public opinion" steered by Nazi propaganda. To give up the attempt to obtain impressions of opinion and concentrate upon "behaviour" appears inadequate to me. Specifically on the "Jewish Question", the *behaviour* of the great majority of the population can only be described as passive. Any probing questions about the nature of the passivity bring us back immediately to the character of the attitudes of the passive majority and what shaped those attitudes.

It was suggested that the element of fear in shaping the attitudes of the non-Jewish population towards the Jews had been missing in my paper. The fear element is at least implicitly present in the paper, as for instance in the remarks about Karl Dürkefälden, and was unquestionably an important factor. However, I was deliberately careful not to place the burden of my explanation upon the fear factor. This can easily be misunderstood as an apologetic of the kind so often heard after the war — that the population had opposed the persecution of the Jews, but had been helpless in the face of totalitarian terror. Further emphasis was laid on the "absolute helplessness" of the population, the implicit presumption being that they *wanted* to help but were prevented by fear from doing so. This seems to me a highly dubious proposition. In my view, although the fear element was no doubt widespread and intense, the weight one attaches to it in evaluating attitudes towards the "Jewish Question" ought to be limited.

Finally, it was felt that I might have underrated the peculiarly German nature of the attitudes I was analysing. The deliberately provocative question I was raising was not, however, meant to be taken in a directly historical sense. Clearly, an evaluation of the obviously different popular attitudes towards the "Jewish Question" in, say, Germany, Italy, and Hungary, would have to take into account a whole array of highly complex developments which had helped to shape those attitudes, and displays of "civil courage" (or the lack of them) would have to be located in the different conjunctural circumstances. The point of my remark, however, was to pose the open question of whether the perceivable German patterns of opinion and behaviour are consonant with what could conceivably take place in other advanced societies, and involving minority groups other than Jews, where, for whatever reasons, a paranoid ideological thrust levelled at a recognisable, and largely unpopular, ethnic minority could be turned into a central focus of government policy.

PART III

The Final Solution in Historiography

IO

Hitler and the Holocaust

Explaining the Holocaust stretches the historian to the limits in the central task of providing rational explanation of complex historical developments. Simply to pose the question of how a highly cultured and economically advanced modern state could 'carry out the systematic murder of a whole people for no reason other than that they were Jews' suggests a scale of irrationality scarcely susceptible to historical understanding.[1] The very name 'the Holocaust', which acquired its specific application to the extermination of the Jews only in the late 1950s and early 1960s, when it came to be adopted (initially by Jewish writers) in preference to the accurately descriptive term 'genocide', has been taken to imply an almost sacred uniqueness of terrible events exemplifying absolute evil, a specifically Jewish fate standing in effect outside the normal historical process — 'a mysterious event, an upside-down miracle, so to speak, an event of religious significance in the sense that it is not man-made as that term is normally understood'.[2]

The 'mystification' and religious–cultural eschatology which has come for some writers to be incorporated in the term 'the Holocaust' has not made the task of Jewish historians an easy one in a subject understandably and justifiably 'charged with passion and moral judgement'.[3] Given the highly emotive nature of the problem, non-Jewish historians face arguably even greater difficulties in attempting to find the language sensitive and appropriate to the horror of Auschwitz. The sensitivity of the problem is such that over-heated reaction and counter-reaction easily spring from a misplaced or misunderstood word or sentence.

The perspective of non-Jewish historians is, however, inevitably different from that of Jewish historians. And if we are to 'learn' from the Holocaust, then — with all recognition of its 'historical' uniqueness in the sense that close parallels have not so *far* existed — it seems essential to accept that parallels *could* potentially occur in the future, and among peoples other than Germans and Jews. The wider problem alters in essence, therefore, from an attempt to 'explain' the Holocaust specifically through Jewish history or even German–Jewish relations, to the pathology of the modern state and an attempt to understand the thin veneer of 'civilization' in advanced industrial societies. Specifically applied to the Nazi Dictatorship, this demands an examination of complex processes of rule, and a readiness to locate the persecution of the Jews in a broader context of escalating racial discrimination and genocidal tendencies directed against various minority groups. This is not to forget the very special place which the Jews occupied in the Nazi doctrine, but to argue that the problem of explaining the Holocaust is part of the wider problem of how the Nazi regime functioned, in particular of how decisions were arrived at and implemented in the Nazi State.

The central issue remains, therefore, how Nazi hatred of the Jews became translated into the practice of government, and what precise role Hitler played in this process. Deceptively simple as this question sounds, it is the focal point of current controversy on 'the Holocaust' and forms the basis of the following enquiry, which attempts to survey and then evaluate recent research and interpretation.

Interpretations

Historians in both parts of Germany after the war came only slowly to concern themselves with anti-semitism and the persecution of the Jews. It was only in the wake of the Eichmann trial in Israel and the revelations of concentration camp trials in the Federal Republic that serious historical work on the Holocaust advanced in West Germany. Even then, historical scholarship and public 'enlightenment' on the fate of the Jews found only a muted echo in the German population, and popular consciousness was reached only through the showing of the American filmed 'soap-opera' dramatization of the Holocaust on West German television in 1979.[4] In the GDR, too, scholarly work on the persecution of the Jews effectively dates from the 1960s, though the subsuming, in the marxist–leninist conception of history, of race hatred within the nature of the class struggle and imperialism meant that down to the upheavals of 1989 few important works specifically on the Holocaust appeared.[5] The publications of Kurt Pätzold, while remaining firmly anchored within the marxist–leninist framework, marked a significant advance in GDR scholarship in this field.[6]

The major impulses to research and to scholarly debate have, therefore, been initiated outside Germany — in the first instance by Jewish scholars in Israel and other countries, and secondarily from non-Jewish historians outside Germany. However, even where the initial stimulant to debate emanated from non-German writers — and the controversies stirred up by Hannah Arendt's publication on the Eichmann trial[7], David Irving's attempt to whitewash Hitler's knowledge of the 'Final Solution'[8], and most recently through the 'Goldhagen debate' provide merely the most spectacular examples — ensuing discussion in the Federal Republic has been strongly influenced by the intellectual climate of German historical writing on Nazism. Hence, the contours of the debate about Hitler and the implementation of the 'Final Solution' are again peculiarly West German, even where valuable contributions have been made by foreign scholars.

The interpretational divide on this issue brings us back to the dichotomy of 'intention' and 'structure'. The conventional and dominant 'Hitlerism' approach proceeds from the assumption that Hitler himself, from a very early date, seriously contemplated, pursued as a main aim, and strived unshakeably to accomplish the physical annihilation of the Jews. According to such an interpretation, the various stages of the persecution of the Jews are to be directly derived from the inflexible continuity of Hitler's aims and intentions; and the 'Final Solution' is to be seen as the central goal of the Dictator from the very beginning of his political career, and the result of a more or less consistent policy (subject only to 'tactical' deviation), 'programmed' by Hitler and ultimately implemented according to the Führer's orders. In contrast, the 'structuralist' type of approach lays emphasis upon the unsystematic and improvised shaping of Nazi 'policies' towards the Jews, seeing them as a series of *ad hoc* responses of a splintered and disorderly government machinery. Although, it is argued, this produced an inevitable spiral of radicalization, the actual physical extermination of the Jews was not planned in advance, could at no time before 1941 be in any realistic sense envisaged or predicted, and emerged itself as an *ad hoc* 'solution' to massive, and self-induced, administrative problems of the regime.

The interpretation of the destruction of European Jewry as the 'programmatic' execution of Hitler's unchangeable will has an immediate (though actually superficial) attractiveness and plausibility. It marries well with the views of those historians who incline to explanations of the Third Reich through the development of a specifically German ideology, where a great deal of weight is attached, as a causal factor in Nazism's success, to the spread of anti-semitic ideas and an ideological climate in which Hitler's own radical anti-semitism could find appeal.[9] There is, of course, no difficulty in demonstrating the basic continuity and inner consistency of Hitler's violent hatred of the Jews — ranging from his entry into politics in 1919 to the composition of his Political Testament in the bunker at the end of April 1945 — voiced throughout in the most extreme language conceivable. The interpretation corresponds, too, to the 'totalitarianism' model where state and society were 'co-ordinated' to the level of executors of the wishes of Hitler, the unchallenged 'master of the Third Reich', who determined policy from above, at least in those spheres — like the 'Jewish Question' — where he had a paramount interest. Seen in this light, the logic of the course of anti-Jewish policy from the boycott and legislation of spring 1933 down to the gas chambers of Treblinka and Auschwitz seems clear. In crude terms, the reason why the Jews of Europe were murdered in their millions was because Hitler, the dictator of Germany, wanted it — and had done since he entered politics over two decades earlier.[10] It is in short an explanation of the Holocaust which rests heavily upon an acceptance of the motive force and autonomy of individual will as the determinant of the course of history.

Numerous influential works on the destruction of the Jews have advanced this or similar types of 'Hitlerist' approach. Lucy Dawidowicz, in her widely acclaimed *The War against the Jews,* for instance, declares that Hitler's idea for the 'Final Solution' went back to his experience in the Pasewalk hospital in 1918, and that by the time he wrote the second volume of *Mein Kampf* in 1925, he 'openly espoused his programme of annihilation' in words which 'were to become the blueprint for his policies when he came to power'. She writes of 'the grand design' in Hitler's idea, the 'long-range plans to realize his ideological goals' with the destruction of the Jews at their centre, and that the implementation of his plan was subject to opportunism and expediency. She concludes: 'Through a maze of time, Hitler's decision of November 1918 led to Operation Barbarossa. There never had been any ideological deviation or wavering determination. In the end only the question of opportunity mattered'.[11]

A similar inclination to a personalized explanation of 'the Holocaust' can be found, not unnaturally, in leading biographies of Hitler. Toland has Hitler advocating, as early as 1919, the physical liquidation of Jewry and transforming his hatred of the Jews into a 'positive political programme'.[12] Haffner, too, speaks of a 'cherished wish to exterminate the Jews of the whole of Europe' as being Hitler's aim 'from the beginning on'.[13] Fest relates the first gassing of

Jews near Chelmno in Poland in 1941 to Hitler's own experience in the First World War and the notorious lesson he drew from it, as recorded in *Mein Kampf*, that perhaps a million German lives would have been saved if 12,000–15,000 Jews had been put under poison gas at the start of or during the war.[14] And Binion's 'psycho-historical' study argues that Hitler's mission 'to remove Germany's Jewish cancer and to poison out Germany's Jewish poison' emanated from his hallucination while recovering from mustard-gas poisoning at Pasewalk, when he allegedly traumatized his mother's death while under treatment from a Jewish doctor and brought this in hysterical association with his trauma at Germany's defeat in 1918. Hitler 'emerged from his trance resolved on entering politics in order to kill the Jews by way of discharging his mission to undo, and reverse, Germany's defeat'. This was his 'main line political track' which ran from Pasewalk to Auschwitz.[15]

The same basic premise of the early formulation and unshakeable retention of Hitler's will to exterminate the Jews as sufficient explanation of 'the Holocaust' underlies Gerald Fleming's study, which seeks to document as fully as possible Hitler's personal responsibility for the 'Final Solution'. Though concentrating almost exclusively on the period of extermination itself, the introductory chapters deal with the growth of Hitler's anti-semitism. There, the claim is repeatedly made that 'a straight path' led from Hitler's personal anti-semitism and the development of his original hatred of the Jews to his personal liquidation orders during the war — 'a straight path from Hitler's anti-semitism as shaped in Linz in the period 1904–7 to the first mass shootings of German Jews in Fort IX in Kowno on 25 and 29 November 1941'. Physical extermination, in Fleming's view, was the aim maintained continually by Hitler from his experience of the November Revolution in 1918 down to his end in the bunker, and at the beginning of the 1920s 'Hitler developed . . . a strategic plan for the realization of his political aim'.[16]

Unwavering continuity of aim, a dominance in shaping anti-Jewish policy from first to last, and the decisive role in the initiation and implementation of the 'Final Solution' are also attributed to Hitler in the most influential works of leading West German experts on the Third Reich. Though prepared to accord 'the historical situation a comparatively high rank in the implementation of National Socialist "Jewish Policy"',[17] the 'programmatist' line (as it has been styled) sees Nazi anti-Jewish aims and measures as integrally linked to foreign policy, framed along with foreign policy in terms of long-range 'final goals', and advancing 'with inner logic, consistency, and in stages'.[18] Klaus Hildebrand summarizes the position clearly and concisely: 'Fundamental to National Socialist genocide was Hitler's race dogma. . . . Hitler's programmatic ideas about the destruction of the Jews and racial domination have still to be rated as primary and causative, as motive and aim, as intention and goal (*Vorsatz and Fluchtpunkt*) of the "Jewish Policy" of the Third Reich'.[19] For the Swiss historian Walter Hofer, 'it is simply incomprehensible how the claim can be made that the National Socialist race policy was not the realization of Hitler's *Weltanschauung*'.[20]

Hofer's remarks were part of a particularly aggressive critique of the 'structuralist' approach of 'revisionist' historians. The particular target of attack in this instance was Hans Mommsen, who is accused of not seeing because he does not want to see the obvious connection between the announcement of Hitler's programme (in *Mein Kampf* and elsewhere) and its later realization.[21] Mommsen himself has argued forcefully in a number of essays that the implementation of the 'Final Solution' can by no means be attributed to Hitler alone, nor to purely ideological factors in the German political culture.[22] Rather, the explanation has to be sought in the peculiarly fragmented decision-making processes in the Third Reich, which made for improvised bureaucratic initiatives with their own inbuilt momentum, promoting a dynamic process of cumulative radicalization. In his view, the assumption that the 'Final Solution' had to stem from a 'Führer Order' is mistaken. Though unquestionably Hitler knew of and approved of what was taking place, such an assumption, argues Mommsen, flies in the face of his known tendency to let things take their own course and to put off decisions wherever possible. Moreover, it is not compatible with his conscious attempts to conceal his own personal responsibility, with his more subconscious suppression of actual reality even to himself — for all the violence of his propagandistic statements, he never spoke in concrete terms about the 'Final Solution' even in his intimate circle — nor with maintaining the fiction of 'labour deployment' and 'natural wastage' through work. Accordingly, concludes Mommsen, there could have been no formal 'Führer Order' — written or verbal — for the 'Final Solution' of the 'European Jewish Question'. References in the sources to an 'order' or 'commission' as opposed to a vague 'wish of the Führer' relate invariably to the '*Kommissarbefehl*' complex of orders of spring 1941. Though the mass shootings of Russian Jews derived from the '*Kommissarbefehl*' group of directives, they must be distinguished from the 'Final Solution' proper — the systematic extermination of European Jewry. And that the latter was based on a Hitler order is, in Mommsen's view, neither supported by the evidence, nor inherently likely. Rather, although Hitler was the 'ideological and political originator' of the 'Final Solution', a 'utopian objective' could be translated into hard reality 'only in the uncertain light of the Dictator's fanatical propaganda utterances, eagerly seized upon as orders for action by men wishing to prove their diligence, the efficiency of their machinery, and their political indispensability'.

An essentially similar interpretation was advanced by Martin Broszat in his penetrating analysis of the genesis of the 'Final Solution'.[23] Broszat argued that 'there had been no comprehensive general extermination order at all', but that 'the "programme" of extermination of the Jews gradually developed institutionally and in practice out of individual actions down to early 1942 and gained determinative character after the erection of the extermination camps in Poland (between December 1941 and July 1942)'. In Broszat's view, deportation of the Jews was still the aim until autumn 1941, and it was only in the light of the unexpected failure of the Blitzkrieg invasion of the Soviet Union that problems in the deportation plans and the inability of Gauleiter, police chiefs, SS bosses, and other Nazi leaders in the Occupied Territories to cope with the vast numbers of Jews transported to and concentrated in their domains that led to a growing number of 'local initiatives' being taken to liquidate Jews, which than gained retrospective sanction 'from above'. Following this interpretation, therefore, 'the destruction of the Jews arose, so it seems, not only out of a previously existent will to exterminate, but also as the "way out" of a cul-de-sac into which [the regime] had manoeuvred itself. Once begun and institutionalized, the practice of liquidation nevertheless gained dominant weight and led finally *de facto* to a comprehensive "programme" '.

Broszat went out of his way in this essay (as had Mommsen in his writings) to emphasize that his interpretation could in no sense be seen in moral terms as removing the responsibility and guilt for the 'Final Solution' from Hitler, who approved, sanctioned, and empowered the liquidation actions 'whoever suggested them'. However, it does mean that in terms of actual practice of the implementation of the 'Final Solution', Hitler's personal role can only be indirectly deduced.[24] And morally, this clearly extends the responsibility and culpability to groups and agencies in the Nazi State beyond the Führer himself.

The role of Hitler is reduced still further in the analysis of the GDR historian Kurt Pätzold, who also demonstrates clearly the gradual and late emergence of an extermination 'policy' arising from unco-ordinated but increasingly barbarous attempts to drive Jews out of Germany and German-ruled territory.[25] While his description of the process which led from the aim of expulsion to genocide matches 'structuralist' explanations of western historians, Pätzold relates this to a sense of dynamic 'purpose' and direction of the Nazi regime which sometimes appears to be missing from 'structuralist' accounts. Despite a ritualistic overemphasis upon the functional purpose of anti-Jewish measures in serving the interests of monopoly capital, Pätzold's treatment has the merit, it seems to me, of locating the destruction of the Jews as an element within the overall context of the ruthless and dehumanizing expansionist drive of the Nazi State. This is to turn round the 'Hitlerist' interpretation, where the purposeful direction of Nazism is attributed as good as exclusively to the ideology of the Führer, and where Nazi *Lebensraum* ambitions are regarded as subsumed within and ultimately subordinate to Hitler's manic determination to destroy the Jews.

The lack of a long-range extermination programme has also come to be accepted by leading Israeli experts on 'the Holocaust'. Yehuda Bauer, for instance, writes that 'Nazi policy towards the Jews developed in stages, but that does not mean that at any given turning point there were not other options open to the Nazis that were considered seriously; there developed in Nazi Germany only one clear idea regarding Jews that was accepted by all policy-makers, namely the idea that ultimately the Jews had no place in Germany'.[26] Such a position is a recognition of the findings of detailed historical research on the course of anti-Jewish policy during the 1930s, where thorough analysis has suggested that the 'road to Auschwitz', was a 'twisted' one and not at all the 'straight path' which Fleming and others have seen.[27] Karl Schleunes's conclusion was, in fact, that 'the figure of Adolf Hitler during these years of search is a shadowy one. His hand appears only rarely in the actual making of Jewish policy between 1933 and 1938. One can only conclude from this that he occupied his time with more important concerns. In part the vagaries and inconsistencies of Jewish policy during the first five years of Nazi rule stem from his failure to offer guidance'.[28] Absence of clear objectives led to varying and rival 'policies', all of which ran into difficulties. But there was no turning back on the 'Jewish Question', and it was in this fashion that Hitler's known ideological obsession with the Jews had the objective function — without Hitler having to lift a finger — of pushing a failure in one direction (boycott, legislation, 'Aryanization', or emigration) into a renewed effort to 'solve the problem'.[29] Once again, there is no doubting Hitler's moral responsibility, nor the role his intentions — real or *presumed* — played. But of a consistent implementation of ideological prerogatives, there is little or nothing to be seen: 'The Final Solution as it emerged in 1941 and 1942 was not the product of a grand design'.[30]

The exploration of Uwe Dietrich Adam, which had the added advantage of continuing the investigation into the wartime period down to the implementation of the 'Final Solution' itself, arrived at similar conclusions: 'The empirical facts confirm first of all that there can be no talk of a planned and directed policy in this field, that a comprehensive plan for the method, content, and extent of the persecution of the Jews never existed, and that the mass killing and extermination, too was most probably not striven after *a priori* by Hitler as a political aim'. Unlike Broszat, Adam attributes the commencement of the 'Final Solution' to a personal order of Hitler in autumn 1941. However, in his view this has to be placed in the context of 'an inner development, which bound Hitler too in no small part'.[31]

At the root of the divergence in historical explanations of 'the Holocaust' summarized here lies the basic dichotomy between 'intention' and 'structure'. Was the systematic extermination of European Jewry the direct realization of Hitler's ideologically motivated 'design for destruction', which, after various stages in an exorable process of development, he set into operation through a written or, more likely, verbal 'Führer Order' sometime in 1941? Or did the 'Final Solution' emerge piecemeal, and without any command of Hitler, as 'an imperative result of the system of cumulative radicalization'[32] in the Third Reich? We turn now to a brief evaluation of these positions and an appraisal of some of the available evidence on which an interpretation must be based. Some new perspectives have opened up with the accessibility, since the demise of the Soviet bloc, of sources in eastern Europe.[33]

Evaluation

It seems important to re-emphasize at the outset that, despite claims sometimes made by those adopting a 'Hitlerist' interpretation, Hitler's continuous personal hatred of the Jews, his unique and central importance to the Nazi system in general and to the unfolding of its anti-Jewish policy in particular, and his moral responsibility for what took place are not at stake in the debate.

Historians favouring a 'structuralist' approach readily accept the overwhelming evidence that Hitler maintained a personal, pathologically violent hatred of Jews (whatever its derivation) throughout his political 'career', and recognize, too, the importance of that paranoid obsession *in determining the climate* within which the escalating radicalization of anti-Jewish policies took place. To put the counter-factual point at its crudest: without Hitler as head of the German State between 1933 and 1945, and without his fanaticism on the 'Jewish Question' as impulse and sanction, touchstone and legitimation, of escalating discrimination and persecution, it seems hardly conceivable that the 'Final Solution' would have occurred. This thought itself is sufficient to posit a fundamental link between Hitler and genocide. Moreover, the moral allegation against 'structuralist' historians — that they are 'trivializing' the wickedness of Hitler — is also misplaced. The 'structuralist' approach in no sense denies Hitler's personal, political, and moral responsibility for 'the Holocaust'. But it does broaden that culpability to implicate directly and as active and willing agents large sections of the German non-Nazi élites in the army, industry, and bureaucracy alongside the Nazi leadership and Party organizations. In fact, if anything it is the apparent need to find a supreme culprit which comes close to trivializing *in terms of historical explanation* by diverting attention from the active forces in German society which did not have to be given a 'Führer Order' to turn the screws of Jewish persecution one thread further until extermination became the logical (and only available) 'solution'. The question of allocating guilt thus distracts from the real question the *historian* has to answer: precisely *how* genocide could happen, how an unbalanced, paranoid hatred and chiliastic vision became reality and implemented as horrific government practice.

Rather, the central areas of debate among historians are: whether evidence of Hitler's continued and consistent personal hatred is sufficient explanation in itself of the Holocaust (given a background of widespread racial anti-semitism and ideological hatred of Jews, and a corresponding readiness to carry out 'Führer Orders'); whether physical extermination was Hitler's aim from a very early date or emerged as a realistic idea only as late as 1941 or so — the last remaining option in 'solving the Jewish Question'; and finally, whether it was necessary for Hitler to do more than establish the underlying objective of 'getting rid of Jews' from German territory, and then sanction the unco-ordinated but increasingly radical steps of the various groups in the State who were seeking, often for their own reasons and by no means primarily moti-vated by anti-semitic ideology, to turn this distant objective into practical reality. These are open questions, not foregone conclusions or matters for dogmatic assertion.

A problem with the 'intentionalist' position — in particular with its extreme 'grand design' variant — is an implicit teleology which takes Auschwitz as a starting-point and looks backwards to the violent expression of Hitler's early speeches and writing, treating these as a 'serious declaration of intent'.[14] Be-cause Hitler frequently spoke about destroying the Jews, and the destruction of the Jews actually took place, the logically false conclusion is drawn that Hitler's expressed 'intention' must have *caused* the destruction. In the light of hindsight, it is easy to attribute a concrete and specific meaning to the barba-rous, but vague and fairly commonplace, generalities about 'getting rid' (*Ent-fernung*) or even 'extermination' (*Vernichtung*) of Jews, which were part and parcel of Hitler's language (and that of others on the *völkisch* Right) from the early 1920s onwards. Coupled with this is the problem of establishing em-pirically Hitler's initiation or direct instigation of shifts in policy towards fulfilment of his aims — a problem accentuated by Hitler's obvious desire not to be publicly associated with inhumane and brutal measures, and the secrecy and euphemistic language which camouflaged the 'Final Solution' itself. If 'programme', 'plan', or 'design' in the context of Nazi anti-Jewish policy are to have real meaning, then they ought to imply something more than the mere conviction, however fanatically held, that somehow the Jews would be 'got rid of' from German territory and from Europe as a whole, and the 'Jewish Question' solved. Before 1941, the evidence that Hitler had more than such vague and imprecise convictions is slender. Finally, the moral 'lesson' to be drawn from the 'Hitlerist' position — apart from the 'alibi' it provides for non-Nazi institutions in the Third Reich — is by no means obvious. Fleming's rather jejune moral conclusion based upon his 'intentionalist' account of the 'Final Solution' is that hatred feeds the animal instinct for destruction of human life which resides in us all.[35]

More important than such bland moralization is the question posed by 'structuralist' approaches, of how and why a political system in all its complexity and sophistication can within the space of less than a decade become so corrupt that it regards the implementation of genocide as one of its supreme tasks. The central issue here revolves around the nature of 'charismatic' politics — how Hitler's vaguely expressed 'intent' was interpreted and turned into reality by government and bureaucratic agencies which developed their own momentum and impetus. The 'structuralist' type of interpretation also has some weaknesses. The empirical data are seldom good enough to allow detailed reconstruction of the processes of decision-making, on which much of the argument resides. And the emphasis upon contingency, lack of planning, absence of co-ordination, governmental chaos, and the *ad hoc* 'emergence' of policy out of administrative disorder seems at times potentially in danger of neglecting the motive force of intention (however vaguely expressed) and distorting the focus of the regime's ideologically rooted thrust and dynamic drive. However, the 'structuralist' approach does provide the opportunity of *locating* Hitler's 'intentions' within a governmental framework which allowed the bureaucratic implementation of a loose ideological imperative, turning a slogan of 'get rid of the Jews' into a programme of annihilation. And concentration on the historical question of how 'the Holocaust' happened rather than, implicitly or explicitly, seeking to allocate guilt makes the issue of whether Hitler took the initiative at every turn, or whether a particular decision was his alone, seem less relevant and important.

During the pre-war years, as the evidence assembled and analysed by Schleunes and Adam convincingly demonstrates, it seems clear that Hitler took no specific initiative in the 'Jewish Question' and *responded* to rather than instigated the confused and often conflicting lines of 'policy' which emerged.[36] The main impulses derived from the pressure 'from below' of Party activists, the internal organizational and bureaucratic dynamism of the SS–Gestapo–SD apparatus, the personal and institutional rivalries which found an outlet in the 'Jewish Question', and, not least, from economic interest in eliminating Jewish competition and expropriating Jewish capital.

The national boycott of Jewish businesses which took place on 1 April 1933 was organized chiefly as a response to the pressure of Party radicals, especially within the SA, during the wave of violence and brutality unleashed by the 'seizure of power'. The only 'plans' of the NSDAP for tackling the 'Jewish Question' which had been formulated before Hitler became Chancellor related to measures for legal discrimination and deprivation of civil rights.[37] Such vague and undetailed administrative 'plans' hardly accorded with the wild and dangerous mood of Party activists in the post–'seizure of power' euphoria of spring 1933. In these weeks, in fact, no directives at all on the 'Jewish Question' came either from the Reich Chancellory or from the Nazi Party headquarters.[38] Meanwhile, the SA, whose 'enthusiasm' could hardly now be checked, had started its own anti-Jewish campaign of boycotts and violence. When Gestapo chief Rudolf Diels complained about the excesses of the Berlin SA, he was informed that 'for very human reasons, certain activity must be found which will satisfy the feelings of our comrades'.[39] Under pressure, Hitler reacted towards the end of March with the call for a general boycott against Jewish businesses and professions, starting on 1 April and to be organized by a 14-man steering committee under the direction of Julius Streicher. As is well known, the boycott was a notable failure, and in the light of the negative echo abroad, the lack of enthusiasm among important sectors of the conservative power-élite (including President Hindenburg), and the cool indifference of the German people, it was called off after a single day and a coordinated national boycott was never again attempted. The shameful discriminatory legislation of the first months of the Dictatorship, aimed at Jews in the civil service and the professions, arose in the same climate and under the same pressures. Hitler's own direct role was a limited one dictated by the need he felt, despite his obvious approval of the boycott, to avoid association with the worst 'excesses' of the Party radicals. But the pace was forced by the momentum of the violence and illegalities, which produced their own compulsion to provide *post facto* legitimation and sanction — a process which was to repeat itself in later stages of the persecution of the Jews.[40]

Following a relatively quiet period between the summer of 1933 and the beginning of 1935, a new anti-semitic wave began and lasted until the autumn of 1935. Again, the agitation was set in motion and sustained 'from below' through the pressure at Gau level and from activists in the Party and in Hitler Youth and SA units in the localities. One Gauleiter noted in his report that stirring up the 'Jewish Question' had been useful in revamping the sagging morale of the lower middle class.[41] The agitation was, of course, backed by propaganda from the party and from the State. But other than that, there was remarkably little intervention from either the Party's headquarters or from the Reich government before mid August, when the boycotts and violence were becoming recognizably counter-productive, both in the repercussions for the German economy and on account of the unpopularity of the frequent breaches of the peace. Hitler himself was hardly involved in any direct sense. Despite his radical instincts, he was effectively compelled in this phase — in the interests of 'order', of the economy, and of diplomatic relations — to recognize the necessity of bringing the damaging campaign to a close.[42] This had to be balanced against the need not to lose face with Party activists and the pressure to comply with Party demands for 'action' — particularly for legislation in line with the demands of the Party programme — in the 'Jewish Question'. The resulting 'compromise' was effectively the promulgation of the notorious 'Nuremberg Laws' in September 1935 — at one and the same time according with demands for clear guidance and 'regulation' of the 'Jewish Question', and a further turn of the discriminatory screw.

The creation of the Nuremberg Laws demonstrates clearly how Hitler and the Nazi leadership responded to the considerable pressures from below in their formulation of anti-Jewish policy at this date.

The agitation and violence of the spring and summer 1935 rekindled expectations within the Party of incisive anti-Jewish legislation.[43] Hints and half-promises of measures were made by Reich Minister of the Interior Frick and others, bureaucrats hurried to regulate discrimination which was already taking place, and bans on various Jewish activities introduced independently by the Gestapo also forced retrospective sanctions by the administrators. One area of discontent among Party agitators was the failure to introduce the long-awaited exclusion of Jews from German Citizenship. Despite indications from the Reich Ministry of the Interior, where preparations were under way, the summer brought nothing to satisfy the hotheads. The other major issue whipped up by propaganda and agitation was that of mixed marriages and sexual relations between 'Aryans' and Jews. Again, illegal but sanctioned terroristic actions in cases of 'racial defilement' forced the pace and shaped the atmosphere. The urgent need for legislation was accepted by the regime's leaders at an important ministerial meeting chaired by Schacht on 20 August. Only the timing remained undecided. There were in fact already rumours in the foreign press in late August that the official proclamation might come at the Nuremberg Party Rally in September. Though such rumours turned out to be accurate, it is possible that they were at the time no more than intelligent speculation since it still appears that the decision to promulgate the laws at a special meeting of the Reichstag summoned to Nuremberg was taken only after the Rally had actually started — probably under renewed pressure from 'Reich Doctors' Leader' Gerhard Wagner who, apparently after talks with Hitler, announced on 12 September the intention of promulgating a 'Law for the Protection of German Blood'. From this point, as is well known, things moved fast. 'Experts' on the 'Jewish Question' were suddenly summoned to Nuremberg on 13 September and told to prepare a law regulating marriage between 'Aryans' and Jews. The sudden decision to promulgate anti-Jewish laws during the Rally seems to have been predominantly determined by questions of propaganda, presentation, and image. The Reichstag had been summoned to Nuremberg, where Hitler originally intended, in the presence of the Diplomatic Corps, to make an important statement on foreign policy, exploiting the Abyssinian conflict to articulate German revisionist demands. On the advice of Foreign Minister von Neurath, this plan was dropped on 13 September. A suitable replacement programme for the Reichstag and for Party consumption had rapidly to be found.[44] The rather undramatic 'Flag Law' hardly matched the demands of the occasion. Hence, the 'Blood Law', now being frantically drafted, and a Reich Citizenship Law, drafted in an hour on 14 September, were brought in as a substantial offering to the Reichstag and the assembled Party faithful. Hitler himself, who chose the mildest of the four drafts of the 'Blood Law' presented to him, apparently preferred to remain in the background during the drafting, pushing the Racial Political Office to the forefront. His role was a characteristically vague and elusive one in the question of how to define 'a Jew', when a conference for this purpose met at Munich at the end of the month. Hitler confined himself to a long monologue on the Jews, announced that the definitional problem would be sorted out between the Reich Ministry of the Interior and the Party, and adjourned the conference. It was mid November before State officials and representatives of the party could iron out a compromise solution — after Hitler had cancelled a further planned meeting in early November at which he had been expected to resolve the matter.[45]

Hitler continued to take no initiative in the 'Jewish Question' during the relatively quiet years of 1936–7, in which the rivalries mounted between the various agencies with an interest in Jewish affairs — the Ministry of the Interior, the Economics Ministry, the Foreign Ministry, the Four Year Plan Administration, the Rosenberg Agency, and, not least, the SS and Gestapo apparatus. A clear line of policy was as distant as ever. To go from Goebbels's informative diary record of these years, Hitler appears to have spoken directly about the Jews only infrequently, and then in general terms, as in November 1937, when, in a long discussion with Goebbels about the 'Jewish Question', he allegedly said: 'The Jews must get out of Germany, yes out of the whole of

Europe. That will take some time yet, but will and must happen'. According to Goebbels, the Führer was 'firmly decided' on it.[46]

These comments followed only a few weeks after Hitler had made his first public attack on the Jews for some time in a rhetorical propaganda tirade against 'the Jewish–Bolshevik World Enemy' during the Party rally in September 1937.[47] This was enough to set the tone for a renewal of anti-semitic activity on a large scale. However, Hitler himself needed to do no more in order to stimulate the process of 'aryanization' of Jewish concerns in the interests of 'big business', which set in at the end of 1937 and where Göring was the chief driving-force, nor to direct the escalating wave of violence which followed the *Anschluß* and became magnified during the Sudeten crisis of the summer. The agitation and terror of the Party rank-and-file in the summer and autumn of 1938, together with the expulsion in October of some 17,000 Polish Jews living in Germany — a move itself prompted by actions of the Polish government to deny them re-entry into Poland — shaped the ugly atmosphere which exploded in the so-called 'Crystal Night' pogrom of 9–10 November. And, as is generally known, the initiator here was Goebbels, who sought to exploit the situation in an attempt to re-establish his waned favour and influence with Hitler. Other than giving Goebbels the green light verbally, Hitler himself took care to remain in the background, and to accept no responsibility for actions which were both unpopular with the public and castigated (though of course not from humane motives) by Nazi leaders.[48]

Previously missing sections of Goebbels's diaries, discovered in archives in Moscow, cast new light on the instigation of the pogrom, and on the respective roles of Hitler and Goebbels. 'I put the matter before the Führer', Goebbels noted, in his description of the gathering of the Party faithful in the Old Town Hall in Munich on the evening of 9 November 1938. 'He decides: let the demonstrations carry on. Pull back the police. The Jews should for once be made to feel the full fury of the people.' 'That is right', continued the Propaganda Minister. 'Straightaway I give directions along those lines to police and Party.' Immediately afterwards, Goebbels gave his rabble-rousing speech to the Party leaders, who then raced to the telephone to set the 'action' in motion. 'Now the people will act', wrote Goebbels. Hitler, it is clear from the diaries, also gave the order that night for the immediate arrest of 20,000–30,000 Jews.[49] The following morning, 10 November, when Goebbels reported on the progress of the pogrom, Hitler showed full agreement: 'his views are very radical and aggressive', commented Goebbels. Hitler also approved 'with minor alterations' the decree which Goebbels prepared once it was felt the time had come to break off the 'action', and also indicated his wish for 'very sharp measures' against the Jews in the economic sphere — for the compulsory restoration of their businesses within any insurance contributions, and their subsequent gradual expropriation. Again, Goebbels then gave out the 'secret decrees' to put this into practice.[50]

'Crystal Night', concludes Schleunes, 'was a product of the lack of co-ordination which marked Nazi planning on Jewish policy and the result of a last-ditch effort by the radicals to wrest control over this policy'.[51] In propaganda terms, it was a failure. But, as usual, Nazi leaders, differing in their proposals for tackling the problem, concurred in the view that radical measures were needed. Jews were now excluded from the economy, and responsibility for 'the solution of the Jewish Question', though formally entrusted to Göring, was effectively placed in the hands of the SS. Emigration, which had significantly increased in the panic after the pogrom, remained the main aim, and was to be channelled through a central office set up in January 1939. The start of the war did not alter this aim. But it did alter the possibilities of its implementation.

The war itself and the rapid conquest of Poland brought about a transformation in the 'Jewish Question'. Forced emigration was no longer an option, and plans, for instance, to try to 'sell' Jews for foreign currency were not now feasible. After working on the idea of making German territory 'free of Jews' the Nazis now of course had an additional three million Polish Jews to cope with. On the other hand, there was now little need for consideration of foreign reactions, so that treatment of Polish Jews — as 'eastern Jews' particularly despised and dehumanized, the lowest form of existence in a conquered enemy itself held in contempt — reached levels of barbarity far in excess of what had taken place in Germany or Austria. Moreover, the more or less free hand given to Party and police, untrammelled by legal restraints or worries about 'public opinion', provided wide scope for autonomous individual 'initiatives' in the 'Jewish Question'.

Before considering the debate about whether the 'Final Solution' was instigated by a single, comprehensive 'Führer Order', and when such an order might have been given, it seems important to glance briefly at the process of radicalization as it gathered momentum between 1939 and 1941.[52]

An administrative decree of 21 September 1939, in which Heydrich laid down the general lines of Jewish persecution in Poland, distinguished between a long-term 'final aim' or 'planned overall measures' — not further elucidated and to remain strictly secret — and short-term 'preliminary measures' with the intention of concentrating the Jews in larger cities around railway junctions.[53] It would be mistaken to draw the conclusion that the vaguely indicated 'final aim' meant the programmed annihilation of the actual 'Final Solution' which later evolved. Clearly, however, the operative part of the decree related to the provisional concentration of Jews for further transportation. On Himmler's order a few weeks later, on 30 October, all Jews in the western part of Poland, now called the Warthegau and annexed to the Reich, were to be deported into the so-called *Generalgouvernement* — the core of German-occupied Poland under the governorship of Hans Frank — in order to make housing and jobs available for the Germans to be settled there. Hans Frank had accordingly to be prepared to receive several hundred thousand deported Jews and Poles from the Warthegau.[54] The policy of forced expulsion led unavoidably to the establishment of ghettos — the first of which was erected at Łódź (Litzmann-stadt) in December 1939. Almost at the same time, compulsory labour was introduced for all Jews in the *Generalgouvernement*. The twin steps of ghetto-ization and forced labour provided part of the momentum which was later to culminate in the 'Final Solution'.[55] For the present, it was presumed that the deportations from the annexed areas would bring about the rapid end of the 'Jewish Question' there, and that in the *Generalgouvernement* those Jews (including women and children) incapable of work should be confined to ghettos, and Jews available for hard labour should be assigned to forced la-bour camps. This decision, taken at a meeting of top SS leaders in January 1940, and accepting the inevitable deaths of thousands through exhaustion, hunger, and disease, marks a point at which 'the murderous anti-semitic idea, previously existing in a general, abstract form, began to take the shape of a concrete project. The decision to murder millions had at this point still not been taken.' But in thought and practice a step in that direction had been taken.[56]

In early 1940 there were still substantial differences of opinion on finding a 'solution to the Jewish Question', and there was no sign of any clear or com-prehensive programme. Obviously not anticipating an early 'solution', Hans Frank indicated in a speech in March that the Reich could not be rendered 'free of Jews' during the war.[57] A few months later, Frank was faced with a demand to receive a quarter of a million inhabitants of the Łódź ghetto, whom Gauleiter Greiser of the Warthegau wanted to be rid of from his domains. Frank refused, at which one of Greiser's team declared ominously that the 'Jewish Question, would have to be solved in some sort of way'.[58]

'Jewish policy' in mid 1940 — by which time West European Jews had also fallen into German hands and the real possibility of an overall European 'solution' had arisen — was still in a state of confusion. Eichmann still nur-tured ideas of a comprehensive programme of emigration to Palestine.[59] At-tempts to further the emigration of Jews from Germany itself (mainly via Spain and Portugal) continued to be promoted well into 1941.[60] However, arbitrary deportation of Jews from eastern areas of the Reich into the *General-*

gouvernement was banned by Göring in March 1940, after Hans Frank had refused to accept any further deportees.[61] And for the 'eastern Jews' — by far the majority under German rule — emigration was in any case not an option. In June 1940 Heydrich informed Foreign Minister Ribbentrop that the 'overall problem' of the approximately three and a quarter million Jews in German-ruled territory could 'no longer be solved through emigration' and that 'a territorial solution' was therefore necessary.[62] Jewish representatives were told that a reservation in an as yet undefined colonial territory was what the government had in mind.[63] A few days earlier Franz Rademacher, head of the Jewish desk of the Foreign Office, had presented plans to create the reservation in Madagascar — a suggestion apparently approved by Himmler, mentioned by Hitler in talks with Mussolini and Ciano that same month, and finally laid to rest only at the start of 1942.[64] The reservation plans were certainly taken seriously for a while, and in the light of recent research cannot be regarded as simply a camouflage for the early stages of the 'Final Solution' itself — though undoubtedly any reservation plan would have led to physical extermination, amounting to genocide by a different route.[65]

Towards the end of 1940 there was no end of the Jewish ghettos in Poland apparent in the foreseeable future. At the same time, the condition of the inhabitants was worsening daily, and coming to resemble the appalling caricature of Jewish existence portrayed in the nauseating propaganda film of 1940, *The Eternal Jew.*[66] From the point of view of the Nazi overlords, the acute problems of hygiene, food provision, accommodation, and administration attached to the ghettos called out for 'a relief from the burden and a solution'. Possible ways out were already being mooted: in March 1941 Victor Brack, a leading official in the Führer Chancellory who had been in charge of the so-called 'Euthanasia Action' which had liquidated over 70,000 mental patients and others in Germany between 1939 and 1941, proposed methods for sterilization of between 3,000 and 4,000 Jews a day.[67]

By this time, spring 1941, the Nazi and military leadership were fully engaged in the preparations for the invasion of (and expected rapid Blitzkrieg victory over) the Soviet Union. In the war against the Bolshevik arch-enemy, the 'Jewish problem' was to enter a new dimension — the last phase before the actual 'Final Solution'. The mass shootings of Russian Jews by the SS-*Einsatzgruppen* marked a radicalization of anti-Jewish policy, which Christopher Browning justifiably labelled 'a quantum jump'.[68] This brings us back to our central concern of Hitler's personal role in the genesis of the 'Final Solution'.

The inadequacy of the sources, reflecting in good measure the secrecy of the killing operations and the deliberate unclarity of the language employed to refer to them, has led to historians drawing widely varying conclusions from the same evidence about the timing and the nature of the decision or decisions to exterminate the Jews. Eberhard Jäckel hints in one place that a Hitler order for the extermination of the European Jews might have been given as early as summer 1940 — on the basis of a source, which he himself admits is not a good one (the memoirs of Himmler's masseur and *confidant* Felix Kersten). However, he adjudges spring 1941 to be the period when the first key decisions were taken, in the context of preparations for the Russian campaign, with further decisions extending the killing to German Jews at the end of September, then to Polish Jews, and finally (probably in November) to all European Jews.[69] Richard Breitman takes the view that by early 1941 'Hitler had already made a fundamental decision to exterminate the Jews'.[70] Helmut Krausnick writes of a 'secret decree . . . that the Jews should be eliminated' being issued by Hitler not later than March 1941, in the context of the directives to shoot the political commissars of the Red Army.[71] Andreas Hillgruber points to a verbal order of Hitler to either Himmler or Heydrich by at the latest May 1941 for the systematic liquidation of Russian Jews, and implies the issuing of an order extending this to all European Jews before the end of July 1941, when Heydrich received from Göring the commission to undertake preparations for 'a total solution of the Jewish Question' in the German sphere of influence and to submit an overall plan of measures necessary 'for the accomplishment of the final solution of the Jewish question which we desire'.[72] Most leading accounts (for instance of Reitlinger, Hilberg, Dawidowicz, and Fleming) concur in indicating a decision by Hitler to implement the 'Final Solution' during the spring or more likely the summer of 1941, and seeing this incorporated in the Göring mandate of 31 July.[73] Christopher Browning, too, emphasizes the centrality of Göring's order as reflecting a decision which Hitler had taken in the summer to extend the killing to all European Jews. However, he relativizes Hitler's decision by seeing it more in the shape of a prompting initiative rather than a clear directive, which the Führer approved and sanctioned in October or November.[74] Adam argues for a decision by Hitler in the autumn rather than the summer, at a time when the German advance in Russia had halted and vague ideas of a 'territorial solution' east of the Urals had obviously become totally illusory.[75] A more radical position is adopted by Broszat, Mommsen, and Streit, who reject altogether the existence of a single, specific, and comprehensive 'Führer Order' — written or verbal — and place the emphasis upon the cumulative 'sanctioning' of '*de facto*' exterminations, initiated by other agencies and wildly escalating, between the summer of 1941 and early 1942, out of which the 'Final Solution' proper — the systematic gassing in the extermination camps — 'evolved'.[76] A similar interpretation seems implicitly offered by Hans-Heinrich Wilhelm at the end of an exhaustive study of the *Einsatzgrup-*

pen, when he writes of a Hitler decision in the summer of 1941, but only relating to 'eastern Jews', with gradual later extension and radicalization, though not without Hitler's express agreement.[77]

Some studies support the case for a later date — at the earliest by the late summer or autumn of 1941 — for the shift into all-out genocide, while reaching quite different conclusions about Hitler's role. Arno Mayer sees the threshold to systematic mass murder crossed only once the Nazi 'crusade' against Bolshevism ran into difficulties, broadly beginning around September 1941. Even at the Wannsee Conference of 20 January 1942, the Nazis were, in Mayer's view, still only feeling their way towards the 'Final Solution'.[78] Hitler plays no specific role in Mayer's treatment, in contrast to that of the Swiss historian Philippe Burrin, who places Hitler at the center of his interpretation while according full weight to the circumstances in which the push for a territorial solution was transformed into systematic genocide. In Burrin's analysis, the increasing difficulties of 'Operation Barbarossa' are again seen as the spur to the lurch into genocide — a move he dates to around mid August in the Soviet Union, extended to the whole of European Jewry about a month later by Hitler's reversal of his earlier position that Jews could only be deported to the east following the defeat of the Soviet Union.[79]

More recent studies have tended to look to distinct phases of racialization rather than to one comprehensive decision, and have increasingly come to date the extension to all-out genocide no earlier than autumn 1941. Götz Aly, for instance, points to 'clear leaps in development (*deutliche Entwicklungssprünge*)' in March, July, and October 1941.[80] But in a striking — and controversial — reassessment, Christian Gerlach goes so far as to pinpoint a 'basic decision (*Grundsatzentscheidung*)' by Hitler, extending the killing of the Jews already raging in the east to the whole of European Jewry, to a meeting of his Gauleiter on 12 December 1941, the day after Germany's declaration of war on the USA.[81] Peter Longerich, on the other hand, rejects the elusive search for a single decision (and thus also Gerlach's precise dating) to instigate the 'Final Solution'. Rather, he views the programme to exterminate the Jews of Europe as the culmination, reached only during spring and summer of 1942, of a number of stages of escalation, all bearing genocidal intent.[82]

As these varied interpretations of leading experts demonstrate, the evidence for the precise nature of a decision to implement the 'Final Solution', for its timing, and even for the very existence of such a decision is circumstantial. Though second-rank SS leaders repeatedly referred in post-war trials to a 'Führer Order' or 'Commission', no direct witness of such an order survived the war. And for all the brutality of his own statements, there is no record of Hitler speaking categorically even in his close circle of a decision he had taken to kill the Jews—though his remarks leave not the slightest doubt of his approval, broad knowledge, and acceptance of the 'glory' for what was being done in his name.[83] Interpretation rests, therefore, on the 'balance of probabilities'.[84] We need briefly to consider the evidence in this light.

Hitler did not need to issue directives or take clear initiatives in order to promote the process of radicalization in the 'Jewish Question' between 1939 and 1941. Rather, as we have seen, the momentum was largely stimulated by a combination of bureaucratic measures emanating from the Reich Security Head Office (whose administrative consequences were not clearly envisaged), and *ad hoc* initiatives taken 'on the ground' by individuals and agencies responsible for coping with an increasingly unmanageable task. Typical of Hitler's stance was his wish, expressed towards the end of 1940, that his Gauleiter in the East should be accorded the 'necessary freedom of movement' to accomplish their difficult task, that he would demand from his Gauleiter *after 10 years* only the single announcement that their territories were purely German, and would not enquire about the methods used to bring this about.[85] His own direct role was largely confined to the propaganda arena—to public tirades of hatred and dire but vague prognostications about the fate of the Jews. The most notorious of these is his Reichstag speech of 30 January 1939, when he 'prophesied' that the war would bring about the 'annihilation (*Vernichtung*) of the Jewish race in Europe'—a prophecy to which he made frequent reference in the years to come, and which he significantly post-dated to 1 September 1939, the day of the outbreak of war.[86] This itself reflected Hitler's mental merger of the war and his 'mission' to destroy the Jews, which reached its fateful point of convergence in the conception of the 'war of annihilation' against the Soviet Union.[87]

The barbarous preparations for the attack on the Soviet Union, which implicated the *Wehrmacht*, too, in the series of criminal directives associated with the *Kommissarbefehl*—the ordered shooting of political commissars in the Soviet army—included briefings of the leaders of the *Einsatzgruppen,* and their subunits, the *Einsatzkommandos,* by Heydrich on the role they were to play in the wake of the advancing army. A number of *Einsatzkommando* leaders claimed after the war that it was during these briefings that they heard of the Führer order to exterminate the Russian Jews.[88] Most historians have accepted that some blanket empowering directive from Hitler to kill the Russian Jews lay behind Heydrich's verbal instructions, and that Heydrich's more limited written order to the Higher SS and Police Leaders in the Soviet Union of 2 July 1941 targeting the liquidation of 'radical elements' in the conquered population, among them 'Jews in party and state positions' was aimed at giving some sort of justification to the *Wehrmacht* or other authorities for the mass shootings.[89] Certainly the *Einsatzgruppen* killings were from the beginning far from confined to those in party and state offices. Already on 3 July, for example, the head of the *Einsatzkommando* in Luzk had around 1,160 Jewish men shot in order, as he said, to put his stamp on the town.[90] The death-squads of *Einsatzgruppe A* in the Baltic placed a particularly liberal interpretation on their mandate.[91] The *Einsatzgruppen* ultimately came to make a major contribution to the murder of in all over two million Russian Jews; *Einsatzgruppe A* alone reported the 'execution' of 229,052 Jews by the beginning of January 1942.[92] Their detailed monthly 'reports of events' belong to the most horrific surviving relics of the Third Reich.

The vast numbers of Russian Jews massacred speaks plainly in favour of a general commission from above, rather than simply local initiatives on the part of trigger-happy units of the *Einsatzgruppen*.[93] At the same time, there was in the early stages of the invasion evidently a lack of clarity among the heads of the *Einsatzgruppen* and other leaders of SS, Party, and police in the eastern occupied territory about the precise scope of their task and about the nature of any long-term solution to the 'Jewish problem'. It seems likely that during the various pre-invasion briefings of the *Einsatzgruppen* there had been talk of exterminating the Jews in the Russian territories to which they were about to be sent, but that such talk was couched in ambiguous terms capable of being understood in different ways.[94] At any rate, the evidence assembled by Alfred Streim and extended in Philippe Burrin's analysis is hard to reconcile with the transmission of a specific Führer order for the extermination of Russian Jewry *before* the beginning of 'Operation Barbarossa' and suggests that the killing instructions to the *Einsatzgruppen* were initially limited, probably indeed along the lines of Heydrich's directive of 2 July 1941.

The early post-war court testimony of *Einsatzkommando* leaders about the prior existence of a Führer order has been shown to be demonstrably false, concocted to provide a unified defence of the leader of *Einsatzgruppe D*, Otto Ohlendorf, at his trial in 1947.[95] More reliable subsequent testimony by those directly involved has indicated with a high degree of plausibility that there was no knowledge of a general liquidation order before the march into the Soviet Union, and that such a mandate was provided only several weeks after the beginning of the Russian campaign.[96] There was little logic, as Streim has pointed out, in trying to stir up the local population to unleash pogroms against the Jews (which had been part of Heydrich's verbal briefings) had a general extermination order already been in existence. Moreover, at the beginning of 'Barbarossa' the guidelines of Heydrich's written order of 2 July were for the most part *broadly* adhered to.[97] Compared with the scale of the killing from around mid August onwards, the numbers shot by units of the *Ein-*

satzgruppen in the first weeks after the invasion were *relatively* small and overwhelmingly confined to male Jews. For example, the exceptionally brutal *Einsatzkommando 3* operating in Lithuania killed 4,239 Jews, of which 135 were women, during the month of July 1941. In August, this rose to 37,186 killed, as many as 32,430 of them after the middle of the month, while in September the victims totalled 56,459, including 26,243 women and 15,112 children.[98] The actual practice of the *Einsatzgruppen* corresponds, therefore, to the significant indicators of post-war testimony and to a number of pieces of documentary evidence that the 'Führer order' was transmitted to the *Einsatzkommandos* sometime during the month of August.[99] However, the mandate to extend the killing now to all Jews irrespective of gender and age — with its notorious culmination in the mass shooting of 33,771 Jewish men, women, and children at Babi-Yar near Kiev on 29–30 September 1941 — was not, it seems, given at a specific time in a single centralized meeting addressed by Heydrich or Himmler. Rather, it seems to have been conveyed by Himmler in discussions with the Higher Police and SS-Leaders in the eastern territories, passed by them to the leaders of the *Einsatzgruppen,* and further transmitted in individual briefings of the heads of the *Einsatzkommandos.*[100] That the extension of the killing in August 1941 had Hitler's approval seems unquestionable. The nature and form of the 'Führer order', and whether it amounted to an initiative by Hitler himself or was any more than the granting of approval to a suggestion — itself, in all probability, emanating from the local commanders of the killing units and broadened into a wider remit — by Heydrich or Himmler, is impossible to establish.

A hint that the possibility was being mooted, even before the *Einsatzgruppen* had begun their massacres of Russian Jews, of a 'solution' involving all European Jews is given in Eichmann's circular of 20 May 1941, advising of Göring's ban on Jewish emigration from France and Belgium (in order not to block any further possible emigration of German Jews) and mentioning the imminent proximity of the 'Final Solution of the Jewish problem' which was 'doubtless to come'.[101] It was, however, over two months later, after the death-squads had been rampaging in the Soviet Union for almost six weeks, that Heydrich received an order from Göring to prepare for 'a total solution of the Jewish question'.[102] As we noted earlier, this authorization, initiated by Heydrich and drafted for him by Eichmann for Göring's signature in the context of the expected imminent victory over the Soviet Union,[103] has frequently been interpreted as giving voice to a Hitler directive marking *the* order for the 'Final Solution'. This interpretation seems unconvincing.

Whether Hitler was directly consulted about the Göring order to Heydrich is itself doubtful. Since the order technically amounted to no more than an extension of the authority which Heydrich had been granted by Göring in 1939, Hitler's further approval was not strictly necessary.[104] In any case, as Burrin has convincingly argued, it seems almost certain that this order did *not* mark the shift to all-out genocide, but still formed part of the intention to bring about a comprehensive territorial 'solution' once the war in the east was over.[105] At the end of July 1941, victory over the USSR seemed a matter of weeks rather than months away, and Heydrich was doubtless keen to establish beyond question his authority in the administration of the 'Jewish Question', which had initially derived from the mandate Göring had given him on 24 January 1939. For his part, Hitler still adhered throughout August 1941 to the view that Jews would be deported to the east only after the end of the Russian campaign.[106] In mid September, Hitler then changed his mind and ordered the earliest possible deportation of Jews from Germany, Austria, and Czechoslovakia. The reasons for the *volte face* are unclear. Demands were certainly being made by Rosenberg among others to deport Jews to the east. And Hitler seems to have been gloomy around this time about the slowing advance in the east, with the mounting possibility of a prolonged struggle. He reverted in his inner circle in precisely these weeks to the lessons to be drawn from Germany's defeat in 1918 and the need to destroy the 'elements' which had undermined Germany's chance of victory in the First World War.[107] And by September of course, as we have noted, full-scale genocide had already been embarked upon by the *Einsatzgruppen* in the Soviet Union. The case, then, for a linkage between the physical extermination which was already comprehensively taking place in the east, the inability to bring about a territorial solution in the foreseeable future, and the mandate which Heydrich had already obtained to organize an overall solution to the 'Jewish problem' in all areas under German occupation was by September 1941 becoming a compelling one. Even so, a comprehensive programme of extermination for the whole of European Jewry had not yet fully emerged.

The summer and autumn of 1941 were characterized by a high degree of confusion and contradictory interpretations of the aims of anti-Jewish policy by the Nazi authorities. It was a period of experimentation and resort to 'self-help' and 'local initiatives' in liquidating Jews, particularly once the transportations from the Reich and from the west of Europe had (in this case clearly on Hitler's orders) started rolling eastwards in autumn 1941, persuading Nazi bosses in Poland and Russia to adopt radical *ad hoc* measures — liquidation — to cope with the countless numbers of Jews from the west pouring into their domain and randomly deposited on their doorsteps.[108] Meanwhile the killing process was escalating rapidly — and not just in the 'Jewish Question'. Christian Streit has demonstrated how the *Wehrmacht* willingly collaborated in the multiplying barbarity of the 'war of annihilation' through its close co-operation with the *Einsatzgruppen* and by its direct involvement in the liquidation of almost two-thirds of the Soviet prisoners-of-war to fall into German hands.[109] It was initially to house Soviet captives that the then small concentration camp at Auschwitz was expanded, and the first experiments with the gas chambers there had as their victims not Jews but Soviet war prisoners.

The confusion, contradictions, and improvisations of the summer and autumn 1941 are, however, compatible with a gradual — though steep — descent into the full-scale genocidal programme known to history as the 'Final Solution', which fully emerged only in spring 1942, in the weeks following the Wannsee Conference. Rudolf Höss (the Commandant of Auschwitz), it is true, recalled after the war receiving the extermination order from Himmler in the summer of 1941. But Höss's testimony cannot be relied upon, and in this case much points to the conclusion that he had erroneously pre-dated events by a year and was really referring to the summer of 1942.[110] Eichmann's testimony in Israel in 1960 was also at times inaccurate. He claimed to remember vividly Heydrich communicating to him two or three months after the invasion of the Soviet Union that 'the Führer has ordered the physical extermination of the Jews'.[111] But his memory was frequently wayward when it came to precise dates and times. In this case, too, it is as well not to build too much on such dubious evidence.[112]

Browning concludes from this confused evidence that Hitler approved in late October or November 'the extermination plan he had solicited the previous summer'.[113] Burrin's interpretation, from the same evidence, is that the Führer order to kill the Jews of Europe was given about September 1941, and was probably synonymous with the order to deport the Jews to the east.[114] Gerlach provides good grounds, however, for believing that these dates for a Führer order are premature.

The uncertainties registered during the autumn by some Nazi leaders in the east — such as Reich Commissar for the Eastern Region (*Ostland*) Hinrich Lohse in Riga and General Commissar for Belorussia (*Weißruthenien*) Wilhelm Kube in Minsk — about the mass liquidation of Jews arriving in their areas from the Reich, and the inconsistencies in Nazi barbarity during these weeks, do not suggest that a central, comprehensive decision to exterminate the Jews of Europe had already been taken. Lohse and Kube were far from alone in seeking clarification from the Reich Ministry for the Occupied Eastern Territories (the *Ostministerium*) and the Reich Security Head Office (*Reichssicherheitshauptamt*, RSHA) about whether deported Reich Jews — Kube viewed the Jews from his own 'cultural sphere (*Kulturkreis*)' as different from the 'native brutish hordes (*bodenständigen vertierten Horden*)' in the conquered eastern territories — were to be killed,[115] and if so whether exceptions were to be made for 'Mischlinge' (part-Jews), Jews with war decorations, or Jews with 'aryan' partners. The unease about such issues, leading to numerous protests reaching the Eastern Ministry and RSHA, prompted Himmler, on 30 November 1941, to prohibit the liquidation of a transport of 1,000 Jews to Riga from Berlin. The order came too late: the Jews had been shot on arrival, as had two transports of Jews from Germany and Austria to Kovno in Lithuania a few days earlier.[116] With the Nazi authorities incapable of coping with the problems — which they had, of course, created for themselves — of housing and feeding the deported Jews, and with a plainly genocidal policy operating in the occupied parts of the Soviet Union, killing the Jews deported into their areas was increasingly seen by local police chiefs and party leaders as the solution.

Some developed local extermination programmes: the beginning of construction in November of the extermination camp in Belzec in the Lublin District in the General Government (the province of SS Police Chief Odilo Globocnik) started out as one such initiative.[117] Another was the killing of Jews in gas vans at the beginning of December at Chelmno in the 'Warthegau' — the large tract of western Poland now annexed to the Reich — the domain of Gauleiter Arthur Greiser and Police Chief Wilhelm Koppe.[118] These local genocides, however, did not yet form part of a comprehensive programme: by the beginning of December 1941, then, Nazi anti-Jewish policy was still evolving, still transitional. The step into outright genocide had been taken in some areas, though there was as yet no co-ordinating programme to link together the various killing actions.

Broadly, the position was as follows. The overall aim of the RSHA appears still to have been a mass deportation of Jews 'to the east' (meaning to the inhospitable regions of the former territory of the Soviet Union), where those capable of work would have died of exhaustion, cold, starvation, and disease, while those incapable of working would have immediately been liquidated.[119] Such a 'territorial solution' to the 'Jewish Question' — itself outrightly genocidal — had been vitiated by the inability of the German army to attain rapid victory over the USSR. Nevertheless, Jews from the Reich were now being deported to the east, despite the continuation of the war and the absence of any territory that might serve as a 'Jewish reservation'. Meanwhile, the *Einsatzgruppen* and their subunits had been slaughtering Jews in their tens of thousands for months in the former territories of the Soviet Union, and Nazi leaders in some areas of the east were increasingly resorting to 'self-help' and developing their own killing programmes. Despite the evident escalation of genocidal actions, there was still a lack of clarity about the treatment of the deported Reich Jews and a need to define any possible exclusions from the deportation programme and liquidation actions.

The need to provide co-ordination and clarification of the deportation programme, particularly concerning the Reich Jews, was the basis of Reinhard Heydrich's invitation, issued on 29 November 1941, to a meeting of state secretaries from government ministries, along with representatives of the RSHA and other agencies directly concerned, to take place at the Wannsee, in the west of Berlin, on 9 December. In the event, the meeting was postponed — almost certainly on account of both the implications of the Japanese attack on Pearl Harbor on 7 December and the opening of the Red Army's major counter-offensive two days earlier, with its inevitable drastic effect on Heydrich's large-scale deportation plans.[120] According to Gerlach's interpretation, by the time the Wannsee Conference was reconstituted, on 20 January 1942, the crucial step in the transition to a comprehensive programme of genocide had taken place; by then, Hitler had given his 'basic decision' to kill all the Jews of Europe.

With the Japanese attack on Pearl Harbor — which prompted Hitler in his Reichstag speech on 11 December to announce the German declaration of war on the USA — the war was indeed now a 'world war' — a term hitherto reserved in Germany for the war of 1914–18; and Hitler, in the notorious speech he made to the Reichstag on 30 January 1939, had 'prophesied' that, in the event of another world war, the Jews of Europe would be annihilated.[121] On 12 December 1941, the day after the war, in his view, had truly become a 'world war', Hitler addressed party leaders (Reichsleiter and Gauleiter), a group of around 50 persons, in his private rooms in the Reich Chancellory; among other topics, he spoke of the Jews. According to Goebbels's summary of this part of his address, he referred to his 'prophecy', and to his view that the 'annihilation of Jewry' had to be the 'necessary consequence' of the fact that the 'world war' had arrived. In Goebbels's chilling account, 'the instigators of this bloody conflict will thus have to pay for it with their lives (*so werden die Urheber dieses blutigen Konflikts dafür mit ihrem Leben bezahlen müssen*)'.[122] This amounted, according to Gerlach, to Hitler's announcement of his decision to exterminate the Jews of Europe.[123]

During the following days, Hitler had private meetings with a number of Nazi leaders who had a direct interest in the 'Jewish Question'. No record survives of what was said at them, but a cryptic note in the recently discovered desk-diary of Heinrich Himmler indicates that the treatment of the Jews was discussed with Hitler at a meeting in his headquarters on the afternoon of 18 December 1941. 'To be exterminated as partisans (*Als Partisanen auszurotten*)' was all that was entered alongside 'Jewish Question', as the outcome of the meeting.[124] Interpretation is clearly not straightforward. Gerlach sees the entry not — as might at first sight be presumed — as referring to the Soviet Union, where the murder of the Jews had by this time been long in full swing, but to 'imaginary "partisans", the alleged "Jewish threat"'. Though accepting that the entry is unclear, it points, in Gerlach's view, 'to a global meaning of Hitler's statement, which in its verbal form can only be understood as a directive'.[125]

The 'Jewish Question' had also arisen at a discussion on 14 December, two days after his address to the Gauleiter, between Hitler and his Minister for the Eastern Territories, Alfred Rosenberg. When Rosenberg gave him the manuscript of a forthcoming speech to glance over — in itself a somewhat unusual occurrence — Hitler commented that the speech had been composed in the circumstances prevailing before Japan had entered the war. Rosenberg's note on the meeting continued: 'About the Jewish Question, I said that the comments about the New York Jews ought perhaps now, after the decision, to be somewhat altered. My standpoint was not to speak of the extermination (*Ausrottung*) of Jewry. The Führer approved this stance and said they had burdened us with the war and brought about the destruction so it was no wonder if they should be the first to feel the consequences.'[126] Gerlach sees this as another piece of evidence for Hitler's 'basic decision', announced two days before his talk with Rosenberg. It is certainly additional evidence that his 'prophecy' about the destruction of the Jews as a consequence (as he saw it) of causing the world war was at the forefront of Hitler's mind in these days.

As a further indication that a momentous decision had been taken by Hitler on or around 12 December, Gerlach cites the reply made by Dr Otto Bräutigam of the Eastern Ministry to a request from Hinrich Lohse, Reich Commissar for the *Ostland,* as to whether all Jews in the east, irrespective of age, sex, and economic requirements, should be liquidated: 'The Jewish Question has probably been clarified by now through verbal discussions. Economic considerations are to be regarded as fundamentally irrelevant in the settlement of the problem.'[127]

A final strand of evidence in support of a basic decision being taken by Hitler in December 1941 to kill the whole of European Jewry is found by Gerlach in the comments of Hans Frank to leading figures in the administration of the *Generalgouvernement* on 16 December, four days after Hitler's address to his party leaders. Frank alluded to Hitler's 'prophecy' (making yet a further appearance in these days), using phraseology which, based on Goebbels's account, had been deployed by Hitler at the meeting with the Gauleiter. Frank spoke of the war as only a partial success if Jews in Europe should survive it. The Jews had to disappear, he declared. He had begun negotiations about deporting them 'to the east', and referred to the forthcoming Wannsee Conference to discuss the issue. 'But what should happen to the Jews?', he asked. 'Do you believe they will be housed in settlement-villages in the *Ost-*

land? They've said to us in Berlin: why are you giving us all this trouble? We can't do anything with them in the *Ostland,* or in the Reich Commissariat [Ukraine]. Liquidate them yourselves!' Frank encouraged his audience, as Hitler has done, to put all sympathy aside. 'We must destroy (*vernichten*) the Jews wherever we meet them, and wherever it's at all possible to do so, in order to uphold the overall structure of the Reich here,' he added.[128]

Gerlach unquestionably makes a compelling case for a sharp intensification, in the immediate aftermath of Germany's declaration of war on the USA, of the drive for a comprehensive and radical genocidal solution; and the significance of December as an important juncture in the evolution of genocidal policy is heightened still further if it is recalled that the crisis that had developed on the eastern front in the advance on Moscow was at this very time approaching its climacteric. Where Gerlach is less persuasive, however, is in his claim that, in the days following the Japanese attack on Pearl Harbor, Hitler arrived at — and announced to his party leaders at their meeting on 12 December — a 'basic decision'.

None of those present later referred to Hitler's meeting with his Gauleiter as carrying any special significance with regard to a solution to the 'Jewish Question', let alone singled it out as the meeting where the key decision for the 'Final Solution' had been reached.[129] The passage in Goebbels's diary — nine lines in a summary covering almost seven printed pages[130] — describing Hitler's comments on the Jews in his speech on 12 December was not highlighted in any way by the Propaganda Minister as of special importance. There was in any case little or nothing in what Hitler said that Goebbels and the others had not heard many times before. The remarks on the Jews occurred, according to the summary, around three-quarters of the way through Hitler's address. They formed, it seems, a minor section in a lengthy speech largely devoted to a commentary on the war situation, the reasons for the declaration of war on America, and bolstering the morale of Hitler's lieutenants in the party — the most important task in such meetings, which were not infrequent during the war and invariably followed important events.[131] Moreover, the improbability of Hitler using this forum to announce a 'decision' to have all the Jews in Europe exterminated is magnified by the fact that the 'Final Solution', other than in the horrific but vague generalities he often made about the destruction of the Jews, remained a taboo subject in his presence, even among his immediate entourage.

Rosenberg's note about his meeting with Hitler on 14 December is of doubtful value as evidence of a key decision by Hitler about the 'Final Solution'. His reference to changed circumstances — 'now, following the decision' — occurs in direct juxtaposition to the views he had expressed in his speech about New

York Jews. Since Goebbels's account of Hitler's address to the Gauleiter on 12 December contains no references to anything resembling a 'decision', but a vital 'decision' — namely to declare war on the United States — had indeed been announced to the Reichstag on 11 December, it seems perverse to presume that this latter was not the 'decision' to which Rosenberg was alluding.[132] Nor does Bräutigam's reply to Lohse provide evidence of a basic decision on the 'Final Solution' taken by Hitler in mid-December. Bräutigam does not mention Hitler or any other specific individual, but refers only to clarity being created 'through verbal discussions' — presumably in the *Ostministerium* or the RSHA, and not necessarily involving Hitler directly. Even Bräutigam's clarification for Lohse of basic policy guidelines did nothing to prevent continuing deliberations between the Lohse's officials and police leaders about the handling of the Jews, nor, beginning in mid-December, the halting of the killing of Jews for some months in the Reich Commissariat *Ostland*.[133]

Hans Frank's remarks to his subordinates in the *Generalgouvernement* are certainly consonant with an extensification and radicalization of genocidal measures in December 1941. Hitler's drastic comments to his party chiefs, which Frank had heard, unquestionably served once more as a spur to outrightly murderous action. They offered what amounted to an invitation from the highest authority in the Reich to make the Jews pay with their lives in revenge for the war. Hearing Hitler's tirade in the explosive climate accompanying the drama of war against the USA and crisis on the eastern front was more than enough for party leaders to go away knowing, as on so many occasions, how to 'work towards the Führer', not needing any explicit order or directive. But there is nothing in what Frank said, appallingly brutal though his words were, to suggest that he had witnessed a key moment where the decision to kill the Jews had been announced.

Finally, the entry in Himmler's desk diary for 18 December 1941 is too terse to allow for more than speculative interpretation. It certainly links Hitler explicitly with extermination policy: it plainly shows him approving of the extirpation of Jews. But there is nothing in it which offers obvious support to Gerlach's view that it is to be equated with the actual decision for the 'Final Solution', with a decision to extend the extermination from Soviet Jewry to the Jews of the rest of Europe under the rubric of combating 'partisans'. However allergic he was to the threat of internal subversion, Hitler never, as far as is known, used the term 'partisan' in connection with Jews in the Reich or in western Europe.[134] On the other hand, both he and Himmler were being made acutely aware in autumn 1941 of the scale of the 'partisan problem' in the Soviet Union.[135] The close identification of Jews with partisans, presumed by many Wehrmacht units since the early weeks of 'Operation Barbarossa', had been emphasized in September both in military guidelines and in an exhortation by Arthur Nebe, head of *Einsatzgruppe B,* in a lecture to officers from Army Group Centre.[136] It seems most likely that discussion of the 'Jewish Question' on 18 December by Hitler and Himmler took place within this context, and was aimed at liquidating the remainder of the Jews in the occupied Soviet territories under the rubric of radical action to combat the 'partisan' problem. A report presented by Himmler to Hitler at the end of 1942 on 'bandit' activity of 'partisans' in southern Russian and the Ukraine for the three months September–November 1942 shows what this could mean. Those 'executed' for their presumed connection with such activity included 363,211 Jews. Others 'executed' for the same reason totalled 14,257.[137]

As the fragments of documentary evidence, whatever their ambiguities, reveal, the open genocidal intent displayed by leading Nazis in December 1941 was unmistakable. But it is also plain that there was as yet no concept of how an immense deportation and extermination programme might be carried out, with what methods, and in what timescale. Hans Frank admitted, when speaking in mid-December 1941 of the need to liquidate the Jews of the *Generalgouvernement,* that he did not know how this could be done: 'We can't shoot these 3.5 Million Jews,' he declared, 'we can't poison them, but will have somehow to take steps leading somehow to a success in annihilation (*Vernichtungserfolg*) in connection with the large-scale measures under discussion by the Reich.'[138] The last comment was a further reference to the deliberations at the forthcoming Wannsee Conference.

Gerlach suggests that the purposes of the Wannsee Conference had changed sharply during the period of its lengthy postponement between 9 December and 20 January 1942. He hints, in fact, that the very postponement — or at any rate its inordinate length — was caused by the changed situation following Hitler's speech on 12 December, and the need now to prepare a full-scale extermination programme which had not been the case when initial invitations to the conference had gone out at the end of November 1941.[139] But whether the conference had undergone a fundamental change of purpose might be doubted. Rather, it seems (to follow Peter Longerich's interpretation) better to view the Wannsee Conference as taking place at a time of rapid transition and shifting perspectives in the 'solution to the Jewish Question' — a time when the intention to undertake an enormous deportation programme leading to total annihilation in work camps in occupied Soviet territory after the end of the war was rapidly giving way to the realization that the Jews would have to be destroyed during the war, and in the territory of the General Government.[140] Viewed in this way, the Wannsee Conference was not the orchestration of an existing plan of the 'Final Solution'; rather it ushered in the final stage of escalation of the extermination policy — the incorporation of the whole of German-occupied Europe in a comprehensive programme of systematic annihilation of the Jews.[141] The evolution of such a programme, once initiated as a planned operation, rapidly gathered pace in the spring. Decisions to widen the killing from the districts of Lublin and Galicia to the whole of Poland, in what was now coming to be called '*Aktion Reinhard*' (linking the three extermination camps of Belzec, Sobibor, and Treblinka), and to liquidate practically all Jews deported from the Reich and other parts of central Europe, were taken around the end of April and beginning of May 1942. By early June a programme had been drawn up for the deportation of Jews from western Europe to begin in July.[142] Most were transported to the largest of the extermination camps by then in operation, Auschwitz-Birkenau. By the summer of 1942, then, the 'Final Solution' as history knows it was fully under way. By the end of 1942, a high proportion of the victims of the Holocaust — according to the SS's own calculations, close to four million — had already been murdered.[143]

In Gerlach's view, 'the presumption that there never was a central decision by Hitler about the murder of European Jews' is 'not sustainable'.[144] The arguments he himself advances for such a decision being taken in December 1941 do not, however, compel. Rather, Hitler's speech to party leaders on 12 December (and his private discussions around the same time with Himmler and other key figures) can probably best be interpreted as providing crucial sanction from the highest authority, through his tirade of genocidal hatred at a time of momentous significance for the Reich and in a context he had long 'prophesied' would result in the destruction of the Jews, for the murderous policies desired or indeed already being put into operation by local Nazi rulers in the eastern territories. At the same time, Hitler's renewed attack on the Jews gave added impetus to the quest by the RSHA leadership to provide the necessary co-ordination for what Heydrich still termed, with justification, at the Wannsee Conference, 'the coming final solution of the Jewish Question (*die kommende Endlösung der Judenfrage*).[145]

Leaving aside Gerlach's insistence on a 'basic decision' by Hitler in December 1941, his overall interpretation fits well into what appears to be emerging somewhat tentatively and still with numerous points of unclarity or dispute — unsurprising given the complexity of the evidence — as a consensus in recent research on the genesis of the 'Final Solution'. This consensus amounts to an increasing readiness among scholars working in the field to accept that no single decision brought about the 'Final Solution', but that a lengthy process of radicalization in the search for 'a solution to the Jewish Question' between spring 1941 and summer 1942 — as part of an immense overall resettlement and 'ethnic cleansing' programme for central and eastern Europe, vitiated through the failure to defeat the Soviet Union in 1941 — was punctuated by several phases of sharp escalation. Hitler's express approval and sanction of the stages of escalation in the killing of the Jews is nowhere in question. The most important stages in this process were spring 1941 (in the planning of 'Barbarossa'), summer 1941 (the move to full-scale genocide in the Soviet Union), autumn 1941 (the consequences of Hitler's decision to deport Reich Jews and those of Bohemia and Moravia to the east), December 1941 (the aftermath of the declaration of war on the USA), and spring 1942 (the emergence of the co-ordinated programme of extermination).[146] Though Gerlach is dismissive of arguments which suggest that the last key decision fell only in the spring of 1942,[147] the piecemeal development of the 'Final Solution' — something intuitively put forward by Martin Broszat as long ago as 1977[148] — seems to be the most significant conclusion arising from an array of recent important regional studies of genocidal policy (including, not least, Gerlach's own).[149] Hitler's precise role in these key phases remains for the most part hidden in the shadows.[150] But that does not mean it was unimportant. On the contrary: the impetus Hitler provided in the framing of the barbarous plans for the invasion of the Soviet Union, his approval of Himmler's widening of the genocidal remit in the Soviet Union in the summer, his eventual agreement in September to have the German Jews deported to the east, and his overt encouragement of extermination actions in December were all crucial strands of authorization for the emerging 'Final Solution'. The Führer's authorization of the vital steps into genocide was indispensable. That there was a single, all-encompassing 'Führer decision' seems very doubtful, and is in any case a secondary issue.[151]

Relating this discussion of the genesis of the 'Final Solution' to the polarized 'Hitlerist' and 'structuralist' interpretations — the one emphasizing a Hitler order as the culmination of a planned long-term programme directed towards extermination, the other stressing a process of permanent improvization as a way out of self-made administrative difficulties — one would have to conclude that neither model offers a wholly satisfactory explanation.

For all the paralleled barbarity of his language, Hitler's direct actions are difficult to locate. Though his hatred for the Jews was undoubtedly a constant, the relationship of his hatred to actual policy changed considerably over time as the policy options themselves narrowed. Hitler himself took relatively little part in the overt formulation of that policy, either during the 1930s or even the genesis of the 'Final Solution' itself. His major role consisted of setting the vicious tone within which the persecution took place and providing the sanction and legitimacy of initiatives which came mainly from others. More was not for the most part necessary. The vagaries of anti-Jewish policy both before the war and in the period 1939–41, out of which the 'Final Solution' evolved, belie any notion of 'plan' or 'programme'. The radicalization could occur without any decisive steerage by Hitler. His influence was, however, all-pervasive, and his direct intervention in anti-Jewish policy was on occasion crucial. Above all, his dogmatic, unwavering assertion of the ideological imperative — 'getting rid of the Jews' from Germany, then finding a 'Final Solution to the Jewish Question' — which had to be translated into bureaucratic and executive action, was the indispensable prerequisite for the escalating barbarity and the gradual transition into full-scale genocide.

Without Hitler's fanatical will to destroy Jewry, which crystallized only by 1941 into a realizable aim to exterminate physically the Jews of Europe, the Holocaust would almost certainly not have come about. But it would also not have become reality, as Streit has emphasized,[152] without the active collaboration of the *Wehrmacht* — the one force still capable of checking the Nazi regime; or, for that matter, without the consent ranging to active complicity of the civil service bureaucracy, which strived to meet the requirements of spiralling discrimination, or the leaders of Germany's industries, who manufactured the death machinery and set up their factories at the concentration camps. And within the SS–SD–Gestapo organizational complex, it was less the outright racial fanatics so much as the ambitious organizers and competent administrators like Eichmann and ice-cold executioners like Höss who turned the hellish vision into hell on earth.[153]

The lengthy but gradual process of depersonalization and dehumanization of Jews, together with the organizational chaos in the eastern territories arising from the lack of clear central direction and concept, the hording together in the most inhumane circumstances of increasing masses of 'non-persons', provided the context in which mass killing, once it had been instigated in the Russian campaign, was applied *ad hoc* and extended until it developed into full-scale annihilation. At the same time, the 'Final Solution' did not simply emerge from a myriad of 'local initiatives': however falteringly at first, decisive steps were taken at the centre to co-ordinate measures for total extermination. Such central direction appears for the most part to have come from the Reich Security Head Office, though undoubtedly the most important steps had Hitler's approval and sanction.

Hitler's 'intention' was certainly a fundamental factor in the process of radicalization in anti-Jewish policy which culminated in extermination. But even more important to an explanation of the Holocaust is the nature of 'charismatic' rule in the Third Reich[154] and the way it functioned in sustaining the momentum of escalating radicalization around 'heroic', chimeric goals while corroding and fragmenting the structure of government. This was the essential framework within which Hitler's racial lunacy could be turned into practical politics.

This examination of the complex development of racial policy, lying at the very heart of Hitler's *Weltanschauung,* has shown that, while it would be meaningless to speak of him as a 'weak dictator', it is also misleading to regard the Third Reich as a dictatorship with a coherent, unitary command structure providing for the regulated and centrally directed consistent implementation of Hitler's will.

Notes

1. Lucy Dawidowicz, *The War against the Jews 1933–45* (Harmondsworth, 1977), p. 17. For the following remarks, see Geoff Eley, 'Holocaust History', *London Review of Books,* 3–17 March 1982, p. 6.

2. Yehuda Bauer, *The Holocaust in Historical Perspective* (London, 1978), p. 31. The chapter from which the quotation is taken is an attack on the 'mystification' (as Bauer put it) of the Holocaust. Bauer himself distinguished (pp. 31–5) between genocide — 'forcible, even murderous denationalization' — and the 'uniquely unique' Holocaust — 'total murder of every one of the members of the community'. I have to confess that I do not find the definitions or distinction very convincing or analytically helpful.

3. Dawidowicz, *War,* p. 17.

4. See the excellent historiographical survey by Konrad Kwiet, 'Zur historiographischen Behandlung der Judenverfolgung im Dritten Reich', *MGM* (1980), Heft 1, pp. 149–92, here esp. pp. 149–53; and the valuable study by Otto Dov Kulka, 'Major Trends and Tendencies of German Historiography on National Socialism and the "Jewish Question" (1924–1984)', *Yearbook of the Leo Baeck Institute* 30 (1985), pp. 215–42. For other, thorough analyses of the, by now, massive extent of research on most aspects of the Holocaust, see the essays by: Saul Friedländer, 'From Anti-Semitism to Extermination. A Historiographical Study of Nazi Policies towards the Jews and an Essay in Interpretation', *Yad Vashem Studies* 16 (1984), pp. 1–50; and Michael Marrus, 'The History of the Holocaust. A Survey of Recent Literature', *JMH* 59 (1987), pp. 114–60. Most comprehensively, there is the fine study of Michael Marrus, *The Holocaust in History* (London, 1988).

5. See Konrad Kwiet, 'Historians of the German Democratic Republic on Antisemitism and Persecution', *Yearbook of the Leo Baeck Institute* 21 (1976), pp. 173–98.

6. See Kurt Pätzold, *Faschismus, Rassenwahn, Judenverfolgung* (East Berlin, 1975), and 'Von der Vertreibung zum Genozid. Zu den Ursachen, Triebkräften und Bedingungen der antijüdischen Politik des faschistischen deutchen Imperialismus', in Dietrich Eichholtz and Kurt Gossweiler, eds., *Faschismusforschung. Positionen, Probleme, Polemik* (Berlin [East], 1980), pp. 181–208.

7. See Hannah Arendt, *Eichmann in Jerusalem. A Report on the Banality of Evil* (London, 1963).

8. David Irving, *Hitler's War* (London, 1977). See the devastating critique by Martin

272 The Final Solution in Historiography

Broszat, 'Hitler und die Genesis der "Endlösung". Aus Anlaß der Thesen von David Irving', VfZ 25 (1977), pp. 737–75, esp. pp. 759 ff. Engl. trans., 'Hitler and the Genesis of the "Final Solution": An Assessment of David Irving's Theses' in H. W. Koch, ed., Aspects of the Third Reich (London, 1985), pp. 390–429.

9. E.g. George L. Mosse, *The Crisis of German Ideology* (London, 1964). The debate engendered by the publication of Daniel Goldhagen's controversial book, *Hitler's Willing Executioners* (New York, 1996), has helped to refocus attention on the significance and extent of popular anti-semitism in Germany, and has breathed new life into interpretations which view this as the prime cause of the Holocaust. For an excellent re-evaluation of the levels of anti-Jewish violence during the Weimar era, see Dirk Walter, *Antisemitische Kriminalität und Gewalt: Judenfeindschaft in der Weimarer Republik* (Bonn, 1999).

10. Tim Mason, 'Intention and Explanation: A Current Controversy about the Interpretation of National Socialism', in Gerhard Hirschfeld and Lothar Kettenacker, eds., *Der 'Führerstaat': Mythos und Realität* (Stuttgart, 1981), p. 32. See also the 'explanation' of the Holocaust given by Sarah Gordon, *Hitler, Germans, and the 'Jewish Question'* (Princeton, 1984), p. 316: the reasons Jews were killed in their millions was 'that power was totally concentrated in one man, and that man happened to hate their "race"'.

11. Dawidowicz, *War*, pp. 193–208.

12. John Toland, *Adolf Hitler* (New York, 1976), pp. 88–9.

13. Sebastian Haffner, *Anmerkungen zu Hitler* (Munich, 1978), English trans., *The Meaning of Hitler* (London, 1979), pp. 178–9.

14. Joachim C. Fest, *Hitler. Eine Biographie* (Berlin, 1973), Engl. trans., *Hitler* (London, 1974), vol. 2, p. 930 (Ullstein edn., Frankfurt am Main/Berlin, Vienna, 1976); Adolf Hitler, *Mein Kampf* (Munich, 1943 edn.), p. 772.

15. Rudolph Binion, *Hitler among the Germans* (New York, 1976), p. 85 and chs. 1, 4; Toland, p. 934.

16. Gerald Fleming, *Hitler und die Endlösung, 'Es ist des Führers Wunsch'* (Wiesbaden/Munich, 1982), pp. 13–27 (where Hitler's 'straight path' is mentioned at least four times). An English translation is available: *Hitler and the Final Solution* (Oxford, 1986).

17. Klaus Hildebrand, *Das Dritte Reich* (Munich/Vienna, 1979), Engl. trans., *The Third Reich* (London, 1984), p. 178.

18. Andreas Hillgruber, *Endlich genug über Nationalsozialismus und Zweiten Weltkrieg? Forschungsstand und Literatur* (Dusseldorf, 1982), p. 64–6 and p. 52 note 88.

19. Hildebrand, *Das Dritte Reich*, p. 178.

20. Walther Hofer, '50 Jahre danach. Über den wissenschaftlichen Umgang mit dem Dritten Reich', *GWU* 34 (1983), p. 14.

21. Hofer, p. 14.

22. See Hans Mommsen, 'Nationalsozialismus oder Hitlerismus?' in Michael Bosch, ed., *Persönlichkeit und Struktur in der Geschichte* (Dusseldorf, 1977), pp. 66–70; 'National Socialism: Continuity and Change', in Walter Laqueur, ed., *Fascism. A Reader's Guide* (Harmondsworth, 1979), p. 179; 'Hitler's Stellung im nationalsozialistischen Herrschaftssysten', in Gerhard Hirschfeld and Lothar Kettenacker, eds., *Der 'Führerstaat': Mythos und Realität* (Stuttgart, 1981), p. 61 ff., and esp. his outstanding essay 'Die Realisierung des Utopischen: Die "Endlösung der Judenfrage" im "Dritten Reich"', *GG* 9

(1983), pp. 381–420, here esp. pp. 394–5 and notes 48–9, 399, 416–18. An extended version of this last essay is published in English translation, 'The Realization of the Unthinkable: the "Final Solution of the Jewish Question" in the Third Reich', in Gerhard Hirschfeld, ed., *The Policies of Genocide* (London, 1986), pp. 97–144 and in Hans Mommsen, *From Weimar to Auschwitz* (London, 1991), pp. 224–53.

23. Broszat, 'Genesis' (see note 8, this chapter), pp. 753–7.

24. Broszat, 'Genesis', pp. 756–7.

25. Pätzold, 'Vertreibung'.

26. Bauer, p. 11.

27. See particularly the works of Karl A. Schleunes, *The Twisted Road to Auschwitz. Nazi Policy toward German Jews, 1933–1939* (Urbana/Chicago/London, 1970), and Uwe Dietrich Adam, *Judenpolitik im Dritten Reich* (Düsseldorf, 1972).

28. Schleunes, p. 258. This interpretation has been directly called into question in a well-researched article by David Bankier, 'Hitler and the Policy-Making Process in the Jewish Question', *Holocaust and Genocide Studies* 3 (1988), pp. 1–20. Bankier succeeds in demonstrating that Hitler did intervene in the 'Jewish Question' more often than has been thought, and that he showed from time to time interest even in the minutiae of anti-Jewish policy. Even so, Bankier takes the thrust of his findings too far in claiming that Hitler 'conceived, initiated, and directed the entire process' (p. 17), and his argument appears to be based in part on a misunderstanding (or exaggeration) of the structuralist (or functionalist) case he is attacking. No one, for example, doubts Hitler's pragmatism and opportunism in the 'Jewish Question', which Bankier is rightly keen to emphasize (pp. 5–8). Bankier's attack on the view (attributed to me among others) that Hitler was 'a moderate' in anti-semitic policy rests on a misunderstanding. Even the most ardent 'structuralist' would regard Hitler as the most radical of the radicals in sentiment and any 'moderation' — a term, incidentally, which Bankier himself uses on one occasion (p. 16) — as merely deployed for tactical purposes, a point I myself sought to emphasize in *The 'Hitler Myth'* (Oxford, 1987), e.g. pp. 236, 239, 250–1. Nor has it ever been in dispute that Hitler's 'profound interest in all matters concerning Jews served as a guideline for state policy in the Jewish Question' (p. 11), or that 'Hitler's ideology was an undeniably powerful factor in the shaping of Nazi antisemitic policy' (p. 16). Within this framework, on which there can be little disagreement, the evidence cited by Bankier interestingly reveals instances of contradictions (p. 13) in Hitler's stance, as well as 'non-decisions' (pp. 10–11). Cases which Bankier cites of Hitler's intervention more often than not arise from points of contention where he is asked to settle a problem, and the generalization that 'it was in fact Hitler and not others who initiated radical measures' (p. 7) is overdrawn. Hitler's own words on 25 October 1941, which Bankier cites (p. 7, from H. R. Trevor-Roper, ed., *Hitler's Table Talk* [London, 1953], p. 90; see Werner Jochmann, *Adolf Hitler, Monologe im Führerhauptquartier 1941–1944* [Hamburg, 1980]), that 'even with regard to the Jews, I have found myself remaining inactive' — for tactical reasons, let it again be stressed — are themselves an indication that radicalization in the 'Jewish Question' could occur in the absence of his close involvement in the direction of policy.

29. See Schleunes, p. 259.

30. Schleunes, Introduction, p. 2.

31. Adam, *Judenpolitik*, pp. 313, 357–60. See also Uwe Dietrich Adam, 'An Overall

Plan for Anti-Jewish Legislation in the Third Reich?', *Yad Vashem Studies* 11 (1976), pp. 33–5, here pp. 34–5. The lack of a long-term 'extermination plan' is fully upheld in two later analyses, by Arno Mayer and Philippe Burrin. Though their interpretations differ in important respects, both argue that physical extermination arose as a comprehensive 'solution' during the course of the Russian campaign. See Arno J. Mayer, *Why did the Heavens not Darken? The 'Final Solution' in History* (New York, 1989) and Philippe Burrin, *Hitler and the Jews: The Genesis of the Holocaust* (London, 1994; orig. French edn. 1989).

32. Mommsen, 'Realisierung', p. 399 note 65.

33. For an important study exploring the genesis of the 'Final Solution' in the light of the findings of recent research, including that in East European and Russian archives, see Peter Longerich, *Politik der Vernichtung: Eine Gesamtdarstellung der nationalsozialistischen Judenverfolgung* (Munich, 1998). A summary of developments in research on the emergence of the 'Final Solution', and in a number of important regional analyses of extermination policy as it unfolded are bought together in Ulrich Herbert (ed.), *Nationalsozialistische Vernichtungspolitik 1939–1945: Neue Forschungen und Kontroversen* (Frankfurt am Main, 1998); English edition: *National Socialist Extermination Policies. Contemporary Perspectives and Controversies* (New York/Oxford, 2000).

34. Mommsen, 'Nationalsozialismus oder Hitlerismus?', p. 67.

35. Fleming, p. 206. See also p. 204 for his conclusion that those implementing Hitler's orders acted out of opportunism, servility, lack of character, and 'the petty-bourgeois zeal of a following whose idealism was abused'.

36. In his recent fine study of anti-Jewish policy during the 1930s, Saul Friedländer, *Nazi Germany and the Jews: The Years of Persecution, 1933–1939* (London, 1997), while accepting significant impulses deriving from other sources, emphasizes more strongly the personal role of Hitler and the function of his ideology in the escalating persecution, feeling that (p. 3), 'over time, the contrary interpretations have . . . gone too far'.

37. Schleunes, p. 70; Adam, *Judenpolitik*, pp. 28 ff.

38. Schleunes, p. 71.

39. Cited in Schleunes, p. 74.

40. Schleunes, pp. 92–102; Adam, *Judenpolitik*, pp. 64 ff., esp. p. 68.

41. Marlis G. Steinert, *Hitler's Krieg und die Deutschen* (Düsseldorf/Vienna, 1970), p. 57.

42. Adam, *Judenpolitik*, p. 121.

43. This account of the genesis of the Nuremberg Laws is primarily based upon Adam, *Judenpolitik*, pp. 118–22, 126; Schleunes, pp. 120–1; and, especially, upon the analyses of Lothar Gruchmann, ' "Blutschutzgesetz" und Justiz. Zur Entstehung und Auswirkung des Nürnberger Gesetzes vom 15. September 1935', *VfZ* 31 (1983), pp. 418–42, here esp. pp. 428–33, and Otto Dov Kulka, 'Die Nürnberger Rassengesetze und die deutsche Bevölkerung im Lichte geheimer NS-Lage- und Stimmungsberichte', *VfZ* 32 (1984), pp. 582–624, here esp. pp. 614–20.

44. Mommsen, 'Realisierung', p. 387 and note 20. See also, for this section, Adam, *Judenpolitik*, pp. 125 ff., and Schleunes, pp. 121 ff.

45. Adam, *Judenpolitik*, pp. 135–40; Schleunes, p. 128. Bankier (p. 14) points out that the first implementation ordinances to the Nuremberg Laws, legally defining a Jew, were

reshaped to conform with Hitler's view. But Hitler's uncertainty, then anxiety to reach a compromise solution, are confirmed by Goebbels's diary notes — *Die Tagebücher von Joseph Goebbels*. Sämtliche Fragmente, ed. Elke Fröhlich (Munich, 1987), vol. 2, pp. 520–1, 536–7, 540–1, entries of 1 Oct., 7 and 15 Nov. 1935.

46. *Die Tagebücher von Joseph Goebbels*, vol. 3, p. 351, entry of 30 Nov. 1937.

47. Adam, *Judenpolitik*, p. 173.

48. See Adam, *Judenpolitik*, pp. 206–7; Schleunes, ch. 7 (esp. pp. 240 ff.). In general, for the pogrom and its aftermath, Rita Thalmann and Emmanuel Feinermann, *Crystal Night: 9–10 November 1938* (London, 1974). A later, well-researched if journalistic, account is Anthony Read and David Fisher, *Kristallnacht. Unleashing the Holocaust* (London, 1989). A good brief analysis, locating the pogrom in the historical context of anti-semitism and discrimination against Jews in Germany, is provided by Hermann Graml, *Reichskristallnacht. Antisemitismus und Judenverfolgung im Dritten Reich* (Munich, 1988). Engl. trans., *Antisemitism and its Origins in the Third Reich* (Oxford, 1992). An excellent collection of essays, brought out on the 50th anniversary of the pogrom and summarizing much recent research, is: Walter H. Pehle, ed., *Der Judenpogrom 1938. Von der 'Reichskristallnacht' zum Völkermord* (Frankfurt am Main, 1988). Engl. trans. *November 1938. From 'Kristallnacht' to Genocide* (New York/Oxford, 1991).

49. *Die Tagebücher von Joseph Goebbels*, ed. Elke Fröhlich, Pt. I, *Aufzeichnungen*, vol. 6 (Munich, 1998), pp. 180–1, entry of 10 Nov. 1938.

50. *Die Tagebücher von Joseph Goebbels*, Pt. I, vol. 6, p. 182, entry of 11 Nov. 1938.

51. Schleunes, p. 236.

52. An outstanding analysis of the way the complex developments in anti-Jewish policy were interwoven with Nazi resettlement plans, relating both to ethnic Germans and to the subjugated people of the conquered areas of eastern Europe, is provided by Götz Aly, *'Final Solution': Nazi Population Policy and the Murder of the European Jews* (London, 1999), first published in German as *'Endlösung: Völkerverschiebung und der Mord an den europäischen Juden* (Frankfurt am Main, 1995).

53. Peter Longerich, ed., *Die Ermordung der europäischen Juden. Eine umfassende Dokumentation des Holocaust 1941–1945* (Munich, 1989), pp. 47–8.

54. Kurt Pätzold, ed., *Verfolgung, Vertreibung Vernichtung. Dokumente des faschistischen Antisemitismus 1933 bis 1942* (Leipzig, 1983), pp. 239–40.

55. Pätzold, 'Vertreibung', pp. 196–7; Mommsen, 'Realisierung', p. 406.

56. Pätzold, 'Vertreibung', p. 196.

57. Werner Präg and Wolfgang Jacobmeyer, eds., *Das Diensttagebuch des deutschen Generalgouverneurs in Polen 1939–1945* (Stuttgart, 1975), p. 147 (entry of 4 March 1940).

58. *Das Diensttagebuch des deutschen Generalgouverneurs*, p. 264 (entry for 31 July 1940).

59. Mommsen, 'Realisierung', p. 407.

60. Pätzold, 'Vertreibung', pp. 199–200; Christopher Browning, *The Final Solution and the German Foreign Office* (New York, 1978), p. 44; Helmut Krausnick *et al.*, *The Anatomy of the SS State* (London, 1968), p. 67.

61. Browning, *Final Solution*, p. 46; Mommsen, 'Realisierung', p. 407; Pätzold, *Verfolgung*, p. 262.

62. Pätzold, 'Vertreibung', p. 201.

63. Mommsen, 'Realisierung', p. 407.

64. Browning, *Final Solution*, pp. 38, 79.

65. Mommsen, 'Realisierung', pp. 395 note 52, 408; Pätzold, 'Vertreibung', p. 206.

66. See David Welch, *Propaganda and the German Cinema 1933–1945* (Oxford, 1983), pp. 292 ff. and, for the best analysis of the film, Stig Hornshøj-Møller, '*Der ewige Jude*'. *Quellenkritische Analyse eines antisemitischen Propagandafilms* (Göttingen, 1995).

67. Pätzold, 'Vertreibung', p. 204.

68. Browning, *Final Solution*, p. 8.

69. Eberhard Jäckel, 'Hitler und der Mord an den europaischen Juden' in Peter Märthesheimer and Ivo Frenzel, eds., *Im Kreuzfeuer: Der Fernsehfilm 'Holocaust'*. *Eine Nation ist betroffen* (Frankfurt am Main, 1979), pp. 151–62, here p. 156; Eberhard Jäckel, *Hitler in History* (Hanover/London, 1987), pp. 51 ff; Eberhard Jäckel, *Hitler's Herrschaft* (Stuttgart, 2nd edn., 1988), pp. 99 ff, 120; and Eberhard Jäckel and Jürgen Rohwer, *Der Mord an den Juden im Zweiten Weltkrieg* (Stuttgart, 1985), pp. 9–17, 190–1.

70. Richard Breitman, *The Architect of Genocide: Himmler and the Final Solution* (London, 1991), p. 153.

71. Krausnick, *Anatomy*, p. 60 (and see also p. 68).

72. Andreas Hillgruber, 'Die ideologisch-dogmatische Grundlage der nationalsozialistischen Politik der Ausrottung der Juden in den besetzten Gebieten der Sowjetunion und ihre Durchführung 1941–44', *German Studies Review* 2 (1979), pp. 264–96, here p. 273, and also pp. 277–8; Andreas Hillgruber, 'Die "Endlösung" und das deutsche Ostimperium als Kernstück des rassenideologischen Programms des Nationalsozialismus', in Manfred Funke, ed., *Hitler, Deutschland und die Mächte* (Düsseldorf, 1978), pp. 94–114, here pp. 103–5. The text of Göring's order is in Hans Buchheim *et al.*, *Anatomie des SS-Staates* (Olten/Freiburg, 1965), vol. 2, pp. 372–3.

73. Gerald Reitlinger, *The Final Solution*, Sphere Books edn. (London, 1971; first published 1953), pp. 82–6. Raul Hilberg, *The Destruction of the European Jews* (New Viewpoints edn., New York, 1973), pp. 177, 257, 262; Dawidowicz, *War*, p. 169; Fleming, p. 59. Hilberg has more recently been inclined to date the Hitler order to the two weeks or so immediately following the Göring mandate. See Jäckel and Rohwer (see ref. in note 69 this chapter), pp. 125–6, 137–8.

74. Browning, *Final Solution*, p. 8, and Christopher Browning, 'Zur Genesis der "Endlösung". Eine Antwort an Martin Broszat', *VfZ* 29 (1981), pp. 97–109, here pp. 98, 108 (also in Engl. trans.: 'A Reply to Martin Broszat regarding the Origins of the Final Solution', *Simon Wiesenthal Center Annual* 1 (1984), pp. 113–32). For Browning's position, see above all his *Fateful Months* (New York, 1985), ch. 1, 'The Decision Concerning the Final Solution'.

75. Adam, *Judenpolitik*, pp. 312–13. A similar date is favoured in a recent article by Shlomo Aronson, 'Die dreifache Falle. Hitler's Judenpolitik, die Alliierten und die Juden', *VfZ* 32 (1984), pp. 51–2.

76. Broszat, 'Genesis', pp. 753 note 26, 763 ff.' Mommsen, 'Realisierung', pp. 416 and note 148, 417; Christian Streit, review of Helmut Krausnick and Hans-Heinrich Wilhelm, *Die Truppe des Weltanschauungskrieges. Die Einsatzgruppen der Sicherheits-*

polizei und des SD 1938–1942 (Stuttgart, 1981) in *Bulletin of the German Historical Institute, London* 10 (1982), p. 17. In his earlier book, *Keine Kameraden. Die Wehrmacht und die sowjetischen Kriegsgefangenen 1941–1945* (Stuttgart, 1978), p. 126 and p. 355 note 274, Streit appears to favour Adam's argument, though he found Broszat's then recent 'Genesis' article also 'convincing'.

77. Krausnick and Wilhelm, pp. 634–5. The decision-making process in the 'Final Solution' was the subject of a major international conference at Stuttgart in 1984, at which all interpretations were discussed. See Jäckel and Rohwer (ref. in note 69 this chapter).

78. Mayer (see ref. in note 31, this chapter), chs. 8–9.

79. Burrin (see ref. in note 31, this chapter), chs. 4–5.

80. Aly, 'Final Solution', pp. 258–9 (*'Endlösung'*, p. 398).

81. Christian Gerlach, 'Die Wannsee-Konferenz, das Schicksal der deutschen Juden und Hitlers politische Grundsatzentscheidung, alle Juden Europas zu ermorden', *Werkstattgeschichte* 18 (1997), pp. 7–44. The essay is reprinted, with some amendments, in Christian Gerlach, *Krieg, Ernährung, Völkermord: Forschungen zur deutschen Vernichtungspolitik im Zweiten Weltkrieg* (Hamburg, 1998), pp. 85–166. The same volume contains (pp. 264 ff.) Gerlach's replies to criticism levelled at his arguments.

82. Longerich, *Politik*, esp. pp. 468–72, 476, 513–16, 581–6.

83. See Mommsen, 'Realisierung', pp. 391 ff. It is uncertain whether and how far Hitler was directly informed about the actual details of the killings in the East (see p. 409 and note 117), even though directives had been given to keep him in the picture regarding the 'progress' of the *Einsatzgruppen* (see Fleming, p. 123; Krausnick and Wilhelm, p. 335). For Hitler's public references to the 'Final Solution', see Kershaw, *The 'Hitler Myth'*, pp. 243–4.

84. Broszat, 'Genesis', p. 753; Browning, 'Zur Genesis', pp. 98, 105, 109.

85. Cited in Krausnick and Wilhelm, pp. 626–7.

86. Hillgruber, 'Die ideologisch-dogmatische Grundlage', pp. 271, 285 ff.; Jäckel, 'Hitler und der Mord', pp. 160–2.

87. See esp. Hillgruber's essays on this point, references note 72 this chapter.

88. Alfred Streim, *Die Behandlung sowjetischer Kriegsgefangener im 'Fall Barbarossa'* (Heidelberg/Karlsruhe, 1981), pp. 74–80.

89. Krausnick, *Anatomy*, pp. 60–4; Krausnick and Wilhelm, pp. 150 ff., 634; Hillgruber, 'Die ideologisch-dogmatische Grundlage', p. 243; Heinz Höhne, *The Order of the Death's Head* (Pan Books edn., London, 1972), pp. 329–30. For controversy about the nature of the orders given to the *Einsatzgruppen*, see Browning, *Fateful Months*, pp. 17–20. The text of the order of 2 July 1941 can be found in Peter Longerich, ed., *Die Ermordung der europäischen Juden* (Munich, 1989), pp. 116–18.

90. Streim, p. 89 note 333.

91. Burrin, pp. 122–3.

92. Krausnick, *Anatomy*, p. 64; Krausnick and Wilhelm, p. 619. Wilhelm's conservative estimate of the total number of murdered Russian Jews, on the basis of the most exhaustive analysis possible of incomplete evidence, is 2.2 million (Krausnick and Wilhelm, pp. 618–22). The large proportion of these killed specifically by the *Einsatzgruppen* cannot be precisely determined.

93. Krausnick and Wilhelm, p. 634.

94. Krausnick and Wilhelm, p. 627; Streim, pp. 88–9.

95. Streim, p. 80.

96. Streim, p. 83.

97. Streim, p. 84.

98. Burrin, p. 110.

99. Streim, pp. 85–6.

100. Streim, pp. 89–93. The extension of the killing was accompanied by a huge increase in the summer of 1941 in the manpower attached to the security police units operating in the east. See Yohoshua Büchler, 'Kommandostab Reichsführer–SS: Himmler's Personal Murder Brigades in 1941', *Holocaust and Genocide Studies* (1986), pp. 11–26, and Christopher Browning, *The Path to Genocide: Essays on Launching the Final Solution* (Cambridge, 1992), pp. 100–6.

101. Pätzold, *Verfolgung*, pp. 288–9; Krausnick, *Anatomy*, p. 67; Reitlinger, p. 84; Fleming, p. 57.

102. Longerich, *Ermordung*, p. 78; Reitlinger, p. 85.

103. See Jäckel and Rohwer, p. 15.

104. See Mommsen's comments on the Göring order, 'Realisierung', pp. 409 and 417 note 149; and Browning, 'Zur Genesis', p. 105 and *Fateful Months*, p. 22.

105. Burrin, pp. 129–31.

106. Burrin, pp. 137–8.

107. Burrin, pp. 138–9, 164–5, 168–9, 173–4.

108. Broszat, 'Genesis', pp. 750 ff.; see also Mommsen, 'Realisierung', pp. 410–12.

109. Streit, *Keine Kameraden* (see note 76 this chapter); see the review of Streit's book by Hans Mommsen, *Bulletin of the German Historical Institute, London* 1 (1979), pp. 17–23. On the behaviour of the German troops on the eastern fronts, see esp. Omer Bartov, *The Eastern Front, 1941–45, German Troops and the Barbarisation of Warfare* (London, 1985); and Omer Bartov, *Hitler's Army* (Oxford, 1991).

110. Burrin, p. 193 note 15.

111. Jochen von Lang, *Das Eichmann-Protokoll, Tonbandaufzeichnungen der israelischen Verhöre* (Berlin, 1982), p. 69.

112. See Gerlach, *Krieg, Ernährung, Völkermord*, pp. 270–2. The outstanding study of Eichmann's role in the 'Final Solution' is that of Hans Safrian, *Eichmann und seine Gehilfen* (Frankfurt am Main, 1995).

113. Browning, 'Zur Genesis', p. 107. See also the balanced account of Wolfgang Scheffler, 'Zur Entstehungsgeschichte der "Endlösung" ', *APZ* (30 October 1982), pp. 3–10.

114. Burrin, pp. 139–41. The best analysis of the background to the deportation order of September 1941 is now Peter Witte, 'Two Decisions concerning the "Final Solution to the Jewish Question": Deportations to Łódź and Mass Murder in Chelmno', in *Holocaust and Genocide Studies* 9 (1995), pp. 293–317.

115. Cited in Gerlach, 'Wannsee-Konferenz', p. 17.

116. Gerlach, 'Wannsee-Konferenz', pp. 12–13.

117. See Dieter Pohl, *Von der 'Judenpolitik' zum Judenmord. Der Distrikt Lublin des Generalgouvernements 1939–1944* (Frankfurt am Main, 1993), pp. 105 ff.; Adalbert Rückerl, *Nationalsozialistische Vernichtungslager im Spiegel deutscher Strafprozesse* (Munich, 1977), p. 106 ff., 132 ff.

118. See Ian Kershaw, 'Improvised Genocide? The Emergence of the "Final Solution" in the "Warthegau"', *Transactions of the Royal Historical Society*, 6th Series, 1992, pp. 51–78; Rückerl, *Nationalsozialistische Vernichtungslager*, pp. 253 ff.

119. Permission had been granted in October 1941 to the Reich Commissar for the Ostland, Hinrich Lohse, to liquidate Jews incapable of work by carbon-monoxide gassing in extermination vans devised by Viktor Brack of the Chancellory of the Führer, who had developed the gassing techniques while head of the 'euthanasia action'. See Helmut Krausnick, 'Judenverfolgung', in Hans Buchheim et al., *Anatomie des SS-Staates*, vol. 2 (Olten/Freiburg im Breisgau), 1965, pp. 409–12. Browning, 'Zur Genesis', pp. 101–2; Fleming, pp. 81–4. Plans (later abandoned) in November 1941 to erect big crematoria near Mogilew, some 200 kilometres east of Minsk, were almost certainly connected with the intention of killing Jews incapable of work who were to be transported into the region. See Aly, *'Endlösung'*, pp. 342–6; Christian Gerlach, 'Failure of Plans for an SS Extermination Camp in Mogilev, Belorussia', in: *Holocaust and Genocide Studies*, 11 (1997), pp. 60–78; Jean-Claude Pressac, *Les Crématoires d'Auschwitz* (Paris, 1993), pp. 31–3 (though, as Aly, *'Endlösung'*, p. 344, and Gerlach, 'Failure', pp. 61–2, point out, Pressac is overready to accept the SS's own explanation for the order of the crematoria, as needed to dispose of the bodies of typhus victims).

120. Longerich, *Politik*, p. 466.

121. Hitler had said, 'today I will once more be a prophet: if the international Jewish financiers in and outside Europe should succeed in plunging the nations once more into a world war, then the result will not be the Bolshevising of the earth, and thus the victory of Jewry, but the annihilation of the Jewish race in Europe!' *Documents on Nazism*, ed. J. Noakes and G. Pridham (London, 1974), iii.1049, Doc. 770. For the context of the speech, see Hans Mommsen, 'Hitler's Reichstag Speech of 30 January 1939', *History and Memory* 9 (1997), pp. 147–61.

122. *Tagebücher von Joseph Goebbels*, Part II, vol. 2, pp. 498–9; Gerlach, 'Wannsee-Konferenz', p. 25.

123. Gerlach, 'Wannsee-Konferenz', pp. 25–8.

124. *Der Dienstkalender Heinrich Himmlers 1941/42*, ed. Peter Witte u.a. (Hamburg, 1999), p. 294 (where n. 60 interprets the entry in accordance with the hypothesis of Gerlach's article — Gerlach is a co-editor of the volume — though without any indications that the hypothesis is highly speculative and controversial).

125. Cit. Gerlach, 'Wannsee-Konferenz', p. 22.

126. *IMT*, vol. 27, p. 270 (Document PS-1517); cit. Gerlach, 'Wannsee-Konferenz', p. 24.

127. *IMT*, vol. 32, pp. 436–7 (Documents PS-3663 und PS-3666); Gerlach, 'Wannsee-Konferenz', pp. 28–9; trans. Noakes and Pridham, iii.1098, Doc. 821.

128. *Das Diensttagebuch des deutschen Generalgouverneurs in Polen 1939–1945*, ed. Werner Präg and Wolfgang Jacobmeyer (Stuttgart, 1975), 457. Noakes and Pridham, iii.1126–7, Doc. 848 has a translation with insignificant variations. Gerlach, 'Wannsee-Konferenz', p. 30 and n. 131, points out that Frank had had private discussions with Hitler as well as with the *Ostministerium* while he was in Berlin.

129. A telling point made in Ulrich Herbert's assessment of Gerlach's argument, 'Eine "Führerentscheidung" zur "Endlösung"?', *Neue Zürcher Zeitung*, 14–15 March 1998, pp. 69–70. Gerlach's reply to Herbert's criticism on this and other points seems to me to be unpersuasive. See Gerlach, *Kreig, Ernährung, Völkermord*, pp. 280–86.

130. *Tagebücher von Joseph Goebbels,* Part 11, vol. 2, pp. 494–500; the passage on the Jews is on pp. 498–9.

131. See also Martin Moll, 'Steuerungsinstrument im "Ämterchaos"? Die Tagungen der Reichs- und Gauleiter der NSDAP', *Vierteljahrshefte für Zeitgeschichte,* 49 (2001), pp. 239–43.

132. See on this point, Longerich, *Politik,* p. 711 n. 233; and Herbert, 'Führerentscheidung'. Gerlach's reply, *Kreig, Ernährung, Völkermord,* p. 286 n. 70 strikes me as unconvincing.

133. Gerlach, 'Wannsee-Konferenz', p. 29 and n. 129.

134. See Longerich, *Politik,* p. 467 and p. 712 n. 234.

135. The Soviet partisan movement, ineffective in the first months following the German invasion of the USSR, was sufficiently significant by September 1941 to persuade the Oberkommando der Wehrmacht to issue a new, brutal edict to attempt to combat the growing threat. See Alexander Dallin, *German Rule in Russia, 1941–1945* (London, 1957), 2nd edn., 1981, pp. 74–6, 209. The halt of the German advance in December 1941 gave the partisan movement a boost. This was precisely around the time that Hitler and Himmler were speaking of using the partisan struggle to eradicate the Jews.

136. Hannes Heer, 'Killing Fields: the Wehrmacht and the Holocaust in Belorussia, 1941–1942', *Holocaust and Genocide Studies* 11 (1997), pp. 79–101, here pp. 87, 89–90.

137. Berlin Document Center, SS-HO/1238, RFSS, 29.12.42: '*Meldungen an den Führer über Bandenbekämpfung*'.

138. *Das Diensttagebuch des deutschen Generalgouverneurs in Polen,* p. 458.

139. Gerlach, 'Wannsee-Konferenz', p. 32.

140. Longerich, *Politik,* pp. 470–1.

141. Longerich, *Politik,* pp. 476, 513–16, 583–6.

142. Longerich, *Politik,* pp. 514–15.

143. *Dienstkalender Heinrich Himmlers,* p. 73 (citing the 'Korherr-Bericht' of 23 March 1943).

144. Gerlach, 'Wannsee-Konferenz', p. 44. Gerlach's attack here is particularly directed at Hans Mommsen, 'Realisierung', pp. 416–17, who was among the first to emphasize a process of continuing escalation rather than a long-term pre-formulated programme in the development of the 'Final Solution'.

145. Longerich, *Die Ermordung,* p. 85; Noakes and Pridham, iii.1129, Doc. 849.

146. While varying approaches put emphasis on different phases (see, e.g., Aly, p. 398, Longerich, *Politik,* pp. 579–84), there appears to be wide acceptance of such a process of escalating radicalization.

147. Gerlach, 'Wannsee-Konferenz', p. 44.

148. Broszat, 'Genesis', p. 63.

149. Among the most important such studies are the study of the Distrikt Lublin already cited by Dieter Pohl, *Von der 'Judenpolitik' zum Judenmord,* and his *Nationalsozialistische Judenverfolgung in Ostgalizien. Organisation und Durchführung eines staatlichen Massenverbrechens* (Munich, 1996); Thomas Sandkühler, *'Endlösung' in Galizien. Der Judenmord in Ostpolen und die Rettungsinitiativen von Berthold Beitz* (Bonn, 1996); the study of anti-Jewish policy in the 'Warthegau' by Peter Witte, men-

tioned earlier. The forthcoming study by Christian Gerlach on extermination policy in Belorussia will be a significant addition. Peter Klein's work on the 'Warthegau' and Christoph Dieckmann's on Lithuania will provide further important insights into regional development. See also the contributions to Herbert (ed.), *Nationalsozialistische Vernichtungspolitik*.

150. Gerlach, *Krieg, Ernährung, Völkermord*, p. 278, accepts that this is the case in autumn 1941.

151. And is seen as such by Gerlach, *Krieg, Ernährung, Völkermord*, pp. 286–7.

152. Streit, *Keine Kameraden*, esp. chs. 3, 6, 13.

153. Hannah Arendt's controversial report of the Eichmann trial ended: 'The trouble with Eichmann was precisely that so many were like him, and that the many were neither perverted nor sadistic, that they were, and still are, terribly and terrifyingly normal' (Arendt, *Eichmann* [see this chapter note 7], p. 253; see also pp. 18–31). According to their editor, Höss's autobiographical recollections reveal him as a 'petty-bourgeois, normal person' rather than a sadistic brute: Martin Broszat, ed., *Kommandant in Auschwitz. Autobiographische Aufzeichungen des Rudolf Höß* (dtv-edn., Munich, 1978), p. 15. Ideological anti-semitism seems at best to have provided a secondary motive in these cases, as it does in the career of Franz Stangl, Commandant at Treblinka death-camp: see Gitta Sereny, *Into that Darkness* (London, 1974). However, it has to be added that there is no intrinsic contradiction between ideological conviction and managerial talent.

154. An attempt to view from a sociological perspective the links between the charismatic nature of Nazi rule and genocide is provided by Uta Gerhardt, 'Charismatische Herrschaft und Massenmord im Nationalsozialismus', *GG* 24 (1998), pp. 503–38.

'Normality' and Genocide:
The Problem of 'Historicization'

The problem of the so-called 'historicization' (*'Historisierung'*) of National Socialism, a term which first entered serious discussion when advanced by Martin Broszat in an important and programmatic essay published in 1985,[1] revolved around the question of whether, nearly half a century after the collapse of the Third Reich, it was possible to treat the Nazi era in the ways that other eras of the past are treated — as 'history' — and what new perspectives such a shift in conceptualization and method would demand. In intellectual terms, the controversy which Broszat's article provoked raises distinctive theoretical and methodological problems, involving consideration of the contribution and potential of what has, in many respects, proved a most fruitful approach in research on the Third Reich, that of *'Alltagsgeschichte'* ('the history of everyday life').

Since the 1970s, new and exciting avenues of research have been explored in a massive outpouring of studies ranging over most of the important aspects of the impact of Nazism on German society. Yet just as the time seemed ripe — many years after the appearance of Schoenbaum's wide-ranging social history of the Third Reich, seen as 'Hitler's social revolution', and Dahrendorf's equally influential interpretation of Nazism as 'the German revolution'[2] — for a new full-scale study which would synthesize and incorporate much of this work and offer a revised interpretation of German society under Nazism, the 'historicization' controversy cast doubt upon even the theoretical possibility of constructing such a social history without losing sight of the central aspects of Nazism which provide it with its lasting world-historical significance and its moral legacy. The first part of this chapter offers an outline of this important controversy, while the second part seeks to evaluate its implications for a potential history of German society in the Third Reich.

The 'Historicization' Approach

A major breakthrough in deepening awareness of the complexity of German society in the Third Reich, it is universally recognized, was the research undertaken and published between the mid 1970s and early 1980s within the framework of the 'Bavaria Project', which helped to offer an entirely new dimension to the understanding of relations between state and society in Nazi Germany.[3] The project, it seems clear, was an important impulse, among others, in the rapid development of the 'everyday life' approach to the Third Reich. The very concept of '*Alltagsgeschichte*' ('the history of everyday life'), and the methods deployed by its exponents, have provoked much stringent criticism — some of it well justified — particularly from the leading protagonists of the 'critical history' and 'history as social science' ('*historische Sozialwissenschaften*') approach.[4] Such criticism has, however, not been able to stem the continued spread of '*Alltagsgeschichte*', and some of the sharpest critics have accepted that, properly conceptualized, '*Alltagsgeschichte*' can have much to offer in deepening understanding.[5] The remarkable resonance of the 'everyday life' approach, exploring subjective experiences and mentalities at the grass roots of society, presumably reflects in part, not least through the opening up of previously taboo areas of consideration, a need, particularly strong among the younger generation, to come to grips with the Third Reich not just as a political phenomenon — as a horrific regime providing a resort for political and moral lessons in a post-fascist democracy — but also as a social experience, in order to understand better the behaviour of ordinary people — like their own relatives — under Nazism. By making past behaviour and mentalities more explicable, more understandable, more 'normal' — even if to be condemned — it is arguable that '*Alltagsgeschichte*' has contributed to deepened awareness of the problems of historical identity in the Federal Republic, and of the relationship of the Third Reich not just to political continuities and discontinuities, but now also to social strands of continuity pre-dating Nazism and extending well into the post-war era. This further prompts the need to locate the Third Reich as an integral component of German history, not one which can be bracketed out and detached as if it did not really belong to it. These were some of the considerations behind Martin Broszat's 'plea for the historicization of National Socialism', premised upon the assertion that the history of the Nazi *era*, as opposed to that of the political system of the dictatorship, still remains to be written.[6]

Broszat's use of the term '*Historisierung*' ('historicization') relates to the problems of historians, and specifically West German historians, in dealing with the Nazi past. Even decades after the end of the Third Reich, the distance which the historian puts between himself and the subject matter of Nazism provides, in Broszat's view, a major obstacle to the possibility of approaching the scholarly study and analysis of Nazism in the same way that other periods of history are tackled — with the degree of intuitive insight which 'normal' historical writing demands. Yet, without the proper integration of Nazism into 'normal' historical writing, he saw the Third Reich remaining an 'island' in modern German history,[7] a resort for lessons of political morality in which routine moral condemnation excludes historical understanding, reducing Nazism to an 'abnormality' and serving as a compensatory alibi for a restored historicism ('*Historismus*') with regard to the more 'healthy' epochs before and after Hitler.[8] The position is summed up in the following way:

> A normalization of our historical consciousness and the communication of national identity through history cannot be achieved by avoiding the Nazi era through its exclusion. Yet it seems to me that the greater the historical distance becomes, the more urgent it is to realize that bracketing the Hitler era out of history and historical thinking also occurs in a way when it is only dealt with from a political-moral perspective and not with the same differentiated applied historical method as other historical epochs, when treated with less carefully considered judgement and in a cruder, more general language, or when, for well-intentioned didactic reasons, we grant it a sort of methodological special treatment.[9]

A 'normalization' of methodological treatment would mean the application of the normal rigours of historical enquiry in a meticulous scholarship deploying 'mid-range' concepts subjectable to empirical investigation in place of bland moralization, whether from a liberal-conservative perspective or from sterile economistic determinant theories of a marxist–leninist or 'new Left' variety.[10] This in itself would refine moral sensitivity through the increased understanding derivable from greater differentiation, as in the relativization of 'resistance' through its 'de-heroization' and recognition of the chequered grey nature of the boundaries of opposition and conformity between the 'Other Germany' and the Nazi regime.[11] It would allow, too, Nazism's function as the exponent of modernizing change comparable with that in other contemporary societies to be properly incorporated in an understanding of the era, and hence a deeper awareness of the social forces and motivation which the Nazi Move-ment could mobilize and exploit.[12]

The relevance of the 'Bavaria Project' and the emphasis upon '*Alltags-geschichte*' to this line of thought is self-evident. The underlying notion behind the whole concept of 'historicization' is that below the barbarism and the horror of the regime were patterns of social 'normality' which were, of course, affected by Nazism in various ways but which pre-dated and survived it. The role of Nazi ideology hence becomes 'relativized' in the context of a 'normality' of everyday life shaped for much of the time by non-ideological factors. Nazism can be seen to accelerate some and put the brake on other trends of social change and development which form a continuum from pre-Nazi times into the Federal Republic.[13] Beneath the barbarity, society in Nazi Germany can thus be more easily related to other eras in German history, and more easily compared with other contemporary societies. The long-term structural change and mod-ernization of German society becomes thereby more explicable, as does the role of Nazism — deliberate or unwitting — in relationship to that change. This per-spective challenges — and in some ways displaces — the traditional emphasis upon the ideological, political, and criminal terroristic aspects of Nazism. One of Broszat's critics has, for example, suggested that the approach which he is advocating looks to a comparison with the modernizing tendencies of other advanced western societies at the expense of neglecting the crucial differences in the essence of their development. From such a perspective, therefore, 'the racialist aspect . . . and particularly the "Final Solution of the Jewish Question" seem to be regarded as somehow irrelevant' since the 'unique duality' of the German modernizing experience is ignored.[14]

The suggested 'historicization' can, therefore, be summarized in the follow-ing claims: that Nazism should be subjected to the same methods of scholarly enquiry as any other era of history; that social continuities need to be much more fully incorporated in a far more complex picture of Nazism and the em-phasis shifted away from heavy concentration upon the political–ideological sphere as a resort for moral lessons (since moral sensitivity can only arise from a deeper understanding, which 'historicization' offers, of the chequered com-plexities of the era); and that the Nazi era, at present almost a dislocated unit of German history, — no longer suppressed but reduced to no more than 're-quired reading' (*Pflichtlektion*)[15] — needs to be relocated in wider evolution-ary development.[16]

Criticism of 'Historicization'

The main critics of Broszat's 'historicization' plea were the Israeli histo-rians Otto Dov Kulka, Dan Diner, and, especially, Saul Friedländer. They recognized the problem of 'historicization' as expounded by Broszat as an important methodological and theoretical issue, as representing in some respects a legitimate perspective, and as raising a problem which 'belongs within the realm of a fundamental scholarly-scientific dialogue' between historians who 'share some basic concerns as far as the attitudes towards Nazism and its crimes are concerned'. As such, they were anxious to distinguish it from the apologetics advanced by Ernst Nolte in the '*Historikerstreit*'.[17] Even so, it was noted in passing that the exhortation to treat the Nazi era like any other period of history was also Nolte's starting point.[18] Leaving Nolte completely to one side, there were still the implications of Andreas Hillgruber's approach to the historical treatment of the German army on the Eastern Front for the concept of 'historicization', to which we will return.[19]

The most direct and structured critique of Broszat's 'historicization' plea was advanced by Saul Friedländer.[20] He saw three dilemmas in the 'historicization' notion, and a further three problems which the approach raises.

The first dilemma he pointed to is that of periodization and the specificity of the dictatorship years themselves, the period 1933–1945.[21] The 'historicization' approach seeks to incorporate the Third Reich into a picture of long-term social change. Broszat himself uses the example of the wartime social planning of the German Labour Front both as an episode in the development of social welfare schemes which pre-dated Nazism and extended into the modern system of the Federal Republic, and as a parallel to what was taking place under entirely different political systems, as in the British Beveridge Plan.[22] These various long-term processes of social change, in this instance in social policy, can be seen, therefore, as taking place in detachment from the specifics of Nazi ideology and the particular circumstances of the Third Reich. The emphasis shifts away from the singular characteristics of the Nazi period to a consideration of the relative and objective function of Nazism as an agent forcing (or retarding) modernization.

The question of the intended or unintended 'modernization push' of Nazism has, of course, been at issue ever since Dahrendorf and Schoenbaum wrote. Friedländer accepted that recent studies have extended knowledge on numerous aspects of this 'modernization'. However, in his view, when taken as a whole such studies reveal a shift in interest from the specificity of Nazism to the general problems of modernization, within which Nazism plays a part. The issue is, therefore, one of 'the relative relevance' of such developments in an overall history of the Nazi era.[23] And, in Friedländer's judgement, the danger — in fact, the almost inevitable result — is the relativization of the political–ideological–moral framework peculiar to the period 1933–45.[24]

The second dilemma rose from the recommended removal of the distance,

founded on moral condemnation, which the historian of Nazism places between himself and the object of his research, and which prevents him from
treating it as a 'normal' period of history. This raises, said Friedländer, inextricable problems in the construction of a global picture of the Nazi era, since if
few spheres of life were themselves criminal, few were completely untouched
by the regime's criminality. Separation of criminality from normalcy is, therefore, scarcely an easy task. No objective criteria can be established for distinguishing which areas might be susceptible to empathetic treatment, and which
still cannot be handled without the historian's distance from his subject of
enquiry.[25]

The third dilemma derived from the vagueness and open-endedness of the
concept of 'historicization', which implied a method and a philosophy but
gave no clear notion of what the results might be. The implications of 'historicization' were, however, by no means straightforward, but might be interpreted in radically different ways — as indeed Nolte and Hillgruber demonstrated in their controversial interpretations of the Nazi era which provoked
the 'Historikerstreit'.[26]

Friedländer was prepared to discount Nolte's writings in this context. But
he used the illustrations of Hillgruber's essay on the Eastern Front to demonstrate the potential dangers of 'historicization', and linked this squarely with
the problems of the 'everyday history' approach itself, and with the open-
ended nature of the 'Resistenz' concept used in the 'Bavaria Project'.[27] Not
only the relativization of distance from the Nazi era, he argued, but also the
emphasis in 'Alltagsgeschichte' on the ordinariness of many aspects of the
Third Reich, on the non-ideological and non-criminal spheres of activity, and
on ever more nuanced attitudes and behavioural patterns, created significant
problems. Friedländer accepted that 'criminality' was not necessarily excluded, and that a continuum could be constructed involving 'criminality' in
everyday life and normality in the regime's 'criminal' system. However, he
suggested that in an overall perspective of the Third Reich premised upon the
relativization and normalization of the Nazi era advocated in the 'historicization' approach, the tendency to overweigh the 'normality' end of the continuum could scarcely be avoided. Despite Broszat's disclaimers, feared Friedländer, the passage from 'historicization' to 'historicism' ('Historisierung' to
'Historismus') in regard to the Third Reich was a real danger.[28] Hillgruber
defended his controversial empathizing and identification with the German
troops in the east by comparing his approach with that of 'everyday history',
as applied to other areas of research.[29] Accepting that there is some force in
this defence, Friedländer suggested that one might justifiably apply the concept of 'Resistenz' to the behaviour of the German soldiers defending the

Eastern Front in the final phase of the war. Hence, many units were relatively immune to Nazi ideology and were only doing their job like soldiers in any army in defending the Front. On the other hand, of course, the *Wehrmacht* was system-supporting more than almost any other institution. This revealed to Friedländer not only that '*Resistenz*' was 'much too amorphous a concept to be of any great use',[30] but also the vacuous nature of 'historicization', which 'implies many different things' so that 'within the present context it may encourage some interpretations rather than others'.[31]

From the dilemmas arose, in Friedländer's view, three general problems. The first was that the Nazi past was still too overwhelmingly present to deal with it in the 'normal' way that one might, for example, tackle the history of sixteenth-century France. The self-reflection of the historian necessary to any good historical writing was decisive in approaching the Nazi era. The Third Reich simply could not be regarded in the same way or approached with the same methods as 'normal' history.[32]

The second general problem was what Friedländer called 'differential relevance'.[33] The history of Nazism, he said, belongs to everyone. The study of everyday life in the Third Reich might indeed be relevant to Germans in terms of self-perception and national identity, and thereby be a perspective which commends itself to German historians. But for historians outside Germany, this perspective might be less relevant in comparison with the political and ideological aspects of the Third Reich, and in particular the relationship of ideology to politics.

The same point was made in slightly different fashion by other critics of 'historicization'. Otto Dov Kulka saw the emphasis upon the 'normal' aspects of the Third Reich as a reflection of the present-day situation and self-image of the Federal Republic as an affluent, modern society — an image into which Nazi ideology and the 'criminality' of the regime could scarcely be accommodated. From this present-day West German perspective, he accepted the examination of, for example, long-term trends in the development of social policy as both justified and important. But the world-historical uniqueness of Nazism, he emphasized, resided specifically in the duality of a society where 'normal' trends of modernization were accompanied by the slave labour and extermination 'in industrially rational fashion' of those ideologically excluded from the 'national community'. And in the event of a victorious Third Reich, modern German society would have looked very different from the democratic welfare state of the Federal Republic and from the socialist German Democratic Republic.[34]

The third — and most crucial — problem was, therefore, how to integrate Nazi crimes into the 'historicization' of the Third Reich. In Friedländer's view

— and he accepted that this was a value-judgement — the specificity, or uniqueness, of Nazism resided in the fact that it 'tried "to determine who should and
who should not inhabit the world" '.[35] The problem — and the limits — of 'historicization' lay consequently in its ability to integrate into its picture of 'normal' development 'the specificity and the historical place of the annihilation
policies of the Third Reich'.[36]

Evaluation

The objections to the 'historicization of National Socialism' raised by
Friedländer, Kulka, and Diner cannot lightly be dismissed. They touch upon
important philosophical and methodological considerations which have a direct bearing on any attempt at writing the history of German society under
Nazism.

Friedländer's concern about the omission or down-playing of the political,
ideological, and moral aspects of Nazism permeates his critique. But it could
at the outset be queried whether the traditional concentration on the political–
ideological–moral framework could lead to further major advances in the
depth of that understanding which provides the basis of enhanced moral
awareness. This 'traditional' emphasis, epitomized perhaps most clearly in the
work of Karl-Dietrich Bracher, produced many lasting gains.[37] A 'historicized'
treatment would not need to discard them. But rigidly to confine scholarship
to the traditional framework would be sterile and perhaps ultimately even
counter-productive, since it would put a block on precisely the approaches
which have led to much of the most original — and most morally sensitive —
research in recent years. Moreover, the implications of 'historicization' might
be less serious both in theory and in practice than Friedländer fears.

It seems questionable whether the first dilemma posed by Friedländer — the
incompatibility of doing justice to the specific character of the Nazi era in a
treatment which concentrates upon the unfolding of long-term social change —
is a necessary one. It might in fact, be countered that the specific features of the
period 1933–45 can only be highlighted by a 'longitudinal' analysis crossing
those chronological barriers and placing the era in a development context of
elements of social change which long preceded Nazism and continued after its
demise. Friedländer's fear is that there would be an inevitable shift in focus to
the problem of modernization, and that a 'relativization' of the dictatorship era
by its new location in a long-term context of 'neutral' social change would be
bound to lose sight of, or reduce in emphasis, crucial events or policy decisions
in the period of Nazi rule itself.

The fear does not appear to be borne out by studies dealing with social change, some of which have adopted a long-term perspective and have deliberately addressed the issue of modernization and the 'social revolution' argument. Obviously, the 'criminal' side of the Third Reich is not the dominant focus in such works. But in the stress on Nazi social policy, the significance of ideology is by no means underplayed, and the relationship of this ideology to the core racial–imperialist essence of Nazism is made abundantly plain. For instance, the wartime social programme of Robert Ley — to take the example, from Marie-Louise Recker's study of wartime social policy, which Broszat cites and Friedländer sees as an example of the dangers implicit in 'historicization' — indeed reveals a number of superficial similarities to Beveridge's social insurance provisions in Britain. But what is most striking in Recker's analysis — though, admittedly, not in Broszat's reference to her findings — is the specific and unmistakable Nazi character of the programme.[38] Not only is it legitimate (and necessary) to deploy a 'longitudinal' and also a comparative perspective in analysis of Ley's programme, but such a perspective contributes directly to a clearer definition of the peculiarly Nazi essence of social policy in the years 1933–45. The same can be said of Michael Prinz's admirable analysis of Nazi attempts to eradicate the status barrier between white- and blue-collar workers, in which the long-term perspective serves to depict particularly clearly both the specific features of Nazi social policy towards white-collar workers, and the anchorage of this policy in Nazi ideological precepts.[39]

Applied to other subject areas, the 'longitudinal' approach highlights precisely the political–ideological–moral framework which Friedländer suspects will be ignored or downplayed — if in ways different to, and often more challenging than, the traditional approach. An instance would be Ulrich Herbert's excellent analysis of the treatment of foreign labour in Germany since the nineteenth century, which allows both the continuities which cross the Nazi era, but also the specific barbarities of that era itself, to come more clearly into view.[40] Herbert was, of course, a leading participant in the Ruhr oral-history project which was so closely linked to perceived experiences of the 'normality' of 'everyday life'. It is all the more significant, therefore, that he was the historian to contribute an outstanding monograph on foreign workers which offers the first major analysis of one of the most barbarous aspects of the Third Reich, and that he not only brings out fully the ideologically rooted nature of the regime's policy towards foreign workers, but also the extent to which 'racism was not just a phenomenon to be found among the Party leadership and the SS, . . . but a practical reality to be experienced as an everyday occurrence in Germany during the war'.[41]

The moral dimension is also more than evident in recent research on professional and social groups — such as the medical, legal, and teaching professions, technicians and students.[42] And there has been little difficulty in such studies in blending together long-term patterns of development and change (into which the Nazi era has to be fitted) and specific facets in such processes peculiar to Nazism. The same is abundantly true of research on the position of women. Continuities in anti-feminism have not prevented an elaboration of the specific contours of the 1933–45 era, as in Gisela Bock's work, for example, in which a direct association is made of Nazi anti-feminism and racial policy by way of an analysis of compulsory sterilization.[43] As in this instance, most other recent publications, many of them excellent in quality, on women in the Third Reich have placed particular emphasis upon the central issue of race — precisely the issue that Friedländer feared will lose significance through a social rather than political history perspective.[44]

It is difficult to see how any scholarly attempt to construct an overall picture of society under Nazism could ignore the findings of such important research. We still face, however, Friedländer's second dilemma: the inability of the historian, having removed the previously automatic 'distance' from Nazism, taken the epoch out of its 'quarantine', and abolished the 'syndrome of "required-reading"', to apply objective criteria to separate 'criminality' from 'normalcy' in the construction of a 'global' picture of the Nazi era.

Friedländer's worry was evidently that spheres of empathetic understanding might now be found in the 'normality' of everyday life under Nazism. The previous general consensus resting upon a total and complete rejection of this era would thereby be broken. But the historian, now faced with a choice other than rejection,[46] would have no objective criteria for drawing distinctions. In the context of the philosophy of 'historicism' ('Historismus'), and in the realm of pure theory, the problem of 'distance' or 'empathy', which Friedländer poses, does indeed appear insoluble. But even at the theoretical level, the problem is hardly peculiar to the Third Reich, and poses itself implicitly in all historical writing. In many areas of contemporary history in particular, one might think, the problem seems hardly less acute than in the case of Nazism. Whether the historian writing on Soviet society under Stalin, on the society of Fascist Italy or Franco's Spain, on the Vietnam war, on South Africa, or on British imperialism faces a fundamentally different dilemma might be questioned. Objective criteria resting on the historian's 'neutrality' arguably play no part in any historical writing. Selection on the basis of subjectively determined choices and emphases is inescapable. A rigorous critical method and full recognition of subjective factors shaping the approach deployed and evaluation of the findings provide the only means of control. The historian of Nazism is in no different position to any other historian in this respect.

Broszat's writings were in places certainly less clear and unambiguous than they might have been on the difference between the method he advocated and the traditional or 'restored' historicism which he contrasted with it.[17] He explicitly presented 'distance' and intuitive insight or 'empathy' ('*Einfühlen*') as opposites and spoke of the possibility of 'a degree of sympathetic identification' ('*ein Maß mitfühlender Identifikation*') both with victims and with 'wrongly invested achievements and virtues' ('*fehlinvestierten Leistungen und Tugenden*'). At the same time, however, he made sufficiently plain that the counter to an uncritical, positive identification with the subject matter lay precisely in the critical historical method, applied to Nazism as to other periods of history, and ultimately promoting enhanced moral sensibility precisely through meticulous scholarship which included but did not uncritically embrace it.[48] The result is the methodological tightrope which all historians have to walk, in which the choice between empathy or moral distance is reshaped by the critical method into the position which characterizes a great deal of good historical writing — that of rejection through 'understanding'. This, the premise that 'enlightenment' ('*Aufklärung*') comes through 'explanation' ('*Erklärung*'),[49] seems the basis of Broszat's approach in his collected papers, and certainly in his own work on the 'Bavaria Project' and elsewhere.

The best work arising from '*Alltagsgeschichte*', in fact, clearly demonstrates that a concern with everyday behaviour and mentalities by no means implies empathetic treatment. Detlev Peukert's work, in which 'normality' is rooted in a theory of the 'pathology of modernity', provides an outstanding example.[50] The dilemma posed by Friedländer is scarcely visible here. 'Everyday normality' is not presented as a positive counter-point to the 'negative' aspects of Nazism, but as a framework within which 'criminality', arising from a 'pathological' side of 'normality', becomes more readily explicable. Nor is the concern that a continuum from 'normality' to 'criminality' inevitably means in practice that the dominant emphasis falls upon the former upheld in Peukert's work, which is all the more impressive in that he has offered so far practically the only wide-ranging attempt to synthesize research emanating from a wide variety of monographs falling within the 'history of everyday life' approach to German society in the Third Reich. And, though Peukert deliberately excluded it from his consideration in his book, there is no reason why the 'road to Auschwitz' could not be fully incorporated into an analysis premised on such an approach to 'normality'. By expressly linking 'daily life and barbarism', through association with the destructive potential built into modern society's emphasis upon advances in production and efficiency, he himself indicated how an 'everyday history of racism', which is still in its beginnings, could contribute to a deeper understanding of the behaviour and mentalities which made the Holocaust possible.[51] Here, too, the dilemma of empathy or distance would be premised upon a false dichotomy and would not in practice present itself.

Friedländer's third dilemma arose from the vagueness and open-endedness of the term 'historicization', which was subject to different — some unattractive — interpretations. It can be readily conceded that 'historicization' is indeed an imprecise and unclear concept.[52] In some respects it is ambiguous if not outrightly misleading. The proximity of the term to 'historicism', which is the opposite of what it denotes, does not help clarity. And it seems related to 'normal' in at least three different ways: to the proposed 'normalization' of 'historical consciousness'; to the application of 'normal' historical method in approaching the Third Reich; and to the 'normality' of 'everyday life'. As an ordering or analytical concept, it has no obvious value, and is purely suggestive of a method of approach. The discarding of the term would arguably be no great loss. It confuses more than it clarifies. But the approach and method signified by 'historicization' could not be dispensed with. Even so, it would be necessary to distinguish the three different uses of 'normal'. The application of 'normal' historical method, and the extension of the sphere of analysis to the 'normality' of 'everyday life' can be more easily defended than can the inclusion of the Nazi era in a supposed 'normalization of historical consciousness'. This last usage, as the 'Historikerstreit' demonstrated, and as Friedländer and others feared, indeed appears either to elide the Nazi era altogether, or to erase or dilute the normal dimension by shifting the spotlight to parallel (and allegedly 'more original') barbarities of other 'totalitarian' states, particularly those of Bolshevik Russia. It is in the context of such distortions that Friedländer posed his third dilemma, by pointing to the use of the same term, 'historicization', in the context of an intended 'normalization' of historical consciousness in the face of a 'past which will not pass away', by Nolte and, implicitly, by Hillgruber.[53]

The argument that the notion of 'historicization' advanced by Broszat, with its connotations of heightened moral sensitivity towards the Nazi past, might be misused 'in the present ideological context'[54] to result in the diametrically opposed 'relativization' of the regime's criminality, as in Nolte's essays which prompted the 'Historikerstreit',[55] is certainly a serious criticism of the vagueness of the concept, but not convincing in itself as a rejection of the approach — largely based on an 'everyday history of the Nazi era' — which Broszat's concept is meant to denote.

If, however, as Friedländer himself suggested, Nolte's eccentric argumentation is left on one side, there still remains the question of Hillgruber's declared adaptation of the approach of 'Alltagsgeschichte' to the problem of the troops on the Eastern Front, with the dubious conclusions he drew.[56] Friedländer astutely pointed out that the empathetic approach could produce startling results, and suggested that Hillgruber's essay demonstrated how Broszat's supposed 'historicization', aimed precisely at avoiding traditional 'historicism', could lead to a return of 'historicism', now dangerously applied to the Third Reich itself.[57] But the point about Hillgruber's essay was that it was squarely rooted in a crude form of the 'historicist' tradition which presumed that 'understanding' (*'Verstehen'*) could only come about through empathetic identification. It was precisely the claim that the historian's only valid position is one of identification with the German troops fighting on the Eastern Front which invoked such widespread and vehement criticism of Hillgruber's essay.[58] The critical method, which in his other work — not excluding his essay on 'the historical place of the extermination of the Jews' in the same volume as the controversial treatment of the Eastern Front — made him a formidable historian whose strength lay in the careful and measured treatment of empirical data, entirely deserted him here and was wholly lacking in this one-sided, uncritical empathizing with the German troops. Though Hillgruber claimed to be applying the technique of *'Alltagsgeschichte'* and the approach advocated by Broszat and others to experience events from the point of view of those at the base of society directly affected by them, it was precisely the absence of critical reflection which provided the gulf between his depiction and the work of Broszat, Peukert and others, who indeed looked to 'grassroots' experiences, but did not detach these from a critical framework of analysis.

The example of Hillgruber appears, therefore, misplaced. What, apart from the dubious value of the actual term 'historicization', it illustrated, was that, in his zeal to emphasize the need for greater empathetic understanding of 'experience', Broszat appeared to have posed a false dichotomy with the 'distance' which is an important control mechanism of the historian of any period, not just of the Nazi era. In reality, Broszat's own historical writing — even his last short book in a series founded on the necessity to 'historicize' German history — plainly did not abrogate 'distance' in the interests of uncritical empathy. Neither here, nor in Broszat's other recent writing, could it be claimed that the narrative approach (*'Erzählen'*) which he missed in historical treatment of the Third Reich[59] had come to dominate or to replace critical, structured analysis and reflection. 'Distance' as well as empathetic understanding might be said to be vital to the historian of any period.

The preservation of a critical distance in the case of National Socialism is, in fact, far from being dispensable, a crucial component of the new social history of the Third Reich. But it is precisely the virtue of this new social history located in description and structured analysis of 'everyday' experience, that it breaks down the unreflected distance which has traditionally been provided by abstractions such as 'totalitarian rule' and compels a deeper comprehension through greater awareness of the complexity of social reality.[60] If I understand it correctly, this was the essence of Broszat's plea for 'historicization', and for a structured 'Alltagsgeschichte' as the most fruitful method of approach. And the findings of the 'Bavaria Project' alone demonstrated how enriching such an approach can prove.

It seems plain that Friedländer was correct to stress that the Nazi era, from whichever perspective it is approached, cannot be regarded as a 'normal' part of history in the way that even the most barbarous episodes of the more distant past can be viewed. The emotions which rightly still colour attitudes to Nazism obviously rule out the detachment with which not only sixteenth-century France (Friedländer's example) but also many more recent events and periods in German history and in the history of other nations can be analysed. In this sense, Wolfgang Benz is quite right when he claims: 'Detached concern with Nazism as an era of German history among others and work on it devoted to purely scholarly interest seems then not so easily possible. The mere distance of 40 or 50 years does not yet make the Nazi era historical'.[61] But of course this does not rule out the application of 'normal' historical methods to the social, as well as to the political, history of Germany in the Nazi era. Even if wide-ranging interpretative analysis of the Nazi era based on such methods will, as Benz adds, naturally be unable 'to do justice to the longing of the citizens of the post-war society to be released from the shadow of the past', this does not mean that it cannot be written.[62] And, while the historian's relationship to his subject of study is different in the case of Nazism than, say, in that of the French Revolution, it could be argued that, even accepting the uniqueness of the Holocaust, the problems posed by 'historicization' are little different in theory to those facing the historian of, say, Soviet society under Stalin.

Like the French and Russian Revolutions, the Third Reich embraces events of world-historical importance. Its history can certainly be approached as part of the pre-history of the Federal Republic (and of the German Democratic Republic), but, as Friedländer rightly says, 'the history of Nazism belongs to everybody'.[63] Perspectives inevitably vary. The polarization in German and Jewish collective memory of the Nazi era — epitomized in the films Heimat and Shoah — was plausibly advanced by Friedländer as an important element in the current debates about approaches to the Third Reich.[64] The differences in emphasis are unavoidable, and each has its own legitimacy. It is difficult to see how they can satisfactorily be blended together in any history which, purely or largely based upon the notion of 'experience' and constructed upon a narrative method ('Erzählen'), attempts a 'global' description of the Nazi era. Even if one suggests that in some ways the historian who shares neither collective memory possibly has an advantageous perspective, the attempt seems in any case bound to founder on the assumption that it is theoretically possible to write the 'total' history of an entire 'era' based upon collective 'experience'.[65] Equally impossible is the construction of a history built solely around the actions or 'experiences' of the 'historical actors' themselves and detached from the other impersonally structured conditions which on good measure shape or predetermine those 'experiences'.[66] Only the application of constructs, concepts, and even theories which reside outside the sphere of historical experience can provide order to make sense of experience in a historical analysis which is bound to be less than 'total' or 'global'.[67] If this appears to stand in contradiction to Broszat's 'historicization' plea, it is scarely out of synchronization with his practice in his own writing on the history of the Nazi era.

If the assumption is abandoned that the history of the Nazi era (or any other 'era'), in the sense of any 'total' grasp of the complexity of all the contradictory and often unrelated experiences which occur in a given period of time, is theoretically and practically possible, then it becomes feasible to conceive of a history of German society under Nazism which could incorporate in a structured analysis the findings of recent social historical research, in particular of '*Alltagsgeschichte*', but which at the same time would embed this in the political–ideological–moral framework which Friedländer is anxious not to lose. Such an approach would have to jettison notions of the 'historicization' of Nazism in terms of regarding it as any other period of history or 'relativizing' its significance. But it would find indispensable the normal methodological rigour of historical enquiry, deployed as a matter of course in dealing with other eras (and already, one might add, deployed in countless scholarly works on Nazism). Applied to the social sphere of 'daily life' as well as to the political–ideological domain, conventional critical historical method would be sufficient to eliminate the modern antiquarianism which has rightly been criticized as a feature of the poorer strains of '*Alltagsgeschichte*'. Finally, it would not only be legitimate, but essential, to proceed in such an approach by way of critical exploration of the continuum which stretches from 'normality' to barbarism and genocide, in order better to comprehend the social as well as political context in which inhumane ideologies become implemented as practical policies of almost inconceivable inhumanity. 'Auschwitz' would, therefore, inevitably form the point of departure from which the thin ice of modern civilization and its veneer of 'normality' could be critically examined.[68]

The last, and ultimately fundamental, issue preoccupying Friedländer seems resolvable in such an approach. The integration of Nazi crimes against humanity into a 'global' interpretation of society in the Third Reich ought to become, in fact, more rather than less possible in the light of the developments made in the empirical social history of Nazism in the past decade. Peukert's synthesis has, in many respects, pointed the way towards an integration of 'normality' and 'barbarism'.[69] I have attempted in my own work explicitly to relate lack of humanitarian concern with regard to the 'Jewish Question' to spheres of dissent and protest in 'everyday' matters.[70] My working hypothesis in such research was the notion that, especially under 'extreme' conditions, 'normal' daily and private concerns consume such energy and attention that indifference to inhumanity, and thereby indirect support of an inhumane political system, is significantly furthered. Robert Gellately, building upon the work of the late Reinhard Mann, has extended such suggestions to the areas of social consensus and active support for 'policing' measures in racial issues.[71] To posit a clear divorce between the concerns of 'Alltagsgeschichte' and the political–ideological–moral framework which focuses upon the genocidal criminality of the Nazi regime is to adopt a misleading perspective. Out of recent work on the social history of the Third Reich, which Broszat did more than most to promote, emerges the realization that there can be a social context in 'civilized society' in which genocide becomes acceptable. Research on the 'grassroots' history of the Nazi era has significantly deepened awareness of the troublesome reflection that 'many features of contemporary "civilized" society encourage the easy resort to genocidal holocausts'.[72]

Notes

1. Martin Broszat, 'Plädoyer für eine Historisierung des Nationalsozialismus', *Merkur* 39 (1985), pp. 373–85, reprinted in Martin Broszat, *Nach Hitler. Der schwierige Umgang mit unserer Geschichte* (Munich, 1986), pp. 159–73. All references which follow are to the latter version. An English translation is available in Peter Baldwin, ed., *Reworking the Past. Hitler, the Holocaust and the Historians' Debate* (Boston, Mass., 1990), pp. 77–87.

2. David Schoenbaum, *Hitler's Social Revolution* (New York/London), 1966; Ralf Dahrendorf, *Society and Democracy in Germany* (London, 1968), ch. 25.

3. Martin Broszat *et al.*, eds., *Bayern in der NS-Zeit*, 6 vols. (Munich 1977–83).

4. See e.g. Hans-Ulrich Wehler, 'Königsweg zu neuen Ufern oder Irrgarten der Illusionen? Die westdeutsche Alltagsgeschichte: Geschichte "von innen" and "von unten"', in F. J. Brüggemeier and J. Kocka, eds., *Geschichte von unten — Geschichte von innen'. Kontroversen um die Alltagsgeschichte*, Fernuniversität Hagen, 1985, pp. 17–47. And for a lively debate about the merits and disadvantages of 'Alltagsgeschichte' see *Alltagsgeschichte der NS-Zeit. Neue Perspektive oder Trivialisierung?*, Kolloquien des Instituts für Zeitgeschichte, Munich, 1984.

5. See e.g. the thoughtful assessment of the limitations but also possibilities of 'Alltagsgeschichte' by Jürgen Kocka in reviews in *Die Zeit* Nr. 42 vom 14. Okt. 1983 ('Drittes

Reich: Die Reihen fast geschlossen') and *taz* vom 26. Jan. 1988 ('Geschichtswerkstätten und Historikerstreit').

6. Broszat, *Nach Hitler,* p. 167.

7. See Broszat, *Nach Hitler,* pp. 114–20 ('Eine Insel in der Geschichte? Der Historiker in der Spannung zwischen Verstehen und Bewerten der Hitler-Zeit').

8. Broszat, *Nach Hitler,* p. 173. See Georg Iggers, *The German Conception of History* (Middletown, Conn., 1968) for the philosophy of historicism in Germany.

9. Broszat, *Nach Hitler,* p. 153 (and back cover). As one who wrote extensively and with great sensitivity about Nazi concentration camps, in which the term 'special treatment' ('*Sonderbehandlung*') was a euphemism for murder, Broszat's use of the term in the present context was a remarkable and unfortunate linguistic lapse.

10. Broszat, *Nach Hitler,* pp. 104 ff, cf. also pp. 36–41. In his exchange of letters with Saul Friedländer, Broszat spoke of a 'plea for the normalization of method, not of evaluation'. — Martin Broszat, Saul Friedländer, 'Um die "Historisierung des Nationalsozialismus". Ein Briefwechsel', *VfZ,* 36 (1988), pp. 339–72, here p. 365 (henceforth cited as 'Briefwechsel'). This letter exchange is published in translation in Baldwin, *Reworking the Past,* pp. 102–34. All references in this chapter are, however, to the German version.

11. Broszat, *Nach Hitler,* pp. 170–1.

12. Broszat, *Nach Hitler,* pp. 171–2.

13. For an excellent collection of essays summarizing much valuable research and locating Nazism within a context of long-term social change, see W. Conze and M. R. Lepsius, *Sozialgeschichte der Bundersrepublik Deutschland* (Stuttgart, 1983).

14. Otto Dov Kulka, 'Singularity and its Relativization. Changing Views in German Historiography on National Socialism and the "Final Solution" ', *Yad Vashem Studies,* 19 (1988) pp. 151–86, here p. 170.

15. Broszat, *Nach Hitler,* p. 161.

16. See Saul Friedländer, 'Some Reflections on the Historicization of National Socialism', *Tel Aviver Jahrbuch für deutsche Geschichte,* 16 (1987), pp. 310–24, here p. 313.

17. Friedländer, 'Reflections', pp. 310–11, 318; Kulka, 'Singularity and its Relativization', pp. 152, 167. The two contributions by Ernst Nolte, which were at the forefront of the '*Historikerstreit*' are reproduced in '*Historikerstreit*'. *Die Dokumentation der Kontroverse um die Einzigartigkeit der nationalsozialistischen Judenvernichtung* (Munich, 1987), pp. 13–35, 39–47.

18. Friedländer, 'Reflections', pp. 317–18; Kulka, 'Singularity and its Relativization', pp. 167 ff.

19. Friedländer, 'Reflections', p. 320; Dan Diner, 'Zwischen Aporie und Apologie', in Dan Diner, ed., *Ist der Nationalsozialismus Geschichte? Zu Historisierung und Historikerstreit* (Frankfurt am Main, 1987), pp. 62–73, here p. 66. An English translation is available in Baldwin, *Reworking the Past,* pp. 135–44. The work referred to is the first essay ('Der Zusammenbruch im Osten 1944/45 als Problem der deutschen Nationalgeschithe und der europäischen Geschichte') of Andreas Hillgruber's, *Zweierlei Untergang. Die Zerschlagung des Deutschen Reiches und das Ende des europäischen Judentums* (Berlin, 1986).

20. Friedländer, 'Reflections'.

21. Friedländer, 'Reflections', pp. 314–16.

22. Broszat, *Nach Hitler,* pp. 171–2.

23. Friedländer, 'Reflections', p. 315.

24. Friedländer, 'Reflections', p. 314. Kulka's criticism in 'Singularity and its Relativization', pp. 168–73, ran along similar lines. Diner ('Zwischen Aporie und Apologie', p. 67) also criticized the inevitable loss of the specifics of the period 1933–45 when, as in the '*Alltagsgeschichte*' approach, the emphasis was placed on 'normality'. With reference to the oral history project directed by Lutz Niethammer on the experiences of Ruhr workers, he pointed out that 'the good and bad times' in subjective memory by no means accord with the significant developments of the period 1933–45. A 'considerable trivialization of the Nazi era' was allegedly the consequence. The reference is to Ulrich Herbert, 'Die guten und die schlechten Zeiten', in Lutz Niethammer, ed., '*Die Jahre weiß man nicht, wo man die heute hinsetzen soll.*' *Faschismuserfahrungen im Ruhrgebiet* (Bonn, 1986), pp. 67–96.

25. Friedländer, 'Reflections', pp. 316–17.

26. Friedländer, 'Reflections', p. 317.

27. Friedländer, 'Reflections', pp. 317–21.

28. Friedländer, 'Reflections', p. 318.

29. Friedländer, 'Reflections', pp. 319–21; and see Diner, 'Zwischen Aporie und Apologie', pp. 66, 69.

30. Friedländer, 'Reflections', p. 319.

31. Friedländer, 'Reflections', p. 321.

32. Friedländer, 'Reflections', p. 321–2.

33. Friedländer, 'Reflections', p. 322.

34. Kulka, 'Singularity and its Relativization', pp. 169, 171–2, and as cited by Herbert Freeden, 'Um die Singularität von Auschwitz', *Tribune,* 26, Heft 102 (1987), pp. 123–4.

35. Friedländer, 'Reflections', p. 323. The phrase is taken from the closing lines of Hannah Arendt, *Eichmann in Jerusalem* (London, 1963), p. 256.

36. Friedländer, 'Reflections', p. 323. Diner ('Zwischen Aporie und Apologie', pp. 67–8, 71–3) was even more unyielding in his criticism, emphasizing the centrality of Auschwitz as a 'universalist point of departure from which to measure the world-historical significance of national Socialism', the impossibility of 'historicizing' Auschwitz, the diametrically opposed experiences of 'perpetrators' and 'victims', and the theoretical impossibility of combing the 'normality' experiences of the former and the experiences of the latter of an 'absolutely exceptional situation' in one narrative history. He added (p. 68) that any notion of 'daily routine' ('*Alltag*') has of necessity to begin from its conceptual opposite of the 'specifically exceptional'. Apparently accepting (p. 71) that some synthesis might after all be possible, he drew the conclusion with reference to the Holocaust that 'only proceeding from this extreme case allows one to make that divided simultaneity — divided, that is, by the close-up perspective into everyday history and mass murders — of the banality of the unreally shaped real normal situation on the one hand and its monstrous upshot on the other hand even approximately comprehensible'.

37. Most classically in Karl-Dietrich Bracher, *The German Dictatorship* (New York, 1970).

38. Marie-Louise Recker, *Nationalsozialistische Sozialpolitik im Zweiten Weltkrieg* (Munich, 1985). See Broszat, *Nach Hitler,* p. 171.

39. Michael Prinz, *Vom neuen Mittelstand zum Volksgenossen* (Munich, 1986).

40. Ulrich Herbert, *Geschichte der Ausländerbeschäftigung in Deutschland 1880 bis 1980* (Bonn, 1986).

41. Ulrich Herbert, *Fremdarbeiter. Politik and Praxis des 'Ausländer-Einsatzes' in der Kriegswirtschaft des Dritten Reiches* (Berlin/Bonn, 1985), back cover. See also Herbert's essay, 'Arbeit und Vernichtung. Ökonomisches Interesse und Primat der "Weltanschauung" ', in Diner, ed., *Ist der Nationalsozialismus Geschichte?*, pp. 198–236.

42. Not surprisingly, moral issues are particularly close to the surface in research, which has made considerable strides forward in recent years, on the place of the Third Reich in the professionalization of medical practice. For surveys of the literature see: Michael H. Kater, 'Medizin und Mediziner im Dritten Reich. Eine Bestandsaufnahme', *Historische Zeitschrift*, 244 (1987), pp. 299–352; and Michael H. Kater, 'The Burden of the Past: Problems of a Modern Historiography of Physicians and Medicine in Nazi Germany', *German Studies Review*, 10 (1987). See also the monographs by Robert Jay Lifton, *The Nazi Doctors* (New York, 1986) and Michael H. Kater, *Doctors under Hitler* (Chapel Hill/London, 1989).

43. Gisela Bock, *Zwangssterilisation im Nationalsozialismus* (Opladen, 1986).

44. See particularly Renate Bridenthal, Atina Grossman, and Marion Kaplan, eds., *When Biology became Destiny. Women in Weimar and Nazi Germany* (New York, 1984); and Claudia Koonz, *Mothers in the Fatherland. Women, the Family, and Nazi Politics* (New York, 1986).

45. Friedländer, 'Reflections', p. 316.

46. Many years ago, Wolfgang Sauer pointed out that a characteristic feature of writing on Nazism was that the historian faced no other choice than rejection. Wolfgang Sauer, 'National Socialism: 'Totalitarianism or Fascism?', *AHR* 73 (1967–8).

47. See Broszat, *Nach Hitler*, pp. 120, 161, for the phrases cited in the following sentence, and pp. 100–1, 173 for comments on 'historicism' ('*Historismus*').

48. See, in particular, the essay: 'Grenzen der Wertneutralität in der Zeitgeschichtsforschung: Der Historiker und der Nationalsozialismus', in Broszat, *Nach Hitler*, pp. 92–113.

49. Broszat, *Nach Hitler*, p. 100. See also 'Briefwechsel', p. 340, where Broszat re-emphasizes his dependence upon a 'principle of critical, enlightening (*aufklärerischen*) historical understanding which . . . is to be clearly distinguished from the concept of understanding (*Verstehens-Begriff*) of German historicism in the nineteenth century . . .'

50. See Detlev Peukert, *Volksgenossen und Gemeinschaftsfremde. Anpassung, Ausmerze und Aufbegehren unter dem Nationalsozialismus* (Cologne, 1982) (Engl. trans., *Inside Nazi Germany. Conformity and Opposition in Everyday Life*, London, 1987). Friedländer offers a qualified acceptance of the merits of *Alltagsgeschichte* in 'Briefwechsel', pp. 354–5, though this is far from satisfying Broszat (see 'Briefwechsel', pp. 362–3).

51. Detlev Peukert, 'Alltag und Barbarei. Zur Normalität des Dritten Reiches', in Diner, ed., *Ist der Nationalsozialismus Geschichte?*, pp. 51–61, esp. pp. 53, 56, 59–61.

52. See the comments of Adelheid von Saldern, which offer some support to Friedländer's objections, in her critique, 'Hillgrubers "Zweierlei Untergang" — der Untergang historischer Erfahrungsanalyse', in Heide Gerstenberger and Dorothea Schmidt, eds., *Normalität oder Normalisierung? Geschichtswerkstätten und Faschismusanalyse* (Mün-

ster, 1987), esp. pp. 164, 167–8. Broszat himself came to accept ('Briefwechsel', pp. 340, 361–2) that the 'historicization' concept is 'ambiguous and misleading'.

53. Friedländer, 'Reflections', pp. 317–21. Nolte's article, 'Vergangenheit, die nicht vergehen will', is in *'Historikerstreit'*, pp. 39–47. Hillgruber's work referred to is the first essay in *Zweierlei Untergang*.

54. Friedländer, 'Reflections', p. 324.

55. See *'Historikerstreit'* pp. 13–35, 39–47. Klaus Hildebrand, for example, praised Nolte in a review for the way in which he undertook 'to incorporate in historicizing fashion (*historisierend einzuordnen*) that central element for the history of National Socialism and of the "Third Reich" of the annihilatory capacity of the ideology and of the regime, and to comprehend this totalitarian reality in the interrelated context of Russian and German history'. — *Historische Zeitschrift*, 242 (1986), p. 465.

56. See Hillgruber's remarks in *'Historikerstreit'*, pp. 234–5.

57. Friedländer, 'Reflections', pp. 320–1. See the further debate between Broszat and Friedländer on this point in 'Briefwechsel', pp. 346, 355–6, 360–1.

58. See Diner, 'Zwischen Aporie und Apologie', pp. 69–70, and von Saldern, 'Hillgrubers "Zweierlei Untergang" ', pp. 161–2, 168 for comments on Hillgruber's argument in the context of the 'historicization' problem. The most devastating critique of Hillgruber's position can be found in Hans-Ulrich Wehler, *Entsorgung der deutschen Geschichte?* (Munich, 1988), pp. 46 ff, 154 ff. See also the excellent review article by Omer Bartov (whose own book, *The Eastern Front 1941–45. German Troops and the Barbarisation of Warfare* [London, 1985], offers a necessary and an important counter-interpretation to that of Hillgruber): 'Historians on the Eastern Front. Andreas Hillgruber and Germany's Tragedy', *Tel Aviver Jahrbuch für deutsche Geschichte*, 16 (1987), pp. 325–45.

59. See Martin Broszat, *Die Machtergreifung* (Munich, 1984) (Engl. trans., *Hitler and the Collapse of Weimar Germany*, Leamington Spa, 1987). For Broszat's remarks on the concept behind the series *Deutsche Geschichte der neuesten Zeit*, see *Nach Hitler*, p. 152. And for his advocation of narrative (*Erzählen*) as historical method, see Broszat, *Nach Hitler*, pp. 137, 161.

60. See Broszat, *Nach Hitler*, pp. 131–9, 'Alltagsgeschichte der NS-Zeit'.

61. Wolfgang Benz, 'Die Abwehr der Vergangenheit. Ein Problem nur für Historiker und Moralisten?' in Diner, ed., *Ist der Nationalsozialismus Geschichte?*, p. 33.

62. Benz, p. 19. Norbert Frei's book, *Der Führerstaat* (Munich, 1987) (Engl. trans., *Nazi Germany. A Social History* [Oxford, 1992]) offers some pointers towards the potential of such an approach.

63. Friedländer, 'Reflections', p. 322.

64. Saul Friedländer, 'West Germany and the Burden of the Past: The Ongoing Debate', *Jerusalem Quarterly*, 42 (1987), pp. 16–17. And see also 'Briefwechsel', pp. 346, 366–7, on the 'dissonance between memories'.

65. See here the pertinent remarks of Wehler, 'Königsweg', p. 35. On the potential, but also substantial problems, of 'experience analysis' (*Erfahrungsanalyse*) with reference to the Third Reich, see von Saldern, 'Hillgrubers "Zweierlei Untergang" '. Friedländer emphasizes the limits of narrative as a method in 'Briefwechsel', pp. 370–1, while Diner ('Zwischen Aporie und Apologie', p. 67) is adamant that 'experienced everyday routine and existential exception can theoretically no longer be narrated as one history'.

66. See Wehler, *Entsorgung*, p. 54, referring to the problem involved in Hillgruber's identification with the German troops on the Eastern front.

67. See the comments by Klaus Tenfelde and Jürgen Kocka in *Alltagsgeschichte der ZS-Zeit* pp. 36, 50–4, 63–4, and by Kocka — on the need for theory in '*Alltagsgeschichte*' — in a review in *taz*, 26 Jan. 1988 (see note 5, this chapter).

68. See Peukert, 'Alltag und Barbarei', p. 61; and Diner, 'Zwischen Aporie und Apologie', pp. 71–2.

69. Peukert, *Volksgenossen und Gemeinschaftsfremde*. Engl. trans., *Inside Nazi Germany* (see note 50, this chapter); see also his 'Alltag und Barbarei' (see note 51, this chapter).

70. Ian Kershaw, *Popular Opinion and Political Dissent in the Third Reich* (Oxford, 1983).

71. Reinhard Mann, *Protest und Kontrolle im Dritten Reich* (Frankfurt am Main/New York, 1987); Robert Gellately, 'The Gestapo and German Society: Political Denunciation in the Gestapo Case Files', *Journal of Modern History* 60 (1988), pp. 654–94; and, especially, *The Gestapo and German Society. Enforcing Racial Policy* (Oxford, 1990).

72. Leo Kuper, *Genocide* (Harmondsworth, 1981), p. 137.

I2

Shifting Perspectives: Historiographical Trends in the Aftermath of Unification

By the mid 1980s, the self-image of the Federal Republic of Germany had become increasingly schizophrenic: on the one hand, the material success-story of the post-war era — prosperous, stable, highly-developed; on the other hand, doomed it seemed forever to live under the shadow of the crimes committed in Germany's name during the Third Reich. It was little wonder that conservative politicians and publicists came to feel it more and more necessary to draw a line under the Hitler era, to emerge — as one leading politician put it — from 'the shadows of the Third Reich', and be proud to be Germans again.[1]

Times have changed more rapidly than anyone in the mid 1980s could have imagined. Now, in a unified Germany within a transformed Europe, drawing the line under the Nazi past appears less easily possible. The reawakened problems of fascism, racism, and nationalism straddle the decades and ensure a continuing preoccupation with the Hitler era. Nazism truly remains 'a past which will not pass away'.[2]

Historical perspectives are, however, never static. They quite properly and naturally change over time. Those on the Nazi era are more than most affected by a variety of influences outside the strict bounds of historical scholarship. One substantial impact on historiography of the political changes in eastern Europe can be noted at the outset: the effective demise of marxist analyses of

Nazism. These have lost, at best, a good deal of their former appeal; at worst they have lost credibility. The orthodox, strait-jacketed marxism–leninism which underpinned the official state ideologies in the GDR and other former Soviet bloc states falls into the latter category: it now finds few willing to defend its manifold and fundamental flaws as a theoretical framework of interpretation. It is rare to find historians of the Third Reich (or other historians) who regret its demise. More regrettable (though not every scholar would agree) is the current dismissiveness shown towards *all* variants of marxist analysis, even those (such as Bonapartist and Gramscian approaches) which at the very least have been intellectually fertile and heuristically stimulating approaches.

What this means is that the marxist contributions to the debates on Nazism no longer enjoy major currency, and that the continuing debates are all conducted within the framework of liberal historiography, now facing — for the first time since political and scholarly analysis of fascism began in the early 1920s — no serious challenge from a fundamentally opposed, alternative philosophy.

Of course, many of the genuine advances in scholarly understanding of the Third Reich will stand the test of time, whatever the political climate. But past and present cannot be clinically separated; conflicting interpretations of Nazism are inextricably bound up with the continuing reappraisal of the political identity of the Federal Republic and the changing ways in which it attempts to cope with the moral burden of the past. It would have been remarkable, therefore, had the unification of the divided Germany in 1990 left no influence on historiographical trends. In the midst of a vast transformation whose eventual outcome we still cannot foretell, it is possible only to hint at some changes which are visible. But it appears that the issues which surfaced in the debates of the mid 1980s still, if in a different context, provide the framework for the current historiographical agenda.

The trends highlighted in what follows focus, firstly, on the ways in which perceptions of the location of Nazism in German history might be refashioned in the light of a changing sense of German identity since the recent unification; secondly, on the place of Nazism in the long-term modernization of Germany and how this could alter the perspective on Nazi barbarism; and, thirdly, on how the end of Soviet Communism could influence attitudes towards the horrors of the Third Reich. The link between the three trends selected for discussion is the continuing preoccupation — reflected in different ways — with 'historicization'.

I. Nazism and National Identity

A key theme in the *Historikerstreit,* particularly in the contributions of Michael Stürmer, was the role of history in creating a positive sense of national identity, and the blockage imposed by the Third Reich on that identity.[3] The long span of German history, rather than the negative concentration on the Third Reich, was in his view the key to finding that identity — an identity capable of uniting, not dividing and morally repelling. He spoke of the Germans in a divided Germany needing to find their identity, which had to be a national identity — though a national identity which, as it seemed at the time, had no prospect of deriving from a German nation-state.[4]

The diametrical opposite to this view was the 'critical history' approach associated above all with Hans-Ulrich Wehler and Jürgen Kocka and intellectually dominant in the decade before the *Tendenzwende* — the political and intellectual challenge to the social-liberal values which had prevailed in the previous two decades or so — set in around the end of the 1970s and early 1980s. It was this approach — emphatic in its self-conscious, politically and morally informed critical approach to the national past, vehemently upholding a sense of post-nationalist identity formed through 'constitutional patriotism' and bonds with western liberal values, and methodologically wedded to applied social science techniques affording a comparative history of society — which was represented in the dispute by Jürgen Habermas.[5]

Application of the 'critical history' approach has not been confined to the Third Reich. In fact, more of the scholarly analyses and monographs influenced by this approach — and many of the most important works of its chief exponents — have focused on nineteenth- rather than on twentieth-century history.[6] However, implicitly if not explicitly, the search for an explanation of how Hitler's triumph in 1933 was possible has been central to the work of the 'critical' historians. And the legacy of the Nazi abomination was pivotal to the socio-political as well as historical philosophy which underpinned the 'critical approach'. As Habermas expressed it, 'a commitment to universalist constitutional principles rooted in conviction has only been feasible in the cultural nation of the Germans after — and through — Auschwitz. . . . Anyone wishing to recall the Germans to a conventional form of their national identity destroys the only reliable basis of our bonds with the West'.[7]

The contrast between the two approaches to the German past could scarcely be plainer. An attempt to create a sense of national identity through an approach to the national past which does not attempt to conceal the crimes of Nazism but to transcend them by 'historicizing' them into a longer-term and wider perspective embracing a multiplicity of facets of national history is confronted by an approach which sees Auschwitz as the essential starting-point of all that is positive in a post-national form of identity.

At the time of the *Historikerstreit,* many thought that the critics of the 'revisionist' positions of Stürmer, Hillgruber, and Nolte had enjoyed the better of the rancorous exchanges. German unification has, however, inevitably altered perspectives on national identity and, therefore, on how the national past could be viewed. The effect has been, it appears, to place the 'critical history' approach even further on the defensive than it had already become during the *Tendenzwende* of the 1980s and to offer greater encouragement than ever possible during the 1960s and 1970s to an emphasis upon German nationality as the cornerstone of historical analysis — with the dangers of a neo-historicism which that entails.[8]

The events of 1989–90 gave German conservatives the opportunity to marry what for four decades had seemed irreconcilable alternatives: the Adenauer heritage of the bonds with the West and the accomplishment of national unity. Since then, the deep divisions, problems of integration, and 'identity crisis' within the new German national state formed by the incorporation of the GDR in the Federal Republic have seemed to lend new urgency — and far more obviously than had been the case in the mid 1980s — to attempts to place the emphasis upon national history as a foundation of national identity and, eventually, cultural and political unity. That an attempt to create national identity through history is as philosophically flawed as it is ideologically tendentious will presumably provide no barrier to this shift in perspective.[9]

Different ways of regarding the German past opened up with the fall of the Berlin Wall and the subsequent unification of the two Germanies. Since the War, it had only been possible to see national history in terms of the temporary, imperfect, and ill-fated unity of the German Reich, leading within little over 70 years to catastrophe and seemingly permanent division. The events of 1989–90 brought not only the Cold War and, with it, the post-war era, to a close. They also seemingly restored to Germany the 'normality' of the existence of a nation-state; as Saul Friedländer put it, they have 'given back national continuity to German history'.[10] The presumed German '*Sonderweg*' ('special path') could now be seen to be at the end.[11] The development of the nation-state had no longer been abruptly truncated and irrevocably terminated by the split of the nation into two states. The future might look bleak; but there *was* a future for the nation, and that future was open. History had not been closed off by war and genocide. Hitler's legacy had not, after all, been the end of the German nation, merely a lengthy interruption to the 'normality' of national unity. Within this changed perspective, it is plain, Auschwitz could no longer continue to serve as the reference point for post-war identity, as Habermas had wanted it to remain.

An obvious problem, nevertheless, is the kind of 'normality' which *could* serve as a reference point for national identity. The Reich that existed between 1871 and 1945 can scarcely offer a model; yet it is the only previous experience of a German nation-state. In one of his books, Michael Stürmer poses alternative vantage points, looking to long-term developments since the Thirty Years' War of the seventeenth century for 'national and trans-national traditions and patterns worth cherishing'. These include, in his view, federalism, religious tolerance, civic institutions, and balance between centre and periphery. He regards an emphasis upon such traditions as offering potential for the creation of a German sense of historical identity within an increasingly closely-knit (western) Europe.[12]

Whether such cultural currents are sufficient to outweigh the ideological baggage of the historical nation-state in shaping new forms of German identity might be doubted; and whether Stürmer's vision of the new Europe will come to pass is still no more than a matter for speculation. But his 'bid to prevent Hitler remaining the final, unavoidable object of German history, or indeed its one and only starting point'[13] is both understandable and seems likely, with the passage of time in post-unification Germany, to be increasingly successful.

Whatever aspirations to national identity exist today, they contain only in the strident tones of the radical Right discordant echoes of the nationalist-chauvinist clamour of the 1871–1945 era. In a world of nation-states — whatever the post-national wishes of those, in Germany as elsewhere, who strive for closer European unity — aspiring to a stronger sense of German national identity is in itself certainly not unnatural and must not necessarily prove unhealthy. But German history provides few models for constructing a national identity. Such a presumed German 'national identity' has not been a historical constant, but is a product of only the last two centuries, has fluctuated greatly over time, and been based on shifting sets of 'German' territorial borders since the Napoleonic conquests.[14] Nor, arguably, can any common identity be an artificial product resting solely, or even mainly, upon historical perspectives but will grow, if at all, organically over time out of common cultural experience and common political and social institutions.

Historiographically, however, the 'paradigm shift' in perspective means not only 'historicizing' the Third Reich in the long span of German history and ceasing to treat it as the central point or even end-point of that history. It also means that some elements within the history of the Third Reich become emphasized more than others, as they fit better into the changed perspective. Some implications of this were already evident in the debate over Broszat's 'historicization plea'.[15] The changing perspective comes out particularly clearly in the way 'historicization' is used to treat the question of Nazism and modernization.

II. Nazism and Modernization

In analysis of the question of Nazism and modernization, the central areas of debate — leaving aside the marxist rejection of the modernization question in its entirety — were once whether the Nazi regime had, despite an anti-modern ideology, unwittingly brought about Germany's 'revolution of modernity', or whether it amounted to social reaction. The modernization theme was then taken up in a different way by Broszat in his 'historicization plea' through the suggestion that the social planning of the German Labour Front could be viewed, in a sense, in detachment from the specifics of Nazi ideology and the particular circumstances of the Third Reich, as an episode in the development of social welfare schemes which pre-dated Nazism and extended into the modern system of the Federal Republic, and as a parallel to what was taking place under entirely different political systems, as in the British Beveridge Plan.[16]

The suggestion that the phenomenon of Nazism could be better understood by locating it in the continuities of German development which extended over and beyond the Third Reich, by looking away from the barbarities long established as its hallmark to underlying social 'normality', was avidly taken up by a number of, predominantly younger, German scholars, and 'historicization' provided the cue for examining Nazism and the links with modernization after 1945 in a variety of new ways.[17] But underlying them was an assumption which differs sharply from earlier treatment of the 'modernization' theme: the claim that the Nazi leadership not only brought about a modernizing revolution in Germany, but, in fact, *intended* to do so.[18] Claims that Mussolini's regime (among other fascist-style dictatorships) was a modernizing dictatorship are not new, though they have frequently encountered the criticism that they ignore the essence of fascism by concentrating on the by-product of modernization. In the case of Nazism, that criticism can be reinforced. Placing the emphasis upon 'modernization' unavoidably leads to a shift in perspective on the Third Reich.[19] In turn, this change in perspective can rapidly engender a trivialization of Nazism, whose crimes are not ignored, but nonetheless largely taken for granted and displaced by the image of the Third Reich as an important era of modernization in the long-term historical treatment of German national development.

This new approach to Nazism and modernization, and its implications for the way the Third Reich is viewed, were strongly influenced by the work of the Berlin political scientist Rainer Zitelmann and came out plainly in his study of Hitler's social ideas, published in 1987.[20] Zitelmann explicitly regarded his book as a contribution to that 'historicization' of National Socialism for which Broszat had pleaded. Young Germans, Zitelmann argued, had hitherto been faced only with stark alternatives, both unacceptable, and both rendering Hitler and the generation which supported him utterly incomprehensible: either total moral condemnation — a demonization of Hitler which turned him into the incarnation of evil — or apologetics and distortion of historical reality. His study of Hitler's social aims and philosophy was an attempt to overcome such incomprehensibility and to break down the sense of distant unreality about the Nazi regime and its leader.[21]

Concentrating not, in the conventional fashion, on Hitler's anti-semitic and *Lebensraum* obsessions, Zitelmann saw a logical cohesion to the German dictator's views on social and economic matters and was not dismissive, as most historians have been, of such views. Not only were Hitler's ideas (within the context of his racist-darwinist philosophy) coherent; they were, Zitelmann argues, in many senses distinctly 'modern'. Hitler was not looking backwards (as were Darré and Himmler) to the recreation of an agrarian wonderland, but forwards to a highly developed, advanced industrial and technological society — resting of course on supplies of raw materials and forced labour extracted from conquered territories, but modern for all that. The decadent bourgeoisie would be replaced by upwardly-mobile workers, with abundant chances of enhanced status and opportunities for social advancement. Industry would fall into line or be taken over by the state. A planned economy would in any case follow after the war. The model, as the brutal agent of a modernizing dictatorship, was Stalin, whom Hitler admired. Instead of regarding Hitler's social ideas, whatever coherence one attaches to them, as a means to the end of racial purification and conquest, Zitelmann came close to inverting the order by seeing the racial programme as the means to bring about revolutionary plans for a transformation of German society by a dictator who saw himself — and deserves to be treated by historians — as a social revolutionary.[22]

Since the publication of the book which made his name, Zitelmann, an enormously productive writer, has argued in much the same vein in a plethora of essays, reviews, and newspaper articles. He has also been extremely active in stimulating other young scholars to collaborate on essay collections framed around the themes of modernization and 'historicization'. The core of Zitelmann's argument is that 'modernization' ought to be decoupled from any normative links with 'progress', humanitarian values, pluralist participatory political systems, and democratization, and seen as 'value-free' — simply a pragmatic tool of empirical investigation and scholarly analysis. It then becomes perfectly possible, he suggests, to speak of modernization taking place (intentionally, not just 'accidentally') in totalitarian states, as well as in liberal systems.[23] This was self-evidently the case under Stalinism (a point which most historians would readily accept), and, on analysis of the thought (and practice) of Hitler and other Nazi leaders such as the Labour Front boss Robert Ley or Albert Speer, the conclusion should be reached, he concludes, that Nazism not only unwittingly contributed towards modernization in Germany, but intended to bring it about and strove to do so.[24]

Powerfully argued though the case is, it seems to contain both methodological and conceptual flaws. As regards method, a kind of coherence in Hitler's social views can be found by taking his comments on 'social matters' from speeches in the early 1920s through to monologues in his field headquarters in the war, and piecing them together. But this approach pays little attention to the precise context or intended function of Hitler's comments and is in danger, therefore, both of exaggerating the coherence and, especially, of elevating the importance of such ideas within Hitler's *Weltanschauung*. In the comprehensive collections of Hitler's speeches and writings between 1919 and 1933 which are now available,[25] for instance, the vision of a modern society is largely confined to the monotonous repetition of the aim to wipe out the distinction between 'workers of the brain' and 'the fist' by the creation of a 'national community' based on racial purity, principles of struggle, and strength to ensure survival through territorial conquest attained by the sword. The 'social vision' — essentially an offshoot of the preoccupation with the 'living space question', obsessive anti-semitism, and pervading racial philosophy which dominate the speeches and writings — is a primitive derivative of nineteenth-century racialist and social-darwinist ideologies, not a blueprint for 'modernization'. It is difficult, in particular, to accept Zitelmann's inversion of means and ends, reducing the obsessions with destroying the Jews and the acquisition of 'living space' at the expense of the Soviet Union to the functional purpose of the revolutionary modernization of German society.

Conceptually, the attempt to remove all normative connotations from modernization and to treat the term as value-free makes it analytically as good as unusable.[26] Of course, it is possible to *describe* 'modernizing' elements in Nazism — which, in fact, have seldom been denied in the literature on the Third Reich. But it cannot suffice *analytically,* in a thesis of Nazism as an intentionally modernizing dictatorship, to evade a definition of 'modernization' or 'modernity' on the grounds that 'modernity' is still too recent to distinguish what is 'normal' and 'exceptional' about it, or that, 'in the present state of discussion', a general definition applicable to the time in question would be 'extraordinarily difficult'.[27] In the absence of any attempt at definition, what the modernizing elements present in the Nazi era ought to signify is difficult to see. In any event, as Charles Maier has pointed out, 'a modern labour market imposes structural demands even on governments that have murderous agendas', so there are scant grounds for surprise at many of the 'modernizing' elements in Nazism. 'What are morally significant', Maier adds, 'are the few institutions that were murderous, not the many normal aspects of running a society'.[28]

The main problem with Zitelmann's approach to the alleged 'modernizing' intentions of the Hitler regime is that it comes close to substituting the accidental for the essential in Nazism as a *historical* phenomenon — that is, for Nazism as it actually developed.[29] Also the worry is — as Saul Friedländer has remarked — that, in the new Germany and with the passage of time gradually eliminating those with living experience of the Third Reich, the perspective could become indelibly shifted from the unique characteristics of the 1933–45 era to the more 'comprehensible' — because more 'normal' — elements which can be regarded as the part of the 'pre-history' of the Federal Republic (though it has to be said that there are few, if any, signs of such a trend developing).[30]

Zitelmann has remarked that Broszat's 'historicization plea' had a 'liberating effect' on himself, and on other younger colleagues.[31] His approach reveals, however, that the vague and interpretationally open-ended concept of 'historicization' can lead in directions never intended by Broszat.[32] There is, of course, no suggestion that Zitelmann's motives in advocating a radical break with the way Nazism has conventionally been treated in scholarship, teaching, and public discourse are anything other than scholarly and honourable. And he has much which is correct and important to say about the attractiveness of Nazism to the German population, and the reasons why it could have such drawing power — inexplicable simply on grounds of the persecution of the Jews, the apparatus of repression, or other aspects of the Third Reich which have rightly been central themes of historical research.[33] But when he rhetorically asks: 'How heavily, as opposed to the atrocities perpetrated against the Jews and other minorities, are social-political progress and increased upward mobility chances for "people's comrades" to be weighted?', and 'can one, given the sufferings of the victims, speak at all of those sides of reality which many people have experienced as positive?',[34] and when we take into account that even before the Berlin Wall fell a third of the population of the Federal

Republic thought the Third Reich was too negatively depicted in school lessons, while more than two-thirds of those questioned were in favour of drawing a line under the Nazi past;[35] then the implicit tendency is plain to see.

III. Nazism and Stalinism

A third way in which approaches to the Third Reich have been affected by the changes in Europe since 1989 has different links with the notion of 'historicization'. In sharp distinction to Broszat's use of this concept — and demonstrating once again how unsatisfactory is the woolliness of the term — Ernst Nolte, in the *Historikerstreit*, had sought a rethinking of Nazism's place in German history by regarding it as the reaction and counterpoint to Soviet communism in the 'European civil war' between 1917 and 1945.[36] Nolte's line of argument prompted bitter debate about the singularity of the Nazi genocide against the Jews, and the extent to which it could be seen as comparable to other twentieth-century genocides or even as a response to the Bolshevik 'class genocide' in the Russian civil war. For Nolte, the fates of the Soviet Union and Germany were, therefore, historically intertwined through the 'European civil war': the fight to the last of opposite, but related, ideologies. In his assertion that Nazism was *reactive,* a preventive attempt to stave off destruction by the equal, if not greater, evil of Soviet Bolshevism, Nolte was coming close to turning the Nazis' own justification of the war they launched into scholarly interpretation. But the furore he instigated certainly succeeded in turning the spotlight in a new way on to the intertwined history of Bolshevism and Nazism and the ideological origins of the genocidal war in the Soviet Union.

This theme, still against the backcloth of the notion of 'historicization', but from a wholly different perspective, was soon to be at the centre of another controversial study. In his book on the 'Final Solution' published just before the events of 1989, in which he claimed he was attempting to 'historicize' the 'Judeocide' (more usually called 'the Holocaust'), the American historian Arno Mayer — whose leftist inclinations set him poles apart from Nolte's stance — also took the German-Soviet relationship as the intrinsic element in what he described as a second 'Thirty Years War'.[37] But his approach was diametrically opposed to Nolte's. There was no suggestion of a 'preventive' attempt to stave off destruction by the Bolsheviks. Rather, Mayer saw the German invasion of the Soviet Union and the war of annihilation which followed as an ideological crusade inspired by a widespread and deep-rooted morbid fear of Bolshevism long prevalent in Germany's bourgeoisie and ruling classes and easily able to marry with and subsume paranoid Nazi images of

'Judeo-Bolshevism'. Far from presuming Nazism to be a reaction to prior Bolshevik barbarity, he laid the stress on unprovoked extreme and lethal anti-Bolshevism (extending way beyond Nazi hard-core support) as the prime, more extensive motivator, and interpreted the genocide against the Jews as arising from the war rather than being planned long before it.

For Mayer as for Nolte, therefore, the war with the Soviet Union and the ideological clash between Nazism and Bolshevism formed the core of any attempt at historical understanding of the Nazi phenomenon. In both cases, but from entirely different starting-points and on the basis of opposing interpretations, the emphasis, as Peter Baldwin summed up, had 'shifted away from the Jews to the Soviets'. But whereas 'for Nolte, the Bolsheviks were the main aggressors', for Mayer, they were 'the primary victims'.[38]

Since the fall of Communism and the possibilities of attaining deeper insights into the inner workings of the Soviet system, the relationship between Nazi Germany and the Soviet Union — especially the comparison and contrast of the Hitler and Stalin regimes — has naturally prompted intensified interest. One offshoot has been a revival of the concept of 'totalitarianism'. Although after its hey-day in the 1950s the concept fell into some disuse and discredit, particularly by historians and political scientists who inclined to the Left, it by no means lost all its appeal as long as the Cold War lasted and, in fact, enjoyed something of a revival in the later 1970s and 1980s. Since the collapse of the Soviet system, the rehabilitation of the concept has been well-nigh complete.[39]

This is not a surprising development. The sharpened focus on the scale and nature of repression — especially under Stalin but more generally in the Soviet system and, not least, in the GDR — together with stories that can now be told of deeply moving personal experiences of repression by the police state have given new vitality to the 'totalitarianism' concept.[40]

The danger is that this will provide sustenance to a simplistic popular image which implicitly posits an identification with Nazism not only of the Stalinist regime in the Soviet Union, but of 'Stalinism' — a concept extended to cover the political system of the GDR.[41] Within Germany, this could easily mean that the perfectly understandable preoccupation with the inhumanity of the GDR system, which has only recently disappeared and is therefore much more vivid in memory, increasingly displaces the fading memory of Nazism, trivializing the horrors perpetrated under Hitler by naïve and shallow comparison with the crimes of the Honecker regime.[42] The distance to a relativization of German inhumanity under Nazism, at the centre of the storm provoked by Nolte's contributions to the *Historikerstreit,* is then a short one. Hitler could be viewed as a wicked tyrant — though less wicked than Stalin; and the Holocaust could be seen as no worse than the Stalinist mass-murders, and as no more than a horrible by-product of the life-and-death struggle of totalitarian systems, in which major atrocities were committed by both sides.

Again, however, it should be emphasized that such changes of perspective, anticipated with concern by some, have not materialized. Moreover, the renewed interest in 'totalitarian' systems does not have only a negative side to it. Given the new research into the functioning of Soviet rule and the sophistication of research since the 1960s into the power structures and repressive apparatus of the Third Reich, the comparative analysis of 'Stalinism' and 'Hitlerism' need not be a retrograde step, and holds out the prospect of a deeper understanding of both systems and the societies upholding them.[43]

Reflections
GENERATIONAL CHANGE AND THE 'GOLDHAGEN DEBATE'

What has happened in the past few years, as regards public sensitivities in present-day Germany towards the Third Reich, is at first sight somewhat surprising. The danger appeared evident that the 'revisionist' trends we have described, which first became visible in the 'change of direction (*Tendenz-wende*)' of the early 1980s, came sharply into focus in the '*Historikerstreit*' — the 'historians' dispute' — of 1986, and appeared to acquire renewed impetus following the unification of 1990, would gain ground and lead, within Germany, to a significant shift in perspective on the Third Reich. It looked probable that the end of the Cold War and the sudden accomplishment of German unification in 1990 would effect what Saul Friedländer called 'a transformation in historical consciousness'[44] and that this might well usher in what conservatives in Germany had long wanted: the drawing of the line under the Nazi past. A possible redefining of national identity, the 'historicization' (seen as 'normalization') of the Nazi era, and comparisons with what could be portrayed as the even greater horrors of Stalinism pointed in this direction. It seemed likely that there would be increasing impatience in the new Germany with an image of the Third Reich which placed heavy — at times near exclusive — emphasis upon German atrocities, war crimes, racial persecution, and genocide against the Jews, all symbolized by the name 'Auschwitz'. It seemed not unnatural that many Germans — two-thirds of whom were not even born when the Third Reich collapsed and could feel no personal responsibility for what took place under Hitler — would now want more than ever to shake off the burden of the past.

A changing historical consciousness, it was possible to imagine, might seek mainly to focus upon those elements of the Third Reich that could be understood as part of the development of a post-war modernized, technocratic, economically advanced, social welfare state. Indeed, as regards actual memory of what life was like under Hitler, oral history techniques had revealed the extent to which the Third Reich—particularly the peace-time years between 1933 and 1939—were seen as 'normal years' sandwiched between economic misery and war, and years that had many positive sides to them.[45] 'Strength through Joy' works outings, Hitler Youth rambles, the building of the motorways, the clearing away of unemployment, and the promise of the 'people's car' outweighed in such memory the 'seamier' side of the Third Reich—concentration camps, pogroms, deportations, and the mass murder of designated 'racial inferiors'.

Certainly, the decade since unification has brought significant shifts in historical consciousness. But these have not taken the direction many commentators at the time—myself included—had predicted; rather, this historical consciousness has come to be dominated as never before by the shadow of the Holocaust. Far from receding with the passage of time, the unprecedented crimes against humanity which Hitler's regime perpetrated loom ever larger, more than 50 years since its destruction, in the way Germans view their own past.

This phenomenon has evident connections with generational change—only around one in ten Germans in today's population had any possibility of being involved in the crimes of the Third Reich. The 'Hitler Youth generation', teenagers as the Reich collapsed into ruin, are themselves now of pensionable age.[46] We are, therefore, fast approaching a time where living experience of the Third Reich will have died out. The generation of those who could engage in outright apologetics for their actions under Hitler is gone, or is at any rate rapidly disappearing. Today's young generation, uninhibited about asking the most penetrating questions about the Nazi past, are now openly probing the actions not of their fathers, but of their grandfathers.

In historical scholarship, too, the generational change has left its mark. Those who for many years have dominated scholarship on the darkest episodes in recent German history, roughly those who were just old enough to have been members of the Hitler Youth in the last years of the war and who have regarded their historical work as a part of their political task of ensuring a lasting legacy of social and liberal values in German society, are now of retirement age. Specialists in National Socialism belonging to a new generation, born in the 1950s and 1960s, have, inevitably, brought new perspectives to bear, feel less bound by the perspectives of their predecessors, want in some senses to break free of their hold, at any rate are prepared to ask questions that challenge the older generation. This is, of course, as it should be—a perfectly natural and desirable phenomenon. Each generation must write history if not exactly anew then at least to match its own demands of the past. Advances in historical scholarship are invariably made by pupils challenging the accepted wisdom of their teachers. In the case of such a troubled period as the Third Reich, however, where the moral dimension is so prominent, this can mean not simply revised interpretations or new accents in research, but the moral interrogation of an older generation of historians by a younger.[47]

Meanwhile, there is seemingly no end to public exposure to the legacy of the Hitler era. The Nazi legacy of war and genocide remains part of present-day politics and moral consciousness in Germany. The burder of the Nazi past has not diminished, even for generations that could feel no personal sense of guilt for what happened. Countering the many who have indeed had 'enough of National Socialism'[48] and long for a line to be drawn under the horrors of the Hitler era, are those who are determined that every aspect of those horrors should be laid bare and that the evils concealed, suppressed, or passed over by the post-war generations should now finally come out into the open. German sensitivities were recently exposed, not for the first time, by something touching them from outside the German cultural sphere: in this instance, the publication in 1996 of a book by a young American political scientist Daniel Goldhagen, whose thesis, bluntly put, was that the Jews were murdered because the uniquely anti-semitic German people wanted them murdered. It amounted to the indictment of a nation.[49]

Goldhagen's book created a sensation in Germany. The first printing of the German edition was a sell-out even before it became available in the bookshops. Thousands — most of whom at that point had not read Goldhagen's book and, in all probability, few if any scholarly analyses of Nazism and the 'Final Solution' for that matter — flocked to the debates where the American author confronted his German academic critics. Some of the debates were televised, with substantial viewing figures. Mass-media attention was extraordinary — not least for a book that had emerged from a doctoral dissertation. A 'Goldhagen industry' of reviews, articles, and even books about his book was spawned.[50]

I happened to be in the country during part of Goldhagen's ten-day publicity tour of Germany and had the opportunity to watch one of the television debates. In the studio staging, the fresh-faced, neatly dressed, impeccably polite, telegenic assistant professor from Harvard was seated opposite a battery of stern-looking critics — some of them heavyweight German professors of daunting erudition. It looked as if Goldhagen was on trial, facing a bench of prosecutors determined on gaining a conviction. His fierce critics, on this occasion including Hans Mommsen (who emerged on numerous occasions as

Goldhagen's most tenacious antagonist) and Ignaz Bubis, head of the Jewish community in Germany, destroyed, I thought (as did my German friends watching at the same time), the basis of Goldhagen's argument in a barrage of well-founded attacks. Goldhagen, speaking in English to ensure that he avoided any linguistic *faux pas* on such a sensitive issue, offered what seemed to me to be only inadequate, bland responses. For such a combative, provocative, aggressively argued book, it amounted, in my view, to a weak defence in which Goldhagen often retreated to qualifications not on offer in the text, or to claims of misunderstanding by his critics.[51] But, however little he was able to confound his detractors, it made no difference — the longer the debates continued, the greater, apparently, became public support for Goldhagen. This seemed to be especially the case among younger Germans.

This can be explained neither by the quality of Goldhagen's contribution to the historiographical debate, nor by the intellectual strength of his revised interpretation of the cause of the 'Final Solution'. Rather, apart from the remarkably successful marketing of the book as a wholly novel interpretation of the Holocaust by the original American publishing house, it has everything to do with the way in which the German trauma of the nation's involvement in the Holocaust has been highlighted once more. Goldhagen's book opened up once more, and in the most glaring fashion, the continuing troubled relationship of Germans with their own past,[52] and stirred up overnight a heated debate in wide sections of the population about the complicity of ordinary Germans in the extermination of the Jews. The televising in Germany in 1979 of the American film *The Holocaust*, which personalized the tragedy of Europe's Jews in a drama revolving around fictional Nazi and Jewish families, did more than the countless academic studies already in print at the time to lay bare the psychological scars of a country that, for decades, had avoided confronting head-on the full horror of the murder of the Jews and the role of ordinary people, not just Nazi leaders, in those terrible events. 'A Nation is Stunned' was the subtitle of one of the books on the reception of the film that appeared at the time.[53] Almost 20 years later, *Schindler's List* doubtless stirred deep emotions in a younger generation. This was the climate in which Goldhagen's book was published.

Even so, it is an extreme rarity that a scholarship book rises overnight to the top of the bestseller lists and that an associate professor of an academic department at a university becomes an international celebrity. So, why did the book have such an impact? For one thing, there was the publicity machine: the Harvard PhD thesis, examining the role of the perpetrators in the killing units of the east through analysis of their testimony in post-war trials, was transformed by publishers' hype into what was marketed as the most original interpretation of the Holocaust ever published, one that stood the entire historiography of five decades — massive in quantity, often excellent in quality, greatly varied and nuanced in interpretation — on its head. This publicity machine had already been operating at full capacity in the USA and in Great Britain for weeks before the German translation of Goldhagen's book was published.

I was invited on a number of occasions to write reviews for the press and to debate the book on television and radio. I declined all invitations. An early reading led me to the view later echoed by the leading German historian Eberhard Jäckel that it was 'simply a bad book'.[54] My view was that it contributed little or nothing to a deeper understanding of how the Holocaust came about. By then, it was already rocketing to a place on the non-fictional bestseller lists; I did, therefore, at this point consent to participate in a panel discussion of the book at the German Historical Institute in London. The four historians on the panel were united in their criticism. Few in the audience disagreed, but what was of interest was that the publicity machine had done its work. Of a packed house, it transpired that hardly anyone — other than the speakers — had read the book.

That was certainly the position in Germany, too, in the early stages of the 'Goldhagen phenomenon'. Even before the German edition had been published, *Der Spiegel* had devoted almost 30 pages, under the title 'A Nation of Demons?', to a discussion of the English-language version of Goldhagen's book. The front page of the magazine, under a photo-montage of eager hands reaching out to greet Hitler, framed by a background of the 'gate of death' of Auschwitz-Birkenau, was headed: 'New Controversy about Collective Guilt. The Germans: Hitler's Willing Accomplices in Murder?'[55] Also before any German version appeared, *Die Zeit,* in a largely positive review, had declared that Goldhagen's book would prompt a new 'historians' dispute'.[56] This turned out, however, to be a premature judgement. In the '*Historikerstreit*' of the 1980s, the fault lines on a number of issues of political, ideological, and moral significance were drawn *between* historians, reflected in their differing interpretations of the position of Nazism in German history (and, in particular, of the 'Final Solution'). In the Goldhagen case, most historians were broadly in unison in their fundamental criticism of what they saw as a seriously flawed book. Leading historians took issue with it, often in the most forthright terms.[57] But all this did was to stir interest in the volume. Copies were flown in from England; by the time the German version was ready to appear, members of the public were thirsting to get hold of it.

Clever publicity does not, however, explain everything. The peculiar reception of the book in Germany had other causes. One was the stark — but for

Germans awful—simplicity of Goldhagen's message. His book has a very clear, actually highly simplistic, answer to the question of why the Holocaust happened. In sharp contrast to the vast majority of works in the library of interpretative scholarly studies of the Holocaust, the answer for Goldhagen is straightforward: the German people had been unique in their commitment to an 'eliminationist anti-semitism' from the early nineteenth century onwards and, once given the opportunity under Hitler, they then eliminated the Jews. This certainly (something which may be welcomed) focuses attention again on the role played by anti-semitic ideology in the path to the 'Final Solution', in contrast to interpretations that have played down the significance of ideology in favour of emphasis on the complex structures of Nazi rule and 'functionalist' explanations of the emergence of genocide (though, in truth, no worthwhile work of scholarship had ignored anti-semitism as a significant element in explaining the Holocaust). But of notable importance in the reception of Goldhagen and his book was the startling simplicity of the interpretation compared with what seemed to be tortuous and complicated explanations offered by his critics. The difference was sharpened by Goldhagen's style of writing—the use of detailed descriptions, acting at times as surrogate eye-witness accounts of the most terrible cruelties—which, for all its repetitive use of sociological jargon in places, contrasted diametrically (in its often emotive narrative of the histories of ordinary perpetrators and their victims) with the more detached and abstract academic prose of most historians of Nazi anti-Jewish policy. It was hard not to be moved, gripped, appalled, shocked, horrified by the personalized stories, so vividly told, of the gratuitous cruelty inflicted on the victims by their tormenters and killers.

Even more important was the fact that Goldhagen, himself from a family that had suffered in the Holocaust, was now indicting as never before—leaving aside the understandable, but still misleading, generalizations that had often been expressed in the early post-war period and the implicit tenor of some strands of historical writing in Israel—the entire German people for their crimes against the Jews. He was adamant in his book that 'eliminationist anti-semitism' (feeding directly under Hitler into exterminatory anti-semitism) was an ideology shared by the German people as a whole, not just by a 'nazified' sector, and that the German people were unique in this. His treatment of the behaviour of the perpetrators, describing the cruelties towards the Jews of 'ordinary Germans', as he insisted on calling them, and not just of committed Nazis or members of the SS, drove the message home. No one in Germany with any sensitivity towards the past could ignore the allegation: the reason the Jews were murdered was that Germans were unlike any other people in being a nation of ideological anti-semites—a nation of Hitlers in this regard, one might say — looking for the opportunity to 'eliminate' the Jews; when the opportunity came, they grasped it eagerly.

Could this be true? Just to pose the question meant having to come to grips with Goldhagen's claim. It was a powerful indictment resting on some emotively displayed evidence. Attempts by academics to counter it by more balanced and differentiated analyses could easily seem weak, unconvincing, detached, even apologetic, to mass audiences which, naturally enough, were for the most part little versed or interested in the nuances of scholarly debate. The more the experienced historians tried to combat the broad sweep of Goldhagen's grand accusation, the less effective — even if accurate — their criticisms appeared to be to a generation ready and prepared to think the worst of their grandfathers.

The trauma Goldhagen's book, once again in the most graphic terms, uncovered shows no sign of diminishing. If anything, the greater the distance from the terrible events of the 1930s and 1940s and the more memory is being replaced by memorial as the generation of the victims dies away,[58] the less the psychological scar on national consciousness appears to be fading.

But although it has been an extraordinary phenomenon in highlighting this trauma more than ever before, as an analysis of the 'Final Solution' Goldhagen's book will, in my view, occupy only a limited place in the unfolding, vast historiography of such a crucially important topic — probably at best as a challenge to historians to qualify or counter his 'broad-brush' generalizations.

Some of the criticism of the book has been savage — none more so than the ferocious onslaught on the bases of Goldhagen's arguments by the New York political scientist Norman Finkelstein, claiming that: 'Replete with gross misrepresentations of the secondary literature and internal contradictions, Goldhagen's book is worthless as scholarship', that his work 'adds nothing to our current understanding of the Nazi holocaust'.[59] This is, however, to go much too far, as even Hans Mommsen, one of Goldhagen's most vehement critics, accepts.[60] Whatever its deficiencies, Goldhagen's book poses important questions which, as the reactions to it have shown, still need answers — not least in the eyes of many younger Germans.

More damaging to Goldhagen was the review by Ruth Bettina Birn, now Chief Historian in the War Crimes Section of Canada's Department of Justice, who for a number of years worked at the *Zentrale Stelle der Landesjustizverwaltungen* (Central Office of State Justice Administration) in Ludwigsburg where Goldhagen carried out most of his research.[61] Birn had extensive knowledge, therefore, of the materials that formed the core of Goldhagen's interpretation. Most of the criticism levelled at Goldhagen by historians of different nationalities and persuasions had targeted the earlier parts of his book which provide, in establishing his central thesis, an overview — based largely on secondary sources — of the development of anti-semitism in Germany down to the eve of the Holocaust. Some historians had been more generous about Goldhagen's more detailed findings on the perpetrators and actions of the killing units in the later sections of his book, while remaining for the most part hostile to his overall interpretation.[62] But Birn's review tackled Goldhagen's argument in the place where he had seemed most impervious to criticism: in his analysis of the trial material relating to the killers. In a sustained attack, levelled not only at the essence of Goldhagen's argument but also at his method, Birn accused the American author, among other things, of one-sided use of the trial evidence to uphold his own *a priori* generalizations. She systematically set out to undermine his use of sources and, therefore, to discredit him as a historian, and to deprive his book of all claim to validity as an interpretation of the Holocaust. 'As it stands,' Birn witheringly concluded, 'this book only caters to those who want simplistic answers to difficult questions, to those who seek the security of prejudices.'[63]

Birn's hard-hitting review was, however, itself not free of weaknesses and errors, not least in the misleading way she couched some of Goldhagen's arguments, and Goldhagen was able to provide a lengthy, and heated, rebuttal — without, however, so far as I can see, countering some of the detailed points of criticism of his use of sources.[64]

All in all, the debate about Goldhagen's book has led to some unusually bitter confrontations, of which the author's conflict with Birn (whom at one time he was threatening to sue) and his dismissive comments about Finkelstein (following the latter's unnecessarily aggressive review) are the most glaring manifestations. It often seemed in the debate that emotionality, from whatever motives, had overtaken rationality. Given the subject matter, that was understandable, but still regrettable. Advances in this most difficult, complex, and important of issues — comprehending better the genesis and perpetration of the Holocaust — will ultimately only come about through historical research detached from overheated emotion and bitter polemics. It is, therefore, all the more welcome to find perhaps the most valuable and most thorough critique of Goldhagen's work in a calm and rational analysis, far from aggressive in tone, and ready to see some merit in the book, by one of the outstanding younger historians of the Holocaust, Dieter Pohl.[65]

The great virtue of Pohl's analysis is that it remains free of polemics, and confined to strictly scholarly parameters of analysis. Pohl subjects both Goldhagen's empirical research and his methodological approach to the most rigorous scrutiny in the context of international scholarship on the Holocaust, and finds the work gravely lacking on both counts. Pohl, whose knowledge of the secondary literature and primary sources relating to the 'Final Solution' is highly impressive, and who has extensively researched in archives in eastern Europe which Goldhagen did not begin to tap, revealed inconsistencies and inadequacies in Goldhagen's empirical exploration wherever he looked. As regards Goldhagen's methodological approach, Pohl — as we have seen, by no means the hardest of Goldhagen's critics — speaks of a 'speculative style of questioning' and 'forms of argument in several places which touch the very limit of scholarly practice'.[66] Bearing in mind the major methodological problems Goldhagen faced, Pohl concludes, 'greater reserve in the way of arguing of the author would have been in place. But Goldhagen knows almost nothing but certainties'. Certainly, on the question of the motivation of the perpetrators, Pohl points out, the book has prompted new questions, and contributes some new detail to scholarly discussion. But overall: 'the book belongs . . . to those great simplifying attempts (*Entwürfe*) . . . that ought to be taken as a challenge'.[67] In the light of Pohl's penetrating analysis — there was no shortage of other far-reaching criticism — it may suffice here simply to outline some of what seem to me to be the flaws of the book.

A highly selective use of evidence is employed by Goldhagen to build up a picture of a people whose endemic anti-semitic mentality, deep seated since the Middle Ages, had by the nineteenth century turned into a uniquely German 'eliminationist' brand of anti-semitism, common to the whole of society. This *a priori* crude generalization is then deployed as the answer to all problems raised, only in order to be dismissed. Why, for example, was there no German opposition to the extermination of the Jews? Easy: the Germans were all eliminationist anti-semites. The demonization of the Germans provides, therefore, the 'answer' to all questions. Circularity of argument is the basis of the book. In reality, a mass of literature exists — some of it produced by Jewish historians — demonstrating a wide spectrum of attitudes towards the Jews both before the Nazis came to power and even during the Third Reich itself.[68]

Goldhagen certainly has no difficulty in providing numerous instances of extreme — often gratuitous — cruelty towards Jews by Germans. Whether the members of the police battalions of the *Ordnungspolizei* can so readily be classed as 'ordinary Germans' is, however, open to doubt. The individuals in such units had not only, like the rest of the population, been subjected to years of relentless anti-semitic propaganda but, even if not members of the SS, belonged to an organization (the *Ordnungspolizei*) that was part of a repressive apparatus in which anti-semitism had certainly been internalized, part in fact of a wider police apparatus whose head was none other than Heinrich Himmler. How important, in any case, anti-semitism was as a motive in the killing units is something which, as Christopher Browning's work has shown, needs to be established, not simply presumed, and could vary in intensity.[69] Only comparative analysis of the behaviour of the men in similar circumstances might indicate whether their hatred of Jews was paramount in their killing actions and cruelty towards their victims. There is some evidence to suggest that there was little difference, for instance, in the same setting between their treatment of Jews and of Soviet prisoners of war.[70]

Goldhagen's assumption — for that is what it is — of the uniqueness of German anti-semitism, his key explanation for the Holocaust, is not tested, remarkably for a political scientist (whose dissertation, from which the book emanates, won a prize in the field of comparative politics), by any comparative analysis between Germans and others implicated in the killing. In particular, the extraordinary brutality of Lithuanian, Latvian, and Ukrainian participants in the mass killing operations is never dealt with in any systematic fashion, nor the reasons for their high level of barbarism related to the argument for alleged German uniqueness of 'eliminationist' (then exterminatory) anti-semitism. Also left unexplained is how this presumed unique anti-semitism, embedded in the German mentality for centuries, changed so dramatically, as Goldhagen claims, after the war to make the Germans 'normal'.

Goldhagen's book is unlikely to play any significant part in the important, and ever-deepening scholarly research on the Holocaust. But sometimes the 'great simplifiers' can serve a purpose outside the context of narrower historiographical debate. Scholarly research and popular historical consciousness are frequently out of step with each other, not just in Germany; it can sometimes happen that a book lacking scholarly distinction can nevertheless touch a raw nerve in a way that the findings of more profound academic research do not, and unleash a debate of some importance. This was the case with Goldhagen's book.

At any rate, the reception of the book in Germany demonstrated, yet again, how far removed we are from any 'historicization' of Nazism, from treating it dispassionately as a period of history much as any other. The Goldhagen affair highlights once more the point that, in dealing with the problem of explaining Nazism, historical–philosophical, political–ideological, and — above all — moral issues remain inescapable.

CHANGING PERSPECTIVES IN RESEARCH

It is possible to draw some encouragement from the onward path of recent research on the Nazi era, especially in Germany. It seems as if some significant trends of change can broadly be established.[71]

The debates that raged in the 1960s and 1970s about the nature of Nazism, whether as a form of fascism or manifestation of totalitarianism, have long since lost their vibrancy. The demise of the Soviet system, with its ideologically inflexible, rival framework of interpretation of Hitler's regime, and the corresponding atrophying of interest in more or less all types of marxist analysis, have doubtless been important in this. The debates in any case had largely run their course; they had become sterile; there was little more to be squeezed out of them. Typologies and taxonomies are, of course, the very stuff of political science, and will rightly continue to be discussed in connection with the character of Nazi rule, but recent works on comparative fascism have proved uncontentious in including Nazism (as a peculiar case) within their framework of analysis.[72] As for the totalitarianism theorem, this, as we have already indicated, has enjoyed a renaissance in the 1990s, and — as the success of a recent anthology of work on totalitarian regimes shows — still retains great currency.[73] The heated ideological debates of yesteryear have, however, evaporated; and, for all that there are constant exhortations to undertake it, comparative empirical research on dictatorships has neither been common nor so far, when carried out, has it brought major interpretative breakthroughs in relation to National Socialism.[74]

The heat has also largely gone out of the question of the relationship between the Nazi regime and 'big business'. Here, too, the ending of the east–west divide has defused a previously explosive area of debate. The issue of 'primacy of politics' or 'primacy of economics' has a somewhat dated ring to it today. The deepest complicity and ready involvement of most big firms, businesses, and financial institutions in the inhumane policies of the Nazi regime, leading to war and genocide, is now well established, generally accepted, and no longer needs special emphasis. Knowledge of the integration of 'big business' into the policy making of the regime and collaboration in the direct aspects of Nazi barbarism has been greatly extended through major works on individual firms such as those by Peter Hayes on IG Farben, the impressive study by Hans Mommsen and Manfred Grieger on Volkswagen, and the fine investigation of Daimler-Benz by Neil Gregor.[75]

The part played by economic imperatives in the preparation for and conduct of war is also abundantly apparent. But the full incorporation of 'big business' interests in the ideological drive of Nazism, without that drive being reduced to little more than an expression of such interests, seems today to need far less forceful advocacy than was the case 15 or 20 years ago. Not only does the fully fledged reductionism of orthodox marxism–leninism seem like a remnant of a bygone era. The attention once given in more sophisticated marxist approaches to working-class unrest in Germany and a foreign policy dominated by domestic policy — in particular, by mounting economic pressures — also appears today to arise from a distorted perspective.[76]

Perhaps the most significant shift in perspective, compared with the position in the early or mid-1980s is the seriousness with which Nazi racial ideology is now viewed as a key motivating force for action. Given the rag-bag nature of Nazism's assemblage of phobias and prejudices, it has always proved tempting to see ideology as no more than an amalgam of ideas at the service of propaganda and mobilization. In some ways, this has become almost reversed: propaganda and mobilization are now seen to have served a racial ideology of central importance to the 'cumulative radicalization' of the regime.[77]

The major empirical breakthroughs of the 1960s and 1970s on the inner workings of the regime — for the most part within Germany itself, and largely confined to the pre-war years — had encouraged a perhaps exaggerated tendency to regard ideology as little more than operational, providing a justification for power-political motives and functions of the different competing agencies within the regime. Certainly, ideology *did* serve such functions. More recent studies have, however, seen no need to pose a contradiction between the instrumentalization of ideas and the genuine motivational force of an ideology of racial purity and racial conquest which underpinned the regime's ceaseless dynamic. The ideology of race was, as such studies have shown, sucked in by a generation of well-educated Germans who came to maturity during the years after the First World War and later came to prominence in the leadership of the SS, police, and security apparatus, the ideological executive of the regime and most important motor of race policy.[78]

In looking to the ways in which the racial ideology permeated, in differing degrees, practically all areas of the regime, new perspectives have opened up on the way the regime functioned, and on the role of Hitler. The 'intentionalism–structuralism' (or '–functionalism') dichotomy, which was dominant in the 1970s and 1980s and served for a time a valuable heuristic purpose, has in the process been largely transcended. The work already undertaken, and that still in progress, on the development of genocidal policy has proved pivotal here. It has shown how vital Hitler's pathological anti-semitism, his own 'mission' to 'remove' the Jews from Germany, then from Europe, was to the shaping of the climate of the 'racial state',[79] fuelling the aggression of the activists, and providing legimation for those directing and planning race policy. Not least, it is plain that Hitler's authorization was crucial at decisive junctures. His significance is, therefore, nowhere in question, or diminished;[80] but, at the same time, the type of reductionism that looked almost exclusively to Hitler's ideological 'intentions' as the explanation of the Third Reich's drive to war and genocide has patently been displaced. The complexity of the processes involved cannot be captured by simple 'intentionalist' arguments. Within the framework of the distant goals Hitler embodied and propagated, the radicalization of anti-Jewish policy fed itself, and was driven by genocidal impulses from below as well as by policy-directives from above.

While recent research on the genesis of the 'Final Solution' has done much, therefore, to uphold 'structuralist' (or 'functionalist') arguments, it has not under-rated Hitler's importance to developments. Suggestions today that he was in some ways a 'weak dictator' sound hollow;[81] here, too, a once-heated debate has markedly cooled. Probably the sheer passage of time has contributed to this, but so have the findings of important studies such as Dieter Rebentisch's investigation of the changing structures of the regime during the war-time years — for long a relatively neglected period in this respect — which illustrated Hitler's centrality to decisions often on quite minor matters of domestic policy as well as those affecting military affairs.[82]

The 1970s can be looked back upon not only as a decade in which some of the key debates about the Nazi Dictatorship — fascism or totalitarianism?, primacy of politics or economics?, intentionalism or functionalism? — reached their apogee, but also as a time when the social history of the Third Reich, until then in its infancy, began in earnest. A ground-breaking role in this was without doubt played by the 'Bavaria Project', which set out to explore resistance in Bavaria and ended by revealing not just numerous and disparate forms of dissent but also how these co-existed with areas of wide-ranging consensus behind the Nazi regime's policies.[83] Since then, there has been a veritable plethora of studies on almost every aspect of life in the Third Reich. Many more will doubtless follow. Here, too, there have been important shifts in emphasis.

The interest in 'class' as an analytical concept has declined — another reflection of the diminished engagement with marxist theories in the wake of the collapse of communism. With it has gone the fascination with the working class, in particular, which was such a prominent feature of research into the social history of the Third Reich carried out in the 1970s and early 1980s. Studies of women, gender, and the family have formed important areas of research which have in good measure supplanted the previous concentration on class.[84] In exploring gender issues, the focus shifted inexorably to Nazi biological policies concerning women.[85] This fitted into another trend in social-historical research which was rapidly gathering pace: the investigation of the victims, as well as the perpetrators, of Nazi 'eugenics' policies, ranging from compulsory 'sterilization' to 'euthanasia'.[86] The history of persecution, undertaken 'from below', revealed a truly appalling picture of suffering, but also, frequently, new levels of 'everyday complicity'.

The social history of the Third Reich moved rapidly, therefore, from its early preoccupation with all forms of 'everyday' opposition and dissent, to uncovering the myriad ways in which Nazi policies of racial discrimination and persecution, embracing other minorities as well as Jews, were pushed along from below. Racism was increasingly revealed as something penetrating practically all levels of society. Even before the opening of the archives in eastern Europe, research interest had extended from different social groups within Germany to attempts to analyze the mentalities of ordinary soldiers fighting in Russia and involved in the worst forms of barbarism.[87] Access to former Soviet archives especially has subsequently unfolded a new, rich potential for detailed empirical investigation of the agents of Nazi racial and genocidal policy in the east.

In social history, too, therefore, issues that once dominated debate — did worker opposition pose a major threat to the regime? did Nazism modernize, even revolutionize, German society? — no longer have the importance they once appeared to have. Not surprisingly, perhaps, they have lost some of their currency in the context of the enormity of Nazi crimes against humanity which, research has shown, can no longer be depicted in isolation from the social forces that made those crimes possible. The Holocaust and the Nazi 'race project' in all its manifestations have correspondingly become increasingly central, also to social history, posing searching questions about the approval and complicity of ordinary people. The issues that have arisen from such research doubtless played some part in heightening the sensitivities that Daniel Goldhagen, whatever the simplicities of his argument, was able to touch.

Looking back across more than half a century of research on the Third Reich, it is tempting to see the unique character of the central historiographical debates as arising from a particular conjuncture of circumstances. Leaving to one side for a moment the '*Historikerstreit*', the debates among German historians were probably at their most rancorous in the 1960s and 1970s. They were debates predominantly among West German historians, and for the most part of roughly the same age cohort (the 'Hitler Youth' generation, born around 1925–30, or a few years older). These historians often looked to the recent past for moral and political lessons for the future, breaking with the traditions of 'historicism', exploring systematically for the first time the returned masses of captured Nazi documents. The climate in which they had begun their research had been one of little public discussion of the Nazi past, with publications often tending to demonize Hitler and propagate apologetics, not least on the part of the former *Wehrmacht* generals. The work of the then new generation of historians was, from the start, therefore, politically sensitive and often highly contentious.

Some of this new generation of historians concentrated on foreign policy, war leadership, and the role of Hitler which was so self-evidently bound up in these spheres. Others explored the internal development of the regime, the workings of specific agencies or ministries, or party-state relations. In studies that increasingly revealed the polycratic structures of Nazi rule, emphasizing internal conflicts and administrative confusion, Hitler's role frequently appeared less prominent. The 'intentionalist–functionalist' debate was born in part of this simple division of labour in a climate of increasing moral and political preoccupation with the Third Reich following long years of relative neglect. The sometimes acrid tone of the debates was doubtless affected here and there, too, by personal animosities as well as professional rivalries.

In a climate in which every scholarly position could be seen to have political overtones, the extreme politicization of German universities towards the end of the 1960s, the student demonstrations of 1968, and the new or revived interest among West German students in marxist theories of fascism helped to widen the rift among Germany's leading historians of the Third Reich. Clashes of method between 'traditional' historians, shunning theory and relying heavily upon empiricism, and those attracted by the theoretical bases of history regarded as a social science, also played their part. By the mid-1970s, with the social history of the Third Reich opening new challenges of '*Alltagsgeschichte*' ('the history of everyday life'), the differences — transcending conventional academic disagreements — between German experts on the Hitler regime were acute. They emerged in full force at the notorious Cumberland Lodge Conference, near London, in 1979.[88]

What few of the Third Reich experts assembled there had done up to that time — it was rapidly to change — was to immerse themselves in detailed study of the murder of the Jews. In the wake of the interest stirred by the Auschwitz trial and, before it, the trial of Adolf Eichmann in Jerusalem, the 1960s — in contrast with the previous decade — had certainly seen some impressive research published in the Federal Republic on the persecution of the Jews.[89] The need to provide expert testimony for the Auschwitz trial had, indeed, during the 1960s, involved one of the participants at Cumberland Lodge, Martin Broszat, together with his colleagues at the Institut für Zeitgeschichte in Munich, in important and ground-breaking research on the direct aspects of genocidal policy.[90] But little of the research carried out at that time on the Holocaust (as it was coming to be called) was carried out in universities;[91] the Holocaust scarcely figured on lecture and seminar lists; it had not entered the mainstream of scholarship on the Third Reich.[92] This did not substantially change before the 1980s. But from then on, the change both in scholarly work and in the public domain was rapid, and accelerating. The expanding scholarly preoccupation with the Nazi persecution of the Jews was already starting to take off in the early 1980s. It was partly prompted by awakened popular interest, reflected in reactions to the televising of the film *Holocaust*. But it was partly, too, sparked by changing scholarly awareness. The need to respond to the provocations of David Irving's attempted exculpation of Hitler's role in the 'Final Solution' had directed the attention of both 'intentionalists' and 'structuralists' to the need to clarify the decision-making processes that led to genocide. The seminal works of Adam and Schleunes paved the way for the research that was to follow, furthered by the important articles of Broszat and Mommsen, the influential book by Gerald Fleming, and the papers of the Stuttgart conference on the murder of the Jews in 1983.[93] All this formed the backdrop to the '*Historikerstreit*' that flared up in 1986. That dispute — really a debate about contemporary political and moral consciousness, masquerading as historical conflict — involved almost all the Third Reich experts from the 'Hitler Youth generation', and relatively few from any other. In almost every case, their stance was predictable. It was their last major confrontation.

Ernst Nolte was at least right, in the first sally of the '*Historikerstreit*', in describing the Nazi era as 'a past that will not pass away';[94] but the founding generation of historical scholarship on the Third Reich has itself passed into retirement age, while research into the Nazi past has largely passed into new hands. With this natural development have come changed perspectives and new emphases. The ever-increasing dominance of the Holocaust in scholarship on the Third Reich has been still further underlined, but the opening of the East European archives has shifted the main research concentration from Germany itself to the epicentre of the Holocaust — Poland and the Soviet Union. Historical research on the Third Reich has, therefore, finally come to focus on the heart of Nazi rule: extermination policy, the killing of an intended 11 million Jews and the remodelling of Europe on race lines following a war of planned barbarity to establish race dominance and the brutal subjugation — in some cases eradication — of 'inferior' peoples.

With the generational 'changing of the guard', much of the rancour has left scholarly debate on the Third Reich. Contested interpretations are, of course, the life blood of historical understanding. As recent writing on genocidal race-policy — the very essence of Nazism — indicates, the genuine disagreements in interpretation which will certainly continue now more closely resemble 'normal' historical debate than did the disputes of the 1960s and 1970s, let alone the '*Historikerstreit*' of the 1980s.

The heat has, then, been taken out of many of the most contentious issues of the past 50 years of historical writing on the Third Reich, with greater distance producing less emotive scholarship. The gains arising from research in that time, especially since the 1960s, have been truly impressive. A genuinely international scholarship — if more often than not working to an agenda strongly influenced by inner-German developments and preoccupations — has explored and elucidated numerous aspects of Nazi rule. A great body of specialized knowledge has been accumulated in a vast literature, much of it of a very high calibre. Valuable syntheses and overarching interpretations have also been written, doing much to bring this research to a wider readership.[95]

The Third Reich — and especially the legacy of the Holocaust — will, of course, continue to belong to the realm of public consciousness, and to stir deep emotions amongst those who will have neither the time nor the inclination to follow the path through the labyrinth of scholarly research.

The Nazi past raises passionate feelings of moral denunciation in those who have to confront it. It is right that it does so. Yet, as justified and even necessary as such feelings are, moral denunciation in the long run will not suffice and can easily become the stuff of legend, not understanding.[96] Moral outrage and revulsion need constantly to be reinforced by genuine historical scholarship and understanding. The past does shape the present — in very obvious ways in Germany, and by no means always or only in negative fashion.

Never since the war — with new forms of fascism and racism more menacing than thought imaginable only a few short years ago — has it been more important to understand the disaster which Nazism wrought on Germany and Europe. Doubtless, the contribution of the specialist historian of Nazism to countering the worrying and depressing reawakening of fascism can be only a small one. But it is nevertheless vitally important that the contribution, however modest, is made. Knowledge is better than ignorance; history better than myth. These truisms are more than ever worth bearing in mind where ignorance and myth spawn racial intolerance and a revival of the illusions and idiocies of fascism.

Notes

1. James M. Markham, 'Whither Strauß — Bavaria or Bonn? Premier Campaigns for "Emergence From Third Reich" ', *International Herald Tribune*, 15 Jan. 1987.

2. The title of Ernst Nolte's essay which prompted the *Historikerstreit* ('historians' dispute') of 1986. See *'Historikerstreit'. Die Dokumentation der Kontroverse um die Einzigartigkeit der nationalsozialistischen Judenvernichtung* (Munich, 1987), pp. 39–47. Extensive analyses of the *Historikerstreit* are provided by Hans-Ulrich Wehler, *Entsorgung der deutschen Vergangenheit? Ein polemischer Essay zum 'Historikerstreit'* (Munich, 1988), Charles Maier, *The Unmasterable Past: History, Holocaust, and German National Identity* (Cambridge, Mass., 1988), and Richard J. Evans, *In Hitler's Shadow. West German Historians and the Attempt to Escape from the Nazi Past* (New York, 1989), while important contributions and commentaries were made available in English

in *Yad Vashem Studies,* 19 (1988), pp. 1–186 and Peter Baldwin, ed., *Reworking the Past. Hitler, the Holocaust, and the Historians' Debate* (Boston, Mass., 1990). The number of articles, commentaries, reports etc. on the *Historikerstreit,* within and outside Germany, runs into the hundreds. Bibliographical references to much of the important literature can be found in the notes to Wehler, pp. 212 ff., the commented guide to further reading in Evans, pp. 186–9, the bibliography in Baldwin, pp. 295–304, and in Geoff Eley, 'Nazism, Politics, and the Image of the Past. Thoughts on the West German *Historikerstreit* 1986–87', *Past and Present,* 121 (1988), pp. 171–208, here pp. 177–8 notes 12–13.

3. The writings of Michael Stürmer most relevant to the *Historikerstreit* include: 'Kein Eigentum der Deutschen: die deutsche Frage', in Werner Weidenfeld, ed., *Die Identität der Deutschen* (Munich/Vienna, 1983), pp. 83–101; *Dissonanzen der Fortschritts. Essays über Geschichte und Politik in Deutschland* (Munich, 1986); 'Geschichte in geschichts-losem Land', '*Historikerstreit*', pp. 36–9; 'Was Geschichte wiegt', in '*Historikerstreit*', pp. 293–5; 'Weder verdrängen noch bewältigen: Geschichte und Gegenwartsbewußstein der Deutschen', *Schweizer Monatshefte,* 66 (1986), pp. 689–94; 'Suche nach der ver-lorenen Erinnerung', in *Das Parlament,* 36 (1986), Nr. 20–21, 17–24, May 1986. On Stürmer's metamorphosis from former adherent of the 'critical history' school to publicist of German conservatism, see Volker R. Berghahn, 'Geschichtswissenschaft und Große Politik', *APZ,* B11/87, 14 Mar. 1987, pp. 25–37; Hans-Jürgen Puhle, 'Die neue Ruhelo-sigkeit: Michael Stürmers nationalpolitischer Revisionismus', *Geschichte und Gesell-schaft,* 13 (1987), pp. 382–99; and Hans-Ulrich Wehler, *Entsorgung der deutschen Ver-gangenheit? Ein polemischer Essay zum 'Historikerstreit'* (Munich, 1988), pp. 28–36.

4. Stürmer, 'Kein Eigentum der Deutschen', p. 98.

5. Jürgen Habermas, 'Eine Art Schadensabwicklung. Die apologetischen Tendenzen in der deutschen Zeitgeschichtsschreibung', in '*Historikerstreit*', pp. 62–76 (Eng. trans., 'A Kind of Indemnification', *Yad Vashem Studies,* 19 (1988), pp. 75–92).

6. See, for an overview, Roger Fletcher, 'Recent Developments in West German Histo-riography: The Bielefeld School and its Critics', *German Studies Review,* 7 (1984), pp. 451–80.

7. Habermas, 'Eine Art Schadensabwicklung', in '*Historikerstreit*', pp. 75–6.

8. In a percipient article published in 1984 ('Zur Kritik an der "Kritischen Geschichts-wissenschaft": Tendenzwende oder Paradigmawechsel?', *GWU* 35 [1984], pp. 1–24), Irmline Veit-Brause already saw the wind of change blowing in the replacement of the 'critical history' approach by the new 'paradigm' of 'national identity'. Hans-Ulrich Wehler's deep antagonism to the shift in focus is shown in his attack on Stürmer's ap-proach in *Entsorgung,* pp. 69–78, 138–45, 171–89, and in his ferocious response to an article by Harold James ('Die Nemesis der Einfallslosigkeit', *Frankfurter Allgemeine Zeitung,* 17 Sept. 1990) suggesting that national myths were needed to compensate for material dissatisfaction and could help to create stability. See Hans-Ulrich Wehler, 'Aufforderung zum Irrweg: Wiederbelebung des deutschen Nationalismus und seiner Mythen', *Der Spiegel,* 24 Sept. 1990, and 'Welche Probleme kann ein deutscher Na-tionalismus heute überhaupt noch lösen? Wider die Apostel der nationalen "Normal-ität": Der Verfassungs- und Sozialstaat schafft Loyalität und Staatsbürgerstolz', *Die Zeit* (24 Sept. 1990) and also his review of Harold James's book, *A German Identity* (London, 1989), 'Im Irrgarten des ökonomischen Determinismus', *Die Zeit,* 11 Oct. 1991.

9. For powerful objections to the presumption that identity can be exclusively drawn from history, see Maier, *The Unmasterable Past,* pp. 149–56.

10. Saul Friedländer, 'Martin Broszat und die Historisierung des Nationalsozialismus', in Klaus-Dietmar Henke and Claudio Natoli, eds., *Mit dem Pathos der Nüchternheit. Martin Broszat, das Institut für Zeitgeschichte und die Erforschung des Nationalsozialismus* (Frankfurt am Main/New York, 1991), pp. 155–71, here, p. 159.

11. See David Blackbourn and Geoff Eley, *Mythen deutscher Geschichtsschreibung* (Frankfurt am Main/Berlin/Vienna, 1980), Engl. trans., *The Peculiarities of German History* (Oxford, 1984). For the sharp and polemical debate unleashed by this book, see e.g. the reviews by Hans-Ulrich Wehler, ' "Deutscher Sonderweg" oder allgemeine Probleme des westlichen Kapitalismus?', *Merkur* 5 (1981), pp. 478–87; Hans-Jürgen Puhle, 'Deutscher Sonderweg. Kontroverse um eine vermeintliche Legende', *Journal für Geschichte,* Heft 4 (1981), pp. 44–5; Wolfgang J. Mommsen, in *Bulletin of the German Historical Institute,* London 4 (1980), pp. 19–26; and the discussion forum *Deutscher Sonderweg — Mythos oder Realität* (Kolloquien des Instituts für Zeitgeschichte, Munich/Vienna, 1982). Directly relating to the causes of fascism, and partly in reply to Jürgen Kocka's article, 'Ursachen des Nationalsozialismus', *APZ* (21 June 1980), pp. 3–15, see also Geoff Eley, 'What produces Fascism: Preindustrial Traditions or a Crisis of the Capitalist State?', *Politics and Society* 12 (1983), pp. 53–82. Jürgen Kocka, 'German History before Hitler: The Debate about the German *Sonderweg'*, *JCH* 23 (1988), pp. 3–16, provides an excellent critique of the pros and cons of the *Sonderweg* argument. He concludes that while the term '*Sonderweg'* is itself misleading and dispensable, the notion of a divergence from the pattern of development of other 'advanced' western countries retains its value in explaining why Germany offered so few barriers to the fascist challenge.

12. Michael Stürmer, *Die Grenzen der Macht. Begegnung der Deutschen mit der Geschichte* (Berlin, 1992).

13. Michael Stürmer in an interview with David Walker, *The Times Higher,* 24 July 1992.

14. See on this the excellent introduction by John Breuilly, 'The National Idea in Modern German History' in John Breuilly, ed., *The State of Germany. The National Idea in the Making, Unmaking, and Remaking of a Modern Nation-State* (London, 1992).

15. Martin Broszat, *Nach Hitler. Der schwierige Umgang mit unserer Geschichte* (Munich, 1986), pp. 159–73.

16. Broszat, *Nach Hitler,* pp. 171–2. The comparison with the Beveridge Plan, which Broszat suggested, was apparently first made by Hanz-Günther Hockerts, 'Sicherung im Alter. Kontinuität and Wandel der gesetzlichen Rentenversicherung 1889–1979', in Werner Conze and M. Rainer Lepsius, eds., *Sozialgeschichte der Bundesrepublik Deutschland. Beiträge zum Kontinuitätsproblem* (Stuttgart, 1983), p. 309. It has been more recently repeated in Ronald Smelser, *Robert Ley. Hitler's Labour Front Leader* (Oxford/New York/Hamburg, 1988), p. 307.

17. See Michael Prinz and Rainer Zitelmann, eds., *Nationalsozialismus und Modernisierung* (Darmstadt, 1991).

18. See Uwe Backes, Eckhard Jesse and Rainer Zitelmann, eds., *Die Schatten der Vergangenheit. Impulse zur Historisierung des Nationalsozialismus* (Frankfurt am Main/ Berlin, 1990), pp. 42–3.

19. For powerful rejections of the interpretation of the Third Reich as a form of 'modernizing dictatorship', see Jens Albers, 'Nationalsozialismus und Modernisierung', *Kölner Zeitschrift für Soziologie und Sozialpsychologie,* 41 (1989), pp. 346–65; and Hans Mommsen, 'Nationalsozialismus als vorgetäuschte Modernisierung', in Walter H. Pehle, ed., *Der historische Ort des Nationalsozialismus. Annäherungen* (Frankfurt am Main, 1990), pp. 11–46; see also Manfred Rauh, 'Anti-Modernismus im nationalsozialistischen Staat', *Historisches Jahrbuch,* 108 (1987), pp. 94–121. Further contributions to the debate include Hans Mommsen, 'Noch einmal: Nationalsozialismus und Modernisierung', in *GG,* 21 (1995), pp. 391–402; and the balanced survey of positions and reflective comments of Michael Prinz, 'Ein Grenzfall: Nationalsozialismus und Modernisierung. Zur neueren Diskussion in der Zeitgeschichtsschreibung', in Dieter Breuer and Gertrude Cepl-Kaufmann (eds.), *Moderne und Nationalsozialismus im Rheinland* (Padenborn, 1997), pp. 21–33.

20. Rainer Zitelmann, *Hitler. Selbstverständnis eines Revolutionärs* (Hamburg/Leamington Spa/New York, 1987).

21. Zitelmann, *Hitler,* p. 20.

22. The interpretation summarized in the above paragraph is advanced consistently throughout Zitelmann's study with the main points brought together in the conclusion, pp. 453–66.

23. See Rainer Zitelmann's essays, 'Nationalsozialismus und Moderne. Eine Zwischenbilanz', in Werner Süß, ed., *Übergänge. Zeitgeschichte zwischen Utopie und Machbarkeit* (Berlin, 1990), pp. 195–223; and especially 'Die totalitäre Seite der Moderne', in Prinz and Zitelmann, *Nationalsozialismus und Modernisierung,* pp. 1–20.

24. Zitelmann, *Hitler,* p. 7; 'Nationalsozialismus und Moderne', pp. 221, 223; 'Die totalitäre Seite der Moderne', pp. 12–20. Smelser, *Robert Ley,* p. 305 and note 3, saw his study of the Labour Front leader 'dovetailing' into Zitelmann's interpretation of Hitler as envisaging 'the Nazi revolution as a major tool to push Germany forward into a more modern society'.

25. Eberhard Jäckel and Axel Kuhn, eds., *Hitler. Sämtliche Aufzeichnungen 1905–1924* (Stuttgart, 1980); and Institut für Zeitgeschichte, ed., *Hitler. Reden, Schriften, Anordnungen Februar 1925 bis Januar 1933,* 12 vols. (Munich, 1992–8).

26. For arguments, which I support, that an explicitly stated normative usage, clear definition, and precise instrumentalization are prerequisites for the deployment of the 'modernization' concept as an analytical device, see the contributions by Wolfgang J. Mommsen, Jürgen Kocka, and Hans-Ulrich Wehler to the discussion following the presentation by Matzerath and Volkmann (Horst Matzerath and Heinrich Volkmann, 'Modernisierungstheorie und Nationalsozialismus', in Jürgen Kocka, ed., *Theorien in der Praxis des Historikers* [Göttingen, 1977]), pp. 107, 111–16. Though I have some reservations about its applicability to the Third Reich, the central argument of Matzerath and Volkmann, that, as regards the 'modernization issue', National Socialism was an attempted special route out of a modernization crisis which led into a disastrous blind alley, is one that I share. See, for a similar argument, the penetrating assessment by Gerald Feldman, 'The Weimar Republic: A Problem of Modernization?', *Archiv für Sozialgeschichte,* 26 (1986), pp. 1–26.

27. See the introduction to Prinz and Zitelmann, *Nationalsozialismus und Moderne,* p. x, and Zitelmann's own contribution, 'Die totalitäre Seite der Moderne', p. 11.

28. Maier, *The Unmasterable Past*, p. 96.

29. A good corrective, in concentrating on the racial essence of Nazism, is provided by Michael Burleigh and Wolfgang Wippermann, *The Racial State. Germany 1933–1945* (Cambridge, 1991).

30. See Friedländer, 'Martin Broszat und die Historisierung des Nationalsozialismus', pp. 161–2, 168–72. For some perceptive and sensible remarks on how the continuities across 1945 might be approached, see the interesting review article by Harold James, 'The Prehistory of the Federal Republic', *JMH*, 63 (1991), pp. 98–115.

31. Rainer Zitelmann, 'Vom Umgang mit der NS-Vergangenheit', in Rolf Italiaander *et al.*, eds., *Bewußtseins-Notstand. Ein optimistisches Lesebuch* (Düsseldorf, 1990), pp. 69–79, here p. 76. See the interesting survey of the publications of these historians by Edouard Husson, 'Les historiens de la République Fédérale d'Allemagne (1949–1998), leurs travaux sur l'Allemagne depuis Bismarck et la question de l'identité politique allemande', unpublished doctoral dissertation (Paris, 1998), vol. 3, pp. 685–711.

32. See the critical review of the book co-edited by Zitelmann, *Die Schatten der Vergangenheit* (reference in note 18, this chapter) by Norbert Frei, 'Die neue Unbefangenheit. Oder: Von den Tücken einer "Historisierung" des Nationalsozialismus', *Frankfurter Rundschau*, 5 Jan. 1991.

33. See here, for example, his comments in 'Vom Umgang mit der NS-Vergangenheit', p. 70.

34. Zitelmann, 'Vom Umgang mit der NS-Vergangenheit', p. 72.

35. Zitelmann, 'Vom Umgang mit der NS-Vergangenheit', p. 70.

36. Ernst Nolte, 'Vergangenheit, die nicht vergehen will', in *'Historikerstreit'*, pp. 39–47, originally published in *Frankfurter Allgemeine Zeitung*, 6 June 1986. Some of the more contentious assertions, and a more extended version of the basic argument, were contained in Nolte's earlier essay, 'Zwischen Geschichtslegende und Revisionismus?', *'Historikstreit'*, pp. 13–35. This latter essay was, in fact, the basis of a lecture delivered by Nolte as far back as 1980. It was published in abbreviated form the same year in the *Frankfurter Allgemeine Zeitung* under the title 'Die negative Lebendigkeit des Dritten Reiches. Eine Frage aus dem Blickwinkel des Jahres 1980' (see *'Historikerstreit'*, p. 35), and was subsequently included in revised form (and with editorial interpolations) in English translation, entitled 'Between Myth and Revisionism? The Third Reich in the Perspective of the 1980s, in H. W. Koch, ed., *Aspects of the Third Reich* (London, 1985), pp. 17–38. The full statement of his thesis appeared in Ernst Nolte, *Der europäische Bürgerkrieg 1917–1945. Nationalsozialismus und Bolschewismus* (Berlin, 1987), published about a year after the *'Historikerstreit'*. Nolte's defence of his position in *Das Vergehen der Vergangenheit. Antwort an meine Kritiker im sogenannten Historikerstreit* (Berlin, 1987), further embittered the controversy, producing allegations that he had deliberately distorted (by brief and misleading paraphrasing) the content of lengthy and highly critical letters received from the Israeli historian Otto Dov Kulka, with the effect of making them appear relatively favourable to his own position. See Otto Dov Kulka, 'Der Umgang des Historikers Ernst Nolte mit Briefen aus Israel', *Frankfurter Rundschau*, 5 Nov. 1987, and the letters to the *Frankfurter Rundschau* which followed on 17 Dec. 1987 from Wolfgang Schieder, 15 Jan. 1988 from Ernst Nolte, and 19 Feb. 1988 from Otto Dov Kulka.

37. Arno Mayer, *Why did the Heavens not Darken? The 'Final Solution' in History* (New York, 1988).

38. Baldwin, *Reworking the Past*, p. 26.

39. A good many of the contributions in the extensive collection of essays edited by Eckhard Jesse, *Totalitarismus im 20. Jahrhundert. Eine Bilanz der internationalen Forschung* (Bonn, 2nd edn., 1999) date from the 1990s.

40. The evocation of images similar to those advanced by Hannah Arendt in her path-breaking work of the 1950s is unmistakable. See Hannah Arendt, *The Origins of Totalitarianism* (New York, 1951).

41. For a thoughtful and balanced comparison — legitimate and necessary, however repulsive the task — of the scale and character of the mass murder perpetrated by the regimes of Stalin and Hitler, see Maier, *Unmasterable Past,* 'Preserving Distinction', pp. 71–84.

42. Eberhard Jäckel, 'Die doppelte Vergangenheit', *Der Spiegel,* 23 Dec. 1991, pp. 29–43, offers some pertinent comments on this point.

43. The essays collected in Ian Kershaw and Moshe Lewin (eds.), *Stalinism and Nazism: Dictatorships in Comparison* (Cambridge, 1997), are an attempt to demonstrate this point.

44. Friedländer, 'Martin Broszat und die Historisierung des Nationalsozialismus', p. 159.

45. See Lutz Niethammer, ed., *Die Jahre weiß man nicht, wo man die heute hinsetzen soll.' Faschismuserfahrungen im Ruhrgebiet* (Bonn, 1986), particularly the contribution by Ulrich Herbert which drew sharp criticism from Dan Diner.

46. Norbert Frei, 'Abschied von der Zeitgenossenschaft. Der Nationalsozialismus und seine Erforschung auf dem Weg in die Geschichte', *Werkstattgeschichte* 20 (1998), pp. 69–83, here p. 71.

47. The heated debates at the *Deutscher Historikertag* (German Historians' Conference) of 1998 about the behaviour under Nazism of two of the most important figures in the West German historical profession in the post-war era, Werner Conze and Theodor Schieder, could be seen as an illustration of this. The defence of Conze and Schieder advanced by their one-time pupils — later distinguished and dominant figures themselves in shaping historiographical trends — Jürgen Kocka, Wolfgang Mommsen, and Hans-Ulrich Wehler, was critically received at the Historikertag by a younger generation of historians. See the commentaries in: *Berliner Zeitung, Die Tageszeitung, Frankfurter Allgemeine Zeitung,* and *Suddeütsche Zeitung,* all of 14 Sept. 1998; also the interview with Hans-Ulrich Wehler, 'Wie man in die Irre geht', *Der Tagesspiegel,* 8 Dec. 1998, Wehler's article, 'In den Fußstapfen der kämpfenden Wissenschaft', *Frankfurter Allgemeine Zeitung,* 4 Jan. 1999, and the letter of Wolfgang J. Mommsen to the *Frankfurter Allgemeine Zeitung,* 23 Jan. 1999, p. 11.

48. The provocative title of a book published long ago by Andreas Hillgruber, *Endlich genug über Nationalsozialismus und Zweiten Weltkrieg? Forschungsstand und Literatur* (Düsseldorf, 1982).

49. Daniel Jonah Goldhagen, *Hitler's Willing Executioners* (New York, 1996).

50. Some of the most important contributions to the early stages of the debate, especially from within Germany, are reproduced in Julius H. Schoeps (ed.), *Ein Volk von*

Mördern? Die Dokumentation zur Goldhagen-Kontroverse um die Rolle der Deutschen im Holocaust (Hamburg, 1996). See also Johannes Heil and Rainer Erb (eds.), *Geschichtswissenschaft und Öffentlichkeit. Der Streit um Daniel J. Goldhagen* (Frankfurt am Main, 1999).

51. According to a report, not unsympathetic to Goldhagen, on the public debates about his book in Hamburg and Berlin, in *Die Tageszeitung,* 7–8 Sept. 1996, p. 17, 'Goldhagen did not engage with his critics. As if he were using text-blocks from a computer-program, he answered different questions in Hamburg and Berlin with explanations in identical wording.' See also the later assessment of the debates in an interview with Goldhagen reported in *Neue Zürcher Zeitung,* 26 Oct. 1998, p. 35. 'Notable historians,' stated the article, had found Goldhagen's central argument 'too simplistic and monocausal. Goldhagen reacted to such objections in the discussion with patient understanding and eloquently formulated, but rather diffuse, counter-arguments. He maintained that the critics had not paid sufficient attention to his own relativizations advanced in his book.' Some of the sharpest points of the argument in the original English text had already been watered down for the German version. See *Der Spiegel,* 33/1996, pp. 42 ff.

52. Another recent indication of this is the controversy over the role of the Wehrmacht in war crimes, prompted by an exhibition in Munich and the response this provoked on the political Right. The exhibition had been previously shown, without undue controversy, in Hamburg. It was turned into a political-ideological issue by the intervention of the Right in Bavaria. For scholars, the involvement of the Wehrmacht in crimes against humanity during the invasion and occupation of the eastern territories has long been established. For a public often unaware of scholarly findings, the revelations in the exhibition were evidently deeply shocking to many, and stirred strong emotions on both sides. The catalogue of the exhibition is edited by the Hamburger Institut für Sozialforschung, *Vernichtungskrieg. Verbrechen der Wehrmacht 1941 bis 1944* (Hamburg, 1996).

53. Peter Märthesheimer/Ivo Frenzel, *Im Kreuzfeuer: Der Fernsehfilm Holocaust. Eine Nation ist betroffen* (Frankfurt am Main, 1979).

54. Eberhard Jäckel, 'Einfach ein schlechtes Buch', *Die Zeit,* 17 May 1996, repr. in Schoeps, pp. 187–92.

55. *Der Spiegel,* 21/1996, cover and pp. 48–77.

56. Volker Ullrich, 'Hitlers willige Mordgesellen', with the subtitle 'Ein Buch provoziert einen neuen Historikerstreit: Waren die Deutschen doch alle schuldig?', *Die Zeit,* 12 April 1996, repr. in Schoeps, pp. 89–92.

57. Among the most important of the critical articles and reviews not assembled in Schoeps's book is that of Hans Mommsen, 'Die dünne Patina der Zivilisation', *Die Zeit,* 30 Aug. 1996, pp. 14–15.

58. This can be taken quite literally in the light of the heated and protracted public debates about the form of the Holocaust Memorial to be erected in Berlin. See, as one of many strands of the discussion, *Die Zeit,* 21 Jan. 1999, pp. 4, 33.

59. Norman G. Finkelstein, 'Daniel Jonah Goldhagen's "Crazy" Thesis: A Critique of Hitler's Willing Executioners', in Norman G. Finkelstein and Ruth Bettina Birn, *A Nation on Trial. The Goldhagen Thesis and Historical Truth* (New York, 1998), pp. 4, 87.

60. See his introduction to the German edition of the book by Finkelstein and Birn,

Eine Nation auf dem Prüfstand. Die Goldhagen-These und die historische Wahrheit (Hildesheim, 1998), pp. 17–22. The favourable comments on Finkelstein's article, following its initial publication in the *New Left Review,* July–Aug., 1997, in *Der Spiegel,* 33/1997, pp. 156–8, provoked the response in the German press that Finkelstein had greatly overshot the mark. See *Die Zeit,* 22 Aug. 1997, p. 7, and *Süddeutsche Zeitung,* 23–24 Aug. 1997, p. 13. Finkelstein's anti-Zionist agenda also contributed to the unnecessary aggression of the polemics.

61. First published under the title 'Revising the Holocaust' in *The Historical Journal,* 40 (1997), pp. 195–215; reprinted, with minor amendments and some stylistic alterations, in Finkelstein and Birn, *A Nation on Trial,* pp. 101–48.

62. See, for example, the review by Hans-Ulrich Wehler, in *Die Zeit,* 14 May 1996, reprinted in extended form in Schoeps, pp. 193–209. An English translation, 'The Goldhagen Controversy: Agonising Problems, Scholarly Failure, and the Political Dimension', is available in *German History* 15 (1997), pp. 80–91.

63. Finkelstein and Birn, p. 148.

64. Daniel Jonah Goldhagen, 'The Fictions of Ruth Bettina Birn', *German Politics and Society* 15 (1997), pp. 119–65, and 'Daniel Jonah Goldhagen Comments on Birn', *German Politics and Society* 16 (1998), pp. 88–91.

65. Dieter Pohl, 'Die Holocaust-Forschung und Goldhagens Thesen', *VfZ* 45 (1997), pp. 1–48. For another extended and fair analysis, written by a French specialist on the historiography of the Third Reich, see Edouard Husson, *Une culpabilité ordinaire? Hitler, les allemands et la Shoah* (Paris, 1997).

66. Pohl, 'Die Holocaust-Forschung', pp. 38–9.

67. Pohl, 'Die Holocaust-Forschung', pp. 38, 42.

68. See, for example, Donald L. Niewyk, *The Jews in Weimar Germany* (Louisiana, 1980); and David Bankier, *The Germans and the Final Solution: Public Opinion under Nazism* (Oxford, 1992).

69. Christopher Browning, *Ordinary Men: Reserve Police Battalion 101 and the Final Solution in Poland* (New York, 1992), a highly — and justly — praised study that offers a more differentiated assessment of the behaviour of men in one of the killing units also analysed by Goldhagen. Presentations by both Goldhagen and Browning, forming part of a debate in which both participated, were published in an Occasional Paper, The 'Willing Executioners'/'Ordinary Men' Debate, by the United States Holocaust Memorial Museum, Washington, D.C., 1996. See also the comments (by no means all critical) on Goldhagen's treatment of the motivation in units of the *Ordnungspolizei* by Pohl, 'Die Holocaust-Forschung', pp. 24–9.

70. See Pohl, 'Die Holocaust-Forschung', pp. 28–9.

71. For a good overview, down to the end of the 1980s, see Jane Caplan, 'The Historiography of National Socialism', in Michael Bentley (ed.), *Companion to Historiography* (London/New York, 1997), pp. 545–90.

72. See, for example, Roger Griffin, *The Nature of Fascism* (London, 1991); Roger Eatwell, *Fascism: A History* (London, 1995); and Stanley G. Payne, *A History of Fascism, 1914–45* (London, 1995).

73. The anthology, Eckhard Jesse (ed.), *Totalitarismus im 20. Jahrhundert,* 2nd edn. (Bonn, 1999), has at the time of writing sold some 30,000 copies. For interesting reflec-

338 The Final Solution in Historiography

tions on 'totalitarianism' from a sociological perspective, see Michael Mann, 'The Contradictions of Continuous Revolution', in Kershaw and Lewin, *Stalinism and Nazism*, pp. 135–57. The theoretical value of the concept is thoroughly explored in Marc-Pierre Möll, *Gesellschaft und totalitäre Ordnung* (Bonn, 1998), whose bibliography (extending over 93 pages) conveys an impression of the revitalized interest in the phenomenon in the 1990s.

74. The volume I co-edited with Moshe Lewin, *Stalinism and Nazism*, was compelled, through the deficits and imbalances in empirical research on the two regimes, to contain essays aimed at 'suggesting fruitful possibilities of comparison, rather than providing the finished product' (p. 9). The major project on European dictatorships funded by the Volkswagen-Stiftung seems to have resulted in little comparative empirical work.

75. Peter Hayes, *Industry and Ideology. IG Farben in the Nazi Era* (Cambridge, 1987); Hans Mommsen mit Manfred Grieger, *Das Volkswagenwerk und seine Arbeiter im Dritten Reich* (Düsseldorf, 1996); Neil Gregor, *Daimler-Benz in the Third Reich* (New Haven/London, 1998).

76. See Timothy W. Mason, 'Innere Krise und Angriffskrieg 1938/1939' in F. Forstmeier and H. E. Volkmann, eds. *Wirtschaft und Rüstung am Vorabend des Zweiten Weltkrieges* (Düsseldorf, 1975), pp. 158–88; 'The Legacy of 1918 for National Socialism', in Anthony Nicholls and Erich Matthias, eds., chs. 1 and 6; and 'Labour in the Third Reich', *Past and Present* 33 (1966), pp. 112–41.

77. The concept of 'cumulative radicalization' was devised by Hans Mommsen, 'Der Nationalsozialismus. Kumulative Radikalisierung und Selbstzerstörung des Regimes', in: *Meyers Enzyklopädisches Lexikon* Bd. 16 (Mannheim, 1976), S.785–90. I offered some remarks on the value and application of the concept in ' "Cumulative Radicalisation" and the Uniqueness of National Socialism', in Christian Jansen, Lutz Niethammer, and Bernd Weisbrod (eds.), *Von der Aufgabe der Freiheit* (Berlin, 1995), pp. 323–36.

78. See Ulrich Herbert, ' "Generation der Sachlichkeit". Die völkische Studentenbewegung der frühen zwanziger Jahre in Deutschland' in Werner Johe and Uwe Lohalm (eds.), *Zivilisation und Barbarei* (Hamburg, 1991), pp. 115–44; Ulrich Herbert, *Best. Biographische Studien über Radikalismus, Weltanschauung und Vernunft 1903–1989* (Bonn, 1996); Lutz Hachmeister, *Der Gegnerforscher. Die Karriere des SS-Führers Franz Alfred Six* (Munich, 1998).

79. The title of the book by Michael Burleigh and Wolfgang Wippermann, *The Racial State, Germany 1933–1945* (Cambridge, 1991).

80. Hitler's indispensable role in shaping anti-Jewish policy is particularly stressed, among recent publications related to the genesis of the Holocaust, by Saul Friedländer, *Nazi Germany and the Jews. The Years of Persecution, 1933–1939* (London, 1997), pp. 3–4.

81. For critical assessments, see Manfred Funke, *Starker oder schwacher Diktator? Hitlers Herrschaft und die Deutschen. Ein Essay* (Dusseldorf, 1989); and Herman Weiß, 'Der "schwache" Diktator. Hitler und der Führerstaat', in Wolfgang Benz, Hans Buchheim, and Hans Mommsen (eds.), *Der Nationalsozialismus. Studien zur Ideologie und Herrschaft* (Frankfurt am Main, 1993), pp. 64–77.

82. Dieter Rebentisch, *Führerstaat und Verwaltung im Zweiten Weltkrieg* (Stuttgart, 1989).

83. See Frei, 'Abschied von der Zeitgenossenschaft', p. 77.

84. For a good overview, see Mary Nolan, 'Work, Gender, and Everyday Life Reflections on Continuity, Normality, and Agency in Twentieth-Century Germany', in Kershaw and Lewin, *Stalinism and Nazism*, pp. 311–42.

85. See, for example, Renate Bridenthal, Atina Grossman, and Marion Kaplan (eds.), *When Biology became Destiny: Women in Weimar and Nazi Germany* (New York, 1984); and Gisela Bock, *Zwangssterilisation im Nationalsozialismus. Studien zur Rassenpolitik und Frauenpolitik* (Opladen, 1986).

86. For a good example, see Michael Burleigh, *Death and Deliverance: 'Euthanasia' in Germany 1900–1945* (Cambridge, 1994). Henry Friedlander's *The Origins of Nazi Genocide: From Euthanasia to the Final Solution* (London, 1995), is excellent on the small cogs — bureaucrats and administrators, as well as doctors and nurses — in the killing machine of the 'euthanasia action'. See also Jürgen Matthäus, 'Perspektiven der NS-Forschung. Neuerscheinungen zu "Euthanasie" und "Endlösung"', *Zeitschrift für Geschichtswissenschaft* 44 (1996), pp. 991–1005.

87. See Omer Bartov, *The Eastern Front, 1941–45: German Troops and the Barbarisation of Warfare* (New York, 1986); Omer Bartov, *Hitler's Army: Soldiers, Nazis, and War in the Third Reich* (New York, 1992); Theo Schulte, *The German Army and Nazi Policies in Occupied Russia* (Oxford, 1989).

88. See the Introduction for this conference.

89. See Ulrich Herbert, 'Der Holocaust in der Geschichtsschreibung der Bundesrepublik Deutschland', in Ulrich Herbert and Olaf Groehler, *Zweierlei Bewältigung. Vier Beiträge über den Umgang mit der NS-Vergangenheit in den beiden deutschen Staaten* (Hamburg, 1992), pp. 73–5.

90. See above all, as the outcome of this work, Hans Buchheim *et al.*, *Anatomie des SS-Staates*, 2 vols. (Olten und Freiburg im Breisgau, 1965), and the *Gutachten des Instituts für Zeitgeschichte*, 2 vols. (Munich, 1958, 1966).

91. Wolfgang Scheffler, whose book *Judenverfolgung im Dritten Reich 1933–1945* (Berlin, 1960) had been the first attempt at a comprehensive survey by a West German historian, remained a somewhat isolated figure at this time in his work on the Holocaust at the Technische Hochschule in Berlin.

92. Herbert points out, 'Der Holocaust in der Geschichtsschreibung', p. 75, that the murder of the Jews occupied only 13 out of 580 pages in the 1979 edition of Karl Dietrich Bracher's standard work, *Die deutsche Diktatur*.

93. See Chapter 10 for full references to these works.

94. See note 2 to this chapter.

95. To be singled out in this regard are the works by Hans-Ulrich Thamer, *Verführung und Gewalt. Deutschland 1933–1945* (Berlin, 1986); Norbert Frei, *Der Führerstaat. Nationalsozialistische Herrschaft 1933 bis 1945* (Munich, 1987) (Engl. trans., *National Socialist Rule in Germany* [Oxford, 1993]); Jost Dülffer, *Deutsche Geschichte 1933–1945. Führerglaube und Vernichtungskrieg* (Stuttgart, 1992) (Engl. trans., *Nazi Germany, 1933–1945: Faith and Annihilation* [London, 1996]); Klaus P. Fischer, *Nazi Germany. A New History* (London, 1995); and Ludolf Herbst, *Das nationalsozialistische Deutschland 1933–1945* (Frankfurt am Main, 1996), which rightly places racism and war at the centre of the analysis.

96. See Broszat's pertinent comment (Martin Broszat and Saul Friedländer, 'Um die "Historisierung des Nationalsozialismus". Ein Briefwechsel', *VfZ*, 36 (1988), p. 365): 'The danger of the suppression of this era does not in my opinion consist only of the normal forgetting, but in this case, almost paradoxically, because for didactic reasons people are too much "at pains" about this chapter of history. From the original, authentic continuum of this history, an arsenal of teaching sessions and statuesque images are pieced together, which more and more develop an existence of their own, especially then in the second and third generation coming to take the place of the original history, before being naively misunderstood as the actual history'. See also Broszat, *Nach Hitler*, pp. 114–20.

PART IV

The Uniqueness of Nazism

13

Hitler and the Uniqueness of Nazism

There was something distinctive about nazism, even compared with other brutal dictatorships. That much seems clear. A regime responsible for the most destructive war in history, leaving upwards of 50 million people dead, that perpetrated, on behalf of the most modern, economically advanced, and culturally developed country on the continent of Europe, the worst genocide yet known to mankind, has an obvious claim to singularity. But where did the uniqueness lie? Historians, political scientists and, not least, the countless victims of the nazi regime have puzzled over this question since 1945.

One set of answers came quickly, and quite naturally, after the war to those who had fought against the nazi menace. The German militaristic, *Herrenmensch* culture that for centuries had sought dominance in central and eastern Europe was taken to be the key in this approach. A. J. P. Taylor's *The Course of German History,* written in 1944, might be seen as characteristic of its genre.[1] Its crudity was, in the circumstances, perhaps understandable. But as an explanation, it led nowhere (as could also be said of the most modern variant of the 'peculiarity of German character' interpretation in Daniel Goldhagen's controversial book, emphasizing a unique and longstanding German desire to eliminate the Jews).[2] From the German side came, unsurprisingly, a diametrically opposed position, represented in different ways by Friedrich Meinecke and Gerhard Ritter: that Germany's healthy course of development had been blown completely off track by the first world war, opening the way for the type of demagogic politics that let Hitler into power.[3] The interpretation saw nazism as part of a European problem of the degradation of politics. However, this in turn left open what was unique to Germany in producing such a radical strain of inhumane politics. Stirred by Fritz Fischer's analysis of Germany's 'quest for world power' in 1914, locating the blame for the first world war in the expansionist aims of Germany's élites,[4] and by Ralf Dahrendorf's emphasis on the essence of the 'German problem' as social and political backwardness in tandem with a rapidly advancing capitalist and industrial economy,[5] a new generation of German historians, led by Hans-Ulrich Wehler, now turned the spotlight on a 'special path' (*Sonderweg*) to modernity.[6] Defence of privilege by threatened but entrenched social and political élites provided the focus for this interpretation of the German peculiarities which saw a line of continuity running from Bismarck to Hitler. By the 1980s, however, this interpretation was itself running into a wall of criticism, beginning with the attack on 'German peculiarities' launched by Geoff Eley and David Blackbourn, who undermined much of the case that had been made for the continued dominance of pre-industrial élites and stressed instead the common features which Germany shared with other modern, capitalist economies at the time.[7] Oddly, interpretations have since that time tended to shift back in emphasis to what, if in completely different fashion, Meinecke and Ritter had been claiming so much earlier: that the first world war and its aftermath, rather than deeper continuities with Imperial Germany, explain the nazi phenomenon. Detlev Peukert, for instance, in a superb short study of the Weimar Republic, expressly rejected the *Sonderweg* argument as an explanation of nazism, stressing instead a 'crisis of classical modernity' during the first German democracy.[8] Perhaps, it may be thought, this just reformulates the problem of German uniqueness. Perhaps, the thought lingers, the *Sonderweg* argument, or at least a strand or two of it, has been thrown out too abruptly.[9] My concern here, in any case, is not directly the *Sonderweg* debate, but the uniqueness of nazism itself, and of the dictatorship it spawned. Unavoidably, nevertheless, this raises questions about mentalities, prompting some reconsideration about what was special about Germany that led it to produce nazism.

To demonstrate uniqueness, comparison is necessary. That ought to be obvious, but seems often not to be so. Alongside those theories that looked no further than German development to explain nazism, ran, from the start, attempts to locate it in new types of political movement and organization, dating from the turmoil produced by the first world war: whether as a German form of the European-wide phenomenon of fascism, or as the German manifestation of something also found only after 1918, the growth of totalitarianism. To consider all the variants of these theories and approaches would take us far out of our way here, and would in any case not be altogether profitable.[10] So let me begin to make my position clear at this point. Both 'fascism' and 'totalitarianism' are difficult concepts to use, and have attracted much criticism, some of it justified. In addition, going back to their usage in the Cold War, they have usually been seen as opposed rather than complementary concepts. However, I see no problem in seeing nazism as a form of each of them, as long as we are looking for common features, not identity. It is not hard to find features that nazism had in common with fascist movements in other parts of Europe and elements of its rule shared with regimes generally seen as totalitarian. The forms of organization and the methods and function of mass mobilization of the NSDAP, for example, bear much resemblance to those of the Italian Fascist Party and of other fascist movements in Europe. In the case of totalitarianism, superficial similarities, at least, with the Soviet regime under Stalin can be seen in the nazi regime's revolutionary élan, its repressive apparatus, its monopolistic ideology, and its 'total claim' on the ruled. So I have no difficulty in describing German National Socialism both as a specific form of fascism and as a particular expression of totalitarianism.

Even so, comparison reveals obvious and significant differences. Race, for example, plays only a secondary role in Italian fascism. In nazism it is, of course, absolutely central. As regards totalitarianism, anything beyond the most superficial glance reveals that the structures of the one-party state, the leadership cult and, not least, the economic base of the nazi and Soviet systems are quite different. The typology is, in each case, markedly weakened. It can, of course, still be useful, depending upon the art and skill of the political scientist, historian, or sociologist involved, and can prompt valuable empirical comparative work of the kind too rarely undertaken. But when it comes to explaining the essence of the nazi phenomenon, it is less than satisfying. Whether seen as fascism, totalitarianism, or both, there is still something lacking. Martin Broszat hinted at this in the introduction to his masterpiece, *Der Staat Hitlers,* in 1969, when he indicated the difficulty of placing nazism in any typology of rule.[11] Ultimately, the singular, the unique in nazism, remains more important, if more elusive, than what it has in common with other movements or regimes.

In the eyes of the non-specialist, the ordinary layman, nazism's historic — perhaps metahistoric — significance can be summed up in two words: war and genocide. It takes us back to the self-evident initial claim to singularity with which this article began. By war, we naturally mean here the war of unparalleled barbarity that the nazis launched, especially in eastern Europe. And by genocide, we think primarily of the destruction of the European Jews, but also of the wider-ranging genocidal intent to restructure racially the whole of the European continent. Both words, war and genocide — or perhaps better: world war and murder of the Jews — automatically evoke direct association with Hitler. After all, they lay at the heart of his *Weltanschauung,* his world-view; they were in essence what he stood for. This is the obvious reason why one significant strand of historical interpretation has remained insistent that there is no need to look any further in the search for nazism's uniqueness than the personality and ideas of its leader. 'It was indeed Hitler's "Weltanschauung" and nothing else that mattered in the end', Karl-Dietrich Bracher summed up, many years ago.[12] Nazism's uniqueness was Hitler, no more and no less. Nazism was Hitlerism, pure and simple.

There was a certain easy attractiveness to the argument. At first sight, it seemed compelling. But, put at its most forthright, as so often, by Klaus Hilde-brand, the thesis was bound to raise the hackles of those, prominent among them Martin Broszat and Hans Mommsen, who sought more complex reasons for the calamity wrought on Germany and Europe and found them in the internal structures and workings of nazi rule, in which Hitler's hand was often none too evident.[13] So was born the long-running, everyday story of historical folk: the debate between the 'intentionalists', who looked no further than Hitler's clear, ideological programme, systematically and logically followed through, and the 'structuralists' or 'functionalists', who pointed to an administratively chaotic regime, lacking clear planning, and stumbling from crisis to crisis in its own dynamic spiral of self-destructiveness.

The 'Hitlerism' argument will not go away. In fact, there are some signs, amid the current preoccupation with sexuality in history (as in everything else), that the old psycho-historical interpretations are making a comeback, and in equally reductionist fashion. Hence, we have recent attempts to reduce the disaster of nazism to Hitler's alleged homosexuality, or supposed syphilis.[14] In each case, one or two bits of dubious hearsay evidence are surrounded by much inference, speculation and guesswork to come up with a case for world history shaped fatefully and decisively by Hitler's 'dark secret'. Reduced to absurdity, a rent-boy in Munich or a prostitute in Vienna thereby carries ultimate responsibility for the evils of nazism.

However, the 'structural-functionalist' argument is also weak at its core. In reducing Hitler to a 'weak dictator',[15] at times coming close, it often seemed, to underestimating him grossly, even to writing him out of the script, and in downplaying ideology into no more than a tool of propagandistic mobilization, this line of interpretation left the central driving-force of nazism ultimately a mystery; the cause of the (ultimately unprovable) self-destructive dynamism hard to explain. My own work on the Third Reich since the mid-

1980s, culminating in my Hitler biography, was prompted by the need to overcome this deep divide in interpretation, which was by no means as sterile as is sometimes claimed. The short analysis of Hitler's power which I wrote in 1990, and even more so the biography that followed,[16] were attempts to reassert Hitler's absolute centrality while at the same time placing the actions of even such a powerful dictator in the context of the forces, internal and external, which shaped the exercise of his power. Writing these books clarified in certain ways how I would understand the uniqueness of nazism. I will return shortly to Hitler's own role in that uniqueness.

Let us meanwhile go back to war and genocide as the hallmarks of nazism. Surprisingly, they played remarkably little part, except on the fringes, in the 'intentionalist-structuralist' debates before the 1980s. Only since then, and in good measure via the belated take-off of 'history from below' (as it was frequently called), have the war, in which nazism came of its own, and the murder of the Jews, that emanated from it, become the focus of sustained and systematic research and fully integrated into the history of the nazi regime. This research, given a massive boost through the opening of archives in the former Soviet bloc after 1990, has not simply cast much new light on decision-making processes and the escalatory genocidal phases within such a brutal war, but has also revealed ever more plainly how far the complicity and participation in the direst forms of gross inhumanity stretched.[17] This is, of course, not sufficient in itself to claim uniqueness. But it does suggest that Hitler alone, however important his role, is not enough to explain the extraordinary lurch of a society, relatively non-violent before 1914, into ever more radical brutality and such a frenzy of destruction.

The development of the nazi regime had at least two characteristics which were unusual, even in comparison with other dictatorships. One was what Hans Mommsen had dubbed 'cumulative radicalization'.[18] Normally, after the initial bloody phase following a dictator's takeover of power when there is a showdown with former opponents, the revolutionary dynamic sags. In Italy, this 'normalizing' phase begins in 1925; in Spain, not too long after the end of the Civil War. In Russia, under quite different conditions, there was a second, unbelievably awful, phase of radicalization under Stalin, after the first wave during the revolutionary turmoil then the extraordinarily violent civil war had subsided in the 1920s. But the regime's radical ideological drive gave way to boosting more conventional patriotism during the fight against the German invader, before disappearing almost entirely after Stalin's death. Radicalization, in other words, was temporary and fluctuating, rather than an intrinsic feature of the system itself. So the 'cumulative radicalization' so central to nazism is left needing an explanation.

Linked to this is the capacity for destruction — again extraordinary even for dictatorships. This destructive capacity, though present from the outset, developed over time and in phases; against internal political, then increasingly, 'racial' enemies in spring 1933, across the spring and summer of 1935, and during the summer and autumn of 1938; following this, the qualitative leap in its extension to the Poles from autumn 1939 onwards; and the unleashing of its full might in the wake of the invasion of the Soviet Union in 1941. The unceasing radicalization of the regime, and the different stages in the unfolding of its destructive capacity cannot, however, as has come to be generally recognized, be explained by Hitler's commands and actions alone. Rather, they followed countless initiatives from below, at many different levels of the regime. Invariably, these occurred within a broad ideological framework associated with Hitler's wishes and intentions. But those initiating the actions were seldom — except in the realms of foreign policy and war strategy — following direct orders from Hitler and were by no means always ideologically motivated. A whole panoply of motives was involved. What motivated the individual — ideological conviction, career advancement, power-lust, sadism and other factors — is, in fact, of secondary importance. Of primary significance is that, whatever the motivation, the actions had the function of working towards the accomplishment of the visionary goals of the regime, embodied in the person of the Führer.

We are getting closer to what we might begin to see as the unique character of nazism, and to Hitler's part in that uniqueness. A set of counter-factual propositions will underline how I see Hitler's indispensability. Let me put them this way. No Hitler: no SS-police state, untrammelled by the rule of law, and with such massive accretions of power, commencing in 1933. No Hitler: no general European war by the late 1930s. No Hitler: an alternative war strategy and no attack on the Soviet Union. No Hitler: no Holocaust, no state policy aimed at wiping out the Jews of Europe. And yet: the forces that led to the undermining of law, to expansionism and war, to the 'teutonic fury' that descended upon the Soviet Union in 1941 and to the quest for ever more radical solutions to the 'Jewish Question', were not personal creations of Hitler. Hitler's personality was, of course, a crucial component of any singularity of nazism. Who would seriously deny it? But decisive for the unending radicalism and unlimited destructive capacity of nazism was something in addition to this: the leadership position of Hitler and the type of leadership he embodied.

The bonds between Hitler and his 'following' (at different levels of regime and society) are vital here. A constant theme of my writing on Hitler and National Socialism has been to suggest that they are best grasped through

Max Weber's quasi-religious concept of 'charismatic authority', in which irrational hopes and expectations of salvation are projected onto an individual, who is thereby invested with heroic qualities.[19] Hitler's 'charismatic leadership' offered the prospect of national salvation — redemption brought about by purging the impure and pernicious evil within — to rapidly expanding numbers of Germans experiencing a comprehensive crisis of social and cultural values as well as a total crisis of state and economy. Of course, manifestations of 'charismatic leadership' were far from confined to Germany in the interwar period. But Hitler's was both different in character and more far-reaching in impact than the charismatic forms seen anywhere else — something to which I will briefly return.

There was another big difference. Hitler's 'charismatic power', resting on the invocation of the politics of national salvation, was superimposed after 1933 upon the instruments of the most modern state on the European continent — upon an advanced economy (if currently crisis-ridden); upon a well-developed and efficient system of enforcement and repression (if for the time being weakened through political crisis); upon a sophisticated apparatus of state administration (if at the time its exponents were demoralized by perceived undermining of authority in a disputed and crisis-wracked democracy); and, not least, upon a modernized, professional army (if temporarily enfeebled) which was thirsting for a return to its glory days, for a chance to kick over the traces of the ignominy summed up by the name 'Versailles' and for future expansion to acquire European hegemony. Hitler's 'charismatic authority' and the promise of national salvation fitted, if not perfectly, then nevertheless extremely well, the need to unite the expectations of these varying strands of the political élite. Hitler was, we might say, the intersection point of a number of ideological traits which cumulatively, if not singly, made up the unique political culture of which these élites were a product, and which extended beyond class confines to extensive sections of German society. This political culture was not in itself nazi. But it provided the fertile ground within which nazism could flourish. Among its components were: an understanding of nationality that rested upon ethnicity (and was hence open to notions of restoration of national strength through 'ethnic cleansing'); an imperialist idea that looked not in the main to overseas colonies, but to German dominance in the ethnic mélange of eastern Europe, at the expense of the Slav population; a presumption of Germany's rightful position as a great power, accompanied by deep resentment at the country's treatment since the war and its national weakness and humiliation; and a visceral detestation of bolshevism coupled with the sense that Germany was the last bulwark in the defence of western civilization. Not the least of Hitler's contributions to the spiralling radicalism of the nazi regime after 1933 was to unleash the pent-up social and ideological forces embraced by this short catalogue of ideological traits; to open up hitherto unimaginable opportunities; to make the unthinkable seem realizable. His 'charismatic authority' set the guidelines; the bureaucracy of a modern state was there to implement them. But 'charismatic authority' sits uneasily with the rules and regulations of bureaucracy. The tension between the two could neither subside nor turn into a stable and permanent form of state. Allied to the underlying ideological thrust and the varied social forces which Hitler represented, this created a dynamism — intrinsically self-destructive since the charismatic regime was unable to reproduce itself — which constitutes an important component of nazism's uniqueness.

If this explosive mixture of the 'charismatic' politics of national salvation and the apparatus of a highly modern state was central to nazism's uniqueness, then it ought to be possible to distinguish the unholy combination from the differing preconditions of other dictatorships. This, however briefly and superficially, I shall try to do.

The quest for national rebirth lay, of course, at the heart of all fascist movements.[20] But only in Germany did the striving for national renewal adopt such strongly pseudo-religious tones. Even if we count the Spanish dictatorship as outrightly fascist, its national 'redemptive' element, if important, was nonetheless far weaker than that in Germany, amounting to little more than the quest for the 'true Spain' and the restoration of the values of reactionary Catholicism, together with the utter rejection of all that was modern and smacked of association with godless socialism and bolshevism. In Italy, pseudo-religious notions of national 'salvation' or 'redemption' were even weaker than in Spain, and certainly possessed little or nothing of the apocalyptic sense of being the last bulwark of western, Christian culture against the atheistic threat of Asiatic (and Jewish) bolshevism that was prevalent in Germany. Mussolini's external ambitions, too, like Franco's, were purely traditional, even if dressed in new clothes. War and imperialist expansion in Africa were intended to restore lost colonies, revenge the ignominy of Italian humiliation in 1896 at the hands of the Ethiopians, and thereby establish Italy's glory and its place in the sun as a world power, with the useful side-effect of bolstering the dictatorship within Italy through the prestige of external victories and acquisition of empire. But nothing much resembled the depth of hope placed in national salvation in Germany.

Though it is often played down in historiography these days, the extraordinarily strong fears of a threat to German culture, a profound cultural pessimism in Germany's unusually broad-based intelligentsia, widespread already before the first world war, formed one of the roots of such susceptibility.

Oswald Spengler's widely-read and influential tract on the downfall of western culture, the first volume of which was published a month before the end of the war in 1918,[21] embodied feelings which, in cruder form, had been spread by a multiplicity of patriotic organizations long before the nazis appeared on the scene. In the polarized society of the Weimar Republic, the antagonism of the perceived threat of modernity to what were portrayed as traditional and true German values — a threat focused on socialism, capitalism and, not least, the representative scapegoat figure for both: the Jew — spread both at élite and popular levels. Shored up by the trauma of a lost war, a trauma arguably greater in Germany than in any other land — in a country where the hated socialism had come to power through revolution and where established religion seemed to be losing its hold — an appeal to hopes of national salvation held substantial political potential. Though other countries were also traumatized by the war, the cultural crisis, even in Italy, ran nowhere near so deep as in Germany and, in consequence, was less formative for the nature of the dictatorship. In addition, the length of the crisis and the size of the mass movement *before* the takeover of power were significant.

Only in Italy, apart from Germany, did home-grown fascism develop into a genuine mass movement before the takeover of power. By the time Mussolini was made prime minister in 1922, in the wake of Italy's postwar crisis, the Italian Fascist Party had some 322,000 members, whereas in Spain, amid quite different conditions of the mid-1930s, before the Spanish Civil War, the Falange could only muster around 10,000 members in a country of 26 million inhabitants. If these figures are a deceptive guide to the potential backing for politics of national salvation in those countries, the activist base was in both cases, quite extremely so in Spain, far more limited than it was in Germany. There, the hard core of believers in a party leader who promised national salvation as the heart of his message was already massive, with 850,000 party members and 427,000 SA men (often not members of the party itself), even before Hitler took power.

And, as elsewhere, the first world war had left, as part of its legacy, the readiness to resort to extreme violence to attain political aims. The crusading idea of national salvation, redeeming Germany from its humiliation, purging it of the enemies — political and racial — seen to be threatening its life-blood, championing the cultural fight against the threat of Slavdom, evoking notions of racial struggle to win back lost territories in eastern Europe, heralding an ultimate showdown with godless, 'Asiatic' bolshevism, tapped brilliantly into this new climate of violence. And whereas there was only a three-year period before Italian fascism gained power, after which its élan rapidly waned, the 14 years of 'latent civil war'[22] that preceded Hitler's takeover allowed the prospect of violently-accomplished national salvation to fester and spread, mas-sively so in conditions of the complete collapse of legitimation of the Weimar Republic after 1930.

Not only the street-fighters and beer-hall brawlers in the nazi movement were attracted by the idea of violently-attained national salvation. As much recent research has shown, a new generation of intelligent, middle-class stu-dents at German universities in the early 1920s soaked up *völkisch* ideas, those of extreme racist nationalism, intrinsic to the ideas of national regeneration.[23] In this way, 'national salvation' found intellectualized form among groups which would constitute a coming élite, groups whose doctorates in law com-bined with a rationalized '*Neue Sachlichkeit*' (or 'new objectivity') type of approach to the 'cleansing' of the nation: the excision of its 'life-threatening diseases'. Such mentalities were carried with them, 10 or 15 years after study-ing, into the upper echelons of the SS and Security Police, as well as into state and party planning offices and 'think tanks'. By the early 1940s, some of these 'intellectuals' had their hands covered in blood as they led the *Einsatzgruppen* into the Soviet Union, while others were laying down plans for the racial 'cleansing' of the occupied territories of the east and the new ethnic order to be established there.[24]

That 'national salvation' involved not just internal regeneration, but a 'new order' based on the ethnic cleansing of the entire continent of Europe, also singles out National Socialism from all other forms of fascism. No small part of its uniqueness, in other words, was the combination of racial nationalism and imperialism directed not abroad, but at Europe itself. And, as already indi-cated, though nazism amounted to the most extreme expression of such ideas, the politics of national salvation had every prospect of blending into the cul-tural pessimism of neo-conservatives and the anti-democratic and revisionist-expansionist currents that prevailed among the national-conservative élites.

It is not just the force in themselves of the ideas of national rebirth that Hitler came to embody, but the fact that they arose in such a highly modern state system, which was decisive for their uniquely destructive quality. Other interwar European dictatorships, both fascist and communist, emerged in societies with less advanced economies, less sophisticated apparatus of state administration, and less modernized armies. And, apart from the Soviet Union (where policies directed at creating a sphere of influence in the Baltic and Balkans to provide a 'cordon sanitaire' against the looming German threat took concrete form only by the end of the 1930s), geopolitical aims in Europe generally stretched no further than localized irredentism. In other words: not only did the expectations of 'national salvation' invested in Hitler enjoy a mass basis — 13 million nazi voters already in free elections in 1932, countless further millions to join them over the following years; not only did such ideas correspond to more 'intellectualized' notions of the defence of western culture among the upper social classes and political élites; not only did 'national salvation' involve the reconstruction on racial lines of the whole of Europe; but — something present in no other dictatorship — a highly modern state apparatus, increasingly infected by such notions, existed in Germany and was capable of turning visionary, utopian goals into practical, administrative reality.

Let us return at this point to Hitler and to the implementation of the politics of national salvation after 1933. I have been suggesting that a modern state system directed by 'charismatic authority', based on ideas, frequently used by Hitler, of a 'mission' (*Sendung*) to bring about 'salvation' (*Rettung*) or 'redemption' (*Erlösung*) — all, of course, terms tapping religious or quasi-religious emotions — was unique. (I should, perhaps, add that, in my view, this populistic exploitation of naïve 'messianic' hopes and illusions among members of a society plunged into comprehensive crisis does not mean that nazism has claim to be regarded as a 'political religion', a currently voguish revamping of an age-old notion, though no less convincing for being repeated so persistently.[25]) The singularity of the nazi form of rule was, thus, undeniably bound up with the singularity of Hitler's position of power. Though familiar enough, it is worthwhile reminding ourselves of the essence of this power.

During the course of the early 1920s, Hitler developed a pronounced sense of his 'national mission' — 'messianic allures', as one ironic remark had it at the time.[26] The 'mission' can be summed up as follows: nationalize the masses; take over the state; destroy the enemy within — the 'November criminals' (meaning Jews and Marxists, much the same in his eyes); build up defences; then undertake expansion 'by the sword' to secure Germany's future in overcoming the 'shortage of land' (*Raumnot*) and acquiring new territory in the east of Europe. Towards the end of 1922, a small but growing band of fanatical followers — the initial 'charismatic community' — inspired by Mussolini's 'March on Rome', began to project their own desire for a 'heroic' national leader onto Hitler. (As early as 1920, such desires were expressed by neo-conservatives, not nazis, as the longing for a leader who, in contrast to the contemptible 'politicians' of the new Republic, would be a statesman with the qualities of the 'ruler, warrior, and high priest' rolled into one.[27]) Innumerable letters eulogizing Hitler as a national hero poured into the Landsberg fortress, where in 1924 he spent a comfortable few months of internment after his trial for high treason at Munich, which had given him new prominence and standing on the racist-nationalist Right. A book published that year waxed lyrical (and mystical) about the new hero:

> The secret of his personality resides in the fact that in it the deepest of what lies dormant in the soul of the German people has taken shape in full living features. . . . That has appeared in Adolf Hitler: the living incarnation of the nation's yearning.[28]

Hitler believed this bilge. He used his time in Landsberg to describe his 'mission' in the first volume of *Mein Kampf* (which, with scant regard for catchy, publishers' titles, he had wanted to call 'Four and a Half Years of Struggle against Lies, Stupidity, and Cowardice'). He also learnt lessons from the failure of his movement in 1923. One important lesson was that a refounded nazi movement had, in contrast to the pre-*Putsch* era, to be exclusively a 'Leader Party'. From 1925 onwards, the NSDAP was gradually transformed into precisely this 'Leader Party'. Hitler became not just the organizational fulcrum of the movement, but also the sole fount of doctrinal orthodoxy. Leader and Idea (however vague the latter remained) blended into one, and by the end of the 1920s, the NSDAP has swallowed all strands of the former diverse *völkisch* movement and now possessed a monopoly on the racist-nationalist Right. In conditions of the terminal crisis of Weimar, Hitler, backed by a much more solid organization than had been the case before 1923, was in a position to stake a claim for ever-growing numbers of Germans to be the coming national 'saviour', a redeemer figure.

It is necessary to underline this development, however well-known it is in general, since, despite leadership cults elsewhere, there was actually nothing similar in the genesis of other dictatorships. The Duce cult before the 'March on Rome' had not been remotely so important or powerful within Italian fascism as had the Führer cult to the growth of German National Socialism. Mussolini was at that stage still essentially first among equals among the regional fascist leaders. The full efflorescence of the cult only came later, after 1925.[29] In Spain, the Caudillo cult attached to Franco was even more of an artificial creation, the claim to being a great national leader, apeing the Italian and German models, coming long after he had made his name and career through the army.[30] An obvious point of comparison in totalitarian theory, linking dictatorships of Left and Right, appears to be that of the Führer cult with the Stalin cult. Certainly, there was more than a casual pseudo-religious strain to the Stalin cult. Russian peasants plainly saw in 'the boss' some sort of substitute for 'father Tsar'.[31] Nonetheless, the Stalin cult was in essence a late accretion to the position which had gained Stalin his power, that of Party General Secretary in prime position to inherit Lenin's mantle. Unlike nazism, the personality cult was not intrinsic to the form of rule, as its denunciation and effective abolition after Stalin's death demonstrated. Later rulers in the

Soviet Union did not try to revamp it; the term 'charismatic leadership' does not readily trip off the lips when we think of Brezhnev or Chernenko. In contrast, the Führer cult was the indispensable basis, the irreplaceable essence and the dynamic motor of a nazi regime unthinkable without it. The 'Führer myth' was the platform for the massive expansion of Hitler's own power once the style of leadership in the party had been transferred to the running of a modern, sophisticated state. It served to integrate the party, determine the 'guidelines for action' of the movement, to sustain the focus on the visionary ideological goals, to drive on the radicalization, to maintain the ideological momentum, and, not least, to legitimate the initiatives of others 'working towards the Führer'.[32]

The core points of Hitler's ideology were few, and visionary rather than specific. But they were unchanging and unnegotiable: 'removal of the Jews' (meaning different things to different party and state agencies at different times); attaining 'living space' to secure Germany's future (a notion vague enough to encompass different strands of expansionism); race as the explanation of world history, and eternal struggle as the basic law of human existence. For Hitler personally, this was a vision demanding war to bring about national salvation through expunging the shame of the capitulation of 1918 and destroying those responsible for it (who were in his eyes the Jews). Few Germans saw things in the way that Hitler did. But mobilization of the masses brought them closer to doing so. Here, Hitler remained the supreme motivator. Mass mobilization was never, however, as he realized from the outset, going to suffice. He needed the power of the state, the co-option of its instruments of rule, and the support of the élites who traditionally controlled them. Naturally, the conservative élites were not true believers. They did not, in the main, swallow the excesses of the Führer cult, and could even be privately contemptuous or condescending about Hitler and his movement. Beyond that, they were often disappointed with the realities of National Socialism. Even so, Hitler's new form of leadership offered them the chance, as they saw it, of sustaining their own power. Their weakness was Hitler's strength, before and after 1933. And, as we have seen, there were plenty of ideological overlaps even without complete identity. Gradually, a state administration run, like that of all modern states, on the basis of 'expedient rationality', succumbed to the irrational goals of the politics of national salvation, embodied by Hitler — a process culminating in the bureaucratically-organized and industrially-executed genocide against the Jews, premised on irrational notions of national redemption.

Not only the complicity of the old élites was needed for this process of subordination of rational principles of government and administration to the irrational goals of 'charismatic leadership'. New élites, as has already been suggested, were only too ready to exploit the unheard of opportunities offered to them in the Führer state to build up unimaginable power accretions, free of any legal or administrative shackles. The new 'technocrats of power', of the type exemplified by Reinhard Heydrich, combined ideological fanaticism with cold, ruthless, depersonified efficiency and organizational skills. They could find rationality in irrationality; could turn into practical reality the goals associated with Hitler, needing no further legitimation than recourse to the 'wish of the *Führer*'.[33] This was no 'banality of evil'.[34] This was the working of an ideologically-motivated élite coldly prepared to plan for the eradication of 11 million Jews (the figure laid down at the Wannsee Conference of January 1942), and for the 'resettlement' to the Siberian wastes, plainly genocidal in intent, of over 30 million, mainly Slavs, over the following 25 years. That, in such a system, they would find countless 'willing executioners' prepared to do their bit, whatever the individual motivation of those involved, goes without saying. This was, however, not on account of national character, or some long-existent, specifically German desire to eliminate the Jews. Rather, it was that the idea of racial cleansing, the core of the notion of national salvation, had become, via Hitler's leadership position, institutionalized in all aspects of organized life in the nazi state. *That* was decisive.

Unquestionably, Hitler was a unique historical personality. But the uniqueness of the nazi dictatorship cannot be reduced to that. It is explained less by Hitler's character, extraordinary as it was, than by the specific form of rule which he embodied and its corrupting effect on the instruments and mechanisms of the most advanced state in Europe. *Both* the broad acceptance of the 'project' of 'national salvation', seen as personified in Hitler, *and* the internalization of the ideological goals by a new, modern power-élite, operating alongside weakened old élites through the bureaucratic sophistication of a modern state, were necessary prerequisites for the world-historical catastrophe of the Third Reich.

Notes

1. A. J. P. Taylor, *The Course of German History* (London 1945). 'In the course of a thousand years, the Germans have experienced everything except normality', wrote Taylor. 'Only the normal person . . . has never set his stamp on German history' (paperback edn, 1961, 1). Any positive qualities in Germans were in his eyes 'synonymous with ineffectiveness': 'There were, and I daresay are, many millions of well-meaning kindly Germans; but what have they added up to politically?', he asked (viii–ix). The attack on the Soviet Union in 1941 was, for him, 'the climax, the logical conclusion of German

history' (260). The long pedigree of German abnormality, and its climax in nazism, is also a theme of Rohan O'Butler, *The Roots of National Socialism* (London 1941); William Montgomery McGovern, *From Luther to Hitler. The History of Nazi-Fascist Philosophy* (London 1946); and, in essence, of William Shirer, *The Rise and Fall of the Third Reich* (New York 1960).

2. Daniel Jonah Goldhagen, *Hitler's Willing Executioners* (New York 1996).

3. Friedrich Meinecke, *Die deutsche Katastrophe* (Wiesbaden 1946); Gerhard Ritter, *Europa und die deutsche Frage. Betrachtungen über die geschichtliche Eigenart des deutschen Staatsdenkens* (Munich 1948).

4. Fritz Fischer, *Griff nach der Weltmacht* (Düsseldorf 1961).

5. Ralf Dahrendorf, *Society and Democracy in Germany* (London 1968).

6. Among Hans-Ulrich Wehler's prolific output, *Das Kaiserreich 1871–1918* (Göttingen 1973), serves as a paradigmatic expression of the thesis. He has modified, though maintained, the *Sonderweg* approach in his magisterial work, *Deutsche Gesellschaftsgeschichte, Bd.3, 1849–1914* (Munich 1995), 460–89, 1284–95. Another prominent proponent of the *Sonderweg* thesis, Jürgen Kocka, put the case succinctly in his article, 'German History before Hitler: The Debate about the German *Sonderweg*', *Journal of Contemporary History*, 23, 1 (January 1988), 3–16.

7. David Blackbourn and Geoff Eley, *The Peculiarities of German History* (Oxford 1984).

8. Detlev J. K. Peukert, *Die Weimarer Republik. Krisenjahre der Klassischen Moderne* (Frankfurt am Main 1987), 271 for the explicit rejection of the *Sonderweg* approach.

9. On this point, Peter Pulzer, 'Special Paths or Main Roads? Making Sense of German History', *Proceedings of the British Academy*, 121 (2003), pp. 213–34.

10. I explored these in some detail in the second chapter of my *The Nazi Dictatorship. Problems and Perspectives of Interpretation* (4th edn, London 2000). See also my reservations about the totalitarianism concept in the essay 'Totalitarianism Revisited: Nazism and Stalinism in Comparative Perspective', *Tel Aviver Jahrbuch für deutsche Geschichte*, 23 (1994), 23–40. Among a library of works on fascism, Roger Griffin, *The Nature of Fascism* (London 1991), is outstanding in conceptualization and Stanley G. Payne, *A History of Fascism, 1914–1945* (London 1995), in typology, while Michael Mann's *Fascists* (Cambridge, 2004), offers the most profound comparative analysis undertaken of the supporters of fascist movements, their motivation, and their actions. Roger Griffin, *Modernism and Fascism* (London, 2007), has now extended his interpretation of fascism as a quasi-religious movement of national 'revitalisation'. Recent anthologies on totalitarianism, a concept revived since the fall of Soviet communism, include Eckhard Jesse (ed.), *Totalitarianism im 20. Jahrhundert. Eine Bilanz der internationalen Forschung* (2nd edn, Bonn 1999); and Enzo Traverso, *Le Totalitarisme: le XXe siècle en débat* (Paris 2001).

11. Martin Broszat, *Der Staat Hitlers* (Munich 1969), 9.

12. Karl Dietrich Bracher, 'The Role of Hitler' in Walter Laqueur (ed.), *Fascism. A Reader's Guide* (Harmondsworth 1979), 201.

13. See the directly opposed contributions of Klaus Hildebrand and Hans Mommsen in Michael Bosch (ed.), *Persönlichkeit und Struktur in der Geschichte* (Düsseldorf 1977), 55–71 and further references to the controversy in Kershaw, *The Nazi Dictatorship,*

chap. 4. Martin Broszat's brilliant essay, 'Soziale Motivation und Führer-Bindung des Nationalsozialismus', *Vierteljahrshefte für Zeitgeschichte*, 18 (1970), 392–409, also amounted to a subtle assault on the 'Hitlerism' argument.

14. Lothar Machtan, *The Hidden Hitler* (London 2001), for the argument, which has encountered widespread criticism, that Hitler was a homosexual. The syphilis argument, outrightly rejected by those who have most thoroughly explored Hitler's medical history, notably Fritz Redlich, *Hitler. Diagnosis of a Destructive Prophet* (New York/Oxford 1999), and Ernst Günther Schenck, *Patient Hitler. Eine medizinische Biographie* (Düsseldorf 1989), has recently resurfaced in an investigation — the most thorough imaginable of this topic — by Deborah Hayden, *Pox. Genius, Madness, and the Mysteries of Syphilis* (New York, 2003), chap. 20.

15. A formulation which has become famous, coined by Hans Mommsen and first stated in a footnote to his *Beamtentum im Dritten Reich* (Stuttgart 1966), 98, note 26. The debate ensuing from the term is explored in my *Nazi Dictatorship*, op. cit., chap. 4.

16. Ian Kershaw, *Hitler. A Profile in Power* (London 1991, 2nd edn 2001); *Hitler, 1889–1936: Hubris* (London 1998); *Hitler, 1936–1945: Nemesis* (London 2000).

17. For a summary of the advances in research, see Ulrich Herbert (ed.), *Nationalsozialistische Vernichtungspolitik 1939–1945* (Frankfurt am Main 1998), 9–66. Much of the new research is incorporated in the excellent survey by Peter Longerich, *Politik der Vernichtung. Eine Gesamtdarstellung der nationalsozialistischen Judenverfolgung* (Munich/Zurich 1998).

18. First formulated in Hans Mommsen, 'Der Nationalsozialismus. Kumulative Radikalisierung und Selbstzerstörung des Regimes', *Meyers Enzyklopädisches Lexikon*, Bd.16 (Mannheim 1976), 785–90.

19. I first directly deployed Weber's concept to help explore the shaping of popular opinion in 'The Führer Image and Political Integration: The Popular Conception of Hitler in Bavaria during the Third Reich' in Gerhard Hirschfeld and Lothar Kettenacker (eds.), *Der 'Führerstaat': Mythos und Realität. Studien zur Struktur und Politik des Dritten Reiches* (Stuttgart 1981), 133–61, 'Alltägliches und Außeralltägliches: ihre Bedeutung für die Volksmeinung 1933–1939' in Detlev Peukert and Jürgen Reulecke (eds), *Die Reihen fast geschlossen. Beiträge zur Geschichte des Alltags unterm Nationalsozialismus* (Wuppertal 1981), 273–92, and, more extensively, in *The 'Hitler Myth': Image and Reality in the Third Reich* (Oxford 1987). I deployed it more directly to examine the nature of Hitler's power in *Hitler: A Profile in Power,* op. cit., as well as in a number of essays, such as 'The Nazi State: an Exceptional State?', *New Left Review,* 176 (1989), 47–67 and ' "Working towards the Führer": Reflections on the Nature of the Hitler Dictatorship', *Contemporary European History,* 2 (1993), 103–18. The concept is also used by M. Rainer Lepsius, 'Charismatic Leadership: Max Weber's Model and its Applicability to the Rule of Hitler' in Carl Friedrich Graumann and Serge Moscovici (eds), *Changing Conceptions of Leadership* (New York 1986), 53–66.

20. Griffin, in particular, has made this the focal point of his interpretation of fascism. See his *Nature of Fascism,* op. cit., 26, 32ff.

21. Oswald Spengler, *Der Untergang des Abendlandes* (Vienna/Munich 1918–22).

22. For the term, see Richard Bessel, *Germany after the First World War* (Oxford 1993), 262.

23. See, for this, especially Ulrich Herbert, ' "Generation der Sachlichkeit": Die völk-ische Studentenbewegung der frühen zwanziger Jahre in Deutschland' in Frank Bajohr, Werner Johe and Uwe Lohalm (eds), *Zivilisation und Barbarei. Die widersprüchlichen Potentiale der Moderne* (Hamburg 1991), 115–44.

24. See the fine study by Michael Wildt, *Generation des Unbedingten. Das Führungs-korps des Reichssicherheitshauptamtes* (Hamburg 2002).

25. The perception of nazism as a form of political religion, advanced as long ago as 1938 by the émigré Eric Voegelin, *Die politischen Religionen* (Vienna 1938), has recently gained a new lease of life. Among others who have found the notion attractive, Michael Burleigh adopted it, alongside 'totalitarianism', as a major conceptual prop of his inter-pretation in *The Third Reich. A New History* (London 2000). See also Burleigh's essay, 'National Socialism as a Political Religion' in *Totalitarian Movements and Political Reli-gions*, 1, 2 (2000), 1–26. It has also been deployed for fascist Italy by Emilio Gentile, 'Fascism as Political Religion', *Journal of Contemporary History*, 25, 2–3 (May–June 1990), 229–51, and idem, *The Sacralisation of Politics in Fascist Italy* (Cambridge, MA 1996). See also Gentile's 'The Sacralisation of Politics: Definitions, Interpretations and Reflections on the Question of Secular Religion and Totalitarianism' in *Totalitarian Movements and Political Religions*, 1, 1 (2000), 18–55. For sharp criticism of its applica-tion to nazism, see Michael Rißmann, *Hitlers Gott. Vorsehungsglaube und Sendungsbe-wußtsein des deutschen Diktators* (Zurich/Munich 2001), 191–7; and Griffin, *Nature of Fascism*, op. cit., 30–2. Griffin, once critical, has, however, changed his mind and now favours the use of the concept, as can be seen in his 'Nazism's "Cleansing Hurricane" and the Metamorphosis of Fascist Studies' in W. Loh (ed.), *'Faschismus' kontrovers* (Pader-born 2002).

26. Cited in Albrecht Tyrell, *Vom 'Trommler' zum 'Führer'* (Munich 1975), 163.

27. Cited in Kurt Sontheimer, *Antidemokratisches Denken in der Weimarer Republik* (3rd edn, Munich 1992), 217.

28. Georg Schott, *Das Volksbuch vom Hitler* (Munich 1924), 18.

29. See Piero Melograni, 'The Cult of the Duce in Mussolini's Italy', *Journal of Con-temporary History*, 11, 4 (October 1976), 221–37; Adrian Lyttelton, *The Seizure of Power* (London 1973), 72ff, 166–75; and most recently the excellent political biography by R. J B. Bosworth, *Benito Mussolini* (London 2002), chaps 6–11. It took several years before the customary mode of address and reference to Mussolini changed from Presi-dente to Duce and some among his old comrades never took to the 'heroic' form. See R. J. B. Bosworth, *The Italian Dictatorship. Problems and Perspectives in the Interpreta-tion of Mussolini and Fascism* (London 1998), 62, note 14. A valuable study of the incomparably more dynamic impact of the Führer cult than the Duce cult on state admin-istration and bureaucracy is provided by Maurizio Bach, *Die charismatischen Führerdik-taturen. Drittes Reich und italienischer Faschismus im Vergleich ihrer Herrschaftsstrukt-uren* (Baden-Baden 1991). Walter Rauscher, *Hitler and Mussolini. Macht, Krieg und Terror* (Graz/Vienna/Cologne 2001), provides a parallel biography of the two dictators, though offers no structural comparison.

30. See Paul Preston, *Franco. A Biography* (London 1993), 187ff.

31. See Moshe Lewin, *The Making of the Soviet System. Essays in the Social History of Interwar Russia* (London 1985), 57–71, 268–76; and also Ian Kershaw and Moshe

Lewin, *Stalinism and Nazism: Dictatorships in Comparison* (Cambridge 1997), chaps 1, 4 and 5.

32. For the term, see Kershaw, *Hitler, 1889–1936: Hubris,* op. cit., 529.

33. Gerald Fleming, *Hitler und die Endlösung. 'Es ist des Führers Wunsch'* (Wiesbaden/Munich 1982), shows how frequently the phrase was invoked by those involved in the extermination of the Jews.

34. The memorable, though nonetheless misleading, concept was coined by Hannah Arendt, *Eichmann in Jerusalem. A Report on the Banality of Evil* (London 1963).

14

War and Political Violence in Twentieth-Century Europe

The last volume of the so-called '*New*' — meanwhile fairly old — *Cambridge Modern History*, published in 1960, covered the years 1898 to 1945. It was entitled 'The Era of Violence'. The title was dropped for the second edition, which appeared eight years later, and replaced by 'The Shifting Balance of World Forces'. The editor of the revised edition, C. L. Mowat, thought that 'the era of violence' was appropriate for the earlier version, reflecting as it did the understandable 'spirit of the 1950s'. But by the late 1960s this emphasis had changed. In his introduction to the new edition Professor Mowat remarked that 'As he surveys the twenty years or more since 1945, . . . the historian may feel that violence has not been the main characteristic of this century'. Despite nuclear weapons, Mowat looked optimistically from the vantage point of 1968 to a future greatly improved through advances in science and technology, to which world politics would positively respond. He saw a world 'increasingly bound together by common problems, common aspirations, and the world-wide effects of ever larger advances in science', concluding that 'though public war and private violence still rage, the historian is less likely to see violence as the mark of the age'.[1]

Even if our view is narrowed to Europe, Bosnia and Kosovo prompt us to pause at such a statement. And the merest glance at the wider world, not least events very close to our own time, might make us even more sceptical. Even so, and however pessimistically we look back on world history in recent decades, it is plain that the ultra-violence that characterised the first half of the century had no equivalent in the second half, though the later decades could still witness the horrific episodes of violence in, for example, the Chinese Cultural Revolution, Khmer Rouge Cambodia or Rwanda. This first half of the century — or, more precisely, the years 1914 to 1950 that spanned the period from the beginning of the First World War to the end of the Second World War, embracing also its immediate aftermath, when high levels of violence against civilian populations with the resulting misery of millions continued — has indeed claim, more surely than any other period in history, to be labelled 'the era of violence'. That is to say: in these four decades of the twentieth century, violence had *epochal* character; it determined the age.

A number of questions come immediately to mind. A first is obvious: what *caused* such an earth-shattering explosion of immense, state-sponsored violence in the first half of the twentieth century? Nothing in the previous decades had prepared the world for what was to come. The First World War is obviously a major part of the answer. But it is unlikely to have been the only cause. Epochal forces in history do not usually have just short-term causes. And this, surely, was no exception.

Another question relates to the *propensity* of states and the societies they claimed to represent to violence. If we understand the politics of violence in a wide sense — as violence stimulated by political motives or intentions, within, between, by or against states — or even if we speak more narrowly (though widely enough) of state violence against civilian populations involving physical repression in all its manifestations, then it becomes immediately obvious that, looked at comparatively, nation-states and the political systems that operated within them can be placed in a spectrum running from those presiding over very low levels to those where the levels soared into the stratosphere. Why, to take the question this prompts, were states more — or less — prone to use of extreme violence?

The answer to this question might help with a third. Since, arguably, every century (or even half-century) throughout history has been violent in greater or lesser measure, is it merely the *scale* of violence, made possible by new technologies of destruction, that singles out the twentieth century? Or was there something qualitatively different, essentially *modern,* about this violence?

Returning to Mowat for a moment, and accepting that the second half of the twentieth century — at least in Europe — was immeasurably less violent than the first half, we face the obvious question: why was this the case? Eric Hobsbawm, whose vision in his *Age of Extremes* was nothing if not global, spoke of an 'Age of Catastrophe' spanning the world wars followed by the

'Golden Age' that ran up to the oil crisis of the 1970s. Even the onset after that time of new, structural crises, causing great instability and disturbance, did not, Hobsbawm points out, usher in a new 'age of catastrophe.'[2] But Hobsbawm's brilliant book ends in 1990 and therefore takes no account of the upsurge of violence that began in the 1990s — and still continues. Does this renewed violence, if not so extreme as the period of what Arno Mayer called the 'Thirty Years War of the Twentieth Century',[3] mean that, after all, we should see violence as a hallmark of the whole of the twentieth century, perhaps of modernity itself, and not just of a more limited period?

In what follows I hope to offer some hints of my own highly tentative and superficial answers, though these amount in essence to little more than thinking aloud — often about areas where my knowledge is scant, to say the best — and voicing my reflections on the questions which, I think, are of some importance to understanding the century just gone and the world we live in at present.

Before addressing the questions, however, let us remind ourselves — leaving aside for the moment qualitative differences — of the sheer *scale* of the violence, that is the *quantitative* difference with what had gone before, in the 'era of violence'. Raw statistics tell nothing, of course, of the death, pain and misery of the millions who suffered so grievously through the violence. They shock, nevertheless. Take first the deaths from war — the most extreme form of inter-state violence. In Europe, the century between the Congress of Vienna in 1815 and the First World War in 1914 was probably the most peaceful — that is, war-free — of any hundred-year period to that time. The Crimean War of 1854–6, leaving some 400,000 dead, and the Franco-Prussian War of 1870–1, when 184,000 lives were lost, were the most violent European conflicts of that era.[4] In the First World War, the dead totalled more than eight million military casualties and perhaps, according to some estimates, a further five million civilians (mainly on the eastern front, though including victims of famine in Poland and probably of the continued bitter fighting in eastern Europe after the Armistice); in the Second World War, 40 million military and civilian deaths would be a minimal estimate.[5] Beyond these figures are those of the refugees forced from hearth and homeland: four to five million in 1918–22, as many as 40 million 'displaced persons' between 1945 and 1950.[6] A good number were driven out or deported. Others fled from repression, terror, ethnic cleansing and genocide. How many were affected by ethnic cleansing in this period (even if the horrible phrase was not then in circulation) is not known with any precision. Some estimates of the numbers affected worldwide by ethnic cleansing across the twentieth century put the figure at anywhere between 60 and 120 million.[7]

Another statistic is worth bearing in mind. Whereas the civilian dead in the First World War formed on the highest estimate just over a third of the victims, in the Second a conservative ratio is around two-thirds — from a maximum of five up to some 27 million.[8] This huge increase was not just a reflection of the new technology of mass killing — for instance, through area bombing. It is an indicator, too, that war was changing character. Away from the areas of fighting, earlier wars had not tended to drag in the civilian population. Even the killing grounds of the First World War on the western front were a relatively confined space (though the eastern front was a different matter). Civilian life could continue remarkably unscathed not very far away. Even so, beginning with the French revolutionary armies, the gulf between soldier and civilian was narrowing. Atrocities against civilians had featured in the American Civil War and in the Franco-Prussian War. The scale of such atrocities was enlarged significantly during the First World War. The brutalisation of warfare, now making civilian populations the target of assault and destruction, which would become so prominent a feature of the Second World War, was present, if on a smaller scale, during the First.

Recent research by Alan Kramer and John Horne has demonstrated that 6,427 Belgian and French civilians were deliberately killed, often in highly brutal fashion, by invading German troops from a variety of army units during August 1914, that is, at the very onset of war. Some brutal treatment of civilians by German, Austrian and Russian soldiers, though on a much smaller scale, also took place on the eastern front in 1914. There was a sharp increase the following year as the Russians retreated from Lithuania and western Poland. The death toll is impossible to calculate. But scorched-earth policies and mass deportations were the order of the day. At least 300,000 Lithuanians, 250,000 Latvians, 350,000 Jews (especially singled out for maltreatment) and 743,000 Poles were deported to the interior of Russia.[9] These brutalities were coupled with a intensified paranoia towards 'the enemy within'. In the crumbling Ottoman Empire to the south, this same paranoia was exploited in what became a major genocide involving upwards of 800,000 Armenians.

Myths legitimating massive violence towards civilian populations now became a part of modern warfare. By the Second World War, military front and home front were scarcely divisible; this was now a *popular* war in the sense of the full involvement of the peoples of Europe in the fighting, and the suffering. A country like Poland, therefore, which was part of a shooting war for not much more than a month, suffered the deaths of around a fifth of its population during the six long years that followed and the highest percentage of civilian deaths of any country in the war. This indicates a new feature of war — and of political violence more widely: in contrast to earlier centuries, a whole people could now be regarded as 'the enemy' and therefore as the legitimate target of the politics of violence, backed by what, even then, for their time, were weapons of mass destruction.

This points unmistakably, taking us, perhaps, into our first question, to an ideological component (exploiting existing social and political cultures) in the causes of the explosion of violence in the first half of the twentieth century, and the propaganda methods by which modern governments could orchestrate violence. Plainly, war on such a scale and of such a character as the First World War was a major breeding-ground of such violence, and I shall return briefly to it in a moment. But first we need to be clear that the roots of the violence lie deeper than the war itself.

The glamorisation of violence as a form of social and political protest against decadent bourgeois society, though only institutionalised in fascist movements after 1919, began before the war. The French fascist intellectual Pierre Drieu La Rochelle later looked back at the pre-war years and recalled 'young men from all classes of society, fired by a core of heroism and violence, who dreamed of fighting . . . capitalism and parliamentary socialism'.[10] The Italian nationalist Enrico Corradini used Marxist terminology and analogy to speak in 1910 of Italy as a 'proletarian nation', arguing that 'we must teach Italy the value of the international struggle. But international struggle means war. Well, let it be war! And let nationalism arouse in Italy the will to win a war'.[11] The Italian Futurists, whose leader, Giacomo Marinetti, stayed faithful to Mussolini to the end, advertised their somewhat eccentric views in their manifesto of 1909: 'We want to exalt movements of aggression, . . . the blow with the fist . . . We want to glorify war — the only cure for the world — and militarism, patriotism, the destructive gesture of the anarchists, the beautiful ideas which kill, and contempt for women. We want to demolish museums and libraries, fight morality, feminism, and all opportunist and utilitarian cowardice'.[12] The incorporation of pseudo-scientific race theories into populist politics advocating national assertiveness, particularly prominent in Germany and the German-speaking part of the Austrian empire, brought with it an increasingly shrill and menacing rhetoric of violence. And in some parts of Europe, notably the Balkans, ethnicity had already been decisive in the appalling massacres of Armenians in the tottering Ottoman Empire. The estimated 200,000 Armenian victims of the atrocities of 1894–6, and subsequent massacres, including those of around 20,000 Armenians in 1909, were stepping-stones en route to the genocide of 1915.[13] Meanwhile, well before the First World War, and across Europe, race theories were being advanced to advocate exclusion or repression of 'inferior elements' of society, thought to damage or weaken it.

In different ways, and in different measures, three of the major ideological currents of the nineteenth century paved the way for the violence that would erupt after 1919. Most crucial was the blending of popular sovereignty with nationalist ideology. This began to lead, in contested territory with an ethnic mix, to increased pressure, often accompanied by violence, upon minority or subjugated populations. Trends in this direction, though nowhere near fully expressed, are visible in the later nineteenth century as earlier liberal features of nationalist thinking were sidelined. They came to their full expression, with baleful consequences, in the post-Versailles Europe, erected on the Wilsonian principle — soon to backfire fatally — of self-determination. The second major ideology was colonial imperialism. The leading imperialist powers could before 1914 remain relatively non-violent at home while exercising great violence in colonised territories. But imperialist thinking, centred on repressing and holding down supposed inferior peoples by force for material exploitation, fed directly into the ideologies of violence after 1914.[14] Nazism, which looked to the occupied territories of the east as the German equivalent of British rule in India, is an obvious example of this. The third ideology, socialism, aspiring, in varied forms and expressions, to a utopia where social equality would bring peace, justice and harmony, seems at first sight to be in strange company with nationalism and imperialism. But, paradoxically, it formed another strand that would lead to the mega-violence of the twentieth century. As social tensions grew in rapidly industrialising parts of Europe, state repression against increasingly organised labour correspondingly intensified. Where the chances of engendering substantial social and political change in inflexible authoritarian states, most notably Russia, without revolutionary violence remained minimal, so, unsurprisingly, the doctrine of ends justifying means gained increasing support. More than a decade before the Russian Revolution took place, therefore, Lenin was advocating — to the horror of some of the Menshevik leaders — that change in Russia could only be brought about through the utmost, and ruthless, use of terror. Once, then, towards the end of the First World War, revolution did take place in Russia, in conditions intensely brutalised through the horrific bloodshed, misery and deprivation of the war, it led inexorably both to the extraordinary violence of the civil war and the subsequent spread like wildfire, outside Russia, too, of counter-revolutionary violence, setting the scene for the fundamental ideological conflicts of the inter-war period.

How the currents present in the late nineteenth century and already running in the direction of a far more violent future would have developed without the cataclysm of 1914–18 is, of course, unimaginable. For it goes without saying that without the searing impact on mentalities of those dreadful years it would be impossible to explain the politics of violence and the extent of the appalling inhumanity this would bring in the following decades. Nowhere is this clearer than in the two countries at the epicentre of the explosion of political violence that ensued: Russia and Germany.

In Russia, where a high level of violence had been traditional and endemic in politics and society, the weakness and bitterly contested nature of state power from the final phase of the First World War to the end of the civil war now lent it sharp ideological delineation. Criminality and banditry blended into ethnic violence against Jews in the west or Muslims in the south, and into the most bestial treatment, often justified as 'retaliation', of 'class enemies'.[15] The scale and ferocity of the Stalinist terror seem only comprehensible in the context of a decade or so of living hell (for those who did not perish in it) from the beginning of the First World War to the start of recovery from the unbelievable brutality of the post-revolutionary civil war. These years saw, for millions, living conditions that defy description. Life was cheap, unbounded suffering routine, and death omnipresent amid the mass slaughter at the front, the complete breakdown of the state, and the utter ruthlessness of those who could grab, hold on to, and wield power in the terroristic chaos of the civil war. The Russian dead had numbered some two million during the world war. But between three and five million perished during the civil war.[16] In fact, there was a drop in population on Soviet territory of over eleven million in the years 1918–21, so it is not surprising that the civil war, not the First World War, left the more searing mark on Russian memories.[17] Terror and violence were what prevailed. They set the tone for the unprecedented levels of violence in the Stalinist era. Without this background, it must be questionable whether Russia would have come to experience the full horrors of Stalinism.

The same could be said for the Baltic regions and the Ukraine, later incorporated into the newly created Soviet Union. Levels of violence and ethnic conflict which had long poisoned these areas soared during the First World War and, in conditions of complete state collapse, exploded at its end. The cruelty was massive in scale and gratuitously barbaric in expression. Jews, now commonly seen as the agents of Bolshevism, as usual suffered the most. At least 50,000 Jews were slaughtered — although one contemporary report trebles that figure — in the Ukraine in 1919, many of them in the 1,300 or so pogroms that occurred in that year. But Poles, Belorussians, Ukrainians, Lithuanians, Latvians, White Russians and Bolsheviks also died in great numbers.[18] A legacy of violence was established, a basis for the institutionalisation of terror laid. Stalin was the chief beneficiary.

In Germany, too, the First World War and its legacy marked a caesura. Without the First World War, a Hitler would have been unimaginable as leader of Germany. Without the brutalising effect of that war and the mythologies of violence that accompanied it, the inculcation of violence into the political culture of Germany in the inter-war years, and the dire consequences of that in the Second World War, would have been inconceivable.[19] Before 1914, Germany was a relatively non-violent society. After 1918 violence was one of its main features — if not remotely on the same level as violence in Russia. Ernst Jünger, a literary hero not just on the outer reaches of the right, could elevate and beautify the violence of total war as the image of the coming 'modern', and 'hard' society' — one dependent upon manliness and ruthlessness. The imagery of the war in the east, ingrained in military minds, of 'deepest Russia, without a glimmer of Central European *Kultur,* Asia, steppe, swamps, claustrophobic underworld, and a godforsaken wasteland of slime', as one contemporary description had it,[20] fed meanwhile into the stereotypes that would promote the barbarisation of 1941 and after. Such views were reinforced by the images brought home by the *Freikorps* units which continued the most bitter fighting after the end of the First World War, in Poland and then in the Baltic on the side of the Whites during the Russian civil war. Back home, many *Freikorps* members slotted seamlessly into the paramilitary scene of the post-war years, including the infant Nazi movement, and were responsible for at least 354 political murders between 1919 and 1922 — practically all of them leniently dealt with (in contrast to the smaller number of political crimes committed by the left) by a judiciary prepared to tolerate right-wing violence as long as it was targeting left-wing opponents.[21] The same sentiments were apparent in the acceptance by good law-abiding *Bürger* and pillars of their society of the mounting violence that accompanied the Nazi rise to power after 1930, and particularly in the summer and autumn of 1932. The scene was set for the widespread welcome given to the Nazi assault on the left in 1933, the establishment of concentration camps, attacks on minorities (particularly Jews) and the undermining of legal constraints on state power. When, the following summer, Hitler openly admitted responsibility for the murder of some of the leaders of his own movement, accusing them of treason, corruption and homosexual practices, he could register widespread approval and a surge in his personal popularity.[22]

Meanwhile, a number of Germans too young to have fought in the war, most with a university education, a good number of them with doctorates — who fervently believed in the cold, rational use of violence to purge Germany of its perceived 'unhealthy', racial impurities — were beginning to establish their careers in the security police and the SS. They would later become not just the planners of the Nazi 'new order' in eastern Europe, with a target of eliminating 31 million mainly Slavs over the next twenty-five years, but the leaders of the extermination squads that launched the 'Final Solution'.[23] It was the culmination of a lengthy process in the escalation of political violence, whose starting-point was the First World War.

The impact of that war on existing political culture seems to have been the decisive factor. Indelible though the experience, memory and imagery of the First World War were, not all countries that went through the war turned into politically violent societies. Great Britain (apart from Ireland) and, though their participation in the war was relatively short, the United States, would be two obvious examples. It seems possible, in fact, turning into my second question, to conceive of a spectrum of violence in which the impact of the First World War is placed alongside elements of existing political culture shaping the relative propensity to violence or non-violence in the succeeding decades.

A relatively low level of political violence appears to relate in some way or other to the following: established democratic structures, values and mentalities; being on the winning side in the First World War (or neutrality in that war); muted ideological conflict and a corresponding absence of revolutionary or counter-revolutionary circumstances; lack of disputed territorial claims; satisfied (or non-existent) imperialist ambitions; and, finally, a sense of national identity drawn from constitutional statehood rather than ethnicity and culture. Even if these features were not equally weighted, they seem to apply to the United Kingdom (with the partial exception of Ireland), the Netherlands, Belgium (for the most part), France (with qualifications), Denmark, Norway, Sweden and Switzerland — all countries (apart from Switzerland) on the north-western periphery of Europe.

Exactly the opposite characteristics apply to an array of countries where political violence was highly pronounced in the inter-war period. Here we see in general terms the absence of solidly established pluralist–democratic structures, values and mentalities; defeat in the First World War and a resultant profound sense of national humiliation; major ideological cleavages and the corresponding existence of revolutionary and counter-revolutionary conditions; territorial losses, disputed territorial claims, and unfulfilled imperialist ambitions; also an ethnocultural basis of nationality, frequently going hand in hand with a culturally rooted mentality of ethnic superiority and an aggressive, integral-organic ideology of nationalism which gained definition by exclusion of ethnic minorities, often sharing the same territory. To a greater or lesser extent such features related to much of central, eastern and south-eastern Europe, to Germany, Austria, Czechoslovakia (in part), Poland, Hungary, Romania, Yugoslavia and Russia (where the vicious ethnic conflict of the civil war period was then overlain with the ideological struggle to extirpate class enemies).

A number of the features, though not the heavy weighting attached to ethnicity, also applied to the Mediterranean region, to Italy (despite its nominal inclusion in the victorious powers in 1918), and Spain (with the notable exception of its non-participation in the war). In these countries, too, the weakness of the state and its contested legitimacy opened the door to deep ideological conflict, the politicisation of violence (leading in the case of Spain to bitter and brutal civil war) and, eventually, to the imposition of right-wing authoritarianism and repression. In Italy, the resentment on the nationalist right over frustrated territorial ambitions, together with utopian hopes on the left, soon dashed, of a brave new socialist world, exposed the impotence of the liberal state and created the political space for Fascism to triumph in a climate shaped by political violence.[24] In Spain, despite that country's neutrality, the First World War sharply intensified political violence as existing class tensions and social conflict were heightened in the wake of major economic upheaval, fatally undermining the legitimacy of the liberal–monarchical state and eventually ushering in authoritarian rule. A preview of the battle lines in the Spanish Civil War can be seen in the ideological, political and social fissures opened up during the period of the First World War, even without Spain joining the belligerent powers.[25] Portugal is something of an oddity. It did not suffer defeat, since it had joined the war on the Allied side in 1916, was fairly homogeneous, had no ethnic minorities or frontier revanchist tendencies, and had experienced no colonial amputation. Nonetheless, its parliamentary system was weak and struggled for legitimacy in an underdeveloped country where authoritarianism had strong roots. The First World War brought internal political crisis, strengthened support for integral nationalism with fascist colouring, deepened ideological divisions and saw an increase in political violence (though of mild proportions compared with many other countries). Political as well as economic backwardness hindered the establishment of parliamentary democracy, but also posed a barrier to the worst excesses of authoritarian violence. Lack of wide political mobilisation was the main reason why repressive, though relatively non-violent, conservative authoritarianism eventually prevailed without outright fascism getting a toe-hold on power.[26]

Arguably, it was the combination (with varied weighting) of the factors just outlined rather than any particular one which shaped the character and extent of subsequent political violence. Crucial in promoting extreme violence was, perhaps nonetheless, a disastrous outcome of the First World War, with subsequent state collapse and political instability, often linked to disputed territory in ethnically mixed areas where ethnicity was the basis of nationality. In these regions, nation-building in ethnically mixed, newly created states was combined with the strains of modernisation. As a consequence, populist scape-goating of minorities — usually including Jews — was easy. The potential for what a later age would call ethnic cleansing was unmistakable. Central, eastern and south-eastern Europe, already emerging as the killing-grounds of Europe, amounted in effect, therefore, following the ill-fated territorial settlement of 1919, to a time bomb waiting to explode.

On the north-western periphery of Europe, the major countries had not experienced the trauma of defeat, humiliation and territorial amputation. Here, ethnic divisions (with the partial exception of Belgium, where the divide was, in any case, linguistic and cultural rather than strictly ethnic) played no great role in politics. Ideological conflicts were largely along class, not ethnic, lines, and the ruling elites, backed by adaptable constitutions, could accommodate and institutionalise conflict. In their colonial territories and settler dominions, of course, such states could exercise and back the use of massive violence towards the indigenous populations.[27] Colonialism fostered racist attitudes back in the homeland. But since the ethnic minorities there were small and insignificant, in terms of challenging for political power, or were integrated (as were the Welsh and the Scots, if not the Irish) into the constitutional arrangements of the existing nation-state, ethnically based violence was not to be expected. Nor, from the point of view of the British state, was the violence deployed in Ireland motivated by ethnic considerations.

As the outstanding work of Michael Mann has shown, ethnicity, where rival ethnic groups are involved in a real (or imaginary) contest for state power in disputed territories — not just in Europe and not just in the inter-war period — turned into possibly the most potent element in large-scale political violence in the twentieth century as more and more ethnically split countries sought to push through policies based on organic nationalism aimed at ethnically 'cleansed' nation-states.[28]

Let me turn briefly here to the third question I raised. Was there simply more violence in the twentieth century? Or was it qualitatively different from what had gone before, more *modern?* Most experts on genocide agree in stressing its modernity. Michael Mann, above all, has argued — convincingly to my mind — that the mass killing of civilians (or less murderous brutal persecution and 'cleansings') on ideological grounds 'in the name of the people', whether ethnically driven (as against Armenians, Jews, Bosnian Muslims, Albanian Kosovans or Rwandan Tutsis) or class-driven (as in Stalinist anti-Kulak terror or Pol Pot's 'classicide') forms a crucial component of what makes modern political violence *modern.*[29] Of course, the mass killing of civilians was nothing new. And ideology — of a religious, not secular kind — was also used in earlier times to justify it. Tens of thousands were killed in the Albigensian

Crusade of the early thirteenth century, the French wars of religion of the latter half of the sixteenth century, and the Thirty Years War of the seventeenth century, for example, most of them in the name of religion. The sacking of Magdeburg by Catholic forces in 1631, when possibly as many as 30,000 men, women and children were slaughtered, and Cromwell's ruthless storming of Drogheda and Wexford ten years later, in which some 4,500 people (though mainly garrison soldiers) were put to the sword in God's name, were particularly brutal massacres on the grand scale. But religious violence — or violence in the name of religion — usually stopped at converts. That is to say, conversion to the other side was usually sufficient to prevent or mitigate violence. And sieges did not normally lead to massacres where the garrison readily accepted *force majeure* and surrendered promptly according to given rules. Moreover, ethnicity was seldom, if ever, a sole or prime factor.

How different this became once the idea — in essence, of course, a positive one — of popular sovereignty implanted itself from 1789 onwards. The upturning and abuse of the original ideals of nationalism was a necessary accompanying development, and in the late nineteenth century the ideological forces which would light the conflagration after 1918 were already gathering pace. As noted earlier, traditional or long-standing social resentments, often laden with violence, were now presented with ideological justification. Violence against disliked or supposedly threatening ethnic minorities escalated wildly. Spontaneous outbursts — which on investigation usually turned out to be locally organised 'spontaneity' — could produce huge bloodletting in massacres and pogroms. But for violence to take shape as full-scale genocide a further ingredient was needed: the ideologically driven modern state. Ethnicity or class, depending upon regime, then turned into givens for the sections of the population affected, unchangeable stamps which, irrespective of all other considerations, determined life or death for millions. Being a Jew under Hitler, a Kulak under Stalin, an intellectual under Pol Pot, was tantamount to a death warrant. This was, therefore, a very *modern* feature of modern political violence.

Two other important components, both already touched on, complement this vital feature in the link between modernity and violence. One is bureaucracy and planning; the other comprises science and technology. Both are unmistakable in the Nazi paradigm. One of the most shocking aspects of Nazi violence, to latter-day sensibilities, is that it occurred in such a modern state, with an advanced economy, sophisticated administration, a high level of education and elevated culture. Of course, in a way this comes close to saying that such barbarism might have been expected in a primitive society, but not in a modern, civilised one. Whatever the prejudice in the presumption, it misses the point. Nazi violence could only be so extreme precisely *because* it was so modern. To accomplish it needed the planners and orchestrators in a multiplicity of state and party offices; it needed the academics — a good number of them historians, some later to achieve great renown — who put their intelligence and abilities to working out how to 'de-judify' (their expression) cities such as Warsaw and Cracow;[30] it needed the data-collectors using punch-card machines as a more efficient way of compiling lists of victims;[31] it needed doctors at the forefront of their profession prepared to engage in the most vile of medical experiments in the interests of scientific progress;[32] it needed the chemists of the Degesch company to produce Zyklon-B, first for disinfection, then for human extermination;[33] and it needed the engineers of Topf and Sons, Erfurt, who could design to order the Auschwitz gas chambers and crematoria.[34]

Of course, without the ideology of racial mastery driving the Nazi regime, and without the corrupting allure of all organisational structures in Hitler's Germany, such scientists, academics, doctors, engineers and civil servants would have been going about the more normal pursuits appropriate to their professions in the modern state. But the ways in which modern bureaucracy and science readily put themselves at the service of such an ideology prompted Zygmunt Bauman to assert that the Holocaust, and modern genocide more widely, 'arose out of a genuinely rational concern, and . . . was generated by bureaucracy true to its form and purpose'.[35] It is an overblown claim. It would be a mistake to substitute the instrument for the ideological driving force as the determinant of the Holocaust. And there was little that was bureaucratically rational about some — perhaps most — other instances of twentieth-century genocide. But it is surely correct to claim that without the bureaucracy which is a hallmark of modernity 'the Holocaust would be unthinkable'.[36] When Bauman interprets the Holocaust as 'an element of social engineering, meant to bring about a social order conforming to the design of the perfect society',[37] he touches on a further important strand of the modernity of political violence: its connection with modern utopias in which it is assumed that perfection can be brought about on this earth and by secular means, the ultimate replacement of God by man as the arbiter of life and death. But, again, it would be as well not to concentrate exclusively on political violence as modernity in the sense of a rational pursuit of the perfect society. Much of the violence and killing — including that by the Nazis — used nothing more modern than a rifle, while the phenomenal killing-rate in the Rwandan genocide depended in good measure on weapons no more sophisticated than machetes.[38] The modernity of the killing methods, in other words, was related to the modernity of the state directing them. But what *were* crucially modern were the ideologies underpinning the methods — the actual cause of the violence and killing. And the most important — and lethal — of these has probably been that of integral nationalism, usually demanding ethnic exclusivity.

Why was the second half of the twentieth century less violent? Or is this a mirage — a European optical illusion?

The unbelievably benign decades after 1950 in much of Europe certainly marked the sharpest of contrasts — even allowing for Bosnia and Kosovo — with the apocalyptic first half of the century. A major factor was, of course, the absence of all but regional war (and that not before the 1990s). With Europe bled white and divided between the victorious superpowers of the United States and the USSR, both interested in their different ways in dominating their respective halves of the continent, the massively destabilising forces of the years immediately following the First World War could never replicate themselves. The cold war itself, for all its inherent dangers, served as an integrating and stabilising element. A second factor of the utmost importance, again in contrast to the 1920s and 1930s, was the onset of an era — Hobsbawm's 'golden age' — of unprecedented prosperity. Sometimes we do learn from history, if not always very well. Even in the 1930s, some far-sighted thinkers had seen that tariff barriers hindering the distribution of wealth in Europe, and notably the German claims on a share of that wealth, were asking for trouble. The abolition of tariff barriers, internationalisation of trade within western Europe through the establishment of a common market, and the huge surge in prosperity produced by the post-war consumer boom laid foundations in western Europe on which inter-governmental economic and political co-operation could build — a framework of co-operation likely to prevent political disorder leading to the collapse of state systems and to limit the dangerous growth of extremist movements. A third factor, at least in western Europe, was the absence of the ethnic tensions which had been such a source of violence between the wars. The heated issue of Germany's eastern borders, with the violence the disputed territories had provoked before 1939, was effectively resolved with the massive and brutally executed ethnic cleansings in eastern Europe between 1945 and 1950,[39] and the extension of Soviet control and huge repressive power deep into the territory of Germany itself. Some flashpoints of violence remained. No longer integral nationalism with all its evils, but now breakaway nationalism posed a problem in some places. Northern Ireland and the Basque country have stayed regions in which breakaway nationalist tendencies and political intransigence have produced endemic anti-state violence — mercifully, perhaps now at last calming in Ulster. However, these have been — in a broad European context — peripheral rather than central problems. And they have not generated major violence — at least contrasted with the first half of the century — by the states targeted by the forms of terrorist actions and guerrilla warfare. In general, levels of violence by the state itself throughout western Europe have been low because state-control mechanisms have become more effective, and, especially, because the conditions which prompted such extreme violence in the inter-war period have been largely absent.

In most of eastern Europe the heavy hand of Soviet rule contained for four decades the ethnic tensions and violence which had poisoned this part of the continent before the Second World War. In Yugoslavia, Tito's clever mix of repression and integration had the same effect. Where anti-Soviet insurgency forced its way through, as in East Germany in 1953, Hungary in 1956, and Czechoslovakia in 1968, it was fairly rapidly quelled and repressive calm restored. It was only once drab containment disappeared with the sudden collapse of the Soviet bloc in 1989–90 that ethnic tensions and accompanying violence in some areas of the former USSR, notably the Caucasus, surfaced with vehemence and are far from quietened even now. In ex-Yugoslavia, the destabilisation after Tito's death in 1980 led by the end of that decade to the stirrings of new and violent nationalism, especially among the Serbs, who used nationalist myth to justify modern ethnic cleansing of a most vicious kind in Bosnia, then in Kosovo. Appalling and terrible though this resurgence of ethnic violence within Europe was, it was a spectacular eruption in one region rather than the symptom of a general problem. The proto-genocidal climate and actions of the inter-war period have been generally absent in eastern and central Europe. The remarkable thing is how non-violent the transition since 1990 to new socioeconomic structures in these regions of the continent has proved. The lack of resistance to change by the moribund old order provides part of the explanation for this. The diminished framework for ethnic conflict within the former communist states — even with the two big exceptions of Chechnya and ex-Yugoslavia — coupled with the absence of any clear alternative ideology to that of triumphant, western capitalist liberal democracy, once the organisational and mobilising potential of communism had been removed or emasculated, is a further significant factor.

In other parts of the world, the second half of the twentieth century could hardly be described as benign. Violence towards civilian populations, usually in the context of war, whether from bitter civil conflict or invasion by neighbours related to unresolvable territorial disputes, has been endemic and huge in scale. In the 1960s and 1970s alone, 'massive massacres amounting to genocide' — a phrase used in a speech in 1979 to Amnesty International — took place, according to one listing, in eleven countries, including the mega-horror of Cambodia.[40] The single example of Rwanda in 1994 is sufficient to remind us that genocide spawned by war is by no means confined to a more distant past. The inescapable dangers of the Kashmir and Palestinian conflicts at the present time are there for all to see. And, though Europe is not a direct participant in these conflicts, today's global politics — and perhaps also a lingering historical sense of some moral responsibility — means that it is both involved and affected.

Looked at globally, and unmistakably evident in the European context, the major difference between the violence in the two halves of the century has been the impact of the two world wars. The second of those wars led to the containment, even eradication, of the main sources of state-sponsored violence, on any large scale in Europe. Outside Europe, repressive violence by colonial powers in the first half of the century gave way in the second to anti-colonial violence at first, but then, increasingly, major outbursts of internal violence, particularly where ethnic divides coincided with serious contests for power. Interstate border disputes, often with an ethnic tinge linked to religious divisions, continue to be a major source of violence and the resort to armed conflict. To this, no end is in sight.

This takes me beyond the past, to the present and future. It appears that at the beginning of the twenty-first century, in the aftermath of the attack on the twin towers of the World Trace Center in New York on 11 September 2001, we have entered a new phase of political violence. The atrocity was not a conventional act of war. And yet an act of war it was — a modern manifestation of guerrilla war, and not by any state or state-bound terrorist group, but by a shadowy international and supranational, hydra-like organisation, Al Qaeda, with tentacles stretching into a number of states but binding it to none. The act of unprovoked aggression, quite literally out of a clear blue sky, led immediately to a pronouncement by the United States of a 'war against terrorism' — a misnomer, since this is something which does not correspond to any traditional category of war, and is being fought largely against faceless, nameless and unidentified targets. Though not a 'war of cultures' from a Western point of view, as some have claimed, that is surely how Al Qaeda and its followers view it, in the form of an open-ended conflict apparently (though vaguely) aimed at nothing less than the destruction of Western (especially US) global power, influence and values. Moreover, this shadowy fight against terrorism, which has given rise to a dangerous Manichean friend–foe dichotomy revolving around the declared 'axis of evil', has already drawn Europe into two actual wars, against Afghanistan and most recently — and most controversially on account especially of its pre-emptive nature — Iraq. But here, too, there is no conventional end to the conflict. Military victory is rapidly attained, given an overwhelming superiority in arms. But this cannot bring an end to the political violence which it set out to eliminate. On the contrary: even the sole superpower cannot stop the repeated pinpricks to its might which undermine the effectiveness of its military control. And, meanwhile, Iraq has, perhaps predictably, been turned into a veritable hotbed of the terrorism which the superpower's attack on that sovereign state was meant to destroy.

It is hard to see the so-called 'war against terrorism' being won by the United States, or by anyone else; certainly, it is difficult to imagine this in a military sense. One man's terrorist is another man's freedom fighter. This is another way of saying that the organisations behind terrorism have a constituency, a hinterland of support from people, however misguided they might be, who see the attack on the representatives and even on the civilian population of an overwhelming superior power as the right, perhaps the only, way to defend themselves, their territory, their possessions, and their values. Terrorism is in many parts of the world, however appalling, however reprehensible, however detestable, generally the resort of the weak, not the strong, in an unequal struggle, but one which, from the point of view of the force trying to suppress terrorism with greater violence, cannot be won alone or even mainly through military might. Kalashnikovs are cheap; Semtex is cheap; and—a new, dangerous and more arbitrary feature compared with yesteryear's terrorism—there is no shortage of would-be martyrs for the cause, ready if need be to blow themselves to smithereens along with their targets (who are often innocent civilians, regarded, however, as part of the 'enemy').[41] So the terrorist struggle in disputed territories, or against perceived imperialist enemies, will continue. Its ramifications for Europe are plain to see. Internal controls by states over their citizens are intensifying. One offshoot of the new brand of terrorism is the continued inevitable erosion of civil liberties as alarmed populations are prepared to trade them for apparent safeguards on security.

It is a bleak scenario. Even so, short of circumstances impossible to foresee—following either major war or, maybe more likely, a calamitous crisis of international capitalism—it is difficult to imagine a repeat of the descent into the mega-violence of the first half of the twentieth century. So we can all be relieved at that. We might all even live happily ever after. At this point, as we sink into our pleasant reveries, a truly enormous squadron of pigs flies past . . .

Notes

Preliminary variants of this paper were patiently heard by audiences in Tutzing, Nottingham and Edinburgh. I am grateful for the comments I received, and to Mary Vincent for her reactions to a draft version. I would especially like to thank Michael Mann for the stimulus of some interesting conversations, and for supplying me in advance of publication with copies of some of his important work on related themes. Not least, my warmest thanks are owing to the Leverhulme Trust, whose generosity allowed me the time and space to work on this paper.

1. C. L. Mowat, ed., *The New Cambridge Modern History, Vol. XII, The Shifting Balance of World Forces 1898–1945* (Cambridge: Cambridge University Press, 1968), 2, 9.

2. Eric Hobsbawm, *Age of Extremes. The Short Twentieth Century 1914–1991* (London: Michael Joseph, 1994), esp. ch. 14.

3. Arno J. Mayer, *Why did the Heavens not Darken? The 'Final Solution' in History* (New York: Pantheon Books, 1988), 20, 31ff.

4. David Stevenson, *Cataclysm. The First World War as Political Tragedy* (New York: Basic Books, 2004), 4 (also pointing out that outside Europe, the American Civil War of 1861–5 cost the lives of 600,000 and the Taiping rebellion in China from 1850 to 1864 killed millions). The figure for losses in the Franco–Prussian War is from Mark Mazower, *Dark Continent: Europe's Twentieth Century* (Harmondsworth: Penguin, 1998), 404; Hobsbawm, *Age of Extremes*, 24, has 'perhaps 150,000'.

5. Norman Davies, *Europe: A History* (Oxford: Oxford University Press, 1996), 1328–9; Niall Ferguson, *The Pity of War* (Harmondsworth: Penguin, 1998), 277; Alan S. Milward, *Der Zweite Weltkrieg. Krieg, Wirtschaft und Gesellschaft 1939–1945* (Munich: Deutscher Taschenbuch Verlag, 1977), 211.

6. Hobsbawm, *Age of Extremes*, 51.

7. Michael Mann, 'Explaining Murderous Ethnic Cleansing: The Macro-Level', unpublished paper, 2000, 2.

8. Based on the tables in Davies, *Europe*, 1328–9.

9. John Horne and Alan Kramer, *German Atrocities, 1914. A History of Denial* (New Haven and London: Yale University Press, 2001), 74–84.

10. Cited in Antony Polonsky, *Fascism*, Historical Studies in Film 6 (London: Inter-University History Film Consortium, n.d.), 2–6. Drieu's views are well examined by Robert Soucy, *Fascist Intellectual. Drieu la Rochelle* (Berkeley and London: University of California Press), 1979.

11. Adrian Lyttelton, ed., *Italian Fascisms from Pareto to Gentile* (London: Jonathan Cape, 1973), 147.

12. Ibid., 211–12.

13. Norman M. Naimark, *Fires of Hatred. Ethnic Cleansing in Twentieth-Century Europe* (Cambridge, MA: Harvard University Press, 2001), 22–3.

14. See Enzo Traverso, *The Origins of Nazi Violence* (New York and London: The New Press, 2003), ch. 2.

15. Dietrich Beyrau, 'Der Erste Weltkrieg als Bewährungsprobe. Bolschewistische Lernprozesse aus dem "imperialistischen" Krieg', *Journal of Modern European History*, 1, 1 (2003), 96–124.

16. Davies, *Europe*, 1329.

17. Beyrau, 'Der Erste Weltkrieg', 99.

18. Orlando Figes, *A People's Tragedy. The Russian Revolution 1891–1924* (London: Jonathan Cape, 1996), 678–9; Piotr Wróbel, 'The Seeds of Violence. The Brutalization of an East European Region, 1917–1921', *Journal of Modern European History*, 1, 1 (2003), 125–49, 136–40, 145.

19. See Bernd Weisbrod, 'Gewalt in der Politik. Zur politischen Kultur in Deutschland zwischen den beiden Weltkriegen', *Geschichte in Wissenschaft und Unterricht*, 43 (1992), 391–404. Whilst it is certainly true that most men were not converted by their experience at the front into rabid right-wing paramilitary proto-Nazis, and re-entered civilian life with remarkably little difficulty, some revisionist writing goes too far in underplaying the continuities of brutalisation from the war, across the violence of the *Freikorps,* and into the politics of the Weimar Republic. An example of the newer trend in research is Benjamin Ziemann, 'Germany after the First World War — A Violent Society? Results and Implications of Recent Research on Weimar Germany', *Journal of Modern European History*, 1, 1 (2003), 80–95.

20. Cited in Vejas Gabriel Liulevicius, *War Land on the Eastern Front. Culture, National Identity and German Occupation in World War I* (Cambridge: Cambridge University Press, 2000), 278, and see the similar images discussed in ch. 5.

21. Ralf Dreier and Wolfgang Sellert, *Recht und Justiz im "Dritten Reich"* (Frankfurt am Main: Suhrkampf, 1989), 328.

22. Ian Kershaw, *The 'Hitler Myth': Image and Reality in the Third Reich* (Oxford: Oxford University Press, 1989), 84–95.

23. Michael Wildt, *Generation des Unbedingten. Das Führungskorps des Reichssicherheitshauptamtes* (Hamburg: Hamburger Edition, 2002).

24. Adrian Lyttelton, *The Seizure of Power. Fascism in Italy 1919–1929,* 2nd edn (London: Weidenfeld & Nicolson, 1987), chs. 2–3; Christopher Seton-Watson, *Italy from Liberalism to Fascism 1870–1925* (London: Methuen, 1967), 505ff., 596ff.

25. Franciso J. Romero Salvado, 'Spain and the First World War: The Structural Crisis of the Liberal Monarchy', *European History Quarterly,* 25 (1995), 529–54; Helen Graham, *The Spanish Republic at War 1936–1939* (Cambridge: Cambridge University Press, 2002), 7–12.

26. See António Costa Pinto, *The Blue Shirts. Portuguese Fascists and the New State* (New York: Columbia University Press, 2000), 44–52.

27. Michael Mann, 'The Dark Side of Democracy: The Modern Tradition of Ethnic and Political Cleansing', *New Left Review,* 235 (May/June 1999), 18–45, 25–7.

28. Michael Mann, *The Dark Side of Democracy: Explaining Ethnic Cleansing* (Cambridge: Cambridge University Press, 2005), fully elaborates these points.

29. Mann, *Dark Side of Democracy,* 19. His book takes the modernity of ethnic cleansing as one of its main arguments.

30. Götz Aly, 'Theodor Schieder, Werner Conze oder Die Vorstufen der physischen Vernichtung', in Winfried Schulze and Otto Gerhard Oexle, eds., *Deutsche Historiker im Nationalsozialismus* (Frankfurt am Main: Fischer Taschenbuch Verlag, 1999), 163–82, 163–5. And see Michael Burleigh, *Germany turns Eastwards. A Study of Ostforschung in the Third Reich* (Cambridge: Cambridge University Press, 1988).

31. See Edwin Black, *IBM and the Holocaust* (New York: Little, Brown, 2001).

32. From an extensive literature: Norbert Frei, ed., *Medizin und Gesundheitspolitik in der NS-Zeit* (Munich: Oldenbourg, 1991); Francis R. Nicosia and Jonathan Huener, eds., *Medicine and Medical Ethics in Nazi Germany. Origins, Practices, Legacies* (New York and Oxford: Berghahn Books, 2002).

33. Eugen Kogon, Hermann Langbein and Adalbert Rückerl, eds., *Nationalsozi-*

alistische Massentötungen durch Giftgas. Eine Dokumentation (Frankfurt am Main: Fischer Taschenbuch Verlag, 1986), 282.

34. Kogon, Langbein and Rückerl, 219–21; Robert Jan van Pelt and Debórah Dwork, *Auschwitz: 1270 to the Present* (New Haven and London: Yale University Press, 1996), 177, 269.

35. Zygmunt Bauman, *Modernity and the Holocaust* (Cambridge: Polity Press, 1989), 17.

36. Ibid., 13.

37. Ibid., 91.

38. A point made by Mann, *Dark Side of Democracy,* 241.

39. The high level of violence used is described by Naimark, *Fires of Hatred,* 115–19, 126–30.

40. Leo Kuper, *Genocide. Its Political Use in the Twentieth Century* (Harmondsworth: Penguin Books, 1981), 186.

41. For an elaboration of similar points, see Mann, *Dark Side of Democracy,* 521.

Acknowledgments

I would like to express my warmest thanks to Otto Dov Kulka, whose work on this darkest period of Jewish history has been an inspiration to me over many years, for suggesting this volume, initiating its publication, and selecting the texts. My gratitude is also owing to Bella Gutterman for her kind help with this publication.

The Introduction to this volume was written specifically at the request of Yad Vashem. In addition, the author gratefully acknowledges permission to reprint the following material:

Chapter 1. ' "Working Towards the Führer": Reflections on the Nature of the Hitler Dictatorship', originally published in *Contemporary European History* 2, no. 2 (1993): 103–118. ©1993 Cambridge University Press. Reprinted by permission of Cambridge University Press.

Chapter 2. 'Ideologue and Propagandist: Hitler in Light of His Speeches, Writings and Orders, 1925–1928', originally presented as a lecture at the Institut für Zeitgeschichte in Munich on February 14, 1992, and first published in German in *Vierteljahrshefte fur Zeitgeschichte* 2, no. 40 (April 1992). Appeared also in Hebrew translation. Reprinted here from *Yad Vashem Studies* 23 (1993): 321–334.

Chapter 3. 'Improvised Genocide? The Emergence of the "Final Solution" in the "Warthegau" ', originally published in *Transactions of the Royal Histor-*

ical Society, 6th series, vol. 2 (London, 1992), 51–78. Reprinted by permission of the Royal Historical Society.

Chapter 4. 'Hitler's Role in the "Final Solution"', originally published in Italian in Marina Cattaruzza et al. (eds.), *Storia della Shoah*, vol. 1. (Torino: UTET, 2005). Reprinted here from *Yad Vashem Studies* 34 (2006): 7–43.

Chapter 5. 'The "Everyday" and the "Exceptional": The Shaping of Popular Opinion, 1933–1939', originally published in German as 'Alltägliches und Außeralltägliches: Ihre Bedeutung für die Volksmeinung, 1933–1939', in Detlev Peukert and Jürgen Reulecke (eds.), *Alltag im Nationalsozialismus: Vom Ende der Weimarer Republik bis zum Zweiten Weltkrieg* (Wuppertal, 1981), 273–292. Reprinted by permission of Peter Hammer Verlag.

Chapter 6. 'German Popular Opinion during the "Final Solution": Information, Comprehension, Reactions', originally published in Ascher Cohen et al. (eds.), *Comprehending the Holocaust: Historical and Literary Research* (Frankfurt am Main, 1989), 145–158. Reprinted by permission of Peter Lang GmbH.

Chapter 7. 'Reactions to the Persecution of the Jews', originally published in *Popular Opinion and Political Dissent in the Third Reich: Bavaria, 1933– 1945* (Oxford, 1983), 224–277. Reprinted by permission of Oxford University Press.

Chapter 8. 'Popular Opinion and the Extermination of the Jews', originally published in *Popular Opinion and Political Dissent in the Third Reich: Bavaria, 1933–1945* (Oxford, 1983), 358–372. Reprinted by permission of Oxford University Press.

Chapter 9. 'German Popular Opinion and the "Jewish Question", 1939– 1943: Some Further Reflections', originally published in Arnold Paucker (ed.), *Die Juden im Nationalsozialistischen Deutschland, 1933–1943* [The Jews in Nazi Germany, 1933–1943] (Tübingen, 1986), 365–388. Reprinted by permission of Mohr Siebeck.

Chapter 10. 'Hitler and the Holocaust', originally published in *The Nazi Dictatorship: Problems and Perspectives of Interpretation* (London, 2000), pp. 93–133. Reprinted by permission of Arnold, a member of the Hodder Headline Group.

Chapter 11. '"Normality" and Genocide: The Problem of "Historicization"', originally published in *The Nazi Dictatorship: Problems and Perspectives of Interpretation* (London, 2000), 218–236. Reprinted by permission of Arnold, a member of the Hodder Headline Group.

Chapter 12. 'Shifting Perspectives: Historiographical Trends in the Aftermath of Unification', originally published in *The Nazi Dictatorship: Problems and Perspectives of Interpretation* (London 2000), 237–270. Reprinted by permission of Arnold, a member of the Hodder Headline Group.

Chapter 13. 'Hitler and the Uniqueness of Nazism', originally presented in 2002 as a Trevelyan Lecture at the University of Cambridge, and first published in *Journal of Contemporary History* 39, no. 2 (2004): 239–254. © 2004 Sage Publications. Reprinted by permission of Sage Publications Ltd, www.sagepub.co.uk.

Chapter 14. 'War and Political Violence in Twentieth Century Europe', originally published in *Contemporary European History* 14, no. 1 (2005): 107–123. © 2005 Cambridge University Press. Reprinted by permission of Cambridge University Press.

Index